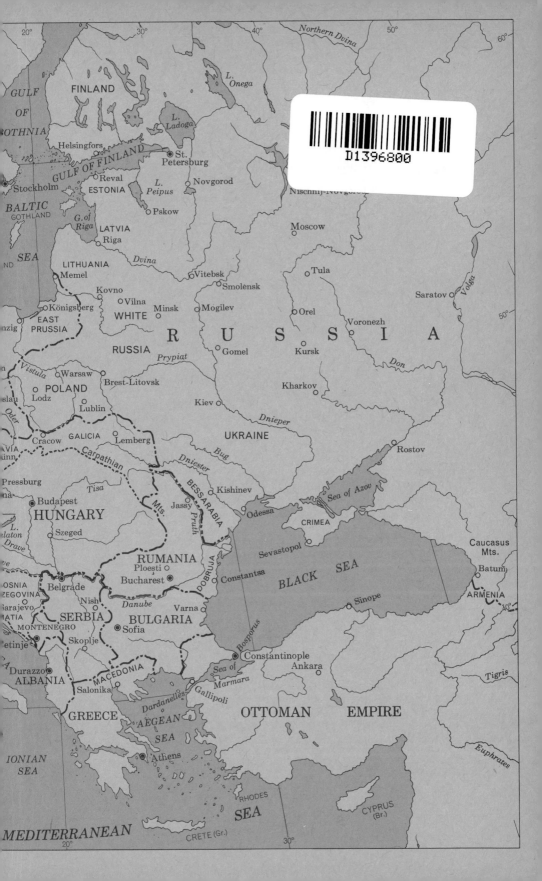

Europe in the 20ᵗʰ Century

A HISTORY

Europe in the 20th Century

A HISTORY

Andreas Dorpalen

OHIO STATE UNIVERSITY

The Macmillan Company, New York
Collier-Macmillan Limited, London

First Printing

Library of Congress catalog card number: 67–18451

The Macmillan Company, New York

Collier-Macmillan Canada, Ltd., Toronto, Ontario

Printed in the United States of America

For Peter and Bruce

Preface

To bring out a new textbook in a field in which a number of very good texts are available requires some justification. The present survey differs in several respects from other books on twentieth century Europe. To a greater extent than most texts on the subject, it relies on a European rather than a nation-by-nation approach in order to throw into sharper relief the European interconnections as well as the national divergences in social, economic, and cultural developments. The book also devotes more space than is customary to the subject of American-European relations in recognition of the fact that this trans-Atlantic relationship has been of considerable importance throughout the entire half-century under discussion. Finally, I have treated cultural developments primarily as historical phenomena, concerning myself not so much with their literary, artistic, or scientific significance as with their relationship to the contemporary social and political scene.

The most difficult problem with which any textbook author is faced, of course, is that of selection from an overabundance of data. I have tried to supply and analyze the basic facts essential to an understanding of the story of Europe during the last half-century, but I have not hesitated to discuss at some length such key situations as the Paris peace conference of 1919, the Soviet social and economic system, or the diplomatic background of World War II since their full impact cannot be understood without a rather detailed examination of their complex intricacies. Beyond all facts and data, however, I have tried to be guided by the realization that this is a story of human beings with all their hopes and anxieties, their strengths and their weaknesses. Since this has been one of my major concerns, I have not shied away from the telling, if unscholarly, anecdote; I hope it has helped to clarify and enliven this account of Europe's endeavors.

I am greatly indebted to my friends and colleagues Foster Rhea Dulles, June Z. Fullmer, and Philip P. Poirier, Ohio State University, Sidney Harcave, Harpur College, State University of New York, and William D. Mallam, St. Lawrence University, who each read parts of the manuscript and made many helpful suggestions. Professors Vernon L. Lidtke, Michigan State University, and John T. Marcus, Hofstra University, read the manuscript for the publisher; I am very grateful to them for their valuable comments and criticisms. Finally, I owe thanks to Hedwig Stoecker, an assistant in the U.S. College Work-Study Program, who gathered some of the data, and to my son Bruce, who assisted me in some of the editorial chores.

A. D.

Contents

Contents

16

17

23

List of Illustrations

List of Maps

Europe in the **20**th Century

A HISTORY

1

The Crisis of the European State System

The European Polity. Europe is, after Australia, the smallest of the seven continents. It is hardly larger than the United States and less than half the size of the Soviet Union. By the standards of physical geography it is not a genuine continent; no natural line of demarcation separates it from Asia. Physically it is but an appendage of the latter, a peninsula jutting out into the Atlantic Ocean and its two branches, the Arctic and the Mediterranean.

That Europe ranks as a continent with such land masses as Asia and the Americas is a tribute to the role it has played in world affairs. For many centuries it was the center of world power and wealth, and its peoples have left their permanent imprint on all parts of the globe. Favored by climate and natural riches, it drew its immense vitality from a cultural tradition in which many strains interacted with each other and evolved that variegated "European" civilization that derived its essential stimulation from its very diversity.

This multifaceted culture could not have survived, however, without a political underpinning, and "Europe," once the term outgrew its geographical connotation, became a political as well as a cultural concept.   **1**

Politically it served to designate that amorphous and often all-but-nonexistent association which the European states evolved in the conviction that ultimately their individual survival depended on a modicum of international order. The size of this polity varied; only after both the Ottoman Empire and Russia had become part of the European state system early in the seventeenth and eighteenth centuries, respectively, did political Europe include the entire continent and extend from the Atlantic Ocean to the Ural Mountains and along the full length of the Mediterranean.

As a political system "Europe" replaced the disintegrating authority of the medieval Church. When Rome could no longer provide the framework for a supranational order the European state system evolved to fill the gap. Its member states sought to preserve their independence by keeping each other from devouring the rest. The conflicts which resulted from this gathering of centrifugal forces account for the looseness of their association; the system drew its unity from a common interest in the existing diversity.

The system did not always live up to its task, and given the unequal distribution of power, it was often abused by the larger powers. Yet it was more than a convenient but meaningless slogan. The Peace of Westphalia, after the Thirty Years War, sought to give it a concrete form—Leopold von Ranke, the German historian, hailed the arrangements as the "fundamental laws, as it were, of a general republic in which all [states] participated." When Louis XIV tried to destroy the system by imposing France's hegemony on the continent, "Europe" rallied against him and put an end to his ambitions. Napoleon I, who challenged it a century later, eventually met with the same fate.

The Changing Temper of Europe.   Under the impact of the Napoleonic challenge, the great powers of Europe agreed on closer and more continuous collaboration to preserve peace and order in Europe. The Concert of Europe which they established at the Congress of Vienna in 1815 was only partly successful; the objectives of its members were too diverse to allow for continuous cooperation. Yet the Concert succeeded in settling some conflicts peacefully, and it was able to localize several clashes which might otherwise have exploded into European wars. Whatever its limitations, it was a political reality, and it reflected a sense of European responsibility on the part of the statesmen who made it work.

The Concert functioned more successfully during the first half of the nineteenth century than during the second. The post-Napoleonic period was a time of comparative quiescence in which national energies were restrained and found outlets at home and abroad without colliding constantly with each other. Where they did clash, settlements could be arranged in most cases. They were more easily reached than in later times because most of the governments could make their decisions on the basis of their own best judgment. Neither Russia nor Austria nor Prussia had to worry about public opinion or parliamentary approval, and where these mattered, as in Britain and France, there was, on the whole, much greater concern with domestic issues than with foreign affairs.

All this changed after the century passed the midway mark. The placidity of the earlier period gave way to a new burst of energies. Industrialization spread across large parts of the continent, increasing immensely its productivity and its wealth and accelerating the search for new markets and opportunities for investment. Fired by a craving for self-assertion, nationalism changed from a sense of community with one's fellow nationals into aggressive feelings of superiority over other nations. At the same time the spread of education and the extension of political rights added a new dimension to international politics. Mass support was now required for the conduct of foreign policy, and the masses on their part began to exercize pressure to influence policies. Emotions were easily aroused and were expressed in the passionate hatreds of chauvinist groups and in the vituperations of a jingoist press. The application of Darwinist precepts gave them a semblance of respectability; whereas earlier thinkers had praised peace as the noblest goal, the supreme objective was now seen increasingly as winning the fight for survival. To many, power became the ultimate aim of politics. In the face of such challenges it proved more difficult to maintain a European perspective, and Europe's state system was subjected to ever-new strains. In the end it could no longer withstand them, and in the summer of 1914 it collapsed.

The disruptive forces of nationalism and imperialism, of racism, and of the cult of brute force were present in all major powers. Britain added large areas to its empire in Asia and Africa, and its imperialist aspirations kept clashing with those of Russia and France. Certain of their supremacy, disdainful of the "lesser breeds without the law," the British had little need to organize mass movements to spur national pride and quicken national energies, but even in Britain important voices— Alfred Tennyson, the poet laureate, for example, and John Ruskin, the critic—hailed war as a mainspring of strength and morality. France, too, enlarged its colonial possessions in many parts of the world, endangering its relations with Italy, Britain, and Germany; at the same time vociferous publicists like Maurice Barrès and Charles Maurras were the spokesmen of a strident nationalism and a new cult of force, and on this latter point they received effective support from their political antipode, Georges Sorel, the anarchosyndicalist, who in his *Reflections on Violence* called violence the world's savior from decay and corruption.

Nationalism, imperialism, and the faith in force left their imprint also on Italy, Russia, and Austria-Hungary. Italy pined for Austria's Italian-

settled lands, which it wished to "redeem" (*Italia irredenta*); it too
embarked on empire-building ventures, while poets like Gabriele D'Annunzio called on Italy's youth to seek release from their sterile lives in
violent action. Russia, in turn, was extending its power deep into Central
and Far Eastern Asia and trying to bring the Balkan Peninsula under its
sway; in these efforts the Russian government had the hearty support of
the Pan-Slav movement and of such widely read publicists as Nikolai
Danilevsky, who gloried in the superiority of Russia over the West and
in the prospect of a long and bitter war between the two from which
Russia would emerge as the victor and the head of an empire embracing
all Slavs. Deeply concerned, Austria-Hungary tried to extend its influence
into the Balkans, thus adding to Russia's anxieties. But Vienna's main
efforts were devoted to keeping together its multinational empire. In
this neither Austria nor the more ruthless Hungary were very successful,
and the existing tensions, carefully watched by their neighbors, created
another source of potential trouble.

The German Challenge.   It was Germany's aspirations, however, that
aroused the greatest concern in Europe. German unification, which had
been completed in 1871, frightened not only France, recently defeated
by Germany, but alarmed Britain and Russia as well. Both countries
feared that Europe's equilibrium was gravely imperiled by this new
concentration of power at the center of the continent. Bismarck, aware
of these misgivings, tried hard to allay them. Carefully planning his
moves, he had unified Germany without provoking a major conflict; he
knew that any further expansion might lead to a European war and
destroy what he had accomplished. His main concern was to preserve
peace, and this he sought to achieve by an intricate system of alliances
into which he brought Austria-Hungary, Russia, and Italy and into
which he hoped eventually to draw Britain also.

As long as he stayed in office, he helped to stave off major clashes. Yet
his policy was not without its own dangers. It was based on the
permanent isolation of France, with whom he considered a reconciliation
impossible. He thus barred any attempt to recreate the old Concert of
Europe and helped to lay the foundation for Europe's division into two
hostile camps. He made an even graver mistake when he failed to help
nurture in his fellow countrymen that sense of political responsibility
which alone could ensure Europe's peaceful development.

In consequence, when Bismarck was dismissed from his post in 1890
by the impetuous young Emperor William II (1859–1941), the country
quickly threw off the restraints which had been the hallmark of the old
chancellor's diplomacy. Proud of its industrial and scientific achievements,
bubbling with vitality and eager to assert rights which it felt misfortune
and the greed of other nations had withheld from it, Germany clamored
for greater might, colonies, and world power status. In its Kaiser it had

an articulate if tactless and indiscreet spokesman who stoutly proclaimed that he intended to lead his people "toward great days." His bluster was seconded by a multitude of scholars and publicists, among them General Friedrich von Bernhardi and the Anglo-German writer Houston Stewart Chamberlain, who extolled the blessings of power and, as the historian Friedrich Meinecke later put it, raised the Machiavellian aspects of politics to the level of a *Weltanschauung*. Organizations such as the Pan-German League, numerically small but extremely vociferous and never officially disavowed, demanded the incorporation of all "Germanic" groups in Europe into Germany and the promotion of Germandom throughout the world. German foreign policy, which had been notable for its conservatism in Bismarck's time, became more aggressive; successive efforts were made to establish footholds in various parts of the world. The search for colonies, reluctantly undertaken by Bismarck in the mid-1880's, was resumed with great vigor, though it netted the Reich only a few new possessions in Australasia and Africa. More significant were attempts to carve out spheres of influence in the Near and Middle East and in Morocco.

There was nothing unusual or especially wicked about these efforts, yet they aroused much greater alarm than those of any other power. The shrillness of German nationalism may help to explain this reaction, and so may the fact that the exaltation of power and war enjoyed a greater respectability in Germany than anywhere else. Yet it was Germany's geopolitical situation that lent its expansionist policies an especially ominous note. Because of its central location, wherever it moved Germany was bound to intrude upon vital interests of some other power. Berlin's actions called forth a general fear that it was trying to establish its hegemony over Europe. This fear was re-enforced by the erratic ways in which the Germans pursued their ambitions. Rather than concentrate their endeavors in one direction, perhaps antagonizing one major power but cultivating the good will of others, they struck out successively, and at times simultaneously, in all directions. Thus they kept making enemies and drove the other powers to join forces against them. Confusing cause and effect, Germany, on its part, complained about being encircled.

The Diplomatic Revolution. It is in this light that the diplomatic developments which took place after 1890 must be understood. Until that year Germany was the focal center of European politics. Austria-Hungary and Italy were allied with Germany in the Triple Alliance; Germany had an alliance with Russia; France was isolated; and Britain, though formally uncommitted, was virtually forced to remain on good terms with the Reich because its relations with both France and Russia were seriously strained. After Bismarck's departure from office, however, Berlin let the German-Russian alliance lapse; it seemed incompatible with the alliance with Austria-Hungary and with a hoped-for rapprochement with Britain. Inevitably, Russia, fearful of Britain and Germany, moved closer to France, and in 1894 St. Petersburg concluded a military alliance with Paris. Significantly, both powers pledged help to each other only in the case of a German attack; no mention was made of Britain, though the possibility of an Anglo-French clash over Egypt or an Anglo-Russian collision along the vast perimeter of Russia's southern boundary seemed much more probable. The troubles with Britain were peripheral issues geopolitically.

The Franco-Russian alliance was defensive in intent, and influential pro-German groups in Russia still hoped for a new rapprochement with Berlin. Their hopes were reciprocated in Germany; William II even dreamed of a vast continental bloc extending from the Atlantic to the Pacific which would challenge the might of the British Empire. But Germany defeated its own purpose by moving into areas which Russia considered its immediate concern. The Germans pressed on with the economic penetration and military development of the Turkish Empire; they established a maritime base at Kiaochow on China's Shantung Peninsula; and they kept backing Austria-Hungary in the Balkans.

Nor did Germany show greater wisdom in its dealings with Britain. Berlin alarmed London, too, by its Middle Eastern activities, which endangered Britain's imperial lines of communication, and the Kaiser infuriated the British by his repeated interference in their quarrels with the Boers in South Africa. And when Britain, beset by disputes with Russia and France, proposed an alliance to Germany, it was curtly rebuffed on the assumption that more favorable terms might be extracted from London as the price for such a commitment. Germany's gravest mistake was to embark on a program of precipitate naval expansion. The decision was hazardous on economic as well as on military and diplomatic grounds. Burdened with one of the largest armies in Europe, the Reich could not hope to build a navy which Britain could not surpass. Nor could a large German navy serve as an effective deterrent, for geography also favored Britain. Commanding the sea routes to and from Germany, Britain could easily close all exits from the North Sea and immobilize the German navy, as indeed it did throughout World War I. To expect, finally, that Britain could be frightened into an alliance or at least be kept neutral in a future war on the continent betrayed a tragic misjudgment of the British character and diplomatic and military resources.

Britain reacted quickly. It embarked at once on a naval expansion program of major proportions. It also decided to end its diplomatic isolation in Europe by seeking a rapprochement with France. Paris, worried about the value of the Russian alliance, was equally anxious to reach an understanding with London. In 1904 agreements were signed by both countries which settled their non-European differences, from fishing rights off Newfoundland and spheres of influence in Siam to customs policies in Madagascar and frontier disputes in Gambia and Nigeria. Above all, they acknowledged Britain's pre-eminent interests in Egypt and those of France in Morocco. Nothing was said about Europe, but the implied understanding (*entente cordiale*) was that with their non-European differences adjusted, the two powers would be able to collaborate more easily in Europe.

Germany, underestimating the significance of this arrangement, attempted to show up its worthlessness. By an ostentatious call of the Kaiser on the Sultan of Morocco in the spring of 1905, France was threatened with a German intervention in defense of that country's independence. The Germans had chosen their moment well; with the Russians paralyzed by domestic unrest and military defeat (at the hands of Japan), and without a clear-cut commitment from Britain, the French were panic-stricken. But the British had been assured that should France seize Morocco, Spain would be allowed to take over the area closest to Gibraltar; thus they preferred a French-run Morocco to one controlled by the Germans and gave their full support to the French. Unwilling to risk a showdown, the Germans allowed themselves to be outvoted at an international conference at Algeciras in Spain and acknowledged France's special rights in Morocco. The Anglo-French *entente cordiale* was notably strengthened by the Moroccan crisis; military staff talks between Britain and France got under way that same year.

There could be no lasting cooperation, however, as long as Britain was at loggerheads with Russia, France's chief ally. Since Russia, too, was anxious for an accommodation with Britain to improve its position in both the Middle and Far East, some major disputes could be settled between the two powers—over Persia, Tibet, and Afghanistan,—and in 1907 the Anglo-French entente became the Anglo-French-Russian Triple Entente. Germany was now almost completely isolated, having as allies only Austria-Hungary, which was torn by internal dissension, and a wavering Italy, which at Algeciras had sided with France. From then on, Britain rather than Germany held the commanding position in European politics; the diplomatic revolution had been completed.

Europe in the Balance. With the creation of the Triple Entente, it has often been said, Europe was divided into two armed camps. This was true as far as the continental powers were concerned. Their respective positions were fixed and two new crises deepened the existing division. One of these occurred in the Balkan Peninsula in 1908 when, to Russia's dismay, Austria gained full control over the two Turkish provinces of Bosnia and Herzegovina. In 1911 another crisis arose over Morocco in which the Germans were forced to accept a French protectorate over that state. Also contributing to the tension, of course, was the armaments race in which all powers were now fully engaged.

Britain, on the other hand, was not yet resigned to the permanence of this chasm. The British Foreign Secretary, Sir Edward Grey (1862–1933), knew the mind of his countrymen. They wished above all not to be drawn into any continental wrangles and this desire he shared wholeheartedly. While Grey was determined to defend his country's position and far-flung possessions, he viewed the Triple Entente not as an agent of division but as an instrument by which Britain might gain sufficient preponderance diplomatically to safeguard the peace of Europe. The two ententes, he maintained, did not commit Britain to anything beyond diplomatic collaboration; in fact, their ultimate purpose was, as he saw it, to give Britain a free hand to choose between two alternate courses. He hoped that the agreements might serve to convince Germany of the need to come to an understanding with Britain as had France and Russia. If, on the other hand, the Germans persisted in their naval expansion and sought to establish their hegemony over Europe, the Triple Entente would be used to align Britain with Russia and France against Germany.

Grey's sincerity cannot be doubted, but his policy could convey an impression of ambiguity, and it was so misread by the Germans. Reich Chancellor Theobald von Bethmann Hollweg (1856–1921), unfamiliar with foreign affairs, stoutly believed that Britain's lack of specific commitment to its entente partners offered a chance to keep it neutral in a future war on the continent. Over this basic misunderstanding talks initiated in 1909 for an Anglo-German rapprochement broke down. But they were doomed in any event since concurrent negotiations about a limitation of naval armaments also ran into a deadlock.

For a fleeting moment it seemed, however, as if Grey's hopes might still come true. New troubles arose in the Balkan Peninsula in 1912. In a short campaign a year before, Italy had shorn the disintegrating Turkish Empire of its North African possessions in Tripoli. Encouraged by this success, several of the Balkan countries now turned on Turkey to strip it of most of its Balkan lands and quickly defeated the Turkish forces. The division of spoils, however, proved difficult, and fighting broke out among the victors. Since Austria and Russia threatened to intervene, an international conference meeting in London worked out a settlement under Grey's skillful guidance. This successful revival of something resembling the old Concert of Europe was shortlived, however, and no steps were taken to establish procedures by which future troubles could be dealt with in the same way. The will to work together existed, Grey noted sadly in his memoirs, but it was ineffectual since almost no one believed any longer in its existence.

Social and Economic Conditions. Grey summed up well the existing dilemma. Although there were individuals in responsible positions in each country who saw war as the only solution to existing difficulties, governments and nations alike hoped to avoid it. For life, on the whole, was improving for increasing numbers of people in the industrialized countries of Europe. The benefits of the Industrial Revolution were spreading to ever-widening circles; real wages increased, living standards improved, scientific and medical advances made life safer and easier, and expanding educational and cultural facilities added to its enjoyment. Political democracy, too, was expanding, and although it was more formal than real in many countries, in others it did help to safeguard the rights and interests of all classes and sectors.

Not all, to be sure, was well; the nationality problem continued to exert its disruptive impact on some of the countries of central and eastern Europe; repression, poverty, and illiteracy remained continuous problems in Russia and the Balkan and Mediterranean countries. Nor were social tensions and economic difficulties absent in the more advanced nations. The growth of socialist and other movements of protest in these countries reflected a continuing discontent of the working class with existing conditions. Yet the tactics of these movements underwent significant changes in the last decades of the nineteenth century. In most European countries erstwhile socialist revolutionaries came to accept evolutionary parliamentary processes as an effective way of realizing their goals, and Marx and Engels themselves allowed in their later years that their program might in some countries be accomplished by parliamentary means.

The general feeling that life was good or could be improved without violent changes helps to explain Europe's failure to realize that its prosperity rested on weakening foundations. This prosperity depended on the effective functioning of the capitalist system; in turn, the latter, by nature a dynamic expansive system, had to keep opening up new markets and opportunities for investment in order to operate properly. Thus, when the homeland was no longer able to absorb the industrial goods and surplus capital the system produced, new outlets had to be found elsewhere. They were provided by increased exports to other countries and by what has come to be known as economic imperialism —the acquisition of colonies and spheres of influence and indirect economic control over other countries and areas. By providing additional jobs for workers in the homeland, these activities also led to an expansion of the domestic market, thus creating new opportunities both at home and abroad. But after the turn of the century foreign outlets were decreasing; countries such as the United States and Japan, which had absorbed much of Europe's surplus production, had developed their own industrial plant, and their production not only satisfied a large part of their domestic demand but also began to compete for foreign markets. In 1860 United States industrial production had constituted about 22 per cent of the world's industrial output, as against Europe's 76 per cent. By 1890 United States production had grown to 37 per cent and Europe's had dropped to 57 per cent; the corresponding figures for 1913 were 42 and 49 per cent, respectively. American exports almost doubled between 1900 and 1914, rising from $1,400,000,000 in 1900 to $2,500,000,000 in 1914; whereas industrial products had accounted for only 35 per cent of the U.S. exports in 1900, their share in 1914 was almost 49 per cent. With all available overseas territories claimed by the various powers, new colonial outlets were no longer available either. Thus Europe's economic expansion began to slow down after the turn of the century, but the effects of this process were not yet sufficiently marked to cause much concern. Europeans continued to look on Europe as the unchallenged and unchallengeable political, economic, and cultural center of the world.

The Desire for Peace.   This basic satisfaction with existing conditions was also reflected in the desire to preserve peace despite all international friction. Peace organizations kept springing up, and the pacifist novel of an Austrian writer, Bertha von Suttner, *Lay Down Your Arms,* became a famous best-seller. Yet mutual distrust and unchecked ambitions barred any genuine understanding. In 1899 and 1907 two Peace Conferences were held at The Hague to secure a reduction of armaments and find ways for the peaceful settlement of international disputes. Beyond establishing an optional system of arbitration and evolving some new rules of war (most of which were quickly discarded during the First World War), the meetings accomplished nothing. Similarly, the success of the London Conference after the Balkan Wars was offset by war preparations in other areas. At the very time the Conference was meeting, Britain and France signed a convention tightening the cooperation of their two navies. Shortly before, France and Russia had agreed on closely concerted action on land and at sea in case of a German attack, and a few months after the conference Germany urged Austria-Hungary, on the occasion of an Austro-Serbian border incident, to insist on a showdown (it was prevented by Serbia's decision to withdraw its troops from the border). Nor was a new Anglo-German rapprochement in 1913–14 more effective. Understandings were reached about Germany's railway projects in the Middle East and about German and English interests in Portugal's African colonies, but six weeks after they had been reached, both countries were at war with each other.

Towards War.   Although few wanted war, almost everyone had come to expect it, and preparations proceeded accordingly. "I only meet people who assure me that an early war with Germany is certain, in fact, inevitable," the Belgian envoy reported from Paris in 1913. "People regret it, but they accept it." This resignation prevailed all over Europe. The growing readiness to glorify force made it easier perhaps to envisage war as an acceptable solution. So possibly did the feeling, widespread among Germans and Slavs, that war was an ineluctable part of human destiny and in the long run inevitable in any event. Whatever the reason, the efforts to prevent it when it was imminent were halfhearted and ineffectual.

The final crisis was touched off by the assassination on June 28, 1914 of the heir to the Austro-Hungarian throne, Archduke Francis Ferdinand, by Serb nationalists. Vienna, suspecting the complicity of the Serb government, considered the murder a challenge to the very existence of the Habsburg Empire. Unless Serbia were dealt a crushing blow, the Empire's non-German nationalities would grow more restless and the Empire might collapse altogether. Yet given the existing military alignments, this was no longer a matter which the Austrians could settle by themselves with the Serbs. The Russians would doubtless come to the aid of the latter; to cope with them, the Austrians needed the help of the Germans. When William II was sounded out, he promised the "full support of Germany" even if the conflict with Serbia should lead to a war between Austria-Hungary and Russia. He was seconded by Bethmann Hollweg who agreed with the Kaiser that Germany could not desert its one reliable ally. Indeed, Berlin was so anxious to see Austria protect its great power status that it urged Vienna to seek a quick showdown with Serbia, hopeful that war, if it came, could be localized by such speedy action. Thus reassured, the Austrians presented to the Serbs a series of demands, several of which the latter could not accept without surrendering their sovereignty. They gave a reply which was conciliatory but evasive; the Austrians rejected it and declared war.

The other major governments attempted belatedly to mediate, but once war had broken out, their endeavors were overruled by the military. The Russian general staff insisted on an immediate mobilization in view of the protracted time this required. In turn, the German generals demanded a speedy mobilization of their own forces when they learned of the Russian intentions, for their war plans were predicated on the defeat of France, Russia's ally, before Russia was ready for combat. Thus, when the Tsar gave in to his generals and ordered a general mobilization, this meant war to the German strategists. On August 1 the Reich declared war on Russia and on August 3 on France. Germany's invasion of Belgium a day later drew wavering Britain into the struggle. Of the major powers Italy alone remained neutral, on the grounds that it need give no aid to the Central Powers since, without consulting it, they had engaged in aggressive actions.

National Moods.   The war was not viewed as a deep human tragedy. Each nation was convinced that it was fighting in defense of vital and legitimate rights. The Triple Entente felt certain that unless checked, the Germans would extend their hegemony over Europe; the Central Powers were just as certain that they were fighting for their survival. In fact, the news of the war was received with some measure of relief; after years of recurring crises the hour of decision finally had arrived.

The risks involved, moreover, seemed small since almost everyone expected the war to last for no more than a few months; the Kaiser, the Tsar, and the King of England were quoted as having stated that it would surely be over by Christmas. In consequence the response to the call to arms was overwhelmingly positive. There had been serious labor unrest in many of the major European countries; political discontent was strong in Russia and was growing in Germany; Britain was plagued by the Irish problem and the clamor for woman's suffrage; and Austria-Hungary was wrestling with its national minorities. But these issues seemed now forgotten; there were no antiwar strikes and demonstrations; except in Austria-Hungary, draftees matched volunteers in their eagerness to defend their country, and even in the Habsburg monarchy the discontented groups acquiesced. It all seemed a gay adventure. Bedecked with flowers, soldiers marched off singing and laughing; German troop trains displayed cheerful signs stating, "Declarations of war still being accepted," and Paris crowds shouted to the departing troops, "Be sure to bring back William's moustache." Many welcomed the war as a badly needed cleansing process, an antidote against the prevailing materialism and selfishness, an opportunity to develop heroism and manliness and restore national unity. Others again thought of it as the beginning of a new era which would bring social and political equality to all. Still others were hopeful that this would be the last war to be fought and that it would usher in an age of freedom, of peace, and disarmament. Hardly anyone had a sense of impending disaster, and there were few who feared that the war would plunge Europe into political and social convulsions. All but a handful would have disagreed with the glum premonition of Sir Edward Grey, "The lamps are going out all over Europe, we shall not see them lit in our lifetime."

2

World War I:
The European Phase

The First World War differed in a number of ways from all earlier conflicts. Militarily it produced far-reaching changes in tactics and strategy both on land and at sea (and to a limited extent introduced air warfare). It also involved more people, caused more casualties, and wrought more destruction than any previous war. But the most revolutionary changes which it initiated were economic and social. Since the struggle was equally a contest of men and matériel, its outcome depended as much the achievements of technicians and scientists as on the accomplishments of the soldiers. This led the governments of all belligerent powers to assume much firmer control over the economic life of their countries than had been the case since the passing of the mercantilist age. The impact of such governmental management of the economy was not quickly forgotten; it pointed the way to the economic planning that became a main theme of the times.

After an initial euphoric phase, the war produced sharp social tensions, destroying the hope that the conflict would usher in an era of greater social cohesion and understanding. Instead, it set the stage for those bitter domestic clashes that would beset Europe in years to come. And **13** if these internal struggles were fought with a new unrelenting ruthlessness, it was because the impersonal character of the war of matériel had left little room for chivalry and restraint and inured men to this type of fighting. Four years of warring in which mass armies and mass matériel proved decisive could only weaken the sense of individual self-respect and responsibility.

THE FIGHTING FRONTS

War Plans. Like the civilians, the military expected the war to be short. The plans of the general staffs were based on the experiences of recent European wars: all of these had been swift wars of movement, lasting at most a few months. The expectation was that a future war would be just as short, if only because of the immense economic strain imposed by mass armies and expensive equipment. The contrary experience of the American Civil War was shrugged off as what one German general called cavalierly a clash of armed mobs. European strategists also discounted the lesson of the Russo-Japanese War of 1904–05 which had bogged down into a war of position: Europe, it seemed, had nothing to learn from campaigns in such distant lands.

Similarly some other lessons of the American and Far Eastern conflicts were largely ignored. Both wars had made clear that close-range fighting was very unlikely in an age in which the rifle could range over hundreds of yards. Yet infantry was sent off to war with bayonets which would rarely be used, and cavalry was equipped with lances which would be used even less. Few recruits, on the other hand, were taught to build breastworks or dig a trench, although the Civil War, as well as the Boer and Far Eastern Wars, had demonstrated the growing need for entrenchments. The Germans did not wish to waste ground on such drills, and the French still believed that attack was the sole key to victory. Victory, French strategists taught, was essentially a matter of morale. "A battle won is a battle in which one will not confess oneself beaten," wrote General Ferdinand Foch (1851–1929), later the commander-in-chief of the Allied forces. A sound rule in hand-to-hand combat, it was, as Foch confessed ruefully after the war, an "infantile notion" in the age of technology. It sent hundreds of thousands uselessly to their death.

The Schlieffen Plan. Since the Germans had the initiative, their strategy determined the early developments on the battlefield. Their plans had been drawn up by Count Alfred von Schlieffen (1833–1913), chief of the Prussian general staff from 1891 to 1906. They grew out of the threat of a two-front war that had confronted the Reich since the Franco-Russian alliance of 1894. Schlieffen hoped to circumvent this calamity by breaking up such a war into two phases. Since Russia presumably would need many weeks to complete its mobilization, he proposed to launch his main forces against France, defeat it in a speedy campaign, then shift his troops to the east and turn upon Russia. His plan provided for a huge wheeling movement through Belgium and southern Holland, outflanking the mountainous and heavily fortified French frontier, a swing southwest around Paris, and a thrust on the rear of the French forces. These would be driven into neutral Switzerland or into Lorraine where another German army would be waiting to close the trap. Schlieffen's successor, Count Hellmuth von Moltke, the undistinguished nephew of an illustrious uncle, retained the plan, but did modify it. The advance through Holland was abandoned to preserve Dutch neutrality, and the left wing in Lorraine was strengthened at the expense of the right in the hope that by an additional advance from Lorraine the French could be more quickly caught in a vise.

The plan was put into operation with the invasion of Belgium. Seemingly, all went well from the German viewpoint. Within three weeks the Germans swept through Belgium into France and drove on toward Paris. By the end of August the French were in full retreat, and the most advanced German units were within twenty miles of the French capital. Yet ten days later the Schlieffen Plan lay buried in shatters.

The plan's chances of success, depending on many unpredictable

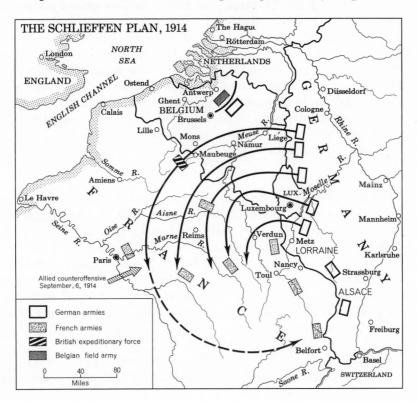

THE SCHLIEFFEN PLAN, 1914

German armies
French armies
British expeditionary force
Belgian field army

Allied counteroffensive
September, 6, 1914

0   40   80
Miles

factors, had never been great; they were reduced further by Moltke's changes which weakened the forces engaged in the sweep through Belgium and France. The German offensive, moreover, ran into unexpectedly stiff Belgian resistance and was also delayed by British forces which entered the fight earlier than had been foreseen. In addition, the advance was slowed down by the loss of two army corps which were dispatched to the aid of the German front in the east. Faulty staff work, inadequate communications, and mistakes by some field commanders created concern and confusion. The final blow was dealt to the plan by the commander of the First German Army who decided to advance east rather than west of Paris to cut off the French forces retreating before him. In doing so, he exposed his flank to a new army which General Joseph Joffre (1852–1931), the French commander-in-chief, had assembled near Paris. This army, part of which was rushed to the front in buses and taxicabs, Joffre now hurled into battle. The Battle of the Marne raged for three days from September 6 to September 9 when the Germans withdrew behind the Aisne River.

Moltke was replaced by the younger and more energetic Prussian Minister of War, General Erich von Falkenhayn (1861–1922). Falkenhayn tried to revive the Schlieffen Plan by strengthening the right wing to envelop the Allied left. The French and the British on their part sought to outflank the Germans, and each side thus spread northward toward the Channel. Regiments of half-trained German volunteers were flung into the battle only to be mowed down by Allied machine guns. Allied losses were heavy, too, and the bulk of Britain's regular army was all but wiped out in the battle of Ypres. Despite these sacrifices the fighting ended in stalemate on reaching the Channel. Deadlocked, both sides settled down to prepare their defenses; trenches were dug, drained, connected, and made habitable as far as weather and subsoil permitted. For the next four years, this was to be home to the millions of men whose interminable lines stretched across France from the Channel to Switzerland.

The Eastern Front.   In the east, the Schlieffen Plan called for delaying actions until victory had been won against France. Meanwhile, the Austrians were to engage the Russians to hamper their mobilization and relieve the pressure on the German defenses. What had not been foreseen was Russia's decision to strike before it had mobilizd fully. The Russians did so in response to a plea from the hard–pressed French. Taking the Germans by surprise, Russian troops crossed into East Prussia on August 17 and three days later defeated them in a hard-fought battle near the town of Gumbinnen.

Panic-stricken, Moltke dispatched to East Prussia one of his most capable staff officers, Major General Erich Ludendorff (1865–1937). Impulsive and headstrong (and of middle-class background), Ludendorff

Hindenburg and Ludendorff. (*U.S. Signal Corps Photo*)

could be appointed only second-in-command of the eastern forces. The top command was given to a retired elderly general, Paul von Hindenburg (1847–1934), distinguished less by his military talents than by his ability to get along with difficult aides. In his anxiety Moltke also upset the Schlieffen Plan and rushed two army corps from the west to the east. By the time they arrived, the Russian tide had already been stemmed. Ludendorff had taken advantage of the planless advance of the Russians and by a quick flanking movement had annihilated one of their armies in the three-day battle of Tannenberg. Two weeks later, in mid-September, a second Russian army that had crossed into Germany was defeated in the battle of the Masurian Lakes. The victories drove the Russians from German soil, and the terrified Germans felt so deeply relieved that they exalted Hindenburg, nominally the victorious commander, into their national hero. For the next twenty years, through good times and bad, the bulk of the nation worshipped the stolid old general with the tall massive frame as its infallible guardian angel.

The Austrians fared less well than the Germans. Like the latter, they were surprised by the speed of the Russian attack. Before they could crush the Serbs, they were forced to rush troops to the Russian front, and the campaign against the Serbs ended, to the amazement of everyone, with the expulsion of the Austrian forces from Serbia. Austrian operations against the Russians were no more successful. After some initial advances the Austrians were driven back, and the Russians advanced into Austrian Galicia. The defeat would have been catastrophic had not the Russians been poorly led and equipped. The most serious result of the setback was its effect on Austria's Slav nationalities. Never enthusiastic about the war, they now sought to escape from it, and desertions of Poles and Czechs became almost daily occurrences.

Once the Russians had been expelled from East Prussia, the Germans dispatched part of their forces to Austria's rescue. But even the redoubtable Hindenburg-Ludendorff team could not break the stubborn Russian resistance. Though short of arms, poorly clothed, and ill–fed, the Russians kept fighting, and although they had to yield ground, they brought the German advance to a halt before Warsaw in early December. It was resumed in May 1915, after reinforcements had been obtained, and over the next few months the German-Austrian forces advanced some two hundred miles on the whole front from the Baltic Sea to the Carpathians.

The War Spreads.   Although both sides expected to win the war quickly, they tried from the outset to find new allies. On Allied prodding Japan declared war against Germany in late August 1914. Its contribution to the war effort was slight, however. The Japanese assigned a few naval units to convoy duty in the Mediterranean and sent some supplies to the hard–pressed Russians. But Tokyo's main concern was to acquire the German Far Eastern possessions and to expand its influence over China while the European Powers were preoccupied in the west.

The other major power to join the Triple Entente was Italy. After coldly bargaining with both sides, Rome decided that it had more to gain from joining the Allies since its principal claims aimed at Austrian territory. In a secret treaty signed at London with France, Britain, and Russia on April 26, 1915, the Italians were promised the Trentino and Southern Tyrol, Trieste and the Istrian Peninsula, a large part of the Dalmatian coast, a share of any territory annexed from Turkey, and some compensation in Africa should Britain and France seize any of Germany's colonies. In return, Italy undertook to wage war "jointly with France, Great Britain, and Russia against all their enemies."

Italy proved little more useful than Japan as an ally. It did declare war on Austria-Hungary within a month, and anti-interventionist deputies got a foretaste of future Fascist techniques when they were terrorized into voting for war by mobs stirred up by D'Annunzio and such lesser tribunes as a young Socialist leader, Benito Mussolini (1883–1945), who had just been converted into a shrill interventionist (supposedly with the help of French money). Anxious for quick territorial gains at Austria's expense, Italy did not declare war on Germany until a year later. Its military contribution was of little significance; it was unready to wage war and was facing an enemy who controlled impregnable mountain positions. Thus some 250,000 Austrians held more than three times as many Italians at bay for two years. By August 1917 the Italians had fought their eleventh battle along the Isonzo River—the starting point of their first offensive.

The Central Powers tried equally hard to gain allies. By a treaty signed at war's outbreak, on August 2, the Turks were pledged to enter the war on Germany's side. Yet when Britain joined Russia and France and the Russians defeated the Austrians, Constantinople shied away from the final commitment. The Germans, however, would not let it stay neutral. With the help of some pro-German government members, they drove the hesitant Turks into the war in late October. A Turkish fleet, led by two German cruisers, bombarded Odessa and other of Russia's Black Sea ports, forcing the Allies to declare war against Turkey.

Once in the war, the Turks plunged headlong into a campaign against Russia's Caucasian front. They suffered a disastrous defeat, but this setback was quickly wiped out by an impressive success. A Russian request for help led the British to draw up plans for forcing the Dardanelles. Their hope was that control of the Straits would take the Turks out of the war and remove any threat to the Suez Canal and Britain's Middle Eastern possessions. It would open also a vital sea route to Russia and might bring other Balkan countries into the war on the side of the Allies. Last but not least, a victory over the Turks would help boost Britain's sagging morale.

There were strong objections to a Dardanelles campaign to which troops required in France would have to be allocated; but under the relentless prodding of the indomitable First Lord of the Admiralty, Winston Churchill (1874–1965), the plan was adopted. In mid-February 1915 the action got under way. It proved to be one of the war's worst bungled undertakings. An initial naval attack destroyed many of the outer fortifications of the Gallipoli Peninsula, but could not be followed up by a land campaign since troops were not yet available. By the time they arrived—a motley force of some British divisions, an army corps of Australians and New Zealanders (Anzac), and some French units— the Turks had rushed reinforcements to Gallipoli. The invading troops, ill organized and supplied with inaccurate maps, had barely established a precarious beachhead when their further advance was blocked by the daring and resourceful General Mustapha Kemal (1881–1938), the future dictator of Turkey. A second landing some months later was no more successful, and the campaign was abandoned. The Dardanelles victory enabled the Turks to tie down in Egypt and Mesopotamia close to 750,000 English, Dominion, and Indian forces which might have tipped the scales on the western front.

The course of the Dardanelles campaign had its immediate effect on the Bulgarians. Anxious to recoup the losses that had been inflicted on them by Serbia and Greece in the Balkan War of 1913, they joined the Central Powers when in October the latter launched another attack against Serbia. With Bulgaria's help the Serbs were quickly defeated.

Greece's course was less clearcut. King Constantine, pro-German and expecting a German victory, favored neutrality while Prime Minister Venizelos, anxious to round out Greece's territory at the expense of Bulgaria and Turkey, sympathized with the Entente Powers. Only after prolonged intrigues which involved engineering the abdication of Constantine, could Venizelos bring Greece into the war on the Allied side in 1917.

Like Greece, Rumania was out for territory, and what she coveted was held by Hungary and Bulgaria. In 1916 the time seemed propitious to seize these areas; the French had just beaten back a German attack on Verdun, the British were mounting a new offensive along the Somme River, and the Russians were routing the Austrians along the Galician front. Yet when Rumania declared war in late August 1916, the British attack had petered out, and the Russian advance had been checked by the Germans. Like the Greeks, the Rumanians contributed little to the Allied war effort beyond diverting some German forces from France. By the end of the year the Germans had overrun almost all of Rumania, including the invaluable oil wells of Ploesti.

The War of Matériel.   Throughout 1915 and 1916 both sides kept trying to end the deadlock on the French front. Yet despite all efforts, neither side was able to break through the front of the other. They failed because the military were slow to appreciate that they were fighting a war of matériel as much as of men and that in order to win it they needed new types of weapons. These weapons existed, but their importance was not understood. A proposal to build tanks to be used against the trench barrier was rejected by the French and English High Commands as wholly impractical. The Allied generals were equally skeptical of the use of machine guns although the Germans had demonstrated their value. Field Marshal Lord Kitchener, the British Secretary of War, finally allowed that their number might be increased from two to four per battalion. It was the mercurial David Lloyd George (1863–1945), newly appointed as Minister of Munitions, who grasped their significance. "Take Kitchener's maximum," Lloyd George told an associate, "square it, multiply that result by two—and when you are in sight of that, double it again for good luck." It was another civilian, Winston Churchill, who sensed the potentialities of the tank and with characteristic contempt for departmental jurisdiction allocated funds of the Admiralty for its further development. In France, War Minister Millerand, an ex-Socialist, ordered the construction of some experimental models over the objections of the military.

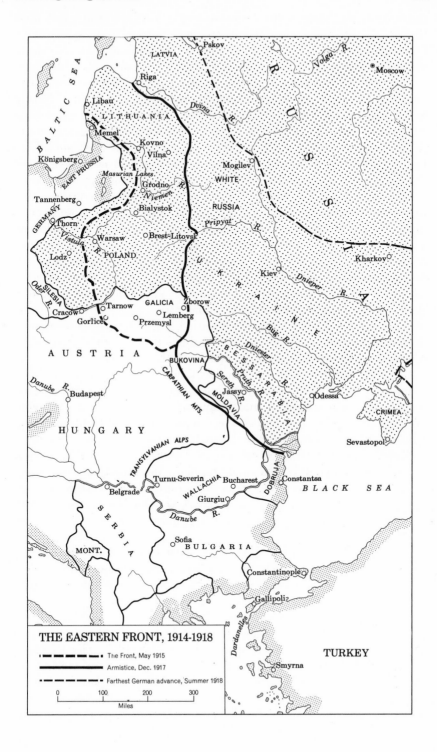

THE EASTERN FRONT, 1914-1918

- ▬ ▬ ▬ ▬ The Front, May 1915
- ▬▬▬▬▬ Armistice, Dec. 1917
- ▬ ▬ ▬ ▬ Farthest German advance, Summer 1918

0   100   200   300

Miles

The Germans were better equipped for matériel warfare and their leaders more inclined to try new techniques. But they, too, failed to take full advantage of the technical innovations that were suggested to them. When the use of gas was proposed to the High Command, it was used without scruple but with doubts of its effectiveness and was applied in insufficient amounts and with inadequate means of projection. Germany ordered tanks even later than the French and the British and never built enough. Unlike the Allied commanders, however, Falkenhayn came to realize in the course of 1915 that frontal breakthroughs were unlikely to be successful. He planned a campaign for 1916 which no longer aimed at piercing the enemy lines, but at inflicting such crushing losses upon the French (whom he considered more vulnerable than the British) that they would finally have to give in. As his objective he chose historic Verdun which he felt the French would never abandon for psychological as well as strategic reasons. By limited advances he hoped to draw them into the meat chopper of his artillery until their reserves would be exhausted and the country, bled white, would sue for peace. Verdun withstood the assaults, but this bloodiest of all battles on the western front cost each side some 300,000 casualties.

On the Russian front too fighting settled down into a war of position during the winter of 1915–16, but in the following spring movement returned to the east. A Russian attack on the Austrian lines early in June under the able General Brusilov drove the Austrian forces back some fifty miles. The defeat was due as much to the Austrians' poor morale as to poor leadership and equipment. Entire regiments fled without fighting or, if they were Poles or Czechs, went over to the Russians, who took some 250,000 prisoners. What saved the Austrians from total collapse was Brusilov's lack of adequate reinforcements and a critical shortage of ammunition and other supplies. In August German forces rushed to the help of the Austrians, and in the ensuing battles the Russians suffered close to a million casualties. By October the Brusilov offensive had turned to disaster.

The War at Sea.   At sea the war revolved almost wholly around the Allied blockade and Germany's counterblockade. German and Austrian merchantmen were quickly swept from the seas; a few naval units which the war caught away from their bases were captured or sunk. Except for some isolated forays, the German surface fleet remained bottled up in its home ports. One major battle was fought between the English and German fleets off the Jutland Peninsula in May 1916. The Germans, sinking twice as much tonnage as the British, won a tactical victory, but the British were the ultimate victors since their blockade remained unbreached.

Under the circumstances the Germans came to rely on the submarine as their main naval weapon. Unable to gauge its value before the war, they had few undersea craft at the outset. U-boat exploits in the first weeks convinced them that submarines were a highly effective weapon. In February 1915 they expanded submarine operations and gave notice that U-boats would sink any enemy merchant ship in the waters surrounding Great Britain and Ireland. Neutrals were warned to stay away from that area lest their ships be sunk by mistake. American reaction was especially bitter, and bitterness rose to fury when on May 7, 1915, the British liner *Lusitania* was sunk by a U-boat and many Americans perished. Perturbed by the growing hostility of the United States, the Germans decided to limit their submarine warfare. The campaign had not had the desired results in any event since there had not been enough boats to enforce the counterblockade (twenty-four at the outset of which only eight were at battle stations at any one time). The Allies, moreover, developed defenses which were exacting their toll—armed merchantmen, submarine nets, and the so-called Q-boats, which were freighters with concealed guns.

In the course of 1916, however, the German U-boat campaign was gaining momentum. Construction of submarines had been stepped up, and they were roaming the seas now in greater numbers. In August Allied shipping losses amounted to 126,000 tons, they rose to 150,000 tons in September, and averaged 176,000 tons for the last three months of the year. In the face of these successes the demand grew in Germany for unrestricted submarine warfare. Chancellor von Bethmann Hollweg, however, spurned the demand, fearful that an all-out U-boat campaign would draw the United States into the war on the Allied side.

Bethmann had to give up his resistance when Hindenburg and Ludendorff, after assuming command over all German forces in August 1916, joined in the clamor. The two generals had reached the conclusion that the war could no longer be won on land and that victory depended on starving Great Britain into surrender. The Admiralty assured them that the U-boats, if given a free hand, could attain this objective within five months. The danger of America's entry into the war was foreseen, but discounted on the grounds that the United States would require one or two years to build up an army, and by that time the war in Europe would long have ended. On February 1, 1917, Germany embarked on an all-out U-boat campaign.

THE HOME FRONTS

Civil-Military Relations. The unexpected course of the war confronted the belligerent countries with serious internal problems. In their first enthusiasm they had entrusted their fate to the military and had given them money and men to fight the war as they wished. Easing further the task of the soldiers, parliaments abdicated many prerogatives and granted their governments special emergency powers—martial law, censorship, and rule by decree—that all but freed the governments and the generals from legislative control. To channel all national energies into the war effort, party and class strife was shelved in political truces—France's *union sacrée,* Germany's *Burgfrieden,* Russia's "perfect union." This done, everyone settled back in expectation of early victories.

Where no such victories could be announced, inevitably a reaction set in. Losses in territory could not be hushed up, nor could casualties be fully concealed from the home front. The growing numbers of mourners, the endless hospital trains, the recurring recruiting drives told their own eloquent story. There were, moreover, alarming reports of shortages of arms and ammunition which rumor inflated beyond their tragic reality. Doubts arose as to the competence of the leaders, and within the limits of censorship and other restrictions demands were voiced for reforms and new faces. But there was no agreement as to who ought to go. The politicians blamed the defeats on the generals, and the generals blamed the politicians; the public, to the extent that it could voice any views, tended to side with the military.

France: The Joffre Phase.　France was among the first to face this problem. At the outset it had handed General Joffre almost unlimited powers. As long as the German advance swept on, the wisdom of this decision was not questioned, but once the front had been stabilized, both government and parliament decided to reassert themselves. But Joffre would not tolerate any civilian interference, and his position was virtually unassailable; despite all setbacks the portly general with the ruddy contented face remained to the nation the irreplaceable "savior of France." Verdun finally proved the General's undoing, and gave his civilian opponents their long-sought chance to remove him. Even then it took careful maneuvers before Joffre was replaced by General Robert Nivelle and the political leaders could reassert their prerogatives.

Britain: Kitchener vs. Lloyd George and Churchill.　Britain's experiences were not unlike those of France. Against all tradition a soldier, Field Marshal Lord Herbert Kitchener, was appointed Secretary of War when the war broke out. The appointment of this distinguished soldier who was something of a legend already in his lifetime was greeted with relief and approval. Kitchener's achievements were great; within less than a year he raised and trained a new army of over a million men. Yet he was as unwilling as Joffre to have civilian advice even in technical matters of supply and production. Unlike Joffre, however, he was confronted with ministers whose restless energies could not be ignored. Lloyd George, investigating the arms production which he was financing as Chancellor of the Exchequer, saw very quickly that it was antiquated and inefficient. He kept urging changes, and when Prime Minister Asquith converted his Liberal government into a National Coalition of Liberals, Conservatives, and one lone Laborite during the ill-fated Dardanelles campaign, Lloyd George was put in charge of a newly created Ministry of Munitions. With the help of Britain's top production and management experts and endowed with dictatorial powers over British industry, the indefatigable Lloyd George expanded arms output with remarkable speed. Supplemented by vast purchases in the United States, it grew sufficiently within less than a year to meet the army's voracious needs.

Lloyd George's cabinet colleague, Winston Churchill, restless, intuitive, bursting with plans and ideas, was another civilian unwilling to defer to the military in all matters concerning the war. Churchill was appalled at the casualty lists that resulted from the futile attempts to break through the German lines. "I think it quite possible," he wrote as early as December 1914, "that neither side will have the strength to penetrate the other's lines in the Western theater. . . . My impression is that the position of both armies is not likely to undergo any decisive change—although no doubt several hundred thousand men will be spent to satisfy the military mind on the point." He proposed to engage the enemy on some other front that was less well defended. The Dardanelles campaign followed, but since it was undertaken by inadequate forces, it failed, and the attempts to break through the German front were continued.

Public opinion tended to blame the politicians for whatever went wrong. Faith in Kitchener and the other military leaders was not easily shaken; Churchill, moreover, assumed full responsibility for the Dardanelles disaster and resigned from the government. Thus Kitchener stayed on in the War Office though many who worked with him questioned his ability to grasp the exigencies of matériel warfare.

The conflict between government and military continued after his death in May 1916. Lloyd George took his place as Secretary of War. The new minister found himself quickly at odds with Sir William Robertson, chief of the Imperial General Staff, who insisted on keeping the war effort focused on the French front. The ensuing dispute led to the resignation of Asquith's government in December 1916. Lloyd George was appointed Prime Minister as the man best equipped to win the war. He formed another all-party cabinet and happily plunged into his new responsibilities, only to discover that as Prime Minister he still had to acquiesce in campaigns which, as he put it, would repeat "the bloody stupidities of 1915 and 1916."

Germany: Victory of the Generals. In Germany the military had always been in a strong position since they enjoyed complete independence from government and parliament and were responsible only to the Kaiser. Their standing was greatly enhanced by the victories in both east and west in 1914. Nor did the subsequent western stalemate impair their prestige, for it was overshadowed by the successes in the Balkans and Russia, by the exploits of the U-boats, and last but not least by the fact that everywhere German troops stood deep in enemy territory.

Under these circumstances the government's position was weak from the outset. The supremacy of the military over the government was sealed when the immensely popular Hindenburg-Ludendorff team replaced Falkenhayn as co-chiefs of staff after the failure of the Verdun offensive. From their new post the two men dictated major policies and drafted laws that they wished enacted. They overruled Bethmann Hollweg on social and political questions and on the issue of unrestricted submarine warfare. More than once they overrode also the Emperor's wishes; but if they were guilty of insubordination towards their Supreme War Lord, no one dared to take them to task for their disobedience. In July 1917 they forced the monarch to dismiss Bethmann Hollweg whom they thought too conciliatory towards the left. Ludendorff himself handpicked the new Chancellor, an innocuous Prussian official, Georg Michaelis.

Austria-Hungary and Italy: Civil-Military Truce.   Austria-Hungary and Italy were less troubled by conflicts between civil and military authority. In the former a virtual military dictatorship was established which was not challenged until after the death of old Emperor Francis Joseph I in November 1916. When his successor, Charles I, subordinated the military to the political leadership, the soldiers were too discredited to resist the move. Italy was the one country in which military and government coexisted without major friction. Rome's main political problem was the existence of a substantial antiwar party, and both army and government had to devote much time and effort to problems created by the disaffected and the defeatists.

Russia: The Fight of the Duma.   In Russia tension between military and government was kept within bounds. Large parts of western Russia were administered by the army as "military zones," and this area was extended eastward as the Russian forces retreated. Civil authorities, overwhelmed by problems for which they were ill-prepared, were not unhappy to be relieved of part of their responsibilities. The military also suffered from lethargy and indifference. Though handicapped by shortages of arms and ammunition, they were content with warnings and pleas, but made no effort to take over the supply system. Tsar Nicholas II (1868–1918) on his part was too weak-willed and apathetic to intervene.

Demands for changes came from the Russian parliament, the Duma. With the exception of some of the Socialists, the Duma had pledged its support to the Tsar at the outbreak of the war. But the deputies' enthusiasm turned to anxiety as they watched the bureaucracy wrestling helplessly with its problems. Others, too, worried about its incompetence, and a multitude of volunteer organizations sprang up to engage in relief work and a host of related activities which should have been the concern of the government.

When the Duma met again in February 1915, the deputies' criticisms roused the Tsar into action. Nicholas replaced the most reactionary and incompetent cabinet members with younger, more capable men and agreed to the creation of special councils consisting of officials, businessmen, and parliamentarians to supervise the manufacture of ammunition, the supply of fuel and food, the care of refugees, the administration of transport and defense. Sparked by fresh blood, the councils achieved some improvements, especially in the area of arms production.

The victory of the Duma proved to be short-lived. In August 1915 Nicholas took over the post of Commander-in-Chief in the field in the hope of improving the army's morale. When he left for the front, the Tsarina became the virtual ruler of Russia. A religious mystic convinced of the divine nature of the Tsarist regime, she followed blindly the advice of her spiritual and political mentor, Gregory Rasputin (1871?–1916). This illiterate and debauched lay monk who was endowed with a kind of animal magnetism had gained her confidence when he had applied his curative powers to her ailing son, the Tsarevich. The Tsarina looked upon Rasputin as a "holy man" sent her by God; when she took over the government after the Tsar's departure, Rasputin became her closest adviser.

Rasputin had a shrewd peasant's common sense, but he was corrupt, vindictive, and dissipated. He arranged government contracts for bribes; he sold confidential information; he drove from office men he disliked and replaced them with unqualified favorites. His continuous interference in governmental affairs disrupted and demoralized the bureaucracy and deprived it of what little initiative it still had. In 1916 food and fuel shortages assumed catastrophic proportions, and in parts of the country the transport system all but broke down. The restiveness of the nation exploded into strikes and bread riots in the cities and manifested itself in sullen non–cooperation in rural areas. The Duma demanded the removal of Rasputin and the formation of a government that enjoyed the confidence of the country. But the Tsar, bowing to the will of his wife, refused to remove Rasputin from the imperial entourage or to appoint a new government. Unrest increased; cries of "Down with the war, down with autocracy" could be heard everywhere. Revolution was in the air, one diplomatic observer noted, and the only question was whether it would come from above or below.

For a moment it seemed that it might come from above. Hoping to stop the drift towards revolution, a group of aristocrats assassinated Rasputin. There was talk of replacing the Tsar with a military dictator; but no one was ready to act. Nor were Tsar and Tsarina. Rather than make any changes, they insisted on governing the country in Rasputin's spirit. Their sole confidant, Minister of the Interior Protopopov, was rumored to commune with Rasputin in daily seances. Insensitive to the signs of approaching trouble, the Tsar contented himself with proroguing the Duma.

War Economics. The demands of matériel warfare compelled the belligerents to pay increasing attention to their economic resources. As months lengthened into years, problems of supply and production became more pressing and complex; government controls were extended to make certain that the dwindling resources of manpower, raw materials, foodstuffs, and transportation were allocated in accordance with a carefully worked out system of priorities.

The Germans were the first to put their economy on a war footing. Germany was no better prepared economically for the war than the Allies although, landlocked and surrounded by potential enemies, it was far more vulnerable. A few individuals, however, were quick to grasp the impact on Germany of the British blockade. The most important of these was Walther Rathenau (1867–1922), board chairman of Germany's General Electric Company and a widely traveled and knowledgeable student of world affairs. Rathenau had been one of the few men to foresee at the outset that the war would be long and difficult. In Falkenhayn, the Prussian War Minister, he found a soldier who shared these fears. The General put him in charge of a newly established department in his ministry which assumed control over the procurement and allocation of all strategic materials. Rathenau also initiated the manufacture of substitute materials to replace those in short supply; among the first ersatz products developed under his auspices were synthetic nitrate and cellulose, both indispensable for making explosives. Later, rayon, plastics, and synthetic rubber were also produced. Strict import and export controls were established; food, clothing, and other consumer goods were rationed; and prices were controlled. As shortages became more stringent, two meatless days were decreed, potatoes and turnips were admixed to bread flour, coffee was made from acorns, wooden soles replaced leather ones, and homes were heated with peat. Under a National Service Act the allocation of labor was assigned to the War Ministry to meet more efficiently the manpower needs of armed forces and industry. Gradually, almost the entire economy was subjected to governmental direction. Whatever the hardships such planning inflicted, it enabled the country to withstand the British blockade for four years.

The Allied nations also assigned to their governments increasing authority over their economic resources. The British government assumed at once control over all transportation both on land and at sea. In March 1915 Parliament empowered it also to take over factories for the manufacture of war materials, sequester housing facilities for workers, and cancel contracts that pre-empted needed production facilities. As Minister of Munitions Lloyd George obtained dictatorial powers over the economy, including the allocation of manpower, compulsory arbitration of labor disputes, and eventually, food rationing. Similarly France and Russia imposed government controls on their economies, but Russia's were gradually worn away by the inefficiency, corruption, and demoralization of the bureaucracy and the breakdown of the transport system. While the other belligerents could always ensure the supply of the basic necessities, Russia's armed forces were almost continuously underfed and underequipped, and after 1915 large parts of the urban population also were near starvation.

Peace Moves. As the war wore on, year after year, enthusiasm gave way to resignation, and resignation turned to war weariness. The food, clothing, and fuel shortage, rising prices, and wartime restrictions weighed most heavily on the members of the working classes, who were unable to ease their lot by patronizing the flourishing black markets. Not unnaturally these groups, reverting to their prewar pacifism and internationalism, were among the first to call for an early peace. By 1917 that demand had considerable support in most belligerent countries, and Socialist conferences in Switzerland and in Stockholm attempted to coordinate these efforts on an international plane.

The call for peace was less widespread in Britain where relatively few wished to end the fighting by negotiations. It had greater support in France and in Germany. In France the Socialist Party and some of the Radicals, appalled at the bloodshed and its futility, wished the war ended on the best possible terms. In Germany too the quest for peace issued from Socialists, who saw that the war was no longer fought in defense of their country, but for territorial and economic gains. The demand was taken up by the liberal bourgeoisie once the latter had doubts that Germany could win the war. Both groups joined forces in July 1917 and passed a resolution in the Reichstag in support of a negotiated non-annexationist peace settlement. In Russia the call for peace gathered strength as the nation sensed that the war was lost irretrievably and that the hardships and deprivations to which the country was being subjected could not serve any useful purpose. In Italy the Socialists opposed the war from the outset.

Yet the governments and the groups from which they derived their support were firm in their determination to fight through to victory. None of them fought the war any longer for purely defensive purposes; they all had their economic and territorial objectives, although most of them kept these aims secret. The French leaders wished to recover Alsace-Lorraine and to acquire the Saar territory and the Rhineland, and they and the English also planned to divide up between them Turkey's Arabian possessions. The Italian government had its eyes on

Austrian territories, the Russian cabinet demanded Constantinople and the Straits, and the German leadership planned to take over, directly or indirectly, Belgium and northeastern France in the west and Russia's Baltic provinces and the Ukraine in the east. These goals could be realized only through the defeat of the enemy. The French and the British, moreover, felt certain that Germany could be eliminated as a military threat only by the complete destruction of its armed forces. The German leaders on their part wished to keep fighting lest a negotiated peace, without annexations, lead to a weakening of the country's social and political structure and to democratic domestic reforms. Thus, whatever peace proposals were made by one side were unacceptable to the other and were advanced mainly to convince public opinion at home and abroad of the intransigence of the enemy camp. For the same reason the peace moves attempted by neutrals, President Woodrow Wilson and Pope Benedict XV, ended in failure.

The one government genuinely anxious to obtain peace was Austria-Hungary. By the end of 1916 Emperor Charles and his advisers were aware that both army and people had reached the limit of their endurance. Through relatives of his wife, a Bourbon princess, the Emperor established secret contacts with the French government, but the negotiations came to an end when Italy refused to modify its claims on Austrian territory.

THE RUSSIAN REVOLUTIONS

Collapse of the Tsarist Regime.   The long-expected Russian revolution broke out in the capital, Petrograd (present-day Leningrad), on March 8, 1917.[1] It grew out of a series of strikes and bread riots which had kept the city in constant turmoil. Troops called out to suppress the unrest refused to fire on the crowds and joined the rioting masses. The Tsar, in his customary apathy, remained unconcerned. "I order that the unrest in the capital . . . be liquidated by tomorrow," he wired to the hapless city commander. Unable to grasp the gravity of the crisis, he would not send reinforcements nor would he return to the capital. When finally he dispatched a small force to put down the riots, its advance was blocked by the revolutionaries. By then even the most devout monarchists were convinced that Nicholas' position was untenable, and the military leaders too favored his abdication. Informed of the generals' attitude, the Tsar bowed to the Duma's request and abdicated in favor of Grand Duke Michael, his younger brother. But Michael was aware of the strong anti-

---

[1] According to the Russian calendar then in use, the revolution began on February 23, 1917, and the Russians speak of it as the February Revolution. Correspondingly, the Bolshevik Revolution, according to the Russian calendar, broke out on October 25, 1917, and is known as the October Revolution in Soviet Russia. In January 1918 Russia adopted the Western calendar.

monarchist sentiment in the capital and would not accept the crown until it were offered to him by a constituent assembly. The throne thus stayed vacant, and the monarchy came right then to an end, though formally it was not abolished until September.

The Provisional Government and the Petrograd Soviet. The Duma had meanwhile set up a committee to which it entrusted the task of restoring order. Its authority was not unchallenged, however. Socialist deputies, workers' spokesmen, and delegates of the soldiers in the capital had formed their own council (soviet) to give voice to the demands of the masses. Though backed by the Petrograd crowds, the soviet did not feel ready to take over the government, but preferred to play the role of the watchdog guarding the rights of the workers and soldiers.

With the soviet's consent the Duma set up a provisional government to guide the country until a constituent assembly had decided on a permanent system of government. The new government was headed by a moderate conservative, Prince George Lvov, and a liberal, the historian Paul Milyukov, became Foreign Minister. With one exception all other ministers, were liberals or conservatives. The exception was a young lawyer named Alexander Kerensky (1881–   ), a vice-president of the Petrograd soviet, who took the Justice portfolio. A leader of the moderate wing of the Socialist Revolutionary Party, which wanted all land turned over to peasants' communes. Kerensky was to serve as a liaison man between soviet and government.

The new government was never able to govern Russia in the accepted sense of the word. In few places did its authority extend to the local level; in most cities soviets sprang up on the Petrograd model, and in time they were formed in small towns and rural areas as well. The soviets were in much closer touch with the masses than the government, and their control over local garrisons, public utilities, railways, and postal services gave them a great deal of power. The government, moreover, did not wish to exercise any powers beyond those required to attend to the most pressing tasks since major reforms were to await the decision of the constituent assembly. It did, however, proclaim full freedom of speech, press, and assembly; abolished religious, ethnic, and social discrimination; amnestied all political, religious, and military prisoners; and introduced universal and equal suffrage. Under pressure from the Petrograd soviet it also enacted such social reforms as the eight-hour work day. But it would not withdraw from the war or initiate land reforms, thus shying away from those very measures that were closest to the heart of the war-weary, land-hungry masses. Soldiers and peasants soon felt disappointed in the Provisional Government, and the suspicion gained ground that the continuation of the war and the retention of the existing system of land ownership suited best the interests of the industrial and landowning groups represented in the Lvov ministry.

The authority of the government was also impaired by the fact that it never gained control of the army. One of the first moves of the Petrograd soviet was to order the formation of soldiers' committees to be attached to all military units in the capital. In all political matters the soviet and the committees claimed full jurisdiction; orders of the government were to be obeyed only if they did not conflict with theirs. They also assigned control of all arms to the committees—a move that all but destroyed the authority of the officers. Other soviets followed Petrograd's lead, thus hastening the disintegration of the armed forces.

In April soviets and government clashed over the question of pursuing the war. The Petrograd soviet objected to statements of Milyukov who wished to fight on in the hope of securing control of the Dardanelles after Turkey's defeat. Lvov was compelled to dismiss Milyukov, and the Minister of War, Alexander Guchkov. To obtain the soviet's support, five additional Socialists were appointed to cabinet posts, and Kerensky took Guchkov's place in the hope that his oratorical talents could revive the morale of the soldiers.

The Emergence of Lenin.   Among the political exiles who came back to Russia when the amnesty had been proclaimed was Vladimir Iljich Uljanov (1870–1924), better known under his cover name Lenin. The son of a superintendent of schools, Lenin had forsaken the security of a bourgeois home and career when an elder brother was executed for his part in a plot to assassinate Tsar Alexander III. This traumatic experience led him to dedicate himself to the radical overhaul of Russia's state and society. He joined the Marxist movement as a student. Endowed with a brilliant mind, self-confidence, and great forcefulness, he soon achieved prominence in St. Petersburg's revolutionary circles. Lenin was exiled to Siberia in the late 1890's, and after his release lived abroad, except for a few months during the Revolution of 1905. His main concern in his exile was to develop an effective revolutionary technique and organization. Marx had had little to say on such matters: he had been satisfied in his belief that as industrialization progressed under bourgeois auspices, the means of production—the factories, banks, mines, and land—would be concentrated in fewer and fewer hands and at the same time the ranks of the proletariat would be swelled by the growth of the working class and the influx of those middle-class members who had been deprived of their livelihood by this process of concentration. In the end, when exploitation and misery had become unendurable, the proletariat, properly organized, would turn on the bourgeoisie and, vastly superior in numbers, overthrow it without much difficulty.

Lenin had no such confidence. He believed that the masses required strong leadership lest they sell their revolutionary birthright for a pottage of economic reforms. Nor did he consider it likely that a revolutionary mass movement could easily be organized under the Tsarist autocracy. The task of preparing the way would have to be entrusted to leaders "engaged in revolution as a profession," ready to dedicate themselves wholly and unreservedly to that cause. In a pamphlet, *What Is to Be Done?* (1902), he outlined the kind of party organization that would be required under Russian conditions: it would have to be based on strictest secrecy and tight discipline, select its members with great care, and train them in the "art of combating the political police."

A year later, at a congress of the Russian Social Democratic Labor Party, Lenin sought to incorporate in the party statute his concept of the party as a specially selected and highly disciplined elite. His proposal was defeated after a heated debate and led to the division of the party into a Lenin-led "Bolshevik" wing ("bolshevik" meaning majority man, for at the end of the congress, because of walkouts, the Lenin faction had a majority), and a minority, "Menshevik," wing headed by one of Lenin's earliest associates, Julius Martov, who wished to establish a mass party.

The split between Bolsheviks and Mensheviks was deepened by disagreements on substantive issues. The Mensheviks felt that after the overthrow of the Tsarist regime Russia would have to go through a bourgeois phase of industrialization before it would be "ripe" for a socialist revolution of the proletariat. Lenin, on the other hand, was convinced that the Russian bourgeoisie was too weak to overthrow Tsarism by itself. It would need the help of the workers and peasants, and the latter could and should therefore move on to the socialist revolution as soon as the bourgeois-democratic revolution had been achieved. The overthrow of Tsarism, moreover, would "set fire" to Europe and rouse Europe's workers, and these, after having rid themselves of their own bourgeoisie, would come to the help of their Russian brethren.

Lenin arrived in mid-April 1917 from Switzerland where he had been spending the war years. Since the first day of the war he had assailed the conflict as an "imperialist adventure" and had called on all soldiers to lay down their arms. Because of his antiwar stand Britain and France had tried to prevent his return to Russia; the Germans, however, had let him go back via Germany in the hope that this antiwar agitation would hasten the collapse of the Russian army.

From the moment of his arrival Lenin attacked the Provisional Government. Being a bourgeois capitalist government, he argued, it could not help being imperialist and continue the fight; peace could be attained only by the soviets. Mensheviks and Socialist Revolutionaries were subject to bourgeois influences and willing to tolerate the government; therefore, the Bolsheviks would have to gain control of the soviets to usher in the socialist phase of the revolution and bring peace and reforms to Russia. At first few took Lenin seriously, but his forceful insistent arguments quickly converted most Bolshevik leaders to his position. It became increasingly clear, moreover, that he had gauged better than they the country's true temper. The declining morale of the workers expressed

Street battle in Petrograd, July 1917. (*Reprinted courtesy Brown Brothers*)

itself in the growing number of strikes; the peasants, in turn, impatient of the postponement of land reform, began to seize land on their own. Above all, the government's determination to stay in the war met with increasing opposition. In early May a Bolshevik party conference adopted Lenin's position—at the very moment at which several Mensheviks and Socialist Revolutionaries joined the Provisional Government and by accepting such key portfolios as War and Agriculture, became identified with those policies which the masses found most objectionable.

The July Crisis and the Kornilov Coup. The Bolshevik stand met with growing approval. Bolshevik candidates were winning most by-elections to city soviets. By June the Bolsheviks were the largest group in the Moscow soviet, and they had a majority among the workers' deputies in the Petrograd soviet. When later that month an all-Russian congress of soviets organized a street demonstration, most of the placards carried Bolshevik slogans.

Early in July, at the government's and the Allies' prodding, Brusilov launched another attack on the Germans. It ended quickly in a disastrous rout of his forces. The campaign touched off a rising in Petrograd— against the advice of the Bolshevik leaders, who opposed it as premature. Prince Lvov and his conservative colleagues resigned, and Kerensky became Premier of a liberal-socialist coalition. With the help of some loyal troops he arrested the Bolshevik leaders, except for Lenin, who escaped to Finland. Among those caught in the dragnet was Leon Trotsky (1879–1940), next to Lenin the most prominent Marxist, who had just taken his following into the Bolshevik Party.

Hardly had Kerensky dealt with the Bolsheviks when he was threatened by a coup from the right led by the commander-in-chief of the army, General Kornilov. Determined to end the growing disorder, Kornilov planned to abolish the Petrograd soviet, hang the Bolshevik leaders, and establish a military dictatorship. But his march on the capital collapsed before it reached Petrograd. Kornilov and some of his fellow generals were arrested by pro-government forces.

The government's victory was short-lived. Food and other shortages had reached catastrophic proportions. The dissatisfied masses were getting more restless. Land seizures by the peasants increased; strikes grew more violent; in some cases workers' committees took over plants. Under the slogan, "All power to the soviets," the Bolsheviks kept gaining ground. Reports of growing unrest in other belligerent countries suggested that they, too, were moving toward socialist revolutions. In mid-September Lenin decided that the time had come to seize power by armed insurrection.

The Bolshevik Revolution. Early in October he slipped back into Petrograd to rally his associates. The party's central committee expressed its support on October 23 by a vote of 10 to 2, the two opponents, Leo Kamenev and Gregory Zinoviev, rejecting the plan as precipitate. Preparations could be made almost openly since the Petrograd soviet in which the Bolsheviks now had a majority had decided to take over the defense of the capital against the approaching Germans. Trotsky, released from jail, was elected President of the soviet and under the guise of his new authority organized shock troops of workers known as "Red Guards." The date of the rising was set for the opening day of a new nation-wide congress of soviets to convene in Petrograd in early November.

Kerensky knew of the Bolsheviks' plans, but in the three months since he had assumed the premiership he had stumbled from crisis to crisis and was almost paralyzed from exhaustion. To halt the revolutionary tide, he had set a date in late November for the long-delayed elections to the constituent assembly, and pending its formation had established a Council of the Republic to formulate policies. But unable to find loyal troops, he could do little else. When finally he tried to take action on November 6, a day before the Bolshevik rising, his attempt to close down the Bolshevik press was blocked by a detachment of Red Guards. The following morning he left for the front, but there he found only a few hundred men prepared to support him, and these were no match for the Bolsheviks.

That same day, November 7, the Bolsheviks struck. They seized bridges, railroad stations, postal and telegraph offices, and other key points in the capital. There was virtually no resistance. By evening Petrograd was in their hands, and at the opening session of the Second All-Russian Congress of Soviet Lenin could proudly announce, "We shall now proceed to construct the socialist order." An all-Bolshevik government, called Council of People's Commissars, was set up. Lenin became its chairman and Trotsky its Commissar of Foreign Affairs. Joseph Stalin (1879–1953), still one of the lesser leaders, was appointed Commissar of Nationalities.

Although the Bolsheviks seized power almost without bloodshed in Petrograd, Moscow fell to them only after a week's fighting. In most other cities the Bolsheviks took control without difficulty, but in small towns and rural areas their hold was precarious, and many of the outlying regions refused altogether to accept their authority.

In compliance with the party's promise, Lenin addressed himself at once to the question of peace and land. At the meeting of the Congress of Soviets he proposed and the Congress accepted a Declaration on Peace and a Decree on Land. The latter will be discussed in its proper context (see p. 167); only the Declaration on Peace pertains to this chapter concerned with the course of the war. It called on all belligerent peoples to start negotiations at once for a "just and democratic peace," based on the principle of national self-determination, without conquests and annexations. A special appeal was made to the workers of the major European powers; as Lenin explained, "this proposal will meet with resistance on the part of the imperialist governments. . . . But we hope that revolution will soon break out in all the belligerent countries; that is why we address ourselves especially to the workers of France, England, and Germany."

On December 3 the new government signed an armistice with the Central Powers, and after resorting unsuccessfully to delaying tactics (in the hope that the revolution would spread to Berlin and Vienna), it accepted the German peace terms. The peace treaty of Brest-Litovsk, concluded on March 3, 1918, deprived Russia of its Baltic provinces and the Ukraine, which became nominally independent, and of some Caucasian borderlands that were given to Turkey. In economic terms the surrender of these territories meant the loss of one-third of Russia's arable lands, one-fourth of its railroads, three-fourths of its iron and coal mines, and over one-third of its factories. Harsh though the treaty was, Russia could not reject it. Above all else, the country needed a respite and had to withdraw from the war.

3

World War I:

The Atlantic Phase

Until the entry of the United States into the war, the conflict was essentially a European one. Most non-Europeans—Canadians and Australians, Indians and Senegalese—fought in it under the leadership of one or the other of the European powers; military action outside of Europe, in Asia and Africa, was of minor significance, and so was the role of non-European countries like Japan which had come into the war on their own initiative. Only with America's entry did the conflict outgrow its European confines.

America's participation meant more than a mere quantitative expansion of the war. It soon became evident that but for that participation the European state system might not survive. Military developments in 1917 indicated that Europe was no longer strong enough to defeat by itself the challenge of Germany to this system—a fact brought home still more forcefully by Russia's withdrawal from the war. At the same time the developments leading up to America's entry into the war make it clear that the United States, whether it wished to or not, was closely involved in the European conflict. Thus its part in helping restore the European order was dictated by its own national interests and was not merely inspired by a sense of mission to make the world "safe for democracy." **37**

THE UNITED STATES ENTERS THE WAR

British Blockade and Submarine Warfare.   When the war broke out, few Americans felt any sense of direct concern. The great majority thought themselves shielded from Europe by the Atlantic, and this supposedly impregnable barrier gave them a sense of security which the European crisis could not affect. Nor did the European belligerents hope for America's participation in the war; neither the Allied nor the Central Powers evinced any interest in seeing the United States enter the war on their side. On both sides of the Atlantic there was general agreement that the United States ought to stay neutral.

Yet almost from the very beginning American neutrality proved difficult to maintain. The Allies resorted at once to a naval blockade of the Central Powers, and the blockade inevitably infringed on American trade. However the United States reacted to Britain's blockade operations, its stand would help one side at the expense of the other. Rigid insistence on the trading rights of a neutral power would aid the Germans, acquiescence in a broad interpretation of Britain's enforcement of its blockade would help the Allies. The United States chose the latter alternative—a decision somewhat facilitated by Britain's policy of tightening the blockade only gradually and with due regard to American public opinion and property rights (in doubtful cases the British indemnified owners for the seizure of cargoes or ships).

Inevitably Germany decided to fight the British blockade with a counterblockade to cut off Allied imports of needed supplies. Early in February 1915 the Germans announced that they might inadvertently sink neutral ships within a specified zone around Great Britain and Ireland. This time the American reaction was much sharper, and the German government was warned that it would be held to "strict accountability" for any destruction of American lives and ships due to submarine action. When a U-boat torpedoed the *Lusitania,* causing the death of 128 Americans, President Wilson warned that a recurrence of such ruthless action would be regarded as "deliberately unfriendly" by the United States. The matter was temporarily settled when the Germans promised not to sink any passenger ships without warning and due regard for the safety of passengers and crew.

The Dilemma of American Neutrality.   Wilson's ambivalent course reflected anew the difficulties which beset America's policy. On the one hand, the President wished to protect American rights on the high seas; on the other, he did not want to become embroiled in the war. Yet these two aims were basically incompatible. The definition and enforcement of America's rights as a neutral, it was seen, did have a direct effect on the war, favoring one side and injuring the other and thus risking the danger of retaliatory action. As it was, Wilson's insistence that the U-boats observe the traditional rules of war favored the British against the Germans. Drawn up for nineteenth century cruiser warfare, these rules could scarcely be applied to the submarine. The latter risked sinking by gunfire or ramming, or capture by enemy warships or even armed merchantmen if it did not at once torpedo its prey but instead surfaced and waited until passengers and crew had debarked. It could also be argued that Americans ought not to travel on belligerent ships, or that the loss of American lives and property in the sinking of such a vessel could not be considered an intentional infringement of American rights, but was the incidental result of an attack on a non-American ship.

Wilson rejected these arguments because the ultimate issue was, in his view, moral rather than legal. Allied interference with American shipping might affect property which could be paid for; U-boat warfare, however, killed human lives for which there could be no compensation. "The Government of the United States," he asserted, "is contending for something much greater than mere rights of property or privileges of commerce. It is contending for nothing less high and sacred than the rights of humanity." By thus raising his judgments onto a higher plane, Wilson was able to resolve the contradictions of his neutrality policy. At the same time this policy of morality expressed best the sentiments of most of his countrymen. Shocked by the invasion of Belgium, the execution of women, the submarine sinkings, Americans were deeply resentful of Germany's tactics—the more so because the Germans were much less adroit than the British in presenting their case to the American public.

While moral revulsion overshadowed all other aspects of the American position, material considerations did nonetheless play a decisive role in evolving this stand. The interpretation which Wilson gave to American rights was dictated also by the cold fact that British sea power controlled the ocean lanes and the United States thus could trade only with the Allies. To limit this trade would have hurt the American economy just after Allied orders had produced a remarkable business revival. Trade with the Allies quadrupled from $824 million in 1914 to $3,214 million in 1916 (whereas trade with Germany and Austria dropped from $169 million to $1 million during that same period). Wheat exports rose from $39 million in 1913 to $300 million in 1917, munition exports from $5 million to $803 million. Buttressed by American loans, the lion's share of steel, cotton, and food exports went to the Allies. The continued prosperity of the American economy thus came to be geared increasingly to the success of the Allied war effort.

Since moral imperatives and economic interests dictated the same course of action, the country never faced clearly the fact of its growing material involvement in the war and, correspondingly, its increasingly unneutral attitude. Similarly the nation paid little attention to the possible impact of a German victory on its security, even though German-

American relations had been frequently troubled in prewar years and there was evidence in 1915 and 1916 that Germany was attempting to provoke a conflict between the United States and Mexico. As time went by, a growing number of individual Americans came to feel that a German victory, implying the domination of Europe by an unfriendly power, could constitute a threat to the security of the United States; among them were Wilson's two most important advisers, Colonel Edward M. House, the President's confidant, and Robert Lansing, the Secretary of State. To the bulk of the nation, however, balance-of-power considerations remained very remote. Moreover, Wilson himself was convinced that a policy of morality was also more realistic than any other. He was aware that America's future would be directly affected no matter who won, and from this fact he concluded that its interests could best be safeguarded, not by the victory of one or the other of the belligerents, but by his insistence on the preservation of international law and morality.

Wilson's Efforts at Mediation.   Since war destroys law and morality, Wilson was anxious to help end the fighting in Europe as quickly as possible. Were it fought to the finish, he feared, the victors would demand punitive peace terms that would breed new hatred and discontent. He proffered his good offices as a mediator as soon as the war broke out, but both sides were resolved to fight the war through to victory and rejected his offer.

The determination of both camps to defeat the other greatly concerned Colonel House. While he considered an Allied defeat a serious misfortune from America's viewpoint, he did not wish to see Germany shorn of all power lest this leave Europe at the mercy of Russia. In the summer of 1915 he devised a plan by which the United States and the Allies would work out terms for a reasonable peace settlement which would then be presented to the Central Powers. With Wilson's consent House sounded out Sir Edward Grey. Grey was interested, but he wanted more than American participation in peacemaking. The course of the war had convinced him that Europe no longer was able to fight off by itself all assaults on its equilibrium, and he wished to have an American pledge of support against future aggression. If Britain agreed to House's proposal, he inquired, would the United States help protect Europe's peace in the future and join a "league of nations" that would uphold law and order? Wilson accepted the idea of such a league; but while Grey viewed the league as a means of committing America permanently to the preservation of peace in Europe, the President hoped, by accepting it, to keep the United States from becoming involved in Europe. Nothing came of these negotiations, for when House called on Grey early in 1916, he found the Foreign Secretary opposed to peace talks. All the Colonel achieved was a vague agreement with Grey that when France and Great Britain considered the time opportune, Wilson would propose the calling of a peace conference. Should Germany cause difficulties, either by refusing to attend or by asking for unreasonable peace terms, the United States would "probably" enter the war on the side of the Allies.

Yet no matter how much the United States wished to dissociate itself from the conflict, it was drawn ever deeper into it. In the course of 1915 the British tightened their blockade (over muted American protests, which were toned down even further when the British bought most of the cotton that would normally have gone to the Central Powers). In an effort to intensify its counterblockade, the German government announced in mid–February 1916 that it would sink armed merchantmen without warning. Soon afterwards an unarmed Channel steamer, *Sussex*, was sunk without warning with several Americans among the victims. Wilson threatened to break off relations with Berlin unless Germany abandoned at once the attacks without warning on merchantmen both armed and unarmed. Berlin submitted to this request, but warned him it would not feel bound by this pledge if Britain continued its illegal practices.

If Wilson refrained from breaking off diplomatic relations at once, he was guided in part by the nation's as well as his own aversion to war. But he feared also that once this country became a belligerent, it would be unable to help bring about that just and enduring peace which alone could ensure the world's and America's well-being. In May 1916 the President outlined in a public address the kind of peace to which he aspired. It would be based on the principles of national sovereignty and self-determination and on guarantees against future aggression to be enforced by a "universal association of nations." To the nation Wilson explained that more was at stake in the war than the lives, the liberties, and property of individual citizens: "We are participants, whether we would or not, in the life of the world. The interests of all nations are our own also. We are partners with the rest. What affects mankind is inevitably our affair as well as the affair of the nations of Europe and of Asia." But trying to impress upon his American audience the loftiness of his aspirations, he also said of the war, rather cavalierly, "With its causes and its objects we are not concerned," thus confusing his own people and infuriating the Allies.

Not surprisingly the speech was coolly received in both Paris and London. Neither capital was willing to negotiate with the Germans—the less so because both expected the Germans to resort sooner or later to unrestricted U-boat warfare. The United States would then be forced into the war on their side, making an Allied victory possible. Even if Britain and France had been prepared to follow up Wilson's proposal, what guarantees did they have that the United States would help to enforce the peace settlement that Wilson was advocating? The course of the Presidential campaign of 1916, with its emphasis on America's dissociation from the conflict, could but reinforce these doubts.

By the time he was re-elected Wilson faced a situation that was rapidly worsening. The British had further tightened their blockade rules: unless they desisted from these practices, the Germans were bound to step up their U-boat campaign. Once more Wilson offered himself as a mediator, but again he failed. The Allied answer, though conciliatory, was non-committal, while the Germans rejected the offer outright. Confident that they could win the war if they resorted to unrestricted submarine warfare, they notified Wilson on January 31, 1917 that on the following day they would launch a U-boat campaign against all shipping, both neutral and enemy, within a specified zone around Britain, France, Italy, and the eastern Mediterranean.

Towards War.   After the warning contained in the *Sussex* note, Wilson had no choice but to break off diplomatic relations with Germany. Any lesser move, he was certain, would gravely impair America's standing, and if the United States lost the respect of the world, it would have no say in the settlement of the war. In late February the President learned that the Germans could not be deterred. The British turned over to him an intercepted dispatch from German Foreign Secretary Arthur Zimmermann to the German envoy to Mexico instructing the latter to propose an alliance to Mexico in the event of war between Germany and the United States. As a reward Mexico was to recover its "lost territory in Texas, New Mexico and Arizona." Mexico was also to ask Japan to join Mexico and Germany against the United States. Published in the American press, this overt defiance of the Monroe Doctrine aroused the country to bitter anger; the bulk of the nation came to understand how seriously America's future might be affected by a victory of the Germans. In the course of March five American ships were torpedoed by U-boats. It was clear that unless Wilson gave up the defense of American lives and property, the country would have to enter the war. But when the President asked Congress for a declaration of war, he mentioned only briefly the U-boats, the Zimmermann Note, and German espionage and sabotage on American soil. Once again he saw the issues at stake in a wider perspective.

It is a fearful thing to lead this great peaceful people into war, but the right is more precious than peace, and we shall fight for the things which we have always carried nearest our hearts—for democracy, for the right of those who submit to authority to have a voice in their own governments, for the rights and liberties of small nations, for a universal dominion of right by such a concert of free peoples as shall bring peace and safety to all nations and make the world itself at last free. To such a task we can dedicate our lives and our fortunes, everything that we have, with the pride of those who know that the day has come when America is privileged to spend her blood and her might for the principles that gave her birth and happiness and the peace which she has treasured. God helping her, she can do no other.

These were noble thoughts, and they expressed the sentiments and beliefs of most Americans. But they ignored the impelling imperatives of national interest and the fact, above all, that America's fortunes were so closely interwoven with those of Europe that the United States could not remain at peace while Europe's fate was hanging in the balance.

Wilson's failure to point out to the country its national stake in the war did not affect America's willingness to enter the fight. Congress responded readily to his call, and on April 6, 1917, the United States declared war against Germany.

CRISIS IN THE WEST

The U-boat Campaign. The United States expected its contribution to the war effort to consist primarily of money, materials, shipping, and naval protection. Plans had been made for the formation of an expeditionary force, but that force was to be limited to 500,000 men and would be composed of regulars and volunteers. To replace them at home, Congress passed a Selective Service Act in May 1917; there was no thought, however, of sending draftees overseas. Yet it soon became clear that the plight of the Allies was such that they required all-out assistance in the fighting both on land and at sea.

In the naval campaign help was needed immediately. The unrestricted U-boat offensive was exacting a fearful toll of Allied and neutral shipping. Sinkings increased from 365,000 tons in January 1917 to 536,000 in February, 590,000 in March, and 865,000 in April (the British losses alone amounted to 526,000 tons in April, little less than the 539,000 tons of merchant shipping British shipyards had built throughout all of 1916). Shipping facilities were further reduced by the refusal of neutral ships to sail through the danger zone. As a result, Britain's stock of grain dwindled to six weeks' supply at the end of April, and official estimates warned that unless the food situation improved, the country would reach the limit of its endurance by early November.

Here American help could be given immediately. Prodded by the persistent Lloyd George and assured of United States naval support, the British Admiralty decided to try out the convoy system. American destroyers were at once assigned to convoy duty, and helped make the convoy system an effective defense against U-boats. Sinkings dropped from a high of 865,000 tons in April to 574,000 tons in May, and after a rise to 660,000 tons in June fell thereafter fairly continuously. By December they were down to 385,000 tons, and after March 1918 they never again reached the 300,000 mark.

Allied Setbacks on Land. Except for some token forces, no American troops could be dispatched to Europe in 1917 to assist the Allies. Yet on land the war was not going well for them either. A spring offensive launched by Joffre's successor Nivelle failed as disastrously as all earlier attacks on the western front. Worse, the defeat touched off a wave of mutinies in the French army. Nivelle was replaced by General Henri-Philippe Pétain (1856–1951), who the year before had distinguished himself in the defense of Verdun. Pétain restored discipline by improving the soldiers' material conditions and staying on the defensive, a strategy for which the cautious Pétain was well–suited both by temperament and military experience.

In late July the British commander Sir Douglas Haig (1861–1928) sent off his forces against the Germans in Flanders. On the second day continuous heavy rain turned the battle area into a quagmire—a contingency of which Haig had been forewarned, but which he chose to ignore. Slogging through the morass of the Flemish plain, his men were mowed down by the German machine guns. Thousands more drowned in water-filled shell holes or were smothered to death in the mud. Although Haig had promised to close down the attack if casualties should be heavy, he persisted in pressing on for another three months. At a loss of 300,000 men he captured a few square miles of territory—a vulnerable salient from which he withdrew at once when the Germans in turn launched an offensive the following spring.

To add to the Allies' troubles, Italy suffered a catastrophic defeat in October. A combined Austro-German force broke through the Italian positions at Caporetto on the Isonzo River. Italian resistance collapsed, and the Italians might have capitulated, had the Germans and Austrians pressed their pursuit. Unprepared for their overwhelming success, they let a large part of the Italian army escape. The latter established a new front some sixty miles back along the Piave River, northeast of Venice. British and French troops were rushed to their aid and helped them beat back a renewed Austro-German offensive.

The Rally of the West.   Under the impact of these setbacks public morale declined sharply. France's uneasiness, fed by the military defeats of the spring, was further aroused by charges of treason that were leveled against prominent French politicians. Other political scandals and squabbles also kept Paris in turmoil. In November 1917 the government fell. France's ability to stay in the war was now in grave doubt, and all depended on who would become the new Premier. President Poincaré chose the man most closely identified with a fight to the finish—the militant ex-Premier Georges Clemenceau (1841–1929). This one-time Jacobin radical, whose political career spanned the life of the Third Republic, assumed his new task with a vigor that belied his seventy-six years. His program was very simple: "Domestic policy? I wage war! Foreign policy? I wage war! I wage war all the time!" His appointment revived the self-confidence of the nation; under his forceful leadership

France weathered the ordeals which still lay ahead until victory was won a year later.

Italy, where defeatism had long been widespread, witnessed a similar closing of ranks. The very disaster that brought the Germans and Austrians close to Venice put an end to Italian disunity. With the nation's survival at stake, the major parties rallied around a new government headed by the veteran lawyer-statesman Vittorio Emanuele Orlando (1862–1952).

In Britain pacifists and defeatists were still rather few in 1917, but there was a marked growth in the number of those who favored a negotiated peace, not because they despaired of ultimate victory, but because they believed the price—the nation's impoverishment and its consequent dangers—too costly. Their best known spokesman was a one-time Foreign Secretary and Viceroy of India, Lord Henry Lansdowne, who expressed these views in a letter to the London *Daily Telegraph* in November 1917.

The letter was well received in the Labor and part of the Liberal press, but most Englishmen rejected Lansdowne's proposal. Lloyd George spoke for them when he stated a few days later: "I warn the nation to watch the man who thinks there is a half-way house between victory and defeat. . . . Victory is an essential condition for the security of the free world." His confidence in ultimate victory stemmed from his knowledge that American aid would make itself felt before long on land as it had at sea and that with this help Germany could be dealt the decisive defeat which had so far eluded the Allies.

The Role of the United States. American military preparations were by then proceeding on a grand scale. A draft army of over two million men was being trained to provide reinforcements for the French front. The need for American troops became still more pressing when Russia withdrew from the war in December 1917. There was a symbolic significance in the fact that shortly after the Russian departure the United States participated for the first time in an Allied war conference—as if to redress the balance.

While military cooperation between Americans and Europeans became increasingly closer, the United States did not join the European alliance, but merely "associated" itself with the Allied war effort. Wilson insisted on this distinction, partly in deference to the American aversion to "entangling alliances," but mainly because he still viewed America's role as basically different from that of the European powers. As he saw it, the latter aimed at the restoration of the traditional balance of power and considered the defeat of Germany their ultimate aim. He, on the other hand, kept hoping for a peace settlement by which he would create that new world order built upon a community rather than a balance of power, which to him was the only enduring foundation of peace and stability.

The President came to stress this theme with particular force when the Bolsheviks proclaimed their own peace program after their seizure of power. With its demand for a peace without annexations and indemnities, arrived at by open negotiations and based on the principle of national self-determination, Lenin's Declaration on Peace appeared to resemble Wilson's own thought on the future peace. Wilson was confident that these views expressed the "voices of humanity," but he feared that the Bolshevik leader was merely a tool of the Germans who were exploiting this "just idea" through Lenin to win the war. For this reason the President did not welcome the latter's proposals.

Wilson changed his mind when his advisers suggested that Germany was close to a social upheaval and the Soviets might be of help to deal it the *coup de grâce*. Since he hoped himself for the overthrow of the German regime, he seems to have seen little difference between Lenin's aims and his own. In his famous address to the Congress on January 8, 1918 in which he outlined his own peace objectives, he praised the Soviets for the concreteness of their program and the sincerity of their spokesmen. If the West did not join them in the peace talks at Brest-Litovsk, he explained, it was not because it was not as anxious as they to have peace, but merely because it did not wish to treat with the present rapacious masters of Germany.

Wilson proceeded to outline his peace plan to reaffirm the sincerity of Western war aims (which had recently been called into question by Trotsky's disclosure, from Russia's archives, of the Allies' secret territorial agreements). In its Fourteen Points the program called for national self-determination, and the creation of a "general association of nations [to afford] mutual guarantees of political independence and territorial integrity to great and small states alike." But the Fourteen Points were also addressed to the enemy powers. One of the points urged Vienna to accord the "freest opportunity of autonomous development" to its nationalities, but assured the Austrians at the same time that America wished to safeguard Austria's "place among the nations." The Germans, in turn, were told that Americans were not jealous of German greatness nor did they wish to impair it. "We wish [Germany] only to accept a place of equality among the peoples of the world . . . instead of a place of mastery." Though Wilson disclaimed any intention of suggesting a change in Germany's internal structure, he made it clear that he would negotiate only with those who spoke for the peace-minded Reichstag majority.

The immediate response to the Fourteen Points program was disappointing. It was answered evasively by the German and Austrian governments and failed to set off a revolution in Germany. Austria's subject nationalities were dissatisfied since the Fourteen Points did not promise them full independence. Nor was the plan welcomed by Britain and France. Lloyd George who had announced shortly before a less generous program was cautious in his reaction, and Clemenceau refrained altogether from expressing his views. Italy's response was blatantly hostile since it felt that the Fourteen Points rejected most of its territorial demands.

But thoughts of peace soon receded into the background. The treaty of Brest-Litovsk enabled the Germans to shift to the west the bulk of their eastern armies, and in March they renewed their attacks on the western front.

THE COLLAPSE OF THE CENTRAL POWERS

Domestic Problems of the Central Powers in 1917. 1917 was as full of disappointments for the Germans as it was for the Allies. The U-boat campaign failed to bring Britain to its knees, and victory seemed as remote as before. War-weary and frustrated, left-wing Socialists broke away from the Social Democratic Party to press more insistently for a peace without annexations. To the left of this new Independent Socialist Party a small radical group founded the Spartacus League, which aimed at transforming the war into a socialist world revolution. The workers of Berlin, Leipzig, and other industrial centers struck repeatedly in protest against inadequate food rations, restrictions on civil liberties, and the unwillingness of the government to abandon its annexationist aims and call for an end to the fighting. Unrest also spread through the High Seas Fleet which lay marooned in its home ports; crews went on hunger strike to get better food, defied shore leave restrictions, and published demands for an early peace. In the wake of mass strikes in Vienna and Budapest a general strike broke out in Berlin in late January 1918 and spread to Hamburg, Leipzig, Cologne, Munich, and other cities; within two days over a million workers had left their jobs. The strikes were readily crushed by the army, but they served to lay bare the internal strains from which the Reich now was suffering.

The longing for peace was even stronger in Austria-Hungary. Emperor Charles kept putting out peace feelers to avert the collapse of his empire and of his dynasty which he was warned were bound to occur unless the war were soon brought to an end. Yet a prisoner of his ambitions and of Germany's military preponderance, Charles could not meet the terms of the Allies, and they turned down his approaches. He was equally unsuccessful in his attempts to consolidate his position by domestic concessions—internal reforms could no longer satisfy the nationality groups which now wanted complete independence. Bulgaria and Turkey too were in difficulties; the Turks in particular were hard–

Franco-American war council, 1918. Left to right: General Pershing,
André Tardieu, French special commissioner to the United States (premier,
1929–30 and 1932), Premier Clemenceau, Marshal Foch, General
Mordacq, Major General McAndrew. (*Reprinted courtesy Brown Brothers*)

pressed by the British who were pushing them out of Mesopotamia and
Palestine.

The German Offensives of 1918 and the First Allied Breakthrough.
During the winter of 1917–18 Ludendorff made preparations for a huge
spring offensive that would defeat the English and French before large-
scale American reinforcements could come to their aid. Of the two and
one-half million men in the east, he transferred one and one-half million
to France; the rest was left in the Baltic states and in the Ukraine to
enforce the Brest-Litovsk treaty. The Germans thus were only slightly
superior to the Allies in numbers, and while they assembled strong forces
at the points of attack, they lacked the reserves to maintain their offensive. With a sufficiency of tanks the scales might still have been tipped
in their favor, but the High Command had not much faith in tanks paving the way for the infantry. The German offensive launched in March
1918 petered out after a notable initial advance, and the same fate
befell two subsequent thrusts in April and May. On July 15 a fourth
attack was opened against the French on the Marne south of Rheims;
the latter, forewarned, evaded the blow, and three days later General
Foch counterattacked the western flank of the Germans. Shielded by
600 tanks and supported by several American divisions, the French drove
the Germans back across the Marne; once more a German offensive was
brought to a halt at that river.

Foch, since April the Commander-in-Chief of the Allied armies (though without real power of command), decided to keep up the pressure on the Germans. On August 8 British tanks overran the German defenses at Amiens, creating confusion and panic among the tired and ill-fed German troops. Since Haig was not ready to pursue this success, Ludendorff was able to close the gap in his front, but he knew what this breakthrough portended: "August 8th was the black day of the German army in the history of the war. . . . [It] demonstrated the decline of our fighting power and . . . given [the demoralization of our] replacements ended all hope of improving our position by some new strategy. . . . The war had to be brought to an end."

The German government was advised to secure an armistice at the first opportune moment, but no suitable opening presented itself. The position of the Central Powers grew worse almost daily. Several hundred thousand American troops moved up to the front, and together with the Anglo-French forces kept pressing forward. During August and September the Germans, exhausted and beset by malingering and disobedience, were slowly pushed back some thirty miles. The plight of their allies was even worse. At the end of September Bulgaria was overrun by French forces operating from Salonika and concluded an armistice. With Bulgaria in Allied hands, Rumania could not be held, and the loss of Rumania meant the loss of its oil wells which fueled Germany's U-boats, airplanes, and trucks. The Turks too were close to collapse; in headlong retreat from Mesopotamia, their armies melted away in mass desertions. Austria-Hungary faced similar troubles, with the breakup of its armies hastened by the empire's political disintegration. In July a Czech National Committee was established in Prague to challenge Austria's supremacy, and in August a Yugoslav National Council was set up in the Slovenian city of Ljubljana. Desperate for a respite, the Austrians announced a plan for a peace conference, but the proposal was rejected by both the United States and the Allies.

Soon afterwards the Germans were forced to acknowledge defeat. On September 26 Foch launched a multipronged offensive against their defense line. Although in most places the attacking armies advanced only slowly, Ludendorff was deeply alarmed at their progress. His forces had dwindled from three and one half to two and one half million men and were facing armies almost double their size, well-rested and fed, and incomparably better equipped. Haunted by fears that the German retreat might suddenly turn to a rout, he demanded on September 28 that Germany at once seek an armistice.

The Armistice. In this hour of crisis the German leaders recalled Wilson's Fourteen Points. They decided to approach him in the hope that tolerable peace terms might be obtained based on that program and the various additional statements Wilson had made in the course of the year. A new government was formed, headed by the liberal Prince

Max von Baden and including some moderate Socialists and members of the left-liberal parties. Such a government, it was hoped, would be able to maintain domestic control in the face of the military defeat; representing the Reichstag majority, it was also more likely to come to an understanding with Wilson. (The parliamentarization of the German government system was formalized three weeks later by a constitutional amendment according to which the chancellor and his deputies were made responsible to the Reichstag. Other prerogatives of the Kaiser such as the declaration of war and the conclusion of peace were also entrusted to the Reichstag.)

On October 3 the request for an armistice and a peace settlement based on the Fourteen Points was sent off to Wilson. But the hope of obtaining a peace from which Germany would emerge with its status intact proved illusory. Shocked by the peace terms imposed by the Germans on Rumanians and Russians, Wilson had given up hope for a "peace without victory" as the means to attain his aims. Instead, he was now convinced that only a clearcut defeat of the Germans, that "force and force alone [would] decide whether justice and peace shall reign in the affairs of men." He insisted not only on an unqualified acceptance of the Fourteen Points and his subsequent statements, including an immediate end to the U-boat campaign, but called also for military and territorial armistice arrangements that would further increase the military supremacy of the Allies. In addition, he asked for assurance that the new German government was backed by a Reichstag majority and spoke for the German people. Only after he had satisfied himself on all these points did he take up the German request with the governments of the Allies.

The latter had followed his exchanges with Berlin with growing concern, for they did not consider the Fourteen Points an acceptable basis for a peace settlement. Consulted now, they objected to a great many points which they felt did not meet their security needs or ignored their economic and territorial demands. Colonel House, who had hurried to Paris, warned that the United States might sign a separate peace with the Germans should the Allies refuse to agree to the Fourteen Points. (As an "associate power," and not an ally, the United States had retained its freedom of action.) In the face of this threat a compromise was worked out: the peace settlement would be based on the Fourteen Points with two reservations—the concept of the freedom of the seas was left open to subsequent interpretation (in accordance with the wishes of the British who did not want to give up their right to resort to naval blockades), and reparations were to cover not only property damage but also all other losses suffered by Allied civilians (again, in order to satisfy the British, whose civilian population had suffered little property damage). French, Belgian, and Italian objections, on the other hand, were sidestepped and came to plague the peace conference later.

On November 5 the German government was informed that the United

States and the Allies were prepared to conclude a peace treaty based on the Fourteen Points, except for the two reservations, and were ready also to propose terms for an armistice. By this time the Germans were close to collapse. Turkey and Austria-Hungary had meanwhile surrendered, and Prince Max was trying to stave off a revolution at home. Impatient with the slow progress of the discussions with Wilson, the German masses were demanding the abdication of William II, whose continued presence at the head of the state was suspected of delaying a speedy agreement. The crisis was aggravated by the decision of the German Admiralty to stage a naval sortie into the Channel in a frenzied attempt to vindicate the honor of the navy by a last act of heroism. On October 29 and 30 the crews of two battleships, unwilling to prolong the war by this desperate scheme, refused to take orders. The revolt spread quickly to other ships and from there to the shore and inland. Bavaria proclaimed itself an independent republic on November 7, and two days later William II was forced from his throne. The German empire became a republic.

One of the last acts of Prince Max's government was to send an armistice delegation to meet with Foch. Partly from distrust of the military, partly to satisfy Wilson, it was headed not by a soldier, but by a civilian, the Reichstag deputy Matthias Erzberger—a break with custom which was later on to provide a dangerous alibi for the German generals. At Compiègne, in the dining car of Foch's special train, an armistice was concluded on November 11. Its most significant terms provided for the surrender of vast amounts of war matériel (including 5,000 guns, 25,000 machine guns, and all U-boats) and the maintenance of the blockade. The agreement also compelled the Germans to withdraw their armed forces from all occupied territory as well as from all German lands left of the Rhine and from four major bridgeheads on its right bank. Not only were the conditions stringent enough to preclude a resumption of hostilities by the Germans—they also opened the way for attempts by the French to make the Rhine their permanent military frontier, in disregard of the Fourteen Points. Although the prearmistice agreement based on those Points precluded an unconditional surrender, the armistice did amount to a virtual capitulation. "I've got my armistice," Foch reported to Clemenceau, "you can make any peace you want, I can impose it. . . . My work is finished, yours now begins."

Wilson doubtless had his misgivings, for he feared that too much security on the part of the Allies would render more difficult a genuine peace settlement. But having secured the prearmistice agreement which accepted his Fourteen Points, he expected the real decisions to be made at the peace conference. There, he was confident, his ideas would triumph. Of this he was certain not only because the Allies were bound by explicit agreement to make peace on his terms; ultimately his confidence stemmed from his conviction that he rather than Clemenceau or Lloyd George expressed the will of the people and the views of mankind.

4

The Search for
a New Order

The war demonstrated that Europe was no longer strong enough to contain by itself all threats to its system. The victors thus were faced with the task of creating a new international order in which the European nations (as well as the non-European ones) would have a reasonable assurance of peace and security. The measures by which they hoped to attain this goal—the peace settlement with Germany and the establishment of the League of Nations—did not produce such an order. The settlement with Germany foundered on its inherent inconsistencies; the League failed because it was not allowed to develop any strength of its own. Europe was again thrown back onto its own resources, but it was a Europe weaker and less self-confident than that of the prewar era. The ordeal of the war had subjected it to a severe drain on its material and emotional resources; the emergence of independent new nation-states compounded the existing national rivalries; above all, the new states were too weak to help redress Europe's balance of power. Europe continued to be torn by distrust and insecurity—a condition only slightly improved during the more prosperous mid-1920's. Mindful of the lesson taught by the war, various statesmen made the attempt to associate the United

States more closely with Europe in the hope that peace and stability could be maintained more effectively with America's help. Yet, except in the economic field, the United States refused to involve itself in Europe's concerns, and the European order continued to rest on a tenuous basis.

THE PARIS PEACE CONFERENCE

Wilson and the Allies. The peace conference opened at Paris on January 18, 1919, some ten weeks after the signing of the armistice. If the leading statesmen had approached the prearmistice and the armistice negotiations with differing views, the intervening period had done nothing to reconcile their positions. Indeed, once the enemy had been defeated, the need to settle their differences had become much less pressing. Consequently, the European leaders were more inclined to listen to the demands of their own peoples clamoring for revenge and indemnities than to the exhortations of Wilson. Against his better judgment, Lloyd George failed to disabuse his countrymen of their belief that Germany could and should foot the entire war bill; he won a Parliamentary election in December 1918 by accepting a mandate to "hang the Kaiser" and "squeeze the [German] orange until the pips squeak." The French asked with equal insistence for retribution and, above all, military security; when doubts were voiced whether Clemenceau, at his age, would insist on these demands with sufficient forcefulness, the Premier dispelled these fears by telling a wildly cheering Chamber of Deputies that, as far as he was concerned, no League of Nations could ever serve as a substitute for solid military alliances and a well–guarded frontier. The Italians, finally, kept pressing for large areas of Austrian territory, and this they did with a fervor that even a stronger man than Premier Orlando could not have ignored. The European statesmen felt the more justified to depart from their prearmistice agreement because Wilson's own countrymen did not seem to feel bound by the Fourteen Points. On November 6, 1918, elections in the United States produced Republican majorities in both houses of Congress; since Wilson had appealed to the voters to express their approval of his peace policies by supporting the Democrats, the outcome was considered, rightly or wrongly, as a repudiation of his advocacy of lenient peace terms for Germany.

In spite of these ominous portents Wilson remained unshaken in his conviction that he was the true spokesman of the peoples of the world. He felt confirmed in this conviction by the rousing receptions with which he was greeted when he traveled through Europe in December 1918. In his illusion he mistook the ovations, which were tendered to him as the symbol of victory, as an approval of his plans for a new world order. Despite this misconception, Wilson was fully aware that his ideas would not easily triumph. He decided to attend the peace conference in person, because he was deeply distrustful of Europe's statesmen and feared that they might bypass his program unless he were there to defend it. "I want to say very frankly to you," he cautioned an English audience, "that [the United States] is not . . . interested in European politics. But she is interested in the partnership of right between America and Europe. . . . We are not obeying the mandates of parties or politics. We are obeying the mandates of humanity."

The Participants in the Conference. The delegations which assembled at Paris came from all parts of the world. Every one of the six continents was represented; in addition to the European participants and the United States, there were delegates from China, Japan, Siam (present-day Thailand), Hedjaz, Liberia, Brazil, Bolivia, Peru, and Ecuador, to name but some. The British Dominions, Canada, Australia, New Zealand, and the Union of South Africa, acting as separate states, also sent delegations, and so did India. There were finally countless unofficial spokesmen, representing the Irish, Koreans, Ukrainians, Zionists, Arabs, and other suppressed nationalities.

The two major absentees were Russia and Germany. Russia was plunged into civil war between Bolsheviks and anti-Bolsheviks, and the conference could reach no agreement as to whom to invite as the spokesman of Russia. The Germans, too, had been expected to attend—after the victor powers had reached a preliminary agreement on the terms of the treaty. However, the negotiations among the victors proved so difficult—at one point Wilson threatened to leave, and the Italian delegation in the end did walk out—that the plan of inviting the Germans was dropped. For the same reason the Austrians, Turks, and Bulgarians were excluded.

The Work of the Conference. The Paris Peace Conference has often been compared to the Congress of Vienna, but the resemblance between the two gatherings was superficial. The two meetings differed not only in their composition, which was European in one case and worldwide in the other, but also in their basic objectives. While the statesmen at Vienna saw their main task in the re-establishment of a balanced European state system, of the leading actors at Paris only Clemenceau wished to create a new European balance of power. Wilson was thinking in terms of a world order in which there would be no room for regional power balances, whereas Lloyd George, mindful of Britain's European and imperial commitments, oscillated between these two positions. (Orlando and Baron Makino, the chief Japanese spokesman, were interested mainly in the fulfillment of their territorial demands.) These disagreements touched off some bitter disputes over the application and interpretation of the Fourteen Points; they were also the main source of the ambiguities of the final peace treaty. The dissensions were deepened

The Big Four at Paris. Left to right: Orlando, Lloyd George, Clemenceau,
Wilson. (*U.S. Signal Corps Photo*)

by the differences in character and outlook of the three main protagonists:
Wilson—austere, withdrawn, and driven inexorably by his faith in man
and his vision of a rational world order; Clemenceau—cold, cynical, and
chiefly concerned with France's security; Lloyd George—not insensitive
to Wilson's ideals, but mercurial and opportunistic, and forever anxious
to have a majority on his side.

The impact of the personal element must not be exaggerated, however; the problems which the peacemakers faced were beyond the control
of any three individuals. The statesmen at Paris were not free agents,
but were bound by the views and hopes of their nations. Wilson was in
a specially vulnerable position, for he seemed to have lost domestic
support for his program of conciliation. Lloyd George and Clemenceau,
on the other hand, were backed by their fellow countrymen. Their
demands for territorial and economic rewards thus could not be simply
dismissed as incompatible with the Fourteen Points. Nor could Wilson **55**

impose his ideas any longer by threats as he had during the pre-armistice negotiations. Besides, some of the Fourteen Points had been overtaken by the march of events; the Austro-Hungarian Empire, for example, had broken up into several states, and its "place among the nations" could no longer be "safeguarded," as Point No. 10 had promised. Other demands, such as that for "open covenants˙ of peace, openly arrived at," were clearly impractical, and Wilson had to acquiesce in their violation. Some, finally, like the promise of a Baltic harbor to Poland, were incompatible with the principle of national self-determination. Yet the Fourteen Points were not simply discarded, as has sometimes been charged. Many were fully carried out, others were observed as far as this could be done realistically.

The Drafting of the League Covenant.   In accordance with Wilson's wishes the first Point to be taken up was the Fourteenth which asked for the creation of a League of Nations "to promote international co-operation and to achieve international peace and security." Here the views of the American and French delegation collided at once. The Americans envisaged a universal association of all states of the world, based essentially on voluntary cooperation and the support of world public opinion. The French, on the other hand, haunted by their fear of a German resurgence, wished the League to include only the Allied and Associated Powers to whom might be added the neutrals. They also called for an international army and general staff to bolster the strength of the League. France's military demands were rejected by both Britain and the United States. The two powers abhorred standing conscript armies and the far-reaching political and military commitments implied in the French proposal. Instead, a League was created which was to rely on good will and moral pressures, but could, if it so decided, resort to forcible measures. However, in compliance with France's request, Germany and its former allies were not to be admitted to League membership until they had proven themselves "civilized nation[s] which [could] be relied upon to promote [the League's] objects."

Once work had been completed on the draft of the Covenant, Wilson returned briefly to the United States where opposition to his policies was gathering strength. Fearful lest the Senate reject the League Covenant, he felt compelled on his return to Paris to ask for several amendments which would remove from the Covenant all supranational features: one barred the League from intervening in matters solely within the domestic jurisdiction of one of the disputants (it was vehemently opposed by the French who feared that it would enable the United States to dissociate itself from European affairs); another recognized the overriding validity of regional understandings such as the Monroe Doctrine; a third gave League members the right to withdraw from the League upon two years' notice.

To secure the acceptance of the League Covenant, Wilson had to yield also on other issues. The British Dominions and Japan wished to annex Germany's former colonies in Africa, Australasia, and Asia and opposed the plan of placing them under League jurisdiction. In the end the territories were turned over to France, Britain, Japan, and the Dominions to be administered by them as League mandates. Similar arrangements were made for most of Turkey's Arabian possessions, which became mandates of Britain and France. If the practical differences between mandate and outright possession seemed slight, Wilson could at least hope that the League might later attain a more equitable solution, for it was to be one of its functions to review treaties and situations that were potential sources of trouble. This hope made it also easier for him to yield on others of his objectives.

The Territorial Settlement for Germany. Wilson was forced to make the greatest concessions in the treaty that was being drafted for Germany. The French, ever aware of the fact that their population was less than two-thirds that of Germany (40 million against 62 million) and their industries, too, much inferior, wished to strip the Germans not only of Alsace-Lorraine as provided for by the Fourteen Points, but of the Rhineland as well. This region, important as the center of Germany's armament industries and a main source of German mineral wealth (coal), was to become a French-sponsored buffer state between France and Germany. To so flagrant a violation of the principle of nationality Wilson would not agree; he was backed by Lloyd George who opposed the French plan as a threat to the Continental balance of power. The two leaders consented, however, to an Allied military occupation of the Rhineland for fifteen years and to the permanent demilitarization of the area. A French demand for the outright annexation of the coal-rich Saar Basin was also rejected; although German in character, the basin was, however, separated from Germany and included in the French customs zone, with a plebiscite to decide its fate after fifteen years. As part of the reparation settlement, moreover, the coal mines of the Saar territory were turned over to France. Pending the establishment of an effective League, Wilson and Lloyd George also offered Clemenceau a treaty of guarantee by which the United States and Great Britain were to come to France's defense in case of a German attack. The treaty was not ratified by the United States Senate, however, and since the British guarantee was to become effective only if America were committed, the French were left without this additional safeguard.

The largest territorial losses the Germans suffered in the east. Here too efforts were made to draw the new boundary lines in accordance with the nationality principle. The difficulty was that Germans and Poles had so closely intermingled in the course of time that no clear dividing lines could be drawn. As a result the territories included in the new Polish

EUROPE AFTER WORLD WAR I

lost by Germany
lost by Austria-Hungary
lost by Bulgaria
lost by Russia

0   100   200   300   400 Miles

state—West Prussia, Poznan, and large parts of Upper Silesia—contained substantial German minorities. Application of the nationality principle also led to the creation of the Polish Corridor, a strip of territory assigned to Poland which cut off the German-inhabited province of East Prussia from the rest of Germany. In these as well as all similar cases arrangements were made to protect the political and cultural rights of the newly created minorities, and the League was charged with the supervision of these arrangements.

Special difficulties arose over the implementation of the promise, contained in the Fourteen Points, to give the new state of Poland "free and secure access to the sea." Geographically the only available harbor was Danzig, at the mouth of the Vistula River; yet Danzig's population was 90 per cent German, and thus Danzig could not be assigned to Poland. The problem was solved by transforming the city into a separate state under League supervision, with Poland enjoying special customs and port privileges in it. Under the circumstances it was probably the most equitable solution, but it was to be a source of continuous trouble. Including areas ceded to Belgium, Denmark, and Lithuania, Germany lost 13 per cent of its territory and 10 per cent of its population. The lost lands contained 15 per cent of its arable soil, 75 per cent of its iron ores, 26 per cent of its coal deposits, and 25 per cent of its steel production.

Disarmament, Reparations, and War Guilt Clause. One of the foremost concerns of the Fourteen Points was the worldwide limitation of armaments. The over-all implementation of this Point was left to the League of Nations, but the peace conference took up the disarmament of the Central Powers. Here again Anglo-American views collided with those of the French. Disagreement arose over the questions as to whether the Germans were to have an army of 200,000 draftees serving a year (which Britain and the United States, averse to conscription, opposed) or a small professional army of long-term volunteers (to which the French objected as providing ready made officer cadres for future expansion—a warning which proved remarkably prescient). In the end the Germans were allowed a professional force of 100,000 men whose enlisted men would serve for twelve years and its officers for twenty-five. This army was to have neither tanks nor planes or heavy artillery, and German manufacture of arms was accordingly limited. Similarly, the navy was reduced to a small surface fleet for coastal defense and the air force completely abolished.

The British had only reluctantly agreed to the reduction of the German army to 100,000 men. With France, Poland, and Russia free to maintain large armies, they were worried lest Germany's unilateral disarmament might make it impossible to recreate a Continental balance of power. At their suggestion German disarmament was linked up with worldwide disarmament and was expressly described in the treaty as being undertaken "in order to render possible the initiation of a general limitation of the armaments of all nations"—a stipulation which became a serious embarrassment to the victor powers in later years.

The reparations issue also required prolonged negotiations. In this case Clemenceau and Lloyd George were aligned against Wilson. They first insisted that Germany pay the entire cost of the war, but in the face of heavy American opposition they scaled down their claims to the payment of damages and war pensions. Wilson acquiesced, hoping to limit the actual amount to a reasonable lump sum equivalent to the physical damage. However, the conference did not fix the amount, and when this was done two years later, the United States had no influence on the final decision, having withdrawn from the Reparations Commission. The total amount was set at $33,000,000,000. Part of this was to be paid in kind— by the surrender of the bulk of the German merchant marine, large shipments of coal, and other deliveries.

Whatever the sum the Allies would collect from the Germans, it was clear that the amount would never approach the astronomical figures which the Allied peoples believed they could claim. Fearful of public opinion at home, Clemenceau and Lloyd George proposed the insertion of a clause in the treaty which established Germany's obligation to pay all costs of the conflict on the grounds that the aggression of Germany and its allies had caused the war. Their hope was that if Germany acknowledged at least its moral responsibility, the Allied nations would more easily resign themselves to a merely partial fulfillment of their expectations. The "war guilt clause" aroused bitter resentment in Germany and provided the Germans with inexhaustible ammunition for attacks on the treaty. In effect, it weakened rather than strengthened the moral position of the reparation creditors.

Germany objected with equal vehemence to another section of the treaty which called for the surrender of the ex-Kaiser and other persons "accused of having committed acts in violation of the laws and customs of war." These "war criminals" were to be tried by an Allied military tribunal. Little came of that plan. The Netherlands refused to extradite William II who had been granted asylum by the Dutch government, and the German government rejected the request that it turn over to the Allies some 900 "war criminals," among them Hindenburg, Ludendorff, and Bethmann Hollweg. The Allies did not press their demand and accepted a German proposal to try the accused before the German Supreme Court at Leipzig. Few, however, were prosecuted, and of these, most were acquitted while the rest received nominal sentences.

Ratification of the Treaty.   The Germans were called to Versailles, near Paris, in late April 1919 to receive the treaty. The Allies barred all negotiations, but gave the German delegation fifteen days within which to submit a written reply. In due course the latter submitted counter-proposals most of which were rejected; one major concession, the grant-ing of a plebiscite in Upper Silesia, and a few minor revisions were made. The immediate German reaction was to reject the treaty, but the German National Assembly decided to accept it except for the "articles of shame," which dealt with the war guilt, and the surrender of the "war criminals." When the Allies refused to accept these reservations and threatened to resume hostilities, the Assembly ratified the treaty without reservations. It was signed in the Hall of Mirrors of the Versailles Palace on June 28, 1919.

The Other Peace Treaties.   The treaty with Austria, signed in the Paris suburb of St. Germain-en-Laye on September 10, 1919, ratified the breakup of the Austro-Hungarian empire. Czechoslovakia, established in October 1918, was confirmed in its territorial possessions, including the German-speaking Sudeten area; Poland was likewise confirmed in its control of Galicia. To Italy, Austria ceded the region around Trieste and the Tyrol south of the Brenner Pass; Rumania and the newly formed kingdom of Yugoslavia acquired Austria's Balkan possessions. Reduced to the German-speaking parts of the old empire, Austria survived as a purely German state, but the peace treaty denied it the right to unite with Germany lest the latter become too strong. Like the Germans, the Austrians had to pay reparations, justified by the "war guilt clause," and their army was reduced to a professional force of 30,000 men.

The treaty with Hungary stripped that state of two-thirds of its territories, which were annexed by Czechoslovakia, Rumania, and Yugoslavia. Hungary too had to pay reparations, based on the "war guilt clause," and its army was limited to 35,000 men. Owing to a Communist interlude in the spring of 1919 and to the ability of the Hungarians to draw out the negotiations, the peace treaty with them was not signed until June 4, 1920, at Trianon, near Versailles. Meanwhile the Bulgarians had concluded their treaty with the Allies at the Paris suburb of Neuilly in November 1919. Their main territorial loss was the surrender of Western Thrace to Greece, which cut them off from the Aegean Sea. Bulgaria also was subjected to severe armament limitations and to the payment of reparations.

Drafting a treaty for Turkey proved the most difficult. Turkey was forced to surrender to Greece a large part of its European territory. To put an end to the age-old struggle over control of the strategic Turkish Straits—Bosphorus, Dardanelles, and the Sea of Marmara—it was proposed to place them under an American mandate. When the United States rejected the plan, the Straits were internationalized and their shores demilitarized. Most of Turkey's Middle Eastern possessions were turned over to Britain and France as League mandates, but parts of Arabia were given statehood. In Asian Turkey (Anatolia), Greece was allowed to occupy the Greek-settled port of Smyrna, and eastern Anatolia was broken up into separate states. The Turkish government accepted these terms at Sèvres on August 10, 1920, but Turkish nationalist forces, led by Mustafa Kemal, rejected the partition of Anatolia and soon set out to undo it.

Evaluation of the Versailles Treaty. The peace treaties of 1919–20 preserved peace in Europe for only twenty years, and during most of these years that peace was at best an uneasy one. The future of the European system depended primarily on Germany's role in Europe, and an explanation of the Paris peacemakers' failure to give Europe a more lasting order must therefore focus on an evaluation of the treaty concluded with Germany.

Much has been written about the "harshness" and the "softness" of that treaty. These are relative concepts, and a case can be made for both judgments, depending on the interpretation of the purpose of the treaty. It was clearly too stringent if it was to help integrate Germany as a self-respecting cooperative member into the European community; it was too lenient if it was to keep Germany under the prolonged control of the victor powers. No real agreement was ever reached at Paris on the treaty's basic objective and this lack of agreement accounts for the fact that the treaty contains side by side the humanitarian League Covenant and the punitive terms of the reparations provisions. This ambiguity was perpetuated during the postwar years because Britain and France, the chief executors of the treaty, could rarely agree on a common policy toward Germany. The British, whose security needs had been met by the destruction of the German navy and the transfer to them of a major portion of the German merchant marine, became more conciliatory; yet without American backing they lacked the strength and the determination to make their viewpoint prevail. The French, on the other hand, remained as anxious as ever to keep the Germans in check, but on their part lacked the self-confidence and economic independence to take the measures which they considered essential to their security. The result was a diffident policy of half-measures, severe enough to discredit Germany's new democratic regime, which was willing to meet the Allies halfway, but not stringent enough to suppress the oppositional forces of nationalism and noncooperation.

Thus Europe continued on its troubled course; but truncated and economically disarrayed, it lacked the strength and the self-reliance to develop a new equilibrium.

THE IMBALANCE OF THE EUROPEAN SYSTEM

The Fighting Continues. The upheavals caused by the war were so great that neither the armistice nor the peace treaties ended the fighting in Europe. In the spring of 1918 civil war broke out in Russia between the Bolshevik government and anti-Bolshevik forces. After the armistice of November 1918 German troops fought side by side with the British and Balts against the Red Army in defense of the newly created Baltic states of Lithuania, Latvia, and Estonia. At the same time Rumanians were battling Hungarians, and the Poles were fighting Germans and Lithuanians. Somewhat later an Italian band led by the poet Gabriele D'Annunzio seized the disputed Adriatic port of Fiume.

In April 1920 war broke out between Poland and Soviet Russia. Since Russia had not attended the Paris Peace Conference, the frontier between Russia and the new Polish state had not yet been fixed. A boundary line proposed by the Western Powers, the Curzon Line, was rejected by the Poles on the grounds that it deprived Poland of territories that had been Polish before the partitions of the eighteenth century. Taking advantage of the Russian civil war, the Polish leader, Joseph Pilsudski (1867–1935), launched an attack on the Ukraine to

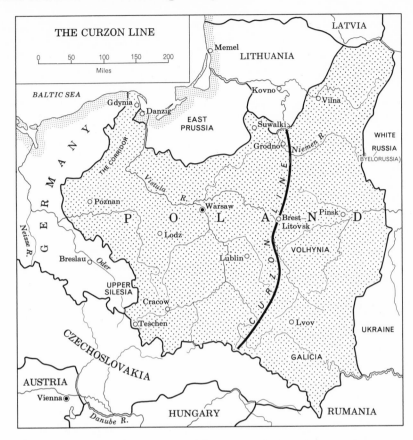

THE CURZON LINE

secure this land for his country. The Poles scored some initial successes and captured Kiev, but were then driven back by the Red Army, which advanced to the gates of Warsaw. Bolshevism, it seemed, was on the verge of inundating eastern and central Europe. The French, anxious to preserve Poland as an outpost against both Soviet Russia and Germany, rushed a military mission to Warsaw; with its help Pilsudski defeated the exhausted and overextended Red forces. He imposed upon Soviet Russia a peace treaty that gave Poland large parts of Byelorussia and the Ukraine—territories which the Soviets reclaimed as rightfully theirs during the Second World War.[1]

Large-scale fighting also broke out in Turkey over the implementation of the peace treaty of Sèvres. Supplied with war matériel by Soviet Russia, Mustafa Kemal first recovered eastern Anatolia and then turned on the Greeks. The latter had occupied Smyrna in 1919, and hope-

---

[1] The British and American governments considered the Polish annexations as unjustified because they ignored the ethnic distribution of the local population. They refused at first to recognize the transfer of the territory and for some time would not establish consulates in that area.

ful of Allied backing, had advanced into the surrounding area, ruthlessly massacring the local Turkish population as they proceeded. Allied support was not forthcoming, however. Kemal defeated the Greeks in a campaign equally noted for its brutality, and in September 1922 the Turks recaptured Smyrna. At the peace conference of Lausanne in July 1923, the Greeks were not only forced to renounce all claims to Anatolia, but had to surrender also all territories in Europe which they had acquired from Turkey.

The American Withdrawal from Europe. To Americans who had entered the war confident that their participation would help to create a better world, postwar Europe presented a disillusioning picture. The wrangles at the peace conference, the re-emergence of old rivalries and anxieties, the continued fighting in central and eastern Europe, all suggested that Europeans had learned nothing from the recent catastrophe. It was an argument effectively used by those who wished the United States to dissociate itself from European and world affairs and who opposed in particular America's entry into the League of Nations.

Most Americans would probably have approved the Versailles Treaty and American membership in the League had the treaty been submitted for ratification in the spring of 1919. But there were many delays, ·and the popular mood in favor of treaty and League Covenant was not clearly enough articulated to contend effectively with the gathering opposition. Many who had approved America's part in the war were beginning to wonder whether Wilson was not plunging them too deeply into the vortex of world affairs. There was a widespread fear, unjustified but strongly encouraged by League opponents, that the Covenant was impinging on American sovereignty and depriving Congress of its prerogative to declare war. Others again saw no need for a permanent association of the United States with the rest of the world—an attitude explained by the traditional aversion to foreign "entanglements" and by the absence of any visible threat to American security. Only a minority understood fully the close interrelationship between the United States and Europe; most Americans had already forgotten that the United States had entered the war, not in pursuit of an abstract ideal as they now believed, but in defense of its national interests. The ensuing apathy and inertia along with an increasing preoccupation with domestic problems, diverted attention from the peace treaty and the Covenant.

Still, the bulk of the American people continued to favor America's entry into the League, a minority accepting the Covenant as it was, the majority calling for modifications. But a bitter conflict had meanwhile arisen between the President and the Senate over the terms of American membership in the League. Wilson insisted on the unqualified acceptance of the treaty lest other countries asked for amendments, and he would not compromise on what he considered a matter of principle. His Senatorial opponents were equally adamant and demanded the inclusion in the treaty of a series of reservations re-emphasizing American sovereignty and Congressional rights. Other factors such as Wilson's physical breakdown and his subsequent isolation from the outside world, Republican partisanship that would not tolerate an unqualified Democratic success, and the personal antagonism existing between Wilson and Senator Henry Cabot Lodge, the leader of the Republican opposition, further reduced the chances of an accommodation. When the treaty came up for a vote in November 1919, it failed to secure the needed two-thirds majority, with or without reservations. Public opinion, still favoring its ratification, forced a reopening of the issue, but a second vote in March 1920 again failed to produce a two-thirds majority for any of the proposed versions.

By the time the Presidential election was held in November 1920, the nation was fully absorbed in its domestic problems, and the election did not produce a pro-League decision either. President Harding, who had been ambiguous on the League issue in the election campaign, now rejected expressly American membership in the League. A separate peace treaty concluded with Germany in August 1921 awarded the United States all the rights provided for in the original peace treaty, but released it of all of its responsibilities. Similar treaties were signed at the time with Austria and Hungary, the other two countries with which the United States had been at war.

The European nations followed the American debate on the League with anxious concern. Britain wished the United States to share the responsibility for maintaining order in Europe and elsewhere throughout the world; France considered America's entry into the League important to its security. The smaller nations, in turn, saw in the United States a potential counterweight against Britain and France and an impartial arbiter of Europe's disputes. Prudence forbade any open attempt to influence America's final decision, but to ensure America's entry, both Britain and France let the President and the Senate know that they would agree to the reservations proposed by the Senate. Britain also dispatched Sir Edward Grey, now Lord Grey of Fallodon, to Washington to persuade Wilson to assume a more flexible attitude. Since Grey had been one of the original proponents of the League, his counsel was believed to carry some weight with the President. But the latter refused to receive him. On his return, Grey published a letter in the London *Times* in which he expressed the view that America's League membership with reservations was greatly to be preferred to a League without American participation—a statement he would hardly have made, given his special status, without the consent of the British government. (Lloyd George, in fact, expressed his approval of Grey's remarks in a press interview a short time later.)

Whatever beneficial effects Grey's letter and Lloyd George's statement might have had on American public opinion, they were offset by the publication at that very moment of a sharp attack on the reparations settlement as unjustified and unrealistic. The book, *The Economic Consequences of the Peace,* by the English economist, John Maynard Keynes (1883–1946), became an immediate best seller in the United States, and by predicting new troubles for Europe, strengthened the case of the League's opponents.[2] They remained the ultimate victors.

The League of Nations.   The League of Nations was formally established when the Versailles Treaty became effective on January 10, 1920. It consisted of three organs, the Assembly in which every League member would be represented, the Council, an executive committee on which the great powers would sit permanently and four (later six and eventually nine) small countries would serve for three-year terms, and a Secretariat. Except for some nonsubstantive matters, all decisions of Assembly and Council required unanimous agreement. The unanimity principle, a concession to the sovereignty of the League members, made it difficult to arrive at any decisions; such decisions, moreover, could only recommend, not prescribe, a course of action. Wilson of course had been aware of these shortcomings, but had felt confident that the League would generate its own moral momentum and that this momentum would be given an additional impetus by the participation of an impartial America.

It would be pointless to speculate on the role the United States would have been able (and willing) to play in the League if it had joined it, yet it is clear that America's abandonment of that body dealt it a very grave blow. In the eyes of the world the League was Wilson's creation, and the prestige of the League was greatly affected when the United States did not become a member. America's nonparticipation weakened the League in other ways too. The British, who had always favored an organization primarily consultative and mediatory in nature, became more reluctant to accept the League's enforcement procedures. They were fearful that punitive measures such as economic sanctions would be ineffective without America's cooperation, whereas a naval blockade might even lead to a head-on collision with the United States. One of the first changes which Britain and the Dominions requested was a restrictive application of economic sanctions. The French, too, became more skeptical of the League when the United States dissociated itself from that body. France concluded military alliances with Belgium, Poland, and Czechoslovakia, openly demonstrating its lack of faith in the League.

America's absence from the League was only one of the factors contributing to its weakness. On more than one occasion Britain and France by-passed the League and settled directly such issues as the Greco-Turkish War and a Greco-Italian dispute over the island of Corfu. At other times either Britain or France blocked League intervention, as in

---

[2] A French economist, Etienne Mantoux, has since shown that Keynes' conclusions were based in part on erroneous assumptions. *Cf.* Mantoux's *The Carthaginian Peace or the Economic Consequences of Mr. Keynes* (1946). Yet some of Mantoux's arguments are not entirely convincing either.

the case of the French occupation of the Ruhr. Once or twice both powers virtually nullified League actions. Albania, which owed to the League its survival in the face of Italian, Greek, and Yugoslav claims, eventually was taken over by Italy because Britain and France insisted on entrusting to Italy the protection of Albania's territorial and economic independence.

The British concept of the League as mainly an instrument of international cooperation and the French view of the League as primarily a bulwark against aggression also interfered with the League's task of preserving peace and limiting armaments. The French sponsored two efforts to strengthen the League's authority. A draft treaty of mutual assistance proposed in 1923 committed every signatory country to give assistance to any other signatory that had been attacked, with military aid limited geographically to the continent of the assisting power. This plan was welcomed by the smaller European countries but was rejected as too comprehensive by the British, the Dominions, and the Latin American countries and was sharply attacked by the United States and Soviet Russia. A second plan, known as the Geneva Protocol, provided for the compulsory arbitration of all disputes between the signatory states, with a refusal to accept arbitration tantamount to an act of aggression. It was adopted by many European and Latin American countries, but was also vetoed by Britain and the Dominions. Again they were fearful that the imposition of economic sanctions might involve them in difficulties with the United States—an attitude encouraged by strong American objections to the Geneva Protocol.

If Britain was a stumbling block in the path of collective security arrangements, France was reluctant to agree to any reduction of armaments as long as it had no explicit assurance of British and American help against future German attacks. As a result, League efforts to initiate any arms reduction remained unsuccessful. The only disarmament agreements that were reached were achieved outside the League, with American participation. The first one was concluded at the Washington Naval Conference of 1921–22, where the United States, Britain, Japan, France, and Italy agreed to limit their capital ships to a tonnage ratio of 5:5:3:1.67:1.67—an agreement facilitated by some doubts about the value of battle cruisers and aircraft carriers in future wars. At another naval conference in London in 1930, the United States, Britain, and Japan reached some limited additional agreements also on the construction of light cruisers, destroyers, and submarines, but the French and Italians rejected this pact. The French demanded as the price for their signature a new Anglo-American guarantee of security, which President Hoover refused.

In some cases, the League did successfully settle political or territorial disputes that otherwise might have ended in war. It resolved a quarrel between Sweden and Finland over control of the Aland Islands; it rescued Albania from its more powerful neighbors, at least temporarily; and it helped settle a Greco-Bulgarian border clash in 1925. None of these issues involved a great power, however, and their significance ought not to be overstressed. Yet their solution did help to create what was called the "spirit of Geneva"—"a sharpened vision of interests common to all men and all nations," in the words of F. P. Walters, the League's historian. It was perhaps no mere coincidence that soon afterwards the League began to attack problems outside of Europe. It took on some Middle and Far Eastern problems, such as the dispute over the oil-rich Mosul territory between Britain, Iraq, and Turkey (which it resolved) and the rehabilitation of China (in which it was less successful, owing to great-power indifference). Later on it also helped settle some Latin American disputes.

The League was most successful, however, in the discharge of its nonpolitical functions. This work was performed by a number of auxiliary agencies attached to or affiliated with the League. Among them were the Economic and Financial Organization, the Health Organization, and the International Labor Organization. Their work rarely commanded the headlines, but it was effectively implemented on a worldwide scale— largely because no questions of national power or prestige were involved and most countries found it to their advantage to take part in these activities. The Economic and Financial Organization, a clearing house for information on commercial policies, currencies, taxation, and production, helped a number of countries, including Austria, Hungary, Greece, Bulgaria, Estonia, and Albania, solve their financial problems. The Health Organization was active in the fight against epidemics and tropical diseases and through its Epidemiological Intelligence Service collected and disseminated information on the incidence of infectious disease. It also provided technical assistance to national health authorities and sent medical missions to China, Liberia, and several Balkan countries. The International Labor Organization collected data and engaged in research on matters affecting the status of labor; in addition, it sought to improve labor standards by international agreements or by recommendations. Between 1919 and 1939, it was able to obtain, by persuasion and moral pressure, the adoption of sixty-three conventions concerned with minimum wages, Sunday rest, working hours, and social insurance. Of these, forty-four had come into force by March 15, 1939, each having been ratified, on the average, by at least nineteen countries. There is no better testimony to the effectiveness of these agencies than the fact that all of them were retained by the United Nations.

Europe and Soviet Russia. The difficulties of creating a new European order were compounded by the absence of Soviet Russia from the European state system. While the fighting in the West continued in 1918, the Western Powers made several attempts to restore a measure of European balance by intervening in Russia. Troops were sent to the northern ports of Archangel and Murmansk and to Vladivostok in the Far

East to keep out of German hands war matériel that had been dispatched to Russia while it was still an ally. To relieve German pressure on the western front, efforts also were made to prepare the way for a reopening of the Russian front, and support was rushed to the anti-Bolshevik forces which took up arms against Lenin's government. The hope was that the White Russians would not only destroy the Bolshevik regime but also re-enter the war against Germany. Neither hope was fulfilled. Western assistance to the anti-Bolshevik factions came to an end late in 1919 when the latter, disunited and demoralized, succumbed to their Bolshevik foes.

Despite the profound distrust with which Soviet Russia and the European powers looked upon each other, they began soon afterwards to put out political and economic feelers towards each other. By the spring of 1921 Lenin and most of his closest associates had accepted the fact that the Bolshevik Revolution was unlikely in the near future to spread to the West and give Soviet Russia access to the West's industries. Desperately in need of economic assistance, they decided to try to break out of their isolation. Some of the Western countries, in turn, hoped to relieve their own economic difficulties by gaining access to the Russian market. Britain, seriously plagued by overproduction, was especially anxious to export to Russia. These mutual needs led to a rapprochement between the two countries, and in March 1921 they signed a commercial agreement. Shortly afterwards Germany concluded a similar pact, and somewhat later it was followed by Italy and some of the smaller European nations.

The Genoa Conference and the Pact of Rapallo. These separate arrangements could do little, however, to relieve Europe's economic difficulties. Both sides realized that the European economy would have to be revived on a continent-wide rather than a bilateral scale. Western bankers and industrialists drew up a blueprint for an international corporation which would plan and help finance the economic reconstruction of Europe. Lloyd George became the chief advocate of these proposals. He urged the calling of an economic conference of all European states including the former enemy countries. Besides these, he wished to invite Russia and the United States whose financial help would be needed to rebuild Europe's economy. The moment seemed especially opportune because Lenin had shortly before inaugurated his New Economic Policy (see p. 180); Russia seemed to be returning to a capitalist, private-enterprise economy. Lloyd George was seconded by French Premier Aristide Briand (1862–1932) on the need for establishing closer relations with both Germany and Soviet Russia. Preparations were made for a conference to convene at Genoa in April 1922.

By the time the conference met Briand had been forced to resign, and his successor was Raymond Poincaré (1860–1934). Unlike the easygoing and flexible Briand, the new Premier was stubborn and unrelentingly legal-minded. (Comparing the two men, Paris wits liked to quip that Poincaré knew everything and understood nothing while Briand knew nothing and understood everything.) Poincaré was convinced that France's security depended on Germany's strict fulfillment of the Versailles Treaty, and he objected to the admission of Germany as an equal participant in the conference. At his insistence all questions touching on reparations and France's security were excluded from the discussions. Poincaré was equally opposed to an economic rapprochement with the Soviet regime until the question of the repayment of Tsarist debts and the indemnification of the former owners of nationalized property had been settled satisfactorily. These were problems of special concern to France since 80 per cent of Tsarist Russia's foreign loans had been underwritten by French investors, and Frenchmen had also been hardest hit by the nationalization of Russian industrial enterprises.

Thus hamstrung, the conference had little chance of success. It suffered a further setback when the United States refused to attend on the grounds that the conference would be more political than economic and Washington did not wish to become involved in European politics. Moreover, at France's suggestion, the Germans were barred from some of the early negotiations and the Russians were confronted at once with the question of debts and indemnities. Angrily the Russians turned to the suspicious and worried Germans and proposed the conclusion of a separate treaty between their two countries. The Germans consented, and on Easter Sunday 1922 Soviet Foreign Commissioner Georgei Chicherin and German Foreign Minister Walther Rathenau met in deep secrecy at the seaside resort of Rapallo. There they signed a treaty by which they cancelled their respective financial claims, agreed to resume full diplomatic relations, and in order to promote trade expansion, granted each other most-favored-nation privileges.

The Rapallo Pact dealt the death blow to the Genoa Conference. Beyond that, it raised the prestige of Soviet Russia, now recognized by a major power, and gave the Germans a new sense of independence and self-esteem. Under the cover of expanding commercial relations, the pact initiated the military collaboration of the two powers—soon German officers were training the Red Army while German technicians developed in Russian plants weapons the Germans were not allowed to have under the disarmament provisions of the Versailles Treaty. Above all, Rapallo put an end to all hopes, however slim, of bringing Germany back as a full-fledged partner into the European order. Whatever commitment Germany made to the West in the years to come would always be qualified by some reservation intended to safeguard its special relations with Moscow. "[A breakoff of the alliance with Russia] would place us wholly at the mercy of France and Britain," a leading official of the German Foreign Office confided to an American journalist in 1925. "Our interest is . . . to play off East against West, and West against East."

The Reparations Problem and the Occupation of the Ruhr. As John Maynard Keynes had predicted, the reparations arrangement was one of the main causes of Europe's political and economic difficulties. Short of foodstuffs and raw materials, Germany found itself burdened with obligations which even in normal times would have proved to be a severe drain on its economy. The problem of effecting the payments in the currency of the reparations creditors created additional difficulties. The recipient countries were plagued by overproduction and unemployment and were unwilling therefore to buy German goods. In consequence, the Germans found it exceedingly hard to obtain any foreign exchange. They themselves aggravated their difficulties; there was a continuous flight of private capital from the country, which the German government failed to check just as it failed to put an end to the spreading inflation. It was not until August 1921 that Germany paid a first installment of one billion marks which was financed by short-term credits. Another payment of 500 million marks was made in November, but soon afterwards the Berlin government, harassed by budget deficits, tax evasion, and inflation, asked for a moratorium which was reluctantly granted.

Britain's and France's attitudes toward the reparations issue were sharply at variance. By this time the British had second thoughts on the wisdom of the reparations settlement. Their main concern was the revival of trade, and they knew that Germany's reparations, as well as the Allied war debts, prevented an early normalization of commercial relations. They were prepared on their part to renounce their reparations claims and their claims on their wartime allies, provided the United States would cancel its war debt claims. Such an arrangement would have entailed a substantial financial loss to the British, but this they were willing to bear. They also sensed that insistence on full payment was playing into the hands of the German nationalists and was likely to block the stabilization of the new European order in which they saw the only lasting foundation of peace.

Most Frenchmen were just as certain that peace could not be preserved in Europe unless the Germans were forced to fulfill their reparations commitments. Only by keeping Germany economically weak, they believed, could their more populous, more dynamic, and economically more highly developed neighbor be prevented from reverting to its aggressive ambitions. Frenchmen who took this view were also convinced that they could not count on Britain's support in the event of a German resurgence. These fears increased when Britain, to ease France's mind, proposed a new security pact in 1921; to Paris' dismay, London would not commit itself to any specific action should the Germans turn on the French. But the reparations question was also of great economic importance to France. The reconstruction of its war-devastated areas was to be financed by German reparations, and so was the payment of the French war debts. Having suffered the heaviest damage of all reparations creditors, France had been accorded the lion's share, 52 per cent of all payments. France, then, had a far greater stake in reparations than did Britain, which together with the British Empire was entitled only to 22 per cent.

The divergence of the two powers came to a head in January 1923 when Germany was in arrears on its coal and timber deliveries. Poincaré insisted that the delays were unjustified, and the Reparations Commission upheld him by a three to one vote, with Britain the lone dissenter. On January 11, 1923, French, Belgian, and Italian technicians, escorted by two French divisions and a few Belgian units, moved into the Ruhr to secure some "productive guarantees" from which the claims of the three countries concerned could be satisfied. The move was intended not only as a showdown with Germany, but also as evidence of France's determination to act on its own if Britain would not support it. The German government retaliated by enjoining the population of the Ruhr territory not to collaborate with the occupation authorities. What Poincaré had envisaged as a minor operation in which a small force would protect the technical experts sent to the Ruhr grew into a major military and technical enterprise. At great cost French engineers, workers, and railroaders who were rushed to the scene managed to revive parts of the area's industries. But the policy of passive resistance proved even more costly to Germany. In September 1923, after the strike had all but wrecked the country's inflation-ridden economy, it was called off by a newly formed German government. The decision marked the emergence of Gustav Stresemann (1878–1929). The new German Chancellor understood that Germany could hope to master its difficulties only by compromises and not by recalcitrance, and he agreed to resume coal deliveries as scheduled by the Reparations Commission.

Poincaré won only a Pyrrhic victory. The occupation of the Ruhr increased France's economic difficulties and further weakened its currency. Many Frenchmen, moreover, felt uneasy about their country's growing alienation from Britain and the hostility of world public opinion. Despite its success they decided to abandon Poincaré's policy of force and unilateral actions and to attain security and reparations by more conciliatory means and in close concert with Britain.

ATTEMPTS AT A NEW EUROPEAN ORDER

The Dawes Plan. Obviously there was no hope of an economic recovery without a settlement of the reparations problem. Bowing to the inevitable, Poincaré agreed that a committee of financial experts examine the issue as purely an economic one, removed from all politics. He insisted, however, that there could be no question of a reduction of the total amount, but only of a lighter schedule of payments.

The nonpolitical nature of the committee made possible also American participation in its deliberations. American business and government leaders knew that the prosperity of the United States was closely related to the economic well-being of Europe, and while shying away from foreign *political* "entanglements," were prepared to assist in Europe's *economic* rehabilitation. Secretary of State Charles Evans Hughes had been the first to propose the formation of just such a committee of technical experts (including Americans) as was now established, and after the committee had done its work, Hughes went himself to Europe to urge the acceptance of its proposals. The Europeans on their part acknowledged America's vital role in the reordering of the European economy and elected Charles G. Dawes, a Chicago banker, chairman of the committee.

The "Dawes Plan" which the committee worked out established a schedule of annuities closely geared to the condition of the German economy. As a further concession, the Germans were no longer asked to make their payments in the currencies of the creditor countries; the task of conversion was entrusted to a special Agent-General of Reparations, again an American, who was to effect the transfers in such a way that they would not endanger the newly stabilized German currency. A loan of $200,000,000 was to help protect further the German mark and facilitate payment of the first reparations installment. The plan was accepted with some reluctance by Germany and more readily by its creditors. Since it did not reduce the overall reparations debt to a realistic amount, it was, however, no more than a temporary arrangement. As such it did offer a breathing spell and new hope for the future. The plan worked well during the five years of its operation— thanks chiefly to the continued flow into Germany of foreign, mainly American, loans.

The Inter-Allied War Debts. Like the reparations, the Allies' war debts hampered Europe's economic recovery. The hope had been that they could be paid back out of Germany's reparations, but when this proved illusory, efforts were made to obtain a cancellation of all inter-Allied debts. The United States rejected these proposals, and an embittered trans-Atlantic debate ensued. Americans felt that having gained no territorial or other material advantages out of the war, they were entitled at least to the repayment of their loans; Europeans retorted that the loans had helped to expand the American economy and that in any event they had been spent in a common cause to which the United States had contributed much less than its debtors.[3] The loans, moreover, were not commercial self-liquidating loans; the proceeds did not

[3] In 1917 the American government had used these same arguments to justify the granting of loans to the Allies. A Treasury bulletin issued in the latter part of that year pointed out that by lending money to the Allies, the United States was helping not only them, but also American soldiers and sailors; such assistance would lessen "the work and danger and suffering of our own men in bringing the war to an

increase the productive wealth of the borrowers but were used for such uneconomic transactions as the purchase of arms, ammunition, and other noncapital goods. The United States remained unconvinced. In fact, by raising its tariffs (Fordney-McCumber Act, 1922) America compounded the difficulties of its debtors and made it still harder for them to sell on the American market and obtain the dollars they needed to repay their debts.

Bowing to American pressure, the Allies agreed in the end to negotiate the settlement of their war debts. During the years 1923–1926 funding agreements were concluded by the United States with Britain, France, Italy, and the smaller European debtors. Even though the American government wrote off large parts of its claims, Allied repayments might have proved difficult if the Germans had not been paying their reparations to America's debtors. Since these payments were serviced with American capital pouring ceaselessly into Germany, this meant in effect that American investors underwrote the repayment of the Allied war debts owed to their own government.

The Locarno Treaties. With the economic climate improved, the European powers turned their attention to the political scene. In February 1925 the Germans proposed that both they and the French accept their common frontier as permanent and that Britain act as a guarantor of this agreement.[4] The British government had recently rejected the Geneva Protocol; feeling the need for some gesture to help ease France's fears, it welcomed this more modest proposal. The French response, on the other hand, was not favorable. A few weeks later, however, France was faced with revolts in Morocco and Syria, and its need for a European settlement became pressing. By this time, Briand had returned to the French Foreign Office. Convinced that France had neither the strength nor the will to protect itself against potential German ambitions, he took up in earnest the negotiations for the proposed security pact. He wished to extend it, however, to eastern Europe and asked for a guarantee of the German-Polish and German-Czech boundaries as fixed by the Treaty of Versailles. His demands were unacceptable to both Britain and Germany. The British did not wish to assume a commitment as far

---

earlier close." The statement added that since the American economy was producing more goods than could be consumed by its own people, American prosperity depended on the sale of the excess production to its allies. In a similar vein Secretary of the Treasury Carter Glass wrote in 1919: "The service of these loans in assisting to hold the battlefronts of Europe until the might of our heroic army could be felt effectively, made possible, beyond the shadow of a doubt, the ending of the war in the fall of 1918. Without this aid to the Allied governments, the war unquestionably would have been prolonged, if not lost, with the resultant additional cost in life and treasure." See Harold G. Moulton and Leo Pasvolsky, *War Debts and World Prosperity* (New York, 1932), p. 49.

[4] In a similar plan presented in 1922, the United States was to have been the guarantor.

Locarno Conference, October 1925. Seated at the table in clockwise
direction, center of side closest to viewer: Stresemann (Germany), Luther
(Germany), Grandi (Italy). Two seats to left: Mussolini (Italy). Two seats
from Mussolini: Chamberlain (Britain). At center of far side: Briand
(France). (*Reprinted courtesy Brown Brothers*)

removed from Britain's strategic interests as eastern Europe appeared
to be; the Germans would not accept as unchangeable their eastern
frontiers. France also insisted that Germany join the League of Nations
to bind it further to peaceful behavior by the rules of the League
Covenant. To this condition the Germans objected on the grounds that
German League membership might impair German-Russian relations.

In the end all difficulties were patched up, and in October 1925 the
negotiations were concluded at Locarno, the picturesque Swiss resort on
the Lago Maggiore. A Treaty of Mutual Guarantee signed by Britain,
France, Germany, Belgium, and Italy declared as inviolate the Franco-
German and Belgian-German frontiers and the demilitarized zone of the
German Rhineland. Britain and Italy pledged themselves to help the
three countries concerned to uphold the agreement, promising to come
to the aid of Belgium and France in case of a German attack and to
that of Germany in the opposite event. Disputes between Germany,
France, and Belgium were to be settled by arbitration, with refusal to
submit to arbitration to be considered an act of aggression. Germany
also signed arbitration treaties with Poland and Czechoslovakia, avowing
that it would seek territorial changes on its eastern frontiers only by
peaceful means. The way was also prepared for the entry of Germany
into the League of Nations: Germany agreed to apply for membership

provided it received a permanent seat on the League Council and would not be asked to take part in any League action against Soviet Russia.

The Locarno Treaties were widely hailed as harbingers of a new era of peace and international collaboration, and for a moment even most Germans and Frenchmen shared the general sense of relief. Reflecting these feelings, the Swedes awarded the 1926 Nobel Peace Prize to the architects of Locarno, Stresemann, Briand, and Sir Austen Chamberlain, the British Foreign Secretary.

Relations between France, Britain, and Germany did improve after Locarno. The Allied evacuation of the occupied Rhineland got under way, Germany entered the League of Nations, and Allied controls of German disarmament were brought to an end (even though Germany had not fully complied with the disarmament provisions of the Versailles Treaty). German and French business, professional, and cultural leaders also began to collaborate more closely with one another. But the underlying tensions were not removed. Limited to western Europe, the Guarantee Pact failed to recreate the kind of balanced European system which might have given France and its eastern allies the hoped-for assurance that German ambitions could be contained. As it was, with Germany unreconciled to the loss of Danzig and the Polish Corridor, the French and their allies still felt uneasy and tightened their military alliances. Their anxieties grew when in April 1926 Berlin and Moscow signed a new friendship and neutrality pact; conceivably the treaty could open the door at some future date to another partition of Poland.

The Germans on their part objected to the discriminatory treatment to which they were still subjected despite Locarno and their membership in the League. Part of their territory remained occupied by foreign troops; they were not allowed to rearm though no one else had disarmed; and they still had to pay reparations. They considered any new Allied concessions merely their due, and at that quite inadequate. The British and French resented Germany's lack of appreciation, and the French became even more reluctant to make any further concessions.

A. J. P. Taylor, the English historian, is probably right when he observes that the Franco-German conflict could not have been resolved either by more or fewer concessions; since it proved impossible to recreate a balanced European order and thus contain the Franco-German rivalry, it may well be, as Taylor contends, that only the fear of some common danger could have brought the two countries together. On occasion Briand's policies seem to have been dictated by premonitions of such a threat. "We'll soon find ourselves encircled by two formidable powers, the United States and Russia," he warned in 1922. "You can see it is absolutely essential to create the United States of Europe."[5]

---

[5] Quoted in Jacques Chastenet, *Histoire de la Troisième République* (Paris, 1952–62), V, p. 91.

Yet neither the Soviet Union nor the United States seemed likely to threaten Europe, and the relative power position of France and Germany remained one of the crucial issues of European and world politics.

The Kellogg-Briand Pact. The Franco-German conflict continued to smoulder while Europe enjoyed on the surface the benefits of peace and prosperity. German nationalists were losing ground in the elections of the mid-twenties, but they remained as strident as ever in their demands for the repudiation of the war-guilt clause, the recovery of the lost eastern territories, and German rearmament. Similarly all German governments, whether they tended to the left or the right in their political coloration, acted as spokesmen for these demands. French fears of German intentions thus never subsided, and Briand continued his quest for additional safeguards. In 1926, just a few months after Locarno, he negotiated treaties of friendship with Yugoslavia and Rumania to draw them closer into the French orbit.

Briand's most ambitious effort was an attempt to associate the United States, if ever so loosely, with the French security system. On April 6, 1927, the tenth anniversary of America's entry into World War I, he addressed a "Message to the American People" in which he announced that France was ready, in view of the "common inspiration and identity of aims which exist between [it] and the United States . . . publicly to subscribe, with the United States, to any mutual engagement tending, as between these two countries, to 'outlaw war,' to use an American expression." And bypassing deftly France's reluctance to disarm, he added that the two countries could in this manner best illustrate "this truth that the accomplishment most immediately to be attained is not so much disarmament as the practice of peace."

The reaction of the American government to Briand's proposal was markedly cool. The State Department viewed it as a "negative military alliance"; it might not only give France a free hand in Europe by committing the United States to neutrality if France went to war, but it might also prevent the United States from asserting its rights as a neutral should France violate these rights as Britain and Germany had done in World War I. Just at that time, however, Franco-American friendship received a powerful stimulus from Charles Lindbergh's nonstop flight from New York to Paris; popular sentiment in favor of Briand's peace plan soon grew so strong that the proposal could not be shelved. In December Secretary of State Frank B. Kellogg countered it with a plan of his own by which all countries of the world were to join in the "outlawry of war." This proposal in turn alarmed France, for it threatened to undermine France's military alliances. Kellogg explained that the pact he envisaged was to outlaw aggressive wars only and that wars fought in self-defense or in defense of such vital interests as the Monroe Doctrine would still be permissible. Each nation, moreover, would be the judge of whether "circumstances require[d] recourse to war in self-defense." Thus reassured, fifteen nations signed the pact in Paris on August 27, 1928, and subsequently forty-nine more acceded to it.

Like the Locarno Treaties the Kellogg-Briand Pact was greeted with widespread enthusiasm. Peace appeared more securely established than ever before. If not legally, at least morally the United States seemed committed to help preserve peace in the world, and so, for that matter, did the Soviet Union, one of the first to announce its adherence to the pact. Yet unless implemented by specific obligations, moral commitments have proved to be of uncertain value in international relations. The Kellogg-Briand Pact contained no enforcement provisions, nor did it provide consultation or arbitration procedures to replace war "as an instrument of national policy." Above all, it was hedged in with innumerable reservations and "explanations" which could render it meaningless. Many governments seemed to think so. While the crowds of Paris greeted the German Foreign Minister with gay shouts of "Long live Stresemann" when he arrived to sign the pact, the French cabinet was completing its plans for the Maginot Line of fortifications to be built along the Franco-German frontier. At the same time the German government gave its final approval to the construction of a series of new pocket battleships. And a month after the United States Senate had ratified the pact, it passed a naval appropriations bill providing for the construction of an aircraft carrier and fifteen new cruisers.

But Briand was undismayed. To him the pact was not an end, but a beginning, and he maintained that it held out "precious promises for the future." Despite all the evidence to the contrary he remained hopeful that it might lead, with American help, to the eventual creation of a positive system of collective security.

The Young Plan. There were indeed constant reminders that the interests of the United States and Europe were irretrievably intertwined. By 1928 it was generally agreed that the time had come for a permanent settlement of the reparations question. The Germans were pressing for it, hopeful that their burden could thus be eased; the Allies thought it desirable because their American war debts had meanwhile been fixed and they wished to coordinate Germany's and their own obligations. They insisted that reparations be high enough to service their payments to Washington, but were prepared, in return, to consider the German demand for a withdrawal of their troops from the Rhineland.

The close economic connection between war debts and reparations and their dependence on American loans was by then clearly established. But to avoid being drawn into European politics, the American government still refused to acknowledge officially any correlation between the two obligations. American financiers, on the other hand, concerned with their German investments, were vitally interested in an equitable reparations arrangement; when a new committee of experts set out to re-examine the problem early in 1929, it was again headed by an American business leader, Owen D. Young, who had already served on the Dawes Committee.

The committee produced the "Young Plan," which reduced the overall debt to about $9 billion and provided quick relief by cutting the first few annuities from $600 million to $400 million. Payments were spread over fifty-nine years to 1988, the terminal date of the war debt payments. War debts and reparations thus were coordinated; their interrelationship was also acknowledged by the provision that in the event of a reduction of Allied war debts, reparations would be reduced correspondingly.

In its inception the Young Plan had been a by-product of that era of international collaboration that had been ushered in by the Dawes Plan. The hope was that the new plan would make its contribution to the easing of tensions. It did away with all foreign controls over Germany's economy; it was coupled with the evacuation, ahead of schedule, of the Allied forces from the occupied Rhineland; and it lightened Germany's financial burden and provided for the suspension of payments in case of economic difficulties.[6] But the plan did not fulfill the hopes for an improvement of the international atmosphere. When it was ratified in the spring of 1930, the world was in the grip of the Depression and in Germany Nazism was in the ascendence. Stresemann, worn out and ill, had died in October 1929, a few weeks after he had obtained the Allies' promise to withdraw their last occupation forces by June 30, 1930. His death marked the end of an era. When Germany celebrated the liberation of the Rhineland in July 1930, Reich President von Hindenburg would not even mention Stresemann's name in the official ceremonies.

There were other signs of a change in the political climate. A few weeks before Stresemann's death, in September 1929, Briand launched a proposal for closer association of the countries of Europe to strengthen cooperation among them and in this way enhance their security. Stresemann welcomed the plan in his last address to the League, and other statesmen also expressed their approval. Briand was asked to submit a detailed plan in consultation with the other European League members. Yet when the League met again in September 1930, the project was quietly shelved. In the atmosphere of growing distrust second thoughts had aroused strong misgivings, and almost every state now had reservations. Halfway through the League session the Nazis won their first major victory at the polls. Their success put an end to what hopes there still were for a closer union of Europe.

---

[6] It was widely assumed, moreover, that a large part of the settlement was academic since it was unlikely that reparations payments would be continued for another two generations.

5

Economy, Society, Culture
in the 1920's

Although the efforts to create a new European polity were not successful, the European states remained linked to each other by a multitude of social and economic concerns. To some degree all European nations, neutrals as well as former belligerents, shared these problems—an indication of the pervasiveness of the war's repercussions. Essentially these problems centered around three major issues: the need to restore viable economies; the expectations of an aroused working class that had borne the hardships of war in the hope of a better future; and the opposition of upper and middle class to the aspirations of labor which threatened the traditional elitist order. Many of these issues were European, if not world-wide, in nature, and the tasks of economic reconstruction in particular transcended national boundaries; but rather than view them as such, most countries attacked these questions as separate national problems and thus failed to solve them. Only those more perceptive observers of the contemporary scene, Europe's writers and artists, sensed fully how closely the European nations were linked in their fundamental concerns. Their literary and artistic creations showed a remarkable similarity in their outlook and approach to the issues of the time—a fact that heightened the tragedy of Europe's failure to find common solutions for its common troubles.

THE ECONOMIC SITUATION

The Decline of the European Economy.　At the end of the war Europe's economy was faltering in severe disarray. Physical destruction had laid waste large areas of Belgium and northern France, the major battlefields in the west. In the east Poland, Hungary, and the Baltic and Balkan states bore the scars of wartime action and postwar fighting; similarly, much of western Russia lay in ruins after three years of war, with the ravages of the Russian civil war adding to the desperate plight of the country.

Physical destruction, however, was not the main cause of Europe's economic difficulties. Dislocation of production and disruption of trade were even more important factors. They affected not only the actual battle zones, but also countries like Britain and Germany which had remained physically all but untouched by the fighting. Industries had been converted to the manufacture of war matériel, merchant shipping diverted to military purposes, manpower drafted into the armed forces or into war-essential work. Strategic industries had expanded far beyond peacetime needs; others of little or no military significance had been allowed to fall into disrepair. Raw material stocks were depleted and production techniques in nonessential areas had become antiquated. By the end of the war Europe's industrial production had dropped to two-thirds of its 1913 volume. Moreover, the weakened economies of the European belligerents were burdened with either immense domestic and foreign debts or huge reparations.

Europe's most pressing economic need was the speedy expansion of its industrial and agricultural production to satisfy the needs and expectations of its people, repay the obligations incurred or imposed, and restore prewar prosperity. This, it was felt, could best be achieved by a return to the methods that had proved effective before the war. "By comparison with 1919," Sir Arthur Salter, a British financial expert, later recalled, "the world of 1913 seemed to most of us a paradise from which we had for a time been excluded by a flaming sword. It seemed a sufficient goal for our efforts to win our way back to what we lost, and an attempt was made to do so."

When the war ended, domestic government controls were stripped away as quickly as possible to give free scope again to private enterprise and free competition. This precipitate return to a domestic laissez-faire policy was in many respects unfortunate. Immediately after the fighting ended, it is true, the victor countries enjoyed a brief boom period, stimulated by the accumulated backlog of consumers' needs and partly fueled by British and American credits. This boom subsided, however, after a few months when the most pressing needs had been met and spiraling prices brought demand to an abrupt end. Meanwhile, the relaxation of government controls increased the inflationary pressures on currencies that were already unstable because of the war. The removal of governmental controls also prevented the allocation of resources on the basis of equitable priorities, adding to the sharp social tensions. Above all, the elimination of all governmental restrictions precluded any systematic attempt to adjust postwar reconstruction to the changes that had occurred in the world economy. The European nations let themselves be guided by their presumed national interests and proceeded to rebuild their economies along prewar lines. Constrained by this parochial nationalism, they recovered but slowly from the after-effects of the war.[1]

The war had wrought many changes which blocked Europe's economic expansion. That expansion, which had slowed down already before 1914, now faced the loss of the vast Russian market and of investments in Russia amounting to $3.5 billion, or 10 per cent of all European investments abroad. Intra-European trade was further impeded by the break-up of the Austrian and Russian empires which fragmented Europe into 27 separate customs units as compared to the 20 of prewar Europe. In world trade Europe faced a United States whose total productive capacity had increased by one-seventh between 1914 and 1918 (as against a reduction of Europe's industrial output alone by one-third). The United States and Japan had, moreover, captured many of the overseas markets which the European belligerents had been unable to service during the war; the Europeans lost other markets as the British Dominions and some of the Latin American countries built up industries of their own.

Europe took little if any account of these developments. Behind high tariffs and aided by subsidies, wheat and beet sugar production was increased beyond prewar levels, although the United States, Argentina, Canada, and Australia had stepped up their own wheat production and overseas cane sugar output had quadrupled. Coal production collided with the increased use of oil and hydroelectric power as sources of fuel and energy. There was also a great deal of duplication of effort as a result of postwar territorial changes. As long as Alsace-Lorraine was German, Lorraine's iron ore had been melted down on the spot and the finished steel was produced in the Ruhr; however, when Alsace-Lorraine went to France, the French built steel mills in Lorraine and the Germans built pig-iron furnaces in the Ruhr.

The breakup of the old Austro-Hungarian Empire touched off similar developments. Whatever its political difficulties, that empire had been a

---

[1] War debts played no role at this time since repayment did not begin until the mid-1920's and interest payments had been suspended. The Germans alone did make two cash payments on reparations account in 1921, which accelerated the depreciation of the mark. They also made regular deliveries in kind.

well-balanced state economically, with the industrialized western parts (Austria and Bohemia) and the agricultural and raw material producing eastern parts (Hungary, Slovakia, Galicia, and Transylvania) complementing each other. Hungary had been Bohemia's most important textile market before the war; after the dissolution of the Habsburg Empire, Hungary expanded its textile industries and by 1933 met almost all of its textile needs out of its own production. And while Austria's and Bohemia's textile plants had supplemented each other until 1918, with most of the spindles located in Austria and the weaveries in Bohemia, after 1918 the Austrians built their own weaveries and the Czechs set up their own spinning mills. These small-scale industries produced at high cost and on the whole were confined to their limited domestic markets. Worse, their products were often inferior in quality to competitive foreign products. Thus living standards did not improve, and the Central European economies stagnated from lack of consumers. Even Czechoslovakia, comparatively the most prosperous of the so-called successor states, never attained prewar levels in some of its industries. Hungary's industrial production grew little more than 1 per cent per year in the period from 1913 to 1937, as compared to an annual growth rate of 8 per cent between 1898 and 1913. Yet when Reporter John Gunther suggested to a Hungarian that a mutual 10 per cent reduction of Hungarian-Czech tariffs might somewhat relieve the economic difficulties of Hungary, his Hungarian host was indignant: "Do you imagine we rate our hatred of the Czechs at only 10 per cent!"

In the face of such obstacles a return to the self-regulating ways of prewar international trade proved impossible. Wartime tariffs were retained and often increased, and industries of strategic importance were protected by special measures. The war had demonstrated the decisive importance of economic self-sufficiency, but efforts to maintain or achieve a large measure of autarky were incompatible with the attempts to restore normal international commercial relations. Related to this form of economic nationalism were endeavors to keep a potential enemy economically weak—a policy that France pursued towards Germany and that helps to account for the adamant opposition of the French to any reduction of German reparation payments.

The fact remained that because Europe's industrial production was geared to substantial exports, prosperity could not be restored until international trade had been greatly expanded. It was in recognition of this need that the Genoa Conference met in 1922 in an unsuccessful attempt to restore trade relations on a scale vast enough to encompass Europe, Soviet Russia, and, if possible, the United States.

The United States and Europe. As in the diplomatic arena, Europe looked for help to the United States in its economic difficulties. During the immediate postwar period the American government continued to grant substantial loans to the Allied powers to help them restore their economies. After 1920, however, government aid was discontinued as economically unhealthy. Washington warned the European nations that their continuing troubles were largely due to their inadequate tax policies, inflated currencies, and obsolete trade restrictions. It urged them to reorder their finances, stabilize their currencies, and increase their exports. This was helpful advice as far as domestic policies were concerned, but of little use in regard to exports that were barred by high tariffs from the United States and faced with increasing American competition in other parts of the world.

United States-European economic relations had undergone far-reaching structural changes in the course of the war. Since the outbreak of the conflict the United States had evolved from a debtor into a creditor nation in world trade. In July 1914, American foreign indebtedness exceeded its international assets by $3.7 billion; in December 1919, American foreign assets surpassed liabilities by $12.5 billion. The United States had become not only the country with the largest productive capacity but also the one with the greatest financial resources. The prewar balance of transatlantic trade—American capital imports in exchange for European imports of foodstuffs and raw materials—had been destroyed. Loans might temporarily even out this imbalance, but in the long run the European nations could finance their imports from the United States and repay their debts only by a substantial increase of their exports. Few Americans were cognizant of these economic facts of life, and the nation as a whole was not prepared psychologically or materially to undertake the far-reaching readjustment of its domestic economy that the creation of a new transatlantic balance of trade demanded.

The problem might have been met halfway by the cancellation of all intergovernmental war debts, but this solution the United States found unacceptable.[2] The American government did take one step, however, to ease Europe's plight. In September 1919 the Treasury Department suspended for a three-year period all interest payments due on debts to the United States government. But the beneficial effects of this measure were offset by the increase in American tariffs in 1921 and 1922. The increases were made to aid the declining economy—a decline brought on in large part by Europe's inability to maintain its purchases in the United States.

Inflation and Stabilization.   Meanwhile inflation weighed heavily on many of the European economies. In some countries—France, Italy, Belgium—it was kept under control; in others—Germany, Austria, Hun-

---

[2] Unlike the large-scale shift to increased imports, the cancellation of these debts would not have entailed a major economic reorientation—all it would have required would have been a moderate increase in taxes to service the bonds issued to finance the government loans to the Allies.

gary, Poland—it was not, with results that were catastrophic. The German inflation which was solved primarily by the Germans themselves will be discussed later in the context of German domestic developments. (see Chapter 8). More pertinent in the present context is the story of Austria's currency troubles, the settlement of which is a notable example of international cooperation. A rump state of six-million inhabitants of whom one-third were crowded into Vienna, Austria was unable to adjust its economy to the new circumstances. Without adequate food supplies, raw materials, and capital, it could not feed itself or export enough to meet the basic needs of its people. Political unrest rendered the task of rehabilitation still more difficult, and so did administrative inefficiency.[3] For a time Austria lived on "relief credits" provided by the former enemy powers, but these were spent on immediate needs and proved insufficient to rehabilitate the economy of the country. By August 1922 the Austrian crown was worth one fifteen-thousandth of its normal value, and it was clear that the country would never be able to reorganize its economy and develop its resources without substantial outside help.

The League of Nations was charged with the task of devising a plan for Austria's rehabilitation, and it did so with the help of Britain, France, Italy, and Czechoslovakia. (Britain was concerned with Austria's recovery for economic reasons, France and Czechoslovakia were anxious to keep Vienna from turning for help to Germany, and Italy, with an eye on the Balkan Peninsula, did not want it to seek aid from the so-called Little Entente—Czechoslovakia, Yugoslavia, and Rumania.) The plan called for the slashing of public expenditures, tax reforms, and the stabilization of the currency. A loan of $130 million, underwritten by a consortium of private banks, was floated; a portion of it was guaranteed by the above-mentioned countries and some neutral governments, and the whole issue was secured by Austrian taxes especially earmarked for this purpose. In return, Austria had to accept League control of its use of the loan and had to pledge itself to remain independent—that is, not to seek union (*Anschluss*) with Germany.

The League plan was highly successful, and a similar plan, although without international guarantees, was worked out subsequently for Hungary. Germany stabilized its currency late in 1923, and Belgium and France followed in 1926.

Economic Reconstruction. With currencies stabilized and budgets balanced, the European economy began to expand again; after 1924

---

[3] Sir Arthur Salter recalls, "When I came to Vienna [in the fall of 1922], I noticed that the clerks in my office were using the back of crown notes as scribbling paper; it was the cheapest paper they could get. I looked at the date of the notes; it was quite recent; it was in fact by that time costing about sixty times as much to print a note as the note was worth when printed. But the blind routine of printing even the smallest denomination continued."

production increased more rapidly, although still at a slower rate than before the war. By 1929 output exceeded prewar capacity by some 10 per cent.

The revival of the European economy was due in large part to the influx of American loans. As inflation was checked and currencies stabilized, Americans found Europe an attractive field for investments. Not only did American investments facilitate the payment of reparations and war debts, they also permitted countries whose liquid capital resources had been wiped out by inflation to finance imports without corresponding exports. Relieved of the need to accumulate capital by their own savings, these countries were able to maintain high internal consumption levels that kept their economies moving. Germany modernized and expanded its industrial plant, yet enjoyed at the same time a fairly high living standard. A large part of its increased production was sold in Latin America and the Far East, which bought these goods with American loans of their own. Another portion of German exports went to Russia on credits financed by American capital that Germany had received. Not a few American loans, finally, were used to underwrite public work projects—municipal buildings, hospitals, stadiums, and other recreational facilities—that provided job opportunities for men who otherwise would have remained unemployed.

Offered on a limited scale and on terms that assured economic and efficient use, American capital could have made a lasting contribution to Europe's prosperity. As it was, it was granted indiscriminately and in excessive amounts. States, counties, municipalities, and industrial enterprises were flooded with offers of loans. One Prussian finance minister later recalled that not a week passed without the agent of an American bank calling on him to offer financial aid; and there was the famous case of a Bavarian village in need of $125,000 which was in the end persuaded to borrow $3 million. Loans of this kind merely concealed the existing maladjustments in the European economies—excessive tariff barriers, wasteful duplication, rigid price structures, and restrictions on output imposed by cartels. They also blurred the maldistribution of wealth that left a disproportionately large amount of purchasing power in too few hands and impeded the growth of domestic markets. Obviously the American loans could be no more than temporary expedients, but neither Americans nor Europeans considered them such. The loans were the more dangerous because they allowed many countries to develop economies which they could never hope to sustain out of their own resources. Some economies became wholly geared to the continued influx of American capital, much of it short-term credits, and this dependence made them especially vulnerable.

Not all fields of economic activity could be revived, even with the help of American capital. The iron and steel, shipbuilding, and textile industries remained in a state of continued depression. They had been vastly expanded to meet the needs of the war, but found no comparable peace-time demand. These were the industries on which Britain's economy had been built up; Britain never overcame the resultant difficulties, in spite of its efforts to adjust its industrial output to world market needs (see p. 112). After 1919 there were increasing demands for protective tariffs in this last refuge of free trade, and calls for domestic planning. Not only the socialist Labor Party but such confirmed Liberals as Lloyd George and John Maynard Keynes urged a more active government role in the guidance of the economy. Keynes first advanced these views in a lecture titled prophetically *The End of Laissez-Faire*.

The World Economic Conference of 1927. It became increasingly clear that many of the existing economic difficulties could be solved only on the international plane. For that purpose a world economic conference met under the auspices of the League of Nations in May 1927 at Geneva. Fifty countries were represented, among them the United States and the Soviet Union. There was general agreement that the existing productive facilities could provide a much higher level of prosperity and that the disparity between productive capacity and standard of living was especially marked in Europe. The conference blamed Europe's troubles, apart from internal problems in various countries, on the lack of economic coordination and of an international division of labor. Such collaboration, the final report concluded, required the lowering of tariff barriers and the removal of such other obstacles to international trade as import quotas and export duties. The response was highly favorable. Twenty-nine countries expressed their readiness to take part in any joint move to adopt the proposals of the conference, and a number of commercial treaties, calling for reciprocal tariff reductions, were concluded within the next year. But the movement towards tariff reductions soon petered out, one of the reasons being, as a League report noted in 1929, "the prospect of still higher duties in the United States." In many cases, the main obstacle to the removal or lowering of tariffs was the pressures of special interests that had flourished behind high tariff barriers. Sir Arthur Salter wrote at the time:[4]

These private interests are better organized, more vocal, and more politically effective than the general public interests on the other side; and are much more conscious of what they would stand to lose than the other business interests (such as exporting industries) of what they would gain. Exporters and industries which would certainly gain by a reduction in tariffs, even those of their own country, have been disappointingly indifferent when their support might have been decisive.

As the American economist J. B. Condliffe put it, "The battle for freer trade was lost not on the international, but on the home front."

[4] Quoted in George L. Ridgeway, *Merchants of Peace* (New York, 1938), p. 258.

THE SOCIAL SCENE

Reforms vs. "Normalcy."   The end of the war had been greeted with a mixture of relief and expectation, not only by the belligerents but by the neutrals as well. The belligerents, both victors and defeated, were physically and emotionally exhausted; weary of the hardships of war, they longed to return to an ordered civil existence. The neutrals, greatly dependent on foreign trade, also had suffered severe deprivations, and were anxious to end them. Yet the masses did not want simply to return to prewar conditions; the war had touched off aspirations that called for fulfillment. In the wake of the Fourteen Points political democracy spread across Europe—women were granted the right to vote in Germany, Britain, and Sweden, and special voting qualifications were dropped, as in Belgium and Prussia, the largest state in the German Republic. Even in eastern Europe where political apathy and illiteracy were still widespread, democratic suffrage provisions were introduced almost everywhere.

How meaningful these changes were to the beneficiaries is hard to determine. The immediate concern of the great majority was the improvement of their social and economic lot, and not all of them saw a connection between political rights and the realization of their material expectations. They felt simply entitled to a better life after four years of hardships and sacrifices. Lloyd George had promised to make Britain a land "fit for heroes" and Britons were determined to take him at his word. Similarly, French and Italian labor expected comprehensive reforms from their governments, as did their German and Austrian counterparts and those of the neutral nations. Labor's demands extended from calls for shorter working hours, better pay, and improved systems of social insurance to capital levies to pay off war debts and the nationalization of banks and key industries. Confidence in the power of governments to effect reforms had greatly increased; governments had assumed so many functions and wrought so many changes during the war that they were expected to meet these postwar demands without difficulty. There was also the example of Soviet Russia, whose government seemed to have done a great deal for its workers.

The postwar era thus got under way on a note of sharp social tensions; whereas middle and upper class wished to return as quickly as possible to the "normalcy" of prewar conditions, workers insisted on far-reaching social reforms. Neither position took into account the needs of the hour which called for the curtailment of domestic consumption and strict allocation of resources. In the supercharged atmosphere of the postwar period such concerns were ignored; moreover, to labor its demands were an effort to end age-old inequities and, as such, were concerned with issues that were moral as much as social and economic, and moral positions are not easily influenced by practical considerations.

While almost all of Europe was troubled by social conflicts in the 1920's, these struggles differed in character from country to country. In some of them—Germany, Italy, and Spain—they came close to touching off civil wars; in others—France and Austria—they led to occasional outbreaks of violence. On the other hand, Britain and the Scandinavian and Low Countries were spared bloodshed and violence. These differences, of course, were not accidental. The countries in which violence was most widespread were those least experienced in self-government and in the give-and-take of negotiations across social and political barriers. Clashes were avoided more easily by nations with a self-assured middle class able to adjust to changing conditions without fear of losing its status. Labor on its part was less unyielding where upper and middle class did not attempt to evade their share of the common hardships. This proved true, for example, in Britain. In that country the financial burdens of the war were distributed more equitably than in any of the other belligerent nations; of all the participating powers, Britain financed the largest portion of war expenditures by direct taxes. Nor did Britain suffer an inflation that wiped out the savings of middle and working class, as happened in Germany and in Austria, while the great fortunes, invested in land or industrial stock, remained intact or increased. Resort to violence was also more likely to occur in countries like Germany and Italy where respected scholars and publicists hailed violence as a healthy manifestation of vitality and created a mental climate in which the use of brute force was accepted more readily.

Communism. The war also inured many to violence and aroused a new militancy in the workers. Revolutionary factions that had been held back by prewar prosperity and muted by wartime controls made themselves heard again. In Germany the Communist-oriented Spartacists advocated a social revolution; in France revolutionary syndicalism renewed its call for violent action, the takeover of factories, and that ultimate weapon, the general strike; in Italy left-wing Socialists cast off the restraint they had observed since Italy had entered the war. Similar stirrings aroused the ranks of Danish and Dutch labor and caused considerable agitation among the workers of Norway.

All these groups took much of their inspiration from the Bolshevik Revolution, which appeared to have secured political power and social justice for Russia's workers. As they witnessed the economic difficulties of their own countries and the reluctance of middle and upper class to concede them more than a few limited reforms, they concluded that the caution and circumspection of the moderate Socialists could do nothing to improve the lot of the workers; what was needed to secure labor its due was a complete overhaul of the socioeconomic system like that performed by the Bolshevik leaders. Breaking away from the Socialists, Communist parties sprang up in every country of Europe.

Few of those who embraced Communism had ever studied the writings of Marx or Lenin, whose works, to be understood, required a solid background in history, economics, and sociology; what impressed recruits to Communism was the militancy and self-certainty of Communist views and predictions. In their mood of frustration and bitterness the Marxist program offered them the guidance and reassurance that in earlier times religion would have provided. They embraced it, on faith, like a religion, and their faith in it was the more fervent because it gave them a sense of mission, making them, the downtrodden and underprivileged, the vanguard of the revolution that was to usher in a better world.

Communism drew the bulk of its following from the working classes, but it attracted individual followers from other strata as well. Some intellectuals became Communists, either because their personal hopes and aspirations had not been fulfilled in the capitalist system or because orthodox Marxism with its "scientific" laws and predictions offered them a firm intellectual foundation which they had not found anywhere else. Others joined from a genuine idealism which saw in Communism the promise of a better life that they wanted to help create. Well-educated, informed, used to thinking in long-range terms, many of them assumed positions of leadership in the Communist parties just as their less radical-minded fellows helped guide the Socialist parties.

The radical upsurge receded in the mid-1920's. In Germany, where the bulk of the workers remained Socialists, the Communists were checked by armed force; in France the Communist tide petered out because of internal dissensions and a doctrinal and tactical inflexibility that repelled large parts of French labor; in Italy the rigid admission requirements of the Communist Internal (see p. 180) led to a three-way split of the Italian Socialist Party. There were similar split-ups of Marxist parties elsewhere, with the Communists retaining rarely more than the support of a minority.

Communism also suffered setbacks on other fronts. In the fall of 1920, at the height of the Russo-Polish War of 1920–21, the advance of the Red Army was stopped before Warsaw. The defeat of the Soviet forces put an end to the hope that Communism might conquer Europe in the wake of Red military victories. Unlike Russia, moreover, most European countries had a large middle class determined to stop the advance of Communism. Contrary to the expectation of Marx, that middle class was not forced into the ranks of the proletariat by a growing concentration of economic power in fewer hands; in fact, the middle class increased in numbers as the demand grew for managers, engineers, scientists, teachers, and accountants. Discontent with existing conditions was widespread in the ranks of the middle class, but whatever solutions the disaffected embraced, the remedies were all anticommunist.

Continued Social Tensions.   While the revolutionary wave had spent itself by the end of 1923, social tensions ran deep even during the era of prosperity from 1924 to 1929. Though hopelessly isolated and frequently torn by factional disputes, the Communists continued to draw some 10 per cent of the vote in the French and German elections of 1924 and 1928, and the number of votes cast for them increased 15 to 20 per cent, respectively. The fact was that workers benefitted but little from the economic revival. The real wages of French labor increased less than 10 per cent between 1914 and 1928 while productivity grew 40 per cent during that same period. In Germany real wages in 1928 were 6 per cent higher than in 1913 while the annual national income was estimated to have grown almost 50 per cent compared to 1913. The very existence of a Communist Party, moreover, forced the moderate Socialists to assume positions that made cooperation with bourgeois parties more difficult. Their stand in turn served to deepen the distrust with which large parts of the bourgeoisie looked on the Socialists. Here socioeconomic apprehensions were reinforced by emotional qualms. Middle and upper classes were not only alarmed at the demands for social and economic reforms; they also rebelled against the Socialists' challenge of the existing social and political order in which the educated and propertied classes held the commanding positions. To be governed by a one-time harnessmaker like Friedrich Ebert, the Weimar Republic's first President, was a humiliating experience to large parts of the German bourgeoisie, and the diffidence and ineptness of many Socialist leaders encouraged this social antagonism and heightened it into bitter contempt. Parliamentary exigencies produced occasional coalitions between bourgeois parties and Socialists, but these were precarious arrangements that never lasted for long. A deep social and political gap kept dividing labor and bourgeoisie in many countries; it made these nations especially vulnerable when the Depression struck.

In some countries social tensions were kept in check. Britain weathered a nationwide strike in 1926 because both labor and government leaders were determined to prevent outbreaks of violence. The strike was broken off by the labor leaders when bloodshed seemed imminent, and Prime Minister Stanley Baldwin in turn insisted that business ought not to exploit its victory. If Baldwin was only partly successful in his effort to bind up the wounds which the strike had inflicted, the wounds nonetheless did heal, even though they left scars. The Scandinavian and Low Countries also emerged from their postwar troubles with their social fabric intact. They, too, were afflicted with internal antagonisms which various bourgeois-Socialist coalitions failed to bridge, but they were able to ease the existing tensions by a number of constructive social and economic reforms.

Whatever domestic tensions existed in eastern Europe, they rarely were openly noticeable. The peasantry of the Balkan countries distrusted the landed gentry and the professional and business groups that dominated the political stage, but they were too cowed or too apathetic to translate their grievances into political action. The only exception was Bulgaria where the peasant leader Alexander Stambolisky made a short-lived attempt to improve the lot of the peasants. Some of the more active peasants supported the Communists as a gesture of protest as long as the latter could operate legally, which was never for long. While the Socialist parties were not outlawed as a rule, none of them attracted a significant following, partly because of the lack of a large working class and partly because of the Socialists' inability to appeal to the peasants. In the wake of the Depression parts of the peasantry were attracted to fascist organizations such as the Iron Guard in Rumania.

International Ties. While labor and bourgeoisie found it difficult to establish common ground within their own countries, Socialist parties collaborated more easily with their counterparts in other nations. After some delay, they revived the Second International, defunct since 1914 and now officially known as the Labor and Socialist International.[5] They made some attempts to work out an equitable solution of the German reparations problem, but lacking political influence in their own countries, they were unable to translate these proposals into official policy. Similarly, when French and Belgian forces occupied the Ruhr in 1923, the Socialist International, on a motion of the French and Belgian delegates, condemned that move as unjustified and economically irresponsible; however, this action had little, if any, effect, on the eventual settlement.

No concerted action on an international scale was attempted by middle or upper classes whose political orientation was primarily national. However, some individuals and economic interest groups sponsored anticommunist and, more generally, antilabor activities across national boundaries. In its early days the Nazi Party seems to have been a beneficiary of such endeavors, but the extent of these foreign contributions to the party treasury has never been clearly established and probably never will be.

The Rise of Fascism. As those workers who were distrustful of capitalism and parliamentarism turned to Communism, some elements of middle and upper class who lacked faith in democracy and the capitalist system embraced fascism.[6] Fascism crystallized out of ideological and philosophical currents that had existed already before the First World War

[5] The First International, an association of socialist and anarchist groups and some labor unions, was set up by Marx in 1864 and disbanded by him in 1876. The Second International, an organization of Socialist and Labor parties, was founded in 1889. The Communist International (Comintern), set up in 1919, was the Third International.

[6] The term is used here in its generic meaning. When used with reference to the Italian movement, it will be capitalized.

but had been kept in check by the strength and stability of prewar society. Protesting against the shallow materialism and cold rationality of that society, the forerunners of fascism had urged their contemporaries to let their actions be guided by their emotions rather than by their intellect and to accept violence as a natural and constructive force.

The war had extolled these very values, and in the social and spiritual chaos left by the war, they exerted a greater appeal than they had in the ordered and stable conditions of prewar life. Fascist movements were led by men who had never fitted into a peaceful ordered society, and most of their early followers consisted of those whom the war and its aftermath had made unfit for a disciplined civil life. Hitler and Mussolini, both social outcasts, recruited their first supporters from rootless adventurers, disgruntled war veterans, brawlers, and other such misfits. But they also attracted some idealists who despised the shallowness of their own existence and saw in fascism a positive force that promised to fill the void in their life.

When the fascist parties grew into mass movements, they were appealing to those who saw threatened all those values on which their life had been founded—order, property, social status. These people found themselves caught by forces which seemed overpowering: white-collar employees and officials watched helplessly as inflation wiped out their savings and with them the security that money had always provided; small merchants and artisans felt trapped between big business and labor unions that threatened to crush them; peasants were fearful of the growing importance of urban labor and of being outpaced by merchanized large-scale farming. These groups also were haunted by fears of a social revolution that would drive them into the ranks of the working class. They felt that the state—government, parliament, courts, police—was as helpless and bewildered as they themselves, and unable to discharge its task of protecting and helping them. Nazis and Fascists reinforced this feeling of insecurity by murders and street fights, mass demonstrations and beerhall brawls, and a silent terror which helped to create an atmosphere of permanent near-civil war.

Fascist movements sprang up in almost all European countries during the 1920's, but they acquired significance only in those that had no tradition of responsible self-government. Apart from their economic difficulties all these nations were nursing some major foreign political grievances that made them especially receptive to appeals to emotions and prejudices. Nazis and Fascists also capitalized skillfully on social frustrations by picturing material success as the product of fraud and deceit and by brushing off humanitarian impulses, respect for law, and concern for property as bourgeois timidity. In turn, they held out to their followers the ideals of a life of dedication and heroism in which the individual would serve state and nation and find his reward in the security of his assigned post and in his historical role as a fighter against greed and envy at home and abroad. In a world in which law-abiding, hard-working men seemed unable to hold their own, the fascist view that life was an unrelenting war against the forces of darkness and evil made sense to many. Disenchanted, they were ready to join this struggle; if it meant continued hardships and sacrifices, as the fascists defiantly warned, that fight imparted at least a new purposefulness to their life. Nor were they deterred by the fact that the avowed objectives of the fascists were vague and contradictory. Their allegiance was as much an act of faith as was that of the Communist masses to Communism. What mattered more than any clearcut coherent program was the self-assured activism of the fascists which seemed a more adequate response to the deepening crisis than the cautious calculations of the traditional parties. In effect, the lack of any coherent and clearcut program enhanced the position of the fascist leader: his decisions could not be evaluated against the promises and principles of a concrete program, and he was entirely free to determine action and policy.

Fascism thus sought to appeal to all those who were deeply dissatisfied with the existing political system of parliamentary democracy and its economic correlate of private-enterprise capitalism but who were also opposed to the equalitarianism of Socialism and Communism. These elements fascism proposed to forge into an aggressive striking force organized tightly along military-elitist lines, propelled by a combination of dedicated idealism, shrill nationalism, and moral cynicism, and contemptuous of individual rights and economic interests. However, to be successful, fascist movements depended also on the support of upper-class elements strategically placed in army, business, and government. These groups disliked fascist uncouthness and radicalism but provided aid and protection in the hope of using the fascists in defense of their own social and political privileges. (In the initial stages army and government aid was more important; business leaders objected to the "socialist" aspects of fascism and, except for a few, hesitated at first to give help.) Individually fascist movements displayed variations; unlike National Socialism some fascist parties did not make racism part of their ideology, and fascist attitudes toward religion differed from country to country. Above all, national characteristics left their mark on the individual movements. Italian Fascism was never a match to the inexorable all-encompassing ruthlessness of German Nazism.

The success of any political movement depends not only on the persuasiveness of its aspirations and on its strength and determination but also on the attitude of its opponents. The opposition to Communism was determined enough in the 1920's to block a Communist seizure of power in Europe. Opposition to fascism was never as strong—at least not in countries like Italy and Germany where fascism became a significant movement. In both countries the antifascist forces greatly outnumbered the Nazis and Fascists when these two parties were making their bid for power in 1922 and 1923, but this numerical superiority was never effectively mobilized. Many who sincerely believed in reason and law, in human values and individual rights, refused to take seriously movements that were so crude and irrational. Others were torn between their opposition to the fascists and their awareness that the fascist charges of self-interest and materialism were not without justification; while they condemned the brutality and lawlessness of the fascists, they could not bring themselves to oppose them. Still others were too indolent or too tired to express their hostility in active opposition. Labor was so absorbed in its internal feuds or so demoralized that it failed to put up any effective resistance even though fascism was openly hostile to it. Thus the anti-Fascist forces in Italy failed to block Mussolini's rise to power, and the advance of Nazism in Germany in 1923 was checked, not by the democratic forces of that country, but by conservative elements which sympathized with Hitler but considered his bid for power inopportune. In France the Catholic Church, no supporter of the anticlerical Third Republic, played a similar role. The Church dealt a major blow to the *Action Française,* the movement closest to a French fascist organization in the early 1920's, when it asked all Catholics to withdraw from it and put its newspaper on the Index.

Ineffectiveness of the antifascist opposition in countries where fascism was gaining ground was as significant a sign of the times as the fact that fascism was able to obtain widespread support. The inaction of the opposition in the face of fascist lawlessness and brutality underlined the weakness of public morality and political responsibility in large parts of postwar Europe.

CULTURAL LIFE

The Impact of Science. The cultural scene of postwar Europe reflected the uncertainties of the contemporary world. Science too was drifting away from its moorings and could no longer rely on the reassurance of immutable laws. Physics had undergone a far-reaching revolution since the turn of the century when the German physicist Albert Einstein (1879–1955) demonstrated that time and space were not absolutes, but were relative metaphysical concepts dependent on the position of the observer. His fellow countryman, Max Planck (1858–1947), showed energy to be, not a continuous force, but rather an intermittent spurt of separate units called *quanta* (quantum theory), and the Dane Niels Bohr (1885–   ) developed the principle of discontinuity in physics. Another German physicist, Werner Heisenberg (1901–   ), demonstrated that the law of cause and effect was not universally valid in the physical world. Heisenberg underscored the uncertainties inherent in the physical world by showing that place and momentum of a particle

Albert Einstein. (Reprinted
courtesy Wide World Photos)

could not be jointly determined as precisely as possible, but only at the
price of the accuracy of one or the other. The natural scientist, too, faced
a world that was subject to unpredictable forces and circumstances and
lacked the cohesion that the Newtonian view of the universe had assumed.

Most laymen were hardly aware of these changes in scientific theory.
They were much more impressed with the great contributions of science
to medicine, both preventive and curative. Dietary research and the
discovery of vitamins improved eating habits; new vaccines offered protection against diphtheria, yellow fever, and tetanus; and improved techniques in anesthetics and surgery made possible delicate operations on
brain, heart, and lungs. Scientific advances also benefited technology and
added to the comforts of life: radio came into mass use; the talking picture replaced the silent movie; electrical appliances eased household
chores. There were continuous improvements in the construction and
operation of automobiles and in the range and speed of the airplane.
Less happily, the contemporary observer noted also that many of these
advances improved the ability to wage war.

One discipline which had a very direct impact on European life in the
1920's was psychology. Its influence is associated primarily with the
psychoanalytic teachings of the Austrian neurologist, Sigmund Freud
(1856–1939). Freud had worked out his theory and method of treatment
before 1914, but he became a major clinical and cultural force only
after World War I. Prewar Europe, seemingly secure and well ordered,
had little interest in a theory which taught that man was driven by in-

Sigmund Freud. *(Reprinted courtesy The Bettmann Archive, Inc.)*

stinctual impulses and that the repression of these drives produced frustrations and emotional maladjustments. The war led to a great increase of emotional disturbances, especially in the form of "shell shock," and spurred the interest in psychiatry. It also shattered the self-assured faith in human rationality; in consequence, Freud's thesis that the subsoil of the human mind harbored powerful irrational forces was more readily accepted after the war. By stressing the importance of personal self-realization and happiness, Freud offered release from discontent and anxiety. If democracy was to assure man's liberation on the political plane, psychoanalysis proffered freedom to the emotionally disenfranchised.

Freud was only one of many who were probing the human psyche. Before him Henri Bergson (1859–1941), the French philosopher, had achieved fame and some influence by acknowledging the limitations of reason and intellect; Bergson had singled out the *élan vital*, the impetus and movement of life, as the fundamental reality of human existence. But since he relied on intuition rather than intellectual analysis to understand this basic force, he remained in the long run unconvincing. Following Freud, some of his disciples, Alfred Adler (1870–1937), a fellow Viennese, and Carl Jung (1875–1961), a Swiss psychologist, developed their own psychoanalytic theories. Freud's emphasis on the sexual drive as the prime human impulse has since come under attack and so has his neglect of environment as a psychological factor. None of this can impair his historical significance. It was he more than anyone else who directed attention to the workings of the human mind and provided insights that have left a lasting impact on our knowledge and thinking, on art and literature, education and criminology, or at a more profane level, on advertising techniques and public relations. "His name is no longer the name of a man," the critic Alfred Kazin has written, "like 'Darwin,' it is now synonymous with a part of nature. This is the very greatest kind of influence that a man can have."

Literature. As sensitive barometers of prevailing trends and concerns, the major writers and artists reflected the moods and preoccupations of postwar Europe. Their dominant themes dealt with the banality of human existence and the disintegration of traditional values, with individual consciousness and experience and the related problem of reality and illusion, and with the difficulty of meaningful communication from man to man. These questions were taken up by authors and artists of all European countries; indeed, the most striking aspect of the major literary and artistic creations of the 1920's is the remarkable consonance of their views of the human condition, transcending all national barriers. While politically the European comity was drifting apart, as a cultural community it survived the war and, if anything, emerged strengthened from it. Something of the supranational character of Europe's cultural concerns is suggested also by the fact that many European writers and artists lived in other than their native lands—James Joyce, the Irish novelist, in Italy; Hermann Hesse, the German novelist, and Rainer Maria Rilke, the Austrian poet, in Switzerland; the Swiss painter, Paul Klee, in Germany; and the Spanish artist, Pablo Picasso, and the Swiss architect, Charles LeCorbusier, in France. Not surprisingly many of the writers and artists also were in the forefront of movements advocating the political union of Europe.

Immediately after the war the artistic concern with the human condition was expressed in a flood of bizarre and abstruse poems and paintings intended as protests against the conformity that war had imposed upon life. By their very extravagance these creations sought to hold up a mirror to the irrationality of a civilization engaged in its self-destruction. The most extreme of these movements of protest was dadaism. It originated in Switzerland and had some adherents in France and in Germany. Sterile and self-defeating, dadaism's systematized nonsense was soon superseded by the surrealist school. Surrealism shared the dadaists' distrust of human sagacity and under the impact of Freud sought to give expression to subconscious feelings and instincts. The techniques of the surrealists, both in their literary style and their mode of painting, were experimental, frequently incoherent, and often unintelligible to all but the initiated; they reflected a reality that did not fit into any preordained pattern and could never be fully grasped. Although surrealism soon lost ground as a movement, it nonetheless left its imprint on art and literature; the works of James Joyce, T. S. Eliot, Picasso, and Salvador Dali attest to its influence.

As the novelty of these literary and artistic excesses wore off, they gave way to more traditional styles and techniques. But the mood of uneasy bewilderment and introspection survived, as did the concern with the subconscious mind. The individual and his emotional conflicts has always been a major theme of the artist and writer; Freud, in Alfred Kazin's word, "brought, as it were, the authority of science to the inner promptings of art, and thus helped writers and artists to feel that their interests in myths, in symbols, in dreams was on the side of 'reality,' of science itself." The stream-of-consciousness technique which predated psychoanalysis as a literary device now came fully into its own in the work of James Joyce, Virginia Woolf, and the German novelist-physician Alfred Döblin.

The malaise of those years was succinctly expressed in the work of the American-born poet and critic T. S. Eliot (1888–1965). His dark forebodings are summed up in his poem, *The Waste Land,* that "place not merely of desolation, but of anarchy and doubt, [representative of] our postwar world of shattered institutions, strained nerves and bankrupt ideals [in which] life no longer seems serious or coherent," as the critic Edmund Wilson has described it. The structure and diction of Eliot's poetry with its abrupt rhythmic changes and obscure allusions are suggestive of life's incoherence and man's inability to grasp its meaning. A similar uneasiness, though expressed more conventionally, pervades the poetry of Rainer Maria Rilke (1875–1926), but he, unlike Eliot, rejoices in the "terribleness of life"—a difference suggestive of the contrast that separated the Germanic from the Anglo-Saxon outlook on life.

The artist's disenchantment is also reflected in the work of James Joyce (1882–1941); his novel *Ulysses* depicts in its over 700 pages the events of one day in the banal life of Mr. Average Man. In probing the deepest recesses of human existence, Joyce resorts to linguistic experiments that served to accentuate the opaque, many-layered structure of life—at times almost to the point of unintelligibility. The French novelist Marcel Proust (1871–1922) explored the meaning of human existence on a different social level (aristocracy and upper bourgeoisie) in his great work, *Remembrance of Things Past*. Its nostalgic melancholy, its relentless probing of the subconscious mind, its picture of the empty life led by the highly placed and the well-to-do bore out the general feeling of futility. "We are always feeling with Proust as if we were reading about the end of something," Edmund Wilson has written. "Not only do his hero and most of his other characters pass into mortal declines, but their world itself seems to be coming to an end." This mood struck a responsive chord in many a reader; while the first volume, published in 1913, went

Marcel Proust. (*Reprinted courtesy The Bettmann Archive, Inc.*)

largely unnoticed in the confident atmosphere of prewar France, the second volume, issued in 1919, was an immediate sensation and received the *Prix Goncourt,* France's most distinguished literary award.

Franz Kafka (1883–1924), an Austro-Jewish novelist living in Prague, also was haunted by the feeling that man was helplessly trapped in a hostile world. In Kafka's novel *The Trial* the accused never confronts his prosecutor or his judge and in *The Castle* the newcomer to the village fails to gain access to the castle or its lord—man does not know his role or his destination in an unfeeling mechanized world run by bureaucrats and alienated from God, and he must keep struggling without hope of redemption. To Kafka man's insignificance was such that he did not bother to give names to the heroes of some of his novels, but simply called them by the initial K. (for Kafka).

The problems of the individual lost in a welter of conflicting values dominate also the work of the German author, Thomas Mann (1875–1955). Mann's heroes are not the main actors—developments are never set in motion by the central figures; instead, the protagonists are carried along by forces to which they submit. This was already one of the major themes of Mann's first novel, *Buddenbrooks,* a melancholy story of bourgeois decline. The theme recurs in Mann's major work of the 1920's, *The Magic Mountain.* This novel centers on a community which is diseased both physically and morally: in a tuberculosis sanatorium a liberal humanist, indulging in a barren rationalist optimism, and an irrational authoritarian, hailing the glories of the totalitarian future, confront each other in efforts to win over a young apolitical German engineer. Occasional passages hint that Mann's sympathies lie with the humanist, but in the last analysis the novel is inconclusive. In his noncommittal attitude Mann may have viewed himself simply as the impartial artist standing above the battle, but the lack of decision was also expressive of the uncertainties of the author and his fellow countrymen.

Another of the significant authors of the postwar decade was the Italian playwright, Luigi Pirandello (1867–1936). In *Six Characters in Search of an Author* and others of his plays, Pirandello explored the relationship between reality and illusion, the meaning of concepts, and the difficulties of communicating personal experiences.[7] "How can we ever come to an understanding," one of his characters asks, "if I put in the words I utter the sense and value of things as I see them, while you who listen to me must inevitably translate them according to the conception of things each one of you has within himself. We think we understand each other, but we never really do."[8] The resulting complications Pirandello exemplifies in the inner conflicts of individuals anxious for social respectability who find themselves trapped in unconventional situations. Unable to cope with their troubles, they shy away from reality and take shelter in the world of illusion. As the historian H. Stuart Hughes has written:[9]

In Pirandello, the spiritual disarray of the immediate postwar period is delineated in its bleakest form. Yet the attitude of the author himself is not without pity: there is simply no trace of sentimentality in it. Nor is there a trace of political ideology, national allegiance, or any other conscious social doctrine. The great plays of the early 1920's have reached an unprecedented extreme of abstraction: social cohesion, the familiar world of sense experience, even the individual self—all these have been dissolved. The lack of human communication has become almost total. All that is left is an infinitely poignant

[7] Problems of communication and understanding were also one of the major concerns of contemporary philosophy, as evidenced by the work of Bertrand Russell, G. E. Moore, and Ludwig Wittgenstein in Britain, Edmund Husserl in Germany, and Rudolf Carnap in Austria. Semantics became a significant field of study.

[8] A contemporary illustration of this point has been provided by an economist: "The history of war debts and reparations and of their absurd and catastrophic results cannot be understood on the basis only of financial and economic factors, such as difficulties of transfer and balance of payments. The intricacy of this problem and the final impossibility of arriving at a really satisfactory solution seem to be due even more to differences of opinion on the political, legal, and moral aspects of the problem than to the opposition of material interests. This fact is one of the most convincing examples in history of the deep psychological meaning behind the maxim of Luigi Pirandello, the famous Italian playwright: "Everybody has his own truth." Paul Alpert, *Twentieth Century Economic History of Europe* (New York, 1951), p. 53.

[9] H. Stuart Hughes, *Consciousness and Society: The Reorientation of European Social Thought: 1890–1930* (New York, 1961), p. 391.

awareness of *la condition humaine*—and with it a disappointed longing for a better humanity.

All of these works are heavy intellectual fare, and to make their point, they deal with extreme, sometimes bizarre situations. Yet they did find large audiences and many of them were translated into other languages. They touched on concerns that were widely shared and whose exploration was welcomed. Novels and plays that probed these questions in simpler language and in less demanding form intellectually enjoyed even wider circulation—the novels of John Galsworthy (*The Forsyte Saga*) and of Martin Roger Du Gard (*The Thibaults*), which explored the fortunes of the bourgeoisie in a changing society, or Jules Romains' massive series of novels, *Men of Good Will*, which analyzed the problems of contemporary society in a wider setting. In a similar vein the works of George Bernard Shaw, D. H. Lawrence, André Gide, Robert Musil, and Jakob Wassermann, to name but a few, examined the conflicts between social pressures and personal integrity. Although the problems explored during the 1920's were of general rather than national interest, the treatment often differed significantly between English and Continental writers. The former were concerned with the moral, social, or psychological significance of their material, the latter tended to inject political or ideological issues—a difference reflecting the comparative serenity of the British scene as distinct from the tense political and ideological battles that were fought on the Continent.

There was of course also an important body of literature of purely national concern and impact; it will be discussed in the context of developments in the individual European countries.

The Creative Arts.   The restlessness of the times was reflected also in the works of the painters, composers, and sculptors. Here too the break with tradition, the search for new modes of expression, the impact of psychology and technology helped to set the tone and provide the themes. Some of it was frivolous and absurd, but where experimental impulses were guided by artistic imagination and skill, some notable works of art were created. The portraits of the Austrian painter, Oskar Kokoschka (1886–   ), reflected the new psychological insights; the cubist school injected mathematical and industrial elements into painting. It also tried to introduce a fourth dimension, the motion in time and space, by superimposing several layers of movement upon each other or by depicting an object from different angles in the same picture. The work of Pablo Picasso (1881–   ) has been influenced by each one of these trends at one time or another and sometimes simultaneously. Overwhelmed by such variegated influences, he found it difficult to present a coherent picture of life and many of his paintings and sculptures, as one critic has observed, do not try to re-create life but are merely notes and commentaries on it. On the other hand, Russian-born Wassily Kandinsky (1866–1944) and the Swiss painter, Paul Klee (1879–1940), turned their backs on reality altogether and no longer depicted identifiable objects but sought to capture movements, rhythms, or visual impressions. (Interestingly, this "abstract" art proved to have its practical uses; its patterns influenced textile and furniture design and had its impact also on advertising art.) The outstanding representative of more traditional techniques was Henri Matisse (1869–1954), though he too went through a cubist and "abstract" phase. Depicting the joyous, uplifting aspects of life, his work is distinguished by bright colors and traditional subject matter. But even Matisse's paintings of the 1920's reflected something of man's absorption into his environment: the individuals who people Matisse's work are not the center of interest; the painter's concern is focused on the overall color scheme or the entire scene of which people are merely a part, like a bowl of goldfish or a vase of flowers. Human faces, if they are outlined at all, are wholly lacking in individuality.

Among sculptors American-born Jacob Epstein (1880–1959), who made his home in England, achieved distinction during this period with his massive creations in stone and bronze suggestive of the animalist crudity of man barely disguised by the veneer of civilization; the experimental works of the Englishman, Henry Moore (1898–   ), and of Russian-born Alexander Archipenko (1887–   ) seek to represent visual impressions of shape, motion, or other abstract concepts; they are made of metals and other materials that technology has put at the artist's disposal. In music Arnold Schoenberg (1874–1951) and Igor Stravinsky (1882–   ) have broken with established traditions and developed new theories whose dissonance and atonality seem to many suggestive of the chaotic state of the world. If the general public of the 1920's was little impressed with the works of Picasso or Klee, it found "modern" music even more baffling, and the classical composers continued to dominate the musical stage.

Unlike the other creative arts, architecture developed a new style along strictly rational and functional lines. Here the impact of industrial technology, the need for efficiency and economy made themselves felt. Postwar building developments were associated primarily with two names in Europe—that of the German architect, Walter Gropius (1883–   ), and his French-Swiss contemporary, Le Corbusier (1887–1965). In his famous *Bauhaus* school Gropius, who owed some of his ideas to the inspiration of the American architect, Frank Lloyd Wright, developed a new style marked by simplicity, lightness, and efficiency, in which special attention was paid to the particular function which the building was to serve. Full advantage was taken of the new building materials that had become available—steel, glass, concrete—and of advances in engineering techniques. While other artists were haunted by pictures of a disintegrating, chaotic world, architects were determined to make the most of scientific and technological progress to make life more healthy and comfortable. Gropius and his fellow countryman Ludwig Mies van der Rohe (1886–), interested in designing inexpensive hygienic dwellings for workers, also planned a variety of housing projects.

An entirely new artistic medium was developed in the motion picture. A product of the age of technology, the film, relying on speed and movement to tell its story, could simplify and telescope involved plots and developments into one or two hour shows. The closeup of a face conveyed psychological insights that could be easily understood, a special symbolism translated abstract ideas into descriptive pictures—the legs of a galloping horse, the rotating wheels of a car signifying speed or the passage of time, or the heavy boots of marching soldiers suggesting a war machine inexorably pushing ahead on its deadly mission. In its simple pictorial language the film was a "democratic" art catering primarily to mass audiences. It provided excitement, played on emotions, and allowed the viewer to lead vicariously a life of romance and glamor, of adventure and heroism. As a welcome escape from the drabness of everyday life, inexpensive and easily available, movie-going became part of the ordinary routine—no special event like a visit to the theatre for which one dressed up, but a habit indulged in unceremoniously.

To a lesser extent, radio, which was just coming into its own, fulfilled the same function. Both film and radio offered, moreover, unrivaled opportunities to reach vast audiences, and the political potentialities of both media were soon to play an important role in public affairs.

6

Domestic Politics in the 1920's: The Western European Democracies

The following two chapters deal with individual developments in the Western European countries during the first postwar decade. The basic issues that confronted these countries were on the whole rather similar; they revolved, it will be recalled, around the restoration of the economy and the establishment of a new political and social equilibrium after the war had weakened or destroyed the prewar balance. The response of the various countries to these tasks showed considerable uniformity in economic matters, but varied sharply in the social and political domain, depending on political experience, tradition, and, to no small degree, moral values. The policies that were adopted covered the whole spectrum of governmental practices—parliamentary and dictatorial, civil and military, peaceful and violent. If any overall trend was discernible here, it was that it became increasingly difficult for any government to act without mass support. This, however, did not necessarily herald the rise of an age of universal democracy; as the experience of Italy demonstrated, such mass support could also be generated within the framework of an authoritarian regime.

BRITAIN: BETWEEN PAST AND PRESENT

The Problem of Labor.   The British people greeted the end of the war
with a deep sense of relief. Hardships and sacrifices seemed at an end,
and there was a general expectation that the nation could now enjoy the
comforts of peace and prosperity. Because the last parliamentary election
had been held in 1910, Lloyd George decided to capitalize on this mood of
happy expectancy and called for new elections at once. He conducted
a whirlwind campaign in which he promised to make Britain a land
"fit for heroes" and seemed to suggest that Germany would pay the
entire cost of the war. On the strength of these pledges his Conservative-
Liberal coalition won a sweeping victory in the "khaki" elections of
December 1918.

If Lloyd George drove the country into an election before it had time
to catch its political breath, he did so also because of his fear that the
end of the fighting would plunge the war-geared economy into a serious
decline. To his happy surprise his anxiety proved unfounded; domestic
demand, pent up during four long years, provided industry with a ready
market. British goods were also in great demand in the many countries
whose productive capacity had been impaired by the war.

This very prosperity, however, brought with it new problems. Labor
was restive after four years of hardships and demanded its share of the
new abundance. By a series of strikes it secured shorter hours and
increases in wages, but pay never kept pace with the rising prices. Social
reforms, however, were few since labor's representation in parliament
was too weak to compel legislation. In consequence, there was some talk
of "direct action" and of a general strike to force the hand of the government. Nothing came of such threats because of the calmer counsels of
labor's leaders; but with revolution rife in many parts of the world, this
agitation caused upper and middle class considerable anxiety.

Toward the end of 1920 the boom abruptly gave way to a severe
depression. Exports were halved within a year from 1920 to 1921 and
steel production reduced by three-fifths of its volume. In the face of
mass unemployment the workers had to submit to new wage cuts. The
government, moreover, embarked on a rigorous policy of retrenchment
which not only led to a further contraction of the labor market, but put
also an end to such social innovations as a nationally subsidized housing
program. New relief legislation tried to alleviate the lot of the unemployed; the measures taken, however, were inadequate and gave help
on terms that were often humiliating. Hunger marches were organized
in angry protest and mock raids staged on relief agencies. The authorities
quickly took countermeasures, but excesses of the police aroused widespread sympathies with the demonstrators. When their plight received
wider attention, relief was granted on more liberal terms.

The Crisis of the British Economy. Few people understood at the time that these developments were not simply phases of the regular business cycle that had accounted for the ups and downs of the prewar economy. Britain's economy was in fact suffering from a severe structural crisis. The war had greatly accelerated the decline of the British position in world trade and manufacturing. Many of Britain's overseas customers had developed industries of their own, or, like the United States, had vastly expanded their industrial plant. Competition was especially strong in those fields in which the British had long held the lead—steel, shipbuilding, textiles, and coal. The coal industry was also affected by the growing importance of oil and electric power, while German reparations in coal reduced further French and Italian purchases. Moreover, Britain was hampered by the inefficiency of its coal industry which kept it from competing successfully with cheap coal producers such as Poland and Spain. Britain's "invisible" exports—shipping, banking, insurance—also suffered sharp setbacks. They were most marked in shipping which had been reduced to almost half of its prewar volume and now was faced with a newly built American merchant marine and the expanded activities of the wartime neutrals. These were alarming trends for a country dependent on exports to pay for the foodstuffs and raw materials it had to import.

Lloyd George sought to overcome the depression by the traditional means of wage cuts and the reduction of public expenditures, but the resulting deflation merely compounded the difficulties. Abroad he hoped to revive world trade by an economic rapprochement with Russia and by the cancellation or reduction of war debts and reparations. Even if he had been wholly successful, these policies could have provided only partial relief, for they bypassed the structural weaknesses of Britain's economy. One step, however, was taken which meant a sharp break with the past: in 1921 Parliament passed the "Safeguarding of Industries Act," imposing protective tariffs on some types of imports. It was Britain's acknowledgement that its industrial supremacy had come to an end.

The Irish Problem. There were other signs of declining strength. In 1914 Ireland had been granted home rule by Parliament, but the implementation of the Home Rule Act had been suspended until the end of the war. Distrustful of Britain's sincerity, the extremist Sinn Fein ("Ourselves Alone") Party decided to secure independence while Britain's military strength was committed in France. On Easter Monday 1916 the Sinn Feiners staged a rising in Dublin, but it was quickly suppressed by the British. As soon as the war was over, the struggle for independence flared up again. The seventy-three Sinn Feiners elected to the British Parliament in December 1918 convened their own Parliament in Dublin, proclaimed Ireland an independent republic, and elected the only sur-

viving leader of the Easter Rebellion, Eamon De Valera (1882–   ),
its first president.[1]

There followed two years of guerrilla warfare between the "Irish
Republican Army" (I.R.A.) and British regular forces bolstered by
volunteer units known as the "Black and Tans" from their black hats
and khaki uniforms. Both sides fought with brutal savagery; yet British
public opinion was more shocked by the outrages of the Black and Tans
than by those of the I.R.A. The feeling was widespread that British
government forces ought not to stoop to the lawless methods of the Irish
insurgents. Most Englishmen, moreover, either sympathized with the
Irish demand for independence or were indifferent and felt that the
activities of the Black and Tans only rendered more difficult an early
and equitable settlement.

Late in 1920 Parliament passed a new Government of Ireland Act. It
separated Protestant North Ireland (Ulster) from the rest of the island
and gave each a parliament for internal affairs. Both parts also were
given representation in the British Parliament since they were to be kept
in the United Kingdom. North Ireland accepted the plan and is still
governed by it; the Dublin Irish rejected it. Since the British people were
unwilling to engage in an all-out war against the Sinn Feiners, Lloyd
George entered into negotiations with them. After prolonged discussions
an Irish Free State was established as an autonomous Dominion within
the British Empire. But De Valera and other advocates of a united
Ireland and complete independence rejected the treaty. Fighting broke
out between the new state and the De Valera faction, which had the
support of large parts of the I.R.A. For almost a year civil war raged in
Ireland (spilling over as well into Ulster). The De Valera forces finally
surrendered in May 1923, but they remained unreconciled, and the issues
of a united Ireland and full independence continued to plague Anglo-
Irish relations.

From Lloyd George to MacDonald.   In the face of these recurrent
difficulties, the Conservative-Liberal coalition began to weaken. Lloyd
George tried to improve his slipping fortunes by his gigantic project of
Europe's economic rehabilitation, but his hope of thus solving his troubles
collapsed with the failure of the Genoa Conference. In September 1922
it even seemed for a moment as if he were pushing the country into a
war against Turkey. When Mustafa Kemal, in his campaign against
Greece (see p. 63), threatened to drive a small British force from
Chanak in the neutralized zone at the Dardanelles, the Prime Minister
called on France, Italy, and the British Dominions to help Britain resist

---

[1] De Valera had escaped execution because, born in New York, he was technically
an American citizen (which he disclaimed) and Britain did not wish to add to
Anglo-American tension, already sharp because of British blockade actions, by the
execution of De Valera.

the Turks. His stand helped to safeguard Britain's Middle Eastern position, but to the bulk of his countrymen he seemed like a reckless gambler. The country had grown tired of his dazzling vitality, his improvisations, the abrupt turns of his policies. "He is a dynamic force," Stanley Baldwin complained at the meeting at which the Conservatives decided to withdraw from the coalition, "and it is from that very fact that our troubles, in our opinion, arise. A dynamic force is a very terrible thing; it may crush you."

Lloyd George resigned at once, and the leader of the Conservatives, Andrew Bonar Law, formed a new all-Conservative government. Bonar Law was the very opposite of his predecessor, quiet and cautious, and these very traits appealed to the country. When new elections were held in November 1922, the Conservatives obtained a substantial majority on a platform of "tranquillity and freedom from adventures and commitments both at home and abroad." At the same time, the Laborites more than doubled their representation in Parliament, outdistancing the faction-ridden Liberals and becoming the official opposition.

Bonar Law, stricken by cancer, resigned his office after a few months. He was succeeded by Stanley Baldwin (1867–1947), like him a moderate and averse to experiments. Behind an unimpressive exterior and a marked penchant for indolence, Baldwin concealed a keen flair for politics and a great deal of shrewdness—"he is the most extraordinary ordinary man I know," as one acquaintance described him. Though closely identified with industrial interests, Baldwin knew that the country's stability depended on labor's cooperation, and he made some attempts to mitigate social tensions. On the other hand, he lacked all interest in foreign affairs; except for one painful conference with the redoubtable Poincaré, he seems to have had only social contacts with foreign statesmen during the more than ten years during which he guided the fortunes of Britain. In the years of Hitler's ascendancy this proved a dangerous failing.

Baldwin's first administration was short-lived. Faced with persistent mass unemployment, he concluded that it could not be dealt with without all-out tariff protection. But when he called new elections on this issue in December 1923, the Conservative majority declined to a plurality, while the Laborites and the reunited Liberals, who both opposed tariffs, scored major gains.

In the new House of Commons the Liberals held the balance of power. Because of the tariff issue they could not enter a coalition with the Conservatives, but a coalition with Labor was ideologically just as unacceptable to them. They decided that the time had come for the Labor Party to assume governmental responsibility and offered to support a Labor government without joining it. As they saw it, Labor's dependence on the Liberal vote would force it to steer a moderate course; should it indulge in any socialist schemes it could at once be removed. There seemed little danger of radical changes since J. Ramsay MacDonald

(1866–1937), Labor's Prime Minister-designate, had no interest in socialist ventures. Far from being rigid and doctrinaire, MacDonald's political views were in fact rather blurred. But he was a skilled negotiator and an able parliamentary strategist of considerable presence and eloquence, and these were important qualifications for one whose task it would be to maintain the Labor-Liberal association.

Owing to its short-lived existence (January–October 1924) and the confining influence of the Liberals, the first Labor government had an undistinguished domestic record. In foreign affairs, on the other hand, MacDonald, who doubled as Foreign Secretary, was notably active. He improved relations with France, accepted the Dawes Plan, helped draft the Geneva Protocol (which his successor rejected), and accorded the Soviet government formal recognition. Subsequently he concluded with Moscow a commercial treaty which granted both countries most-favored-nation privileges. An additional agreement suggested the possibility of a loan to the Russians once the question of the Tsarist debts and nationalized properties had been settled. Though this was a rather unlikely prospect, the very hint of a loan brought down on MacDonald the wrath of both Liberals and Conservatives. His difficulties were compounded by a bitter controversy over the prosecution of an obscure Communist editor on charges of having advocated sedition. On the advice of his cabinet, MacDonald decided to appeal to the country. New elections were held and produced a Conservative landslide. Labor lost almost one-fourth of its seats (though its popular vote increased by over one million), while the Liberals, reduced to a mere forty seats, lost three-fourths of their representation (and 1.3 million votes).[2] The bulk of the country obviously wished to return to the safe, steady "normalcy" of Baldwin's conservatism.

The Baldwin Era.   To most Englishmen a return to normal conditions meant a return to prewar conditions, the era of British supremacy. This did not seem a utopian dream. A marked improvement of the economy, a drop in prices, and a slight rise in wages appeared to herald the approach of the time when Britain would once more be the center of world trade and finance. To speed up this trend and restore confidence in the pound, the Baldwin government restored the gold standard (abandoned during the war) and fixed the price of the pound at its prewar level. Economically the move was unwise, for it put British goods at a competitive disadvantage on the world market; since Winston Churchill, then the Chancellor of the Exchequer, was the moving spirit

---

[2] During the last days of the election campaign a letter purportedly written by Gregory Zinoviev, the head of the Communist International, to the British Communist Party was published in the press. The letter, most likely a forgery, contained instructions on how to conduct subversive activities. Since it obviously made a mockery of MacDonald's efforts to normalize relations with the Soviet Union, it was widely believed to have had an important effect on the outcome of the election. This seems unlikely, however, considering the increase in Labor's popular vote.

behind it, it was perhaps inspired more by visions of Britain's imperial prestige than by economic considerations.

The industry most directly affected by the revaluation of the pound was coal mining. After a brief boom in 1923 when the pits of the Ruhr were closed down during the French occupation, the industry was once more in great difficulties. A government-sponsored investigation some years earlier had concluded that the industry was in need of so vast a reorganization that only a nationalization of the mines could provide a solution. At the time the proposals had been rejected by both the industry and the government, and since the industry was still unwilling to reorganize to improve its efficiency, the mine owners proposed a new cut in wages and an increase in hours. They also asked that future wage negotiations be conducted locally, thus depriving the miners of what in effect had been a national minimum wage. The miners rejected a proposal that placed the penalty for the industry's inefficiency so one-sidedly on their shoulders. The government sought to prevent a collision by appointing another investigating commission, but neither mine owners nor miners would accept the compromise proposed by that body. The owners now called for a showdown and on May 1, 1926 locked the miners out of the mines.

The dispute was followed with anxious concern by labor throughout the country, for its outcome, it was believed, would affect the entire labor force. On May 3 workers in most major industries struck in support of the miners, but their hope to bring pressure to bear on business and government was disappointed. In anticipation of a general strike the government had made preparations to maintain the essential services, and with the help of the army and thousands of volunteers it ensured food supplies, transportation, and communications. The labor leaders had made less adequate plans, possibly because most of them hoped to the last that the strike could be avoided. They dreaded bloodshed and violence, and this fear continued to haunt them once the strike did get under way. Efforts were made to keep the strikers off the street by arranging community sings, games, and other activities. On the whole the strike was remarkably peaceful; in Plymouth police and strikers even met in a soccer game (which the latter won 3 to 1). When there was a danger of violence after nine days, the labor leaders called off the strike, much to the dismay of the workers. Only the miners kept struggling on for another six months.

By refusing to take an active hand in settling the original dispute, Baldwin bore a large share of the responsibility for the strike; but anxious to bind up the wounds of the struggle, he now exerted himself on behalf of the strikers and in most industries secured their return to work on prestrike terms. The major exception was the coal industry, where the miners had to accept in the end the original demands of the owners.

The remaining years of the second Baldwin government passed quietly.

In 1927 the government, under pressure from the Conservative right wing, pushed through Parliament a Trade Disputes and Trade Union Act which outlawed "general" strikes and curbed the political activities of the unions. Although the law was deeply resented by labor, it did not touch off serious trouble; after their recent setback the workers were anxious for peace. A marked improvement in the economy also helped to ease tensions. Industry, adjusting itself to world market conditions, was shifting to fields in which it could compete more effectively. There was a steady increase in the export of automobiles, aircraft, electrical goods, chemicals, and precision instruments. Banking and shipping services were again on the rise.

Yet large-scale unemployment continued, and it was the more noticeable as it was concentrated in the areas of the old staple industries—coal, steel, shipbuilding, and textiles—in South Wales, West Cumberland, large parts of Scotland, Tyneside, and Lancashire. The government lacked both initiative and imagination to cope with these "distressed areas"; Baldwin, by nature passive and indolent, preferred to let matters take care of themselves. Paradoxically, his very passivity kept him at the head of the government, for by taking no stand, he remained an acceptable leader to the various factions within the Conservative Party.

The one man who did produce a new and constructive program was Lloyd George. He proposed to eliminate mass unemployment by large public works, some state supervision of the country's key industries, and an economic planning board assisting the government. His plans received widespread support in business circles, and the Labor Party, convinced of their soundness, blandly incorporated them in its own party platform. Thanks to them, when elections were held in 1929, Labor emerged once more as the largest, though not the majority, party. Lloyd George's Liberals, on the other hand, remained a small minority group, and his hopes for a political comeback were disappointed. He had to take what comfort he could from the fact that his program became from then on a central issue of British politics.

From Empire to Commonwealth.   The decline of Britain's world power status was reflected also in its changing relationship with the Dominions. The Dominions had long enjoyed a large measure of domestic self-government, but since the war London's control of their foreign and defense policies had also come to an end. The Dominions had had their own representation at the Paris Peace Conference; they had joined the League of Nations individually; they had begun negotiating treaties with other countries and had established their own consular services. When Britain signed the Locarno Pact, the Dominions (and India) were expressly exempted from all obligations unless they voluntarily adhered to the Pact. Economic ties between mother country and Dominions also were weakening, and so was military collaborations, as was made clear by Canada's refusal to support Britain in the Chanak crisis of 1922.

In 1926 an imperial conference redefined the relations between mother country and Dominions in the light of these changes. A conference committee on interimperial relations produced a definition whose awkwardness was in itself descriptive of the amorphous nature of the surviving ties. Britain and the Dominions, according to this statement, "are autonomous communities within the British Empire, equal in status, in no way subordinate one to another in any aspect of their domestic or external affairs, though united by a common allegiance to the Crown, and freely associated as members of the British Commonwealth of Nations." The one formal tie, then, that held together these sovereign states was the powerless British monarch; except for this tenuous legal bond, the British Commonwealth of Nations was to rest on mutual interests, political, economic, and military. The arrangement was formalized by the Statute of Westminster, enacted by Parliament in 1931, and it proved enduring and useful. If British statesmanship was less than inspired in the 1920's, it could claim credit at least for having contained the centrifugal forces in the Dominions.

The Social and Cultural Scene. Inevitably the war called forth changes in Britain's social and cultural life as well. Wartime exigencies had done away with many established mores, and these were not restored when peace returned. Women remained at their jobs, and their economic independence brought with it their social and political emancipation. Women's fashions reflected this change; short hair, shorter skirts, and a somewhat boyish appearance were symbolic of their new freedom. The lessening of social restraints also led to greater sexual freedom, and preoccupation with sex became in turn an important feature of postwar literature.

The 1920's saw also some narrowing of the gap between the classes, at least on the material plane. Income distribution underwent significant changes; between 1911 and 1924 income from wages and salaries rose from 55.1 per cent to 67.5 per cent of the national income. Movies, radio, improved housing, and inexpensive attractive clothes, all of them within the reach of low-income groups, made life more pleasant and comfortable for the great majority of the people.

Yet not a few were dismayed by these changes and worried about the social and moral condition of the country. They account for the continued popularity of such prewar luminaries as John Galsworthy, Arnold Bennett, and Rudyard Kipling. For those who longed for the stability and greatness of prewar Britain, Galsworthy's nostalgic *Forsyte Saga*, the settled world of Bennett's novels, and Kipling's tales of imperial splendor offered reassurance or escape from their concerns. On a more philosophical plane William Ralph Inge, the "gloomy Dean" of St. Paul's

Cathedral, whose pithy essays and books enjoyed a great vogue in the 1920's, fulminated against the moral and social atomization of Britain.

FRANCE: POLITICS AND POCKETBOOK

The Postwar Economy. The domestic scene in postwar France was in many ways not unlike that of Britain. There was the economic boom touched off by the backlog of consumer demand, there was the call of the workers for better pay and working conditions, reinforced by a wave of demonstrations and strikes (and in France's case also by serious outbreaks of violence), and there were, in answer to it, some social reforms. And just as the British tired of Lloyd George's dynamism, the French found that Clemenceau's inexhaustible energies would not allow them to enjoy the relaxed life for which they were longing. When Presidential elections were held in 1920, Clemenceau, the victorious wartime Premier, seemed the logical choice for the Presidency. But the National Assembly preferred the innocuous speaker of the Chamber of Deputies, Paul Deschanel, who promised to be a less active head of state than the indefatigable "Tiger."

France, on the other hand, was spared Britain's subsequent business slump and the concomitant problems of mass unemployment. The task of rebuilding and rehabilitating the war-ravaged regions provided work for hundreds of thousands of men. Some 20,000 factories had been destroyed, 200 coal mines flooded, thousands of miles of railroad tracks and highways torn up. In addition, 200,000 residential buildings were destroyed completely and over 300,000 in part. The country plunged into the staggering reconstruction job with remarkable dispatch; plants, offices, homes were repaired and rebuilt, roads and bridges restored, and the farmland brought under cultivation again. By 1926 rehabilitation of the devastated areas was largely completed, and war cemeteries and memorials remained the main vestiges of the battles that had been fought there for four long years.

The task seemed less overwhelming at first because the Germans were expected to pay for it. German prisoners of war did provide manpower until 1920, and there were reparation deliveries of coal, timber, and cattle. But with the exception of two small installments paid in 1921, no cash payment was made until 1924. The immediate burden of financing the reconstruction work thus fell on French shoulders.

The soundest way of raising the needed funds would have been by increased taxation. Yet in a world of reluctant taxpayers the French rank among the most unwilling ones, and the French Chamber of Deputies, responsive to the electorate, kept voting down year after year all governmental requests for higher levies. Besides, the nation remained convinced that ultimately the Germans would foot the bill. A temporary loan seemed a more appropriate expedient than additional taxes, and no one in authority disabused the country of this illusion. The government thus was forced to borrow the required amounts, and a spate of bond issues were floated both at home and abroad. They inflated further the already huge public debt; moreover, they left intact the vast purchasing power stored up during the war which taxation would have reduced. Thus the demand for consumer goods kept competing with the reconstruction program for manpower and raw materials and helped drive up prices; by the end of 1919 the franc was reduced to less than half of its prewar value.

Reparations and Politics. Inevitably political developments centered on the deterioration of the country's financial condition, and governments were judged by their ability to extract reparations from Germany. Elections to the Chamber of Deputies in November 1919 produced a rightist majority loosely coordinated in a *bloc national* which was determined to make the Germans pay for the reconstruction of the war-devastated regions. The intransigence of the *bloc* on this point contributed to Clemenceau's failure to be elected to the Presidency some weeks later. Apart from its preference for a less demanding head of state, the *bloc* rejected him because it believed that he had not pressed with sufficient vigor France's claims at the peace conference. This of course was an inconsistent position to take: on the one hand, the *bloc* insisted on reparations and security which could be had only at the price of sustained vigilance; on the other, it dismissed as too exacting the man best qualified to attain these objectives.

This inconsistency was to plague the Republic throughout those years, and most governments fell because they violated one or the other of the nation's conflicting wishes. Several of the Premiers who followed Clemenceau were forced from office because of their willingness to make concessions in the reparations issue. One of them was Briand who agreed to a temporary suspension of reparation payments (in return for a British promise of military aid in case of German aggression). He was succeeded by Poincaré who announced that the reparations problem took precedence over all other questions and that France would take all appropriate measures should Germany default on its obligations. Poincaré's statement was received with unprecedented applause by the Chamber of Deputies and that body expressed its confidence in the Premier by a vote of 472 to 107. But this mood changed when Poincaré sent troops into the Ruhr a year later, an undertaking that proved unexpectedly costly. In the elections of May 1924 Poincaré was repudiated; in the new Chamber a more conciliatory coalition of moderate and leftist parties including the Socialists (*cartel des gauches*) obtained a majority.

The new government headed by the Radical Socialist Edouard Herriot (1870–1957), with Briand as Foreign Minister, tried to steer the country out of the diplomatic impasse into which Poincaré's Ruhr policy had led it. While tightening and expanding France's alliance system, it also inaugurated a policy of close collaboration with Britain and strove for better relations with Germany. The Dawes Plan and the Locarno Pact were the most noteworthy milestones of this new policy. At the same time Herriot and Briand sought to strengthen the prestige of the League of Nations, and they established diplomatic relations with Soviet Russia. All these steps aimed in one way or another at the containment of Germany, yet were also to enlist its cooperation. The hope was that this multipronged strategy would ease France's financial and military commitments and yet ensure its security.

Taxes and Politics.   France's financial condition worsened rapidly after the Ruhr occupation. Long-term loans could no longer be placed, and the price of the franc continued to fall. In the spring of 1924 Poincaré prevailed on the Chamber to grant him a 20 per cent increase of all taxes to balance the budget; the measure was deeply resented and contributed to his defeat at the polls. The Herriot government was no more successful in its efforts to deal with the crisis. In the election campaign the *cartel des gauches* had advocated a policy of retrenchment and a balanced budget; yet not a few of its candidates had also promised the repeal of Poincaré's tax increases. The two pledges could be reconciled only by an increase of the taxes imposed on the higher-income groups; together with the Socialist demand for a capital levy and the consolidation of government bonds to reduce the public indebtedness, the proposal touched off a near panic which aggravated the existing difficulties.

The Herriot government, forced to resign, was followed by seven different cabinets in fifteen months, each one proposing some new form of taxation which proved its undoing. It was not that parliament did not see the need for new taxes; as one historian has written, "Most deputies were willing to vote additional taxes; they simply could not agree as to which Frenchmen should pay them."[3]

The Poincaré Era.   By mid-1926 inflationary price rises, the flight of gold from the country, and the persistent cash difficulties of the government had all reached dangerous proportions. The franc had dropped to one-tenth of its prewar value, and the Bank of France, a private institution over which the government had no control, threatened to withhold further credits. There were mass withdrawals of savings and panicky buying sprees, driving prices up even more quickly. Signs of unrest were increasing in Paris; crowds gathered in front of the Chamber of Deputies in a mood that portended trouble. In a countermove, fascist groups,

[3] Gordon Wright, *France in Modern Times* (Chicago, 1960), p. 455.

subsidized by industrial money, sprang up on the right, and there was a widespread call in conservative circles for a dictator who alone could save France.

Thoroughly alarmed, Parliament realized that the settlement of the crisis could not be postponed any longer. With the *cartel des gauches* unable to agree on a solution, a "Government of National Union" was formed, extending from the moderate conservatives on the right to the left-of-center Radical Socialists (who were actually neither one nor the other, but reform-minded liberals). To head the new government, Poincaré was selected; financially a conservative, he was yet a loyal supporter of the Republic and thus acceptable to both camps. Moreover, his tireless energy and unchallenged integrity assured him the necessary authority to apply the drastic remedies required by the emergency.

Poincaré was given the special decree powers which the Chamber had been unwilling to grant to any one of his predecessors. With his authority thus reinforced, he balanced the budget—public expenditures were sharply cut and taxes increased to a point where they claimed over one-fifth of the national income. Above all, he tightened the system of tax collection. These measures had immediate salutary effects; the franc rallied quickly, panic buying came to an end, and most important, private capital was being repatriated and reinvested at home in government bonds and in business. Poincaré also benefited from the influx of German reparation payments and from the completion of the restoration of the war-devastated areas, which relieved the public treasury of one of its heaviest burdens. Soon the currency could be stabilized—at 20 per cent of its prewar value. The low level of the new parity was a boon to French exports.

The years of the Poincaré administration, from 1926 to 1929, were years of apparent prosperity. In many sectors of the economy production surpassed prewar levels; industrial output was almost 50 per cent greater than in 1913. This expansion was due in part to the acquisition of Alsace-Lorraine, rich in iron ore deposits and textile and steel plants, and to France's temporary control of the Saar Basin and its coal mines. In part it resulted from the forced modernization of the country's industrial plant; during the war new factories had been built in unoccupied France to replace those that had fallen into German hands, and after the war many of those latter had to be rebuilt from scratch because they had been either completely destroyed or damaged beyond repair.

Yet compared to the industrial progress of other countries, France kept lagging behind. One major obstacle to its industrial growth was the lack of good coking coal (which accounted for France's continuous interest in the Ruhr and Saar Basins with their abundant supplies). But the main reason was the deeply ingrained penchant of the French people for a modicum of economic independence. Clinging to the traditional ways of their forebears, most Frenchmen, as the French publicist

André Siegfried has pointed out, tried to attain this independence by acquiring a little income from investments, a little farm, or a little business. This self-limitation was incompatible with the demands of the twentieth century; it discouraged expansion and experimentation and broke up the economy into a multitude of small inefficient and uneconomical units. Yet these weaknesses were apparent to few contemporary observers. Most Frenchmen were content with Poincaré's economic accomplishments, and they approved of him the more readily because he mitigated his old militancy and supported Briand's moderate foreign policy. In the elections of 1928 they gave his coalition a large majority in the Chamber.

Nevertheless, with the economy stabilized, political divergences reasserted themselves. If the Radical Socialists, in André Siegfried's famed phrase, carried their pocketbooks on the right, their hearts were politically on the left. As investors, farmers, and businessmen they had been alarmed by the Socialist proposals of a capital levy and had welcomed Poincaré's less radical measures. But now they began to feel uncomfortable in their alliance with the moderate right and agreed with the Socialists that the coalition impeded social and political progress.

In November 1928 the Radical Socialists withdrew from the government in protest against a cabinet-approved bill that permitted some missionary religious orders to open novitiates in France—to the Radicals' mind an unwarranted concession to the Church. Poincaré had no difficulty forming a new cabinet of rightist and center parties. Whatever misgivings the conservatives had about the Premier's republicanism, they were even more alarmed at what they considered the financial recklessness of the left and welcomed the chance to keep it out of the government.

Poincaré remained in office for only a few more months. Worn out by the struggle over the Young Plan and the war debt settlement with the United States which the Chamber accepted with an eight-vote majority in mid-July 1929, he suffered a physical breakdown. Although still a senator, he withdrew from political life and during his remaining years devoted himself to his memoirs which he spun out, with his usual industry, into a ten-volume opus.

The Maginot Line.   French military policy during those years reflected the self-contradictory goal noted above—the attainment of a maximum of security against a German attack at a minimum of public expenditure and individual inconvenience.

Military service was reduced from three years to eighteen months in 1923, and in 1928 it was cut further to one year. With this last reduction the French ceased to have an effective army in peacetime. The great majority of the men under arms were nothing more than recruits in training. Earlier these men had been retained for another six months to two years after their training had been completed, thus constituting the actual army; from now on, however, they would be discharged as soon as they had been trained. The available forces were not even considered sufficient to hold off a German attack until the reserves had been mobilized, should Germany call up both its army and armed police. Parliament was compelled to increase the army's professional contingent to form such a border guard. Critics objected to this fragmentation of the army organization and warned that one year of service would not suffice to develop the proper soldierly spirit in the trainees. They also worried about the effect which an organization so clearly geared to defense operations would have on the fighting will of the troops and on their readiness to launch counteroffensives and carry the war into enemy territory. But the nation was essentially defense-minded in those days of Locarno and the seeming ascendancy of the League, and despite its abiding distrust of German intentions it refused to heed these warnings.[4] It seemed even to have forgotten that it might some day be forced to launch an attack against Germany in fulfillment of its obligations to its allies. "Our military organization must meet two requirements," War Minister Paul Painlevé told the Chamber of Deputies when he introduced the army reorganization bill in 1927. "A present requirement: to protect our colonies; a potential requirement: to put into the field quickly a military organization capable of defending our borders." There was no mention of France's military commitments to its allies.

In view of the drastic reduction of France's peacetime effectives, Painlevé proposed the construction of a line of fortification along the eastern frontier to provide a better defense against any German attack. Fearful of the expenditures involved, the Chamber did not act on the plan at the time. It changed its mind a year later when France, Britain, and Belgium consented to withdraw their remaining forces from the occupied Rhineland. Without an occupation army to help cover its mobilization, France felt compelled to reinforce the defenses on its own soil. Provisions had also to be made for those years in the mid-1930's when the country, because of the decline of the birth rate in World War I, would suffer from a serious manpower shortage. In December 1929 the Chamber appropriated the sums required to build the "Maginot Line."[5] It was soon to become a symbol of that resigned diffidence that was pervading French life.

Labor Problems. Under the impact of the war the nation had developed a sense of community that augured well for the solution of the

---

[4] The army reorganization bill of 1928 was supported as fully by the right as by the traditionally antimilitarist left; the vote in the Chamber of Deputies was 410 to 23.

[5] By that time Painlevé had been replaced as Minister of War by André Maginot after whom the Line was named.

country's perennial social problems. In the early months of 1919 Parliament enacted laws establishing the principle of the eight-hour day and sanctioning collective bargaining. But labor pressed for other speedy reforms. Like its British counterpart, labor followed with passionate interest the emergence in Soviet Russia of what appeared to be a genuine workers' state. Aroused by the Russian example, the unions intensified their demands, and a wave of strikes swept the country. In Paris there were outbreaks of violence that had to be crushed by armed force. After this clash quiet returned; but when labor, hard-pressed by inflationary price rises, called in vain for higher wages, unrest flared up again. In the spring of 1920 there was an attempt at a general strike. Poorly prepared, it was quickly suppressed by the government. The swift collapse of the strike and the harsh punishment meted out to the strikers (some 20,000 railroad workers were dismissed, and there were similar mass dismissals in industry) dealt a heavy blow to the labor movement; the membership of the *Confédération Générale des Travailleurs* to which most unionized workers belonged was reduced from 2,000,000 to 600,000.

Labor's deep disillusionment was manifested at the national congress of the Socialist Party later that year. A large majority of the delegates, determined to adopt a more militant course, decided to establish a Communist party and join the Comintern. The new party took over the Socialists' party apparatus and newspaper and secured the support of most of the members. However, it lost its initial momentum in a welter of internal quarrels, and the Socialists soon outnumbered the Communists.

If labor remained quiescent through the decade, it was nonetheless dissatisfied with existing conditions. The substance of the few gains it had made was quickly eroded; collective bargaining became rare, and since the implementation of the principle of the eight-hour day was left to agreements between employers and unions, it too was widely ignored. Large sections of upper and middle class kept worrying about a Bolshevik take-over unless labor was curbed. Thus the nation remained split into two camps deeply suspicious of each other's intentions.

The Religious Issue.   The Church problem that had beset the Republic in the prewar era lay dormant during most of the 1920's. The war had helped to smooth over the differences between the Catholic faithful and their opponents. The clergy had shown great courage and patriotism on the battlefield and in the occupied areas, and devout Catholics had fought as bravely in defense of their country as had anticlericals, many of whom had, under the stress of war, felt the need for religion and had returned to the Church. When a new government was formed after the elections of 1919, the anticlerical moderates had no difficulty forming a coalition with the proclerical conservatives. The new government resumed relations with the Vatican, broken off since 1904, and the elevation to sainthood of Joan of Arc eased further the rapprochement between Church and nation. It is possible that the revival of the clerical issue in the election campaign of 1924 contributed to the success of the *cartel des gauches;* if it did, its effect was short-lived. At that time Premier Herriot tried to extend the separation of state and Church to Alsace-Lorraine, but the reaction was so hostile throughout the country that the plan was immediately dropped. In 1928 the Radicals dredged up the clerical issue once more to justify their break with Poincaré. Poincaré, however, bypassed parliament with impunity, and the controversial missionary novitiates were permitted to operate without express legislative sanction.

In fact, the Church was now welcomed by many former opponents as an ally against the Communist threat. It responded to this new role by organizing Catholic labor unions and Catholic Action groups that catered to workers and peasants. It also turned against rightist extremists and ostracized its ally of prewar days, the *Action Française* (see p. 95). None of these efforts were sufficient, however, to bridge the existing social cleavages and help re-establish national unity.

Social and Cultural Trends. As in England, women took on many new functions in France during World War I, and of these they relinquished but few when the fighting ceased. Their greater economic independence was accompanied by their social emancipation, but efforts to secure them political rights remained unsuccessful. In May 1919 the Chamber of Deputies, by a large majority (329 to 95), passed a bill granting women the suffrage, but the Senate with its rural preponderance blocked its enactment. Another attempt in 1924 was equally unsuccessful, as was a more modest endeavor in 1926 to give women the vote in municipal and cantonal elections. Opposition to woman suffrage, however, was not solely a matter of traditionalism. Among the opponents were Radical senators who feared that the Church might re-enter politics by way of the influence it still exerted on women in rural areas.

Radical deputies in the Chamber with its larger urban representation had no such fears, for the Church kept losing ground in the cities and larger towns. The growth of religious indifference was clearly reflected in some social trends—divorces increased from 13,500 in 1913 to 20,000 in 1925 and the birth rate rose only slightly from 193 births per 10,000 people in 1913 to 196 in 1925, in spite of a marked increase in the number of marriages (353,000 in 1925 compared to 299,000 in 1913) and a lowering of the marriage age (from 26 to 25 years). The virtually unchanged birth rate cannot be explained merely by the loss in the war of over one-tenth of the male population of propagative age; it suggests also the widespread adoption of birth control.

Owing to the acquisition of Alsace-Lorraine and a large influx of immigrants, there was no population decline in the 1920's, yet France was just holding its own while Germany's population kept growing.

Immigration, moreover, created problems of assimilation and was viewed with dismay by French labor. To make up militarily for its manpower shortage, the country was forced to rely on its African colonies as a manpower reservoir for the army.

France's demographic stagnation was another reflection of the country's disspirited attitude. Inevitably French contemporary literature reflected the same self-centered, diffident outlook that molded French social and political life. This was even more evident in the work of the lesser literary figures who explored specific French problems than in that of the great writers of the period, discussed earlier, who probed situations of universal concern. As documents of their time, if not as novels, the books of writers like George Duhamel, Jules Romains, and Roger Martin du Gard are still of considerable interest. Duhamel, shocked by the horrors of World War I, turned his back on industrial society and tried to capture the spirit and values of nineteenth-century bourgeois France. Romains started out by accepting his age and believed in its basic goodness (*Men of Good Will* is the title of his magnum opus); but the optimism of the first volumes of this multivolume cycle later gave way to despair as the national and international horizon darkened. Standing between Duhamel and Romains, Martin du Gard neither affirmed nor rejected what he saw, but simply probed its meaning and potentialities. A detached analyst, he explored in his major work, *The Thibaults*, the fate of two generations of the French bourgeoisie. The contrast was striking: while the parents felt secure in their social status and religious beliefs, their children, having lost faith in these values, were trying to find new moral and social footings in a disintegrating society. That they failed in these efforts added to the realism of the story, in the disillusioned judgment of contemporary readers.

THE PERIPHERAL COUNTRIES

The Low Countries.   Postwar developments in the Netherlands and in Belgium bore a marked resemblance to those in Britain and France, respectively. Despite its wartime neutrality, the Netherlands did not escape the effects of the war. The country suffered no physical damage, except for some shipping losses, but as a nation largely dependent on foreign trade it was greatly affected by the disruption of the world markets. Unemployment was a constant concern of the Dutch throughout the interwar period. They tried to alleviate its severest effects by an extensive social security system.

Whereas the Netherlands' position was not unlike Britain's, conditions in Belgium resembled those in France. Like France, Belgium had been a battlefield and had to repair and rebuild its war-devastated regions. It, too, had to finance the reconstruction itself and as a result was likewise beset by inflation. Its currency was stabilized at only one-seventh its prewar value, after as many delays as in France. Yet Belgium experienced fewer of the social and political troubles that plagued postwar France. During the critical period immediately after the war its governments rested on coalitions embracing all three major parties, Catholics, Socialists, and Liberals. As a result, a number of far-reaching social reforms could be enacted. Unions were granted full freedom of organization; restrictions on strikes were removed; the eight-hour day was legalized; and the social insurance system expanded. In both countries, moreover, the monarchs, Queen Wilhelmina of the Netherlands (1880–1962) and King Albert I of Belgium (1875–1934), performed important services as mediators.

Belgium did face a more serious issue in its nationality problem. Fifty-one per cent of its people were Dutch-speaking Flemings and 43 per cent French-speaking Walloons (the remainder spoke German). Since the Walloons had led the independence movement in 1830, French became the country's official language when the kingdom of Belgium was founded. Flemish objections were fanned into open discontent by the Germans while they occupied Belgium in 1914–18. Woodrow Wilson's call for national self-determination further encouraged the agitation for linguistic equality. After the war efforts were made to meet the demands of the Flemings. The country was divided into two linguistic sections in which French and Flemish, respectively, became the official language. In the army Flemish and French regiments were formed, the school system was reorganized, and the University of Ghent was transformed into a Flemish institution. Some Flemish nationalists were not satisfied with these concessions, however, and demanded greater political autonomy or even a union of Flanders with the Netherlands. Of little significance in the 1920's, they gained in importance in the mid–1930's when they joined forces with the fascist movement in Belgium.

Switzerland. Faithful to its traditional policy of neutrality, Switzerland emerged from the war with its democratic institutions intact. The exigencies of the war had forced it, however, to strengthen the powers of the federal government at the expense of the cantons. The postwar slump created new difficulties which could be solved only on the national level, and the process of centralization continued. At the same time new democratic safeguards were introduced into the federal system; the use of popular initiative and referendum was expanded and proportional representation adopted for elections to the National Council, the lower house of the Federal Assembly.[6]

Except for these modifications of existing practices, Switzerland shied away from political changes. It did not follow the general trend and give

---

[6] The upper house is the Council of States, representing the cantons. It is the prerogative of each canton, as a sign of its sovereignty, to determine the mode of election, term of service, and pay of its delegates to the Council.

women the vote. The Swiss were slow to enact reforms since they lived in a state embracing three different cultures (German, French, and Italian) and four national languages (the above and Romansh, a Latin-derived idiom spoken in the Engadine), with religious divisions (between Protestantism and Catholicism) creating additional problems. Given these divergences, it was feared that frequent and far-reaching changes might endanger the union.

In fact, all important new policies were submitted to the electorate for its approval. Switzerland's entry into the League of Nations was decided by popular referendum, and its social security system expanded by a constitutional amendment that required the support of both the electorate and the cantons. Similarly, when the federal government wished to assume control over agriculture to make Switzerland more self-sufficient in foodstuffs, it had to obtain the needed authority by another constitutional amendment in 1929. Admittedly this was a cumbersome process, but it did not block changes and allowed Switzerland to solve its problems without weakening its internal cohesion. In emergencies, moreover, the Federal Assembly could enact needed legislation without consulting the people. A federal income tax thus was introduced by emergency legislation in 1933.

The Scandinavian Countries. The Scandinavian countries, too, escaped the ravages of the First World War except for some shipping losses, but all three found life in the postwar world filled with new problems. Their monarchs were able, conscientious men and proved to be elements of stability. Extensive social reforms also cushioned some of the shocks. Nevertheless, Denmark and Norway, highly dependent on foreign trade, suffered severely from inflation and unemployment. Denmark was troubled by serious unrest in 1919, culminating in a nationwide lockout and general strike and the call for a republic on the part of the workers. A last-minute compromise, relating wage rates to living costs, averted a major crisis. The government also cut military expenditures in order to improve the social insurance system. Norway's difficulties led to frequent government changes and induced the Norwegian Labor Party to join the Communist International. The party soon withdrew from the Comintern in protest against Moscow's controls, but it remained the most militant of the noncommunist labor parties in Europe. Norway's domestic difficulties were compounded by the retention of prohibition, which had originally been introduced as a temporary wartime measure; not only was there widespread smuggling and illegal distilling, but the country's exports were also impaired. Spain and Portugal, for example, refused to buy from a country that would no longer purchase their wines. Prohibition was repealed in 1927, but the exporting industries failed to recapture all of their markets.

Sweden, economically more resilient than its two neighbors, suffered a brief postwar depression, but was able to absorb its unemployed into a large public works program. After 1923 it was one of the first countries to reach a new level of prosperity. Its recovery was aided by its expanding cooperative movement which helped to distribute more evenly the nation's resources. By preventing the formation of a few large concentrations of wealth, the cooperatives also softened the effects of the Great Depression on Sweden. Both Denmark and Norway, which had less well developed cooperative systems, felt the full severity of the crisis, but their greater dependence on world trade also made them more vulnerable.

In foreign affairs the Scandinavian countries set a noteworthy example of constructive collaboration. Sweden submitted to the decision of the League of Nations when that body awarded the disputed Aland Islands to Finland. A quarrel over Greenland between Norway and Denmark was decided in Denmark's favor by the International Court of Justice at The Hague and Norway acquiesced. In a strife-torn world the Scandinavian countries succeeded in holding their peace. But this happy state of affairs came to an end with Hitler's accession to power.

7

Domestic Politics in the 1920's: The Western European Dictatorships

In the countries of southwestern Europe the social and economic struggles touched off by the after-effects of the war led to the breakdown of all parliamentary institutions. Popular representation, never very effective in any of them, was replaced by dictatorships. In Italy where political awareness was most widespread, the dictatorship rested on a virulent mass movement supported by business, agrarian, and army circles; yet while mindful of the special interests of these groups, the Fascist regime was never controlled by them and charted its own totalitarian course. In both Spain and Portugal, on the other hand, the dictatorships were traditional ones, created for the benefit of army, upper classes, and Church and resting on the support of the armed forces. Again unlike Italian Fascism, the Iberian dictatorships contented themselves essentially with controlling the political life of their countries, although Portugal's soon moved somewhat closer to the Italian model and adopted certain of the organizational features and external paraphernalia of a fascist regime.

ITALY: THE RISE OF FASCISM

The Failure of Parliamentary Government.   Italy came out of the war
as it had entered it—torn by dissension. The anti-interventionists
blamed the country's postwar difficulties on its participation in the war;
the interventionists blamed them on the hapless Prime Minister Orlando,
who, in their view, should have secured all the territorial spoils of victory to which they felt Italy was entitled by the London Treaty of 1915.
They lamented their "mutilated" victory and forced the government's
resignation in June 1919.

Harassed by inflation and mass unemployment, restless and disillusioned, the frustrated, impoverished nation was in desperate need of
imaginative, purposeful leadership. What it got was an able but colorless
administrator, Francesco Nitti (1868–1953), who was singularly lacking
in political flair and attractiveness. His authority was challenged at once
by that flamboyant warrior-poet, Gabriele D'Annunzio, who took it upon
himself to rectify the injustices which he felt had been inflicted on Italy
at the Paris Peace Conference. With a small band of regular forces, war
veterans, and youthful adventurers, he seized the city of Fiume in
September 1919 and claimed it for Italy.

Fiume was a small Austrian port on the Adriatic which straddled the
ethnic boundary line between Slavs and Italians. Of little material value
to Italy, its control seemed important as a matter of prestige. At Paris
Orlando had asked for its cession to Italy in lieu of Dalmatia, which had
been promised to Rome by the Treaty of London but was given to
Yugoslavia. Orlando had walked out of the conference when Wilson
refused to yield. Since neither side was willing to compromise, the question was still unsettled when the peace treaty with Austria was signed
in September 1919. Two days later D'Annunzio took over the city.

Premier Nitti made no attempt to oust D'Annunzio from Fiume
although he disapproved of the coup; the Prime Minister did not dare
incur the ire of those who acclaimed the foray as a patriotic deed. On
the other hand, he did not yield to their demands that he annex Fiume.
His ambiguous attitude served to dissipate further the dwindling moral
and political authority of the government.

The prestige of parliament was also declining. In November 1919 the
first postwar elections took place. Unlike the French and British elections, they produced a sharp swing to the left—an indication of the
country's unwillingness to return to prewar conditions. The two largest
parties were the Socialists and the Catholic Populars, who between them
controlled half of the seats of the new Chamber. The Socialists spoke for
the industrial proletariat, whereas the Populars made the lot of the landless peasants one of their major concerns. The programs of the two par-

ties thus were in agreement on basic aspects of social policy and differed mainly on the methods of implementation. Nevertheless doctrinairism, inexperience, and irresponsibility kept them from entering a coalition. Distrustful of the bourgeois parties, the Socialists refused altogether to take part in the work of the parliament. Thus Nitti, a moderate Liberal, stayed in office, governing chiefly by special decree. But the weakness of both government and parliament appeared to bear out the warnings of those who denounced parliamentary governments as irresponsible and ineffective.

As if to lend further support to these charges, political action was shifting increasingly from cabinet room and parliament hall into the streets and the countryside. The nation was kept in constant turmoil by demonstrations and strikes of the workers and seizures of land by the peasants. Armed clashes occurred between the Socialists and their foes and between peasants and landowners organized in self-help battalions. A disastrous crop failure placed further burdens on the economy strained to the utmost already by wartime destruction and dislocation. In June 1920 Nitti was forced from office. When he had been appointed the year before, as one observer has noted, "the search had been for a government which could make the best of the new democratic forces; in 1920 the search was for one which could solve day-to-day problems by any means at all."[1] The choice fell upon an experienced practitioner of political expediency, Giovanni Giolitti (1842–1928), who had governed the country by clever maneuvers for over ten years in the prewar era.

Giolitti, coldly appraising the situation, concluded that the forces of discontent were too strong to permit the restoration of governmental authority by a show of force. When Milanese workers resisted a lockout by occupying the factories and maintaining production as best they could, he did not intervene but waited until the lack of supplies and of expertise forced them to withdraw from the plants in return for a vague promise of remedial legislation. Nor did he interfere in the unending fights between the Socialists and the newly emerging Fascists. Only in the case of Fiume did he resort to force after his usual method of parleys and bargains had failed to dislodge D'Annunzio. A few naval salvoes were sufficient to remove the poet from his "Regency." Fiume became an independent city-state in accordance with a treaty concluded with Yugoslavia.

New elections held in May 1921 failed to give Giolitti a viable majority, and he resigned. The following eighteen months, until the Fascists' assumption of power, were a period of continuous moral and political disintegration. The government stood by passively while large parts of the country were plunged into near-civil war.

[1] Cecil J. S. Sprigge, *The Development of Modern Italy* (New Haven, 1944), p. 182.

Benito Mussolini, in Fascist black shirt, addressing an open air meeting in Turin. (*Reprinted courtesy Wide World Photos*)

The Beginnings of Fascism. Fascism was the outgrowth of postwar Italy's disillusionment and of its ensuing moral and political cynicism. Only in a society devoid of ideals and purposes and incapable of upholding law and order could a movement gain ground that was identified with an attitude of mind—force, action, militancy—rather than with a substantive program. In Benito Mussolini, moreover, it had a spokesman whose own restlessness and belligerency expressed well the mood of his followers. Undisciplined and rebellious, this son of a poor blacksmith and a schoolmistress had become interested in socialism in early youth, and after a checkered career as a teacher in Italy and an agitator and journalist in Switzerland (where he went to evade the draft), he had risen quickly through the ranks of the Socialist Party. A man of strong personal magnetism and a rousing speaker and writer, he became one of the leaders of the party's radical wing. He was an early advocate of Italy's entry into World War I and was expelled from the anti-interventionist Socialist Party in 1915. He served for some months as a corporal at the front; when the war ended, the 35-year-old ex-teacher, ex-journalist, and ex-Socialist faced an uncertain future.

In March 1919 Mussolini formed his first *fascio di combattimento* (combat troop). The step seems to have had some business support, for the charter meeting took place at the "Club for Industrial and Commercial Interests" at Milan. Despite the rightist make-up of its supporters, **129** the first appeal of this "healthily Italian" movement, as it called itself proudly, was vaguely socialist in its tenor, except for its advocacy of a nationalist foreign policy. With conditions so much in flux, Mussolini preferred to keep all doors open rather than commit himself ideologically. Less than a month after its formation the Milan *fascio* broke up a Socialist rally and wrecked the printing plant of the Socialist paper, *Avanti;* but when Milanese workers took over and ran a factory by themselves, Mussolini praised "this creative strike that does not disrupt production." As he himself stated with cynical frankness, "we allow ourselves the luxury of being aristocratic and democratic, reactionary and revolutionary, legalistic and illegalistic, according to the circumstances of place, time, and environment in which we are compelled to live and act."[2]

However, playing off proletariat and property owners against each other proved an impossible undertaking, and Fascism made little headway at first. In the elections of 1919 not one of its candidates was elected; Mussolini himself suffered an ignominious defeat in Milan. The one element of his movement, however, which he did not disappoint, the blackguards and brawlers who could not adjust to an orderly life, continued to rally behind him and form new *fasci* to battle the "Reds." They attracted the support of frightened industrialists and landowners and of some parts of the middle class. Anxious to put an end to the strikes and seizures of land, these circles supported the black-shirted Fascist squads with money and arms. The army too helped to equip them, for it saw allies in them against the pacifist left. Similarly, the Fascists had the sympathetic support of the police, which often stood by while the Blackshirts gave battle to Socialists or to the newly organized Communists. In the election campaign of 1921 Giolitti even made an agreement of mutual support with Mussolini. The Premier encouraged the Fascists to obstruct the campaign of the Socialists and the Populars, and as a result the country was treated to an unprecedented spectacle of organized violence. It did not produce the hoped-for majority for Giolitti, but it helped to elect some thirty-five Fascists and give them official status.

Despite its limited electoral success, the movement seemed irresistible, at least in northern and central Italy. *Fasci* sprang up wherever there were Socialists or Communists to be fought, and in some areas the Blackshirts were in virtual control of the local government. They derived their strength from their own local following and acknowledged Mussolini as leader (*duce*) only as long as he adhered to the course of brute force, which was the only policy they knew and accepted. When he concluded a truce with the Socialists in August 1921, the Fascists denounced it and continued their campaign of savage brutality. Their disobedience did not discredit Musolini, but rather established him as a moderate with whom non-Fascists could do business.

[2] Quoted in Laura Fermi, *Mussolini* (Chicago, 1961), p. 156.

The appeal of the Fascists did not lie only in their opposition to the radical left. Large parts of the nation were attracted to Fascism by Mussolini's call for a vigorous foreign policy. The Duce fired the national imagination by vistas of an Italy pursuing its rightful claims under Fascist leadership and securing the territories which had been withheld from the country. To Italian national pride, still smarting under the setbacks suffered at the Paris Peace Conference, these were inspiring prospects.

By mid-1921 leftist radicalism had clearly been defeated. "To say that there still exists a Bolshevist peril in Italy," Mussolini wrote in July 1921, "is to substitute certain insincere fears for the reality. Bolshevism is vanquished. Nay, more, it has been disowned by the leaders and by the masses."[3] Fascist attention turned to seizing the government, and by the fall of 1922 the country seemed ripe for a Fascist take-over. Many saw in Mussolini the only man able to restore public order which in reality he and his squads had done their best to destroy. He made open preparations for the seizure of power; a Fascist militia was organized, and at a mass meeting at Naples in October he announced blandly that if the government were not turned over to him, "we shall take it, descending upon Rome." Arrangements were made for such a "March on Rome" to take place on October 28, with *fasci* converging upon the capital from all directions.

During the events that followed, however, Mussolini was the led rather than the leader. He threatened to march on Rome, hoping to frighten the government into yielding to him, but hesitated to order his squads to move on the capital. Anxious, in fact, to avoid a forcible show-down, he approached Giolitti and Nitti and proposed the formation of a coalition government. And while the Blackshirts were mobilized every-where for the march on the capital, he remained in Milan (close to the Swiss border), waiting to see what government and army would do.

In a last-minute show of determination the government decided to impose a state of emergency; but King Victor Emmanuel III (1869–1947), on the advice of the army, refused to proclaim it—the first time in his twenty-year reign that the King would not sign a decree proposed by the government. The road thus was cleared for Mussolini's assumption of power, and on October 30, 1922, he was appointed Premier.

The Consolidation of Fascist Power. At the time few people were aware of the significance of his appointment. Mussolini's beginnings seemed quite innocuous; his new cabinet rested on a coalition of Fas-cists, Nationalists, Liberals, and Populars, and of its fourteen members only four were Fascists. The Duce himself became Premier and Foreign

[3] *Popolo d'Italia*, July 2, 1921, quoted in G. A. Borgese, *Goliath: The March of Fascism* (New York, 1937), p. 213.

Minister and took over also the Ministry of the Interior which controlled the police, but this did not seem noteworthy either, for his primary task was the restoration of public order. Similarly two other measures he took received only little attention. One was the creation of the Fascist Grand Council, composed of Fascists and government members whose task it was to coordinate the work of Fascist Party and government; in effect, however, the former was superimposed upon the latter, charting all basic policies. The other measure taken by Mussolini merged all Fascist squads into a state-supported Voluntary Militia for National Security which owed its allegiance, not to the King, but to Mussolini.

The nation was much more impressed with the new impetus which Mussolini imparted to the governmental machinery. After years of strife and confusion, peace seemed to return to the country. Political clashes and street battles came to an end, and there were no more lockouts and strikes. The government launched public works projects and embarked on long overdue educational reforms. Its drive for efficiency even succeeded in having the trains run on time. Fascist terrorists were still stalking the country, but their actions were explained away, if they were admitted at all, as the excesses of local bosses who were abusing the trust of the Duce.

By 1924 Mussolini felt strong enough to dissolve the Chamber, in which the Fascists held less than 10 per cent of the seats, and to arrange new elections. One of the last acts of the old Chamber was the passage of a new electoral law by which the largest party would automatically receive two-thirds of all seats provided it polled at least one-fourth of the vote. The measure was justified on the grounds that the multiparty system had been largely responsible for the country's political confusion. On the strength of that argument many non-Fascist Deputies voted for it; others were subjected to various pressures to secure a majority. The elections in April 1924 gave the Fascist 65 per cent of the vote. In spite of terror and violence 2.25 million out of 7 million voters voted for non-Fascist parties.

Among those denouncing the election results and demanding new and genuinely free elections was a Socialist Deputy, Giacomo Matteotti. Shortly after his attack on the government he disappeared, and two months later his battered body was found in a wood near Rome. Whether Mussolini ordered the murder of Matteotti has never been ascertained, but there was widespread agreement on his moral guilt and he himself assumed what he called the "historical responsibility" for the deed. The opposition parties withdrew from the Chamber, vowing that they would not return until law and order had been restored, and many newspapers likewise assailed Fascism and the government with unusual vehemence. But the oppositional forces remained divided and leaderless, and Mussolini, who was panic-stricken at first by this unexpected reaction, quickly reasserted himself and tightened his hold on the country.

He destroyed all freedom of press by authorizing local authorities to suppress newspapers which published objectionable material. This post-publication censorship proved far more effective than the traditional pre-publication control, for it created even greater uncertainty as to what it was permissible to print. Early in 1926 the Chamber surrendered its legislative functions and empowered the government to issue decrees that would have the force of law. There followed the elimination of all non-Fascists from the cabinet and the conversion of the bureaucracy into an out-and-out Fascist tool. All oppositional groups and activities were suppressed and oppositional deputies barred permanently from the Chamber. Any remaining opposition was fought by a newly created secret police, special courts, and consignment without trial to detention camps and penal islands where bread-and-water diets, solitary confinement, and physical torture could be inflicted. Nongovernmental organizations—labor unions, professional associations, sports clubs—were either brought under direct governmental control or forced to accept appointment of active Fascists to all leading positions. Members of the professions, writers, and artists had to belong to their respective Fascist-controlled organization to pursue their calling and lost that right if they were expelled, as they might be for lack of "national loyalty."

The economic life of the country was controlled by syndicates or corporations in which employers and employees were brought together under the ultimate supervision of the Fascist Grand Council. While labor lost all freedom in this arrangement, business retained some measure of independence as the result of a special understanding between Mussolini and the business community. Fascist control became total when the Chamber of Deputies was dissolved in 1928 and new elections were held in March 1929. This time the candidates were selected by the Fascist Grand Council from lists compiled by the corporations. After such preparations the elections produced returns virtually 100 per cent in support of the government.

The Fascist Party. In paving the way for these developments, the Fascist Party played a decisive role. It was never a party in the traditional European sense, identified with special social and economic interests and performing its main tasks in parliament. In fact, it always took pride in being instead a national movement opposed to the traditional parties. For some time it would not even organize itself as a party and remained a loose association of *fasci*. When it did constitute itself as a party in November 1921 to tighten cohesion and discipline, it continued to see its primary function in its extraparliamentary activities.

Once Mussolini had attained power, the Fascist Party gave up all pretense of normal party concerns. It assumed the special role of a party in a modern dictatorship that constantly must shape and control the will of the people and generate support for the government. This the Fascist Party did by ideological indoctrination, press campaigns, and mass rallies in which the country was prepared for major policy shifts, and government policies were explained and extolled. The party also was instrumental in organizing the nation into professional and cultural associations that kept the individual citizen under surveillance. Party members who were government officials helped to control the bureaucracy; others again performed similar functions in the armed forces and in the police. The party thus infiltrated the nation's political, social, economic, and cultural life and injected Fascist views and demands into all its sectors. In these pursuits it was assisted by a number of affiliated organizations. Youth groups such as the *Balilla* for those between eight and eighteen years and the *Fasci Giovanili* for the eighteen to twenty-one year olds inculcated the Fascist spirit in the minds of the young. *Dopolavoro*, the "After-Work" organization, provided free or at minimal rates sports facilities, adult education, entertainment, and other activities to keep the workers happy (and under control) in their leisure time. There was finally the Fascist militia which along with secret police, special courts, and detention camps helped to ensure the security of the regime.

Fascist Ideology.   For the exalted role of state and party Fascist ideology provided the spiritual underpinning. In keeping with the origins of Fascism as a revolt against reason and intellect, this ideology was haphazardly put together rather than worked out systematically and was more concerned with mental attitudes than with specific objectives. "As an anti-individualist idea," according to Mussolini's definition, "[Fascism] believes in the state. . . . Liberalism negates the state in the interest of the individual; Fascism looks upon the state as the only true reality of the individual. For Fascism everything is part of the state. In this sense Fascism is totalitarian, and the Fascist state as the sum total and embodiment of all values lends significance to the life of the entire nation, helps it develop and strengthens it." Fascism dismissed as unimportant material hardships: "It rejects the equating of well-being with happiness which turns men into animals since they have only the one thought of being well-fed and fattened and are being debased into a purely vegetative life." The good life was not one of comfort of riches, but one "in which the individual attains by self-denial, by the sacrifices of his special interests, by death even that truly spiritualized existence on which rests his dignity as a human being." Life, then, was duty and struggle; Fascism, Mussolini boasted, "does not believe in the possibility or utility of eternal peace. It rejects pacifism which implies a renunciation of fighting and cowardly avoidance of sacrifices. Only war develops fully all human energies; . . . all other tests are substitutes because they do not confront man with the alternative of life or death." Or as he put it even more bluntly: "The Fascist state is will to power and domination. . . . To Fascism the drive towards empire, that is the expansion of the nation, is a sign of vitality. . . . Peoples that rise or rise again are imperialist, only decadent peoples are prepared to renounce."

The responsibility for the implementation of these precepts belonged to those who by their heroism, their sacrifices and dynamism, were part of a natural elite destined to wield power. Among these Mussolini, who supposedly had displayed these qualities to the highest degree, was the unchallenged leader, and he was exalted by an untiring propaganda apparatus into a superman of inexhaustible energies and infallible wisdom. Rising to lyrical heights in depicting Italy's greatness and unsparing in his invectives when raging against bourgeois smugness or foreign rapacity, he presented himself as the dedicated leader of his people and evoked confidence and submission. Thus there were many who saw nothing absurd in the claim which press, radio, and party speakers kept blaring forth that "Mussolini is always right." They ignored his egotism and self-indulgence, his opportunism and irresponsibility, and seemed unaware of his deep contempt of their individual worth and intelligence.

The Popularity of Fascism. The effectiveness of this indoctrination is attested by the fact that Fascism enjoyed widespread support in the 1920's. Its popularity was the more noteworthy because material conditions, far from improving, declined for large parts of the nation. Mussolini's innumerable public work projects, launched regardless of cost, produced inflationary pressures, and his efforts to make Italy self-sufficient drove prices still higher. Wages never kept pace with the increase in the cost of living. Social insurance and social services were severely curtailed, and unemployment remained a continuous problem. At the same time taxes were raised to meet the insatiable needs of the armed services and the bureaucracy, and everyone, whether party member or not, was forced to make contributions to the Fascist Party and its affiliated organizations.

Yet Fascism did not rest merely on coercion and propaganda. It enjoyed a great deal of spontaneous support, partly from genuine enthusiasm, partly from fear of potential alternatives, and partly from apathy. It had restored order, it was injecting a new purposefulness into the life of the nation, it was embarking on ambitious melioration plans— land reclamation, highway construction, and public building—, and with its much-publicized "Battle of Wheat" it proposed to, and eventually did, make Italy self-sufficient in breadstuffs. Agriculture did benefit from the measures taken in its behalf; production of most major crops was expanded, and by 1933 over 500,000 farm workers had become independent cultivators, as owners or tenants. That the country had to pay an excessive price for many of these achievements was either not seen or minimized by a nation which had but unhappy memories of pre-Fascist times.

Mussolini also could claim credit for ending the dispute between State and Church that went back to the unification of Italy in 1870. In 1929 he concluded the Lateran Treaty with Pope Pius XI by which Italy acknowledged the secular sovereignty of the Pope over the Vatican grounds (Vatican City) while the Pope recognized formally the Kingdom of Italy and gave up all claims to the former Papal States. A concordat agreed to at the same time sought to settle a number of questions concerning education and marriage, but was less effective, and the right to educate the young remained a permanent source of friction between the Church and the Fascist regime.

Mussolini's foreign policy also had the country's approval. In 1923 he seized Fiume and incorporated it into Italy, and in that same year he occupied the Greek island of Corfu after the murder (by unknown assailants) of an Italian general and his staff at the Greco-Italian border. He demanded a large indemnity and a humiliating apology from Greece although Greece's responsibility for the crime was not proven. Because of Anglo-French intervention he was forced to evacuate Corfu, but only after the Greeks had paid the indemnity. It was thus not difficult for him to claim a great victory.

His most important achievement, however, was the improvement of Italy's status as a great power. This was strikingly demonstrated by its inclusion as one of the guarantors of the Locarno Pact, and less conspicuously but no less clearly by the unending pilgrimage of foreign statesmen to Rome to pay their respects to the Duce. Not only Italians but foreign observers as well were greatly impressed by Fascism. They admired the apparent order and discipline which it had brought to Italy and the purposiveness and vitality it inspired. Moreover, the easy-going ways of the Italians (and widespread corruption) somewhat tempered the harsh demands of Fascist orthodoxy and made it appear less formidable. As for Mussolini's glorification of war and expansion, these effusions were discounted as meaningless in view of Italy's limited potentialities and its poor fighting record.

Except for the Fiume and Corfu ventures, moreover, Mussolini's actual foreign policy seemed unobjectionable during the 1920's. His most conspicuous activity consisted in signing friendship pacts; he concluded at least eight between 1926 and 1930. "No country ever signed so many pacts and treaties as Mussolini's Italy," recalled one of the Duce's diplomats, "he never refused his signature to any convention that was proposed to him, even those most contrary to his ideas and purposes."[4] Few understood that what seemed to be efforts to promote peaceful cooperation were in effect moves to avoid any clearcut alignment and keep conditions in flux in the hope that eventually Italy might by some swift stroke benefit from this instability.

Cultural Trends. In the confining atmosphere of Fascist controls no writers of real distinction emerged. Some of them went into exile; of these Ignazio Silone deserves to be mentioned as the author of two

---

[4] Quoted by H. Stuart Hughes, in Gordon A. Craig and Felix Gilbert, eds., *The Diplomats: 1919–1939* (Princeton, 1953), p. 225.

deeply felt novels (*Fontamara* and *Bread and Wine*) that explored the problem of human freedom and man's control of his fate in a totalitarian state. Pirandello remained, but was soon out of favor and fell silent. Several of the older established writers, however, continued to publish in Italy; the best known of these was the novelist Grazia Deledda, winner of the Nobel Prize for Literature in 1926, who cast her work in an apolitical human and regional framework that was unobjectionable to Fascist censors.

At least one dissenter was never silenced. This was Benedette Croce (1866–1952), the historian-philosopher. Despite some misgivings he had at first welcomed the advent of the Fascist regime, hopeful that it would invigorate the disspirited nation. He soon became disillusioned with Mussolini's authoritarianism, and in 1925 he openly broke with Fascism. As a senator he spoke out against its repression of freedom in parliament; later he shifted his fight to the literary plane and published a number of works (among them, *History of Italy from 1871 to 1915* and *History of Europe in the Nineteenth Century*) in which he described "history as the story of liberty." Less impressive from the viewpoint of scholarship, these books bespoke his courage and moral integrity—qualities which he also displayed in the editorship of his journal, *La Critica,* and in his assistance to opponents of the regime.

Under the circumstances it was a grave blow to Croce that one of his disciples, the philosopher Giovanni Gentile (1875–1944) became the leading academic supporter of Mussolini. Gentile saw in the Duce and his movement the embodiment of that "activist idealism" around which he had built his philosophical system. Despite some disappointments Gentile always retained his faith in Fascism, even though the Fascists never felt fully at ease with this erudite scholar who did not quite fit into their anti-intellectual world.

Devoid of esthetic values, Fascism was as uncreative in the arts as it was in the humanities. In architecture Mussolini favored a massive neoclassical symmetry expressive of order and strength and therefore the favorite style of all totalitarian rulers. His taste in painting was no more subtle. Somewhat less rigid than Hitler and Stalin, however, he would tolerate an occasional straying into modern functionalism in public buildings.

THE IBERIAN DICTATORSHIPS

Political Chaos in Spain. Spain had remained neutral during the First World War. Pro-German and pro-Allied forces were rather evenly balanced, and neither camp felt that it had much to gain from entering the war. Moreover, neutrality proved highly profitable; there was an enormous demand for Spain's foodstuffs and raw materials, and the country was able to redeem most of its national and industrial debt and almost quadrupled its gold reserve. Prosperity failed, however, to ease the existing social and political tensions and in fact sharpened them. Its benefits accrued mainly to landowners and industrialists and to a lesser extent to the middle class. The workers made no notable gains since wage increases were quickly absorbed by the rising cost of living. Labor's discontent exploded into strikes, frequently verging on civil war. The army which was called out to suppress the strikes became the mainstay of public order and a factor of increasing importance in politics. With one officer to every ten men, the officers were left with much time on their hands, and found their forays into politics a welcome release for their energies. The army's encroachment on the civil domain was encouraged by King Alfonso XIII (1886–1941), who was anxious to rid himself of parties and parliament (Cortes). It also had the support of landowners and industrialists determined to block labor's ascendance. Allied with them was the Church, which feared for its spiritual influence and as a major owner of banks and industrial enterprises shared their material concerns.

During the immediate postwar years a number of governments struggled hard to reduce the increasing tensions. While essentially conservative, they saw nonetheless that the growing unrest could not be dealt with by armed intervention. Yet every governmental attempt at conciliation was sabotaged by a coalition of employers and army leaders, tacitly abetted by King Alfonso. Inevitably industrial warfare became more embittered, with both sides resorting to the use of armed gangs and assassinations to terrorize the other into surrender.

Political tension was heightened by a series of defeats the army suffered in its campaign against the rebellious Riffs in Spanish Morocco. In the summer of 1921 a Spanish force was all but annihilated by a much smaller Riff force; 10,000 Spaniards were killed and the remaining 4,000 were taken prisoner. The King, who had ordered the campaign without consulting the general staff, was largely responsible for the disaster. To safeguard the monarchy, both he and the army were determined, however, to conceal his involvement, and when the Cortes set up a committee of inquiry, they decided to intervene. They were the more anxious to curb the Cortes because recent elections had produced a solid majority for the government, presaging a better functioning of the parliamentary system. Preparations were made for the abolition of the constitutional regime, and in September 1923, General Miguel Primo de Rivera (1870–1930), Captain-General of Catalonia, was appointed head of the government with dictatorial powers.

The Dictatorship of Primo de Rivera. An intense patriot, well-intentioned and not without generous impulses, Primo de Rivera had no political program except that he wished to save his country. He has been described as a latter-day Haroun-al-Raschid, eager to bestow his bountiful favors on one and all. Though his background was that of a hard-drinking, pleasure-loving grandee, he was concerned with the plight of the landless peasantry and anxious to ease its lot. But he was dependent on the support of the landlords, which precluded any agrarian reforms —an imperative task in a country in which one per cent of the population owned half of the arable land and let much of it go to waste. He did inaugurate an ambitious public works program which gave Spain an excellent network of roads and improved its railways, brought additional land under cultivation, and modernized the country's public utilities. Above all, it almost did away with unemployment. Primo also suppressed the Riff rebellion (with France's help), salving the country's hurt pride and relieving it of a heavy drain on its resources. "Had Primo retired in 1925, after the successful termination of the Moroccan War," wrote one observer, "he would have gone down to history as one of the saviors of Spain."[5]

His dictatorship rested, however, not on a national movement, but on Church, army, and upper class. He became increasingly dependent on these groups as he closed the Cortes, banned all political parties, and subjected the press to a rigid censorship. Primo never obtained the support of middle class and intelligentsia, and since he was unable (and unwilling) to undertake any major social reforms, the working class, too, eventually turned against him. As opposition spread, he tightened his policy of repression. King and army, perturbed by his growing unpopularity, began to conspire against him. The effects of the Great Depression undermined his position still further and in January 1930 he was driven from office.

Primo was succeeded by another general, Damaso Berenguer, who tried to return to constitutional practices. But antimonarchist feeling had grown so strong by this time that Alfonso feared for his throne. He would not consent to new Cortes elections and allowed only the holding of local ones. They took place on April 12, 1931 and resulted in a sweeping victory of the republican parties in almost all cities and towns. The army, anxious to extricate itself from a hopeless impasse, withdrew at once its support from the King. Alfonso left the country two days later, and Spain was proclaimed a republic.

Portugal. A republic since 1910, Portugal was unable to establish a functioning parliamentary government. As in Spain, the bulk of the population was made up of illiterate, landless peasants. Politics thus was the domain of the small upper and middle class, but this exclusiveness did not make for poltical unity. While the republicans were in the majority, they were badly split, and the resulting instability led monarchist

[5] Gerald Brenan, *The Spanish Labyrinth* (New York, 1943), p. 82.

groups to make repeated attempts to overthrow the Republic. Of the six Presidents who were elected between 1910 and 1926, only one served out his four-year term. During the same time span the country had over forty different governments, among them several dictatorships.

As the result of this instability Portugal's economy kept declining. Budget deficits grew, and in 1923 the government was forced to float a loan at a discount of 50 per cent, owing to the lack of confidence in its fiscal policies. A gigantic fraud perpetrated upon the country in 1925 increased the inflationary pressures. With the help of forged orders a group of financial manipulators had the official printer of the Portuguese currency print half a million 500-escudo notes ($230,000,000). The notes were circulated through a bank founded especially for that purpose in Lisbon. Perhaps because of their brazenness the operations went undetected for many months and unbalanced further the country's precarious finances.

At the height of these difficulties, in May 1926, the army overthrew the government and established a military dictatorship. General Antonio Oscar de Fragoso Carmona became Provisional President of the Republic and was later elected (and re-elected three times) to the Presidency. It was a civilian, however, Dr. Antonio de Oliveira Salazar (1889–   ), who emerged as the central figure of the new regime. This ascetic, deeply religious professor of economics was strongly opposed to the erratic ways of Portuguese parliamentarism. Elected a deputy in 1921, he resigned his seat after attending parliament for only one day. Similarly, he accepted the appointment as Minister of Finance only after having been granted full and exclusive control over the country's financial policies. Salazar became quickly the actual head of the government, and in 1932 he became Premier in name also. He entrenched himself further by giving the country a new constitution which transformed Portugal into a corporate state somewhat on the Italian model. Censorship, a secret police, a green-shirted militia, and a one-party system made his position wholly impregnable.

Salazar balanced the budget within a year by increasing taxes, suppressing graft, and pruning the badly inflated bureaucracy. The public debt was consolidated and interest rates cut by up to 50 per cent. The savings he thus achieved were invested in public works projects; transportation, communications, and electrification were improved and expanded. Wheat production was increased to reduce the importation of foodstuffs. There was, however, little direct improvement of living conditions for the great mass of peasants and workers. Wages remained very low and taxation was still primarily indirect, placing a major share of the tax burden on those who could least afford to pay taxes. Nor did Salazar enact any important social and educational reforms. The bulk of the people thus had to pay the price of continued poverty for the outward order and financial stability that the dictator brought to the country.

8

Domestic Politics
in the 1920's: Central
and Eastern Europe

In 1918–19, inspired or urged on by the messages and exhortations of President Wilson, most of central and eastern Europe introduced democratic, parliamentary regimes. Yet whatever high hopes accompanied these changes—and in many cases expectations were not great to begin with—democratic self-government collapsed quickly in almost all of these countries. Beset by economic, social, and ethnic difficulties, their peoples were ill-prepared to assume the demanding responsibilities of representative government. Where parliamentary government kept functioning, as in Germany, Austria, Poland, and Yugoslavia, it was repeatedly threatened by internal upheavals. The domestic history of these states is filled with clashes between the democratic and antidemocratic forces, with authoritarian regimes evolving everywhere in the end. Since in nearly every case the nondemocratic governments were the agents of special social and economic interests, these regimes deepened the existing domestic cleavages. Yet, sharpening grievances and weakening internal cohesion, they also stirred longings for new and better societies which would be founded on unity and remain untainted by economic concerns. **141**

GERMANY: THE WEIMAR REPUBLIC

Early Difficulties. The revolution which swept Emperor William II from his throne in November 1918 owed its success to the brittleness of the monarchy rather than to its own dynamism. A spontaneous outburst, born of war weariness and demoralization, it had no long-range goals, no leaders anxious to seize political power, and no armed force to back up its authority. The men who took over the government did so because no one else was available. They were the leaders of Germany's largest political party, the moderate Social Democratic Party, and of its more radical offshoot, the Independent Socialist Party. On November 10, 1918 they formed a new government, the so-called Council of People's Commissars, composed of three representatives each of the two parties.

The dominant figure in the Council was its chairman, Friedrich Ebert (1871–1925). A one-time harnessmaker and innkeeper, Ebert had risen through the ranks of the Social Democratic Party and had become one of its chairmen in 1913. He was a hardworking, dedicated man, conciliatory and of great personal dignity, but without any flair for the external trappings of political leadership. As a moderate Socialist, Ebert was opposed to violent revolution and aroused at once the opposition of the Spartacist League, which wished to establish a dictatorship on the Soviet model and called on the starving, embittered masses to overthrow the "traitors of the revolution." Numerically small, the Spartacists derived their strength from their concentration in the industrial centers; they were supplied with money and arms by the Soviet government, which hailed them as the vanguard of the German dictatorship of the proletariat. Ebert, lacking an armed force of his own, could not check their activities unless he had armed support. Such support could be provided only by the old monarchist army, but all depended on whether Field Marshal von Hindenburg, the commander-in-chief, would come to the rescue of a socialist government. Fortunately for Ebert the army on its part needed the support of the government to maintain discipline in its own ranks, and on November 10, Ebert and General Wilhelm Groener, the successor of Ludendorff as Hindenburg's right-hand man, concluded an agreement by which army and government promised to help each other fulfill their respective tasks.

The agreement was indicative of the weakness of the Republic. Government and army faced each other as equals, with the army retaining its traditional autonomous status under the arrangements that were made between Ebert and Groener. The Spartacist threat was crushed by the military with the help of volunteer units; these so-called Free Corps were composed of specially selected veterans and other militant elements opposed to parliamentarism and democracy and contemptuous of the new state. Appalled at seeing these forces fight a workers movement with the approval of a socialist government, the Independents withdrew from the Council of People's Commissars in December 1918.

The Independents objected also to Ebert's gradualism in the implementation of the socialist program. The new government introduced direct, secret, and equal suffrage, gave women the vote, established freedom of press and assembly, proclaimed the eight-hour work day, and provided for unemployment relief. The Independents, however, called also for the immediate nationalization of the major means of production lest the old social elements retain their economic power and undo the gains of the revolution. Ebert and his party associates feared to disrupt further the badly disordered economy by any measures of nationalization; they also thought it undemocratic to initiate such incisive steps without an express mandate. They insisted that a popularly elected, genuinely representative parliament ought to decide these questions.

The Weimar Constitution. On January 19, 1919 a national assembly was elected to draft a constitution for the new state. It met early in February in Weimar, a quiet residential town in Thuringia. Weimar was chosen because it was feared that in strife-torn Berlin attempts might be made to disrupt the discussions by demonstrations and strikes. Moreover, Weimar, the home of Goethe and other great German minds in the eighteenth and nineteenth century, was a symbol of humanist culture and cosmopolitanism, and its choice as the seat of the constituent assembly was to be suggestive of the new spirit guiding the young Republic.

The elections were in many ways inconclusive. The Social Democrats obtained 163 seats while the Independents got a mere 22. (The Spartacists, now absorbed into the newly formed Communist Party, did not take part in the elections.) With 185 seats (out of 421) the socialist parties failed to secure a majority in the assembly. The bourgeois parties, on the other hand, did have a majority with a total of 236 seats, but this majority ranged from the left-of-center Democrats to the reactionary German National People's Party. Of the four major bourgeois parties, the Democrats and the bulk of the Catholic Center Party supported the Republic while the German Nationals and the right-of-center German People's Party wished to restore the monarchy. There could be no doubt, however, that the majority of the German voters accepted the establishment of the democratic Republic. On the basis of a provisional constitution that was quickly drawn up, the assembly elected Ebert Reich President and approved a new government composed of Social Democrats, Democrats, and Centrists. This done, it settled down to its main task of drafting a permanent constitution.

The Weimar constitution was completed some five months later, in July 1919. It was an elaborate document of 181 articles, placing ultimate political power in the hands of the German people and its representative body, the Reichstag, elected by universal, secret, and direct suffrage. The government was to be responsible to the Reichstag and could stay in office only as long as it had the confidence of the Reichstag. Germany remained a federal state composed of some 20 member states which were represented on the Reich level by a Reichsrat, a body that had chiefly advisory functions. At the head of the Republic stood the Reich President, who was popularly elected. He was envisaged as a supraparty figure symbolizing the unity of state and nation, but he was to be no mere figurehead. He appointed the Reich chancellor and Reich ministers, and he could override the Reichstag by dissolving it or by calling for a referendum on a Reichstag-enacted bill. He could also intervene with armed force against states derelict in the fulfillment of their constitutional duties, and in serious emergencies he could take whatever measures were needed to restore public order and safety. This latter right of a temporary Presidential dictatorship, embodied in the now famous Article 48 of the constitution, was to assume decisive importance in the last years of the Weimar Republic. The constitution contained a detailed bill of rights guaranteeing all basic civil rights and liberties; to satisfy the socialist parties, it also provided the legal authority for the socialization of "suitable" business enterprises. (However, the bourgeois majority in the assembly blocked any actual measures of socialization.)

The Weimar constitution was the product of compromises designed to contain the many centrifugal forces dividing the nation and to make the new state acceptable to people of the most diverse political views. In this endeavor the constitution-makers adopted the system of proportional representation by which a party could send a deputy to the Reichstag for every 60,000 votes cast for it in one of the large electoral districts (each district had an electorate of at least 1,000,000 voters). Minority groups thus were to be given a voice in the Reichstag, but this arrangement also encouraged the formation of innumerable splinter parties, which impaired the efficiency of the parliament. In the 1928 Reichstag elections, 31 parties participated, of which 16 elected deputies; in 1930 the figures were 26 and 13 respectively.

In the same spirit the problem of the national flag was solved by a compromise. The original draft of the constitution had proposed the adoption of black-red-and-gold, the flag of the Revolution of 1848, as the national colors. The change was to demonstrate the break with the past and the new emphasis on democratic liberalism. Many Germans, among them sincere supporters of the Republic, rejected this plan; they thought it a betrayal of Germany's past and demanded the retention of the old Imperial colors of black-white-and-red. In the end black-red-and-gold was adopted as the national colors, but black-white-and-red, the flag of the monarchy, was retained for the commerce flag, with the new national colors shown in the upper inner corner—a concession justified on the rather disingenuous grounds that black-white-and-red could be seen better at sea. The compromise was symbolic of the division and the lack of perception of the republican forces; by failing to give the nation one flag around which it could rally, the two-flag solution helped to deepen the conflict between the republican and antirepublican camps.

In addition to these intrinsic difficulties, the constitution suffered from its association in many minds with the lost war. In June 1919 the Weimar Assembly was called upon to decide whether or not to ratify the Peace Treaty of Versailles. That treaty came as a bitter shock to the Germans since it was much more severe than they had expected. After long deliberations the assembly decided reluctantly to accept the treaty except for the war guilt clause and the war crimes trials. When the Allies insisted on an unqualified acceptance, a majority consisting of Social Democrats and Centrists voted to ratify the treaty. However, they did so only after a member of the rightist opposition had publicly acknowledged on behalf of his political friends that those who accepted the treaty were acting from patriotic motives. Nevertheless, once the treaty was signed, nationalist propaganda lost no time in branding the ratifiers as cowards and traitors. Since the ratifiers also supported the constitution, the antirepublicans found it easy to show that acceptance of both constitution and peace treaty were inspired by the same un-German spirit. The constitution thus was burdened with heavy political and psychological liabilities from the day it became the law of the land in August 1919.

The Kapp Putsch. A major weakness of the German Republic was its lack of leaders who could capture the country's imagination and state the case of the new state in convincing terms. The colorless, unpretentious ways of the republican leaders, their diffidence and tolerance, aroused the contempt of their rightist opponents and confirmed these in their conviction that only a social and economic elite was equipped to assume the leadership of the country. "The Marxists," wrote the philosopher Oswald Spengler in 1919, "had the power, they could have dared anything. A great man [rising] out of the depth, and the entire nation would have followed him. Never was a mass movement dragged more miserably into the mud by the inadequacies of its leaders and followers." Nor was the new leadership able to retain the confidence of the workers. Many mistook the government's inability to enact further social reforms as a betrayal of labor's interests and shifted their allegiance to the Independents and Communists.

Unrest and discontent were kept alive also by those rootless and jobless war veterans who were unable, after four years of war, to return to normal civil pursuits. Some joined militant organizations of the radical left, but the majority entered the Free Corps and other paramilitary groups on the right. They threw themselves into the brawling and fighting inside and outside of Germany, sometimes defending legitimate national interests, as in the case of Polish assaults on Upper Silesia, but more often harassing political opponents and not infrequently fighting simply for fighting's sake. They had the financial and moral support of parts of the aristocracy and bourgeoisie, who planned to use these paramilitary units in their endeavors to return to an authoritarian regime in which the upper classes would enjoy again their one-time social and political prerogatives. Thus street fighting, demonstrations, and strikes became permanent features of the political scene and heightened the general feeling of insecurity. Many who had first accepted the Republic in the hope that it would secure the country a lenient peace and solve its internal problems felt disappointed and looked for other solutions.

Rightist discontent culminated in the Kapp Putsch, which attempted to establish a dictatorship in March 1920. The rising, led by a Prussian official and one-time Pan-German annexationist, Wolfgang Kapp, was ill-prepared and started precipitately. It was backed by some Free Corps that the government was about to disband at the insistence of the Allied Powers. The Reichswehr, pursuing its own autonomous course, refused to defend the Republican government, but except for some local units would not support the conspirators either. The legal government escaped from Berlin and established itself in South Germany. Most government officials remained loyal to it and refused to acknowledge Kapp's government. A general strike proclaimed by the labor unions brought the economic life of the nation to a virtual standstill. Four days after its seizure of power, the Kapp regime collapsed and Kapp fled to Sweden.

The Kapp Putsch touched off mass risings of workers in central Germany and the Ruhr Basin against the forces supporting Kapp. The Ruhr rising turned into a savage Communist revolt after the collapse of the putsch. It was suppressed with equal brutality by Reichswehr units dispatched into the demilitarized Ruhr territory. This violation of the Treaty of Versailles in turn led to the French occupation of Frankfurt-on-the-Main and several other cities. France's move added to the difficulties of the German government and enhanced again the position of the rightist nationalist elements so recently embarrassed by the ill-fated Kapp Putsch. Since labor, moreover, was widely discredited by the Ruhr insurrection, the Republic's victory over the putschists did little to consolidate the new state. Judges sympathizing with the Kappists saw to it that the few who were tried on charges of treason were either acquitted or received nominal sentences. Kapp's Minister of the Interior, a retired police commissioner named Traugott von Jagow, was the only one who was briefly imprisoned before he was amnestied. On his release he sued the Prussian state for illegally withholding his pension and won his case.

Reparations and Inflation. The trend of public opinion was disclosed in the returns of the first Reichstag election held under the new constitution in June 1920. Of the moderate republican parties, the Social Democrats lost almost half of their vote and the Democrats 60 per cent. The

Center's following was reduced by nearly 40 per cent; the bulk of the Centrist defections occurred in Bavaria where most former Centrists supported the newly formed Bavarian People's Party, which aimed at the restoration of the Bavarian monarchy. On the far left the Independent Socialists more than doubled their vote, while on the right the German People's Party tripled its following and the reactionary German National People's Party, despite its recent embarrassment by Kapp's foray, increased its vote by one-third.

After lengthy negotiations a new exclusively bourgeois government was formed. The Social Democrats, fearful of losing more of their followers to the Independents and Communists, did not wish to bear the responsibility for the unpopular measures that would have to be taken to cope with the country's mounting difficulties. The parties which formed the new government coalition—Democrats, Center, and German People's Party—had no majority in the Reichstag, however, and the government depended for its continued existence upon the tolerance of the Social Democrats. This left little leeway for action, and one of the government's major concerns was to reconcile the conflicting interests of the right-wing German People's Party, the main spokesman of industry, *in* the cabinet with those of the Socialists, labor's chief spokesman, *outside* of it. It was a task that was to absorb the energies of most subsequent governments of the Weimar Republic; of the sixteen cabinets formed between June 1920 and the formation of the Hitler government in January 1933 only four were based on majority coalitions. All others depended on the support of parties outside the government, which accounts for the short-lived existence of most of them.

One of the most pressing problems faced by the new government was that of reparations. It made strenuous efforts to obtain an easing of the reparations burden but failed to take the one step that might have induced France to make some concessions. To the French the formation of the numerous semimilitary organizations was evidence of Germany's continued militarism, and they insisted on Germany's fulfillment of its reparations obligations, hoping to curb its military resurgence by keeping it economically weak. The German government on its part did little to restrain these militant groups, partly because it depended on rightist and army support and partly because it had no police power of its own and many of the state governments refused to intervene against "national" organizations. Thus Franco-German relations were caught in a vicious circle: France, fearful of German militant nationalism, rejected all thoughts of revising the reparation arrangements, while France's failure to make concessions confirmed German nationalists in their conviction that a conciliatory attitude would not relieve Germany of its difficulties and that only defiance promised success.

In the spring of 1921 the Allies set the definite amount of reparations that Germany would have to pay. The sum was fixed at $33 billion, payable over 42 years—an enormous amount, given Germany's economic condition, but in fact $1 billion less than John Maynard Keynes had thought feasible (see p. 66). In early May, impatient of further delays, the Allies presented Berlin with an ultimatum: unless it accepted the amount and the schedule of payments within six days and reduced German armaments without further delay to the levels set by the Treaty of Versailles, the Allies would occupy the Ruhr Basin.

This ultimatum touched off a new political crisis in Germany; even moderates counseled rejection on the grounds that Germany could not possibly meet the Allied terms and that the Allies would therefore move into the Ruhr Basin in any event. But a newly formed government, including once more the Social Democrats, decided to accept the ultimatum. Its hope was that if it tried to live up to its reparations obligations and then defaulted, the Allies themselves would be willing to re-examine the settlement.

A peaceful settlement seemed imperative also because the German economy was in desperate need of stabilization. Postwar shortages had aggravated the inflation bequeathed by the war, and the constant disruption of business by risings and strikes had further undermined the economy. If it was to recover, it had to be relieved of the uncertainties and upheavals that kept plaguing it. Yet the first reparations payment in cash, in August 1921, accelerated the fall of the mark and the "fulfillment policy" of the government came under renewed rightist attack. Members of a secret nationalist organization murdered the two most prominent protagonists of that policy, the Centrist deputy Matthias Erzberger, the signer of the armistice in 1918 and one of the few dynamic leaders in the republican camp, and Foreign Minister Walter Rathenau, who as a Jew was the special target of nationalist hatred. Attempts were made also on the lives of other republican leaders.

The inflation spread meanwhile almost unchecked despite some government efforts to increase taxes and control foreign exchange. While a minority of businessmen, landowners, and speculators knew how to benefit from the continued depreciation of the mark, officials, workers, and employees saw their real income reduced to a fraction of its former purchasing power and their savings dwindle away altogether. By early 1922 a dollar was worth over 200 marks as against its parity value of four marks and twenty pfennig. As money kept losing its value, people bought up what they could with their cash, driving prices still higher and further devaluing the currency. Helpless in the face of this overwhelming catastrophe, they searched frantically for solutions to the disaster that engulfed them. Many answers were offered—Marxist, nationalist, religious; among those who proposed solutions the strident voice of a new party, the National Socialist German Labor Party, began to be heard. Its leader was a 32-year-old war veteran, Adolf Hitler (1889–1945), a lonely, asocial individual, by appearance and background very much a man of the masses, undistinguished and without means, a failure by all conventional standards. The son of an Austrian petty customs official, Hitler was a would-be artist who had been refused admission to Vienna's Academy of Fine Arts and had eked out a pitiable living in odd jobs in Vienna and Munich before the war. He had volunteered for the German army in 1914 and served honorably in the frontline throughout the four years of the struggle. At war's end he had remained in the army, and as a forceful speaker with a consuming interest in politics had been used by his superiors to build up the Nazi Party into a mouthpiece for their antipacifist and antiparliamentarian concerns. Hitler was endowed with an unerring sense for the deep-seated weaknesses of Germany's social and political structure. Gifted with a marked personal magnetism, ruthless willpower, and exceptional oratorical talents, he became an effective spokesman, not so much of the army as of those who saw their social and economic existence disintegrate. By blaming their misfortune on a worldwide Jewish conspiracy, Hitler provided a simple explanation for their difficulties; this explanation could be understood the more easily because it capitalized on deeply ingrained prejudices. Beyond that, his immense self-confidence conveyed the impression that here at last was one man strong enough to master those demonic forces that seemed to overpower everyone else (see p. 222).

1923: The Year of Crisis. In January 1923 Poincaré sent French troops into the Ruhr. The German government retaliated by proclaiming a policy of passive resistance, the effect of which was to cripple Germany's most important industrial region. The unemployed Ruhr population had to be supported out of government funds; these relief payments were financed by the printing of additional money which increased the imbalance between money and goods, now vastly increased by the loss of the Ruhr's production. At the beginning of the year the dollar had been worth about 10,000 marks; by the end of January 1923 it bought 50,000. In June its price rose to 100,000 and in August to almost 4,000,-000 marks. Debtors were able to pay off their obligations at a fraction of their original value while owners of savings accounts, bonds, mortgages, and insurance policies found their claims reduced to nothing. "A man who thought he had a small fortune in the bank might receive a politely couched letter from the directors: 'The bank deeply regrets that it can no longer administer your deposit of sixty-eight thousand marks since the costs are out of all proportion to the capital. We are therefore taking the liberty of returning your capital. Since we have no banknotes in small enough denominations at our disposal, we have rounded out the sum to one million marks. Enclosure: one 1,000,000-mark bill.' A canceled stamp for five million marks adorned the envelope."[1]

[1] Konrad Heiden, *Der Fuehrer* (Boston, 1944), p. 127.

Wages never kept pace with the money depreciation, and strikes trying to ensure more adequate adjustments merely increased the existing difficulties without providing relief. In July Berlin almost ran out of potatoes and fats because the agrarians would not sell their products in return for the worthless paper currency. Bread riots and raids on foodstores occurred in several cities, and attempts were made to hold up food transports.

The inflation could have been halted by rigid exchange controls, taxation, and the slashing of public expenditures. Allegedly the stabilization of the currency was blocked by industrialists and landowners who benefited from the inflation and by nationalist elements who wished to demonstrate the irrationality of the reparations arrangement. The government was also believed unwilling to cut expenditures since this would have meant a curtailment of social services and would have caused trouble on the left. There may be some truth in these claims, but the overall impression is that of helpless bewilderment on the part of the government. Stabilization of the currency also would have been predicated on an end to passive resistance in the Ruhr region, an act that in view of the mood of the country required great courage and statesmanship. The Chancellor at the time was a shipping director, Wilhelm Cuno, an able administrator but no statesman to rise to the emergency. Nor were his finance and economic ministers men of vision and outstanding talent; the president of the Reichsbank, a well-versed technical expert, saw his main function as printing sufficient amounts of money to meet the growing demand.

The government was beset by other difficulties. Bavaria, openly defiant of he Reich government, tolerated the increasingly unlawful activities of the Nazi Party and seemed to approve when Hitler, inspired by the example of Mussolini, began to talk of a march on Berlin. In Saxony and Thuringia, Socialist governments challenged the authority of the Reich; in the Rhineland, French-sponsored separatist movements made plans to establish a Rhenish state. Threatened with territorial dismemberment, internal risings, and economic chaos, the Cuno cabinet drifted along, incapable of any positive action. It resigned readily in August 1923 when the Social Democrats refused to support it any longer.

The government that succeeded it was led by Gustav Stresemann, the head of the German People's Party. The 45-year-old Stresemann, son of a Berlin beer brewer, had been a vociferous Pan-German and annexationist during the war and had voted against both the Peace Treaty of Versailles and the Weimar constitution. However, he was subtle and more open-minded than his political confreres and was not burdened with their self-centered pessimism and arrogance. His attitude during the Kapp Putsch had been ambiguous; at heart he remained always a monarchist, but he concluded soon after the putsch that stubborn opposition to the republican regime and to France would leave Germany permanently prostrate. Ready to adjust to realities, Stresemann formed a cabinet extending from his own right-of-center German People's Party to the Social Democrats so that he would have the widest possible backing for the unpopular measures he knew he must take. The first of these was to call off passive resistance in the Ruhr—a step bitterly attacked by the nationalist opposition, which still considered the Ruhr struggle an effective defiance of the French despite its catastrophic effect on the German economy. Bavarian opposition to the Reich government also became more intense, and a nationalist politician, Gustav von Kahr, was given special emergency powers in Munich. Near Berlin some units of the illegal "Black Reichswehr" prepared for a march on Berlin that was stopped only at the last moment by the regular army. In a countermove Saxony and Thuringia made preparations to block a Bavarian march on Berlin and prevent the establishment of a rightist dictatorship in the capital.

By a comprehensive enabling act the government was given authority to enact quickly all measures needed to stabilize the country's financial position. By that time the dollar was worth 160 million marks; in October the price rose to 200, 500, 800 million marks, and in November it climbed to one billion and beyond. A new currency was created; it was covered by the real property of the Reich and was to be introduced on the basis of one new mark for one trillion of the old marks. Its circulation was strictly limited, and so was the government's authority to borrow money. The implementation of the shift to the new currency was entrusted to Dr. Hjalmar Schacht (1877–   ), a prominent Berlin banker, who was to play a significant role in both politics and economy from then on.

Meanwhile political unrest reached new heights. Bavaria refused to heed Berlin's urgent requests to curb the Nazis, and the local Reichswehr commander would not obey orders to enforce the demands. In Saxony and Thuringia, Communists entered the state governments in preparation for a nation-wide rising for which the two states were to serve as the springboard; in the Rhineland, Rhenish separatists tried to establish a "Rhineland Republic."

At this very moment, however, the threats to the republican government began to subside. The separatist efforts were stillborn for lack of popular support, and the Comintern called off as hopeless the proposed risings in Saxony and Thuringia; a Reichswehr force sent to assert the authority of the Reich government encountered little resistance. Stresemann felt too weak to intervene in Bavaria, but as it turned out, armed intervention was no longer needed to restore order in Bavaria. The liquidation of the Communist threat, the Reich's determination to put its financial house in order, a growing demand for domestic peace had their effect on Kahr and his associates; realizing that they could no longer count on allies in northern Germany should they rise against the

Berlin government, they hesitated to act. Hitler, however, would not be stopped, and on November 8, 1923 he staged a putsch in Munich, proclaiming in one of the city's beer cellars a new Reich government of which he was to be the Chancellor and General Ludendorff the military commander-in-chief. Neither the Reichswehr nor the Bavarian government would support him, however, and a day later the putsch collapsed. Except for Hitler's fateful re-emergence a few years later, the rising would be forgotten today like all the other innumerable insurrections of those days.

Hitler's putsch was the last of these revolts. The unrest that had kept the country in constant turmoil for five turbulent years had spent itself. Tired of the unceasing strife and confusion, the nation longed for peace and stability. The new currency was issued on November 15 and was readily accepted by business as well as by the public at large. A week later an agreement was reached with France by which the Ruhr industry regained its freedom of action in return for a resumption of reparations deliveries of coal and other materials; after another week Poincaré agreed to a re-examination of Germany's reparations payments by a committee of experts. Yet on the parliamentary plane the political struggle continued. On the very day on which the Ruhr agreement was signed with France, the Reichstag rejected by a substantial majority (231 to 156) Stresemann's request for a vote of confidence. The Social Democrats would not forgive him his differential treatment of Saxony and Bavaria, and the German Nationals still thought him a traitor for having ended passive resistance in the Ruhr. Despite the notable achievements which Stresemann had attained in the three brief months of his chancellorship he was forced to resign.

Recovery. Stresemann's successor was William Marx (1863–1946), the head of the Center Party. A judge on Prussia's highest court, Marx was an amiable man, judicious and tolerant, and anxious to bind up old wounds. In his conciliatory, flexible attitude he was representative of the republican bourgeoisie, and during the next five years he headed several governments. Throughout that period Stresemann remained Foreign Minister.

The stabilization of the currency was an important step toward the restoration of the German economy. But financial stability required also an adequate tax system, and the Reichstag gave the Marx government special decree powers to revamp that system. A full and lasting recovery depended finally on an easing of the reparations burden. This was achieved by the adoption of the Dawes Plan in August 1924, and it was indicative of the changed political atmosphere that a large number of German National Reichstag deputies voted in support of the plan to help provide a majority for its acceptance. The new reparations settlement, buttressed by a substantial Anglo-American loan, served to restore confidence in the German economy.

With customary energy, and aided by foreign loans, the country plunged into the rehabilitation of its industry. By the end of 1925 industrial production had reached prewar levels, and in 1929 production surpassed the prewar volume by more than 15 per cent; steel production alone increased by 38 per cent compared to 1913. Wages rose, living standards improved, and everything seemed to suggest that prewar prosperity had once more been restored. Yet, although exports in 1929 exceeded those of 1913 by 29 per cent, the German trade balance remained passive throughout this period, and the deficit could be covered only with foreign credits, the larger part of which were repayable on short notice. Similarly, while wages increased, 90 per cent of those employed gainfully earned less than $50 a month in 1928; they did enjoy the benefits of a comprehensive social security system, but with their earlier savings wiped out by the inflation and their present earnings too small to permit significant savings, they had no economic reserves to meet any major emergency.

Economic stability led also to greater political stability. New Reichstag elections in December 1924 produced substantial gains for the moderate parties at the expense of the extremists of both the right and the left. The first action of the new parliament was to proclaim an amnesty for political offenders as an indication of the changed atmosphere; one of the beneficiaries of this measure was Hitler who had been sentenced by a sympathetic Bavarian court to a minimum five-year term of imprisonment in a military fortress (a sort of honorable confinement which he spent dictating the first volume of *Mein Kampf*); he was released after having served less than eight months of his sentence. In January 1925 the German Nationals entered the Reich government at the insistence of their agrarian and industrial backers, who had grown impatient of the party's sterile obstructionism; but they were taken into the government only after they had expressly acknowledged the legality of the Republic and had pledged themselves not to oppose Stresemann's foreign policy.

The Election of Hindenburg. In February 1925 Reich President Ebert died unexpectedly. A first Presidential election produced no majority for any one of the many candidates. For the second election the republican parties selected Marx as their joint candidate, and the Communists nominated their party leader, Ernst Thälmann. The rightist parties, after considerable soul-searching, chose the 77-year old Hindenburg. They had little confidence in the old Marshal's political experience and determination, they worried about his age and his caution, and they wondered uneasily whether his serving as republican Reich President would not strengthen rather than weaken the Republic; but Hindenburg, the nation's hero, seemed the only man on the right who could possibly defeat Marx. Hindenburg did beat Marx by the comparatively narrow margin of 900,000 votes; his victory was variously attributed to the lone-wolf tactics of the Communists, who wasted their votes on Thälmann's hopeless candidacy, and to the defection of the Bavarian People's Party, which preferred the monarchist Protestant Hindenburg to its fellow Catholic Marx. The fact is, however, that Marx would have won the election despite the Communist and Bavarian tactics if some 500,000 Centrists and Democrats had not turned against him, the candidate of their own parties, preferring to vote for Hindenburg. Thus there stood now at the head of the Weimar Republic a devout monarchist and nonpolitical soldier who had never made any secret of his dislike of the republican regime and his deep distrust of parliamentary democracy.

Still, behind a façade of rigid conservatism, Hindenburg was a man of some flexibility, ready to accommodate himself to prevailing conditions. While he would not swim with the republican current, he was willing to let himself be carried along by it. He accepted the Republic, swore an oath on its constitution, and on the whole allowed himself to be guided by the advice of the government. Those who had hoped that he would prepare the way for the establishment of a new authoritarian regime and the restoration of the monarchy found themselves disappointed. But although Hindenburg rejected any such plots, he did nothing to stop them, leaving the plotters with the impression that at heart he was on their side. His position in other matters was equally ambiguous: although not enthusiastic about Stresemann's foreign policy, he appreciated the gains achieved by the Locarno treaties and the benefits that might accrue from Germany's membership in the League of Nations. Yet what he was willing to concede in the privacy of his study, he refused to state in public, and the rightist parties interpreted his silence as an approval of their opposition.

Republican Blunders. The republican parties on their part did nothing to impress Hindenburg with the accomplishments of parliamentary democracy. Three government changes took place between 1925 and 1928, and at least two of the resulting crises were settled only after many weeks of futile negotiations, with the Social Democrats bearing a large share of the responsibility for the delay. On both occasions Hindenburg had to intervene and insist on a settlement before a new government was finally formed.

Nor did the republican forces handle other critical issues with greater skill. In May 1926 the Reich government tried to settle the ever-smouldering flag dispute by requesting all diplomatic missions and consulates overseas and in European ports to display both the national black-red-and-gold and the black-white-and-red commerce flags. Of dubious constitutional validity, the decree aroused the fury of the republican parties and led to the resignation of the government. But Marx, who formed the new government, proceeded to implement the decree so as not to irritate Hindenburg, and the republican parties, despite their earlier strenuous protests, tacitly acquiesced.

Later that year the Social Democrats made some attempts to curb the autonomy of the Reichswehr. Agreements were reached between the government and the Socialist leaders concerning changes in the army's recruiting practices and its relationship with the paramilitary organizations. The way seemed prepared for the formation of a bourgeois-Socialist government that would command a substantial majority in the Reischstag. At this moment the *Manchester Guardian* published a report on Germany's secret rearmament and the Reichswehr's military collaboration with the Soviet Union. A Socialist party spokesman subjected the army to a blistering attack in the Reichstag and demanded far-reaching reforms in its financial and organizational structure. However justified the charges were, the speech put an end to the plan of a bourgeois-Socialist coalition. Marx now looked to the right for support and formed a new cabinet that included once more the German National People's Party and whose composition was weighted strongly in favor of the antirepublican elements. In every one of these crises the republicans thus were the losers.

Antirepublican Uncertainties. Yet if the supporters of the Weimar Republic failed to consolidate their position, their opponents did not strengthen theirs either. The German National People's Party entered Marx's cabinet lest its agrarian wing break away; once more it seemed wiser to cooperate with the Republic in order to have some say in matters of taxes and tariffs. As it turned out, Marx's right-of-center government introduced more significant social reforms, including a comprehensive system of unemployment insurance, than most other governments of the Weimar Republic. Nationalist attacks on foreign policy continued, however; Stresemann was assailed for his inability to obtain the Allied evacuation of the occupied Rhineland, and for his collaboration with Britain and France in the League of Nations.

Increasing numbers of Germans, however, much as they disliked Weimar politics, preferred to concern themselves with their material well-being rather than with political and ideological disputes. This became very evident in the Reichstag elections of 1928. The parties that scored gains in the elections were those identified with special economic and social interests—the Social Democrats and Communists, the Economics Party, a middle-class party catering to small business, and the *Landvolk* Party which represented small farmers. Outwardly, the elections constituted a striking success for the Social Democrats; they gained 15 per cent over the elections of 1924, and a Social Democrat, Hermann Müller-Franken, became Chancellor of the new government. But given the weakness of the republican leadership and the motivations of the electorate, this could hardly be called a significant victory. Evidently the future of the Weimar Republic was wholly dependent on the trend of economic developments.

Social Conditions.   The civil rights and liberties which the Weimar constitution gave to the nation produced some incisive changes in the country's social conditions. Women not only were given the vote and became eligible as deputies to the Reichstag and other parliamentary bodies; they were also appointed to official positions as administrators and judges and played a more significant role in education and the professions. Much was done to improve the status of labor. Collective bargaining, compulsory arbitration, and a vast network of labor courts helped to ensure industrial peace. Despite a substantial growth of the labor force, fewer working days were lost by strikes after 1925 than in prewar years.

In keeping with the new spirit, attempts were made also to modernize education and to adapt it to the requirements of the new times. To bridge class differences, common educational facilities were provided at least for the first years of schooling, and new types of secondary schools were set up for those who lacked the resources or the ability to go on to the regular high schools. Social services for underprivileged groups were likewise expanded; the excellent public health facilities served as a model for many other countries. In the field of penology, and especially in the treatment of juvenile delinquency, some of the states enacted important reforms. Yet greater social freedom, like greater political freedom, led also to serious abuses, and Germany's larger cities became notorious for the increase in homosexual practices, obscene literature, and moral scandals.

Cultural Life.   The cultural life of the Weimar Republic reflected the deep split that divided the nation into two increasingly hostile camps. Those authors who, like Thomas Mann and Jakob Wassermann, were concerned with human rather than national problems have been discussed in Chapter 5; facing them was a group of national-oriented writers of whom Hans Grimm was a representative spokesman. His widely read novel, *People Without Space*, appealed to the nation's sense of frustration; it described the desperate struggle of German settlers holding on to their land in German Southwest Africa after that territory had been taken from Germany by the Versailles Treaty. More influential in the long run was the writer Ernst Jünger (1895–   ) (*Storm of Steel, War as a Spiritual Experience*), who also saw man trapped in a mechanized world. Jünger urged his countrymen to accept their fate instead of grieving about it, to serve as warriors and workers, fighting for the sake of the fight and doing their duty for the sake of that duty, unconcerned with values and purposes.

Like Jünger, the philosopher Oswald Spengler (1880–1936) saw man caught up in the stream of history: civilizations, he maintained in

The Decline of the West, develop in cycles comparable to the seasons of the year; Western civilization was approaching its last (winter) phase, after which it would perish. This last phase would supersede the autumn phase of democracy and the rule of money; it would be one of dictatorial Caesars in which blood rather than money would determine the course of events and the warrior would defeat the merchant. At the end, however, Western culture would succumb to a new stronger culture. "In view of this fate there exists only one *Weltanschauung* worthy of us . . . : rather a short life full of deeds and glory than a long one without contents. . . . Time does not stop; there is no prudent return, no wise renunciation. Only dreamers believe in escape. Optimism is cowardice." Neither Jünger nor Spengler was or ever became a National Socialist in the formal sense of the term. But their writings did help to create that atmosphere of moral nihilism in which Nazism could flourish.

THE SUCCESSOR STATES: AUSTRIA, HUNGARY, CZECHOSLOVAKIA

The Successor States. As Austria-Hungary broke up in 1918, three new states—Austria, Hungary, and Czechoslovakia—emerged from the fragments of the old Habsburg Empire. In economic terms the dissolution of that empire meant the destruction of a healthy, well-balanced if underdeveloped economy. Politically it demonstrated the failure of the Habsburg regime, not only to integrate its several parts into a viable polity, but also to develop common political values and governmental processes. Indeed, the three so-called successor states evolved three quite different political systems, ranging from a semifeudal landowning oligarchy in Hungary to a parliamentary democracy in Czechoslovakia, with Austria drifting from such a democracy toward a regime of clerical authoritarianism.

These differences tended to accentuate the ethnic and national differences that distinguished the three states, and imparted a special significance to their divergent external orientations: Austrian foreign policy was focused on the tenuously democratic Weimar Republic; Czechoslovakia looked to democratic France for support; and Hungary was Fascist Italy's protégé. The successor states thus constituted a mosaic of conflicting interests; while the foreign political implications of these differences were concealed in the comparative quiet of the diplomatic scene in the 1920's, the internal problems of the three states were a source of recurrent difficulties.

Austria: Vienna vs. the Hinterland. Austrian politics during the 1920's centered on the conflict between metropolitan Vienna and the rest of the country. Vienna was the domain of the Social Democratic Party, a somewhat more dynamic replica of its German counterpart, while elsewhere the Christian Social Party, a clerical-conservative party, held sway. The Socialists, who controlled Vienna's municipal administration, were remarkably successful in providing that city with excellent public health services, schools, and workers housing that became world renowned for its cleanliness and attractiveness. They were less successful on the national plane. Heading the government during the first two years after the war, they failed to effect the economic adjustments required by the diminished size and resources of the country. They gave way to the Christian Socialists, and in 1922 Monsignor Ignaz Seipel (1876–1932), who combined the detachment of the religious ascetic with the astuteness of the worldly wise politician, succeeded in putting Austria's financial house in order. With the help of a loan of $130,000,000 from the League of Nations he stabilized the currency, balanced the budget by determined retrenchments, and attracted foreign capital to Austria. Until 1929 Seipel dominated Austrian politics. Under his aegis the country's economy made a notable recovery, and its political life became, at least on the surface, more stable. Actually Socialist Vienna and the Christian Social hinterland continued to view each other with deep distrust. Their political and ideological differences were fought out mainly in parliament and in the press, with the acid polemics between Seipel and the Socialist leader, Otto Bauer, adding a personal touch to the feud. Both sides also had their own private armies, the Socialist *Schutzbund* and the *Heimwehr*, respectively, ready to transfer the rivalry from press and parliament to the streets should the occasion arise. Even union with Germany, a national concern in 1918–19, became a partisan issue, with the Socialists advocating *Anschluss* and the Christian Socialists, fearful of "Prussia-Germany," opposing a merger. As the differences between the two camps grew sharper, Seipel's regime became increasingly authoritarian.

Hungary: Kingdom of the Magnates. Like Austria's, Hungary's political pendulum swung over to the left after the breakup of the Habsburg monarchy. A Socialist government headed by Count Michael Karolyi took power in November 1918, but unrealistically pacifist and ineffectual, it gave way in March 1919 to a Soviet regime under a disciple of Lenin, the journalist Bela Kun. Bela Kun in turn was overthrown four months later by Rumanian forces that had come into Hungary to seize its southeastern province of Transylvania. In November 1919, after the Rumanians had withdrawn from Budapest, Admiral Nicholas Horthy von Nagybanya (1868–1957) entered the capital at the head of a newly formed Hungarian army. Some months later a National Assembly, having decided to retain the monarchy with the throne left vacant, elected Horthy Regent of the Kingdom of Hungary—a post the gruff, outspoken admiral was to hold until the defeat of the country in World War II.

Horthy was a member of Hungary's old landed gentry, and his Prime

Minister for the next ten years, Count Stephen Bethlen, was one of the country's wealthiest landed magnates. The regime catered openly to the interests of Hungary's landowning aristocracy. One of its first decrees curtailed the suffrage so as to ensure the dominance of the large land-owners: the right to vote was predicated on strict educational and residence requirements, and in rural districts secrecy of the vote was abolished, virtually disenfranchising the peasantry. Under the circumstances only very limited land reforms were enacted; less than 1,500 large landed proprietors continued to own one-third of the arable land while 750,000 small owners had to make do with less than half of the cultivable soil. The remaining 3.7 million of Hungary's rural population —that is, over 80 per cent—eked out a pitiable existence as agricultural proletarians.

Land reform, however, could have provided only a partial solution for the plight of Hungary's rural population. What was needed was a comprehensive government-sponsored program of industrial development; yet industrialization proceeded but slowly because of Hungary's limited markets. It was also opposed by the landowning aristocracy, which did not wish to see its prerogatives challenged by a growing class of industrialists. However, the landowners did promote industries such as textiles and leather goods that processed raw materials produced on their land. At the same time, parliament enacted some significant social reforms such as the eight-hour day and a national system of social insurance in industry—somewhat reminiscent of England's nineteenth-century factory laws which Britain's landed gentry supported in order to curb the growing wealth of the manufacturers.

Czechoslovakia: Democracy and Nationalities. Of the three successor states, Czechoslovakia had the least troubled history during the 1920's. In Thomas Garrigue Masaryk (1850–1937), a historian-philosopher turned statesman, it had an able and judicious President; in his disciple Eduard Beneš (1884–1948), a skillful, hardworking Foreign Minister. Czechoslovakia developed a parliamentary democracy that on the whole functioned well; it carried through a fairly satisfactory land reform and fostered its industries by intelligent financial policies. Benefiting from the Allied stake in this "Western" outpost in central Europe, Czechoslovakia also buttressed its economy by profitable commercial treaties with Britain and France. Unlike Austria and Hungary, moreover, it was not burdened with reparations.

The country's most serious domestic problem concerned its various nationality groups. Of the 13.5 million people within its borders 6.5 million were Czechs; 2.2 million, Slovaks; 3.1 million, Germans; 750,000, Hungarians; and one million belonged to various other minorities. Czechoslovakia's nationality legislation was enlightened and more tol-

Masaryk. (*Reprinted courtesy The Bettmann Archive, Inc.*)

erant than that of other European states, but it did not eliminate all difficulties. Slovaks and Germans complained about their inadequate representation in the bureaucracy and judiciary, discrimination against the use of their mother tongues, and pro-Czech favoritism in the agrarian reforms. There was also a good deal of social friction, with Czechs looking down on Slovaks, and Germans on Czechs. In time many of these troubles were settled. In 1926 the Germans entered the national government and from then on were represented in every cabinet. What helped reconcile the German minority to life in Czechoslovakia was the benefits it derived from Czechoslovakia's commercial ties with France and Britain. The Czech Germans sold to the British and French their textiles, glassware, and costume jewelry, whereas these markets were much less hospitable to the Reich Germans producing these same goods on the other side of the border. Whatever difficulties remained between the German minority and the Czechs did not seem irremediable.

POLAND: THE PILSUDSKI ERA

The Early Years. Like the successor states the new state of Poland was plagued by a variety of ethnic, agrarian, financial, and ideological problems. Almost one-third of its population of 30 million was non-Polish—Ukrainian, White Russian, German, and Jewish. A landed gentry making up less than 5 per cent of the population owned half of the land, and only one-fourth of all land holdings were self-supporting. Inflation added to the troubles of the war-devastated country; by December 1923 the dollar was worth 6,400,000 Polish marks. In the political arena socialists and conservatives were irreconcilable foes, and parliamentary and authoritarian aspirations were locked in an unending battle. In addition, Poland had at least two problems peculiarly its own: domestically the young state consisted of three regions that until recently had been parts of three widely divergent empires and still reflected these divergences in their political, economic, and cultural standards; externally Poland was wedged in between two major powers, Germany and Soviet Russia, with a long history of aggressive designs on Polish territory and now smarting also under the loss of lands of their own to Poland.

Not surprisingly, then, the early history of the new state was one of continued internal tensions and governmental crises. Between November 1918 and September 1926 Poland had no less than seventeen different governments. The main political battles revolved around the bitter conflict between the Socialist Party—revolutionary, given to violence, with a strong anti-Russian tradition—and the National Democratic Party—conservative, authoritarian, clerical, and primarily anti-German. In March 1921 the Polish parliament (Sejm) adopted a constitution that established a democratic regime with all basic powers lodged in the Sejm and the President reduced to a figurehead—a measure intended to keep the redoubtable Marshal Pilsudski, the most likely first President, from becoming too powerful. With its reliance on a well–functioning parliamentary system the constitution proved wholly unsuited for a country without political traditions and experience and lacking also a well-integrated expert bureaucracy that might have provided an underpinning for the shifting parliamentary majorities and government coalitions. Pilsudski refused to run for the presidency, and for the next five years Poland presented a melancholy picture of political intrigues and crises, many of them provoked by the embittered Marshal, who remained active behind the scenes. Nor did the economy improve as much as expected. While the currency was stabilized, overvaluation of the zloty hampered exports, and heavy government subsidies to agriculture and industry created new inflationary pressures. Land reform, moreover, suffered delays for political and economic reasons, and the plight of the peasantry was hardly alleviated.

The Pilsudski Regime. In 1926 Poland's external position also began
to decline. Germany and the U.S.S.R. concluded a treaty of friendship
which the Poles viewed as a threat to their security (see p. 76). That
same year Germany, having been admitted to the League of Nations,
was given a permanent seat on the League Council but Poland was not.
Germany also raised its agrarian tariffs, reducing its imports from
Poland, but Polish retaliation proved ineffective; if the British miners
strike had not opened up new markets for Polish coal, the economic
effect of the German-Polish tariff war might have been catastrophic. The
position of the government thus was precarious; when it tried to check
Pilsudski's backstage intrigues by removing his supporters from command
positions in the army, the Marshal decided to strike. Aided by some army
units, he led his supporters, mostly war veterans, in a march on Warsaw,
and after three days of street fighting in the capital took over the government.

Already something of a legend by then, Pilsudski had been a revolutionary socialist in his youth since Marxism had seemed the most promising way of attaining Polish independence. Now almost 60, a veteran of
several armed risings and full-fledged wars, the Marshal had turned into
an imperious martinet—ruthless, erratic, and inordinately crude, even
for a dictator, in his personal relations. Still, as the foremost fighter for
Polish freedom he was idolized by the nation, and his immense prestige
outweighed all personal failings. Pilsudski forced through the Sejm a
series of constitutional amendments that strengthened the power of the
executive, and for a time headed the government as Prime Minister. But
he was unable to reduce the Sejm to complete subservience, and in 1928
he resigned as Premier. He withdrew to the war ministry from which
he could still control the army, the ultimate instrument of political
power. Though increasingly senile in his last years, Pilsudski remained
the central figure of Polish politics until his death in 1935.

The semidictatorial regime which he set up succeeded in stabilizing
conditions and attracting foreign capital, and until the outbreak of the
Depression, Poland enjoyed a fair measure of economic prosperity. To
steer industrial development into the desired channels the government
itself invested heavily in industrial undertakings; gradually it came to
control a substantial sector of the Polish economy. On the eve of World
War II the Polish state owned the entire armaments industry of the
country, 80 per cent of its chemical industry, and almost 50 per cent of
all metallurgical enterprises. By such governmental direction of its industrial development Poland was also able to alleviate the imbalance
between agriculture and industry that had long plagued its economy
and was one of the major causes of its continued unemployment problem. Between 1929 and 1939 the share of industry and mining in the
national output increased from 32 to over 50 per cent per year.

THE BALKAN STATES

Political Developments. In the wake of the First World War the Balkan states, too, adopted democratic constitutions or amended existing ones along democratic lines. As elsewhere in politically inexperienced and largely illiterate Eastern Europe, these new constitutions proved unsuited to the Balkan nations, and one after another they reverted to dictatorial regimes in the late 1920's or early 1930's. Substantive political issues also were largely the same as in other East European states. One major source of friction was the treatment of national minorities: the Croats and Slovenes of Yugoslavia objected to that country's strongly centralized government that favored the Serbs; Rumania's Hungarians and Bulgarians bore similar grievances against the Rumanians. Most of the Balkan countries were rent also by rivalries between town and country; the hard-pressed peasantry resented the comparative affluence of the urban upper and middle class which controlled the government and by legal maneuvers or corruption lived well at the expense of the hapless rural populace.

Only once did the peasantry gain political power. In Bulgaria in 1919 the peasant leader, Alexander Stambolisky (1874–1923), became Premier and enacted a series of incisive agrarian and social reforms, including compulsory education and labor service and a progressive income tax. But Stambolisky's autocratic ways and the abuses of some of his associates did much to discredit him; in 1923 he was assassinated in a coup staged by a coalition of bourgeoisie, army leaders, and IMRO, the nationalist-terrorist Internal Macedonian Revolutionary Organization. Elsewhere the peasant parties lacked spokesmen genuinely concerned with agricultural problems. Most of their leaders were business and professional men less interested in improving the lot of the peasantry than in using the peasant movements to pursue political aims, such as obtaining autonomy for Croatia, or to promote urban programs of trade expansion and industrialization.

Nor did the monarchs of the Balkan states help to integrate their respective nations and serve as arbiters of their ethnic and social problems. King Alexander I of Yugoslavia was identified with Serb interests; Carol of Rumania discredited his throne by his amatory exploits and had to abdicate in favor of his son Michael; and Greece was proclaimed a republic after the disastrous Turkish-Greek War of 1921–23. Even though both Carol of Rumania and George II of Greece were eventually restored to their thrones, the prestige of their monarchies was greatly impaired. Political frustrations, religious and national prejudices, and a desire for effective leadership brought forth various fascist and terrorist organizations—the Iron Guard in Rumania, the Ustasha in Croatia,

IMRO in both Bulgaria and Yugoslavia—which looked for new ways to settle their countries' problems.

Economic Developments. All of the Balkan countries suffered from serious economic difficulties, and the basic cause in each case was an increasing agrarian overpopulation. Everywhere the bulk of the people were trying to make a living on land that was inadequate, both in quantity and quality, to provide such a living. Land redistribution helped to alleviate the problem but could not solve it; even after agrarian reforms had been enacted in Rumania, Bulgaria, and Yugoslavia in the 1920's, 80 per cent of Rumania's farms and 68 and 62 per cent, respectively, of Yugoslavia's and Bulgaria's still were holdings of less than twelve acres, too small to support their owners.

Because of restrictions emigration no longer provided an adequate outlet for excess manpower; thus only industrialization could provide jobs for those who could not live on the land. Yet in the Balkans industrialization expanded but slowly in the interwar period. Lack of capital was a major obstacle to the needed industrial development. Some foreign capital did flow into Greece, Yugoslavia, and Rumania, but it was mainly invested in the exploitation of mineral resources. The bulk of the profits, moreover, were taken out of these countries rather than reinvested in processing or manufacturing industries. This policy was dictated partly by the existing political instability, which made limited risks and quick profits advisable, but it was also encouraged by the lack of skilled manpower, which made investments in the processing and manufacturing industries unattractive. This was a major problem of Yugoslavia, of all the Balkan countries the most richly endowed with mineral resources (copper, lead, zinc, bauxite); it was not until the late 1930's that a copper refinery and an aluminum plant to process bauxite were built in that country. Most of the mined ores, however, had still to be exported and the finished metals imported. Rumania, on the other hand, did have a sufficient number of refineries to handle its oil, its most important mineral asset. Consumer good industries, requiring less capital and skilled manpower, were more highly developed, with the textile and food industries holding the lead positions.

Given the lack of industrialization, steel, metals, chemicals, machinery, and other capital goods all had to be purchased abroad, and these imports in turn were financed by the exportation of foodstuffs and raw materials. Yet the need for the importation of vast amounts of industrial products and the high tariff protection of what few domestic industries existed created a wide disparity between industrial and agricultural prices, compounding the difficulties of the Balkan peasants. The precarious economy of the Balkan states, moreover, was closely tied up with the state of the world market; once the latter was no longer able to absorb their ores and agricultural products, the Balkan countries were likely to face economic disaster.

Balkan Federation. When the Balkan states shook off the domination of the Turkish Empire in the nineteenth century, the peninsula became the scene of unending territorial and ethnic disputes. The peace treaties after World War I solved some of these difficulties, but also created new ones, and the 1920's were again filled with clashes over national boundary lines. Bulgaria, Yugoslavia, and Greece quarreled over control of Macedonia; Hungary would not resign itself to Rumania's annexation of Transylvania; Bulgaria refused to accept the loss of the Dobrudja to Rumania; Greece coveted some districts of southern Albania; and Albania in turn claimed the Yugoslav area of Kossovo.

Attempts were made to stabilize conditions by a number of diplomatic agreements. The main obstacle to these endeavors was Bulgaria, which would not resign itself to the territorial losses that had been imposed upon it after World War I. Stambolisky wanted to solve Bulgaria's problems by the creation of a union of all South Slavs, and he worked hard for close relations between Bulgaria and Yugoslavia. (He also promoted an international federation of all peasant parties, the so-called Green International, in the hope of strengthening the position of the peasantry by collaboration across national boundaries.) Among those who engineered Stambolisky's assassination were Bulgarian nationalists who objected to his rapprochement with Yugoslavia and resented his unwillingness to pursue Bulgaria's revisionist claims. For the time being, his death put an end to all plans for a Balkan union.

The Depression impelled the Balkan countries to renew their attempts at closer collaboration, and beginning in 1930 annual conferences brought Yugoslavia, Rumania, Bulgaria, Greece, and Turkey together for discussions of problems of common concern. These gatherings led to the establishment of a Balkan Chamber of Commerce and Industry, a Balkan Medical Union, and a Chamber of Agriculture. But when King Alexander I of Yugoslavia tried to ease political tensions to keep Hitler and Mussolini from playing off one Balkan state against another, only Rumania, Greece, and Turkey supported his efforts. In February 1934 the four countries concluded a pact which provided for the mutual guarantee of their Balkan frontiers. Bulgaria, fearful of signing away its territorial demands, did not adhere to the treaty, and Albania was not invited. In July 1938 an understanding with Bulgaria seemed finally in the offing, but the Munich Pact, three months later, established Hitler's ascendancy over southeastern Europe and ended all further efforts to form a Balkan Entente.

9

Soviet Russia in the 1920's

Whatever the differences between the countries discussed in the preceding chapters, their views and problems bore some similarities and they considered themselves part of the same world. Practically all of them tried to cope with their problems in customary and tested ways, and to this orthodox approach even Fascist Italy was an exception only with important qualifications. Russia, on the other hand, embarked on a social and economic revolution of unparalleled dimensions after 1917; if the speed of this transformation was accelerated at first by circumstances beyond the control of the leaders, this was a difference in degree rather than substance. The Bolshevik leadership was determined to create a wholly novel society, and it pursued this design, apart from temporary digressions, with relentless persistence. The history of Russia after 1917 is above all that of a stupendous endeavor in social engineering. The effects of this effort were not confined to the Soviet Union; gradually they exerted their impact, directly and indirectly, on the non-Soviet world as well. In particular the European nations, faced with a crisis of their own values, were affected by the Soviet challenge to their traditional way of life.

THE FIRST MONTHS

Bolshevik Politics and the Marxist Program. The Bolshevik coup of November 1917 was but the first step of the Bolshevik Revolution, if by "revolution" we mean the transformation of Russia from a capitalist-agrarian state into a Communist one. All the Bolsheviks secured on that fateful November 7, 1917 when they overthrew Kerensky's Provisional Government was control of the capital. Their government, the Council of People's Commissars, could count on organized support only from their own party members (probably little more than 100,000) and the left wing of the Socialist Revolutionaries. Right Socialist Revolutionaries, Mensheviks, Constitutional Democrats, and Conservatives were opposed to them, and so was the bulk of the bureaucracy, businessmen, land-owners, clergy, and army leaders. And while many workers welcomed the Bolshevik seizure of power, the peasantry was indifferent.

Lenin. (*Reprinted courtesy The Bettmann Archive, Inc.*)

Since the peasants constituted the largest element of the nation, their support was of crucial importance. To gain their backing, the Congress of Soviets, on the day following the Bolshevik coup, issued a Decree on Land which in effect authorized the peasants to help themselves to the land that they had long been demanding. Actually the peasants had been appropriating land for some time already, and it would have been impossible—and suicidal—for the Bolsheviks to try to stop them. Yet these land seizures ran counter to one of Marxism's basic tenets—the abolition of private land ownership. The decree bypassed this difficulty by abolishing all landed proprietorship, but seizing only landed estates and crown and church lands while exempting from confiscation the land of "ordinary peasants and ordinary Cossacks." According to "Instructions" accompanying the decree, the confiscated land was to be distributed for the "use" of those who were "willing to cultivate it by their own labor, with the help of their families, or in partnership, and only as long as they are able to cultivate it by their own efforts." To the peasants the legal difference between ownership and usufruct was meaningless (if they knew at all of these provisions); they seized the available land and divided it up as they pleased.

The government faced the opposite problem in dealing with industry. Here its primary concern was to establish its control over industrial production but not to expropriate industries for the time being lest it aggravate the disruption and destruction caused by war and revolution. It took over factories only when it thought owners or managers uncooperative or inefficient. However, its hand was frequently forced by zealous workers or local soviets who seized plants on their own initiative. (Ironically, workers and employees also took over the railways and postal services, which were already state-owned.) Since only individual factories rather than industries were nationalized in this manner, this haphazard procedure compounded the existing difficulties. In May 1918 it was therefore decided to initiate the orderly nationalization of all major industries. But what was envisaged as a gradual process turned into a quick and sweeping change-over. This reversal of policy was caused by fears that Russian industrialists were planning to sell their properties to German firms since these enjoyed immunity from nationalization, according to the Peace Treaty of Brest-Litovsk. Even without these apprehensions large-scale nationalization would soon have occurred, for the outbreak of the civil war made it imperative for the government to have complete control over all existing resources.

The one branch of the economy that was nationalized almost immediately was banking. When the State Bank refused to grant credits to the Council of People's Commissars and private banks either closed their doors or curtailed their activities, the State Bank was put under direct government control and the larger private banks taken over in December 1917. In the course of the following year all other banks were either nationalized or liquidated. (The noncooperation of the banks was not simply a matter of sabotage, as the Bolsheviks charged; distrustful of the new government, the population refused to make any deposits, leaving the banks without adequate cash funds.) Early in 1918 all government loans, foreign as well as domestic, were declared null and void, except for internal bonds up to 10,000 rubles that were held by small investors.

The Consolidation of the Bolshevik Regime. Since the immediate seizure of all means of production was out of the question, the Bolshevik government had to look for other bases of power in order to assure the victory of the Marxist revolution. As a check on the army a workers' militia was set up with priority claims on all available weapons. A new network of "people's courts" composed of elected judges and "people's assessors" superseded the old judiciary, and "revolutionary tribunals" elected by local soviets were to deal with counterrevolutionary activities, profiteering, sabotage, and "other misdeeds of merchants, manufacturers, officials, and other persons." A special political police force (Cheka) was formed "to make war on counterrevolution and sabotage." In the same vein administrative authority was transferred to the local soviets, but since the Bolsheviks were in the minority in most of them (if they were represented at all), this step merely removed the officials appointed by the Provisional Government without on the whole increasing Bolshevik power.

How precarious the Bolshevik hold on the country was the elections for the Constituent Assembly revealed. They had been scheduled by Kerensky for November 25 and Lenin did not dare cancel them. The Socialist Revolutionaries emerged as the majority party with 410 deputies (out of 707) while the Bolsheviks won only 175 seats, barely 25 per cent of the total. The remaining seats went to various nationality groups, to the Mensheviks, and to the Constitutional Democrats, the only remaining bourgeois party (which was outlawed soon afterwards). Under the circumstances Lenin reluctantly agreed to the inclusion of a number of Socialist Revolutionaries in the government, and after extended negotiations, three left-wing Socialist Revolutionaries joined the Council of People's Commissars, assuming the portfolios of Agriculture, Justice, and Post and Telegraphs.

Given the weakness of the Bolshevik government, its chances of survival were rather uncertain. It was therefore much concerned with establishing a record of social reforms while it remained in power. "The decrees of the first period," Trotsky recalls in his memoirs, "had more propagandist than administrative significance." They were to serve as a beacon to future generations of Marxists should the Bolsheviks fail. One decree provided for a wage raise of 20 per cent for all workers and employees; another entitled them to full pay in case of illness or unemployment, without time limitations. All military ranks and titles, from corporal to general, were abolished: "The army of the Russian Republic from now on consists of free and equal-to-another citizens, holding the honorable stations of Soldiers of the Revolutionary Army." Both marriage and divorce were greatly simplified, the latter being granted on the petition of only one party—a measure that was meant to establish the full equality of both sexes. The right of inheritance was abolished and the property of a deceased person was assigned to the state (with some provision made for needy relatives).

Slowly, however, the Bolsheviks were gaining ground. Control of the central government gave them an important advantage over their many opponents. The Assembly elections, moreover, produced comfortable majorities for them in the key industrial cities and, more important perhaps, in the army units stationed around Petrograd and Moscow, the capital after March 1918. Above all, the Bolsheviks had determined, relentless leaders. With the left Socialist Revolutionaries cooperating with them, they felt strong enough to dissolve the Constituent Assembly when it met in mid-January 1918 on the grounds that it no longer represented the will of the people.

Economic Difficulties. As some threats were eliminated, others arose. Anti-Bolshevik forces were being organized in the Don Basin; the Ukraine proclaimed its independence; Japanese forces seized Vladivostok. In March the Socialist Revolutionaries withdrew from the government in protest against the acceptance of the Peace Treaty of Brest-Litovsk. The most serious crisis, however, developed on the economic front. The peasants in seizing the land thought that they were taking only what was their due and felt no obligation to the new government. With inflation driving up prices for tools and other essentials, they refused to sell their grain at official rates to the state (which had inherited the state grain monopoly from the Provisional Government). Instead, they disposed of their produce more profitably on the black market. But few consumers could afford patronizing the black market, and by the spring of 1918 large parts of the urban population were on the verge of starvation (in Petrograd the daily bread ration was reduced from four ounces to two in May). The Bolsheviks tried to collect food forcibly from the peasants, sending police and workers detachments into the villages on food requisitioning forays. They also mobilized the poor peasants against the more prosperous kulaks;[1] "Committees of the Poor" were empowered to seize grain surpluses of the kulaks for governmental distribution and in return received an allotment from the seized stocks. But this attempt to carry the class struggle to the countryside had little success—possibly because the poorer peasants felt a sense of identity with the kulaks as a result of the land distribution.

The procurement of industrial goods proved equally difficult. Here again conscious opposition and force of circumstance are hard to disentangle. Sabotage there was, but there were also innumerable instances

---

[1] Kulaks were peasants who hired labor and produced food surpluses for the market; "poor peasants" either owned no land or not enough to subsist on it and worked for others. Between these two groups there existed a third, the "middle peasants" who could make a living off their land but did not as a rule produce surpluses or hire labor.

where employers had to stop production for lack of fuel or raw materials or because they were unable to pay the higher wages decreed by the government. All war contracts, moreover, had been cancelled at once by the Bolshevik government, thus increasing industry's disarray. Allied agents, finally, set about crippling arms and munition plants lest they be used by the Germans. But whatever the motives behind these actions, to the Bolsheviks they were all part of the anti-Bolshevik class struggle. Lenin's reaction was quick and incisive: he openly called for the "shooting on the spot" of "wreckers" and "speculators." In addition, businessmen, along with other "unproductive elements," were no longer provided with food by the government; unless they could buy on the black market, they were faced with starvation.

The Fight Against Religion.   Another foe which the Bolsheviks soon were fighting was organized religion. Marxism is opposed to religion as a force apt to divert man from concentrating his energies on the improvement of his earthly life. Marxists also attack religion because it has frequently been abused to block reforms on the grounds that the existing order was divinely ordained. Accordingly, the Bolsheviks looked on the Orthodox Church as a mainstay and tool of the Tsarist regime and as such a dangerous counterrevolutionary element; party fanatics tried to destroy it physically by burning and looting church property and persecuting the clergy. The leaders, however, knew that religion was too deep-rooted in Russian life to be eradicated at once, and they proceeded to strangle it slowly by stripping all religious bodies of their economic foundation. The property of churches and religious societies was nationalized and the compulsory collection of dues, assessments, and fines prohibited. The government sought also to break the social and psychological hold of the Orthodox Church on the people by denying legal validity to religious marriages, separating the state and church, and forbidding religious instruction in the schools. In February 1918 a decree established the principle of "freedom of conscience," leaving it to the individual to decide whether or not he wished to profess a religion. The decree removed all legal disabilities resulting from membership in certain religious groups such as the Jewish community or from nonmembership. Extralegal discrimination continued, however, since religious affiliation made its bearer politically suspect and barred him from a great many posts, including membership in the Bolshevik Party.

The First Soviet Constitution.   These provisions were incorporated in the constitution of the Russian Socialist Federal Soviet Republic (R.S.F.S.R.) that was promulgated in July 1918, as were the nationalization measures that had been taken. They were all milestones on the road towards the "abolition of any exploitation of man by man," the elimination of class divisions, the creation of a socialist society, and the worldwide extension of socialism,[2] which the constitution considered the primary task of the new state. To attain these goals the constitution sought to strengthen the Soviet government, the agent of the dictatorship of the proletariat. Only the workers were assured of freedom of opinion, assembly, and association, and only they were deemed worthy (or sufficiently reliable) to bear arms "in defense of the revolution." The workers also enjoyed a privileged position in the election of the soviets: the All-Russian Congress of Soviets was to consist of representatives of the urban soviets, with one delegate to be elected for every 25,000 *voters*, and of the provincial soviets, with one delegate to be elected for every 125,000 *inhabitants*. Since there were about two inhabitants to each voter, the arrangement was weighted by a ratio of 5 to 2 in favor of the urban vote.[3] Returns could be further controlled by pressures since the voting was open. Corresponding arrangements were made for the election of the regional and provincial soviets. Although there was to be no discrimination on the basis of sex, religion, or nationality, entire social groups such as businessmen, rentiers, clergymen, Tsarist police officials, and members of the Tsarist family were deprived of their voting rights. Those who did not work for a living, moreover, would be compelled to do so on the principle that "he that does not work, neither shall he eat."

Ultimate political power, according to the constitution, was vested in the country's working population as organized in the soviets. Rising from the urban and rural soviets which were elected directly was a hierarchy of indirectly elected soviets on the county, district, provincial, and regional level. At the top of this structure was the All-Russian Congress of Soviets which was to determine the basic domestic and foreign policies of the R.S.F.S.R., serve as its legislative body, and control the Council of People's Commissars. However, since all soviets voted by show of hands and their Bolshevik members were bound by party instructions, they were no counterweight to the government. Moreover, the dividing lines between the Congress of Soviets and the Council of People's Commissars and between them and an Executive Committee that exercised the Congress' functions when the Congress was not in session were blurred; all these organs had executive and legislative powers and could

[2] The term *socialism* rather than *communism* was (and is still being) used in the Soviet Union to indicate that Soviet Russia has reached only the first phase of communism. In this phase private ownership of the means of production has been abolished, but distribution because of an insufficiency of goods takes place according to work performed and not, as is the Marxist goal, according to need (see also Art. 12, par. 2 of the Soviet Constitution of 1936). The Soviet concept of socialism differs therefore from the Western concept which defines socialism as democratically controlled state ownership.

[3] The differing mode of calculation stemmed from the fact that before the amalgamation of all soviets in one All-Russian Congress the delegates to city soviets had been elected proportionately to the size of the electorate, whereas rural soviets had based their elections on the size of the population. It seemed best to retain these usages.

assume each other's specific functions. As it turned out, these were soon concentrated in the hands of the Council of People's Commissars.

The constitution made no mention of the judiciary.

The Communist Party. During the early months of the Soviet regime the Bolshevik Party was one of several parties. Mensheviks and Socialist Revolutionaries were represented in the soviets, and for a short time some left Socialist Revolutionaries were members of the Council of People's Commissars. Policy was made by the Council and the All-Russian Congress of Soviets; the land legislation, for example, bore the Socialist Revolutionary rather than the Bolshevik imprint. For this reason the constitution enacted by the Congress of Soviets in July 1918 made no special mention of the Bolshevik Party or, more accurately, the "Russian Communist Party (Bolsheviks)," as it came to call itself after March 1918, reverting to the original terminology of Marx and Engels and disavowing "social democracy" with its connotations of parliamentarism and compromise.

From the outset, however, the Communist Party played a unique role in the new state. The decision to overthrow the Provisional Government had been taken by its Central Committee; it dominated the Congress of Soviets and the Council of People's Commissars, and its members took over the key positions in the administration and in the economy. Crucial decisions such as whether to ratify the Treaty of Brest-Litovsk were made by the party leadership; gradually the party superseded the soviets as policy maker and ultimate arbiter of all basic problems. Internally the party was tightly structured; its organization consisted of a network of organs spreading down from the party congress through regional, provincial, county, and district units to the local party cells in factories, villages, governmental agencies, and military units. And as in the government, power tended to be concentrated increasingly in the Council of People's Commissars, in the party it shifted from party congress and Central Committee to the latter's five-men Political Bureau (*Politburo*) after that body was set up as a permanent organ in 1919.

The party retained its prerevolutionary character as a highly selective organization. New members were accepted only if some party members in good standing vouched for their integrity and after a probationary period as candidate members. While selectivity had earlier been imperative to protect the party against informers and turncoats, it now was considered essential to maintain the party as an elite, as the "vanguard of the proletariat and of the poorest peasantry—that part of these classes which consciously strives to realize in practice the communist program," to quote the party congress of 1919. The party member was to be a dedicated individual, disciplined and cooperative, ready to undertake any assignment given to him, and a model citizen who by his hard work and austere way of life was to set an example to non-party members.

Party members earning more than a certain minimum were to turn over any excess amount to the party. Similarly, the salary of a People's Commissar was set at the wage level of a skilled worker, with other officials getting correspondingly less. Yet despite all precautions opportunists and blackguards managed to join the party; at the party congress in March 1919 there were bitter complaints about the "drunkenness, debauchery, corruption, and irresponsible behavior of many party workers so that one's hair simply stands on end," as one member of the Central Committee put it. Later that year the party underwent its first purge by which two-fifths of its members, then numbering between 250,000 and 300,000, were expelled for not being "sufficiently communist, or even directly parasitic."

THE CIVIL WAR

The Origins.   Such soul-searching was the more essential because the Soviet regime was engaged at the time in a struggle for its very survival. Organized opposition had gradually crystalized in the early part of 1918. On the right it drew its support from monarchists, from proponents of a military dictatorship, and from officers who refused to accept the Bolshevik surrender to the Germans and formed a so-called Volunteer Army; on the left it consisted of Socialist Revolutionaries and Mensheviks who would not resign themselves to the dissolution of the Constituent Assembly and the suppression of all civil liberties. Between them stood property owners, manufacturers, merchants, and landowners who either hoped to recover their lost possessions or prevent the future forfeiture of their holdings. They were joined by various minority groups such as Ukrainians and Georgians who wished to obtain their independence, and by several foreign powers which came to their help.

Britain, France, and the United States sent troops and supplies, partly in order to keep out of German hands Allied war material that had been dispatched to Russia, partly in the hope of enabling the White Russians who opposed the Peace Treaty of Brest-Litovsk, to re-enter the war against the Germans. All of them also saw in the Soviet regime a threat to their own social and economic system. The Japanese sent an expeditionary force to Siberia to establish a sphere of influence in the maritime provinces of Asian Russia—much to the concern of the United States, which dispatched some of its forces to check Japan's aspirations. There was finally a contingent of Czech prisoners of war trying to make their way out of Russia whose clash with Bolshevik forces first touched off large-scale fighting. The military contribution of most of these foreign forces was minor, but their very presence on Russian soil hampered the Bolshevik war effort and bolstered White Russian morale. The provisioning of the White forces with Allied supplies, on the other hand, was of decisive significance.

The Course of the War. The war went well at first for the Whites. By midsummer 1918 the anti-Bolshevik forces and their foreign allies controlled almost all of Siberia, the Urals, the northern region around Murmansk and Archangel, the middle reaches of the Volga valley around Kazan and Samara (now Kuibyshev), the lower Don valley and the Caucasus. (In addition, German and Austrian forces occupied the Ukraine and the Baltic provinces.) The Bolsheviks retained control only over the central part of European Russia around the Petrograd-Moscow axis. But in the fall the tide began to turn. Under Trotsky, who had been appointed Commissar of War and proved an untiring, resourceful organizer, a new army was assembled and molded into a fighting force. Abandoning the Bolsheviks' earlier ideals, Trotsky insisted on strict discipline, reintroduced military ranks, and abolished the election of officers. Conscription was introduced for workers and peasants, and in late July 1918, at the height of the military crisis, compulsory military service was made universal. To relieve the shortage of competent officers, Trotsky also drafted some 30,000 former Tsarist officers into the Red Army. Communist party members were assigned to keep watch over them and shield the troops under their command from anti-Bolshevik influences. Moreover, the officers' families were held as hostages lest these men desert or commit treason or sabotage. Under Trotsky's personal leadership units of the new army were sent to the Volga valley, and in September the Whites were driven from Samara and Kazan. Stalin hurried to

Trotsky. (Reprinted courtesy Brown Brothers)

Tsaritsyn (later Stalingrad and now Volgograd), whose loss would have cut off Moscow from its last major granary; together with Klimenty Voroshilov (1881–   ), a one-time oil worker turned army commander, he held that city against the attacks of the Don Cossacks and the Whites' Volunteer Army.

The Red position was newly endangered, however, when the armistice at Compiègne brought to an end World War I on the western front. British and French troops were dispatched to the Black Sea coast; other British forces seized control of the oil-rich region along the Caspian Sea in which British financial interests had heavy investments. While militarily of little significance, these moves served to stiffen White Russian resistance. Allied supplies, moreover, could now be sent in increasing

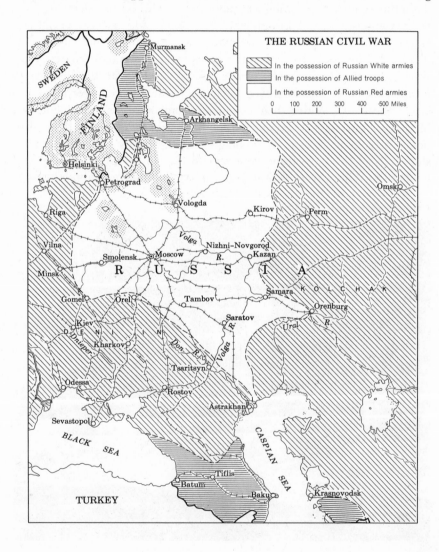

THE RUSSIAN CIVIL WAR

In the possession of Russian White armies
In the possession of Allied troops
In the possession of Russian Red armies

0   100   200   300   400   500 Miles

amounts, and this assistance enabled the Whites to take the initiative once more. Admiral Alexander Kolchak, head of a White regime that had been set up in Siberia, launched an offensive across the Ural Mountains in early 1919 and by April was approaching the Volga valley. Red forces stopped his advance, however, and drove him back into Siberia where, after further defeats and deserted by his troops, he was handed over to the Reds and executed in February 1920.

Just after Kolchak's advance had been halted by the Red Army a new threat to the Soviet position developed in the south. In May 1919 General Anton Denikin, commander of the Volunteer Army, launched an offensive that captured Kharkov, Tsaritsyn, and Kiev and made him the master of all of southern Russia. In October he advanced to Orel, some 250 miles south of Moscow. There his forces were turned back by a Soviet counterattack; with his supply lines endangered by civilian unrest he was forced to withdraw. His retreat soon turned into a rout, and by the end of the year Denikin had lost all the territory he had gained and was compelled to seek refuge in the Crimean Peninsula. A final threat to the Reds developed in the north when a White army under General Nicholas Yudenich, based in Estonia, descended on Petrograd in October 1919. Trotsky himself took over command of the city and drove Yudenich back into Estonia. Yudenich's attack was the last serious White Russian threat that confronted the Soviet regime. Denikin's army, now led by Baron Peter Wrangel, kept fighting in the Crimean Peninsula, but Wrangel's efforts were futile. Had the Red forces not been preoccupied by the war against Poland (see p. 62), his army would have been destroyed even sooner.

Allied military intervention passed its high water mark in early 1919. The French, threatened by mutinies, withdrew their troops from southern Russia in the spring of that year. British forces departed from there in the summer and fall as did the Allied forces in the Murmansk-Archangel region; the last American troops left Siberia in April 1920. Only the Japanese stayed on in Siberia until October 1922.

The Civilian Front. The Reds had some strategic advantages in their campaigns—a unified command and control of the interior lines, which gave them greater mobility—but their victory was not due to military factors alone. The Whites lost much of their initial support because of their political shortsightedness. They antagonized the peasants by allowing former landlords to reclaim their holdings in the areas from which the Reds were expelled. As a result both Kolchak and Denikin were faced in their rear with an irate peasantry which rose against them and regarded the Reds as the only guarantors of the small peasant farms. Liberal and moderate socialist elements were repelled by the dictatorial ways of the military who set the political tone in the White Russian camp. Allied intervention, finally, proved a political handicap to the

Whites, for it gave rise to the belief that the Soviet regime, unlike the Whites, was fighting for Russia's independence from foreign domination —a belief that led many opponents of the Reds to cast their lot with the latter.

War Communism.   The war confronted the Soviet regime with grave economic problems. The economy, already disrupted and inefficient, was weakened further by the loss of the coal and iron ore mines of the Ukraine and the Donets Basin, the oil wells of the Caucasus and Transcaucasia, the cotton of Turkestan, and many of the best food producing areas. Industry thus was plagued by the lack of raw materials (aggravated further by a tight Allied blockade), the lack of incentives for manufacturers to keep up production, let alone expand it, and the wholesale flight of workers to the country to escape starvation in the cities. Agricultural production also decreased, partly because of the lack of equipment and fertilizer, partly again because of the lack of incentives to maintain or increase production. The measures taken against the kulaks further reduced the available food supplies since the kulaks were the ones who produced for the market. Similarly the breakup of the large landed estates into small peasant farms led to a changeover from market production to subsistence farming and rendered food collection more difficult.

The government sought to remedy these difficulties by expanding its control over all branches of the economy under a system known as "War Communism." Grain collection was tightened and armed detachments sent to the villages to requisition all available food surpluses. Nationalization of industrial enterprises was extended to establishments employing more than ten workers or, if they used power-driven machinery, more than five. This still left almost three-fourths of all plants in private hands, but this private sector too was subjected to far-reaching government controls and its production geared to the war effort. At the same time labor was made compulsory and workers were forbidden to leave their jobs without permission. Private trade, both domestic and foreign, was abolished and the distribution of consumer goods taken over by government agencies and cooperatives. Distribution was based on a staggered rationing system that favored industrial workers and soldiers' families.

Given the existing lack of manpower, machinery, and raw materials, War Communism could not halt the decline of production; by 1920 industrial productivity had been reduced to one-seventh of what it had been in 1913, the last prewar year. The decline of agricultural production is harder to determine since the peasants managed to hide part of their produce to sell on the black market—it probably dropped to half of what it had been in 1913. All that War Communism could do, in effect, was to harness available resources and production facilities to the war effort and control the distribution of the remaining goods to the consumer—

an unwieldy process constantly hampered by bureaucratic red tape. Yet whatever its economic and technical shortcomings, the system tided the Soviet regime over this critical period—at the price of immense hardships and growing resentment, especially among the peasants.

The Comintern. Since the outbreak of World War I Lenin had stressed the need for the formation of a more militant socialist International to take the place of the moderate Second International that had broken up as a result of the war. The German revolution of 1918 and the organization of a German Communist Party seemed to bear out the expectation of the Soviet leaders that the Bolshevik Revolution was the initial phase of a worldwide revolution and that the time had come to found a new Communist International to coordinate and lead this world movement, "subordinating the interests of the movement in each particular country to the interests of the revolution on its international scale." In March 1919 fifty delegates representing nineteen different countries met in Moscow; thirty-five were fully accredited and given voting rights, the rest participated in a consultative capacity. Most of the delegates resided in Russia and were Russian citizens, and the Central Committee of the Russian Communist Party had picked, not only its own candidates, but also those who were to represent the Poles, Finns, Ukrainians, and other former minority groups that now had formally gained independence. Only a few of the participants—among them the German, Austrian, Swiss, and Norwegian delegates—had made their way from their homelands to Moscow. The policies and objectives of the Third, or Communist, International (Comintern) thus were shaped from the beginning by the predominance of the Russians; the program adopted by its first congress not only denounced capitalism, colonialism, and bourgeois democracy, but also called on the "proletarians of the whole world" to rally to the support of the Soviet regime, force their governments to withdraw from the Russian civil war, and provide Soviet Russia with economic and technical help.

The response to the establishment of the Comintern varied. The newly formed Communist parties of central and eastern Europe joined it at once,[4] but in Western Europe, apart from some minuscule groups, only two major parties—the Italian Socialist Party and the Norwegian Labor Party—became members.

The second congress of the Comintern met in Moscow in July 1920. This time more than 200 delegates from some 35 countries attended, and many of them represented parties that commanded a substantial following. The meetings took place just when the Red Army had driven the

[4] There is no evidence, however, that the two short-lived Soviet regimes established in Hungary and Bavaria in the spring of 1919 were instigated by the Comintern although the leaders of these movements undoubtedly took their inspiration from Russian developments.

Polish forces from Russian soil and was advancing on Warsaw; the establishment of a Soviet regime in Poland seemed imminent, and from Poland the revolution was expected to sweep across Germany into western Europe. Under the circumstances it was considered imperative to tighten the Comintern's organization and discipline to make it a more effective agent of revolution. The congress adopted a list of twenty-one conditions to which any party would have to subscribe in order to qualify for membership in the Comintern. The more noteworthy of these conditions required the removal of "reformists," that is, the moderate Socialists, from any party that wished to join, the creation of an underground organization in preparation for the approaching civil war, propaganda activities in the armed forces, tight internal party discipline with periodic purges, submission of the party program for Comintern approval, and acceptance as binding of all Comintern decisions.

Paradoxically, when the twenty-one conditions were adopted, the Russian Communist leaders had no assurance that these conditions would redound to their benefit. The expectation was that as the revolution swept westward, Russian influence in the Comintern would be reduced correspondingly. However, since the Soviet advance was turned back at the gates of Warsaw, Russia retained its predominant position in the Comintern, and the effect of the twenty-one conditions was to subordinate all parties accepting them to the dictates of Moscow. Where no Communist parties existed as yet, Comintern agents were dispatched by Moscow to help organize them by promoting the breakup of existing socialist parties and by leading the revolutionary wings into the Comintern camp. The hold of Moscow on these parties was further strengthened by their dependence on Soviet subsidies. Their leaders, moreover, unable as social and political outcasts to make a living, were given jobs in local Soviet consulates, trade offices, or press agencies and thus were dependent on Moscow for their livelihood. However, Soviet control of the non-Russian parties was not based solely on backstairs maneuvers and financial pressures; other Communist parties worked closely with Moscow also from political self-interest, for unless Soviet Russia survived as a Communist state, there was little hope that Communist revolutions would succeed elsewhere.

FROM LENIN TO STALIN

The New Economic Policy. The hardships that War Communism imposed upon the people under Soviet control were grudgingly accepted while the civil war was being fought. As much as the peasants resented the requisitioning of their grain, they did not resist it since a White victory would have meant either the loss of their land or the payment of heavy indemnities to the former landlords. Similarly, the workers suffered the sacrifices imposed upon them in order to assure the victory of the Reds. Once the Whites had been defeated, however, peasant discontent exploded into open unrest. There were uprisings in several of the major food producing areas; hit hard by a severe drought in the spring and summer of 1920, these regions were especially resentful of the forced food collections. Workers went on strike in Petrograd and other industrial centers in protest against the growing food shortage and the widespread unemployment caused by the lack of fuel and raw materials. Discontent spread to the armed forces, and on March 1, 1921 the sailors and soldiers of the Kronstadt naval base mutinied, elected a "provisional revolutionary committee," and demanded the restoration of free speech and assembly, secret elections of new soviets, equal rations for all engaged in productive work, and freedom for peasants to cultivate their land as they wished and for craftsmen to work independently.

Red Army units suppressed the mutiny in mid-March, but the rising enabled Lenin to persuade a reluctant congress of the Communist Party to take drastic measures to cope with the general dissatisfaction. It was decided to halt food requisitioning and to collect only a limited grain tax, wih the peasants free to dispose of their remaining produce as they wished. As a further incentive tax reductions were granted to those who increased their production. Later, peasants were also permitted to rent additional land and to hire labor for limited periods of time. The peasants, however, would not step up production unless they could buy tools and other necessities for their money; it thus was imperative to expand as quickly as possible the supply of such goods. Since small local plants could do this more easily than the unwieldy government-owned large factories, the establishment of small private enterprises was encouraged and existing ones allowed to hire up to twenty workers. Light industries that had been nationalized were returned to private management by means of leases to individuals or industrial cooperatives. Labor conscription was abolished and worker mobility, based on a flexible wage system, restored. To speed up distribution, some private trade and a limited free market economy regulated by the law of supply and demand also were re-established. (Perhaps it would be more accurate to speak of the *legalization* of a measure of private trade, for private trade had been carried on surreptitiously throughout the period of War Communism.) Finally, a new currency was introduced to further stabilize the economy, and concessions were granted to some foreign firms for the development and exploitation of the country's resources.

The New Economic Policy (N.E.P.) achieved some notable economic improvements within a short time. Between 1920 and 1922 the output of consumer goods more than doubled. Food production at first kept declining because of another drought in 1921 (the resulting famine was relieved with American help); but in 1922 agricultural production expanded substantially and amounted to almost three-fourths of the prewar output. Industry, on the other hand, could not keep up with this agrarian expansion, and industrial goods remained scarce. Inevitably prices for them rose steeply while agricultural prices declined. Once more the peasants began to withhold their produce from the market. The government was forced to intervene and lower industrial prices to restore the balance between them and agricultural prices. Thereafter the economy developed more evenly and by 1927 attained prewar production levels.

While N.E.P. expanded the private sector of the economy, it left the state in control of the "commanding heights." All major industries, banking and credit facilities, production of raw materials, and imports and exports remained state owned and controlled. Nevertheless, many Communists were greatly perturbed by the concessions made to private enterprise: as the English author Sir John Maynard reports, not a few party idealists committed suicide over this apparent betrayal of the Marxist creed. To Lenin, however, N.E.P. was simply a temporary tactical retreat from socialism; nonetheless he did see its social and political dangers and took care to consolidate the Soviet position in other areas. The Menshevik and Socialist Revolutionary Parties which had so far survived were suppressed; the new private traders and manufacturers were subjected to special taxation and to political and other restrictions; and Communist Party members were forbidden to engage in private business activities that depended on hired labor.

The Union of Socialist Soviet Republics. One of the planks of the Bolshevik party program had promised national self-determination to the non-Russian groups in the Russian Empire. Once in power, however, the Bolshevik leaders discouraged the political self-determination of the non-Russian nationalities. Instead, they directed non-Russian longings for self-expression to the advancement of native cultures, furthering in particular the use of local languages in schools, press, and literature. While the Ukrainians, White Russians,[5] and Transcaucasians (Georgians, Armenians, and Azerbaidzhani) established formally separate republics, these were linked to the R.S.F.S.R. by economic and military treaties and, more important, by the Russian-controlled Red Army and the All-Russian Communist Party of which the non-Russian parties were merely regional branches. All these republics accepted, moreover, the leadership of the R.S.F.S.R. and its government. For the minorities within the R.S.F.S.R., autonomous republics and regions were created, depending on the size of the group, with formally separate governments and parliaments. In reality the autonomy of these units was virtually nil; lack of competent native personnel precluded also the independent exercise of what separate functions they were allowed.

[5] The term is used here in its geographical connotation and refers to the inhabitants of White Russia (Byelorussia), an area in the westernmost part of European Russia, as distinct from the political concept of "White Russian," the anti-Communist Russian.

In December 1922 the R.S.F.S.R. and the Ukrainian, White Russian, and Transcaucasian Republics formalized their federation by the creation of the Union of Socialist Soviet Republics (U.S.S.R.). The constitution of the U.S.S.R., promulgated in January 1924, assigned foreign affairs, defense, foreign trade, transport, and communications to the Union and made finance, economy, labor, and food the joint concern of Union and constituent republics. All other matters were left to the jurisdiction of the republics, although local autonomy in these areas, as it turned out, was always more nominal than real. The new constitution also provided for a Supreme Court "in order to maintain revolutionary legality." One of the court's main functions was to pass on the constitutionality of laws enacted by the member republics and to examine their compatability with Union legislation. The court had no right, however, to inquire into the constitutionality of federal legislation. The distribution of legislative powers remained as blurred under the new constitution as it had been under the earlier one.

Between 1925 and 1929 three other republics, the Uzbek, Turkmen, and Tadzhik S.S.R.'s, joined the U.S.S.R.

The Rise of Stalin. In January 1924 Lenin died, after a long period of incapacitation. As long as he had been active, his leadership had been unchallenged, and since he was only in his early fifties when he suffered a first stroke in 1922, no one until that time seems to have given much thought to the question of his succession. He himself expressed some inconclusive views on this matter in a statement he dictated in December 1922 when he lay half-paralyzed from his recent stroke. The document, since known as his "testament," predicted that the stability of the Communist Party (and hence of the regime) would depend on two factors—a working agreement between workers and peasants, and good relations between Trotsky and Stalin. He also pointed out some of the strengths and weaknesses of these two men and touched briefly on the leadership qualifications of several others.

No particular perspicacity was required to realize the vital importance of the town-country relationship for the future of Soviet Russia, and political and economic discussions during the next few years did keep revolving around this problem. Few observers, however, would have sensed at the time, as Lenin did, that the succession to Lenin's mantle would center on a contest between Trotsky and Stalin. Of the two, only Trotsky was a well known and popular figure. Next to Lenin, he was the most important Communist leader, he had played an outstanding role during the Bolshevik Revolution and the civil war and was the party's most effective orator and pamphleteer. Stalin, on the other hand, a dull speaker and devoid of intellectual brilliance, was an obscure figure who had never sought the public limelight. Grigori Zinoviev (1883–1936), chairman of the Petrograd soviet and president of the Comintern, Leo

Kamenev (1883–1936), chairman of the Moscow soviet, and Nikolai Bukharin (1888–1938), editor of the party newpaper *Pravda* and chief party theorist, all were far better known and seemed much more likely to assume the leadership of the party.

Compared to the careers and achievements of these men, the life of the forty-five-year-old Joseph Stalin seemed in fact rather undistinguished. Stalin's chief claim to fame prior to the Bolshevik seizure of power was his involvement in raids on banks and other financial institutions to replenish the party treasury. His position as Commissar of Nationalities in the government was of secondary importance (although he made skillful use of it to place his supporters in key positions in the non-Russian areas). During the following years Stalin proved a faithful collaborator with Lenin; unlike most Soviet leaders, who looked down on Stalin as a mediocrity, Lenin seems to have had a high regard for Stalin's organizational abilities. In 1922 Stalin was appointed Secretary General of the party, an administrative rather than a policy-making post, because of his organizing talents. Again he gave this position unexpected significance by staffing the party bureaucracy with his personal followers. By the end of 1923 his hold on the party machinery and the execution of policies was such that Lenin, aware of Stalin's arbitrary use of his powers, added a postscript to his "testament" in which he proposed the removal of Stalin from his post as Secretary General.

While Stalin built up a loyal following in the party, Trotsky made no such effort. Brilliant, abounding in energy and ideas, and deeply convinced of his superior intellectual insights, he was impatient of lesser minds. He does not seem to have realized to what extent he owed his pre-eminence to Lenin's protection and backing. Without this support, however, Trotsky's position was vulnerable. "Old Bolsheviks" resented the rapid rise of this comparative newcomer to the party; others feared him as a potential Bonaparte, because as War Commissar he controlled the Red Army; still others hated him simply because of his self-centered arrogance.

When Lenin's incapacitation required some arrangement about the leadership of the party, the anti-Trotsky forces joined in a common front, and a triumvirate consisting of Zinoviev, Kamenev, and Stalin (in that order) took Lenin's place. Soon a bitter struggle ensued between the triumvirate on the one hand and Trotsky and other oppositional forces on the other. It reached its full force after Lenin's death and ended with the defeat of Trotsky and all other oppositional groups, with Stalin emerging as the unchallenged leader.

Stalin's victory was due largely to his control of the party machinery and his superior tactical skills; Trotsky, on the other hand, plagued by illness and indecision, preferred to go his own way and for a long time would not join forces with other oppositional groups. When he finally did form such an alliance, including Zinoviev and Kamenev, whom Stalin had meanwhile outmaneuvered in consolidating his own position in the Politburo and Central Committee, Stalin's hold on the party was already unassailable. In desperation Trotsky and his allies committed the worst breach of Communist party discipline: they aired the intraparty struggles in a number of public meetings and organized street demonstrations in Moscow and Leningrad (the former Petrograd). As a result they were expelled from the party in December 1927. Zinoviev and Kamenev at once recanted their views and eventually were readmitted into the party, but Trotsky was exiled to Turkestan. Expelled from the U.S.S.R. in 1929 because of continued oppositional activities, he spent the next twelve years moving from one exile to another until in 1940 he was assassinated by a Stalinist agent in Mexico.

The struggle between Trotsky and Stalin was not merely a contest for power between two ambitious rivals but involved basic political and ideological issues as well. The fight exploded at the height of the price crisis in 1923 and touched off a heated debate on policy. Trotsky, critical of N.E.P., warned of the growing economic power of the "capitalist" kulaks and urged increased planning and greater concern with heavy industry to righten the balance between industrial and agricultural production. Stalin, however, sided with those who wished to conciliate the peasantry, and the party decided to stimulate farm production by reducing agricultural taxes and removing restrictions on the leasing of land and the hiring of labor. Yet in the long run Trotsky's warnings could not be ignored by conscientious Marxists, for events seemed to bear him out: village soviets were unable to assert themselves against the pervasive influence of the kulaks; the villagers continued to look to the more successful peasants as their natural leaders, and these men were not inclined to help party and government. Ultimately Stalin adopted Trotsky's proposals, and the very party congress that approved the expulsion of Trotsky and his associates from the party in 1927 charged the party's Central Committee with the drafting of a Five Year Plan that would concentrate on the development of heavy industry (important also to strengthen the country militarily). The congress called also for heavier agricultural taxes (to help finance industrialization and weaken the peasantry economically) and for the encouragement of the collectivization of farms. At the same time the state placed new curbs on private business by means of extortionate taxes, the withdrawal of hired labor, and other discriminatory practices. Having served its purpose, N.E.P. was to be brought to an end.

Another source of conflict grew out of Trotsky's charges that Stalin and his supporters were not showing sufficient zeal in promoting revolutions abroad. Stalin retorted that Trotsky's doctrine of "permanent revolution" was unrealistic in the face of the consolidation of the capitalist countries; coining the slogan of "socialism in one country," he insisted that the Soviet Union concentrate on the socialist organization of its own economy. The policy of "socialism in one country" provided an effective political and ideological underpinning for Stalin's position. By de-emphasizing (though not denying) the importance of world revolution, it seemed to promise peace and stability to a nation which for more than ten years had been plunged into interminable crises. Trotsky found himself assailed as an "adventurer" who wished to commit Russia to the upheavals and uncertainties of "permanent revolution" and who lacked confidence in Russia's ability to develop a prosperous economy without the help of a communist Europe. For "socialism in one country" also expressed faith in Russia's ability to fend for itself; it was a declaration of independence from Europe, a denial of the traditional conviction that ultimately the fate of the Soviet Union depended on the fate of communism abroad. The importance of "socialism in one country" thus reached far beyond the struggle between Stalin and Trotsky: it gave the implementation of the Marxist program a national Russian slant that left its indelible imprint on the further development of Soviet Communism.

SOVIET CIVILIZATION

Education. In the effort to transform backward agrarian Russia into an industrialized communist state, education played a decisive role. "You cannot build a communist state with an illiterate people," Lenin kept stressing. Only through education could the nation be converted to the tenets of communism, and only through education could it develop the skills and experience needed to attain industrialization and modernization. To accomplish the first goal, all of the country's cultural institutions (except the churches) were drawn into the service of ideological education—press, radio, movies, theaters, libraries, and museums as well as schools and other institutions of learning. In addition, more systematic political and ideological education was undertaken by the Communist Party and its affiliated organizations, with the youth organizations— Komsomol for the 14–23-year-olds, Young Pioneers for the 10–14 age group, and Little Octobrists for the 8–11 group—molding the minds of the young.

In order to devolp a skilled and knowledgeable nation, it was above all necessary to wipe out illiteracy, still prevalent among at least half of the population at the time of the Bolshevik Revolution. Systematic efforts to improve formal education could not be undertaken until after the civil war. Thereafter the school system expanded rapidly, but the quality of instruction did not keep pace with its quantity. There was a lack of qualified teachers and adequate teaching materials; admission to secondary schools was often determined by social rather than academic qualifications, with children of workers and poor peasants given preferential treatment over youngsters with a bourgeois background. Much time and effort were spent on experimental methods and on attempts to break away from the rigid school discipline of Tsarist days by an elaborate system of student self-government. Some progress, however, was made: by the end of the N.E.P. period in 1928, illiteracy had been reduced to 44 per cent of the population, and some schooling was available at least to the majority of the inhabitants of the R.S.F.S.R. An ambitious adult education program, including evening schools and educational "clubs" set up by labor unions and village soviets and often staffed by high school or university students, offered some basic instruction to the older generation as well.

Instruction on all levels was coeducational, in keeping with the principle of the equality of the sexes, and free of charge so as to provide equal opportunities to all regardless of economic status.

The Family. The family was of concern to the Soviet leaders because they viewed it as an object of church domination and a symbol of the inequality of women. To curb the influence of the churches, civil registration of marriages was made obligatory and ecclesiastical courts were deprived of their jurisdiction over family law. Women were protected from subjection and maltreatment, still widespread at the time; divorce was made easy; full equality of the sexes was established in all matrimonial relations; and illegitimate children were accorded the same rights as legitimate ones. In 1920 abortion was legalized, and was to remain legal, according to the official decree, as long as women were forced by social prejudices or economic necessity to resort to this operation.

However, the Soviet leaders did not wish to destroy the family as an institution, and they rejected the view of party extremists who considered the family a bourgeois property arrangement for which there could be no place in a socialist state. During the civil war communal kitchens and dining rooms and children's homes were set up to relieve women workers of their domestic chores, but these were products of the emergency rather than of ideological programs, and many of these communal arrangements were discontinued after the war was over. During the N.E.P. period the government made it clear that it was much concerned with stabilizing family life; this policy was meant also to conciliate the peasantry, the object of its special concern at the time, since the peasants had long frowned on all measures that weakened the traditional marriage ties.

Social Services. A comprehensive system of social insurance was established immediately after the Bolshevik Revolution and provided coverage for all forms of disability as well as for unemployment. The cost of social insurance was to be borne entirely by the employers, and insurance benefits thus represented part of the worker's wages. Until the end of the civil war, however, these benefits were nominal rather than real, and unemployment relief payments were suspended altogether. Insurance benefits became available, if only to a limited extent, during the N.E.P. period, but owing to the lack of funds allocations were largely determined by considerations of public policy. Benefits for temporary incapacity due to maternity, illness, or accident were paid out promptly to assure the speedy return of the worker to his job; those permanently disabled, on the other hand, received only half of what they were entitled to, and these partial payments were limited to a maximum of fifteen rubles a month. Similarly, when unemployment payments were resumed in 1921, payments in practice were made only to unemployed skilled workers, and even these payments did not meet minimum subsistence needs. Nor did the situation of the unemployed improve as the economy expanded. In July 1925 most of those on the relief rolls received only 20 per cent of their standard pay, and the highest relief payment amounted to 30 per cent of the normal wage.

Medical services were largely nationalized during the civil war; private medical practice was not outlawed but disappeared from attrition. Like all other social services, the public health program was severely curtailed by lack of personnel and facilities and did not begin to improve until the mid-1920's. The greatest advance was made in the training of physicians, whose number grew to 63,000 by 1928 (as compared to 20,000 in 1913). On the other hand, the number of general hospital beds increased only from 142,000 in 1913 to 217,000 in 1928 and that of maternity beds from 6,800 to 27,300.

As with insurance benefits, low rents for housing were considered part of the worker's "social" wages, but very little housing was available throughout the 1920's. Bolshevik Russia inherited from Tsarist days a serious housing shortage that had been aggravated by world war and civil war. As part of the policy of War Communism all larger apartment houses were nationalized in 1918, which led to a redistribution of the available accommodations and somewhat relieved the lot of the slum dwellers. Yet according to one report 36 per cent of Moscow's population had to make do with half a room or less in 1923. Lack of funds, materials, and incentives accounted for the continued severe housing shortage during the N.E.P. period. When funds did become available, most of them went for repairs to halt the rapid deterioration of existing buildings rather than into new construction projects.

Law, Courts, Police.   The Soviet leaders looked upon law as a defense mechanism designed to uphold the interests of a state's ruling class; correspondingly they expected law to wither away along with the state once the classless society had been established. However, during the transitional period laws would still be needed, but as a bourgeois hangover rather than a socialist creation. Accordingly, an early Soviet decree provided that prerevolutionary laws remain valid unless they were repealed or were incompatible with the "revolutionary conscience and revolutionary conception of right." In November 1918, however, another decree forbade the application of prerevolutionary laws or judicial precedents and in the absence of any pertinent Soviet laws made "socialist consciousness of right" the sole basis of judicial decisions. For the next few years civil law was virtually nonexistent in Soviet Russia; civil law suits all but disappeared from court calendars, and there was even some thought of discontinuing courses in civil law in the universities. Criminal law, on the other hand, received much attention, for its function was to protect the existing order against "class enemies." Little of it was codified during those early years, however, and since most decisions in criminal proceedings had to be based on "revolutionary consciousness," the powers of the professional judges, brought up in the traditional concepts of law, were severely curtailed. The existing courts were replaced with so-called "people's courts" in which the judges could be outvoted or reversed by "people's assessors."

If the absence of civil law was perhaps tolerable during the period of War Communism, it was incompatible with the purposes of N.E.P., which could achieve its objectives only if private property and business activity had the sanction and protection of law. In the early N.E.P. period criminal, civil, agrarian, and labor law was codified to provide this legal security. The criminal code, reflecting the Marxist view of its function, distinguished between crimes committed against a private individual and those perpetrated against the state, with the latter type punished much more severely. The code did not accept the principle of "no punishment without law"; where no legal provision applied to a "socially dangerous" act, it was to be punished on the basis of provisions dealing with offenses "most closely approximating, in gravity and kind, the crimes actually committed." The civil code protected individual rights such as property and contracts "except in cases in which they are exercised in a sense contrary to the economic and social purposes for which they have been established." It also acknowledged the right to bequeath to near relatives property up to an amount of 10,000 rubles. In the application of the new law trained jurists played once more an important role, for codified law rather than "revolutionary consciousness" became again the primary basis of judicial decisions.

During the early phase of the Soviet regime special "revolutionary tribunals" were established to deal with crimes threatening the security of the state. These were abolished after the civil war and the people's courts were charged with the handling of violations of law. In addition, the Cheka dealt with "counterrevolutionary" activities, its procedures and range of action being unhampered by legal restrictions. Felix Dzherzhinsky, the Cheka's head, frankly admitted that the Cheka's main purpose was "organized terror." It was given the right to execute armed insurgents, counterrevolutionaries, and bandits, but its main weapon of repression was the forced labor camp. The Cheka, supposedly a temporary institution to be abandoned once the Soviet regime had consolidated its position, was replaced by the OGPU (Unified State Political Administration) after the establishment of the U.S.S.R. An entire section of the constitution of 1924 dealt with the organization of the OGPU, whose permanent status was thus established. Its jurisdiction, never precisely defined, expanded as repression increased and eventually came to be directed against any activity considered criminal. Correspondingly the OGPU resorted to execution in a widening range of offenses, and conditions in its concentration camps became increasingly bad. There was only one restriction which the OGPU had to accept: it was not allowed to touch members of the Communist Party. Thus, apart from its social stigma and material effects, loss of party membership was dreaded also because the expelled member was no longer immune to arrest by the secret police.

Literature. As Marxists the Soviet leaders considered literature a central aspect and instrument of social policy. However, under the pressures of revolution and civil war, the Soviet regime could pay but little attention to the direction of literary activities. Little was published in any event during these years; the unceasing crises and difficulties did not provide a propitious atmosphere for creative work, and lack of paper and printing facilities reduced the publication of books and periodicals to a trickle. No prose works of merit made their appearance, but some memorable poetry was written by Sergei Essenin (1895–1925), a symbolist, and Vladimir Mayakovsky (1893–1930), a member of the Futurist school. Essenin mistook the Bolshevik Revolution for a movement dethroning urban civilization and liberating the peasant and wrote some deeply felt poems exalting the beauties of nature and the simple rustic life, with religious and mystical overtones. He soon became disillusioned, however, and ended his life when he came to understand the true character of the revolution. Mayakovsky, on the other hand, hailed the revolution as the gateway to material progress, to industrialization and modernization. He and his associates represented the experimental phase of Bolshevik literature. As a Futurist, Mayakovsky had always been interested in developing a literary style adapted to the new industrial society of telephones, cars, and planes by means of broken lines, rapidly changing rhythms, and sound effects—language to him was a tool to be developed into the "best expression of contemporary facts." He now set out to apply his art in the service of the revolution, for he believed that poets, if they were to fulfill their mission, should not be "pontificating creators but master agents of the social order," and literature, in order to be significant, ought to be socially useful. His poetry, singing of the revolution, of machines, government bonds, taxes, and N.E.P., was, as the critic Marc

Slonim has observed, a kind of poetic journalism, but not without the attributes of genuine art in its passionate involvement and its careful verbal and phonetic structure. It was an art for the masses, designed to be read aloud to mass audiences.

Despite his enthusiasm for the revolution, Mayakovsky never completely suppressed a lyrical-romantic strain in his poetry. For this "ideological inconsistence" he came increasingly under attack until frustrated by Soviet censorship and torn by his own inner torments, he too committed suicide. The eccentricities and obscurity of other Futurists whose work was unintelligible to the uninitiated and thus "socially useless" also did much to discredit Mayakovsky's work in Bolshevik eyes. To fight this kind of "intellectual-bourgeois decadence" efforts were made by a group known as "Proletkult" to develop an authentic class literature by training young proletarians to write stories and poetry. These attempts were tolerated rather than encouraged by the Soviet leadership, then preoccupied with fighting the civil war, and ended, inevitably, in failure.

N.E.P. provided a wider scope for literary activity, and as it did in other fields, it allowed noncommunists to put their talents to work for the new state. In the more relaxed atmosphere of the mid-1920's a wealth of new poetry, novels, and plays was published, some of it work of notable literary significance. Those of the authors who were not Communists accepted the Bolshevik Revolution as part of the Russian national destiny and in their writings wove Russia's past and its present into a pattern of historical continuity. They gave Soviet literature a distinctly Russian tenor accentuated by a strong anti-Western slant, and helped prepare the way for that declaration of independence from Europe inherent in the policy of "socialism in one country."

Among the noteworthy works of this period were the novels of Boris Pilnyak (1894–?), who viewed the revolution as a revolt in the tradition of the peasant rebellions led by Stenka Razin and Pugachev in the seventeenth and eighteenth centuries (*The Naked Year*). Pilnyak accepted the Communists as the harbingers of modern enlightenment and industrial progress, but he worried about their "mechanical rationalism" (*The Tale of the Unextinguished Moon*). In consequence he fell into disgrace and vanished in the purges of the 1930's. To Konstantin Fedin 1892–　　), author of the novel *Cities and Years*, the revolution was a manifestation of the traditional Russian spirit which aimed at creative change through violent upheavals. The novel's hero pays with his life for his inability to accept the bloodshed and cruelty out of which the new world is to arise. In a second novel, *The Brothers*, Fedin took up once more the relationship between culture and violence and concluded that in the Soviet state the humanist traditions of the past had been reconciled with the ruthless impersonal ways of the present.

Among the "proletarian" novels of those years, *Cement*, by Feodor Gladkov (1883–1959), deserves mention. This is the story of a worker who after the civil war is instrumental in reopening a damaged and abandoned cement plant despite bureaucratic red tape, lack of materials, general apathy, and counterrevolutionary sabotage. Revolutionary enthusiasm wins out over all obstacles. In struggling to achieve his goal, however, the hero is also faced with a personal problem: his wife, claiming the freedom newly accorded to Soviet women, refuses to take care of household chores, neglects their child, who dies from undernourishment, and indulges in free relations with other men. The answer to the hero's marital disappointments is found in the deep satisfaction he derives from the fulfillment of his social mission. *Cement* has none of the artistry of Pilnyak's or Fedin's novels, yet it became quickly a bestseller, despite its unconvincing denouement. With its simple plot and unpretentious style it could be understood by a large reading public and apparently satisfied a widespread need for moral and social inspiration that Russians have always looked for in their novels.

Art, Music, Theatre, and Film.   Developments in painting, sculpture, and music paralleled those in literature. During the early postrevolutionary years there was much experimentation in a radical break with the past. In the field of music, where the dearth of creative talent was especially marked during the civil war period, older works were adapted to the ideological needs of the times: thus Meyerbeer's opera *The Huguenots* was changed into a dramatization of the Decembrist Revolt of 1825 in St. Petersburg, and Puccini's *Tosca* became the story of the Paris Commune. Painters produced colorful posters which reportedly were highly effective in improving discipline and morale during the civil war and in alerting the nation against the dangers of sabotage and foreign intervention. With the N.E.P. period music and arts also witnessed a return to more traditional techniques.

Unlike other artistic endeavors theater and film continued to flourish even during the darkest days of the civil war. As means of reaching large numbers of people, especially among the uneducated and illiterate, these media enjoyed special government support. The theatre, moreover, had producers of remarkable ingenuity and imagination in Konstantin Stanislavsky and Vsevolod Meyerhold, whose work attracted worldwide attention. In movie-making Sergei Eisenstein developed new photographic techniques that made the screen an especially effective chronicler of the class struggle (*The Battleship Potemkin*).

10

The Great Depression

The Great Depression marks a watershed in the history of the interwar period. If until 1929 the peoples of Europe hoped to go back to pre-World War I ways, it was evident after the economic collapse of 1929–30 that that era belonged to an irretrievable past. The Depression dealt a shattering blow to private-enterprise capitalism, it weakened the internal cohesion of many countries, it shook widely, where it did not destroy altogether, faith in the traditional systems of government. As the crisis deepened, many of the European nations looked for wholly novel solutions to their difficulties. Whatever the differences of these solutions, they had a common denominator in increased government leadership and control. Almost everywhere laissez-faire capitalism was subjected to expanded government intervention; in most of Central and Eastern Europe multiparty systems gave way to military dictatorships or totalitarian regimes, and where dictatorships already existed, their reins were tightened. In Western Europe many governments likewise were given exceptional powers; where they were not, as in France, the crisis was considerably prolonged.

On the international plane the Depression also became the dividing **193** line between two separate periods. Until 1930 the trend of international relations was largely determined by the after-effects of World War I. The major milestones of European developments—Dawes Plan, Locarno, Young Plan, and the Allied evacuation of the Rhineland—all aimed at rectifying and alleviating postwar difficulties and at creating a new and stabler international order. These efforts continued into the Depression; the crisis produced, in effect, the final settlement of the reparations problem and saw a world disarmament conference convene at Geneva. Yet the Depression years witnessed also the first major act of aggression by a great power, Japan's invasion of Manchuria, and the increasing militancy of the Germans—developments that initiated that chain of events which ultimately led to the Second World War. While at the outset of the Depression most major diplomatic efforts were still seeking to liquidate the first war, at its end European diplomacy was becoming concerned with preventing the second.

ECONOMIC DEVELOPMENTS

The Causes of the Crisis. The restoration of Europe's economy had been burdened with many mortgages. Some European countries never outgrew their dependence on American financial aid and kept living beyond their means. Industries tended toward large-scale production, but wages and salaries remained low, and the mass purchasing power that was needed to absorb the expanding output was quickly exhausted. To sustain the economic momentum, the installment plan was developed but it provided no more than a temporary bridge across the gap between supply and demand. Duplication of effort, tariff barriers, war debts, and reparations compounded these difficulties.

Agriculture was the first sector of the economy to be seriously affected by this imbalance. Once Europe had restored its agricultural productivity, American, Canadian, and Argentine farmers found it more difficult to market their crops. Their exports glutted the European markets and forced prices down from 1926 on. Unlike the manufacturers, the farmers were not inclined to reduce production as prices fell, but tended to counteract smaller profits by expanding output and selling more. (Agricultural production, in fact, increased during the Depression.) The disparity between supply and demand thus kept growing, and the decline of prices continued. It assumed catastrophic proportions when the New York Stock Exchange crash touched off a worldwide economic crisis in the fall of 1929. Having lost a large part of their domestic market, American farm products were dumped onto the food-importing markets of Western Europe. Not only did they drive Central and Eastern European farm products from these markets, but they also hurt the farming economy of the Western European countries. These latter protected themselves by tariff increases and import quotas, but the Eastern European countries—Hungary, Poland, and the Balkan states—that depended on their agricultural exports to import manufactures and meet their large foreign debts could fight off overseas competition only by dumping their own products. To add to the plight of European agriculture, Soviet Russia became a large-scale exporter of wheat after 1930 in order to finance its expanding industrial imports under its Five-Year Plan.

The collapse of the American economy also had its immediate effect on Europe's industries. New American loans were no longer available, and earlier credits were withdrawn as soon as they came due. (Of the American loans granted to Europe between 1924 and 1930 about half were short-term and thus subject to early recall.) The resulting lack of liquidity aggravated the inherent weaknesses of the European economies. In addition, enactment of the Smoot-Hawley Tariff Act by the United States in 1930 touched off another round of tariff increases and a further throttling of exports. Added to the imbalance of domestic supply and demand, these developments accelerated the contraction of economic activities. Production cutbacks led to large-scale dismissals of workers, and the increase in unemployment set into motion an unending downward spiral. Since the jobless had to live on their small unemployment insurance or public relief payments, their purchasing power was sharply reduced. As a result domestic demand kept falling off, leading to the further curtailment of production, closing of plants, and additional unemployment. Wages and salaries of those still employed were reduced to cut costs of production and adjust to the fall in prices. With tax revenue dropping off correspondingly, governments also reduced salaries and pared down their various programs, aggravating further the decline in effective demand. The results evidently bore out those who were rebelling against the absurdity of the human condition: whereas an immense reservoir of manpower and production facilities went unused, millions were without many of the basic necessities—a situation not unlike war in its economic effects. The economist Wladimir Woytinsky has indeed estimated that the economic losses incurred between 1930 and 1934 owing to the decline of production, transport, and trade equaled the cost of the First World War.

Economics and Politics. The crisis differed from earlier ones not only in its severity, but also in the close interconnection of economics and politics. This became evident in September 1930 when the Nazis emerged as the second largest party in the German Reichstag elections. The rise of this aggressive, reputedly anticapitalist party touched off a large-scale flight of capital from Germany, reducing further the country's holdings of gold and foreign exchange. When several European countries suffered financial breakdowns the following year, the causes again were partly political.

The first victim was Austria, whose largest bank, the *Oesterreichische Credit-Anstalt,* was compelled to close its doors in May 1931. Its failure was caused by the recall of large amounts of French short-term credits, and these were withdrawn at the news that Germany and Austria were planning to enter a customs union—a project which the French considered (not without reason) a first step toward the dreaded *Anschluss.* The financial collapse of tiny Austria was sufficient to touch off a chain reaction of financial crises throughout Europe. The collapse of the *Credit-Anstalt* proved especially costly to Germany, one of the bank's major depositors. Confidence in the German economy was badly shaken already by growing unemployment and the rise of the Nazis; with most of Germany's Austrian assets frozen, it was undermined further. There was a new flight of capital from that country, and it became clear that Germany would soon be unable to meet its foreign commitments. President Hoover, anxious to safeguard American investments in Europe and concerned about the future of American exports to Europe, proposed a moratorium on all intergovernmental debts (meaning especially war debts and reparations), but once more political tensions aggravated the economic difficulties. Acceptance of the Hoover plan was delayed by the French for whom the growth of Nazism and the increasing stridency of the German right was a source of deepest anxiety. Paris was fearful that any easing of Germany's financial burdens would allow the Germans to increase their military expenditures; French apprehensions increased when Berlin refused to abandon a new naval construction program as the price for the moratorium. When the French did accept the proposal, after some face-saving modifications, valuable time had been lost, and the moratorium came too late to prevent the collapse of the German banking system. In mid-July 1931 the German government was forced to proclaim a bank holiday, and the banks reopened only after tight controls had been imposed on all gold and foreign exchange transactions.

To ease the strain on Germany, French Premier Pierre Laval (1883–1945), who believed an improvement of Franco-German relations essential to the maintenance of European peace, proposed to arrange for a $500 million loan to be guaranteed jointly by the French, English, and American governments. In return Laval asked for the dissolution of Germany's paramilitary organizations, a German pledge not to increase military appropriations for a ten-year period, and a promise not to ask for any revision of the Versailles Treaty during that time. But the German government was too much the captive of the nationalist mood of its people to consider this plan. One wonders also whether French public opinion would have tolerated such a rescue operation for Germany, and whether hard-pressed Britain would have wished to enter so large a commitment. All that was arranged in the end was an agreement on the part of Germany's private creditors not to recall any credits for a period of

London Conference, July 1931, called to help restore Germany's credit and stabilize the financial position of Europe. Front row, left to right: Mellon (United States), Laval (France), MacDonald (Britain), Stimson (United States), Henderson (Britain). Second row, between Laval and MacDonald: Briand (France). Behind MacDonald: Brüning (Germany). Behind Stimson, Grandi (Italy). (*Reprinted courtesy Wide World Photos*)

six months; this "standstill" agreement was periodically renewed and remained in effect until World War II.

Currency Devaluation, Tariffs, and Bilateral Clearing Agreements. In September 1931 Britain's gold holdings had been so drained by withdrawals that a newly formed "National Government," headed by Ramsay MacDonald and ostensibly including all parties, suspended payments in gold and allowed the pound to depreciate by almost one-third of its parity. The move was designed to make British goods less expensive for foreign buyers and thus increase British exports. Correspondingly Britain abandoned its traditional free trade policy and imposed a 10 per cent duty (soon raised to 20 and more on many items) on all imports except food and most raw materials. The devaluation of the pound caused the Scandinavian countries, Spain, Portugal, and several of the Eastern European states to devalue their currencies too. But new tariff increases also occurred in Europe and elsewhere in 1932, and world trade suffered a further decline. Between 1929 and 1933 its volume shrunk by two-thirds. **197**

Tariff increases were not the only measures taken to protect domestic markets, for they were not always effective in shutting off imports. In some cases foreign producers were able to offset them by slashing prices either through a cut of their costs of production or with the help of subsidies from their governments; in others, price rises caused by tariff increases could still be passed on to the consumer. Of additional measures that were taken, government control of foreign exchange as a means of controlling imports (of goods) and exports (of capital) has already been mentioned; following the German example, a great many countries resorted to it. Another device was the institution of import quotas or licensing systems by which no more than a fixed amount of a commodity could be imported.

All of these measures had been taken on earlier occasions, but an entirely new device was developed in late 1931—the bilateral clearing agreement. Used first between Austria and Switzerland, it was quickly adopted by other countries. With gold and foreign exchange increasingly scarce and the latter subject to sudden depreciation, neither one was any longer an adequate means of exchange in international trade. The bilateral clearing agreement eliminated the need for international payments: the importers of country A paid the price of their imports from country B in their national currency into an account in the national bank in A; importers in country B, on their part, paid for imports from country A by depositing the amount due in an account in the national bank in B. A's and B's exporters were paid out of these accounts by their respective national banks.

Besides eliminating the need for foreign exchange, bilateral clearing agreements forced a country, wishing to export, to import on its part goods or services from the country that accepted its exports. In consequence, they made international trade still more inflexible and furthered its fragmentation; goods were imported, not from countries where quality and prices were best, but from those where funds had accumulated from exports. These agreements, moreover, made international trade almost as much a matter of politics as of economics. Since clearing agreements were negotiated between governments, their terms and conditions were frequently dictated, not just by economical, but by political considerations as well. From there it was but one step to the use of these agreements as weapons of economic warfare.

The Lausanne Conference and Other Relief Measures. Efforts to relieve the existing impasse on a multilateral scale were not completely abandoned, however. In June 1932, after several postponements, another reparations conference met at Lausanne, Switzerland. In view of Germany's financial difficulties, the conference extended the moratorium on reparations for another three years. In 1935 Germany was to make a final payment of three billion marks ($714 million) in the form of a bond issue in that amount, but this payment was hedged in with so many reservations that no one expected it to be made. It never was, nor did it have to be paid; legally Germany continued to owe its full reparation debt, for the Lausanne agreement was not ratified. The creditor nations made their ratification dependent on a corresponding readjustment of their own debts to the United States, but no such readjustment was made.

Britain, Italy, and several of the smaller countries resumed payments on their American debts in 1932, but the other debtor nations refused to remit any further installments. In 1933 Britain, Italy, Rumania, Czechoslovakia, and Latvia made another small token payment after which they also defaulted. The one country which continued to meet fully its obligations was Finland; but Finland was in a somewhat better position to repay its debt than the one-time belligerents. As a postwar creation, it had received loans only for rehabilitation purposes and had used them more productively than those states that had spent their American credits on arms and ammunition. Moreover, unlike Poland, Czechoslovakia, and the Baltic countries that also defaulted although they had received American loans under the same circumstances as Finland, only Finland had a favorable trade balance with the United States.

Attempts were also made to solve economic difficulties by regional pacts. In 1930 the Scandinavian states, the Netherlands, Belgium, and Luxembourg signed an agreement at Oslo pledging cooperation in matters of trade and tariffs, and the three latter countries drew up a further convention in 1932 which was to unite them eventually in a customs union. Great Power opposition prevented these agreements from becoming effective; the Belgium-Netherlands-Luxembourg customs union project was, however, revived during World War II and implemented in 1948. In the summer of 1932, at a Commonwealth conference at Ottawa, Britain negotiated an agreement with its Dominions and India by which mother country, Dominions, and Crown Colonies were linked by a reciprocal system of preferential tariffs. Going further, the League's International Labor Office tried to combine a direct attack on the unemployment problem with the promotion of Europe's economic integration: it proposed a number of European public works projects, such as the construction of continent-wide networks of roads, waterways, and electric power. But in the prevailing political and economic climate these plans were little more than utopian dreams.

The World Economic Conference of 1933. The most comprehensive effort was the calling, under League auspices, of a World Economic Conference at London in June 1933. Given the world's economic interdependence, its economic recovery was predicated on the revival of international trade. The conference was arranged to promote that revival by removing the uncertainties and restrictions that kept interfering with commerce. Uncertainty stemmed chiefly from the currency devaluations

that kept taking place; the most serious restrictions were tariff barriers
and import quotas. Currency stabilization proved, however, impossible
since President Franklin D. Roosevelt, anxious to spur American exports,
would not assume a commitment to keep the dollar stable. Without
American cooperation a return to monetary stability was out of the question, and the conference, after some further desultory negotiations, broke
up. Even if it had been possible to agree on currency stabilization, it
is doubtful, given the attitude of many of the participant nations, that
agreements could have been reached on the reduction of tariffs or the
removal of other restrictions on trade. In both economics and politics
national considerations in the narrowest sense remained paramount.

BRITAIN: THE END OF LAISSEZ–FAIRE

The Second Labor Government. The Depression struck Britain shortly
after the second Labor government had come into office in 1929. During
the election campaign the Labor Party had promised to deal with the
perennial unemployment problem by organizing public works projects;
since the Liberals had made similar promises, they could be expected to
support such a program. Yet the steps which the new government took
proved utterly inadequate in the face of the deepening crisis. A Housing
Act provided small government subsidies for slum clearance, and some
assistance was furnished for the building of schools and roads and for
improved social services. But these undertakings provided work for only
a fraction of the growing number of unemployed. As one observer notes,
"Events had become more powerful than the men who had to deal with
them." Prime Minister MacDonald, now in his mid-sixties, lacked energy
and initiative and was increasingly ineffective as an administrator; his
main interest, moreover, had always been foreign policy. J. H. Thomas,
an old trade union leader, had been charged with tackling the unemployment problem; unresourceful and without imagination he proved equally
incompetent. Philip Snowden, finally, the Chancellor of the Exchequer,
was rigidly opposed to any departure from traditional financial practices
as proposed by John Maynard Keynes and others in order to generate a
new economic élan.

One of the country's most pressing problems was the steady increase
in imports; in the desperate quest for gold and foreign exchange, other
countries dumped their goods on the unprotected British market. The
demand for tariffs grew more insistent; Snowden not only ignored it,
but in his first budget eliminated the duties imposed in 1921 to safeguard
some strategic industries. His faith in free trade was unshakable; as the
historian D. C. Somervell has written, if a protectionist Inquisition had
started burning free traders, Snowden would have been prepared to go
to the stake. Meanwhile unemployment increased by over 60 per cent

during the government's first year in office, from 1,200,000 to 2,000,000.

The one member of the government anxious to come to grips with the unemployment problem was a junior cabinet minister, Sir Oswald Mosley (1896–   ). He submitted a plan proposing increased government spending to expand purchasing power and calling also for protective tariffs, the raising of the school-leaving age and lowering of the retirement age, and government control of foreign trade. Mosley had considerable rank-and-file support in the Labor Party, but the plan was ignored by the leaders and he eventually resigned from both government and party. In 1931 he founded the "New Party." It called for action instead of debate and was to be a "movement which grips and transforms every phase and aspect of national life to postwar purposes; a movement of order, of discipline, of loyalty, but also of dynamic progress; a movement of iron decision, resolution and reality." A year later the New Party became the British Union of Fascists.

While unable to reduce unemployment, the government did take steps to provide more adequate relief for the growing number of jobless. Eligibility for benefits was expanded, payments increased, and qualification tests liberalized. But the unprecedented demand on the Unemployment Insurance Fund put a heavy strain on the government's resources. Additional sums had to be borrowed, and the budget was soon out of balance. The financial pressures were aggravated by the adverse balance of payments and by the collapse of the Austrian and German banking systems which froze British assets in these two countries. With Britain's gold holdings dwindling away, these events touched off a severe crisis of confidence and caused large-scale withdrawals of capital in the summer of 1931.

Snowden was fearful lest the collapse of the pound plunge Britain into an inflation similar to Germany's in the early 1920's. To safeguard against this calamity he proposed to balance the budget by a combination of tax increases and economies, including a 10 per cent slash of relief benefits. Many cabinet members rebelled at the thought of thus adding to the plight of the unemployed. They considered the plan a betrayal of the socialist cause and suggested that a revenue raising tariff be substituted for the cut in the dole. The demand for tariffs had by now the support of influential trade union circles and even some Liberal leaders, and could count on strong backing in the cabinet. Nothing came of it, however, because neither the Conservatives nor the Liberals were willing to accept the proposal without a reduction of unemployment expenditures.

The National Government.   The Labor government resigned in August 1931 and was replaced by an ostensibly "National" government. To reconcile Labor, it was headed by MacDonald, and it included Conservatives, Liberals, and a few Laborites. In effect, it was a thinly disguised

Conservative government, and the Labor Party, defying MacDonald and Snowden, repudiated it at once. The National Government adopted Snowden's original budgetary proposals including the reductions in relief benefits, and Britain's financial position was temporarily consolidated with the help of some American credits. In mid-September the pound was subjected to new pressure. While some bondholders, in a patriotic gesture, returned their bonds to the government to assist the national exchequer in its hour of need, not a few of the victims of the new economies took to the streets to voice their dissatisfaction. Teachers demonstrated against the salary cuts; similar protests of the unemployed against cuts in relief payments ended in clashes with the police. What was thought most serious, however, was a public protest against pay reductions by some crews at the Scottish naval base of Invergordon. Magnified into a "mutiny" by the press, the incident caused new anxieties, leading to the withdrawal of some £30 million of gold in three days. The government gave up the fight for a stable currency and at the behest of the Bank of England abandoned the gold standard. Its fear of a financial panic proved unfounded; the country accepted the measure calmly.

It was clear, however, that further steps would have to be taken to cope with the crisis. To carry them out, the government decided to go before the country to obtain a popular mandate. Parliament was dissolved and new elections were held late in October. Although the struggle against the Depression was the basic issue at stake, the campaign was focused more on the past than on the future. The most likely step to be taken after the election was the adoption of a comprehensive protective tariff, yet this topic was still considered taboo by many Liberals. The government preferred, therefore, not to discuss its plans for the future so as not to jeopardize the National coalition. It simply asked for a general vote of support, a "doctor's mandate," as a manifestation of "national unity." The country was willing to entrust its fate to the government on such general terms, and the government won a landslide victory. The bulk of its majority of 556 seats was supplied by 471 Conservatives, but many Liberals and Laborites also voted for it on a National Liberal and National Labor ticket, respectively. The opposition was reduced to 56, 51 Laborites (who polled, however, 6,600,000 votes, or 31 per cent of the total vote), and five Liberals led by Lloyd George. Snowden resigned as Chancellor of the Exchequer and was succeeded by Neville Chamberlain, half-brother of Sir Austen, the one-time Conservative Foreign Secretary. Neville Chamberlain (1869–1940) had been a successful businessman and mayor of Birmingham and had distinguished himself as a tireless and resourceful administrator in various cabinet posts. Long one of his party's financial experts, he was well-prepared for his new task. In the election campaign he had been one of the few to come out openly, though somewhat apologetically, in favor of protective tariffs: "I must frankly say that I believe a tariff levied on imported

foreign goods will be found to be indispensable." Under his guidance
an emergency tariff was enacted at once and a comprehensive tariff
adopted early in 1932. Tariff rates were further increased in the wake
of the Ottawa Agreements to satisfy the Dominions.

The departure from gold standard and free trade marked the formal
end of Britain's role as the world's banker and workshop. Here was the
explicit admission that the return to a self-regulating, gold-based international trade on which Britain's commercial leadership had rested
before World War I had proved impossible.

There were other signs of change. A civil disobedience campaign
organized in India by Mahatma Gandhi in order to secure India's independence from Britain had created so much turmoil in that colony that
some major concessions had to be made to the Indians' demand for
autonomy. In a series of roundtable conferences with Indian leaders both
the Labor and the National Government sought to prepare the way for
the extension of India's self-government. The conferences had the approval of all parties and the bulk of the British people. Among the few
outspoken opponents was Winston Churchill to whom they were intolerable blows to Britain's status as a world power. (For the same reason
he opposed the devaluation of the pound.) Churchill withdrew from the
Conservative leadership early in 1931 and until the outbreak of the
Second World War remained one of its bitterest critics.

Whether the abandoning of the gold standard and the enactment of a
tariff proved economically beneficial is a matter of controversy. Whatever the reason, in 1933 the decline of the British economy came to a
halt. Unemployment, which had reached the three million mark in the
early part of that year, began to recede from then on. A year later
recovery had advanced far enough to permit the restoration of the cuts
in unemployment benefits, and not long afterwards production levels and
living standards surpassed those of 1926–1929.

FRANCE: POLITICAL STALEMATE

The Island of Prosperity. For some two years after the outbreak of
the world economic crisis France was little affected by it. Having
stabilized the franc at a rather low level, the country enjoyed evident
price advantages over its competitors in the international market. Accordingly, the decline of French exports was at first more moderate than
that of other exporting nations. Almost self-sufficient in foodstuffs, France
was also less dependent on foreign trade than Britain and Germany;
when the drop in exports increased, it did not inflict exceptional hardships upon the French people. Moreover, whatever France had to
purchase abroad could be paid out of the large gold reserve the government had accumulated from Germany's reparations. Only in 1931 did

France begin to experience serious economic difficulties. By then tariff increases and import restrictions of other countries had greatly reduced its export markets, and price slashes had deprived it of any competitive advantages. France was also hard hit by Britain's depreciation of the pound, which cut British export prices by almost one-third and raised import prices proportionately. The barrier against French cross-Channel sales was reinforced by Britain's adoption of a tariff; France retaliated by raising its own tariff and establishing import quotas. But Paris did not dare devalue its currency lest any tampering with the franc plunge the economy into another inflation—an especially serious calamity in a country in which the rentier, the man living on his savings, constituted a significant part of the population.

Limited Crisis. Although France was granted a period of grace to prepare for a possible crisis, it had no plan to meet the emergency when it did arise. This was not due to a lack of foresight on the part of its leaders. André Tardieu (1876–1945), who headed three governments between 1929 and 1932, had consistently warned that the country could not forever escape the effects of the world depression. In early 1930 he proposed an ambitious public works program aimed at expanding and modernizing the country's economy, with the government preparing the way by electrification, road building, and harbor improvement projects. At the time a substantial part of the program could have been financed out of public funds that had accumulated in the treasury, but the over-bearing, hard-driving Tardieu failed to persuade a cautious and thrifty parliament to embark on so ambitious an undertaking. Tardieu's proposals were pared down to an ineffective one-fifth of their original scope.

When the Depression struck France, the slump never attained the proportions which it reached in the United States, Britain, and Germany. France's antiquated economy proved better suited to absorbing the shock. There were few giant enterprises whose collapse deprived thousands of workers of their jobs, and the many small farmers and businessmen managed to ride out the storm by tightening their belts. Not a few unemployed workers returned to the family farm which provided a livelihood, however meager; others found work in the construction of the Maginot Line which got under way in 1930 and proved of unexpected significance as a reservoir of employment. Some 100,000 foreign workers, finally, were sent back to their homelands to relieve the labor market. According to the official records, the number of totally unemployed never exceeded 600,000, but it is probable that their actual number (which included those who received no public assistance) was close to one million.

Still, after 1931 the government faced serious difficulties. Its surplus funds had been spent on veterans' bonuses, export subsidies, grants to hard-pressed industries, and bulk purchases of excess farm products such as wine; at the same time government revenues were dropping off, owing to declining taxes and tax write-offs in aid of small farmers and businessmen. But this piecemeal approach to the country's economic ills attacked the symptoms rather than the causes of the Depression. Discontent and apprehensions increased—the more so because governmental assistance was roughly proportionate to the amount of political pressure any interest group could exert. In this contest the small tradesmen and workers were at a clear disadvantage since the right-of center parties representing business and agriculture predominated in the Chamber of Deputies.

Swing to the Left. In the spring of 1932 the four-year term of the Chamber ended and new elections were held. They produced a marked swing to the left. Radical Socialists and Socialists scored substantial gains, chiefly because of the willingness of the Radicals to join forces with the Socialists in the run-off elections. The Socialists refused, however, to enter a government coalition with the bourgeois parties and merely promised to give their support to a Radical government. The new government found itself caught between countervailing pressures from both right and left; trying to balance the budget, it maneuvered uneasily between the Socialists, who opposed economies affecting government pay, unemployment relief, and social services and called for increased taxation of the well-to-do, and the demands of the rightist parties, which opposed new taxes and insisted on greater economies. Moreover, to cover the growing deficits the government was dependent on bank credits which could be secured only at the price of increased retrenchment. (The Bank of France, the chief source of credit, was an independent, privately owned institution; its Board of Regents was composed of bankers and industrialists who considered the Bank's dealings with the government as strictly commercial transactions, with little, if any, concern for the government's social commitments.) Under the circumstances no government could stay in office for more than a few months. Six cabinets followed each other in the twenty months between June 1932 and February 1934, when the moral and political disintegration of the Republic was bared to its full extent by the Stavisky scandal (see p. 257).

Challenges to the Republic. Government and parliament thus presented a picture of indecision and helplessness, interminably arguing and bargaining, and evidently unable to master the crisis. While other countries were emerging from the depression after 1932, no such improvement took place in France. The impression of weakness and incompetence was underscored by a series of diplomatic setbacks. In June 1932 France was forced to abandon its reparations claims against Germany; in December it had to acknowledge, under Anglo-American pressure, Germany's right to equality in armaments; a month later Hitler became German Chancellor; and that same year he withdrew from both the Disarmament Conference and the League of Nations and set out to break up the French system of alliances (see p. 304). It seemed as if all efforts to keep the German menace under control had been in vain.

But not all Frenchmen were frightened by Hitler. Many were also impressed by his quick restoration of domestic order in Germany and by his successful suppression of Communism, without worrying much about the ways by which he had attained these goals. They began wondering whether their democratic-parliamentary system was still adequate to deal with the problems the nation faced, or whether France, too, ought not to adopt an authoritarian regime. Fascist organizations had existed in France since the mid-1920's; they had so far remained inconspicuous, but now their appeal increased. The best known among these "leagues" were the *Jeunesses Patriotiques*, the *Solidarité Française*, and the *Francistes*. More important in terms of numbers was the *Croix de Feu*, a veteran's organization headed by an ex-officer, Lt. Col. Casimir de la Roque, more noteworthy for his good looks than for his political talents. The *Croix de Feu* was not a fascist organization in the strict meaning of the word, but rather a nationalist-conservative movement like the *Action Française*, aiming at a government controlled by the traditional social elites. Lacking strong leadership and the milieu of social disintegration and frustrated nationalism favorable to the growth of a fascist movement, none of these groups ever became a factor of major political importance; but in the uncertain days of 1933–34 no one could have foretold with assurance that they would not sweep the country some day.

On the left, too, a more radical trend made itself felt. The Communist Party suffered some losses in the elections of 1932, but Communist gains in subsequent local elections, larger attendance at Communist meetings, and increased circulation of Communist newspapers indicated that the party was again gaining ground.

ITALY: FASCIST ECONOMICS

The Long Depression. Italy's economic difficulties predated the Depression of 1929. In 1927, after years of inflation, Mussolini had stabilized the lira with the help of an American loan, but for the sake of national prestige had pegged it at too high a level. As a result Italy's export and tourist trade had suffered considerably. Unemployment increased, imports had to be curtailed, and living standards, already low, suffered a further decline. Living conditions were also affected by the government's efforts to make Italy self-sufficient in the production of wheat. With bread the chief item of the Italian diet, increased crops were to relieve the country's dependence on large-scale wheat imports. The "Battle of Wheat" was fought successfully, but the cost of victory was high—bread prices trebled and other sectors of agriculture were badly neglected, above all the production of meat and such essential export commodities as oranges, lemons, and olives (oil).

The Italian economy thus was highly vulnerable when the Depression set in. The crisis accelerated the deflationist trend of the preceding years. Exports and tourism fell off further; remittances of emigrants to their families, long an important source of income and foreign exchange, also dropped to a fraction of their usual volume. Efforts were made to lighten the lot of the taxpayer by a reduction of public expenditures, but these economies were offset by the government's readiness to come to the help of any bank or industrial enterprise that faced bankruptcy. The government bought large amounts of stock of Italy's textile and metallurgical industries and extended help also to shipping and agriculture. In 1934 Mussolini admitted that the government was subsidizing in one form or another "three-fourths of the Italian economic system, both industrial and agricultural." A special Institute for Industrial Reconstruction was set up to administer the state's business holdings.

Some efforts were made to relieve unemployment by public works, but the government would never stray far from its deflationist course, and employment in public works projects failed to keep step with the increasing unemployment. The Fascist dictatorship developed no effective ways of combating the crisis; in fact, the Depression lasted longer in Italy than in most of the democracies. Unemployment receded only when Mussolini's military ventures in Ethiopia and Spain absorbed additional manpower into the armed forces and armament industries. A comprehensive effort, launched at that time, to expand Italy's economic self-sufficiency also helped to reduce the number of jobless, although at a staggering cost to the nation.

GERMANY: THE FALL OF THE WEIMAR REPUBLIC

Economics and Politics. The Depression struck Germany while the country was wrestling with one of its recurrent political crises. The coalition government of Social Democrats, Catholic Centrists, liberals, and moderate conservatives that had been in office since the Reichstag elections of May 1928 had done little to win popular acclaim. Its one major achievement had been the negotiation of the Young Plan and coupled with it, the Allied evacuation of the occupied Rhineland five years ahead of schedule. Even this achievement had been assailed as inadequate by the nationalist opposition. Alfred Hugenberg, manager of the largest German newspaper chain and newly elected head of the reactionary German National People's Party, proposed a law, to be adopted by popular referendum, which not only rejected the Young Plan, but threatened with a stiff jail sentence any minister who would set his signature under that plan.

The referendum campaign failed ignominiously; nonetheless, it had far-reaching consequences. To add to the vigor of the campaign, Hugenberg had entered an alliance with Hitler; while the Nazi Party was still numerically small, it had lost none of its brutal militancy and was considered a useful ally. The partnership with Hugenberg, the spokesman of heavy industry, proved a boon to Hitler; it made him socially "respectable" and provided him with substantial funds. Nazi activities were greatly intensified, and frustrated voters, disgusted with the ineffectiveness of the government and the Reichstag and frightened by the worsening economic crisis, increasingly turned to the Nazis in state and local elections. Nazi charges against the Jews provided a comfortable explanation for the existing difficulties. Nazi promises of a new political and economic order based on soldierly discipline and untainted by selfish material interests had a special appeal for those who saw no chance of a livelihood under the present system.

In the spring of 1930 the government broke up. The brittle bourgeois-socialist coalition came to an end over the question of financing the mounting unemployment insurance claims. The German People's Party, speaking for the employers, wished to reduce benefits to avoid burdening business with further expenditures; the Social Democrats opposed all cuts on the grounds that the unemployed were getting barely enough to meet their minimum needs. Beyond the immediate issue, the right-of-center German People's Party wished to end labor's political influence and drive the Socialists from the government, whereas the Socialists would not make any further concessions lest labor be left completely defenseless as the Depression deepened. A compromise, carefully distributing the burdens for raising additional funds, was finally worked out by the cabinet; it proved unacceptable to the Social Democratic Reichstag delegation, and the government resigned.

The Brüning Government. The new government was a rather novel creation. It was formed, not as a result of negotiations between the various political parties, but by the fiat of Reich President von Hindenburg. As the product of his personal choice the new cabinet was expected to enjoy greater independence from parties and parliament and steer a steadier course than its predecessor. In selecting the Chancellor, Heinrich Brüning (1885–), the Center's financial expert, and the other members of the cabinet, Hindenburg was guided by the advice of Major General Kurt von Schleicher (1882–1934), the army's liaison man with government and parliament. As the Reichswehr's spokesman and a close friend of Hindenburg's son, the sociable, urbane Schleicher enjoyed the special confidence of the Field Marshal-President who never felt fully at ease with his civilian advisers. The General was alarmed by the rapid growth of the Nazi movement and fearful of a civil war between Nazis and Communists which the army would have to suppress; his hope was that a strong conservative government backed by Hindenburg's presidential authority would be able to maintain law and order and lead the country out of its economic difficulties. Thus, for the next three years, the concerns of the army became a decisive factor in shaping the policies of the country.

Contrary to Schleicher's expectations, a large number of rightist deputies would not support Brüning in the Reichstag although he was Hindenburg's man. Most German National deputies were fearful of losing their voters to Hitler and rejected the austerity budget that Brüning submitted to the Reichstag. Since Social Democrats and Communists opposed him too, the Chancellor decided to have a showdown. On his advice President von Hindenburg dissolved the Reichstag and promulgated the budget by decree on the basis of Article 48 of the constitution (see p. 144). Whether this procedure was constitutional was highly doubtful; but in the face of the existing impasse no one was prepared to challenge the legality of the Chancellor's actions.

The elections held in September 1930 revealed that a large part of the electorate was not prepared to back Brüning against the Reichstag. The Nazis emerged as the second largest party in the Reichstag: from 12 deputies their delegation grew to 107. Communist representation increased from 54 to 77, while that of the Socialists declined from 153 to 143; Brüning's Center Party increased from 62 to 68. The main victims were the bourgeois parties, which lost almost half of their following; the delegation of Hugenberg's German National People's Party dropped from 73 to 41 members. Despite the unfavorable returns the Brüning government stayed in office; Hindenburg's (and Schleicher's) confidence in the Chancellor was undiminished, and the Social Democrats decided to "tolerate" him lest a Nazi-German National government take over. But although the Reichstag by a narrow majority allowed Brüning to carry on, it no longer functioned effectively and was unable to produce legislative majorities. Laws were from now on issued by presidential decree, and the center of political gravity shifted increasingly from the parliament to the President.

Economic conditions meanwhile grew worse. The electoral success of the Nazis precipitated further withdrawals of capital from the country— a ruinous drain on the resources of the impoverished economy. A devaluation of the currency might have improved Germany's balance of payments, but Brüning was not permitted under the Young Plan to take such a step. Moreover, any tampering with the currency would have revived memories of the recent inflation and might have touched off a new financial panic. The Chancellor insisted on a policy of rigid financial orthodoxy, balancing the budget by increased taxes and stringent retrenchments, curtailing imports by tariffs and quotas, and increasing exports by drastic price cuts. By this cautious deflationist policy he hoped also to convince Germany's reparation creditors that if Germany could no longer meet its financial obligations, this was due not to economic mismanagement but to conditions beyond its control, and reparations would have to be cancelled.

Brüning, Schleicher, and the Nazis.   If to Brüning, frugal to the point of asceticism, this course seemed wise, politically and economically his policy of deflation proved disastrous. His economies meant wage and salary cuts, discontinuation of public works projects and other governmental activities, and the further reduction of relief benefits. As a result available purchasing power continued to shrink and demand declined correspondingly. Unemployment (including the "invisible," unregistered, unemployed) which had risen from 2,410,000 in 1929 to 3,650,000 a year later grew to 5,640,000 in 1931 and to 7,340,000 in 1932. In their despair increasing numbers turned to the Nazis and Communists who promised quick relief from the existing misery if the government were turned over to them. It was a measure of people's anxieties that the vagueness and inconsistencies of the Nazis' promises did not perturb them. The economist Peter Drucker tells of a Nazi agitator who announced to a wildly

Hitler among the Nazi Party faithful. (*Reprinted courtesy The Bettmann Archive, Inc.*)

enthusiastic peasants' meeting: "We don't want lower bread prices, we don't want higher bread prices, we don't want unchanged bread prices —we want National Socialist bread prices." No one, not excepting the speaker himself, could have told what this meant, but his words seemed to suggest a solution, and his audience accepted his statement as such. Unlike the diffident Brüning and the remote elderly Hindenburg, Hitler seemed to have the strength and the imagination to lead the country out of its impasse to new prosperity and national greatness, and his followers did not worry about his specific plans. Even the increasing violence and lawlessness of the Nazi stormtroopers failed to shake their faith in the Fuehrer.

During 1931 Brüning suffered two serious reverses. His plan to join Germany and Austria in a customs union which was to give him a badly needed foreign political success was vetoed by France and had to be dropped. The furor over this setback had barely subsided when in mid-July, after a renewed run on Germany's gold reserves, one of the largest banks collapsed, and a bank holiday had to be proclaimed. Both crises seemed to bear out Hitler's charges of the incompetence of the government, and the Nazi ranks were swelled by new converts. The government weathered the storm, but General von Schleicher, next to Hindenburg Brüning's main ally, wondered whether the government ought not to come to terms with the Nazis—the more so as Nazi sympathies were by now widespread in the army as well. The Chancellor considered any such collaboration unfeasible, but Schleicher, underestimating Hitler's ruthless ambitions, felt that Brüning was too inflexible. He voiced his misgivings to Hindenburg; Brüning, however, persuaded the President that his course was correct and that if he were allowed to pursue it, Germany would soon be fully relieved of its reparations burden (payments had been suspended thanks to the Hoover moratorium) and might also be granted the right to rearm—concessions that would never be made by the Western Powers if the Nazis were taken into the government.

In the spring of 1932 Hindenburg's presidential term expired. Hitler was the candidate of the Nazis; the anti-Nazi forces could find no one except the 84-year old Field Marshal to run against the Nazi leader with any hope of success. The President won handily over Hitler, but the election did not bring peace to the country. The supporters of the President were united only in their preference of Hindenburg over Hitler; many were otherwise as distrustful of each other as they were of the Nazis, and their coalition broke up as soon as the election was held. Hindenburg himself was much perturbed by the fact that he was the candidate of Socialists, Centrists, and liberals, whereas those to whom he felt closest socially and sentimentally voted for Hitler. The President also resented that Brüning, immediately after the election, induced him to dissolve the Nazi stormtroops and elite guards in the interest of public order and safety, for Hindenburg knew that in doing so he exposed himself to renewed attacks from these same social circles. Thus Brüning's position kept growing weaker, and since the reparations settlement was postponed and no progress made in the question of German rearmament, the President became increasingly dissatisfied with the Chancellor. He was also perturbed when his land-owning friends assailed Brüning as an "agrarian Bolshevik" because the Chancellor proposed to break up into small peasant farms some hopelessly indebted estates that had been subsidized unsuccessfully by the state.

Schleicher meanwhile was negotiating with Hitler behind Brüning's back and in late May 1932 thought he had reached an agreement with him: the Nazi leader would support a new conservative government in return for the readmission of the proscribed Nazi formations and new Reichstag elections. With the ground thus prepared, the General suggested to Hindenburg the replacement of Brüning by a one-time general staff officer and conservative politician, Franz von Papen (1879–   ), who would have the support of the Nazis and be able to stabilize the political situation. Hindenburg agreed, and Brüning was compelled to resign.

The Papen Government.   The Papen government was almost entirely Schleicher's creation. To please Hindenburg, it was composed largely of noblemen; Schleicher who preferred to remain in the background took the post of Reichswehr Minister. To his dismay the Nazis attacked this "cabinet of barons" as bitterly as that of Brüning, although Papen did his best to placate them. The new Chancellor dissolved the Reichstag, he readmitted the Nazi formations, and with the backing of the army removed the Socialist-Center government in Prussia and replaced it by appointees of conservative leanings. Benefiting from Brüning's endeavors, he also obtained the virtual cancellation of all reparations obligations at the Conference of Lausanne in June 1932. Nonetheless Papen satisfied almost no one. The Reichstag elections of July 1932 netted the Nazis 37.4 per cent of the vote and 230 seats, and the Communists obtained 14.9 per cent and 89 seats. The Socialists and the bourgeois parties suffered further reverses; most of the latter were reduced to minuscule splinter parties. Some of Hindenburg's advisers wished to concede Hitler the chancellorship in a new government; but Hindenburg, deeply distrustful of the loud-mouthed, undisciplined Nazi leader, would offer him only the vice-chancellorship in a Papen-led government. This proposal Hitler rejected, confident that the chancellorship would in any event soon be his. Since Papen had no majority in the new Reichstag without the Nazis and no other government could be formed, the Reichstag was again dissolved when it convened in September.

In early November once more elections were held. The Nazis emerged again as the largest party, but they polled over two million fewer votes than in July, and their delegation was reduced to 196 deputies. The Communists, on the other hand, gained 700,000 votes and twelve seats. The bourgeois parties which supported Papen scored some moderate gains. The Nazi setback was due partly to a slight improvement in the economic outlook; it seemed less imperative now to entrust one's fate to the unfathomable ways of Nazi radicalism. But there was also a growing feeling that Hitler's political talents had been overestimated and that he was constantly being outmaneuvered in his quest for government power. However, Papen's position was not improved, and he still faced a hostile majority in the Reichstag. Yet Hindenburg who had taken a liking to the Chancellor clung to him with the stubbornness of old age and would not dismiss him.

To remain in office, Papen proposed a temporary suspension of the Reichstag—a violation of the constitution which he justified by the existing emergency; but Schleicher warned that the army might not be strong enough to defend the government should the Nazis and Communists rise in protest against such a move. The General thought it possible on the other hand to split the Nazi Party, large parts of which seemed dissatisfied with Hitler's leadership, and form a coalition of dissident Nazis, labor unions, Center, and bourgeois parties. Anxious to avoid bloodshed, Hindenburg appointed Schleicher Chancellor in early December.

Papen and Hitler. Schleicher's appointment was welcomed by many with a sense of relief, for he was known to be more social and reform-minded than Papen. The new Chancellor thus could count on greater goodwill and confidence than his predecessor. But the volatile high-strung General was not a strong man; he was unable to break up the Nazi Party; he failed to persuade the Social Democrats to work with him; his contacts with labor antagonized the bourgeois camp; and his revival of Brüning's land reform plans infuriated the agrarians.

While Schleicher was struggling to form a parliamentary coalition, Papen re-established contact with Hitler. Papen had the support of industrial groups anxious to make use of the Nazis against Socialists and Communists who seemed again on the rise. The industrialists hoped that after his electoral setback Hitler would be more accommodating in joining the government. To demonstrate their interest in such an alliance, these same circles collected several million marks to bail the near-bankrupt Nazi Party out of its financial difficulties. Hitler, however, still insisted on the chancellorship—that vantage point from which he expected to revamp the country's political and social structure. On the other hand, he no longer asked, as he had before, that half of the other cabinet posts be given to fellow Nazis. He contented himself with two, the strategic Ministry of the Interior and the Department of Aviation to be newly created. Foreign Office, Reichswehr, finance, and all other ministries he was ready to concede to conservative non-Nazis.

Papen kept Hindenburg informed on his talks with Hitler, but although the President did not discourage the negotiations, he was still unwilling to make Hitler Chancellor. At the end of January, however, Schleicher had to admit that he would be forced from office by a no-confidence vote of the Reichstag unless the parliament were dissolved, and he himself now proposed its suspension. Bewildered by the General's turnabout and warned by Papen that only a Hitler-led government could restore peace and stability, Hindenburg began to waver. Papen assured him that Hitler could easily be controled as Chancellor: in the cabinet he could be outvoted by the non-Nazi majority should he try to engage in any irresponsible ventures, and the Reichswehr also stood ready to curb him. Reluctantly, Hindenburg yielded to Papen's pleas, and on January 30, 1933 Hitler was appointed Chancellor and Papen Vice-Chancellor in a new government composed of 3 Nazis and 9 conservatives. Papen was confident that Hitler was now his captive and that he, Papen, and his conservative colleagues, all men of superior social and educational background, would know how to deal with the uncouth, ignorant Nazi leader. The new Vice-Chancellor assured a worried friend, "In two months we'll have pushed Hitler into a corner so hard he'll be squeaking."

THE DIPLOMATIC FRONT

Franco-German Relations.   The initial phase of the Depression was comparatively quiet on the diplomatic front. The Young Plan was ratified by the participating countries during the winter of 1929–30; Briand's proposal for a United States of Europe was being mulled over by the various Foreign Offices; and in London another naval disarmament conference met from January to April 1930 (see p. 67). In June 1930 the last Allied troops withdrew from the Rhineland.

Their departure did not improve Franco-German relations. The Germans kept calling for the cancellation of reparations, arms equality, and the restoration of the territories surrendered after the war. The French (and to a lesser extent the British) thought this reaction rank ingratitude, and French anxiety about France's security grew. The French became even more reluctant to make any further concessions: they helped defeat the German request that the proposed World Disarmament Conference be held in the fall of 1931 and had it delayed until February 1932; they held up acceptance of the Hoover moratorium; they obtained a postponement of the reparations conference from January to June 1932. They were also largely instrumental in compelling Germany and Austria to abandon their projected customs union.

The history of that project deserves to be explored briefly, for it is illustrative of the pitfalls that beset Franco-German diplomacy. Ironically, the plan was indirectly inspired by Briand's proposal of a United States of Europe: regional economic agreements had been suggested by advocates of European union as a useful first step towards that goal. Chancellor Brüning was fully aware, however, of the risks which he ran—France and Czechoslovakia could be expected to fight the plan as a hidden *Anschluss*. Both could also point to the Peace Treaty of St. Germain and the terms of the League-sponsored reconstruction loan of 1922, according to which Austria was not to enter into any agreement that would jeopardize, directly or indirectly, its political or economic independence. Brüning did not, therefore, commit himself fully to the project, but intended to launch it publicly only after it had been approved by France and the other powers. However, in March 1931 the news of the agreement leaked out, and the Berlin government was compelled to issue an official communiqué; it thus became fully committed to the plan and confronted the world with a *fait accompli*. The secrecy in which the negotiations had been carried on kindled France's suspicions of Germany's real intentions, and by diplomatic and financial pressure France forced Austria and Germany to abandon the plan. The Permanent Court of International Justice from which the League Council had requested an advisory opinion on the legality of the Austro-German agreement upheld the French position, but only by a one-vote majority (8 to 7). Some significance was seen in the fact that all those judges who sided with their French colleague were nationals of countries which had a strong interest in blocking the project (Italy, Poland, Rumania) or belonged to the Spanish-American bloc which habitually voted with France in the League. The Germans in any event denounced the decision as political rather than judicial.

Japan's Invasion of Manchuria. Historical changes never occur from one day to another but are the results of extended developments. To single out a specific event as a "historical turning point" would be misleading, but an incident may properly be considered as *symbolic* of the transition from one historical phase to another. In the case of the changeover from the post-World War I phase to the pre-World War II period in European (and world) developments, Japan's invasion of Manchuria can claim this symbolic significance. That action challenged the existing order; it defied solemn legal and treaty commitments; it laid bare the ineffectiveness of the machinery devised to maintain international law and order; and it demonstrated that aggression, well timed and speedily carried out, could succeed—even against a group of potentially more powerful opponents.

The Japanese seizure of Manchuria grew out of rivalries of long standing between China and Japan over their respective rights in that province. Legally Manchuria belonged to China, but Japan had acquired important interests in it after the Russo-Japanese War. The basic issue dividing the two countries concerned the future control of Manchuria.

In recent years large numbers of Chinese settlers had come to that country which thanks to the Japanese-run railway system and Japanese-financed industrial enterprises and administrative organizations had become a more secure and orderly area to live in than China proper. If allowed to continue, this influx was bound to lead to the full integration of Manchuria into China—a development that Japan was determined to prevent since it was likely to deprive the Japanese of their special rights in that area.

The incident that touched off the Manchurian crisis—the alleged blowing up on September 18, 1931 of a section of the Japanese-owned South Manchurian Railway by the Chinese (denied by the latter)—was probably manufactured by the Japanese. Whatever happened, Japanese troops guarding the railway seized the city of Mukden and within less than a week occupied all major cities along the railway—in order to protect the line and other Japanese property from bandits and other disorderly elements, as the official explanation asserted. During the following year and a half all of Manchuria was brought under Japanese control.

The Chinese appealed to the League of Nations; but when Japan assured the League that it had no territorial designs on Manchuria and would withdraw its forces as soon as order had been restored, the League contented itself with asking both parties to settle their differences as speedily as they could. Despite their assurances, the Japanese kept driving deeper into Manchuria, and the League Council reconvened. Since Japan's actions violated also the Kellogg-Briand Pact and the Nine-Power Treaty of 1922 by which, among others, the United States and Japan had pledged themselves to respect the sovereignty and territorial integrity of China, the United States was invited to take part in the talks of the Council. For the first (and only) time an American representative participated in a League Council session, with strict instructions, however, to speak up only when the discussion turned to the Kellogg-Briand Pact. Although the American delegate was no high-ranking diplomat, but merely the American Consul in Geneva, League supporters hailed his appearance as a milestone in the organization of world peace, and Briand and all other Council members expressed their pleasure in warm welcoming speeches. This enthusiasm, coupled with rumors that the United States had joined the League, frightened Secretary of State Stimson, who was already under heavy attack from isolationist newspapers, and he reduced the American delegate to the status of an observer.[1]

---

[1] This created some technical difficulties, however. Stimson insisted that as an observer Consul Gilbert ought not to sit at the conference table, but was told that there were no seats away from the table in the Council room. In his diary Stimson has left a record of his woes: "There came a telephone call from Geneva from Gilbert, bringing up again this infernal question of his seat at the table. Briand

Meanwhile Japanese aggression continued unabated. But none of the Great Powers was prepared to intervene. Armed action was out of the question since neither the American nor the British people were willing to go to war over a conflict in as remote a country as Manchuria. The imposition of economic sanctions also seemed inadvisable because they would have intensified the Depression. The hard-pressed American South would have suffered a further decline if American cotton exports to Japan had been stopped, and Britain's Far Eastern economy would have incurred serious losses had food exports to Japan come to an end. It was widely feared, moreover, that the imposition of sanctions might drive the Japanese to some retaliatory action such as the seizure of Hongkong. And there was also a feeling that hardworking overpopulated Japan had perhaps a better claim to Manchuria than the inefficient, disorganized Chinese, who were not even able to utilize the vast resources of China proper. The League Council contented itself with the appointment of an investigating commission under Lord Lytton, a former Viceroy of India. Later, following the American lead, the League Assembly also passed a resolution opposing recognition of any forcible territorial and treaty changes in the Far East.

By the time the Lytton Commission submitted its report in September 1932, the Japanese had overrun the major part of Manchuria and had established it as a separate state of Manchukuo. The report tried to maintain an impartial stance between the conflicting claims of Japan and China; it granted that Japan had legitimate grievances against China, but on the whole vindicated the Chinese position and denounced Japan's military actions as going beyond "legitimate self-defense." The commission recommended that Manchuria be given a large measure of autonomy under Chinese sovereignty; all armed forces were to be withdrawn from the province except for a local gendarmerie and all Sino-Japanese treaties renegotiated on a more equitable basis. Yet when the League Assembly endorsed these proposals, the Japanese withdrew from the League and launched new military operations against China proper.

Manchuria may have seemed remote from Europe at that time, but the Manchurian crisis was followed with keen interest by Hitler (and presumably by Mussolini as well). China, unarmed and rent by domestic strife, had been unable to defend itself against Japan, and no one had come to its help; Germany, Hitler warned, found itself in a position not unlike China's, and only rearmament by a strong government could preserve it from a similar fate. Most Germans, non-Nazis as well as

---

seemed to think that if we moved his seat from the table it would upset the whole stability of Europe. . . . Finally I decided that so long as Gilbert kept out of secret meetings . . . I would let him go on sitting at the damned table. He is, however, to keep his mouth shut." Quoted in Robert H. Ferrell, *American Diplomacy in the Great Depression: Hoover-Stimson Foreign Policy, 1929–1933* (New Haven and London, 1957), pp. 142–143.

Nazis, agreed with him. But this was not the essential issue for Hitler. What he really learned from the Manchurian experience was that it would not be too hard to defy the League and the individual Great Powers in starting Germany on the road to rearmament and aggression.

The World Disarmament Conference. At the height of the Manchurian campaign, in February 1932, a World Disarmament Conference convened at Geneva. The obligation to limit armaments had been assumed both by the signers of the Peace Treaty of Versailles and the members of the League of Nations, and the Geneva conference was to implement this twofold obligation. Among the 61 members attending were several, however, who were neither signers of the peace treaty nor of the League Covenant, among them the United States and the Soviet Union. A Preparatory Disarmament Commission had been appointed by the League of Nations in 1925 in those happier days when international understanding and peaceful cooperation seemed to have a genuine chance of success. The commission became involved in long wearisome debates in its efforts to prepare an agenda, and it was not until late in 1930 that a draft convention was worked out. That document was hedged in with so many reservations and qualifications that its main merit was, as one French newspaper put it, that it had been drawn up at all. Even this proved an overstatement, for the draft was not used by the conference.

The fundamental difficulty that beset all efforts to limit armaments was the unwillingness of the Great Powers to give up any of their weapons as long as there existed other powers of similar strength which they distrusted and with which they might find themselves at war some day. (Small countries, on the other hand, were more willing to agree to armament limitations since they could not defend themselves against any comer and felt that they had little to lose from arms limitations.) Any effective limitation thus was possible only where it was based on mutual trust and no outside power threatened the parties concerned; the Anglo-American naval agreements of 1922 and 1930 are a case in point.[2]

In this respect the prospects of the Geneva Disarmament Conference were especially unpromising. Not only did the Manchurian crisis cast its shadow across the conference table, but so did the rapidly growing Nazi movement, whose views did not fail to affect the attitude of the German delegation. The Germans, in fact, were little interested in armaments limitations, but wished to secure the right to rearm on the grounds that no one else had disarmed. The French on their part were, as always,

---

[2] The situation is somewhat different now in the case of nuclear armaments. The Test-Ban Treaty of 1963 may prove effective in spite of the mutual distrust of the signatories because violations of the treaty (which would void it) cannot be concealed.

concerned with their security and tried hard to bar German rearmament. They revived their proposal of an international police force, first advanced at the Paris Peace Conference; it was now to have a monopoly on bombing planes and was to have at its disposal tanks, capital ships, large submarines, and heavy artillery. As before, this plan was unacceptable to both the United States and Britain; it was also rejected by Germany which saw in it merely another scheme to block German equality in arms. The British wished to abolish all "offensive" weapons as distinct from "defensive" ones, but it proved impossible to reach an agreement on where to draw the dividing line. Each state considered armaments most suited to its own needs as defensive and labeled as offensive those weapons which it did not need or considered dangerous to its security. The American and British delegates thought submarines offensive while the Germans and French did not; there were similar disagreements on the functions of tanks. A German proposal called for the abolition of all armaments forbidden to Germany by the Treaty of Versailles. The Soviets, finally, called for total disarmament—a plan which no one took very seriously: Maxim Litvinov, the chief Soviet delegate, is said to have joined in the laughter with which the proposal was greeted. Some months later President Hoover proposed a plan abolishing bombers, tanks, heavy mobile guns, and means of chemical warfare, and reducing all other armaments by one-third; this plan too was quietly shelved as incompatible with the realities of European conditions.

The German government, now headed by Papen, became more insistent in its demand for equal status. Trying to take the wind out of the sails of the Nazis, it withdrew its delegation from the conference in mid-September 1932. In December the Germans returned after a formula embodying both the German and French claims had been worked out: Germany was granted, in principle, "equality of rights in a system which would provide security for all nations." But when the conference reconvened in February 1933, Hitler had become Chancellor, and the chances of reaching any concrete agreement became even slimmer. Prime Minister MacDonald submitted a plan which suggested for the first time specific figures for the effective strength of the various armies, after a gradual reduction of armaments extending over five years—France, 200,000 men at home and 200,000 colonial forces; Germany, 200,000 at home and none overseas; Italy, 200,000 and 50,000, respectively; Poland, 200,000 and none; Czechoslovakia, 100,000 and none; Soviet Russia, 500,000 and none. Negotiations dragged on inconclusively until in June the conference adjourned for the summer.

During the recess the French, thoroughly alarmed at Germany's resurgence, called for the postponement for four years of the armaments reductions proposed by MacDonald. The French request was accepted by the British, American, and Italian delegates, but was rejected by the Germans; when the conference reconvened in October 1933, Germany withdrew from it (and from the League of Nations) on the grounds that the highly armed states were not carrying out their obligation to disarm and would not satisfy Germany's recognized claim to equality of rights.

Germany's withdrawal sealed the fate of the Disarmament Conference. Its general commission convened periodically for another year and then ceased to meet. No one bothered to close the conference formally.

Centrifugal Trends. The unceremonious fading away of the Disarmament Conference was symbolic of the disintegrating effects of the Depression. Distrusting international cooperation, most states were relying increasingly on their own resources to master their difficulties, and the tenuous international ties restored in the 1920's dissolved again. World trade shrank in the face of the drive toward economic self-sufficiency; ideological divergences created new political and cultural barriers; the contrast between nations beset by internal demoralization and those inspired by hope and self-confidence accentuated the existing disparities. By the early 1930's Europe was once again torn by deep fissures, and this external fragmentation was accompanied in many of the European nations by an internal disintegration that reached equally deep.

11

Nazi Germany

Adolf Hitler was the prime beneficiary of those opportunities that the disordered state of Europe and of the world presented. As the child of a fifty-two-year-old father and a twenty-nine-year-old mother, he was himself the product of a fragmented world, and he grew up in the *fin de siècle* atmosphere of the disintegrating Austro-Hungarian Empire. Perhaps for that reason he sensed more clearly than others the hollowness of that prewar world that Europe was trying to re-create in the 1920's; his biographer, Konrad Heiden, has written that Hitler recognized decay wherever he met it, for it belonged to his own nature. Certainly he was deeply aware of the dehumanizing effects of the mass age, of the growing social and economic interdependence called forth by an expanding technology, and of the possibilities this de-individualization presented to the unscrupulous for the manipulation of men. "I have not come into this world to make men better," he blandly declared, "but to make use of their weaknesses." This was the man who rose to power in Germany in 1933 and was to remain from then on the central figure of European and world events until his death in 1945 in the smoking ruins of war-devastated Berlin.

LEADER, IDEOLOGY, AND PARTY

Hitler. The external data of Hitler's life have been summarized in Chapter 8; here they need to be supplemented by an analysis of Hitler's personality and views, for these are basic to an understanding of the developments which will be discussed.

Hitler never fitted into the world in which he lived. In his youth, he had failed to establish roots anywhere; his father, driven by a deep-seated restlessness, kept moving from one home to another. The boy did not learn to form any meaningful personal relationships and at an early age withdrew into himself. Withdrawal, however, did not mean resignation to him but spurred him to replan and reorder the world that rejected him; rather than adjust himself to that world, he wished to remold it in accordance with his own aspirations. At sixteen he already seems to have had a mystical sense of mission that in his view raised him above his fellowmen and gave him the right, because of his superior insights and knowledge, to map out their lives for them. Even then he daydreamed of rebuilding Linz, his home town, and Vienna, and he worked at his architectural blueprints as if driven by some inner compulsion. He showed that same drive when he drafted some ambitious social reform schemes by which he hoped to transform society; yet as August Kubizek, his one friend of those days, later recalled, his planning was inspired not by sympathy with the underprivileged, but by his own personal misery that aroused in him the wish for a total reordering of life. Similarly, as if impelled by some uncontrollable inner force, he would venture out on some hopeless one-man political demonstration, readily risking abuse and physical injury.

In the orderly prewar world Hitler was doomed to spend his days in frustrated isolation. He fitted equally poorly into the tight hierarchy of the German army in which he served during World War I; although a dedicated soldier of undoubted bravery, he never rose beyond the rank of private first-class because his superiors thought that his turbulent nature made him unfit for any command post. However, in the tumultuous conditions that engulfed postwar Germany, Hitler recognized his opportunity to translate his ideas into reality. As he evolved them over the years, he planned to build up a German state that thanks to the biological superiority of its people, its fighting will, and its rigid organization and efficient technology would under his leadership become the dominant power in Europe and evenutally in the world. What he planned was no mere military conquest, however, but a perpetuation of this domination by the creation of wholly new racial hierarchies and the economic enslavement and human degradation of those he considered inferior.

With unshakable confidence in his mission Hitler built up the National Socialist movement as the instrument with which he would attain his objectives. While the masses flocked to him, confident that he was concerned about their cares and frustrations and anxious to help them, he himself saw in them only the "human material," the bricks from which he proposed to fashion his new world. "If a movement has the intention of pulling down a world and of building a new one in its place," he wrote in *Mein Kampf*, "[it] will have to divide the human material it has won into two great groups: into followers and members. . . . I [saw to it] that the organization received only the best material." To be useful, this "material" had to be totally subservient to him; it was organized along military lines and indoctrinated with his views and values by men sharing his cynicism, captivated by him, and willing to serve as his instruments.

Similarly Hitler secured full control over Germany once he had obtained the key post of Chancellor. The structure of German political, economic, and cultural life was overhauled in the same relentless way that had been characteristic even of Hitler's earliest schemes, with human beings considered simply the raw material that went into the building of the new state. Like an architect, moreover, Hitler felt entitled to dispose of these "human bricks" as he saw fit, placing them wherever he wished and destroying those he considered undesirable—political opponents, Jews, the mentally deficient—just as a builder would discard faulty bricks. Later on millions would be transplanted and resettled in order to consolidate his hold over Europe, and others unconcernedly sacrificed in battle, for, as he coolly remarked, "That's what they are there for." Nor did he feel any compunction about abandoning his countrymen to their fate at the moment of Germany's total military collapse; since they had lost the war although he had led them, he was satisfied that the Germans deserved to perish.

Nazi Ideology. National Socialist ideology was officially formulated by the party philosopher, Alfred Rosenberg, but it was basically an expression of Hitler's own thinking. It centered on a few ideas culled largely and indiscriminately from the writings of Houston Stewart Chamberlain, the Anglo-German political publicist, Richard Wagner, the composer, and the philosophers Arthur Schopenhauer and Friedrich Nietzsche (whom Hitler misunderstood). All lumped together, these concepts were to help Hitler mold the German people into the pliable instrument he needed to carry out his plans. One was the "leader principle" (*Führerprinzip*), according to which the Nazi Party and, for that matter, any organization had a hierarchy of leaders each of whom could demand absolute obedience from his subordinates and in turn owed similar obedience to his superiors. At the top of the state and party hierarchy stood *the* leader, the Fuehrer. According to Nazi doctrine, he was entirely independent of all groups and interests; he was the agent of no one but rather the "bearer of the collective will of the people."

Thus Hitler enjoyed complete freedom of action and need not account to anyone, and at the same time exercized full control over his sub-leaders and followers. As for the average citizen, the nonleader, he was to serve his people—that is, its Fuehrer—with total dedication and, if necessary, with the sacrifice of his life. His existence was circumscribed by the principle that the commonweal always took precedence over individual rights and interests.

Racialism was another ideological precept of Nazism. It claimed that race was the basic element of all historical events, of the formation of states and the creation of culture, and that there were peoples of superior racial substance—master races—such as the Germans, who were destined to rule, and inferior ones, such as the Slavs, whose task it was to be servants. Far below these latter groups were the Jews whose racial stock was the lowest. The Jews were considered the greatest racial danger on the grounds that they were engaged in a worldwide conspiracy to corrupt the Aryan race with their inferior racial substance. What was especially significant about this pseudoscientific doctrine was its denial of man's possible improvement through cultural or spiritual influences. Whereas earlier anti-Semites had given the Jew a chance to "redeem" himself by embracing Christianity, the racist rejected any possibility of Jewish redemption. By this reasoning an unbridgeable gap was to be created between the Germans and the allegedly inferior racial groups, so that the Germans could be trained to rule over their inferiors without indulg-ing in misguided sympathy or compassion.

In justice to themselves and in order to fulfill their "world-historical" task, Nazism asserted, the German people were entitled to additional living-space. Expansion, however, was not to be limited to the recovery of the territories lost after World War I ("political nonsense of such a degree . . . as to look like a crime," Hitler fumed) but was to be large enough to assure a growing people adequate space for centuries to come. Such space ought not to be sought in overseas colonies whose racial and military value was dubious, but must border on Germany so that the new settlers would not be lost to the mother country and both mother country and the newly acquired lands could be fused into one mighty power complex. Adequate living space could be found only in the east —in Russia—and fate, Hitler was certain, was assisting Germany by speeding Russia's collapse under Bolshevik rule.

Obviously territorial expansion was bound to involve Germany in war, but war, according to Hitler, was in any event a law of nature, a phase in the never-ending struggle for survival, a testing ground of racial vitality. "He who wants to live should fight," he warned in *Mein Kampf*, "and he who does not want to do battle in this world of eternal struggle does not deserve to be alive." There could be no more sacred war, he added, than one fought for the strengthening of the "racial substance."

The Nazi Party.   The Nazi Party and its affiliated organizations helped pave Hitler's way to power and enabled him to seize full control of the state once he had been appointed Chancellor. Based on the leader principle, the party was organized along military lines with a hierarchy of leaders extending from the national level down to cells in street blocks and plants. Among the affiliated organizations the stormtroopers (S.A., for *Sturm-Abteilungen*) and the elite guards (S.S., for *Schutz-Staffeln*) were the most important. The stormtroopers were "political soldiers," guarding meetings, marching in demonstrations, and fighting street battles. The elite guards were charged with protecting the leaders. In accordance with the Nazi aim of permeating the entire nation, there were also organizations for lawyers, doctors, teachers, farmers, and other professional groups. There was a Nazi women's league, the only party organization in which women could assume leadership functions since their main task was to tend to the home and bear children. Boys between the ages of fourteen and eighteen were organized in the Hitler Youth, girls of that age had their own groups, and still another organization catered to children from ten to thirteen years.

Party members, stormtroopers, and elite guards might well consider themselves linked to the Fuehrer in a special relationship—to Hitler they

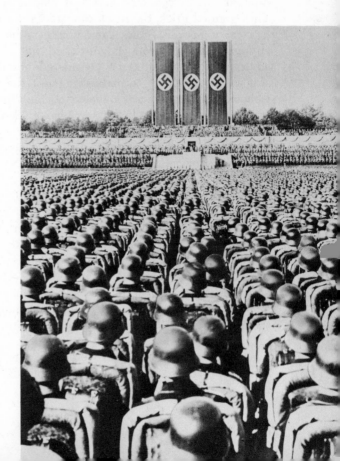

Nazi Party Congress at Nürnberg. *(Reprinted courtesy The Bettmann Archive, Inc.)*

were all mere tools and expendable once they had outlived their usefulness. "Should I come to the conclusion that the party is no longer needed
for the welfare of our people, or unable to appreciate the historical tasks
which I have to fulfill," he once told a party conclave, "I would be the
first to hurl the blazing torch into the political structure of our movement
in order to destroy it in the interest of the future of our people."

THE ORGANIZATION OF THE NAZI STATE

Political Controls. This, then, was the man whom Vice-Chancellor
Papen thought he had made his prisoner in the government formed in
late January 1933. It became at once apparent that the conservative
majority in the cabinet was no match for the ruthless energies of Hitler
and his associates. The non-Nazis were outmaneuvered by the new
Chancellor when they agreed to the dissolution of the Reichstag, which
still had a non-Nazi majority and thus might have served as a brake
on Hitler's ambitions. They were unable to prevent Hitler's second-in-
command, brutal and blustering ex-Captain Hermann Göring (1893–
1946), who was put in charge of the Prussian police, from turning that
force of almost 50,000 men into a compliant Nazi tool by replacing hundreds of police commissioners and officers with S.A. and S.S. leaders.
They granted Frick, the Reich Minister of the Interior, additional powers
to combat Socialists and Communists, without realizing that this new
authority was so loosely circumscribed that Frick could invoke it against
anyone whose activities he considered objectionable. Nor was Papen
able to do anything but protest against the terror which Nazi stormtroopers and elite guards inflicted not only on "Marxists," but on Centrists and liberals as well. Meetings of Centrists and Socialists were
broken up (those of the Communists had at once been forbidden), their
speakers harassed and manhandled, and countless non-Nazi party and
newspaper offices ransacked, with the Nazified police refusing to
intervene.

On February 27, 1933 the Reichstag building was set afire. Apparently
the fire was set, not by the Nazis, as was widely suspected, but by a
half-witted Dutch Communist, Marinus van der Lubbe, as a gesture of
protest against Nazi brutalities. Hitler used the event to obtain additional
powers "for the protection of the German people." At his request Hindenburg signed a decree which gave the Chancellor the authority to suspend
almost all constitutional liberties and to remove obstructive state governments. On the basis of this decree all Communist leaders who could be
found were sent to newly created concentration camps, and so were
great numbers of Socialists and other prominent anti-Nazis. Nevertheless,
when the Reichstag elections were held, the Nazis obtained only 44 per
cent of the vote; despite all terror and blandishments the majority of the

German electorate still was unwilling to entrust its fate to the Nazis. But this majority was powerless, for it was broken up into a multitude of mutually hostile parties; moreover, by this time almost all power resources of the state were concentrated in Hitler's hands. The two agencies not yet under his control, Reich President and Reichswehr, stood by passively, unwilling to curb him.

Under the circumstances Hitler had no difficulty forcing through the Reichstag an Enabling Act that transferred to the government the legislative authority of the Reichstag. On the basis of this act a law was promulgated, "coordinating" state, county, and municipal parliaments by providing for a redistribution of seats proportionate to the recent Reichstag election returns. A second law installed in each state a Reich governor who was to supervise the actions and policies of the state government. Early in April 1933 the civil service and the judiciary were purged of all "non-Aryan" officials (except war veterans), the term "non-Aryan" referring to anyone who had at least one Jewish grandparent. The law permitted also the dismissal of all those officials "who do not give the assurance, due to their previous political activity, that they will always serve faithfully the national state." This provision made possible the removal of anyone objectionable to the new masters; it was widely used to dismiss not only Socialists and Communists, but liberals too, and replace them with loyal Nazis. It served, moreover, to intimidate those who had their reservations about the new regime, and ensured their collaboration.

Another law broke up the labor unions and established the German Labor Front, a Nazi-dominated organization to which every worker and employee had to belong. Similarly, one after another the political parties were either suppressed or disbanded voluntarily in anticipation of such suppression. In July 1933 the National Socialist Party was proclaimed the only legal party, and it became a criminal offense to organize any new party. At the same time several of the conservative ministers in the Reich government were replaced by Nazis; in addition, Joseph Goebbels (1897–1945), the Nazi Party's propaganda chief and an accomplished speaker and editorialist famed for his gift of mellifluous invective, was appointed head of a newly created Ministry of Propaganda and Popular Enlightenment. Goebbels' special task was to supervise press, radio, and entertainment, but his jurisdiction encompassed also all other cultural activities.

Cultural Activities. Goebbels lost no time in establishing his control over Germany's cultural life. The press was the first to be "coordinated." Anyone found guilty of publishing news detrimental to the national interest was liable to severe punishment; daily bulletins informed all newspapers as to what news to report, which to stress and which to play down or ignore. Moreover, all editors, reporters, and other regular contributors had to be members of the Reich Press Chamber; since loss of membership barred them from all journalistic activity, they were doubly careful not to print anything that the Propaganda Ministry might find inappropriate, for such an offense could lead to expulsion from the Press Chamber. Nominally, most German newspapers remained in private hands, but they were subject to controls no less stringent than those exercised in Soviet Russia by government, Communist Party, and other official organizations through their outright ownership of the press.

Writers, painters, and composers were controlled in similar ways. There were Reich chambers of literature, of the creative arts, and of music, which watched that their members chose "German" topics and themes and cultivated a "German" style; a novel dealing sympathetically with Jews or a nonrepresentational painting or atonal music thus was excluded. Inevitably German cultural life, remarkably rich and varied during the Weimar era, became sterile and dull. No less than 250 of the better known writers, among them Thomas Mann, Stefan George, and Alfred Döblin, went into exile; others remained but were silenced or retreated into safe historical themes. A few regional writers produced works of sensitive artistry, but no truly great work could be created in the stifling atmosphere of Nazi Germany. Starved for good literature, the Germans turned to the novels of Thomas Wolfe, Margaret Mitchell's *Gone With the Wind*, and Rachel Field's *All This, and Heaven Too*, which became (in translation) leading best-sellers in Germany. In music the aging Richard Strauss still was at work, but here as well as in the creative arts many of the best talents departed for more hospitable climes.

The Economy.   Hitler had no interest in economic problems as such nor did he have any marked preference for either private enterprise or state ownership. His sole concern was that the economy serve his plans; since these, most likely, could not be realized without resort to war, he had the economy geared to war needs. Collective bargaining and strikes were outlawed and techniques were devised that assured him as effective control of the German economy as if it were government-owned. Care was taken, however, to maintain the outward forms of free enterprise so as not to jeopardize Hitler's claim that he was its champion and Germany's last bulwark against Bolshevism.

Some control devices such as foreign exchange regulations and import and export licenses had already been established by previous governments. These checks were used now to bar purchases abroad of nonessential materials such as luxury goods, but also of less-needed foodstuffs like butter and eggs. Similarly, when a manpower shortage developed after 1935, state employment offices allocated labor only to enterprises whose production furthered the war economy or was otherwise considered important; firms that did not meet these terms were forced either to close or to change to a different line of production. Small businesses which were considered wasteful and inefficient were closed out by means of new taxes and by laws which barred their incorporation, subjecting the owners to the risks of unlimited liability. To finance the war preparations, credits were readily made available. Substantal sums were also obtained from corporations which were forbidden to distribute any dividend above 6 per cent; excess amounts had to be lent to the government "in appreciation of the government's revival of the economy which had made possible the resumption of dividend payments." Wages were frozen at Depression levels to curtail the demand for consumer goods and prices were fixed to check inflationary pressures; savings were encouraged and were invested primarily in newly issued government bonds, which absorbed most of the available capital.

Agriculture was subjected to similar controls, with production even more rigidly supervised (unofficial food rationing was introduced as early as 1935). The main objective was, again in accordance with the requirements of the war economy, to make Germany as self-sufficient as possible in foodstuffs. To render agriculture more efficient and also save manpower, an early Nazi law declared farms of a certain size indivisible; the younger sons of a farmer thus could not hope to inherit any part of the land and were forced to make a living elsewhere. Agricultural production did increase, but never attained self-sufficiency in foodstuffs for Germany.

In 1936 these policies were incorporated into an all-embracing Four-Year-Plan whose main purpose was to make Germany as independent as possible of imports of raw materials and foodstuffs. The plan underwrote the development and mass production of substitute materials such as the extraction of synthetic rubber and oil from coal and lignite, the manufacture of cloth from wood, the expanded production of rayon, the mining of low-grade ores, and the utilization of scrap and waste materials. To counter possible food shortages, substitute flour, fats, and other ersatz products were developed. A determined trade drive which brought the countries of central and southeastern Europe into the German economic orbit (see p. 238) served also to strengthen Germany against any future blockade.

Control by Terror. Hitler established one of the most effective controls over the individual citizen by making his job dependent on loyal cooperation. On the whole the fear of jeopardizing one's livelihood and the need to support a family proved effective checks against any thought of active opposition or of openly criticizing the Fuehrer and his regime. In addition, a ubiquitous secret police, the Gestapo, concentration camps, and special courts stood ready to deal with any elements considered disloyal; the very existence of these agencies served as a further deterrent against oppositional action. A network of informers in apartment buildings, street blocks, plants, and offices also watched the movements and associations of their charges and helped to make control over them truly total.

THE ACHIEVEMENTS OF NAZISM

Full Employment. It would be erroneous, however, to assume that most Germans were being continuously terrorized into serving the Nazi regime. If in March 1933 a majority still cast its vote for parties other than the National Socialist Party, by 1936, according to all indications, a large majority had fully accepted the Hitler regime. Whatever the restrictions and deprivations the rearmament program imposed upon the nation, it did revive the economy. By 1934 the *Autobahn* and related programs provided work for hundreds of thousands of men. The economic momentum accelerated when Hitler tore up the disarmament provisions of the Peace Treaty of Versailles and reintroduced compulsory military service. Other sectors of the economy not connected with the rearmament effort benefited also from the improved employment situation; the demand for consumers goods increased notably even though low wages and salaries set limits to this expansion. Thus life did improve for a large number of Germans, and millions who had been without jobs during the long years of the Depression now had the satisfaction of performing useful work again and of being able to take care of their families. That this was due largely to the rearmament drive mattered to few; if they gave any thought to this matter, they accepted Hitler's recurrent statements that Germany was rearming only in order to be able to defend itself, not to engage in aggression.

Strength Through Joy. While living standards remained on the whole fairly low, the Nazis did provide a great variety of recreational facilities (as does every totalitarian regime). They were run by a subsidiary of the German Labor Front which was descriptively named *Strength Through Joy.* Strength Through Joy offered a varied program of sports, entertainment, education, and vacation trips. Sports and educational facilities varied only in number and size from those arranged before by individual labor unions, but the entertainment and vacation programs surpassed anything the unions had ever been able to offer. Workers could now attend at nominal prices concerts, operas, and plays performed by outstanding artists (drafted into the service of Strength Through Joy by pressure if necessary). At equally low prices they could spend their vacation at the seaside, in the mountains, or on a cruise, in hotels and on liners owned or leased by the organization. Not only did workers and employees appreciate these opportunities, but Strength Through Joy also allowed the regime to keep an eye on them in their leisure time.

Hitler's Political Achievements. Most Germans also were greatly impressed by the apparent stabilization of the German domestic scene. For years Germany had hovered on the verge of civil war, with street clashes and beer hall battles a daily occurrence. By mid-1933, a few months after Hitler's accession to power, public order had been fully restored in Germany. Few remembered that the earlier disorders had been due more to the rowdyism of the Nazis than to the activities of any other party, nor did they reflect that the present order was purchased at the price of their political and spiritual freedom. To most of them this freedom had never been very meaningful, and they considered the totalitarian restrictions at most as an unpleasant inconvenience. They were equally impressed when Hitler proclaimed Germany's right to rearm and reintroduced compulsory military service in 1935. To them the right to rearm was above all a matter of justice since no one else had disarmed, and they agreed with the official rearmament proclamation which stated that "with the present day the honor of the German nation has been restored. We stand erect as a free people among nations. . . . Within two years after seizing power [the Fuehrer] has secured political equality for his people." This admiration increased when Hitler sent his forces into the demilitarized Rhineland in 1936 and when in 1938 he scored two more bloodless victories and seized Austria and the Sudetenland in Czechoslovakia.

OPPONENTS OF THE REGIME

Political Opposition. One of the most striking aspects of Hitler's seizure of power was the fact that he encountered practically no resistance in the Nazification of Germany. The opposition was so divided and so demoralized that it made no attempt to resist the lawlessness of the Nazis. In fact, there occurred what might well be called a wholesale surrender to the new masters. A few leftist underground groups were organized; but without resources and foreign support, they could deal only an occasional pinprick to the regime. Conservative elements formed oppositional groups only some years later.

Some opposition to Hitler's regime developed, however, in his own camp. It centered in the stormtroops led by the retired Captain Ernst Röhm. He wished to transform his forces into a revolutionary people's army to be merged with the regular Reichswehr. He also aimed at greater political influence for the soldierly element in the party. How far Röhm had gone or was prepared to go to achieve his objectives has never been ascertained, but there is little evidence that his plans ever assumed any concrete form. Nevertheless, his attempts to buy arms for his formations and his contacts with foreign diplomats and opponents of the regime such as ex-Chancellor von Schleicher aroused Hitler's fears. Hitler knew, moreover, that the ailing Hindenburg was not expected to live much longer; to assure himself of the Reichswehr's support after Hindenburg's death and to consolidate his position, he decided to eliminate the threat to the army and possibly to himself that Röhm represented. On June 30, 1934 Röhm and several score of high-ranking stormtroop leaders were arrested and executed without trial on charges of high treason; along with them others who had run afoul of Hitler at one time or another and a number of potential leaders of an opposition, among them Schleicher, were shot. Hitler himself admitted to 77 dead, but the number of victims amounted probably to between 150 and 200. The subservient cabinet passed a law some days later proclaiming Hitler's actions as "justified self-defense of the state."

On August 2, 1934 Hindenburg died, and Hitler proclaimed himself head of state. The Reichswehr swore allegiance to him, and a plebiscite formally ratified the step by a majority of 90 per cent of the vote.

The Churches. The most persistent opposition to the Nazi regime came from the churches. To ensure the Germans' unquestioning subservience, Hitler wanted them to be guided by Nazi values; he therefore objected violently to the precepts of Christian morality which taught the equality of all men, brotherly love, tolerance, and forgiveness. Conversely, a political ideology that claimed the superiority of one race over another, arrogated unto itself the right to eliminate undesirable groups, and proclaimed that whatever benefited the nation was ethical, contradicted everything that Christianity stands for.

To bridge the gap between Nazism and Protestantism, a German Christian movement was organized which claimed to be Protestant, but discarded the Old Testament, admitted only "Aryans" as members, and likened Hitler to Jesus. Under its influence other Protestant groups also refused to baptize Jews and excluded baptized Jews from their congregations. A minority, however, refused to bow to the dictates of the Nazis; organized in the "Confessional Church," these ministers continued to preach the gospel in unadulterated form. They established underground seminaries and tried to give aid to Christians of Jewish background, and they maintained their position even though many of them were deprived of their parishes or were sent off to concentration camps or prosecuted on various charges. They could always count on a loyal following that would faithfully attend services and demonstrate its support.

The fight of the Nazi regime against Catholicism was carried on more covertly and with greater caution; because of the worldwide organization of the Catholic Church an open clash might have had serious international repercussions. In fact, in July 1933 the Vatican and the Nazi government concluded a concordat by which the latter promised the Church "freedom of creed and public worship of the Catholic religion," and the Church in return pledged itself to disband all political, social, and professional organizations. But soon difficulties developed; the Catholic Church objected to the sterilization of the mentally defective, it protested against the closing of parochial schools since the concordat permitted expressly the maintenance of such schools, and Pope Pius XI warned against the growing disregard of all moral values in a papal encyclical ("With burning sorrow"). Like their Protestant counterparts, a large part of the Catholic clergy accommodated themselves to the Nazi regime, but individual bishops and priests fought off the Nazis encroachments with great personal courage. The Nazis retaliated with efforts to discredit the clergy by trials of priests, monks, and nuns on charges of perversion and illegal foreign exchange transactions. Yet mindful of Christianity's world-wide following, the Nazis never dared to suppress any of the churches entirely.

The Persecution of the Jews.   Anti-Semitism had been the best known feature of the National Socialist program in the days before Hitler obtained power, and it had attracted many into the party. Yet although it was generally expected that Hitler would impose restrictions on Jewish citizens once he had taken over the government, few realized how deadly serious he was when he spoke of eliminating the Jewish element from German life and to what lengths he was prepared to go to carry out this plan.

During the first weeks of his administration Hitler refrained from official anti-Jewish measures. In many a small town, however, beyond the ken of foreign diplomats and newspapermen, Jews were brutally man-handled and unofficial boycotts organized against Jewish businesses, doctors, and lawyers. The first systematic action was a one-day nation-wide boycott against Jewish businesses on April 1, 1933, allegedly a spontaneous popular reaction to a worldwide Jewish propaganda campaign against Nazi Germany. There followed the laws excluding persons of Jewish descent from government service, the press, the professions, and all other activities except business, and even there "non-Aryans" were soon subjected to increasing restrictions. This legislation culminated in the Nürnberg Laws of September 1935 which deprived Jews of their citizenship and made marriage or sexual intercourse between Jews and "Germans" a criminal offense.

Thereafter, the position of the Jews became ever more precarious. Nothing, moreover, was done to facilitate their emigration, and those without means found it increasingly difficult to find a refuge abroad. In November 1938 a nationwide pogrom was staged, as a "spontaneous" protest against the shooting of a German diplomat in Paris by a desperate Polish Jew who wanted to call attention to the plight of his people. Synagogues were set afire, Jewish stores and homes looted, and thousands of Jews hauled off to concentration camps. With brutal cynicism, the Jews were assessed one billion marks to pay for the damage that had been perpetrated. Soon afterwards they were forced to assume distinctly Jewish middle names and wear a yellow star to mark them permanently as outcasts. The stage was set for the descent into that ultimate inhumanity that led to the mass murder of German and European Jewry in the gas chambers of Auschwitz and Treblinka.

HITLER AND THE ARMY

Inaction of the Army. When Hitler became head of the German government in 1933, it was widely assumed that the army would check him should he indulge in any unconstitutional actions. The generals were known as conservative traditionalists who were contemptuous of the uncouth radical Nazis; moreover, their commander-in-chief was the Reich President, Field Marshal von Hindenburg, and the venerable Hindenburg, the very embodiment of law and order, could be trusted to call out the army to curb all Nazi excesses.

Contrary to these expectations, the army stood passively by as the Nazis established their lawless regime. Hitler knew that the army leaders had feared nothing more in the Weimar era than to be drawn into domestic disturbances; thus he assured himself of their friendly neutrality by promising them that he would never involve the army in what he called his campaign against Marxists. He had allies in Reichswehr Minister General Werner von Blomberg, a Nazi sympathizer, and his chief aide, General Walter von Reichenau, who was outspokenly pro-Nazi in his views. As for Hindenburg, in spite of occasional misgivings, he soon came to regard Hitler as a great and constructive statesman. None of these men thought of intervening against the Fuehrer, and if there were any generals willing to act against him, they would not do so without orders from these superiors. Besides, whatever uneasiness a few of them may have felt, they appreciated the fact that Hitler at last expanded the army and equipped it with all the new weapons it needed. He also earned the gratitude of the generals when he eliminated their most dangerous rival, the S. A. chief Röhm, in the Blood Purge of June 1934. In consequence, the army readily swore an oath of allegiance to the Fuehrer as commander-in-chief after Hindenburg's death a few weeks later.

The Nazification of the Army. With Hindenburg dead and the army tied by its oath to Hitler, the Fuehrer began to interfere more directly in military matters. In March 1935 he introduced military conscription, apparently without consulting the generals. While the latter approved of the principle of compulsory military service, they objected to the speed with which he wished to apply it, for they feared that it would impair the cohesion and homogeneity of the army. But Hitler, driven by his inner compulsions, would not wait; apart from his military ambitions, he welcomed the rapid expansion of the officer corps and rank-and-file because it brought into the army large numbers of loyal Nazis whose very presence would help to assure the cooperation of the armed forces.

The generals were also averse to any foreign political ventures while the army was still in the process of being built up. They objected when they learned of Hitler's plan to remilitarize the Rhineland, but once more they were overruled. They were also concerned about Germany's involvement in the Spanish Civil War and strongly warned against any actions that might lead to a European war. Their reaction seems to have been equally unenthusiastic when at a conference in November 1937 Hitler revealed to them the full extent of his plans. The time had come, he informed them, to secure the preservation and increase of the German "racial substance" by the acquisition of additional living-space—a goal that, as history taught, could be achieved only by armed force. It would have to be accomplished at the latest in the years 1943–1945 before the rearmament of Germany's "hate-driven enemies" would be completed, but might be initiated earlier if social unrest in France were to cripple the French army. For strategic reasons the first steps to be taken would be the seizure of Austria and Czechoslovakia. The generals present, War Minister von Blomberg, and the army chief, Baron von Fritsch, at once raised a number of questions and warned against an underestimation of the French military potential and the strength of the Czech fortifications.

Furious about their negative attitude, Hitler decided to assume direct control of the army. He dismissed Blomberg, seizing on the fact that the War Minister had recently married a woman of dubious background, and in Fritsch's case he accepted as true trumped-up charges of homosexuality against the General. He took over himself the functions of War Minister and appointed as his executive aide a nondescript desk officer, General Wilhelm Keitel, who could be trusted not to question his orders. As successor to Fritsch he selected the equally cooperative General Walter von Brauchitsch. A number of other generals were either pensioned off or transferred to posts of lesser importance. These changes made, Hitler felt sure enough of the army to order the seizure of Austria in March 1938.

Yet when Hitler prepared to move against Czechoslovakia in the fall of 1938, some of the older generals still on active duty decided that he must be prevented from plunging Germany into a war against Britain and France that the German forces were bound to lose. Preparations were made to arrest him as soon as war would break out, but since war was avoided by the Munich agreement, the plan was abandoned. Impressed by Hitler's skill and his unending successes, the generals, with few exceptions, gave up all further thought of resistance. Along with the rest of the nation, the army had been molded into the pliable tool that Hitler required to carry out his vast plans of conquest.

12

Economy, Society, Culture in the 1930's

The Europe that Hitler set out to destroy was plagued, as he sensed, by many social and economic problems not unlike those of the Weimar Republic. Some of these resulted from the Depression, others were due to deep-rooted social maladjustments—products of a rapidly advancing technology with which governments and society had been unable to keep pace. Finally, many difficulties were contrived by Hitler himself to create dissension and demoralization and to facilitate the destruction of the European order and his domination of the continent. Yet the picture was not entirely negative; although diplomacy failed to measure up to the crisis, in the domestic realm governments and nations proved more resourceful. Here new economic approaches were found and cultural responses developed.

THE ECONOMIC SCENE: INCREASING GOVERNMENT INTERVENTION

The Trading Blocs. Economically, as politically, Europe presented a melancholy picture of fragmentation. During the Depression most governments had tried to insulate their economies from the effects of that crisis by tariffs, import quotas, and exchange controls. The World Economic Conference, called to counteract this trend, had failed to halt it. Instead, efforts were made to modify the prevalent national orientation by the formation of trading blocs.

One such bloc was the sterling bloc, the foundation for which was laid at the Ottawa Conference of 1932 with its preferential tariff arrangements. During the following years the British government negotiated bilateral trading agreements with the Baltic and Scandinavian countries, whose currencies were aligned with the pound sterling, and with the U.S.S.R. and Argentina. All of these states were large-scale exporters to Britain and in return had to grant it reduced tariffs and larger import quotas for British goods.

Unlike the sterling bloc, the so-called gold bloc was less well organized and on the whole ineffective. It consisted of those countries which still adhered to the gold standard and had refrained also from introducing exchange controls. Among its members were France, Italy, Poland, Switzerland, and the Netherlands. Although these states made a number of efforts to achieve closer collaboration, most of them, in the end, had to give up the struggle against currency controls and devaluation. In 1936 an effort was made, by a tripartite agreement between the United States, Britain, and France, to merge the sterling and gold blocs with the dollar area into one vast trading domain, but the attempt was unsuccessful. Capital flight from France continued, and Anglo-American commerce failed to expand to any significant extent.

Apart from domestic difficulties a major reason for the failure of these endeavors was that most European countries, fearful of war, tended to gird themselves against this calamity by trying to become more self-sufficient. For the same reason the colonial powers also tended to strengthen their economic ties with their overseas possessions. They encouraged the production of those raw materials and crops which the mother country most needed, and restricted colonial imports from other countries. France so expanded its trade with its colonies that by 1936 it amounted to one third of the entire French foreign commerce. Thus foreign trade never recovered the ground it lost during the Depression. In 1929 world imports had amounted to $35.6 billion and exports to $33 billion; by 1934 imports had dropped to $12 billion and exports to $11.3 billion. Although by 1937, the best pre-World War II year, production in most countries had surpassed the level of 1929, world trade did not attain even half of the 1929 volume; exports rose only to $16.2 billion and imports to $15.3 billion.[1]

The German Trade Drive. Like the British, the Germans sought to extend their foreign trade by bilateral agreements, bartering locomotives

---

[1] Excluding Spain which was then engaged in civil war; but Spain's exports and imports had barely exceeded $100 million each during the preceding years. Dollars are understood here as predevaluation dollars.

for Brazilian coffee, automobiles for Turkish tobacco, and mining equipment for Mexican oil. In accordance with Hitler's plans German trade policy was primarily war-oriented and served to sustain the drive towards autarky. Thus Germany's attention was centered on southeastern Europe, which Berlin hoped to integrate permanently into the German economic orbit. Taking advantage of the desperate plight of that region, the Germans sought to establish their economic ascendancy by buying up at good prices, often substantially above world level, all raw material and food stocks of Hungary, Bulgaria, Rumania, Yugoslavia and Greece, and they even contracted for the purchase of crops for years in advance. Payment was made in machinery and other useful equipment to help these countries expand their production. (Occasionally, Germany claimed to be unable to make such deliveries or pay in cash and offered instead surplus items like bird cages or mouth harmonicas; but such incidents occurred only rarely, contrary to reports widely believed in the West at the time.)

Gradually, the Berlin government also induced these countries to shift to the growing of crops that Germany was importing from overseas and would no longer be able to buy there in case of war. A German-Hungarian agreement concluded in October 1933 provided for the experimental production of 25,000 tons of linseed to be purchased by Germany at a fixed price; the experiment was successful, and production was greatly increased during the following years. Similarly Germany prevailed upon Bulgaria to grow oil seeds and soy beans and upon Rumania to plant soy beans, cotton, and flax. Substantial amounts of German capital also were poured into the extracting and refining industries of these countries: bauxite production was expanded in Hungary, oil output in Rumania, and the mining of magnesite ore deposits in Yugoslavia. Since none of these commodities could be marketed anywhere but in Germany, the economic dependence of these nations on Germany increased correspondingly.

The Balkans countries tried to offset this trend by expanding their trade with the free currency countries; but while they could have bought a great deal from Britain and France, the latter had little need for the foodstuffs and raw materials southeastern Europe produced. Moreover, Britain's hands were tied by the Ottawa agreements which channeled much of its trade to the Dominions. Thus Western commercial contacts with the Balkans decreased rather than increased during the 1930's, and Germany's growing influence in that area remained unchallenged. It was markedly strengthened by Hitler's incorporation into Germany of Austria and parts of Czechoslovakia; as fellow members of the Little Entente, Yugoslavia and Rumania had close commercial relations with Czechoslovakia. By 1939, Germany controlled half of the foreign trade of Rumania and Yugoslavia and almost three-fourths of Bulgaria's.

To advance further its influence, Berlin also made skillful use of political frictions in the countries concerned. Rumania and Bulgaria, it will be recalled, had a long history of town-country tensions. To reduce these countries more fully to satellites, the Germans sought to block their industrialization (except for extracting and refining industries) and let it be known that they sympathized with those who wished to check the influence of industrialists and merchants. When the Balkan peasants learned of these professions, they became even more interested in doing business with Germany. The Iron Guard, Rumania's fascist organization, was made up mainly of peasants; it was they who in 1940 overthrew King Carol II and set up a strongly pro-Nazi government under General Jon Antonescu.

Governments and Domestic Economy.   As in international trade, governments also assumed an increasingly active part in economic affairs at home, even in the nontotalitarian countries. In most cases such government intervention was not the result of socialist inspiration. In Britain most economic reforms were introduced by Conservative governments. In France, too, not only the semisocialist Popular Front government of Léon Blum, but nonsocialist governments as well intervened in the economy, and most of the economic reforms that the Blum government enacted were retained by its non-socialist successors. Where socialist governments were in office, as in Sweden, these governments were guided, not by socialist doctrine, but by independent economic experts, many of whom were staunch advocates of private enterprise.

Thus Britain's National Government took over from the Bank of England control of the currency by means of an Exchange Equalization Fund; it assumed indirect control over prices by its tariff policies, and in the case of such basic industries as coal and steel exerted direct influence on prices and production. Similarly it forced down electricity rates by the establishment of a Central Electricity Board that bought power from private producers and distributed it through a "grid" for retail at a given price; stations producing above grid cost were forced out of business. Subsidies to housing, shipbuilding, and farming; government-sponsored marketing schemes for potatoes, pigs, and milk, guaranteed prices for wheat, oats, and barley made possible a substantial expansion of farming. The British government also took measures to help the unemployed—a Special Areas (Development and Improvement) Act sought to relieve the difficulties of the "distressed areas." (see p. 112)

In some respects French governments intervened more drastically in economic developments than their British counterparts; in other respects they were less active. To reduce France's excessively high prices and make its economy more competitive in the world market, the Laval government was empowered in 1935 to slash costs of production and prices. Laval decreed an across-the-board reduction by 10 per cent of prices and incomes—salaries, wages, rents, and interest payments. As in

Britain, some industries, such as shipping, and certain sectors of agriculture, especially wine and wheat growers, were subsidized to increase exports. Léon Blum's Popular Front government, on the other hand, reversed Laval's deflationary policies; it secured for the workers pay raises ranging from 7 to 15 per cent, and a reduction of the work week from forty-eight to forty hours at the same weekly wage, which amounted to an additional wage increase of 17 per cent. These measures were taken, not only to meet long standing social demands of the workers, but to revive the economy by putting more purchasing power into the hands of the masses. The Blum government nationalized some parts of the armament industries, especially military aviation, a step which was taken, however, for political rather than economic reasons—to "take the profit out of war." More important, by reorganizing the administrative structure of the Bank of France the government strengthened its control over interest and credit policies. And coming to the aid of the farmers, it set up a Wheat Board to stabilize agricultural prices—the one economic reform that proved effective. Finally, in the fall of 1936, Blum belatedly devalued the franc to halt the flight of capital from the country.

One of the countries in which government intervention in the economy was especially marked in the 1930's was Sweden. Here, too, the increased economic activity of the government grew out of efforts to overcome the Depression. Sweden's policies differed, however, from those of Britain and France in their concentration on the direct reduction of unemployment, with business the indirect beneficiary. Government grants and loans were channeled into the building and iron and steel industries which offered the largest possibilities of employment. Few funds, on the other hand, were set aside to bail out other industrial enterprises that had run into difficulties. The government itself developed a vast public works program providing for the construction of town halls, courthouses, hospitals, and fire stations; idle shipyards were reactivated by orders for both merchantmen and warships; harbors were improved and bridges built, swamp land drained and woodland reforested. The plans resembled in many ways those of the New Deal; yet unlike the latter, Sweden's campaign against unemployment was fully successful and unemployment all but wiped out by 1937. The greater success of the Swedish program was partly due to its vaster scope and partly to extraneous circumstances. Sweden's unemployment was never as large as that of the United States and the road to recovery was therefore much shorter. Recovery, moreover, was greatly aided by Britain's housing program for which Sweden supplied the lumber. Similarly, Sweden's highly developed arms industry was a main beneficiary of the armaments boom.

The Economics of Keynes.   Sweden's economic policies differed also from those of other democracies in their more systematic approach to the problems of unemployment and business stagnation. The French Popular

John Maynard Keynes.
(*Reprinted courtesy Brown Brothers*)

Front government, for example, thought that by raising wages and thus creating new effective demand it would also aid business; but failing to expand production, it discovered that price rises quickly wiped out the increase in purchasing power. Britain in turn slowed down its recovery by heavy taxation that impeded the accumulation of new capital. The Swedish government, on the other hand, sought to solve the problems with which it was faced within the framework of an overall plan that took into account the interdependence of all sectors of the economy and thus avoided the pitfalls of a piecemeal approach.

In the preparation of its plans Sweden was guided by the counsel of the "Stockholm school of economics," a group of economists who advocated many of the financial and economic policies which John Maynard Keynes was proposing at the same time in Britain and which are now commonly associated with his name. Like his Swedish colleagues, Keynes was concerned with the preservation of the private enterprise system, but had come to the conclusion that it could survive only if the government played a more active role in economic affairs and lent its help in the maintenance of full production and full employment. To this end he proposed the abandonment in times of crisis of some traditional economic precepts, such as the need for balanced budgets, and called for deficit financing, reduced taxation, and public works projects to stimulate both **241** production and consumption. Keynes' growing influence was due not only to the forcefulness of his arguments and his literary skill; he was listened to because he expressed ideas which were very much "in the air." In fact, he provided the theoretical underpinning for what some governments were already practicing without the benefit of such scholarly sanction. Furthermore, Keynesian economics offered a middle solution between laissez-faire passivity and socialism, attractive to those who realized that government intervention in the economy had become inevitable but were opposed to socialist planning. And by assigning to the consumer an important role in the proper functioning of the economy, Keynes also met the aspirations of those who saw one of the major tasks of the times in the raising of living standards and the more equitable distribution of what was being produced.

THE SOCIAL SCENE: OLD AND NEW TENSIONS

Social Conflicts. The 1920's had been characterized by sharp social friction; these tensions between workers and bourgeoisie continued into the 1930's. They were eventually suppressed in countries in which fascist or semifascist dictatorships were established—in Germany, Austria, and the Balkan countries—but class conflicts kept dominating the domestic stage in France, in Spain where they exploded into civil war in 1936, and in some of the smaller countries. On the whole the position of labor deteriorated during the 1930's, and it lost many of the social and political rights it had secured earlier; where the workers did improve their position as in France and Spain, subsequent developments deprived them again of most of these gains. There were but few exceptions to this trend, in some of the smaller democracies of northwestern Europe.

A number of factors accounted for the decline of labor's position. Except in the Scandinavian countries, the workers were without able and determined leaders; Chancellor Hermann Müller-Franken in Germany, Britain's Prime Minister J. Ramsay MacDonald, France's Socialist Premier of the mid-thirties, Léon Blum, were well-meaning, honorable men, but they lacked resourcefulness and determination and were unable to master the difficulties with which they were faced. In Germany and France the political impact of the working class also was weakened by its split into Socialist and Communist camps. In Britain, labor's morale suffered from the haunting spectre of continuing unemployment, and this mood of dejection persisted although labor's material lot kept improving during the 1930's; unemployment with its demoralizing prospect of idleness, dependence on others, and loss of self-respect remained a cause of constant anxiety which no economic advances could fully remove. Again, while the lower middle class had often joined forces with labor in the 1920's, in the 1930's it tended to cast its lot with the upper classes who stood for the maintenance of the status quo and were averse to social and economic changes. The feeling was widespread that this was no time for experiments—"we were so tired," France's President Albert Lebrun later described the prevalent mood, and a similar feeling of lassitude was noted in Britain by contemporary observers.

Demographic Developments. Unlike the democracies the dictatorships presented a picture of bustling activity and dynamic vitality. They did share with the former, however, the problem of inadequate birth rates— a trend more easily explained in the case of nations with low morale such as Britain and France than in that of Nazi Germany and Fascist Italy which seemed to abound in self-confidence and hopes for the future. Whatever the cause, even after the Depression had run its course, birth rates continued to drop in nearly all European countries until 1937 when most Western European countries began to record slight increases. The one important exception to this decline was Nazi Germany whose birth rate increased from 14.7 per 1,000 in 1933 to 18.0 in 1934 and 18.8 in 1937. Yet even in Germany's case, despite generous subsidies and other tokens of recognition to encourage the bearing of children (including illegitimate ones), the increased birth rate did not attain pre-Depression levels. The Italian government was even less successful in its efforts to encourage large families although it granted liberal allowances and tax privileges to large families while inflicting severe financial and social penalties on the unmarried. Italy's birth rate kept falling throughout most of the Fascist era (29.7 per 1,000 in 1921–1925, 26.8 in 1926–1930, 23.8 in 1931–1935, 22.2 in 1936). A slight increase in 1937 (22.9) did not exceed the rise noted in other European countries at that time.

This decline was not, however, accompanied by a corresponding decrease of Europe's population. On the contrary, with the exception of France, all European countries experienced net population increases. This was due partly to a universal drop of the death rate, as the result of the continued progress of medicine and public hygiene, and partly to prewar fertility, which accounted for the large number of people of child-bearing age. The fertility of the peoples of eastern and southern Europe declined, moreover, less markedly; while the population of the northwestern countries no longer reproduced itself (except in Ireland and the Netherlands), the birth rates of Italy, Poland, Hungary, and the Balkan countries still remained above the replacement level. Finally, overseas emigration which had drained off hundreds of thousands in earlier years was now reduced to a trickle. In absolute figures Europe's population thus continued to grow during the interwar period, from 345 million in 1920 to 399 million in 1939.

The Refugee Problem. The Bolshevik Revolution and the Russian Civil War drove large numbers of Russians from their homeland. According to League of Nations statistics, about 1.5 million Russian refugees sought asylum in Europe between 1917 and 1921. This influx caused no serious problems; the receiving countries had liberal immigration laws, and additional manpower was always needed in France and was welcomed just then in inflation-ridden Germany which enjoyed full employment. A number of charitable organizations also stood ready to help those who could not take care of themselves; large numbers of these latter, moreover, soon moved on to overseas countries. Thus, even though cultural assimilation proved difficult, economically the Russian exiles made quick readjustments. Many with professional backgrounds took up factory work or learned a trade; noblemen were known to make their living as taxi drivers, and generals exchanged their army uniform for that of the doorman at some restaurant or hotel. On the whole the Russian refugees disappeared quickly from the public stage and were soon forgotten.

When Hitler's persecution of political opponents and persons of Jewish descent drove hundreds of thousands from Germany in the 1930's, this new mass migration, although much smaller numerically than the Russian one, caused far more intense repercussions. Few of the Russians who went into exile were men of world renown; but among the German exiles were scientists like Albert Einstein and James Franck, authors of the stature of Thomas Mann, Arnold Zweig, and Alfred Döblin, and creative artists such as Arnold Schoenberg, the composer, and Walter Gropius, the architect of the *Bauhaus*. Moreover, while the political exile was a recurrent phenomenon of recent European history, the Jewish refugee was something unheard of in modern times, at least in the case of a supposedly highly civilized country such as Germany.

Sympathy and compassion for the German-Jewish *émigés* had to contend, however, with countervailing reactions. The migration from Germany got under way at a time when most countries had barely begun to overcome the Depression; hard put to find work for their own people, they were reluctant to receive the German exiles who might easily become public burdens. Others hesitated to accept any Germans, Jewish or Gentile, from ingrained suspicions that would not die down even in the special circumstances of the existing emergency. Above all, however, most governments had misgivings about admitting large numbers of Jewish refugees either because there existed strong anti-Semitic sentiments in their country or because they feared that such sentiments might develop if there were a large influx of Jews.

That the migration of Germany's Jews might become a major domestic issue in the receiving countries was in fact the hope of the Nazis. It was one of the reasons why they kept making life more unbearable for the Jews: they hoped in this way to drive increasing numbers of them into exile. At the same time they allowed the emigrants to take with them only an ever smaller portion of their possessions, and in the end most of them had to depart virtually penniless. Inevitably, other nations were torn by sharp disagreements whether to follow the dictates of their conscience and admit Hitler's victims or whether to bar their admission and spare their peoples the political and economic problems which the admission of Jewish refugees without means would create. The question stirred up bitter debates in many countries; it was the kind of divisive issue on which fascist movements were thriving. It became even more acute as the number of refugees grew with the incorporation of Austria and the Sudetenland into Germany and with the adoption of anti-Jewish legislation by Italy. While many thousands of Jews found new homes, others were unable to leave because of these difficulties. At the same time anti-Semitism, carefully nurtured by Nazi agents, was becoming more virulent throughout Europe and other parts of the world.

THE CULTURAL SCENE: THE TIME OF COMMITMENT

Literature. The literature of the immediate postwar era had been chiefly concerned with social and psychological problems and with new techniques of expression; most of its major representatives had eschewed any direct involvement in the political issues of the time. If they did take a stand, it was rarely reflected in their major works, but was set forth in lectures and articles composed for that special purpose.

Some of them continued to maintain this aloofness during the 1930's. In *Finnegan's Wake* James Joyce pursued his psychoanalytical probings and linguistic experiments and his endeavor to fuse past, present, and future into one all-embracing experience. Jules Romains, Roger Martin du Gard, and Georges Duhamel kept spinning out their massive epics of French society. Their fellow countryman, Jean Giono, acquired a growing audience with novels notable for their earthy simplicity, unencumbered by pessimistic forebodings, and appealing to many because of their outspoken pacifism. Yet in the darkening world of totalitarian challenges, writers felt increasingly that they could not dissociate themselves from the political and ideological struggles of their times. Outwardly, Thomas Mann stayed above the battles of the day in his magisterial work of the 1930's, the tetralogy *Joseph and His Brothers;* but his attempt to show that ancient myths can be treated rationally and explained psychologically and need not lead to fascist brutality and irrationality had clear political implications, as had the very choice of a Jewish theme at the time of Hitler's ascendancy. Above all, Mann was no longer noncommittal in his conclusions, but spoke out unequivocally in defense of humanistic values.

Like Mann's works some of T. S. Eliot's poems of the 1930's were more directly attuned to the issues of the day—the inhumanity of war and the idolization of the military leader (in *Triumphal March*), the statesman wrestling with an uncomprehending bureaucracy (*Difficulties of a States-man*), the quest for peace, the trend towards conformity, the reluctance to act (*Murder in the Cathedral*). Eliot still saw life as essentially futile in a confused and narrow-minded world, but he now held out hope for redemption through divine grace. To convey his message to a wider audience, he chose the drama as a means of communication, and he abandoned the allusive incohesion of his earlier days and wrote straight-forwardly and to the point. Other writers also made religious faith a major concern of theirs in their search for a release from the trials of the time. The religious revival was especially marked in France, where a group of distinguished writers gathered around the newly founded Catholic monthly *Esprit*, and the novelist François Mauriac found a constantly growing public for his tales of individuals tragically caught in the web of fate and ultimately finding release in religious faith.[2]

Other authors again felt that in a world of increasing injustice and oppression they had to engage more directly in the political battles of the day. Anxious to play their part in the fight against the forces threat-ening the freedom and dignity of the individual, they abandoned al-together the apolitical stance of their predecessors. Many of them believed democracy incapable of defending the values they held dear and felt drawn to Communism as a remedy they thought more effective against the evils they found so perturbing. Theirs was a "communism of the heart," arrived at, not primarily through the study of Marx or Lenin, but as an emotional reaction to existing conditions, or, as in the case of André Gide, in search of the lost Christian values of compassion and brotherhood. Among the best known of these writers in France were, besides Gide, the novelists, André Malraux and Louis Aragon, and in England, the poet Stephen Spender, and of the older generation, George Bernard Shaw.

Malraux's novels (*The Human Condition, Man's Hope*) may serve as a representative example of the "engaged" authors of the 1930's. Like his apolitical predecessors of the 1920's, Malraux (1901–   ) saw the loneliness of the individual and the pervasiveness of decay and disease; but he rejected the resignation of Proust or Kafka. He believed, and sought to prove by his revolutionary activities in China and as an aviator for the Spanish Republic during the Spanish Civil War, that meaning could be given to life (and death) by purposeful action. Malraux main-tained that such action would have to be collective and revolutionary since an individual by himself was helpless and only a revolution could

[2] The renewed concern with religion characterizes also the work of the British his-torian, Arnold Toynbee (1889–   ), who began publishing his multivolume *Study of History* in 1934 in reply to Spengler's *Decline of the West*. Like Spengler, Toynbee viewed history in terms of civilizations rather than peoples or periods; but unlike the German philosopher, he did not believe that all civilizations were doomed to perish eventually. Rather, he held that their fate depended on the creative and spiritual resources of their leaders, and he concluded that Western civilization could reach new heights by a return to religious faith and ethical values.

sweep away the absurdities of the existing social and political order. While he thought at the time—he is now a Gaullist—that this goal could best be attained through Communism, "his fidelity," as a recent critic has written, "was not to a single party, but to a set of values which that party might best protect." He was constantly preoccupied with the problem of preserving the valuable attributes of individualism in the face of the demands of collective action, and he was deeply concerned with the question to what extent he ought to accept the ruthless means of the party line to achieve the end of a better human order. (This same theme was taken up later by the Anglo-Hungarian writer Arthur Koestler in his classic novel *Darkness at Noon.*) As Malraux's novels show, he never found a satisfactory answer, and in the end he broke with Communism just as did most of the other authors who had been attracted by it.

A few writers, among them the novelists Louis-Ferdinand Céline in France, and Evelyn Waugh and Wyndham Lewis in Britain, seeing only confusion and indecision around them, were impressed with the discipline and vitality of the Nazis and Fascists, but the latter two soon came to change their views. Another prevalent attitude, pacifism, produced an avalanche of novels and plays depicting the horrors and degradation of war which found a large and receptive audience (Erich Maria Remarque, *All Quiet on the Western Front;* Beverly Nichols, *Cry Havoc;* R. C. Sheriff, *Journey's End*).

The Arts. Painting and sculpture were less affected by the currents of the times than literature. Surrealism and the abstract school continued to flourish; unlike the writers, artists did not modify their techniques to reach a wider audience. Many of them did feel that their unconventional style was as much a liberating force as any political challenge to the old order, but they found themselves under attack from both right and left. Nazi critics denounced their work as cultural Bolshevism, while Marxists retorted that if their work had any political impact, it was reactionary because it catered only to a small select audience, or even fascist, given its emphasis on the irrational. No totalitarian system could accept the individualist independence inherent in the new art, for it defied that rigid conformity on which all totalitarian regimes must rest.

Like their techniques, the artists' choice of subjects was not greatly influenced by the deepening crisis. One notable exception was Picasso's painting, *Guernica,* a striking surrealist protest against Nazi brutality in the Spanish Civil War. (The story is told that when German soldiers visited Picasso's studio in Paris during the occupation of France, he handed them postcard reproductions of Guernica. "Oh, you did this?" they would ask. "No, you did," he would answer.[3]) In many cases, how-

[3] Barbara Ives Beyer, "Art," in Julian Park, ed., *The Culture of France in Our Time* (Ithaca, 1954), pp. 67–68.

The Nightmare of Total War: Picasso's *Guernica*. (On extended loan to The Museum of Modern Art, New York, from the artist, P. Picasso. Reprinted courtesy The Museum of Modern Art)

ever, artistic aloofness was not caused by political indifference, but rather by a refusal to subject the creativity of the artists to political dictates. While painters were willing to enter political commitments in their personal life, their art was to remain untouched by the political and ideological battles of the day.

Science. Science continued to help make life longer and healthier—at least in short-range perspective. The ill effects of poor nutrition in war and depression stimulated increased research in the field of biochemistry, with important results. Much was learned about the substance and functions of vitamins, about hormones and glands, the nature of viruses, and the chemistry of the blood. New medications were developed, among which penicillin and sulfanilamide drugs proved especially effective against various types of infection.

In the field of genetics, as in physics, it was found that nature proceeds by spurts rather than by a continuous process of evolution, as Darwin had thought. Species arose, it was suggested, from the perpetuation of genes and not, as had earlier been assumed, from their fusion. Experiments showed that individual genes which had been dominant for some generations might become less decisive as the particular characteristics which they transmitted did not respond adequately to environmental challenges; in their place, other genes which passed on more responsive characteristics came to be dominant in the adjustment process. These findings were bolstered by the discovery that external stimuli such as radiation could produce genetic mutations. Taken together with the possibility of artificial insemination, this opened up wholly new vistas for controlling the development of the human race.

The dangerous possibilities entailed in these discoveries were more apparent immediately than any potential benefits. At this very time, in the mid-1930's, the Nazis embarked on their efforts to improve the German race by means of mass sterilizations of "asocial" elements, medical experiments on human guinea pigs, and that crusade against "racially inferior" groups which was to reach its inhuman climax during World War II in what was appropriately called "genocide." In 1936, sensing the awesome potentialities of science, the president of the British Society for the Advancement of Science, Sir Josiah Stamp, called on scientists to awaken to their social responsibilities.

Other threats to mankind's existence arose in the field of nuclear physics. Earlier investigations had disclosed that the atom was not an ultimate unit, but a structure composed of a number of constituent particles held together by an enormous amount of energy. Beginning in 1932 with the discovery of the neutron, most of these particles were identified, and this increased knowledge paved the way for the splitting of the atom and the release of the energy stored in it. The feasibility of this process was demonstrated by two German physicists, Otto Hahn and Fritz Strassmann, in 1938. The technological problems involved in the utilization of this discovery were subsequently resolved in the United States.

13

Domestic Politics in
Non-Nazi Europe

Although Hitler's appearance on the international stage aroused uneasiness throughout Europe, most countries remained preoccupied with their domestic concerns. Unemployment, class tensions, and political instability tended to overshadow the international complications arising from Hitler's ascendance. If Nazism affected the life of the average European, it was as an internal problem rather than as an issue of foreign policy: its most immediate effect made itself felt in the Nazi impact upon native fascist movements.

To the extent that Nazism (and Fascism) aroused anxieties as external threats, such concern again created policy problems that were as much domestic as foreign. To see these threats for what they were meant to acknowledge the fact that one might have to suffer hardships and sacrifices in defense of his country. If millions were ready to pay this price if they must, others wondered whether they ought to help safeguard an economic and political system in which they no longer had faith. In consequence the question of whether to react to Hitler by accommodation or arms became a deeply divisive issue.

The problem of relations with Germany created divisions also in fascist and near-fascist countries. Whatever the attitude of their governments, large numbers of Italians, Poles, and Hungarians continued to look on the Germans with strong distrust, and at least the Italians were as anxious as the British and French to stay out of war. Plagued with economic problems not unlike those of the democracies, the authoritarian countries thus faced many of the same difficulties.

BRITAIN: THE QUEST FOR PEACE

The National Government. Preoccupation with domestic concerns was the hallmark of British politics during the 1930's. It was also reflected in Britain's foreign policy, which strove above all for the preservation of peace—a goal inspired not only by a deep-seated aversion to war, but also by the desire to be left alone. This isolationist attitude helps to explain the inconsistencies in the measures proposed to prevent war.

Most Britons viewed peace as the result of disarmament; they refused to listen to those who warned that in the face of Hitler's rearmament peace could be preserved only by increased armaments. In the fall of 1933 several "National" Liberals withdrew from the government on the grounds that it was not working with sufficient energy for disarmament. Students at Oxford arranged a full-dress debate on the motion that "this House refuses to fight for King and Country" and adopted it by a large majority—a performance which may have been no more than a prank, but a type of prank unlikely to have been performed at any other time. A "Peace Ballot" produced an enormous response in favor of armament limitations and collective security; but whereas 90 per cent favored the imposition of economic sanctions on any aggressor, only 60 per cent approved of military measures. Similarly, the feeling was widespread that only the League ought to deal with aggression, but the advocates of League action against aggressors refused to increase their own armaments to lend greater strength to the League.

The government, while uneasy about Hitler's intentions, did nothing to dispel the existing illusions. Ramsay MacDonald, still nominally its head, was both mentally and physically incapable of leadership. Baldwin, the second-in-command, was as always averse to dealing with matters of foreign policy, and Sir John Simon, the Foreign Secretary, was a distinguished lawyer without experience in foreign affairs whose policies were shaped by his detached legalism. The driving force in the cabinet was Neville Chamberlain, the Chancellor of the Exchequer, who retained the outlook of the business executive he once had been and tended to approach problems of politics as if they were business transactions. He favored some moderate rearmament in the face of the growing Nazi menace—within the limits of a balanced budget. "Common prudence would seem to indicate some strengthening of our defenses," he wrote

King George V with his sons, the Prince of Wales (later Edward VIII and Duke of Windsor) and the Duke of York (later George VI). (*Reprinted courtesy Wide World Photos*)

at the time, "and happily we are no longer expecting a deficit at the end of the financial year." But he continued to worry about the economic effects of rearmament, and to Churchill's demand that Britain "must lay aside every impediment in raising her own strength," his answer was that it would be folly to take this advice, for the expenditures involved would impair trade for a long time, undermine confidence in the country's economic stability, and greatly reduce the revenue.

Next to unemployment (reduced from 3 million in 1933 to an apparently irreducible 1.3 million in 1937), the government was primarily concerned with Britain's future relations with India. In 1935 a Government of India Bill was enacted which granted British India a large measure of legislative autonomy on both the federal and provincial level and gave Indians a greater degree of participation in the executive.

If the India Act was a sign of the waning powers of the British Empire, the nation-wide celebrations on the occasion of the Silver Jubilee of King George's reign that same year provided an impressive demonstration of national unity in the mother country. Neville Chamberlain told something of the popular mood when he wrote at the time: **252** "My sentiments were admirably expressed by a stout flower stall holder

in Strutton Ground who said . . . 'Ain't it glorious to be an Englishman?
This'll teach 'em.' Curiously enough the same phrase was reported from
Birmingham by Geoffrey Lloyd [one of Baldwin's aides]. He says the
poorest streets in Ladywood were decked with flags and streamers and
everywhere he was met by the slogan 'This'll show 'em.' " Chamberlain's
interpretation of that slogan is not without interest: " 'Em I conclude
means the foreigner or the Communist or anyone who isn't a true blue
John Bull." Hitler was not singled out among those who needed to be
impressed.

In the fall of 1935 Baldwin, who had meanwhile replaced MacDonald
as Prime Minister, called new elections. The Conservatives ran on a platform of moderate rearmament and collective security and promised, in
somewhat ambiguous terms, to support the League in its efforts to settle
the war between Italy and Ethiopia (see p. 307). Labor asked for more
determined League action against Mussolini without making clear how
far it wanted the League to go. At the same time it criticized the government for spending money on arms rather than allocating more aid to the
unemployed. It pledged itself, if elected, to help the distressed areas,
nationalize banking, coal, iron and steel, transportation, electricity, and
cotton, and to work for worldwide disarmament. The government retained control of the House of Commons, but its majority was reduced:
it won 428 seats, 385 of which went to the Conservatives, while Labor
increased its representation to 154. Opposition Liberals secured twenty-
five seats.

The Abdication Crisis.   In January 1936 King George V died. He was
succeeded by his eldest son, Edward VIII (1894–   ). The new King
lacked the sense of duty and disciplined self-restraint of his father, and
his accession aroused some anxiety among those who knew him well.
"I do hope he 'pulls up his socks' and behaves himself now he has heavy
responsibilities," Chamberlain worried, "for unless he does he will soon
pull down the throne." These fears increased when some months later
the King expressed his determination to marry Mrs. Wallis Simpson, an
American-born divorcée who was about to get a second divorce. Edward's
decision raised serious religious and constitutional questions. As King,
he was the head of the Anglican Church, which disapproved of the marriage of divorced persons. Marriage to Mrs. Simpson thus would have
created a delicate religious problem. Difficulties would have arisen also
over the coronation of the new queen which is a church-conducted cere-
mony. Beyond this, according to British constitutional practice, a King
must not marry against the advice of his ministers. As it was, Prime
Minister Baldwin assumed that the bulk of the British people disapproved
of the proposed marriage, and he informed the monarch that the cabinet
could not give its assent to Edward's marriage plans. He warned the
King that the government would have to resign if its advice were not

heeded. This, in turn, would have drawn the King into a public political controversy and would have gravely impaired the prestige of the monarchy. But the King was not without supporters, among them the large newspaper chains of Lord Beaverbrook and Lord Rothermere. And among prominent individuals, Winston Churchill, stirred by a sense of vassal's loyalty to his liege, rushed to the aid of his monarch.

The "King's matter" thus threatened both Britain's national unity and the monarchy as an institution. But it was not merely a British crisis, for Edward VIII was also King of the several Dominions. The Dominion governments also declared themselves opposed to Edward's marriage to Mrs. Simpson, and they rejected as equally unacceptable the King's suggestion of a morganatic marriage which would have left his wife a private person without royal status and would have barred any children of the marriage from succeeding to the throne.

In the face of this opposition, Edward abdicated on December 10, 1936 and was succeeded by his brother, the Duke of York, who ascended the throne as George VI (1895–1952). Owing to Baldwin's skill the crisis was settled calmly and speedily, without harm to the monarchy, nation, or Commonwealth. As the historian D. C. Somervell has written, "the incident was soon seen to have affected no one but King Edward himself. He disappeared, and in a few months it was exactly as if he had never been, and George VI had succeeded George V."

Rearmament vs. Appeasement. Once the crisis was settled and the coronation of the new King celebrated with the traditional colorful ceremonial, the government could devote itself fully again to other pressing problems. Baldwin, worn out and ailing, retired a few days after the coronation in May 1937, and Chamberlain took his place. The new Prime Minister stepped into a melancholy inheritance. Collective security had proved nonexistent; the Spanish Civil War, raging by then for almost a year, threatened to turn into a European conflagration; Japan was expanding its empire in the Far East; and Germany kept getting stronger while the French were consuming themselves in domestic disputes. Rearmament had proceeded slowly even though armament expenditures had risen from £103 million, or 12.9 per cent of the budget, in 1932–33 to £186.7 million, or 22.4 per cent of the budget, in 1936–37. (Germany that same year was believed, erroneously, to have spent more than five times as much on armaments; the actual rate was a little over twice as much.) The greatest progress was made in the expansion of the Royal Air Force, in recognition of Britain's new vulnerability to air attack. But even here advances were slower than expected, partly because of the lack of industrial facilities, but also because of financial restrictions—rearmament was not to unsettle the economy.

Chamberlain, moreover, was still hopeful of reaching an understanding with Hitler and Mussolini. Having never had any dealings with brutal and unscrupulous cynics like these two men, he remained convinced that they were basically reasonable and concerned with the welfare of their fellow men, whatever their political views and immediate interests might be. He had no faith in the League of Nations, but he felt that he could come to terms with the two dictators in direct negotiations in which their justified grievances would be removed, and these efforts he did not wish to jeopardize by a precipitate rearmament program.

Public opinion on the whole approved of Chamberlain's approach; Churchill's warnings that an inadequately armed Britain would only invite further aggression went unheeded. His impassioned appeals were shrugged off as excessive rhetoric, and the fact that he had been an outspoken supporter of King Edward during the abdication crisis reinforced a widespread feeling that he lacked balanced judgment.

It was not until after the Munich crisis in the fall of 1938 (see p. 321) that rearmament was undertaken on a vast scale and with full public support. In April 1939, after Hitler's occupation Prague, Britain also introduced military conscription. The step had symbolic rather than practical significance since it provided only for the drafting of men aged twenty and twenty-one for a six-months training period; but it was the first time in its history that the country had resorted to conscription in peacetime, and as such the measure was indicative of its changing attitude. Liberals and Laborites rejected the draft as useless and a threat to freedom, yet the bulk of the two parties supported the other rearmament efforts of the government. "The country feels stronger and more united," noted one observer, "had not Munich been tried as a gesture for peace and failed." The nation's sense of danger was now aroused and the need to prepare for war no longer questioned.

Radicalism on Right and Left. Sir Oswald Mosley's British Union of Fascists was active throughout the 1930's. It never had more than 20,000 members, but its unorganized following was considerably larger, and it drew crowds of several thousands in the unending series of meetings it held all over the country. It also had the support of Lord Rothermere's widely read *Daily Mail* and *Sunday Pictorial* and, thanks to the munificence of Mosley himself and some other well-to-do sponsors, had ample financial resources. In June 1934 it staged a mass meeting at London's Olympia Stadium that was attended by some 15,000 people while an overflow crowd of 5,000 had to remain outside. The meeting was marred by brutal beatings of hecklers and other violent incidents that received wide publicity, and many who had sympathized with the Blackshirts now withdrew their support, among them Lord Rothermere. Meetings and marches continued, frequently ending in violent clashes, but except in the London area the movement ceased to grow. Mosley himself, a persuasive speaker of great personal charm, was too much the product of the English public school system to develop that unrestrained toughness that is a prerequisite of successful fascist leadership. Early in 1937 the Union participated in election for the London County Council and received some 20 per cent of the vote in three East London districts; however, in municipal elections six months later it suffered defeats throughout the country—an experience that was repeated in October 1938. After that, the movement, torn by dissension, declined rapidly.

Britain's Communist Party also remained a minuscule group during this period, although the number of its members and sympathizers increased during the Spanish Civil War. Communist efforts, however, to form a "united front" against Nazism and Fascism were rejected by the Labor Party. While some left-wing Laborites approved of the formation of such a "popular front" and eventually were expelled from the party, the party as a whole remained as anti-Communist as it was anti-fascist.

Ireland.   Britain's relations with Ireland were troubled throughout the 1930's. In 1932 De Valera became Prime Minister of the Dublin government and at once took steps to make Ireland entirely independent of Great Britain. A new Irish citizenship was created, judicial ties with Britain were cut, and government debts to Britain stemming from earlier Irish land purchases, repudiated. Britain retaliated by imposing special duties on imports from Ireland; Ireland in turn imposed duties on British coal, iron, steel, and cement. After the abdication of Edward VIII, the Irish Free State withheld official recognition of George VI. A new constitution in 1937 created "a sovereign independent democratic state" of Eire encompassing as "national territory" all of Ireland.

After this, tensions began to subside. An election held in Northern Ireland in February 1938 rejected unification by a large majority, and De Valera abandoned his efforts to bring Ulster into Eire. Shortly afterwards Britain and Eire concluded a number of agreements which rendered relations between the two countries more normal. The most important concession the British government made was the abandonment of three naval bases on Irish soil which Britain had retained until then in order to protect more effectively the approaches to its own shores and to safeguard its lines of communications across the Atlantic.

FRANCE: THE DECLINE OF THE THIRD REPUBLIC

The Sixth of February.   Like Britain, France was relatively little concerned with foreign affairs during the months following Hitler's assumption of power. Internal problems—economic stagnation, unemployment, the budget—claimed most of the country's attention, and this preoccupation was reflected also in the growing domestic unrest. The recurrent changes of government, over seemingly minor questions, the whimsicalities of parliament—what one observer has called the musical chairs atmosphere of French politics—encouraged continued attacks on the parliamentary-democratic regime and sparked the growth of the anti-republican leagues. In February 1934, the growing discontent exploded into large-scale riots in Paris.

The disturbances were touched off by a financial scandal—the shady transactions of one Serge Stavisky who had floated a series of fraudulent bonds on behalf of the municipal pawnshop of Bayonne in southwestern France. The fraud could not have been perpetrated without accomplices highly placed in the government, and letters published in the rightist press established a link between Stavisky and Albert Dalimier, the Minister of Colonies. Further investigations revealed that Stavisky had had numerous brushes with the law, but had never been brought to trial for any of his offenses—evidently because of his good connections with the police, politicians, and members of the judiciary. To rightist groups the Stavisky affair was welcome proof of the corruption of the Republic, and their suspicions deepened when a few days after these disclosures the press reported that Stavisky had comitted suicide in his Alpine hide-out just when the police were about to arrest him. It was widely, though probably wrongly, believed that the police had killed Stavisky on instructions from Paris because his testimony would have embarrassed many prominent persons.

The government of Premier Camille Chautemps, having obtained Dalimier's resignation, hoped to ride out the storm, but in the end was forced to step down. Chautemps' place was taken by Edouard Daladier (1884–   ), a heavy-set, grim-looking Radical Socialist from Provence, who gave the impression of strength and determination, but was in reality a cautious, slow-moving tactician carefully threading his way between right and left. (One of his first acts was to fire the Paris Commissioner of Police, Jean Chiappe, whom the left suspected of pro-fascist sympathies; yet so as not to antagonize the right, he offered Chiappe the highest post in his gift, the Residency-General in Morocco, which Chiappe, however, refused. Daladier compounded his difficulties when he removed the head of the *Sureté*, France's central police authority, and blandly appointed him director of Paris' famous old theater, the *Comédie Française*.)

On February 6, 1934, when Daladier presented his new government to the Chamber of Deputies, the rightist organizations called their followers into the streets. In the course of the evening several thousand demonstrators converged on the Chamber and clashed with the police. The demonstrations grew quickly into a full-fledged riot that raged until after midnight. When order had been restored, total casualties of both sides amounted to 1,450, among them fifteen dead.

The "Government of National Union." It is unlikely that the rioters planned to take over the government; had they intended to seize power, they would doubtless have tried to occupy the ministries, communications centers, and other key spots. Their march on the Chamber suggests that they wished only to remove the Daladier cabinet in favor of one of more rightist complexion. This they achieved. Daladier resigned on the following day to be succeeded by a "Government of National Union," headed by former President Gaston Doumergue and including a number of ex-Premiers such as Herriot, Tardieu, Laval, and Barthou, and as War Minister, Marshal Pétain, the aged hero of Verdun.

With the help of special decree powers, the Doumergue government was able to improve the financial situation; but since it relied mainly on a reduction of expenditures and increased taxes to achieve its objective, unemployment continued to grow. Doumergue's primary concern was a constitutional reform that would strengthen the executive and give France a more stable government. Yet in presenting the plan directly to the nation in a series of radio broadcasts, over the head of some of his cabinet members and the Chamber of Deputies, Doumergue aroused suspicions of dictatorial ambitions, and in November the "Government of National Union" broke up. During the next year and a half there followed another succession of short-lived cabinets, one of which lasted for only a day. At the insistence of the Bank of France which opposed the devaluation of the franc, these governments pursued deflationary policies of price-cutting, reduction of pensions and salaries, and other retrenchments. These measures caused new hardships and resentments without solving the country's economic difficulties. In effect, they helped to pave the way for the victory of the leftist parties in the parliamentary elections of April and May 1936.

The Popular Front.   The victory of the left was due above all, however, to the formation of the so-called Popular Front, an alliance of Socialists, Communists, and Radicals concluded during 1934 and 1935 to check the growth of French fascism and secure comprehensive social and economic reforms. The Communists took the lead in seeking a rapprochement with the Socialists—whether they acted on their own or on instruction from the Comintern is not clear; in any event the Seventh Comintern Congress in 1935 endorsed this policy of collaboration (see p. 295). The Popular Front produced its first noteworthy results in the French municipal elections of May 1935, with the Communists the main beneficiaries.

In the light of this manifest trend to the left, a growing number of Radicals urged that their party join the Popular Front to improve its electoral fortunes in the parliamentary elections in 1936. Only the Popular Front seemed prepared to deal with the increasing violence of the rightist leagues. In sharp contrast to the growing lawlessness on the right, the Communists were careful to act with decorum, making it easier for hesitant Radicals to accept collaboration with them. An electoral program was hammered out jointly by a committee of Socialists, Communists, and Radicals; divided into three sections—(1) defense of freedom, (2) defense of peace, and (3) economic demands—it called under (1) for the dissolution of the fascist leagues and greater freedom for labor unions, under (2) for collective security to be safeguarded by the League of Nations, the nationalization of armament industries, and progressive disarmament, and under (3) for social and economic policies closely resembling those of the New Deal. Agreement was also reached on the collaboration of the three parties in the elections: they would run separate tickets on the first ballot, but in the second round would support joint candidates in those districts in which a rightist might otherwise win. The need for a closing of ranks was further brought home to the left when the Socialist leader, Léon Blum, who as a Jew was the special target of rightist attacks, was brutally beaten by members of the *Action Française;* the incident pointed up, for all to see, the ruthlessness of the radical right.

The election campaign was exceptionally bitter. The Popular Front made the most of the continued large-scale unemployment, the plight of the farmer, and the threat of the leagues; the rightists on their part warned against the Bolshevization of France. Foreign policy played a subordinate role in the debates even though Hitler had marched into the Rhineland less than two months before. Thanks to its electoral alliances, the Popular Front won a clearcut victory over the rightist parties, it secured 62 per cent of the seats although its combined popular vote increased by only 2 per cent over that of 1932. Within the Popular Front, however, some striking changes took place: the Radicals were reduced from 159 to 116 seats, whereas the Socialists increased their representation from 97 to 146 and became the largest party in the new Chamber. The Communists, doubling their popular vote, emerged with 72 deputies (as against 12 in 1932)—in part a tribute to their skillful campaign in which they played down Marxist themes and invoked the spirit of Joan of Arc and the Marseillaise. Corresponding to the shift to the far left in the Popular Front, the extremist groups on the right scored some gains while the moderates were the main losers. The divisions in France's body politic kept growing wider.

The Blum Government. As head of the Socialist Party, which was both the largest party and the one holding a middle position between Radicals and Communists, Léon Blum (1872–1950) was the logical head of a Popular Front government. In his early sixties, the scion of a well-to-do family of silk ribbon manufacturers, one-time theater critic and fastidious esthete, Blum was an unlikely leader of a workers party. Indeed, he never felt quite at home with its rank-and-file, and to the latter he always was "Monsieur Blum" rather than "Comrade." But he was a man of strong social convictions, of courage and unchallenged integrity, and as such he commanded respect.

Blum found it less easy than he had thought to form the new govern-

Premier Léon Blum. *(Reprinted courtesy Brown Brothers)*

ment. The Communists refused to enter the cabinet and would merely pledge their support in the Chamber of Deputies; without responsibility for the government's policies, they thus remained free to criticize any measures and pose as the conscience of the Popular Front. Negotiations with the Radicals also were difficult, and it was not until June 3, a month after the second elections, that the Blum government could take office.

By this time economic life in France was in near-total disarray. Since the last week in May a wave of sit-in strikes had been sweeping across the country. In the main the strikes appear to have been spontaneous, spreading from Paris to the other industrial centers. Their purpose was partly to speed up the formation of the new government, and partly to strengthen Blum's hand and ensure the enactment of the reforms promised in the electoral program of the Popular Front. Although almost two million workers were involved, there was no violence and no physical damage; the strikers observed remarkable discipline, arranged the sit-ins in rotating shifts, and whiled away the time in the plants by dances, games, and community sings. The strikes, moreover, did not involve banks, railroads, and public utilities, and the maintenance of these essential services made tolerable the hardships imposed by the work stoppage.

Blum brought together labor and management to negotiate a settlement, and the frightened employers agreed to the workers' demands for a forty-hour week, wage increases, paid vacations, and collective bargaining. Parliament soon afterwards enacted bills anchoring the forty-hour week, paid vacations (two weeks per year), and the right to collective bargaining in the statutes. Other reforms followed. The management of the Bank of France was reorganized to give the state effective control over the policies of the Bank in accordance with the promise of the Popular Front to turn the Bank of France into France's bank. Similarly the government was authorized to purchase, before March 31, 1937, any enterprise manufacturing or trading in armaments—a power of which the government, however, could make only limited use because of a shortage of funds. In fulfillment of another electoral pledge, the government also dissolved the paramilitary rightist leagues, but did not prevent them from reconstituting themselves as political parties. Finally, concerned with the health and happiness of the lower classes, it developed a series of leisure-time programs, arranged reduced railroad fares and inexpensive hostelries for low-income groups, and sponsored sports and other recreational activities.

Yet these reforms did not bring France the hoped for stability and prosperity. The increased purchasing power of the workers failed to stimulate production and was wiped out by price rises; worse, the wage increases and new fringe benefits undermined further France's competitive position in the world market. Together with the proposed nationalization of armaments plants, they also discouraged arms manufacturers from expanding production, in spite of the darkening international situation. Moreover, frightened by the advent of the Popular Front, much private capital was transferred abroad for safer investments in the United States, Britain, and Switzerland. Finally, there was some deliberate sabotage of the efforts of the Blum government through willful production cutbacks and the refusal to make new investments. But the government also made some serious mistakes. That its reforms were enacted at a very inopportune time is obvious, yet given the mood of the workers, they could not be postponed. Blum could, however, have mitigated their worst effects by devaluing the franc to increase exports and by establishing tight controls over foreign exchange. He hesitated to take these steps, hoping to reconcile the business community by his restraint. When he finally did devalue the franc in September 1936, prices had risen so high that the measure had little effect.

The continued economic difficulties led to renewed political trouble, after a relatively calm summer. The Communists turned against Blum for his failure to effect further reforms. They also assailed him for his refusal to aid the Madrid government in Spain's Civil War, and there were new demonstrations and strikes. This in turn perturbed the Radicals, most of whom were opposed to an intervention in Spain, and they began to attack the Communists. At the same time the rightist extremists maligned the government with new confidence; Blum's Minister of the Interior, Roger Salengro, was driven to suicide by their trumped up charges of wartime desertion.

With the Popular Front disintegrating and the nation divided on most social and economic issues, Blum called a halt to further reforms. But inaction was no solution to the country's difficulties. France's financial condition continued to deteriorate, with strikes curbing production and taxation falling off, and all this at a time when international developments called for increased expenditures and a greater armament effort. When finally in June 1937 Blum asked for authority to impose a capital levy and establish foreign exchange controls, his request was rejected by the Senate. Discouraged and tired, the Premier resigned.

Swing to the Right.   There followed another succession of short-lived cabinets, two of them headed by Chautemps, a nondescript Radical, and a third once again by Léon Blum. The first and the third still were nominally based on the Popular Front, now reduced to an uneasy alliance of Radicals and Socialists, but they no longer had the reformist élan of the early days of Blum's first ministry. Blum's second government in March 1938, immediately after Hitler's annexation of Austria, lasted for only three weeks; its fall marked the permanent end of the Popular Front. Under Daladier as Premier, the Radicals turned to the right to form a new coalition.

The Popular Front collapsed not only because of its internal disintegration, but also because its program with its emphasis on domestic problems no longer was relevant in the face of the deepening international crisis. Until the fall of Austria, most Frenchmen had been comparatively little concerned with foreign affairs—when Hitler annexed Austria in March 1938, the country was finally aroused to face the reality of the Nazi menace. This reaction, however, was not uniform; while there were widespread demands, primarily on the left, for increased armaments and a strong stand against Germany, the bulk of the right called for an accommodation with Hitler. Between these two camps Daladier steered his cautious course, stepping up the armament program, but abandoning Czechoslovakia to Germany.

Domestically the government followed the lead of its Finance Minister, Paul Reynaud (1878–1966), who was mainly concerned with restoring the confidence of the business community in France's economy. The forty-hour week was abolished, overtime pay regulated, incentives offered to those who repatriated their foreign investments, and a 2 per cent surtax levied upon all incomes regardless of size. A general strike called by the unions in protest against these measures petered out quickly; only a minority of the demoralized workers answered the call, and the government, equipped with special emergency powers, dealt with the strikers by drafting workers of railroads and public services into continued service. Economically Reynaud's policies were successful; production increased, the franc which had been devalued twice more in 1937 and 1938 and still kept declining, was finally stabilized, as were prices, and capital that had been transferred abroad did return to France. But since no attempt was made at any structural reforms of the antiquated economy, the revival did not carry France's productivity beyond what it had been prior to the Depression.

The fact was that the country was in the grip of a spiritual and moral paralysis that prevented the reorganization and rejuvenation of its institutions. The nation remained deeply divided socially and politically in the face of the Nazi menace, and defeatism and apathy kept gaining ground. Parliament ceased to function; after Munich it surrendered its legislative prerogatives permanently to the government, granting it special decree powers that were periodically renewed. Militarily, this resigned attitude was reflected in the defense strategy of the Maginot Line and in the reluctance of the French general staff to consider the proposals of Colonel Charles de Gaulle to form armored corps that could take the initiative in military operations. Gertrude Stein, the American writer then living in Paris, noted that people were no longer interested in events, but only in mere existence. In this spirit France entered the war against Germany in 1939.

THE SCANDINAVIAN AND LOW COUNTRIES: OASES OF PROGRESS

The Fight Against the Depression.   In the smaller democracies of northwestern Europe, just as in Britain and France, efforts to overcome the Depression centered around the key question of whether this goal could best be achieved by the traditional policies of retrenchment, balanced budgets, and stable currencies or whether new solutions such as currency devaluation, reduced taxes, public work projects, and other methods of pump priming should be applied. The answers varied, but in retrospect it can be said that the tempo of economic recovery depended on the speed and extent with which the second alternative was adopted. Sweden, as will be recalled, led the way; shortly afterwards Denmark embarked on similar policies of devaluation, subsidized prices, and other forms of relief, and although the Danish approach, unlike Sweden's, was pragmatic rather than systematic, it too scored impressive results. Norway's recovery was slower, propelled chiefly by the gradual improvement of world trade; but when in 1935 the Norwegian government adopted a more active role in fighting unemployment, conditions improved more rapidly. Belgium's experience was similar; its recovery got fully under way only in 1935 when Premier Paul van Zeeland launched a program very similar to the American New Deal. The Netherlands, on the other hand, under the cautious leadership of Hendrik Colijn, who was Prime Minister throughout the 1930's, hesitated to abandon the path of traditional economics, except for a devaluation of the guilder in 1936. Unemployment remained high, and while the devaluation helped to increase exports, as an isolated measure it was of only limited benefit to the Dutch economy.

Domestic Politics.   The experience of the Scandinavian and Low Countries also pointed up the close interrelationship between political and economic conditions. Speed and extent of the recovery were proportionate to the degree of political unity that prevailed in the various countries. The Swedish and Danish governments whose economic policies were the most successful also had the broadest political support while Norway and Belgium were slower to achieve the needed political unity. Collaboration between the major political parties was least satisfactory in the Netherlands, and the failure of the bourgeois and socialist parties to achieve an understanding, as they did in the other four countries, accounts in part for the Netherlands' inability to resolve its economic difficulties.

Neither communism nor fascism played a significant role in these countries during the 1930's, but it is not without interest that fascism acquired some following, for a brief moment, in the two countries whose economic recovery was slowest, Belgium and the Netherlands.[1] In Belgium a young journalist, Léon Degrelle, founded the fascist-oriented Rexist Party. Rexism appealed to the hard-pressed middle class and drew some support from Flemish nationalists; but it was financed chiefly by Belgian business and noblemen who hoped with its help to protect their social and economic prerogatives. In the elections of 1936 the Rexists won 21 seats in the Chamber of Representatives and 12 in the Senate. Flushed with victory, Degrelle challenged Van Zeeland to a direct contest in a Brussels by-election in 1937, but suffered an ignominious defeat. When he was received with much fanfare on visits to Berlin and Rome, he became suspect of being the stooge of Hitler and Mussolini, and he quickly lost a large part of his following. In the elections of 1939 the Rexists retained only four of their seats in the lower house and five in the Senate.

In the Netherlands a National Socialist Movement was founded in 1932 by a civil engineer, Anton Mussert. It obtained 7.9 per cent of the vote in the provincial elections of 1935, but as German Nazism cast its darkening shadow over the Netherlands, the Dutch party declined and in the national elections of 1937 received only 4.2 per cent of the vote. Its main effect was to bring about a rapprochement of the democratic parties, and in 1939 the Social Democrats entered the government for the first time.

[1] A Nazi Party gained some following in the German-settled parts of southern Denmark, but as a localized German phenomenon and small in numbers it need not concern us in this context.

SPAIN: REPUBLICAN INTERLUDE

Early Reforms. The history of the Spanish Republic bears a striking resemblance to that of the Weimar Republic. Like its German counterpart, it owed its inception much more to the internal disintegration of the monarchy than to the efforts of its supporters. Again, as in the German case, the supporters of the Spanish Republic were held together only by tenuous ties, and the future of Spanish democracy depended, as did that of all other European democracies, on whether the middle class and the workers would be able to create jointly a solid foundation for a stable progressive government. Such collaboration required skillful, inspiring statesmanship—a prerequisite all the more necessary in the special circumstances of Spanish politics since Spaniards incline to uncompromising positions. Yet again, like the Weimar Republic, the new Spanish state lacked strong and inspiring leaders around which the people could rally. The ablest of the Republican statesmen, Manuel Azaña (1880–1940), who eventually became President of the Spanish Republic, was a patently sincere, dedicated man, not without eloquence, but self-contained and withdrawn and thus not always aware of the existing realities. By character and taste, Azaña was a blend of Brüning and Léon Blum, with an admixture of Spanish temper, and the tragic role he played in the history of his country was not unlike theirs.

Elections for a constituent Cortes in June 1931 produced a substantial majority for the Republican parties, yet even at this early moment the Republic was already under attack. The opening gun was fired by the Spanish Primate, Pedro Cardinal Segura, who in a pastoral letter praised ex-King Alfonso and warned the Catholic faithful not to remain "quiet and idle" as efforts were made to destroy all religion. His attack touched off a series of Anarchist-organized church burnings in Madrid, Valencia, and Malaga; for these the new regime was held morally responsible by many. This widespread belief was reinforced when the makers of the constitution not only proposed the separation of Church and State, but also subjected religious orders to severe restrictions, outlawed all Church schools, and sanctioned easy divorces in their draft of the new constitution. The anticlerical provisions put a serious strain on the bourgeois-socialist coalition on which the government rested, and led to a cabinet crisis from which a new left liberal-socialist government emerged. The constitution was promulgated in December 1931; apart from its anticlerical articles, it provided for universal suffrage and full civil liberties, subordinated private property to the common welfare, authorizing its expropriation against equitable indemnity, and renounced war as an instrument of national policy.

Implementing the constitution, an agrarian law setting the terms of land expropriation was enacted the following year. If the law had been applied promptly and efficiently, it might have alleviated the worst hardships, but it was not. Because of the Depression, the government lacked the funds to purchase sufficient amounts of land, nor could Socialists and liberals agree as to whether that land was to be turned over to peasant cooperatives or to individual peasants. Little credit could be made available to those who did receive land, nor was money available for adequate irrigation. Thus the agrarian law did little to ease the lot of the peasants while at the same time it embittered the landlords. Anarchist bands meanwhile kept the rural areas in continued turmoil by stirring up local risings.

In the cities conditions were no less chaotic. Unemployment was widespread, partly owing to the worldwide economic slump, partly because of the unwillingness of Spanish business to make new investments under existing conditions. Since the jobless received no unemployment relief, most unemployed workers were facing starvation. In their despair they joined in mass demonstrations, riots, and sabotage acts, and kept the police in a state of constant alarm. Azaña's government, harassed and frightened, often retaliated with a savagery that appalled even its own supporters. In August 1932 it was also confronted with the first open coup of the military which had been plotting the overthrow of the new state since its inception. The ill-planned attempt was quickly suppressed, but it highlighted the precarious state of the Republic.

Swing to the Right. The widespread disillusionment with the new regime was reflected in the stunning defeat which the government parties suffered in the elections of November 1934. For the next two years a center-conservative coalition dominated the political stage. It was equally unable to restore domestic order. Strikes and riots continued in the industrial centers, Catalonia tried to establish itself as an autonomous state within a "federal Spanish Republic," and a miners' rising in Asturias in October 1934 grew into a virtual civil war that was ended only after three weeks of fighting by government troops commanded by General Francisco Franco.

The Asturian revolt deepened the existing political cleavages; it frightened upper and middle class into demands for a military dictatorship and aroused the bitterness of the lower classes because of the cruelty with which the rebels were treated. The government tried to appease both sides: it held up all further land reforms and postponed the implementation of the anticlerical legislation, allowing Church schools to function and restoring the payment of clerical salaries by the state; at the same time the sentences of leftist political offenders were commuted or altogether suspended. But these efforts to ease the existing tensions came to a sudden end when the President of the Republic, Alejandro Lerroux, became involved in a major financial scandal. Quarrels within the center-right coalition prevented the formation of a new government, and the Cortes was once more dissolved.

The Popular Front. Following the French example, the leftist parties from the liberal left to the Communists, at that time still a rather small group, gathered in a Popular Front. Although they received only a minority of the popular vote, they did win, thanks to their electoral alliance, a solid majority of the seats in the Cortes. The assumption of power by a Popular Front government headed by Azaña led to new outbreaks of violence, bombings, and church burnings. Many of these acts were perpetrated by supporters of the Popular Front who hoped to speed up the enactment of various reforms; others were the work of the fascist Falange Party, still small in numbers, but well-equipped and financed by industrialists and landowners who were anxious to pave the way for a rightist dictatorship by having the Falangists increase the existing turmoil. Strikes and land seizures by peasants added further to the disorders.

In the face of these unending disturbances the new government proved helpless. It pushed a number of industrial and land reform measures through the Cortes, but these failed to check the industrial warfare or the rural unrest. Bombings, arson, assassinations, street battles between Falangists and leftist extremists, between Anarchists and Socialists, and even between rival wings of the Socialist Party became daily occurrences. Militant Socialists and Anarchists on the left, army officers, Falangists, monarchists on the right, all plotted the overthrow of the Republic. At this critical moment Azaña, tired of the continuous disorder, let himself be elected to the figurehead presidency. As head of the government he was succeeded by Casares Quiroga, a well-intentioned, but ineffectual middle-class liberal, ill with consumption, who underestimated the gravity of the situation and took only few precautionary measures against further trouble. They proved totally inadequate when on July 16, 1936 a military revolt broke out in Spanish Morocco and quickly spread to the mainland.

The Civil War. The Nationalist generals and politicians who sparked the rising expected no difficulty in overthrowing the government. They counted on the support of the bulk of the army and some paramilitary monarchist groups, whereas the Republican government could rely merely on one small special police force of proven loyalty, the Assault Guards. However, the insurgents managed to seize control of only some two-fifths of the Spanish mainland (mostly in the northwest); in addition they captured Spain's African possessions and most of the Balearic Isles. Southern and eastern Spain, on the other hand, remained in Republican hands. The workers of Barcelona, Madrid, and other industrial centers were armed by the government and successfully defeated all military risings in those parts of the country.

After a few days both sides concluded that they could not defeat their opponents without foreign help. The story of German and Italian assistance to the Nationalists and of Soviet aid to the Republican government will be discussed in Chapter 15; suffice it to state here that thanks to German and Italian help the Nationalists advanced on all fronts, and by September 1936 it seemed only a question of time before Madrid, too, would fall.[2] At this moment, however, Soviet aid began to arrive, and in November the Nationalist attack on Madrid was beaten off.

Republican Politics. The Republican government, a group of middle-class liberals, was never more than nominally in control of its area; the real power rested with the left-radical parties and labor unions and with specially formed local "defense committees" of workers and peasants. The committees were primarily responsible for the retention of large parts of territory under Republican control, but they also acquired a sinister notoriety from the ruthless terrorism by which they suppressed oppositional elements in their midst. Tens of thousands fell victim to these excesses during the first six weeks of the war—among them several thousand priests and monks—and hundreds of churches and monasteries were burned or closed. The Church had had no part in the rising, but was attacked as a symbol of bourgeois hypocrisy and the repression of the poor. The missionary desire to cleanse the country of corruption and insincerity was especially widespread among the Anarchists; they were severely critical of those who would loot churches or middle-class homes rather than merely destroy their contents.

In their determination to prevent pro-Nationalist forces from hampering the Republican war effort, the committees also assumed control of the economic resources in the Republican areas. Their methods varied, depending on whether Socialists, Communists, or Anarchists were the dominant faction in any given area. Both Socialists and Communists refrained from expropriations, except in cases where owners had gone over to the Nationalists, and contented themselves with administering all war-essential industrial plants, paying the proprietors a monthly indemnity in some cases. The Communists opposed any radical changes, on instructions from Moscow which wished to allay the distrust of the Western Powers; they insisted that the Republican forces were a democratic, not a proletarian revolutionary movement. The Anarchists, whose stronghold was Catalonia, maintained, on the other hand, that the war could not be won without a radical social revolution and proceeded to collectivize all land and businesses within their reach.

In September 1936 the impotent Liberal-Socialist government gave way to a Socialist-Communist coalition headed by the Socialist labor leader, Largo Caballero (1869–1946). It was the first time that Communists had ever entered a Western government, and the Spanish Communists did so only on the express orders of Moscow. Stalin wished them

---

[2] General Emilio Mola, the commander of the forces advancing on the capital, was asked at that time by some newspapermen which of his four columns he expected to take the capital. His answer was that it would be a fifth column of Nationalist sympathizers in the city who stood ready to rise at a given signal. Although his prediction did not come true, Mola did give the world a new term for treasonous action.

to supervise the use to which Soviet aid was being put; he also expected their disciplined militancy to stiffen the Republic's resistance. Inevitably tensions developed between them and Caballero, and recurrent quarrels over military and political strategy led to a break between them and the Premier. Caballero resigned and was succeeded by Juan Negrin (1889–1956), a one-time professor of physiology at the University of Madrid and a moderate Socialist who was on good terms with both the Soviet representatives in Spain and the Spanish Communists yet was strong-willed enough to be no mere tool of either. Negrin's dependence on Soviet military aid, however, set narrow limits to his freedom of action; while he improved the judicial system and put an end to the harassment of the Catholic clergy, he also was forced to acquiesce in many Communist abuses of power.

Nationalist Politics. A week after the rising broke out a five-man military junta was established at Burgos to govern the Nationalist-controlled territory. It was as powerless as the Republic's liberal cabinet. The real power rested with a number of regional commanders, primarily General Emilio Mola in northern Spain and General Francisco Franco in the south and in Spanish Morocco. With the military in full control, political life came to an end. Political parties were disbanded, and only "movements" such as the Falange and some monarchist groups were allowed to remain. They helped in rounding up political opponents and like their Republican counterparts indulged in a wave of terror. The number of their victims was far larger, however, since the Nationalists had considerably more enemies among the masses. Many of the executions were carried out with inordinate savagery and the mutilated bodies exhibited to frighten the populace into subservience. As on the Republican side, a great many took part in the massacres, not from vindictiveness, but from a perverted sense of mission, believing that only in this manner could their country be saved from annihilation.

Of the Nationalist generals, Franco emerged as the dominant personality. The son of a naval paymaster, Francisco Franco y Bahamonde (1892–) had had a brilliant military career and in 1925, at the age of thirty-two, had become the youngest brigadier in the Spanish army. Politically uncommitted, he had served the Republic in various posts and had been chief of staff of the army in 1934–1936. Only in 1936, after the victory of the Popular Front, did he throw in his lot with the "forces of order." Thanks to a number of military victories in the early weeks of the war and, perhaps even more important, to his ability to secure aid from Germany and Italy, he gained quickly in stature; thus when it became imperative to establish a central command, he seemed the most suitable candidate for that post. On October 1, 1936 by a mixture of threats and persuasion, he prevailed on the Burgos junta to proclaim him both Generalissimo and head of state. His program,

General Franco. *(Reprinted courtesy Brown Brothers)*

modeled on some of the views propounded by the Falange, was vague; in his inaugural speech he spoke of replacing the popular vote with a "better way of expressing the popular will," of protecting workers against exploitation and peasants against collectivization, and of securing respect for the Church.

Outwardly, political conditions continued quiet in Nationalist Spain during the following months. There was none of that welter of different views and ideologies that kept convulsing Republican Spain, but neither was there any of that popular enthusiasm that inspired the Republican camp. Below this surface calm, however, tensions developed between Franco and the Falange and monarchist movements. The Falange deplored the Generalissimo's lack of interest in its social program, and the monarchists fretted over his opposition to the immediate restoration of the monarchy. In the spring of 1937 Franco put an end to these disagreements by imprisoning and exiling the leaders of both groups; the groups themselves were fused into a new catch-all organization, *Falange Española Tradicionalista*. Franco assumed the leadership of the new Falange, hopeful that it would give him the popular following and the ideological basis that he had lacked so far.

Military Developments. Meanwhile the fortunes of war seesawed, sometimes favoring Republican Spain and sometimes the Nationalists. Madrid withstood their recurrent assaults, and a Nationalist advance south

THE SPANISH CIVIL WAR, 1937

Areas occupied by Nationalists

0   100   200

Miles

BAY OF BISCAY

La Coruña
ASTURIAS
GALICIA
Gijón
Santander
Bilbao
CANTABRIAN MTS.
León
BASQUE
NAVARRE
Bayonne
Bordeaux
Toulouse
PYRENEES MTS.
ANDORRA
Perpignan
Marseilles
Rhone
Garonne R.
Burgos
Valladolid
LEON
OLD CASTILE
Zaragoza
ARAGON
CATALONIA
Barcelona
Oporto
Duero R.
Salamanca
Segovia
GUADARRAMA MTS.
Guadalajara
Tarragona
PORTUGAL
Madrid
Toledo
NEW CASTILE
Teruel
SPAIN
MINORCA
Tagus R.
Alcántara
Valencia
VALENCIA
MAJORCA
Palma
Mahon
Lisbon
Badajoz
EXTREMADURA
Guadiana
IVIZA
BALEARIC ISLANDS
MURCIA
Alicante
Córdova
Seville
ANDALUSIA
Guadalquivir R.
Granada
Cartagena
MEDITERRANEAN SEA
Cadiz
Malaga
Almería
Algiers
Bougie
Algeciras
Tangier
Gibraltar Br.
Ceuta
ALBORAN I. (Sp.)
SPANISH MOROCCO
Melila
Oran
ALGERIA
Rabat
Fez
FRENCH MOROCCO

of the capital was fought to a standstill. A similar advance north of Madrid ended with a rout of the Italian forces that had been thrown into the battle. These successes were merely defensive and failed to recover any territory for the Republic; yet they were politically and psychologically important, for they improved Republican morale and spread gloom in Franco's camp. But in the south the Nationalists won an important victory with the capture of Malaga in February 1937, and in the spring they also gained control of the Basque country. (In the course of this latter campaign the Germans shocked the world by bombing the little unfortified town of Guernica for three hours in order to provide their pilots with bombing practice and to study the effects of such terror attacks.) Both victories were greatly aided by bitter disputes and rivalries in the Republican camp—between Communists and Anarchists in one case, between the central government and the Basques in the other.

What proved ultimately decisive, however, was the large amount of foreign aid that the Nationalists kept receiving while Soviet aid to the Republic fell off rapidly in 1938. This assistance enabled Franco to mount a final offensive against the Republican forces in Catalonia early in 1939 after both sides had been left exhausted and without supplies from a drawn-out campaign in the Ebro valley. What might have ended in a military stalemate and a compromise peace was thus converted into the decisive victory of the Nationalists over the Republic.

The demise of the Republic was anticlimactic. Torn by dissension to the last moment, it collapsed amidst a profusion of plots and risings of various political factions and officer cliques. Most of the Republican leaders managed to escape, carrying their unending quarrels into exile with them. The bulk of their followers were less fortunate, and tens of thousands of them were either shot or sentenced to long years of forced labor for their willingness to defend the Republic.

ITALY: FASCISM VS. THE PEOPLE

The Domestic Impact of the Ethiopian Campaign.   Whereas France and Spain were convulsed by domestic troubles, Italy seemed well ordered and united. Yet underneath that deceptive appearance Italy, too, was beset by grave economic problems and personal hardships which the Fascist dictatorship could not remedy and which in fact it kept aggravating by its imperialist policies. Italy's recovery from the Depression was slow, it will be recalled, and while preparations for the campaign against Ethiopia helped to reduce unemployment, the increased armament program also put a new strain on the country's meager resources. Official salaries had to be cut by 12 per cent, taxes increased, and interest rates raised from 3.5 to 5 per cent. As a further hardship, the belated devaluation of the lira in 1936 caused a 20 per cent increase in the cost of living. Nor did the conquest of Ethiopia alleviate these difficulties. The exploitation of the new colony required considerable investments which yielded but limited returns; in order to underwrite Ethiopia's development, useful domestic projects such as land reclamation had to be abandoned.

To gauge the popular mood in a totalitarian country is a difficult matter, but there are a good many indications that the popularity of Fascism was on the decline in Italy in the 1930's. Its failure to improve the lot of the bulk of the people, its demands for continued and even increasing sacrifices, its constant flirting with war, were disillusioning to many. When Mussolini launched his campaign against Ethiopia, there was widespread grumbling. This resentment gave way to support of the Duce, however, when the League of Nations imposed sanctions on Italy. The nation forgot its misgivings and agreed with the Duce that the sanctions were an attempt of the Western Powers to deny Italy its fair share of colonies. Because few Italians were aware of the inefficacy of the sanctions, they were used as a convenient explanation for the growing domestic shortages. The country accepted the new hardships imposed by the war and willingly contributed its gold and silver (including even wedding rings) to the war effort. The victorious outcome of the cam-

paign seemed to justify these sacrifices, and for a brief moment Mussolini was once again hailed as the nation's hero.

Fascism Loses Its Appeal. When peace did not ease the existing hardships, many people relapsed into their earlier discontent. Mussolini, however, was undismayed. He continued to think that sacrifices would weld
the Italian people into a more closely knit social and national community:
"Socialism used to say, all equal and all rich. Experience has proved this
to be impossible. We say, all equal and all sufficiently poor." What also
caused much resentment was his growing rapprochement with Hitler.
Not only was the diplomatic association with the arrogant and aggressive
Nazis not popular, but many Italians also objected to Mussolini's attempts
to introduce German methods and discipline. The adoption of the goose
step, euphemistically called *passo romano,* aroused considerable indignation. ("People say the goose step is Prussian," the Duce retorted. "Nonsense, the goose is a Roman animal—it saved the Capitol.")

In 1938 Mussolini also introduced anti-Jewish legislation. He had not
been an anti-Semite before and had in fact had close personal and political relations with a number of persons of Jewish descent; obviously he
took the step to please Hitler and perhaps also in order to gain favor
with the Arabs whom he was courting as allies against Great Britain. The
anti-Jewish laws were not as stringent as Germany's, and special provisions exempted about one-third of Italy's Jews from their application,
but to Mussolini's indignation the measure was widely criticized. As
Count Galeazzo Ciano (1903–1944), his son-in-law and Foreign Minister,
records in his diary, the Duce felt himself increasingly at odds with
the nation and raged at its "flabby bourgeois mentality." His hopes of
raising the Italian people into a nation of tough, virile warriors was not
fulfilled. When for one fleeting moment he recovered once more his old
popularity, this was due to his successful efforts to preserve peace in the
crisis over Czechoslovakia.

Whatever their objections to Mussolini's policies, the Italian people
were in no position to force him to change them. His failure, however,
to imbue his countrymen with the proper Fascist spirit of dedication and
discipline placed its own restrictions on his plans and activities. Tax
evasion continued as before and added to the government's financial
difficulties, and inefficiency and carelessness help to account for the
abysmal state of Italy's military preparations when war broke out in
1939. A mortified Mussolini thus had to stand by impotently while
Hitler set out to conquer new lands, but the Italian people, according to
Ciano's diary, felt greatly relieved. And when the Duce did take Italy
into the war in June 1940, his decision, according to that same source,
aroused little enthusiasm even though the prospect of gaining new territory seemed unusually good.

CENTRAL AND EASTERN EUROPE: TIGHTENING OF
THE DICTATORIAL REINS

The Rulers. Developments in most Central and Eastern European countries during the 1930's were strikingly similar. Economically, these nations were unable to extricate themselves on their own from the Depression; lacking capital and trained manpower, they could not resort to public works or other pump priming devices to overcome their economic difficulties. The solution was eventually supplied by Nazi Germany's trade drive which provided the markets for their foodstuffs and raw materials or the jobs for their excess manpower.

Politically, too, these countries were caught up largely in the same trend. Their governments tended to tighten their authoritarian reins in the course of the 1930's and transform themselves into outright dictatorships. In Poland, Hungary, Rumania, Bulgaria, and Greece, parliaments were reduced to complete impotence by suffrage restrictions, terror or bribes, or by simple decree. (Developments in Austria, similar in some respects, were discussed earlier and need not concern us here.) Moreover, as in Western Europe, the caliber of the political leaders during the pre-World War II decade was on the whole inferior to that of those who led these countries in the 1920's. In the case of the East European countries this deterioration concerned more the integrity of the leaders than their sagacity, which had never been high in that part of Europe. Whatever might be said against the political wisdom of Poland's Pilsudski, Hungary's Count Bethlen, or King Alexander of Yugoslavia, these men were sincere patriots, above reproach in the conduct of their personal affairs, and dedicated hard workers. Many of their successors, on the other hand, were unscrupulous and corrupt individuals. Poland, after Pilsudski's death, was ruled by the so called "Government of the Colonels," comrades-in-arms of the Marshal who abused their position to gain honors and wealth. Most of Bethlen's successors in Hungary were opportunists of mediocre ability. Prince Regent Paul of Yugoslavia, who, in lieu of King Alexander's son, eleven-year-old King Peter, took Alexander's place after the latter's assassination, attended to his duties without zeal and interest. King Carol of Rumania, a clever intriguer, managed to establish his personal dictatorship by playing off various political groups against each other; by investing heavily in industrial enterprises he also acquired a large part of Rumania's textile and armament plants, which throve on government subsidies, high tariffs, and other state aid. King Boris III who emerged as Bulgaria's dictator in the late 1930's is still something of an enigma—a gentle, decent, unselfish father of his people to some; a brutal monster to others. Only General Joannis Metaxas, who ruled Greece with an iron hand from 1936 on, seems to have been a man of unchallenged integrity.

The Opposition. The tightening of the East European dictatorships grew out of power struggles between comparatively small political factions and was rarely concerned with substantive political, social, or economic issues. Only in Yugoslavia the contest between government and opposition revolved around a genuine quest for self-government and greater equality for the country's constituent nationality groups. However, there too the official political leaders and their parties represented only small cliques of industrialists, landowners, and other special interest groups and were little concerned with the general welfare. Consequently, in Yugoslavia as well, oppositional sentiments were driven to seek new outlets.

The Communist parties, outlawed almost everywhere, remained small, but "communism," not as a Marxist social and economic system, but as a pragmatic policy supposedly standing for land reforms, freedom, and social justice, aroused some interest among the hard-pressed peasantry of the Balkan countries. The peasants knew little if anything about conditions in Soviet Russia and thought of it simply as a country run by the common people. Finding their own leaders little concerned with their troubles, they were inclined to shrug off the latter's hostility to the Soviet Union. "Our priests and officials tell us that over in Russia the small, humble people are terribly oppressed," the British historian Hugh Seton-Watson was told by Rumanian peasants; "what we cannot understand is why our priests and officials are so indignant at the sufferings of the small, humble people over in Russia when they care so little about their sufferings here in Rumania." Interest in communism could be found mainly in countries of both Slavic and Orthodox background; it was less noticeable in Catholic countries and all but nonexistent in Poland where anti-Russian feelings were strong. At that, it was a vague feeling, amorphous and inarticulate, and given the lethargy of the peasants, presented no direct threat to the powers that were.

Fascism attracted an overt and more activist following. Fascist parties sprang up in Poland, Hungary, Croatia, and Rumania. The Polish National Radical Party, whose program was modeled on that of the Nazis and because of its affinity with the Germans was immediately suspect, had a following only in the Warsaw area. Hungary's Arrow-Cross Party, appealing to students and small peasants, enjoyed greater support, but never gained access to the government. Croatia's Ustasha, though operating illegally, grew in size as Croatians despaired of attaining by legal means full equality with the Serbs. It was involved in the assassination of King Alexander I and after the defeat of Yugoslavia by Germany in 1941 dominated the newly created puppet state of Croatia.

Rumania's Iron Guard, the most important of these movements, became a significant force in Rumanian politics since for many years it enjoyed the financial and moral support of King Carol. Originally a student group intent on the harassment of Jews, strike-breaking, and fights with liberal and leftist opponents, it was fostered by Carol in the hope that with its help he could destroy the two major political parties, the Liberals and the National Peasants, which blocked his dictatorial ambitions. Well supplied with funds, the Iron Guard, under its leader, Corneliu Zelea Codreanu (1899–1938), tried to build up a nation-wide following by means of a program of anti-Semitism, land reform ("one man, one acre"), and an end to corruption. At the same time, shielded by governmental protection, the Guardists instituted a reign of terror that culminated in the assassination in 1933 of Premier Ion Duca, the head of the Liberal Party. Codreanu built up a substantial following among the middle class and the peasantry which was attracted not only by his promise of land reforms (largely illusory) but also by his fulminations against the decadent, un-Rumanian civilization of Bucharest and other large cities. As a token of their deep attachment to the "real" Rumania, the green-shirted Iron Guardists carried little bags of Rumanian soil around their necks.

Unlike other Balkan nations, the Rumanians never were given to violence, and the bloody outrages of the Iron Guard aroused deep resentment throughout the country. The growing resentment was directed not only against the Guard, but also against King Carol who was held morally responsible for the Guard's misdeeds. In the parliamentary elections of 1937 the parties supporting the King received only 38 per cent of the vote; of these the Iron Guard obtained 16 per cent which made it the second largest party in the country. It had, however, outlived its usefulness for the monarch, and since Carol was becoming concerned about Codreanu as a potential rival, he decided to turn on the Guard. After suspending the last remains of parliamentary government, the King had Codreanu and his chief associates arrested, and in November 1938 they were shot while "trying to escape." The Iron Guard, however, would not be cowed. In 1939 it assassinated another Premier, Armand Calinescu, and in 1940, after Carol had been forced by the Nazis to cede part of Transylvania to the Hungarians, it took advantage of the King's unpopularity to frighten him by mass demonstrations into abdicating again. The government which took over after Carol's departure was largely composed of Iron Guardists. Their triumph was only short-lived, however. Indulging at once in a new reign of terror, they were swept from office after a few months.

Czechoslovakia. Of all the countries in central and eastern Europe only Czechoslovakia retained its democratic and parliamentary institutions. It could preserve them partly because the diversified Czech economy established something of a social equilibrium conducive to the maintenance of democracy, partly because the existence within its borders of various sizable nationality groups required that they all have a political voice if they were to be held together. The political instinct of the dominant Czechs and the caliber of Czechoslovakia's statesmen, Masaryk and Beneš, and the Slovak leader, Milan Hodza, also account for the country's ability to meet its mounting difficulties within the established constitutional order until, abandoned by friends and allies, it succumbed to Nazi aggression.

Although the Czech economy did not suffer as seriously from the Depression as the less well-balanced economies of Hungary and the Balkan countries, it did not remain unaffected. Among the worst hit sectors were those industrial areas that produced primarily for the export market, and among these were the border regions in northern and western Czechoslovakia primarily settled by Germans.[3] The economic distress of these Sudeten Germans (so-called from the Sudeten Mountains along which they had settled) deepened their antagonism against the Czechs. The Czechs in turn became increasingly concerned about the loyalty of the Sudeten Germans after Hitler had seized power in Germany. Their alarm was the greater because the Germans lived in those heavily fortified border areas on which the military defense of Czechoslovakia depended. The Prague authorities began to intervene against local Nazi and nationalist organizations, they replaced mayors and other municipal officials belonging to these groups with more moderate Germans, and had Czechs take the place of German police officials. The bitterness among the Sudeten Germans increased, and large numbers joined the newly founded Sudeten German Party which paid lip service to democracy and the Czech constitution, but spread Nazi views and was patterned after the German Nazi Party. Many undoubtedly joined from conviction, but others supported the party mainly from fear lest they be known as anti-Nazis should Hitler take over the area. Whatever their motives, two-thirds of the Germans in Czechoslovakia cast their vote for the Sudeten German Party in the elections of 1935, and the party emerged as the second largest in the Czech parliament. From this time on until the settlement of the issue at the Munich Conference in September 1938, the Sudeten German problem overshadowed all other concerns of Czechoslovakia. But being a foreign more than a domestic problem, its further course will be discussed within the context of international developments in the late 1930's (Chapter 15).

Slovak discontent also increased as a result of the Depression, yet as a purely domestic phenomenon it was of secondary importance compared to the German issue. Moreover, Slovak hostility to the Czechs was not as widespread as German enmity, and a Slovak, Milan Hodza, headed the Czechoslovak government from 1935 to 1938. The deterioration of Czech-Slovak relations deserves mention, however, because it was to play some role in the final hours of Czechoslovakia as a sovereign state.

[3] They were Germans actually only in a cultural sense, having been citizens of Austria-Hungary before the establishment of the Czechoslovak state.

14

The Soviet Union in
the 1930's

The Soviet Union was comparatively little affected by the Great Depression. Domestic needs provided an insatiable market for Russia's agricultural and industrial output, and since the country was suffering from underdevelopment rather than overproduction, it was plagued, not by unemployment, but by a serious manpower shortage. Yet if Soviet Russia did not have to contend with the difficulties that beset the capitalist economies, it was confronted with grave economic and political problems of its own. This was the time of Russia's frenzied changeover into a modern industrial state, and for this transformation the nation paid an awesome price in terms of human suffering and sacrifices. Politics took its own heavy toll in lives and imprisonments as Stalin strove to make his dictatorship wholly impregnable. His willful destruction of human lives invested the hardships endured by the Soviet people with their particular horror; whatever the deprivations borne by the peoples in non-Communist countries, at least in most of these their lives were not endangered— although the spread of fascism was beginning to narrow down the area

to which this distinction applied.

THE "SECOND REVOLUTION"

Agricultural Difficulties. In December 1927 the Fifteenth Communist Party Congress resolved to accelerate the country's industrialization. It was felt that the time had come to put an end to the continuing disparity between agricultural and industrial productivity. A Five-Year Plan to be inaugurated in 1928 was to speed up the expansion of heavy industry in order to assure more adequate supplies of capital goods— machinery, tractors, trucks—and increase the output of armaments for the defense of the country. A drive for the formation of collective farms, to be launched simultaneously, was to undo the detrimental effects of the breakup in 1917–18 of the large estates into small peasant holdings and improve the efficiency and productivity of agriculture. No precipitate changes in the country's economic system were contemplated: Stalin envisaged an annual industrial growth of 15 per cent, considerably less than the average growth rate of 25 per cent that Soviet industry had achieved during the N.E.P. period. As for collectivization, the First Five-Year Plan in its original form provided for a gradual changeover, embracing at the most some 20 per cent of all farms by 1933.

Contrary to these plans, both industrialization and collectivization proceeded at an enormously increased pace during the next few years. The change in tempo was sparked by the failure of the peasants in the winter of 1927–28 to provide the towns with adequate food supplies. Since the harvest had been satisfactory in 1927, the Soviet leaders attributed the food shortage to the unwillingness of the peasants to market their surpluses. While there was some truth in these suspicions, they oversimplified the actual course of events. As on other occasions, the food crisis was caused by a combination of normal self-interest and willful sabotage. As independent producers, the peasants lived better and consumed more of what they raised than they had been able to when working for landlords. But grain was also withheld because industrial output still failed to keep pace with agricultural production and the peasants were unable to buy manufactured goods at reasonable prices. This difficulty the peasants hoped to solve by forcing up agricultural prices.

Noncooperation was especially marked on the part of the kulaks who reduced not only their sales but their production as well. They were deeply resentful of the discriminatory treatment to which they were being subjected. In 1928 their taxes were sharply increased whereas large numbers of poor peasants were exempted from all agricultural taxes. The kulaks were also restricted in their rights to lease additional land and compelled to pay higher wages to hired hands than did the middle peasants. Worst of all, they found it increasingly difficult to obtain credits and purchase equipment, whereas middle and poor peasants joining collective farms received a great deal of state aid. Their resistance stiffened as government agents began raiding their farms to confiscate what supplies they found, and the kulaks themselves were hauled off to jail on charges of hoarding and speculating in grain. The kulaks tried hiding their grain or bribing the agents and as repression grew heavier, they resorted to violence. Collection agents, Party workers, members of village soviets were manhandled or killed or their homesteads burned down in the hope that the government could be forced to relent. A few kulaks may even have thought of bringing about its collapse.

The Collectivization of Agriculture.   Any course on which Stalin embarked to cope with the agricultural crisis was fraught with risks. Had he granted the peasants higher food prices and made other concessions, he would have strengthened the social and economic position of his "capitalist" foes while aggravating the lot of the urban masses, his most important supporters. On the other hand, new forcible measures against the peasants entailed the danger of a further disruption of agricultural production and increased unrest in the rural areas. Still, the latter course seemed preferable socially and ideologically, and Stalin chose it. Collectivization, which had so far attracted mainly the poorer peasants most in need of the financial and technical aid proffered to the collective farms by the state, was to be extended to the farms of the kulaks and middle peasants. The entire peasantry would thus be brought under direct government control and their holdings, dangerous remnants of individual enterprise, eliminated. Collectivization would also increase productivity by fusing uneconomical small farms into more efficient large units. Attaining greater efficiency, it would release manpower from the farms to the expanding industries.

The main thrust of the collectivization drive was directed against the kulaks—a term that was now very loosely applied (see p. 170, n. 1). Their land and equipment were turned over to the nearest collective farm (kolkhoz) or served as the nucleus for the establishment of a new one. The kulaks themselves were exiled to some remote part of the Soviet Union where they were put to cutting timber or toiling in mines or on new building projects; if they were considered less dangerous, they were ordered to cultivate some swamp land or a recently eroded plot in their home district. Poor peasants were enlisted in this campaign of "dekulakization" with promises of aid for their own farms. Together with zealous party officials they enforced collectivization with great ruthlessness, frequently turning as well against middle and poorer peasants who refused to join them, and indulging in orgies of looting. Anarchy spread through the countryside; faced with the prospect of losing their property, the peasants began slaughtering their livestock, and for a few months during the winter of 1929–30 there was an overabundance of meat in the cities. The long-range effects of this wholesale slaughter were catastrophic. For many years afterwards meat and dairy products were in even shorter supply than before; farms suffered from the lack of draft animals, doubly serious since the supply of trucks and tractors never was adequate; and there was a critical shortage of manure that was the more harmful because Soviet plants produced only limited amounts of artificial fertilizer and the government lacked the means to import sufficient quantities from abroad.

In the spring of 1930 Stalin was forced to intervene to prevent the collectivization drive from plunging the rural districts into complete chaos. In a now famous statement published in *Pravda*, the leading Communist party newspaper, he hailed the collectivization campaign as successful beyond all expectations. But carefully shifting the blame for its excesses to others, he attacked those who had become "dizzy from success" and had forcibly driven peasants into kolkhozes rather than rely on arguments and persuasion. Stalin also declared himself opposed to all-out socialization of the collective farms and insisted that "at the present moment" socialization should be limited to the major means of production on the farms—the use of the land, farm buildings, machinery, and draft animals—whereas personal dwellings, small livestock and simple tools ought to remain the personal property of the farmers. As a result, there was an immediate move towards decollectivization, and within two months the number of kolkhozes dropped from 110,000 to 83,000.

The decline of collectivization did not continue for long. Kulak deportations continued, and many of the remaining peasants, though no longer subjected to direct pressures, thought it advisable to join a collective farm. They feared that forcible collectivization had been discontinued only temporarily; moreover, as independent farmers they still suffered discrimination: they kept paying special taxes and found it as hard as ever to buy tools and other equipment. Membership in a kolkhoz also was more attractive now since the farmers were permitted to cultivate small plots of land on their own, and they shared in the profits of the farm in proportion to the amount and kind of work that they did. By 1932 over half of the farms had again been collectivized, and by 1934 three-fourths of all farms had been absorbed into kolkhozes. In 1939 collectivization embraced 93 per cent of all farm land.

Agricultural productivity, however, did not increase according to expectations. Apart from natural causes such as the drought of 1931–32, this was due partly to the tremendous disruption caused by collectivization and partly to the continued shortage of mechanized equipment. To utilize the available machinery as economically and efficiently as possible, it was turned over, not to the individual kolkhozes, but to state-operated machine tractor stations that could service a number of collective farms (and at the same time keep an eye on the operations of these farms). It was not until 1933 that grain crops surpassed the average annual production of the 1920's. Yet while crops on the whole kept increasing during the following years, the growth rate never kept pace with the needs of the population. There was still a serious shortage of mechanized equipment throughout the decade despite a remarkable expansion in the output of tractors and harvester combines, and the deficiency in fertilizer remained equally serious although supplies increased thirteen-fold between 1928 and 1938. However, the main cause of all difficulties was the human factor: the peasants never became fully reconciled to collectivization and would not work as hard and conscientiously on the collective farm land as they did on their own little plots.

Besides the collective farms there existed state farms (sovkhoz), run like industrial plants and worked by wage labor. While many sovkhozes engaged in the usual farming activities, others served as model and experimental farms.

Industrialization.   In 1929, along with the precipitate drive for collectivization, the industrial goals set in the original Five-Year Plan also were sharply raised and the country plunged into a virtual war against technical backwardness. "Shock brigades" of specially selected workers led the attack and millions were drafted into the industrial army that was to wage the campaign. "We are fifty or a hundred years behind the advanced countries," Stalin warned, "we must make good this lag in ten years. Either we do it, or they will crush us." Rapid industrialization was considered imperative, not only in order to strengthen the Soviet Union militarily and render it economically more independent, but also because the success of the collectivization drive depended on the ability of Soviet industry to supply sufficient amounts of farm machinery. The immensity of this particular task becomes clear when it is kept in mind that in 1928, by Stalin's own testimony, there were only 7,000 tractors in all of the U.S.S.R.

Thus mining operations were greatly expanded, machine plants and power stations constructed in many parts of the country, and new industrial centers created in the untapped regions of Asian Russia. Industrial combines were developed such as the Dnieper combine that produced steel, manganese, and other metals. The results were impressive: coal production increased from 40 million tons in 1929 to 76 million tons in 1933; oil, from 13 million to 22 million tons; iron ore, from 8 to 14 million tons; electric power from 6 billion to 16 billion kilowatt hours. Tractor output grew from 3,000 in 1929 to 71,000 in 1933, that of motorcars and small trucks from 1,200 to 26,000 and of heavy trucks from 148 to 23,000. But progress was uneven; unable to move on all fronts at one time, the planners had to select priorities and decided to postpone the development of transportation facilities. Transportation and roadbuilding equipment barely increased; the output of locomotives grew from 575 units in 1929 to a mere 929 in 1933.

If quantitatively industrialization scored remarkable advances, qualitatively it left much to be desired. In their anxiety to meet production quotas, plant managers tended to be concerned more with quantity than with quality. Quality suffered also from the lack of adequately trained managerial and technical personnel; in 1929 half of the posts requiring advanced training were held by people who had never had any theoretical instruction. These difficulties were compounded by the inadequacy of hastily trained rural laborers who failed to handle machinery with proper care and thus were responsible for many production breakdowns.

The industrial campaign was waged as ruthlessly as the collectivization drive. While the latter liquidated the kulaks, industrialization eliminated the remaining independent manufacturers of the N.E.P. period. These private entrepreneurs were forced out of business by ruinous taxes and other discriminatory practices and their plants either closed or seized by the state. The only type of private enterprise that survived, apart from the peasants' small household gardens, were one-man repair and handicraft shops, which were allowed to continue in operation as a matter of convenience.

Businessmen were not the only victims of the industrial campaign. "People were wounded and killed, women and children froze to death, millions starved, thousands were court-martialed and shot," writes John Scott, an American eye-witness, and he concludes that Russia's "battle of ferrous metallurgy" alone involved more casualties than the battle of the Marne. A people given to lethargy, predominantly agricultural and illiterate technically, was called upon to change its way of life overnight, as it were, and to achieve goals which even a more advanced nation would have found difficult to attain in the short time allotted to it. To do the job, party and government exhorted, prodded, even terrorized men into doing their share: slackers were heavily fined; carelessness and absenteeism were dealt with as sabotage; and non-fulfillment of work and production quotas became equally serious offenses. While there were special awards for those who did well, in particular on the engineering and managerial level, life was full of hardships and deprivations for the great majority of the people. All basic necessities—food, clothing, housing, and fuel—were scarce and strictly rationed; prices of many items were exceedingly high and beyond the reach of most people; and to obtain what they could afford often required long hours of waiting in line.

To some extent these shortages were due to inadequate planning, inefficient management, and lack of coordination of the production process. Food shortages also were due to peasant resistance, the disruption caused by collectivization, and such natural disasters as a severe drought in 1931–32. Basically, however, the pitiable state of living conditions was the result of policy decisions made by the Soviet leadership. The First Five-Year Plan purposely concentrated on the development of capital goods and armament industries at the expense of consumer goods industries since it was deemed more important to lay Russia's industrial foundation and build up Soviet military strength than to improve living standards. Thus, consumer goods output not only was not expanded, but in a great many cases curtailed: cotton textiles production, for example, dropped from 3 billion meters in 1929 to 2.4 billion in 1933. Industrialization, moreover, had to be financed out of the country's own resources. Foreign loans were not available to the Soviet Union and if they had been, would have been turned down by the government lest the U.S.S.R. become economically dependent on foreign capitalists. The industrial drive thus had to be paid out of taxes, savings, internal loans, and profits from sales of state-produced goods, and the less the Soviet citizen could buy with his money, the more could be collected from him and invested in industry. Again, imports of tools and machinery had to be financed by exports, primarily foodstuffs and raw materials; since world market prices for primary products were falling more rapidly during the Depression than those for finished goods, the widening gap between world agricultural and industrial prices placed an additional burden on the Soviet economy.

Stalin. The revolution that the Soviet Union underwent during the First Five-Year Plan bears the unmistakable personal imprint of Stalin. He was by now firmly entrenched as Soviet dictator, and it was he who imparted the marked element of inhuman relentlessness to the transformation of Russia into a modern industrial power.

In spite of innumerable attempts to describe and analyze him, Stalin still remains a highly enigmatic figure. Besides his official statements, speeches, and correspondence, little reliable information about him exists; of personal letters, only few have become known in the West. Stalin himself never cared to shed light on his private life, in keeping with the Soviet code of behavior which did not approve of such personal revelations. The recollections of those who came to know him are for the most part officially sponsored, uncritical panegyrics or resentful attacks by frustrated enemies and are hence of only limited usefulness. His daughter, Svetlana Alliluyeva, who published her recollections of him, was close to him only as a very young girl. She pictures Stalin as a playful though erratic and easily irritated father during those early years of her youth; later he became a remote and sinister figure in her life.[1]

The picture which emerges within these limitations is that of a man

---

[1] Psychologists may see some significance in an odd game Stalin liked to play with his little daughter. The all-powerful Soviet dictator insisted that Svetlana, if she wished him to do something for her, send him an order rather than merely express a wish. Across these requests he would scrawl, "I submit," or, "I obey. J. Stalin." His letters to her he would invariably sign as her "wretched secretary, the poor peasant J. Stalin."

of great forcefulness and tenacious perseverance, coldly calculating and unemotional, tough-minded and shrewd, contemptuous and suspicious of men and inordinately ruthless. Stalin's motives are difficult to fathom. Ambitious and lustful for power, he was also driven by a deep-seated hatred of the propertied classes that was not rooted in any sympathy with the underprivileged, but rather in strong personal resentments. Unlike Lenin's socialism, Stalin's does not appear to have been inspired by visions of a "good society"; rarely do his writings and speeches look beyond the problems of the day and invoke the picture of a better future. This is not to say that his decisions were dictated solely by his personal interest—many were forced upon him by the needs of the country—but they were evidently not inspired by generous vistas of a happier future. Having no faith in his fellow men, Stalin was as distrustful of industrial workers as he was of peasants and intellectuals, not to speak of landlords and businessmen, and convinced that only rigid controls and severe penalties could induce most of them to overcome their traditional sloth and irresponsibility. This distrust was reflected in the brutalities he allowed to be inflicted on peasants and workers alike in his drive for collectivization and industrialization and in his resort to terror as a primary tool of government policy. There was no fortress the Bolsheviks could not conquer, he assured his associates—provided, he might have added, they accepted his way of attaining the goal.[2]

No regime, however, can maintain itself on terror alone. Stalin knew how to reward those who were entrusted with strategic tasks in his program—key party and government officials and the managers and engineers on whom depended the success of the Five-Year Plan. They were given additional food rations, priorities on housing and clothing, and other privileges and perquisites. Material rewards were also bestowed as incentives on workers and farmers, but given the shortage of consumer goods, these awards could only be very modest. For this reason special social awards were created—decorations such as the Order of Lenin and titles such as Hero of Socialist Labor and Stakhanovite, after an exceptionally efficient coal miner, Alexis Stakhanov.

Efforts were also made by party and government to enhance Stalin's authority by fashioning around him a kind of Soviet theology. Stalin was exalted into an omniscient infallible leader whose policies were invariably wise and must never be questioned. Blending Orthodox traditions and Marxist doctrine, Soviet Communism assumed a religious flavor, complete with Holy Writ (*Communist Manifesto* and Marx's *Capital*),

[2] As is evident from their self-centered goals and their contempt of their fellowmen, there exists a basic similarity between Stalin's and Hitler's personality. It even extended to such personal idiosyncrasies as their excessive seclusiveness and their habit of turning night into day. Of Hitler it is known that he recognized a kindred mind in Stalin, and there is at least some fragmentary evidence that Stalin shared this feeling.

apostolic interpretations (the writings of Lenin), places of pilgrimage (Lenin's tomb, Stalin's birthplace), and ikons (the ubiquitous pictures of Marx, Engels, Lenin, and Stalin), with Stalin the high priest whose pronouncements became the equivalent of papal encyclicals.[3] The hope was that by clothing ideological and political practices in familiar garments, they would be accepted more readily by the people.

How successful these endeavors were, it is impossible to determine. What may have seemed more attractive to many were the immense opportunities that existed for the ambitious if they worked hard and availed themselves of the increasing educational and training facilities. Others were inspired by the expectation of greater abundance in the not-too-distant future, or by the hope that if they themselves should not be allowed to enjoy the fruits of their labors, at least their children would.

The Second and Third Five-Year Plans. These hopes were encouraged by the Second and Third Five-Year Plans. Now that the industrial foundation was laid, the Kremlin decided to relax the pace of heavy industrial development and reward the nation, if ever so modestly, for its exertions. Imports, moreover, declined as industrialization progressed, and exports could be reduced correspondingly. Between 1930 and 1937 the volume of exports decreased by over two-thirds, releasing substantial amounts of foodstuffs and raw materials for domestic consumption. The hope was that improved living conditions would also increase the productivity of the workers and in particular put an end to their restless shifting from job to job in the never-ending search for a little more food and some better housing. In the Second and Third Five-Year Plans somewhat greater attention was paid to consumer goods than had been the case in the First. Between 1932 and 1937 production of textile goods more than doubled (linen production increased from 135 million square meters to 285 million), and the output of footwear expanded nearly as much (from 84 million pairs to 164 million). But these increases were still very inadequate compared to the needs of a population which by 1939 had grown to 170 million. How desperate the shortage remained in many areas may be seen from the fact that only 540,000 bicycles were turned out in 1937—a fourfold increase over 1932—and the manufacture of home sewing machines expanded from 318,000 to 488,000 (which was still less than the 538,000 produced in 1929).[4]

By 1933 the worst effects of the collectivization drive had also been overcome, and food production was again on the rise. However, as mentioned earlier, it was never entirely adequate, and the shortage of

---

[3] In a more lyrical mood *Pravda* once wrote of him: "The Soviet land has become a vast magnificent garden where the talents of the people blossom and the great Bolshevik gardener nurses them as though they were his private tree."

[4] For figures on industrial output, see Donald R. Hodgman, *Soviet Industrial Production, 1928–1951* (Cambridge, Mass., 1954), pp. 190 ff.

livestock remained especially serious. While direct food rationing was being abandoned after 1934 as evidence of the improved situation, indirect rationing continued by means of high prices for many food items.

In the field of heavy industry the Second and Third Five-Year Plans called not only for a reduced rate of growth but also for the improvement of the quality of production. Both plans also paid greater attention to the development of the transportation system and provided for the expansion of the railroad and highway network, the building of canals, and the extension of civil aviation. Air transportation received special attention because of Russia's vast distances and the difficulties of providing the country with an adequate land transportation system. New industrial centers were developed in Asian Russia beyond the range of possible enemy airplanes; their location in the Asian part of the U.S.S.R. was also designed to facilitate the supply of the Red Army in the event of a war with Japan. Again, the industrial growth of the country was impressive: steel production in 1938 amounted to 18 million tons (as against 7 million in 1933); oil production climbed to 32 million tons (from 22.5 million); coal to 133 million (compared to 76 million); and electric power to 39 billion kilowatt hours (from 16 billion). Tractor output stood at 80,000 per year, and motor vehicles came off the assembly line at an annual rate of 211,000. By 1939 Soviet Russia had overtaken Britain and France and had become the world's third largest industrial power, after the United States and Germany.

The Third Five-Year Plan which was to cover the years 1938 through 1942 was never completed. Beginning in 1939, as war clouds were gathering, it was constantly modified to permit the expansion of the armed forces and accelerate the output of arms and ammunition. Consumer goods industries were at once affected by these changes; in 1939 in a major industrial center such as Magnitogorsk, shoes and suits had become unobtainable, and in 1940 bread, too, was being rationed again.

THE POLITICAL SCENE

Opposition and Purges. With the defeat of the Trotskyite opposition Stalin's hold on the Communist Party had been strengthened materially The extent of his power became evident when less than a year later he broke with some of his most important allies in the struggle against Trotsky—Bukharin, the chief theorist of the party and editor of *Pravda*, Rykov, the chairman of the Council of People's Commissars, and Tomsky, head of the labor unions. The break occurred over the forcible collectivization of the kulak farms. Bukharin and Rykov considered the liquidation of the kulaks economically disastrous and maintained that the gradual absorption of the peasantry into the collective farms was possible and economically and politically sounder. Bukharin also worried that collectivization would further entrench the bureaucracy and stifle individual initiative. Tomsky, in turn, did not want to surrender the right of the labor unions to protect the interests of their members—a prerogative which was bound to interfere with the accelerated industrialization campaign that Stalin was planning. Charging the three with collaboration with capitalist elements (which was untrue) and with attempts to establish a joint opposition bloc with former Trotskyites (which was true), Stalin rallied behind him a majority of both the Politburo and the Central Committee of the Communist Party. The three men were stripped of their policy-making positions, but after having admitted their "errors" and foresworn all future "deviations," they were given appointments of lesser importance.

The defeat of the "right-wingers" did not end all opposition to Stalin. Not every member of the Politburo and the Central Committee was as yet an unreserved Stalinist; on both bodies there still were men who warned against the continued sabotage and conspiracy trials by which Stalin tried to terrorize all opponents, imagined or real, into subservience. These critics also urged a more cautious course in economic matters, and it was possibly due to their pleas that the Second Five-Year Plan paid somewhat greater attention to the output of consumer goods. The plan to give the country a slightly less restrictive constitution also goes back to the period of 1933–34 and may have been the result of their pleadings. According to several sources, some of these critics attacked Stalin bitterly in secretly circulated memoranda and asked for his removal from the top leadership. Whether or not such plans were discussed, mere dissension was sufficient to arouse Stalin's suspicions, and he resolved to eliminate all remaining "moderate" elements. Carefully making his preparations, he managed to appoint some of his most devoted followers to the party's security organs and judicial positions that watched over the loyalty and discipline of the party members.

The opportunity to discredit the moderates presented itself in December 1934 when Sergei Kirov, the secretary of the Leningrad party organization, was assassinated by a disgruntled party comrade. Kirov is believed to have belonged to the moderate faction; a handsome, dynamic young man of great popularity, he seems to have been considered by many as a well-qualified successor to Stalin if the moderates should prevail. Stalin thus may have seen in Kirov a dangerous rival and may well have had a hand in arranging his assassination. Whatever the case, Stalin seized on the murder to rid himself of his opponents, actual and potential. To speed up this process he had the Central Executive Committee issue a decree calling for the completion of any investigation of terrorist plots and activities within ten days, depriving the accused in such cases of the right to counsel, and barring appeals and petitions for pardon.[5]

[5] The decree was issued on December 1, 1934, the very day of the assassination of Kirov, and may well have been prepared in advance—perhaps even in anticipation of the murder of Kirov.

Then Stalin struck. The first victims were non-Communists, so called "White Guards." In their case a connection with Kirov's murder was not even pretended and they were simply charged with terrorist conspiracies. But soon the dragnet of the People's Commissariat of Internal Affairs (the NKVD, into which the OGPU had been absorbed) hauled in thousands of party members who were accused of being associated with a "Zinovievite" center of opposition. Zinoviev, Kamenev, and other one-time oppositionists were secretly tried on charges of false recantations and for having inspired the assassination of Kirov by their ideological attitude; they were sentenced to long terms of imprisonment. Some moderates, among them the writer Maxim Gorky (1868–1936), who had warned Stalin against his terrorist practices, died under circumstances that strongly suggested that their death may not have been due to natural causes.

In the course of 1935 the purges came to an end in the higher party echelons. Such former opponents as Bukharin and the one-time Trotskyites Karl Radek, a prominent party journalist, and Gregory Sokolnikov, a former People's Commissar of Finance, were appointed to the commission charged with drafting the constitution—perhaps in order to give them a false sense of security. The purges continued, however, on the lower levels of the party apparatus. In the Smolensk district, of 4,100 party members, 455 were expelled outright in 1935 and 204 remained under investigation. Of those purged, one-third were engaged in economic work which may bear out the testimony of an American mining engineer, John Littlepage, who found considerable evidence of economic sabotage at the time. To eliminate any possible organized opposition, the Society of the Old Bolsheviks and the Society of One-Time Political Prisoners and Exiles, last outpost of the Old Leninists, were disbanded.

In mid-1936 the attack on the former oppositional leaders was resumed. Zinoviev, Kamenev, and fourteen others were tried publicly on charges of having organized a "terrorist center" on Trotsky's instructions and plotted the assassination of Stalin and other Soviet leaders. All but one pleaded guilty and in the course of their interrogation implicated Bukharin, Tomsky, Rykov, Radek, and other "right-wingers" and Trotskyites. There followed two similar trials in January 1937 and March 1938. In the first, Radek, Sokolnikov, and other one-time greats were charged with treason and readily confessed; in the second, Bukharin and Rykov were among the defendants, and accused of efforts to restore capitalism, in addition to the usual charges of murder plots, treason, and sabotage. Again there were ready admissions of guilt (except that Bukharin refused to admit that he had ever plotted the assassination of Lenin). Most of the accused were sentenced to death; only a few were given long prison terms.

Only those willing to confess (and thus prove Stalin right) were arraigned publicly; a great many more were tried behind closed doors (if they were tried at all). The most sensational of these secret trials involved a number of Red Army commanders, among them the highly popular, much decorated Marshal Michael Tukhachevsky. The generals were found guilty of the betrayal of military secrets to a "certain fascist power" and of conspiring to overthrow the Soviet regime in collaboration with that foreign state.[6] In addition, thousands of officers of army, navy, and air force, mostly of senior rank, were shot or sent to forced labor camps. Care was taken, however, not to destroy the striking power of the armed forces, and the purges took place in intermittent waves to allow the successors of the victims to prepare for their new assignments. At the outbreak of the war against Germany in 1941, many high officers who had been imprisoned were reinstated and given responsible posts.

As Nikita Khrushchev has since revealed in his indictment of Stalin in 1956, there was some opposition to this bloodbath in the Central Committee. Stalin's position, however, was by then so impregnable that no one could stop him, and the critics, in the end, all had to pay with their lives for their objections. Inexorably the purges fed upon themselves: the associates of the immediate victims, the associates of these associates, their aides and protégés, all those who might be linked to the purged by common views or possible ties of gratitude or loyalty, and might perhaps some day become their avengers, were caught up in the holocaust. Khrushchev revealed that of the 1,966 delegates to the Seventeenth Party Congress in 1934, 1,108 were subsequently charged with revolutionary crimes, and of the 139 members and candidates of the Central Committee elected by that Congress, 98 (70 per cent) were arrested and shot, "mostly in 1937–38." Spying, denunciations, mutual recriminations set friend against friend, relative against relative in a desperate quest for self-protection or in the cynical hope for advancement. But as the records of the Smolensk party organization indicate, no one was safe. At one party meeting a speaker, trying to demonstrate his support for Stalin, urged Stalin and the Central Committee to be less lenient toward the "Trotskyite-Zinovievite group" and "finish it for good." He was immediately denounced as "politically disloyal" for having accused the Central Committee and "Comrade Stalin" of being too conciliatory. On another occasion a group of factory workers called for the punishment of those leaders of their plant committee who had admitted Trotskyites and other "accursed" enemies to the party. The local district leader tried to shrug off this request as "the method of the enemy, to discredit the leaders." His inactivity may have been considered a "dulling of vigilance," for although a devout Stalinist of long standing,

[6] The charges are in themselves unconvincing: if Tukhachevsky and his associates had really been involved in such a plot, they would have been arrested as soon as it had been discovered—but they were taken into custody several months after their names had first come up in one of the open trials. There exists, moreover, some evidence that the documents establishing their guilt were forgeries concocted by the NKVD and the German Gestapo and filtered back into Russia by way of Czechoslovakia. President Beneš has confirmed in his memoirs that he passed on to Stalin some incriminating information which Czech diplomats in Berlin had obtained.

the man was removed from his office some months later and presumably shot or imprisoned.

What finally brought the carnage to an end was the fact that, like the forcible collectivization of the farms, the mass executions and deportations wrought havoc with the country's economy and administration. It became increasingly difficult to find replacements for those who had been purged, and when they were found, the new appointees proved reluctant to make any decisions lest these might be held against them at some future time. Such was the dearth of qualified party members that non-party men had to be appointed to important positions in the government and economy. Party strategy was changed in 1938, and it became now a serious offense to be "excessively vigilant." Expulsions from the party were reviewed, investigations discontinued, and some of the prisoners released. There was no rehabilitation, however, of the Old Bolsheviks, nor did Stalin or other top party leaders assume responsibility for whatever mistakes had been made. These were blamed either on the excessive zeal of local officials, on arbitrary procedures of the NKVD, or on traitors who had infiltrated the police and the party.

The Purpose of the Purges. In inflicting this merciless bloodbath on his party comrades, Stalin apparently wished to accomplish several purposes. His immediate goal was to tighten further his hold on the party by the elimination of any potential rivals. The timing of the purges —during the period between the remilitarization of the Rhineland by Hitler and the Nazi seizure of Austria—suggests that Stalin was fearful lest his critics seek to overthrow him in the event of a war with Germany or Japan, perhaps by taking advantage of any reverses that Russia might suffer in such a war. To guard himself against such a danger, he also replaced the leaders of the armed forces, most of them veterans of the Civil War, with men who owed their promotions to him alone and could thus be expected to remain loyal to him, even in a grave crisis. Finally, the purges, and above all the public trials, were to enhance Stalin's standing in the eyes of the nation. He was shown as being ever vigilant and concerned with people and country, ridding the nation of traitors and saboteurs. The public confessions of the defendants served to underline Stalin's patriotism by identifying all opposition to him with treason.

In making these confessions the accused thus rendered him a great service. Why, then, did they plead guilty even though the bulk of the charges were manifestly untrue? (Had they been true, Stalin and his regime could not possibly have survived.)[7] We have it on Khrushchev's authority that many, if not all, of the defendants were subjected to

[7] At a mock trial in Mexico City in 1938, which was to give Trotsky his day in court, it was proved that a Copenhagen hotel, the alleged scene of a clandestine meeting of some of the defendants, did not exist and that an airfield near Oslo at which one of the accused was supposed to have landed on a secret visit to Trotsky was closed to all traffic at the time of the alleged visit.

mental and physical torture. The right of the NKVD to hold as hostages the families of political offenders may have induced some of these men to confess to crimes they had never committed in order to save their wives and children. Others, again, may have hoped for milder punishment, and a few of the most cooperative defendants did escape the death sentence. But some may also have acted from an ineradicable loyalty to the Communist Party, feeling that by their confessions they were helping to restore the unity of the Party and thus rendering it a last service. In their eyes a united party, even if led by Stalin, was preferable to one rent by discord and unable to fight off Nazi Germany and Japan. Bukharin, one of the most courageous of the defendants, who refused to be cowed by the prosecutor and whose words for this reason carry special weight, thus justified his confession: "When you ask yourself: 'If you must die, what are you dying for?'—an absolute black vacuity suddenly rises before you with startling vividness. There was nothing to die for if one wanted to die unrepentant. . . . This in the end disarmed me completely and led me to bend my knees before the party and the country."[8]

The Constitution of 1936. In November 1936 the new constitution was promulgated. It was hailed as reflecting the progress towards democracy and socialism that had been made since the enactment of the constitution of 1923. Actually its political sections differed but slightly from the earlier document. The right to vote was now accorded to every citizen above the age of eighteen regardless of social origin, property status, and past activities. Suffrage was to be equal and the weighting of the vote in favor of the urban worker abandoned. Elections of all soviets from the local level up to the Supreme Soviet of the U.S.S.R. were to be direct and secret. But these changes were of little significance since the party selected the one electoral candidate nominated for each seat. The changes thus were hardly more than a liberal gesture that it was hoped would be appreciated at home and abroad.[9]

Correspondingly, the Bill of Rights of the new constitution guaranteed freedom of speech, press, assembly, and organization to all citizens of the U.S.S.R., and not merely to workers as before. Again the change was largely meaningless since these rights were granted only "in conformity

---

[8] This explanation, which probably applies to several of the confessions, was accepted as valid by Trotsky and is the main theme of Arthur Koestler's novel, *Darkness at Noon*.

[9] Voters did have the right, however, to strike out the candidate's name and, if they wished, write in another. If the official candidate did not get 50 per cent of the vote, he was not considered elected. No candidate for the Supreme Soviet or state or provincial soviets has ever been rejected in this manner, perhaps simply because it would be impossible to organize any opposition on a large enough scale without party support, but a few candidates to city and village soviets have each time failed of election—in 1950, for example, 102, or less than 2 per cent of all candidates.

with the interests of the working people and in order to strengthen the socialist system," thus narrowly circumscribing the limits within which these "freedoms" applied. The constitution also reaffirmed the federal structure of the Soviet Union and the right of the member states to secede: but the elaborate provisions governing state-Union relations once more were of little import since both Union and state governments and bureaucracies were bound by the commands and controls of the highly centralized All-Union Communist Party. A similar air of unreality attached to the chapter dealing with the judicial system, for the legal rights of the individual were subject to the same limitations as all political rights.[10]

The main interest of the constitution of 1936 lay in its social and economic provisions. Article 4 established the "socialist system of the economy and the socialist ownership of the instruments and means of production" as the economic foundation of the U.S.S.R.; socialist property was defined as state, cooperative or collective-farm property (Art. 5). Articles 7 and 8 described the organization of the collective farms, adding that every household in a collective farm had *"for its personal use,"* that is, as a tenant, a small plot of land, and could own a house, livestock, and minor tools. Supplementing this exception to the socialist system, Article 9 permitted craftsmen as well to work on their own as long as they did all the work in their shop by themselves and did not "exploit the labor of others." Another provision acknowledged the right to private property in incomes, savings, homes, the above-mentioned small enterprises, and any articles of personal use and convenience. Among the social rights not usually mentioned in constitutions until that time were the right to paid employment, to rest and leisure ensured by the seven-hour working day, paid annual vacations, maintenance in old age, sickness and disability, and the right to free education.

Yet these guarantees were of questionable value. Although the constitution established specific amendment procedures, both the seven-hour working day and the right to free secondary education were modified by simple decree in 1940.

THE COMINTERN

Fight Against Socialists. Throughout the mid-twenties, after the debacle of the German Communist risings, the Comintern refrained from the active promotion of revolution in Europe. Some Communist parties maintained uneasy relations, occasionally growing into a measure of cooperation, with their Socialist counterparts. The policy reflected

---

[10] The constitution (Art. 127) does not expressly make this reservation, but the official *History of the Communist Party of the Soviet Union (Bolsheviks)* made it clear that the reservation applied to these rights too.

Stalin's view that there was no early prospect of overthrowing capitalism and that the task of building up the U.S.S.R. ought not to be jeopardized by international complications. The Comintern was reduced to but another instrument of Soviet policy which Stalin treated with his customary disdain: from the death of Lenin to the Comintern's demise in 1943 only three plenary congresses were held, and none of these he addressed himself.

The uneasy truce which the Comintern observed in the mid-1920's came officially to an end in 1928 at the second of these congresses. Efforts to maintain some measure of collaboration with China's Kuomintang, Britain's labor unions, and some of the socialist parties of Eastern Europe had all ended in failure. Moreover, as was made clear at the congress, the Soviet leaders expected, with what proved accurate foresight, an early economic crisis in the capitalist countries. A slump was bound to sharpen the class struggle, and from such tensions the Kremlin hoped to benefit most by a go-it-alone policy. The Comintern therefore declared war on all socialist parties and denounced them as capitalist tools designed to destroy the working class from within. The change also reflected the political shift in the Soviet Union: by discrediting the moderate Socialists in other countries Stalin hoped also to discredit Bukharin and likeminded "rightwingers" who counseled moderation at home and abroad and against whom he was soon to turn openly.

The Reaction to Nazism.   Abroad the most immediate target of the new policy was the German Social Democratic Party. In the face of the rising Nazi tide the German Socialists were savagely attacked and harassed as "Social Fascists." Social Democratic proposals to form a united Socialist-Communist front against the Nazis were rejected, except on terms that would have destroyed the Social Democratic Party. At times the German Communists even joined forces with the Nazis and supported the latter's assaults on the Weimar Republic; thus, in 1931 they co-sponsored a referendum designed to oust the democratic regime in Prussia. Nazism was viewed as the last desperate attempt of bourgeois capitalism to stave off the proletarian revolution in Germany; it was expected to fail since the uncouth and ignorant Nazis would merely aggravate the crisis of capitalism and thus hasten the Communist takeover. In a sense the advent of Nazism was therefore welcomed in Moscow: "The open dictatorship of fascism," exulted one of the Comintern's journals, "accelerates the speed of Germany's march towards the proletarian revolution," and as late as December 1933, after the German Communist Party had been annihilated by Hitler, *Bolshevik,* the doctrinal journal of the Soviet party, still assured its readers that "in Germany the proletarian revolution is nearer to realization than in any other country."

But in the long run the fact could not be ignored that the Nazis were firmly in the saddle and a Nazi attack on the U.S.S.R. far more likely than the internal collapse of the Nazi regime. This danger appeared to be greatly increased by the conclusion of the German-Polish Nonaggression Pact of January 1934: Moscow suspected the treaty of involving a deal by which Germany would recover Danzig and the Polish Corridor while it would help Poland in efforts to seize parts of the Ukraine. Soviet foreign policy had throughout 1933 insisted on the possibility of maintaining friendly relations with Nazi Germany; the Kremlin now shifted its stand and sought a rapprochement with the West, entered the League of Nations, and concluded military assistance pacts with France and Czechoslovakia.

The Popular-Front Strategy. Inevitably, Comintern strategy was affected by this change, and at a new congress in 1935 the "Popular Front" policy was proclaimed. The congress called on its member parties to cooperate with all antifascist forces, whether socialist, liberal, or conservative, in order to halt the further spread of Nazism or any other form of fascism. Popular Fronts were formed in France, where the front was even set up prior to its official adoption by the Comintern, in Spain, and in a number of non-European countries. While meeting with some success in China and some of the Latin American countries, the Popular Fronts in France and Spain at best delayed the victory of fascism. Mutual distrust of the various partners precluded any prolonged constructive collaboration within the two countries, nor were France and Spain able to work closely with one another while under Popular Front governments. Stalin, too, forever distrustful of Western influences, viewed with misgivings the Popular Front strategy because it called for closer contact between the U.S.S.R. and the West. He did come to the aid of the Spanish Popular Front during Spain's Civil War; but after he withdrew from the war he turned with particular ferocity on those Soviet officials who had served in Spain. Their stay in the West and their association with Western hopes and ideals rendered them suspect. According to some estimates, almost all Soviet citizens involved in the Spanish venture perished in the purges. The Popular Front strategy thus came to an end before it was openly discarded by the conclusion of the Nazi-Soviet Nonaggression Pact in August 1939.

SOVIET CIVILIZATION

Soviet Patriotism. During the early years of its existence the Soviet regime turned its back on Russia's past and sought to eradicate all traces of nationalism as incompatible with the supranational mission of Communism. History was dropped as an independent discipline and became a subdivision of sociology, taught only as the history of class struggle; the *Internationale,* the battle hymn of Marxism, took the place of the national anthem; and members of the Red Army swore allegiance to the cause of "toiling mankind" rather than to their homeland.

Stalin's strategy of "socialism in one country" foreshadowed a change in attitude, and in the mid-1930's the official opposition to all manifestations of national pride was modified; while the term "national" was still being shunned, a feeling very much akin to nationalism, Soviet patriotism, was now encouraged. The change in policy took place in the early part of 1934, when the Soviet government came to understand fully the grave threat that Nazism presented to the U.S.S.R. As the danger of war grew more imminent, it became important to nurture the Soviet peoples' attachment to home and soil in order to strengthen their determination to fight in defense of their country. Soviet patriotism, it was also hoped, would enlist the support of those who still had their reservations about the Soviet regime.

To foster Soviet patriotism, history was restored as a discipline in its own right, and historians who had been removed were reappointed to their university chairs. In the new textbooks that were brought out, Ivan the Terrible and Peter the Great were pictured as progressive social reformers who had replaced the old hereditary aristocracy with a new nobility based on state service. In turn, Tsar Alexander I who defeated Napoleon I in 1812 was acclaimed as the successful defender of his country. Sir John Maynard tells of a school teacher who was dismissed in 1933 for having praised too highly two of Alexander's generals, Kutusov and Bagration, the engineers of Napoleon's defeat; he was recalled in 1938 because what had been condemned earlier as counter-revolutionary teaching was now appreciated as a tribute to a great Russian victory. Similarly poets, playwrights, and novelists took up historical themes, and movie producers and newspaper editors also looked to the past as a source of inspiration and strength. Soldiers of the Red Army swore allegiance to the Soviet Union, and traditional ranks and decorations, detested earlier as symbols of Tsarist militarism, were reintroduced in the armed forces.

The Family. The trend toward traditionalism and stability led also to a reconsideration of the status of the family. Ideology had dictated the legalization of abortions and easy divorces in the early days of the Soviet regime, but the need for greater personal discipline and an increased birth rate called for a change in policy. In 1936 a decree limited the legal performance of abortions to cases in which they were indicated for reasons of health, and declared their performance for other reasons a punishable offense.[11] The same decree provided for increased financial

---

[11] Before the decree was promulgated, it was submitted to public discussion. The discussion was noteworthy because it touched off some very outspoken attacks on the plan in letters to the press which were published. Most of the critics were women who complained that low incomes, lack of housing, and inadequate crèches required the retention of a liberal abortion policy.

assistance to expectant and recent mothers; special grants were to be awarded to mothers with more than six children, with additional bonuses to be paid to those with over ten children. At the same time divorce procedures were rendered somewhat more difficult and divorce fees raised, with further increases imposed in the case of second and third divorces. Parents were admonished that one of their foremost duties was to be the "social educators" of their children and to "prepare good citizens," and youngsters were warned to show respect to their elders. To emphasize this latter point, press and party gave much publicity to a visit of Stalin to his old mother in Georgia although, as a rule, the family life of the Soviet leaders was not considered a matter of public concern.

Education. The educational system was greatly expanded during the 1930's. In consequence, attendance of a four-year school became compulsory for every child throughout the Soviet Union, and seven-year schooling was provided for all children in the R.S.F.S.R. and in all cities outside of Russia proper. Beyond this level, there were available, at least in the larger cities, three years of additional high school training leading to university study, and a variety of trade schools and technical high schools. In line with the general trend toward discipline and traditionalism educational experiments such as school soviets were abandoned, and conventional curricula, homework, examinations, and report cards reintroduced. The fight against illiteracy proceeded successfully; by 1939 the rate of literacy for the entire country had risen to 81 per cent, with the most striking advances recorded among the backward peoples of Asian Russia.

In accordance with the Soviet constitution, education was free on all levels, and most students pursuing university and advanced technical studies received government stipends to meet their living expenses. In return, they had to serve the first five (now three) years after graduation wherever the government decided to send them—as a rule, to remote areas where few professionally trained people were willing to go voluntarily. In 1940, as military preparations were stepped up, the principle of free education was abandoned for all studies beyond the seven-year school that did not pertain directly to these preparations. Except for outstanding students, anyone wishing to pursue such studies had to pay tuition fees. On the other hand, in order to channel students into war-essential training, stipends were also awarded for attendance of vocational and technical schools which provided such training, and during the war large numbers of students were conscripted into these schools. The fact that the children of well-to-do parents were allowed to pursue any studies they wished constituted a sharp departure from the principle of equal educational opportunity regardless of economic status. Many observers saw in such a concession evidence of the emergence of a new Soviet class system.

One of the Soviets' earliest educational reforms had been the introduction of coeducation in order to assure women of full equality in educational opportunities. Coeducation in the schools was, however, abandoned in 1943 on the grounds that separate education adjusted to the different rate of physiological and psychological development of boys and girls would produce better results. As was emphasized also, there would be no danger now of inferior educational opportunities for women since the large number of existing schools would assure girls of educational facilities fully equal to those provided for boys.

Religion. Religious activities continued to be subject to various restrictions throughout the 1930's. In 1929, an amendment to the constitution redefined "freedom of conscience" as the right to engage in religious *worship* or antireligious *propaganda* (rather than both religious and antireligious propaganda), and in this form the concept was incorporated into the constitution of 1936. The amendment was enacted at the height of the first collectivization drive, which Orthodox priests were known to oppose, and was part of an effort, along with the closing of churches, to curb their influence on the peasants. The harassment of the Orthodox Church subsided somewhat after 1932, in keeping with a general relaxation of checks and controls, but efforts to discourage religious activities by educational and political pressures continued. In the course of the purges, persecution of the Orthodox clergy flared up again, and there were wholesale arrests and treason trials of priests. In the Western Oblast, the region around Smolensk, with a population of 6,500,000, only 852 places of worship—churches, synagogues, chapels—remained open in 1936, and 836 clerics tried to minister to the spiritual needs of the faithful. Yet as Yaroslavsky, head of the League of the Militant Godless had to admit, in 1937 almost half of the population still were believers. It was doubtless due to this widespread religiousness that the antireligious campaign was toned down in the late 1930's to ensure the support of religious believers in case of war.

The fight against Mohammedanism and Buddhism proved even more difficult. Here, enforcement of antireligious policies was impeded because a large part of Soviet Russia's Mohammedans and Buddhists were nomads who found it easy to evade government regulations. Jews, on the other hand, could be controlled more easily, and although they were recognized as a special national group and given the Siberian territory of Birobidjan on which to settle, there was continued interference with their religious activities. Zionism became a special target of Soviet wrath, for it turned the attention of its supporters to a land outside the U.S.S.R. and thus was in conflict with Soviet patriotism. It was therefore denounced as an alien anti-Soviet nationalism and harshly suppressed.

Housing. Housing conditions remained inadequate throughout the prewar period. Although all three Five-Year Plans made provisions for the construction of new apartment houses, urban housing space decreased from 67 square feet per person in 1923 to 42 in 1939. Construction could not keep pace with the influx of rural workers into the already over-crowded cities; it was slowed down in particular by the lack of a labor force properly trained in modern building techniques. Moreover, the demand for apartments had to compete with the call for more schools, hospitals, office buildings, and factories, which were given priority, and with the construction of recreational facilities—workers' clubs, movie houses, theaters, and sports stadia—which were considered important to uphold morale. To provide at least a modicum of accommodations for their labor force, factories built their own dormitories; but even these failed to meet the existing needs, and in a city like Magnitogorsk, which in a few years mushroomed from a small village into a major industrial center, thousands of workers were forced to live in tents even in the depth of the Siberian winter.

Medical Services. Between 1928 and 1941 considerable progress was made in the expansion of health and medical facilities. The number of physicians more than doubled from 63,100 to 130,300. Special attention was paid to the establishment of medical centers where teams of doctors consisting of both general practitioners and specialists provided all needed services; the number of centers grew from 13,100 to 27,000. Impressive as these figures were, they meant that there still was only one physician available for every 1,500 people. Least satisfactory was the increase in hospital beds during that period from 217,700 to 661,400, or one bed for every 290 inhabitants. Special efforts were made, however, to improve facilities for maternity cases, and the number of beds in maternity hospitals increased fivefold from 27,300 to 141,800.

All doctors were salaried employees; to make work in rural areas more attractive, rural physicians were paid up to 20 per cent more than their urban colleagues with corresponding responsibilities.

Literature. Like any other aspect of Soviet life, literature reflected the shifts and changes of the Communist party line. The interrelationship between literature and politics was close, for literature was to serve, in Communist parlance, as a "tool in the organization of the masses." Thus, as the N.E.P. period drew to an end, writers were deprived of the comparative freedom they had enjoyed during the mid-1920's and were drafted into the service of party and government. In 1932 the Central Committee replaced the existing literary organizations with a single Union of Soviet Writers to which all authors had to belong if they hoped to achieve any measure of success. Members were to be guided by "socialist realism" in their work, which Stalin's spokesman, Andrei Zhdanov (1896–1948), defined as the depiction of life "not just as 'objective reality,' but . . . in its revolutionary development . . . combined with the task of ideological remolding and re-education of the toiling people in the spirit of socialism." Or, as Stalin put it, the writer was to be an "engineer of human minds." Accordingly, the Union of Soviet Writers pledged its members to create works "saturated with the heroic struggle of the international proletariat, with the grandeur of the victory of socialism, and reflecting the great wisdom and heroism of the Communist Party."

In accordance with this "social command," writers devoted their talents to the support of the Five-Year Plans, and a spate of novels dealing with collectivization, industrialization, and other aspects of the Soviet Union's economic development were published in the 1930's. Boris Pilnyak's *The Volga Flows Into the Caspian Sea* revolves around the building of a dam to make the Moskva river navigable to large ships; Mikhail Sholokhov abandoned his multivolume epic, *And Quiet Flows the Don*, to deal with the collectivization drive in a new novel, *Seeds of Tomorrow;* Valentin Katayev, in *Forward, Oh Time!*, told the story of a group of concrete mixers at Magnitogorsk; two novels by Fedor Gladkov and Leonid Leonov dealt with the construction of an electric power plant and a paper mill, respectively.

But though the topics were remarkably uniform (in accordance with party dictates), their execution showed noteworthy differences. To Pilnyak the construction of the dam was merely a background theme even though, catering to the powers that were, he devotes long pages to its engineering problems. Yet he was obviously much more interested in the conflict between the old impassioned Bolsheviks of the revolutionary period and the new technical-minded, pragmatic Communists of the Stalinist persuasion, and his sympathies lay with the former. Katayev's central concern, on the other hand, was the building of the huge combine around Magnitogorsk, and he shared the enthusiasm and confidence of the Communists that people his novel. Sholokhov stood between Pilnyak and Katayev: he was sympathetic toward the party official sent to collectivize the village of his novel, but he also drew the opponents of collectivization objectively and with understanding, and he did not gloss over the price in human despair and material losses that had to be paid for the victory of collectivization.

Among the works which reflected more closely the self-confidence of socialist realism were Nikolay Ostrovsky's novel, *How the Steel Was Tempered*, the story of a young Communist who by courage, persistence, and resourcefulness overcame many difficulties during the revolutionary and civil war period, and Nikolay Virta's novel, *Lawfulness*, which deals with the treason and sabotage trials of the 1930's, explores the motives of the accused, stresses the lawfulness of party and government, and urges its readers to remain vigilant. Alexei Tolstoy's monumental trilogy, *The Way Through Hell*, combines skillfully historical and psychological ingredients with the dictates of socialist realism and Soviet patriotism.

The central characters, all of them members of the prerevolutionary bourgeoisie, survive many difficulties with great fortitude until finally they come to accept the new Soviet state as the modern embodiment of the old "holy Russia." Among plays one of the most successful was Nikolay Pogodin's *The Kremlin Chimes*—a series of vignettes depicting Lenin, with warmth and humor, as the friend of the poor, the resourceful planner of Russia's greatness, and the charismatic leader who by the forcefulness of his reasoning succeeds in enlisting even bitterly hostile anti-Communists in the service of the Soviet state. (The original version of the play had Stalin assist Lenin in his endeavors, but Stalin's part has since been expunged.)

If socialist realism was to fulfill its educational purpose, its works had to be written simply and straightforwardly in order to be easily understood by the great mass of the Soviet public. As a result, even the better novels and plays of those years were marred by long passages of dull pedestrian writing—a condition aggravated by the confining substantive requirements of socialist realism. A contributing factor to this esthetic deterioration was the baneful influence of Stalin's own literary style, for by the mid-1930's the dictator was setting the tone in matters of art and esthetics. "The style of the ruler," as his biographer, I. Deutscher, has written, "became the ruling style of the nation," and since Stalin's style was appallingly awkward, the national style degenerated into a wooden, repetitive lingo to which even creative writers did not remain fully immune.

Music and Painting. Music too adapted itself to the prevailing trends, and a large number of compositions were inspired by national and historical themes. Sergei Prokofiev (1891–1953) wrote a cantata, *Alexander Nevsky,* extolling the defeat of the Teutonic Knights by that Moscow grand prince in the thirteenth century, and he composed an opera based on Tolstoy's *War and Peace.* Modernist music, on the other hand, was banned, and Dmitri Shostakovich (1906–), perhaps the greatest Russian composer of his time, encountered serious difficulties because some of his works, among them his opera *Lady Macbeth of Mtsensk,* were considered too experimental and hence unintelligible and decadent. Once he returned to symphonic composition, he was widely acclaimed again.

Painting as well reflected the political shifts of the 1930's. While many painters still dealt with social themes, there was a new concern for the beauty of the Russian countryside, and interest in strictly historical subjects also revived. But painting, like the other arts, suffered from the stifling style of the times, and few significant works of art were created.

15

The Destruction of
the European Order

The present chapter constitutes in a sense a concluding summary of the events that were discussed in the preceding sections. The specific form which international developments took in the 1930's grew out of the interaction of frenzied activity and dispirited quietism that characterized the two main camps. While the Western Powers kept shying away from foreign political confrontations, Hitler deliberately sought to provoke them. Counting on the indecision of his opponents, he scored one victory after another, extending Germany's hegemony as he advanced. Europe's setbacks, however, were not only due to its failure to establish a common front against Nazi aggression. The European nations were equally unable, or unwilling, to induce either the United States or the Soviet Union to help contain Germany. In the 1920's the British and French had remembered the lesson of World War I that Germany could no longer be checked without outside help; but in the 1930's they made, if any, only half-hearted attempts to apply that lesson. But this was not Europe's mistake alone. The United States and in the end the Soviet Union as well thought that they could afford to ignore the moral of 1917–18 and leave Europe to shift for itself. In this belief they proved **302** as tragically wrong as did Europe.

HITLER AGAINST EUROPE

Hitler's First Moves.   Hitler's first steps on the international stage were cautious and ostensibly peaceful. He stated in every speech and assured every foreign visitor that he needed peace to accomplish his task of rehabilitating Germany. This was true, although not quite in the sense in which his audiences were led to understand his remarks. Hitler needed quiet in order to build up a "tightly authoritarian," well-armed state. Time was also required to drill into the Germans what he called an "absolute readiness" to fight for their country. Only after his had been done could he risk embarking on his expansionist plans. For this reason Germany continued to attend the sessions of the League and the Geneva Disarmament Conference during the spring of 1933 even though Hitler had always assailed the hypocrisy of the League and the disarmament movement, and the Germans also took part in the World Economic Conference. When Mussolini proposed a Four-Power Pact between Britain, France, Germany, and Italy for the maintenance of peace in Europe in March 1933, Hitler was immediately ready to sign it.

This he could do the more easily because the pact was intended expressly to strengthen Germany. As one of the "revisionist" powers, Italy was anxious to see Germany become a powerful ally in its campaign for a revision of the peace treaties. Unlike the Locarno Pact the proposed Four-Power Pact was not concerned with the preservation of the status quo, but with treaty revision, Germany's right to arms equality, and the redistribution of colonies. The pact was also a direct threat to the League of Nations. While it paid lip service to the League and pledged the signatories to proceed within the framework of the League, in reality it sought to establish a directorate of the four Great Powers and commit them, "so far as Europe was concerned, to make other states conform to their decisions." This last clause was intended to drive a wedge between France and its allies. Indeed, the latter wondered how valuable their alliances with France still were; even after the pact had been rewritten to allay their anxieties, they remained perturbed by the fact that France had considered accepting a pact to which its allies were not a party. The French alliance system thus suffered a first setback; worse, France worried its allies needlessly, for in the end the French government decided against ratifying the pact.

The readiness of Britain and France to bypass the League encouraged Hitler to defy that organization; he withdrew from it in October 1933 after the Disarmament Conference decided to delay Germany's rearmament. But the withdrawal from the League was caused also by the vehement charges of Nazi terrorism and injustice with which the German delegation was confronted at the League session. Hitler's hope to pursue his aims for a time within the European community thus proved futile; isolated and without allies, he now set out to break up what remained of that polity.

Polish Pact and Austrian Coup.   Hitler launched his first move in this campaign almost at once. In January 1934 he concluded a ten-year non-aggression pact with Poland. The pact not only seemed to ease him out of his isolation, but it also served to weaken further France's alliance system. For the Poles, on the other hand, the arrangement promised at least a temporary truce in the battle over the Polish Corridor and other formerly German territories that had been given to Poland after World War I. The accommodation with Germany was also important to Poland because the Poles continued to have serious doubts about France's loyalty as an ally. But if Poland was drawing away from France's orbit, the Soviet Union, alarmed at the German-Polish rapprochement, began to move closer to France. Thus Hitler, who had tried to maintain, at least outwardly, friendly relations with the Soviet Union, saw his isolation increase.

This trend was accelerated in mid-summer 1934 when Austrian Nazis, supported by German money and arms, tried to overthrow the Austrian government of Chancellor Engelbert Dollfuss. To incorporate his homeland Austria into Germany was an old ambition of Hitler, and he devotes much space to it in *Mein Kampf*. Austria, on the other hand, was much less interested in an *Anschluss* since Hitler had seized power in Germany. The Austrian Catholic faithful found the anticlerical, aggressively nationalist character of Nazism repulsive, and the Social Democrats did not wish to share the fate that had befallen their comrades in Germany. Tension between the two countries increased in the summer of 1933 when Dollfuss sought to buttress his dictatorial regime by outlawing the Austrian Nazi Party and Hitler in turn attempted to starve Austria into surrender by barring German tourists from Austria. France, Britain, Italy, and some of the smaller countries came to Austria's aid, acknowledging jointly the right of the Austrians to independence and arranging a substantial international loan. Italy had a special stake in Austria's independence since it did not wish to have Germany as a neighbor; Mussolini therefore dispatched large shipments of arms to help equip the semifascist Heimwehr, Dollfuss' most important domestic support. Both Italy and the Heimwehr demanded a price for their aid, however: the Socialists who were still in control of Vienna's municipal administration must be removed from their last stronghold. This Dollfuss did in February 1934; after some heavy street fighting the Social Democratic Party and all Socialist labor unions were disbanded. Yet in destroying the Socialist movement, Dollfuss deprived himself of a stalwart ally against the Nazis; unlike its German counterpart, the Socialist Schutzbund was a militant group, willing to fight the Austrian Nazis just as it fought off half of the Austrian army equipped with machine guns, armored cars, and artillery before its resistance was crushed.

Late in July 1934, Austrian Nazi formations trained and equipped in Germany tried to overthrow Dollfuss' government. The rebels seized several government buildings, and Dollfuss was killed in his office; but except for isolated local revolts in Carinthia and Styria, the nationwide rising that had been planned did not take place. A new government was formed by Kurt von Schuschnigg (1897–   ), like Dollfuss a Christian Social leader with strong authoritarian leanings. With the help of the army and police force, most of which remained loyal to the government, Schuschnigg restored order after a few days. At the outbreak of the Putsch, moreover, Mussolini had rushed troops to the Austro-Italian frontier, ready to move into Austria should Austria's independence be threatened. Hitler immediately dissociated himself from the rebels, the German minister in Vienna who had had some dealings with the insurgents was dismissed, and the Austrian Nazi formations on German soil liquidated. German press and radio attacks on the Austrian government virtually came to an end.

EUROPE REACTS TO HITLER

France's Diplomacy. The Austrian crisis aroused Europe into more systematic attempts to construct an anti-German coalition. France was the center of these activities. In February 1934, seventy-two-year-old Louis Barthou became French Foreign Minister. Barthou had been a close associate of Poincaré, and he shared the latter's views on how to treat Germany. Barthou proceeded at once to reinforce France's alliance system by closer ties with the Soviet Union and Italy. He sponsored Soviet Russia's admission to the League, and he initiated negotiations for the conclusion of a military assistance pact with Moscow. Barthou also tried to settle some of the problems that had long troubled Franco-Italian relations. However, before Barthou could complete this task, he and King Alexander I of Yugoslavia, who had just arrived on a state visit to France, were killed at Marseilles by a group of Croatian terrorists. Barthou's successor, Pierre Laval, a shrewd negotiator and skilled tactician, but an opportunist without long-range views, continued to pursue the foreign policy of his predecessor, with the accent, however, on the rapprochement with Italy. The outstanding difficulties with the Italians were readjusted. France ceded to Italy some territory in French Equatorial Africa and in French Somaliland, fulfilling belatedly the treaty of London of 1915, and agreement was reached on joint action should Germany violate its disarmament obligations or again threaten Austria's independence. Laval also assured Mussolini that France would not stand in the way of Italy's efforts to strengthen its economic position in

Ethiopia—a pledge that led Mussolini to feel that Laval was giving him a free hand in that country.

In March 1935 Hitler repudiated the disarmament provisions of the Versailles Treaty. Despite widespread alarm Europe's reaction was weak. France lacked the determination to act and did not dare to act in any event without Britain, and Britain was opposed to any military action. There was also a general feeling that Hitler had simply implemented the German right to equality, and while his methods were deplorable, the action as such seemed quite justified. France, Britain, and Italy met at the Italian resort town of Stresa where they "regretfully recognized that the method of unilateral repudiation adopted by the German government . . . had undermined public confidence in the security of a peaceful order." Similarly the League Council stated merely that the German action deserved "condemnation," but it did suggest that any future action endangering peace should be punished by the imposition of financial and economic sanctions on the offending country. A committee was formed to explore the practical problems involved in the application of sanctions.

Hitler's move gave new impetus to the Franco-Soviet negotiations of a military assistance pact which had been lagging since the death of Barthou. In May 1935 a treaty of mutual assistance was concluded by the two powers, and it was supplemented by a similar pact between the Soviet Union and Czechoslovakia. Yet the value of both these treaties was dubious since the U.S.S.R. did not border on either Germany or Czechoslovakia and Poland would not accord it the right of transit; what military aid the Kremlin could give to either of its two treaty partners was uncertain under the circumstances. Moreover, despite their pact, France continued to look on the Soviet Union with manifest distrust: Laval was unwilling to implement the pact with a military convention, and France's ratification of the treaty was not completed until March 1936. Similarly, the Czechs insisted on inserting in their pact the clause that neither side was obliged to come to the aid of the other unless France met its obligation to assist the country attacked. The one immediate advantage France derived from the pact was a directive by Stalin to the French Communists to end their opposition to all French defense measures. Communist opposition to the extension of France's military service to two years ceased at once.

The British Position.   During the first two years of the Nazi era Britain kept largely aloof from the increased diplomatic activities that Hitler's appearance touched off. Preoccupied with domestic and empire problems and still feeling relatively secure, the British did not share the concerns of Germany's neighbors. In fact, many Britons felt more sympathetic toward Germany's demand for arms equality than toward France's insistence on security. Nazi Germany was moreover welcomed as a sturdy bulwark against Communism which was thought a far greater threat than National Socialism. The mood of the country was pacifist, and Britain's leadership was not of a caliber to dispel the nation's illusions.[1]

Britain participated in the negotiations for the Four-Power Pact, it joined in the demand for the preservation of Austria's independence, and protested against Hitler's reintroduction of military conscription; but in accordance with the country's traditional policy of nonalignment in peacetime, the government refused to become a party to France's treaty negotiations with Italy and the Soviet Union. The one concession it made to the reality of Nazi rearmament was to order a substantial increase in the number of planes to be built for the Royal Air Force in 1935.

The Anglo-German Naval Pact. This measure was, however, at once offset by a naval agreement with Germany. The initiative for this pact seems to have come from Berlin; London, although it had just condemned Hitler's proclamation of German rearmament, now sanctioned that move by agreeing to naval discussions. The hope was that by negotiating a treaty Britain could prevail upon Hitler to keep his naval rearmament within bounds compatible with Britain's security needs. The agreement provided for a tonnage ratio of 35 to 100 in Britain's favor, although within that overall ratio Germany was given the right to a submarine tonnage equal to that of the entire British Commonwealth. The arrangement suited Germany well: Hitler was neither able nor anxious to build a surface navy competing with Britain's, but was primarily interested in constructing U-boats whose value for Germany had been demonstrated in World War I. The British Admiralty on its part was confident that newly developed sonar detection devices would greatly reduce the U-boat menace in future wars.

The pact aroused the indignation of France and Italy, who objected to it after a last-minute consultation. Apart from his substantive gains, Hitler had also succeeded in creating friction among his opponents.

THE BEGINNINGS OF AGGRESSION

The Ethiopian War. Tension increased between France, Britain, and Italy as Italy got ready to go to war against Ethiopia. Preparations for that campaign had been under way since 1932; the conquest of Ethiopia was

---

[1] There was also a great deal of misapprehension in government circles about the character of the Nazi dictatorship. As late as 1936 Thomas Jones, a close confidant of Baldwin, was still hopeful that Hitler could be restrained by the power of German public opinion: "I keep on and on and on preaching against the policy of ostracizing Germany, however incalculable Hitler and his crew may be. . . . We have abundant evidence of the desire of all sorts of Germans to be on friendly terms with us. There is still a substantial element of elderly men and women in Germany who have not forgotten the war and its horrors, and who are in no hurry to precipitate another."

to implement Italy's right to imperial expansion as befitted "a fertile nation which has the pride and will to propagate its race over the face of the earth." The time seemed favorable; the manifest impotence of the League, the rapprochement with France, Britain's aloofness from continental affairs—everything suggested to Mussolini that he would encounter little, if any, opposition if he launched his campaign against Ethiopia.

An armed clash at Wal Wal, an oasis on the Ethiopian side of the frontier where the Italians claimed a right of usage, provided the pretext for the subsequent war. While the League tried to settle the incident, Italy proceeded with its military preparations, and when the investigating commission concluded that neither country was responsible for the incident, Rome retorted that a backward and barbarous state like Ethiopia had no right to League protection.

The Italians launched their invasion of Ethiopia in October 1935. League reaction was unexpectedly firm: Italy was branded as the aggressor and for the first time in its history the League imposed economic sanctions. The sanctions were far from complete, however. Coal and oil exports were not embargoed on the grounds that such sanctions would be pointless since Germany and the United States would still be free to sell Italy coal and oil. But the main reason was political. Neither the French nor the British government was anxious for a showdown with Mussolini. To Laval, Italy was above all a newly gained ally against Germany who must not be alienated and driven into Hitler's arms. Sir Samuel Hoare, who had taken Simon's place at the Foreign Office, was worried on his part lest in a collision with Italy, Britain would have to fight by itself, for no other country had forces stationed in the Suez-Red Sea area. Hoare did not wish to commit Britain's limited forces in Africa while Nazi Germany and, even more so, Japan posed their own threats to his country. There also seems to have been some fear that Italy's defeat might lead to the overthrow of Mussolini and the establishment of a leftist-radical government.

Thus Laval could persuade his British colleague that they ought to settle the crisis by allowing Mussolini to take about half of Ethiopia's territory (far more than the Italians had conquered up to that time). The Hoare-Laval proposals were leaked to the press (possibly by Laval) and aroused a storm of indignation in Britain. Hoare was forced to resign and was replaced by the young and popular Anthony Eden (1897–   ), a strong believer in collective security. But Eden could not undo the harm that had been done; the Italian advance continued, aided by poison gas, and in May 1936 Fascist troops entered the Ethiopian capital of Addis Abeba. In emulation of the relationship between Britain and India, King Victor Emmanuel III was proclaimed Emperor, and the Duke of Aosta, his cousin, Viceroy of Ethiopia.

In July the League lifted the sanctions imposed upon Italy; what little prestige it had still retained was now thoroughly shattered.

The Remilitarization of the Rhineland. Among those who had taken notice of the ineffectiveness of the League and the indecision of Britain and France was the German Fuehrer. As a further step in his rearmament drive Hitler had planned for some time to repudiate the demilitarization of the Rhineland, first stipulated in the Treaty of Versailles and reconfirmed in the Locarno Pact to reassure France. Sensing that the moment to act had come, Hitler asked his army leaders to prepare the move militarily. His generals warned him that the fledgling German army was not yet ready for a confrontation with France, but though he knew they were right, Hitler would not be stopped. In a combination of calculation, instinct, and irrepressible impulses, his intuition that France would not fight hardened into an unshakable determination to march into the demilitarized zone.

Hitler's move did not come as a surprise to the French; in preparation against it they had again extended military service to two years in order to have an adequate force of trained men under arms. But Hitler moved before this reform had any effect, and France thus confronted him without an effective striking force. General Gamelin, the French chief of staff, insisted that several classes of reservists would have to be called up before he could move, and he hinted that ultimately there would probably have to be a general mobilization. Faced with dissension and financial troubles at home, the cabinet was unwilling to venture forth without British support but no such aid was forthcoming. The British felt that "the Germans had marched into Germany," and were happy to learn that Hitler proposed signing a 25-year nonaggression treaty with France and Belgium and an air pact to bar air raids on cities, and was also willing to re-enter the League—a clear indication to them that he was anxious to maintain peace. But if the French overestimated the extent of Germany's military preparedness, Hitler on his part overrated France's available striking power. While the world admired his iron nerves, the Fuehrer was in fact deeply worried. "I have never been as scared as in these days of the Rhineland enterprise," he later confided, immensely relieved. "I would not have had one brigade at my disposal to challenge even a mere threat of war from France. Am I glad! My God, am I glad that everything turned out all right. The world belongs to the bold. God is with them!" This was the reaction, not of a statesman who had run a calculated risk, but of a gambler who had bet against heavy odds and had won.

There were as always diplomatic protests, and an emergency session of the League Council noted that Germany was guilty of a breach of its international treaty obligations. Nothing further was done, however, although the repercussions of Germany's move were far-reaching. The militarization of the Rhineland all but destroyed France's alliance system. The French could no longer rush troops into the Rhineland to relieve German pressure on their eastern allies in case of war; instead, French forces would have to fight their way into the Rhine valley and the industrial Ruhr. As Germany built up its Rhenish defenses, France might take weeks and possibly months before it could bring effective relief to its allies, and by that time the latter might well be defeated. This fact was not lost on these countries, and Yugoslavia and Rumania began moving into the German orbit. In the west Belgium decided that its alliance with France had lost its value; the Belgians called off their pact with France and proclaimed their neutrality in a future Franco-German war, hopeful that such a war might by-pass their country. In his efforts to destroy the European community Hitler had taken another stride forward.

At the same time it is evident that the community had already lost most of what little cohesion it still had. Whereas men like Briand and Barthou or Sir Austen Chamberlain had looked beyond their country and seen it as part of a European system of carefully balanced power, however amorphous, their successors no longer did. Stanley Baldwin, Neville Chamberlain, Sir John Simon, and most of their advisers and confidents knew little of Europe and of Britain's relationship to the Continent. They were not guided by that basic principle of British foreign policy that Britain's security depended on a sound balance of power on the Continent and that every threat to that balance was a threat directed also at Britain. Similarly their French counterparts, Pierre Laval and Edouard Daladier, thought they could forgo France's traditional strategy of neutralizing Germany's preponderant power by close military collaboration with Russia. Matters of course were complicated by the circumstance that the confrontation with Germany was superimposed upon the conflict between capitalism and communism which made it even more difficult for these men to see in the Soviet Union a useful ally against Nazi Germany. Those, on the other hand, who were aware of that basic European experience that the challengers of the European order could be curbed only by the concerted action of all nations concerned, men like Winston Churchill in Britain and Paul Reynaud in France, were out of the government; others, like Léon Blum and Anthony Eden, were too weak to assert themselves.

THE SPANISH CIVIL WAR

Foreign Intervention. The continuing disintegration of the European state system became again evident during the Spanish Civil War. Both the Republican government and the Nationalists, it will be recalled, concluded quickly that they needed foreign assistance to defeat their opponents. The Nationalists had no difficulty securing aid from Hitler and Mussolini: within days after the two leaders had been approached, help, mainly in the form of transport planes, was on its way. Fuehrer and Duce both wished for a victory of the Nationalists, for psychological as well as geopolitical reasons: an authoritarian Spain, bordering on France and flanking France's and Britain's lines of communications to Asia and Africa, was bound to strengthen the position of Germany and Italy. Britain and France, on the other hand, seem to have been much less concerned about the effect the conflict might have on their own positions. The British government found both sides equally little to its liking and decided to assist neither one; it also hoped that its nonintervention would help to keep the war localized. France's Popular Front government was more sympathetic toward its counterpart in Madrid, but it gave aid only in roundabout ways, partly because it did not wish to act without Britain, and partly because the French right acclaimed the Nationalists with such vehemence that the government's support of the Spanish Republic would have heightened France's internal difficulties and might have led to the breakup of the Blum government. A Franco-British attempt to localize the conflict by means of a nonintervention agreement of all major powers was unsuccessful; the Italian and German governments continued to assist the Nationalists, while the Soviet Union began just then to dispatch aid to the Republican forces.

The Soviet decision to send help to the Spanish Republic was prompted by the realization that without such aid the Republican cause was lost. The hastily organized workers' militia had been able to suppress Nationalist risings in the streets of Madrid and Barcelona, but it was no match to the well-trained and equipped professional army of the Nationalists. If fascism triumphed in Spain, France and other European countries might also succumb, leaving the Soviet Union to face Hitler alone. The Kremlin thus thought it imperative to save the Republic and dispatched to Madrid matériel, as well as military commanders and instructors. Through the vast network of the Comintern, Moscow also organized and equipped new fighting units known as International Brigades; their members were recruited from non-Soviet Communists and liberals. The first two brigades, composed of Germans, Englishmen, Frenchmen, Italians, Belgians, Poles, and Hungarians, were battle-ready just in time to help beat off the Nationalist attack on Madrid in November 1936. At that very moment, however, the Germans decided to increase their aid to "White Spain"; while the International Brigades were fighting their first battle on the outskirts of Madrid, a German air fleet, the "Condor Legion," was assembled at Seville for an aerial assault on the capital. Later that month Italy dispatched a Black Shirt division to the Nationalists, and both Berlin and Rome recognized formally the Nationalist regime that had been established at Burgos under General Franco.

Foreign aid thus continued to pour into Spain; even after a nonintervention agreement was signed by the powers concerned in 1937, it was never fully observed and soon was openly flouted. As the war wore on, however, an ever-increasing portion of that aid went to Franco. It became more and more difficult for the Russians to send help to the Republic as Italian submarines sank with impunity ships bound for Republican Spain, and France most of the time barred shipments across its territory. (At one point the French government kept the frontier closed during the day, but tolerated large-scale smuggling at night.) The Soviets, moreover, realized that all hope for an Anglo-French intervention against Franco was illusory; feeling very much isolated, they began to dissociate themselves from the Republic to avoid a collision with Germany, and the International Brigades were also withdrawn.

Conversely, Hitler decided in the fall of 1938, after his triumph in the Czech crisis, that he could safely increase his aid to the Nationalists. The Anglo-French surrender at Munich convinced him that London and Paris would not enter the Spanish war, however flagrant a violation of the nonintervention agreement he might commit. In return for mining rights in Spain and Spanish Morocco, he supplied Franco with large amounts of new war matériel, and with this aid the Generalissimo dealt the Republic its death blow.

The European Impact. The outcome of the war was another sharp setback to the cause of democracy. Whatever its failings, the Spanish Republic had remained to untold millions a beacon of human liberty and democratic self-government, and now this bastion had fallen. Its defeat, moreover, was widely attributed to the timidity of the other democracies—a conclusion that weakened further the declining faith in the vitality of the democratic cause. In contrast to the irresolution of Britain and France, the Nazi-Fascist camp had shown itself purposeful and determined and 'had demonstrated its solidarity with the Spanish Nationalists by providing generous assistance. The victory of Franco seemed almost like a matter of historical justice—a part of that irresistible wave that was sweeping country after country into the camp of Hitler and Mussolini. Undoubtedly Hitler felt confirmed in his conviction that he could make himself the master of Europe, and Stalin most likely considered coming to terms with Hitler, partly at least, on the basis of the Spanish experience.

On the other hand, as it turned out, the accretion of material strength that German and Italy derived from the fall of the Spanish Republic was not as great as it seemed at that time. The cautious and circumspect Franco had been able to secure German and Italian aid without bargaining away Spain's independence, and he thus remained able to pursue policies dictated by Spain's national interests rather than by Hitler's or Mussolini's demands.

DIPLOMATIC MANEUVERS, 1936–37

The Rome-Berlin Axis. To Hitler the Spanish war was little more than a side show. Apart from the long-range geopolitical advantages he hoped to derive from the victory of the Nationalists, the immediate benefits of the conflict lay in its diversionary effects: it kept the attention of France, Britain, and Italy focused on the Mediterranean, thus giving him greater freedom to pursue his plans in central Europe. At the conference in November 1937, at which he outlined his expansionist plans to his military leaders (see p. 235), he remarked that he had no interest in an early and complete victory of Franco; he preferred a continuation of the Mediterranean tensions, hopeful that they might lead to war between Italy and the Western democracies.

Outwardly, however, he professed his sincere friendship for Mussolini. Relations between Germany and Italy had much improved since Italy had been at odds with Britain and France over the Ethiopian crisis: Mussolini hoped for Hitler's support in his attempt to build up his Mediterranean-African empire and Hitler wished to assure himself of the Duce's neutrality when he seized Austria. In July 1936 the Fuehrer concluded an agreement with Vienna, restoring normal relations between the two countries and pledging them not to interfere in each other's internal affairs; the agreement was to demonstrate Hitler's peaceful intentions and reassure Mussolini about Germany's acceptance of Austria's independence.

These efforts culminated in a visit of Foreign Minister Ciano to Berlin where agreement was reached on German-Italian cooperation in Austria, Spain, the Danubian countries, and Ethiopia. "The Berlin conversations," Mussolini exulted, "have resulted in an understanding between our two countries over certain problems which had been particularly acute. But . . . this Berlin-Rome line is not a diaphragm but rather an axis around which can revolve all those European states with a will to collaboration and peace." In talks with Schuschnigg, the Austrian Chancellor, some months later, Mussolini assured his visitor that he would come to Austria's help should its independence be threatened again, but he also urged Schuschnigg to accommodate himself with Berlin and avoid any conflict. Schuschnigg came away from the meeting uncertain as to how far he could still count on Mussolini's support.

Further steps to cement the German-Italian friendship were taken in 1937; in September Mussolini himself visited Germany and received a triumphal welcome. Thoroughly impressed, Mussolini came under Hitler's spell during the five-day visit, during which the Fuehrer hardly ever left the Duce's side and kept fussing over his guest's personal comfort. Yet in their talks Mussolini continued to insist that Austria's independence must be preserved, and Hitler remained uncertain as to what Mussolini's reaction would be should the Germans march into Austria.

Britain and Italy.   The rapprochement between Berlin and Rome was viewed with serious misgivings by London. Since the end of the Ethiopian war influential Conservative circles had called for an improvement of Anglo-Italian relations; once the League sanctions against Italy had been lifted, it seemed possible to effect a lessening of tensions. A rapprochement was considered imperative since Italy's intervention in the Spanish war raised the possibility that in return for their help the Italians might acquire a foothold on Spain's Balearic Isles. Protracted discussions led to a "gentlemen's agreement" in January 1937 by which the two countries accorded each other freedom of movement in the Mediterranean, pledged themselves to uphold the territorial status quo, and promised to refrain from any activities liable to impair good relations between them. Yet only two days after the agreement had been signed, another contingent of 4,000 Italian Black Shirts debarked in Spain.

While Foreign Secretary Anthony Eden despaired of reaching a genuine understanding with Mussolini, Neville Chamberlain who became Prime Minister in May 1937 did not. Chamberlain's approach to foreign affairs was determined by a deep-seated, almost religious aversion to war and by his conviction that human beings were all essentially alike in their aspirations, passions, and fears; given good will, they should therefore be able to settle their problems peacefully and in a business-like way. These basic views, more even than the knowledge that an inadequately armed Britain was threatened on three fronts—by Germany close to home, by Italy in the Mediterranean and Africa, and by Japan in the Far East—account for the policy of "appeasement" which Chamberlain pursued until he was to discover, too late, that there existed no common ground between himself and the two dictators.

Chamberlain had no faith in collective security and rather than re-create an alliance system to redress the balance of power, he hoped to settle the growing difficulties by direct contact with Mussolini and Hitler. In pursuit of his preference for bilateral agreements, the Prime Minister proposed to the Duce the conclusion of an Anglo-Italian treaty of friendship. Yet before negotiations could get under way, new complications arose in the Mediterranean where Italian submarines had sunk British ships bound for Republican Spain. Under the impact of his visit to Germany, moreover, Mussolini aligned himself more closely with Hitler. In November 1937 he acceded to the Anti-Comintern Pact that Germany and Japan had signed in 1936 to join forces in their fight against communism. If the original pact seemed aimed at the Soviet Union, Italy's adherence suggested that it might also be used to exert pressure on Britain—in the Mediterranean and the Arab world, or in the Far East where Japan had just launched a large-scale attack on China. In December in a further gesture of defiance against the principle of peaceful cooperation, Italy also withdrew from the League of Nations.

Yet Mussolini did not wish to become too dependent on Germany. He knew by then that Hitler would take over Austria before long. The Duce wanted to strengthen his own position before he would have to face Germany at the Brenner Pass—a disquieting prospect since Hitler, despite his assurances to the contrary, might one day lay claim to the German-speaking Tyrol on the Italian side of the Brenner. Mussolini put out feelers to London for the resumption of talks. Chamberlain was eager to reopen them, but Eden warned against new negotiations unless Mussolini honored his earlier promises and withdrew his forces from Spain. Having long disagreed with the Prime Minister's foreign policy, Eden resigned over this issue; he was succeeded by Lord Halifax (1881– 1959) who shared Chamberlain's views. In April 1938 a new Anglo-Italian agreement was signed. It reaffirmed the agreement of January 1937 and contained understandings on military and propaganda activities in Africa and the Middle East. But the agreement was to become effective only after Britain had recognized Italy's absorption of Ethiopia and Mussolini had withdrawn his forces from Spain, and by the time these conditions were met, at least partly, the pact had lost whatever significance it may first have had.

Britain and Germany.   The arrangements with Italy were in any event of only secondary importance to Chamberlain, for the main adversary was of course Germany. "If only we could get on terms with the Germans," he sighed, "I would not care a rap for Musso." Hitler on his part also was anxious to reach some understanding with Britain which would allow him to pursue his plans on the Continent. His hope was to neutralize Britain by professing himself engaged in an anti-Communist crusade that he was fighting also on Britain's behalf. In August 1936 Joachim von Ribbentrop (1893–1946), a one-time wine merchant who was Hitler's personal adviser on foreign affairs, was sent to London as German ambassador and for the next year and a half tried to persuade Britain's government and British society that they ought to help Germany fight off world communism in France, Spain, and wherever else it threatened the established order. At one point Ribbentrop even asked the startled Eden whether communism was not a serious threat right in Britain.

Again, Chamberlain was more hopeful of a rapprochement with Berlin than was Eden. In November 1937 the Prime Minister seized on a German invitation extended to Halifax as a chance that Halifax might talk to Hitler and learn from the Fuehrer first-hand what his plans and objectives were. Halifax was received by Hitler at his mountain chalet near Berchtesgaden; the conversation, vague and discursive, touched on German membership in the League, disarmament, and colonies—which was, according to Hitler, "the sole remaining issue between Germany and

England," although in reality he was not interested in the acquisition of colonies. At the end they spoke of Austria and Czechoslovakia, and Halifax admitted the possibility of making adjustments in that area, provided they could be accomplished peacefully and without any major disturbances. From this remark Hitler may well have concluded that he need not fear Britain should he move into Austria. Chamberlain on his part was satisfied that the visit created "an atmosphere in which it is possible to discuss with Germany the practical questions involved in a European settlement."

THE SEIZURE OF AUSTRIA

The Austro-German Agreement of 1936. Austro-German relations had been hanging uneasily in the balance since the ill-fated Nazi coup of July 1934. By the spring of 1936 Chancellor von Schuschnigg realized that he would have to seek an understanding with Germany if he were not to be isolated completely. Mussolini, now moving closer to Hitler, advised Schuschnigg that he could help Austria more effectively if the Austrian government improved its relations with Germany. He also warned that in view of Italy's preoccupation with Ethiopia, Austria could not count on all-out support from Rome in case of new difficulties. Since Paris and London had remained passive when Hitler marched into the Rhineland, the Austrian Chancellor knew that he could not rely on French and English assistance either. The Austrian economy, moreover, was hard hit by the trade war with Germany; a repeal of the German embargo on tourism was therefore of vital importance to Vienna. Hitler on his part was ready to mend his relations with Austria in order to reassure Mussolini, and an agreement was concluded between the two countries in July 1936.

In addition to the official document already discussed, the negotiations produced a secret agreement which provided for the free exchange of newspapers and periodicals, the resumption of normal economic relations, an amnesty for political prisoners, and for the inclusion of some representatives of the "National Opposition in Austria" in the Austrian government. Except for the ending of the trade war, Germany was the main beneficiary of these arrangements, and Berlin used its advantage at once to intensify its surreptitious campaign against the Schuschnigg government. Tension reached a critical stage when in January 1938 the Vienna police discovered Nazi plans calling for the provocation of internal disturbances that would give Germany a pretext to march into Austria.

The Agreement of February 1938. Schuschnigg realized that he would have to make further concessions, and a meeting with Hitler took place in February 1938. The Fuehrer confronted the Austrian Chancellor with a virtual ultimatum: if Schuschnigg wished to avoid a military showdown he would have to acknowledge that National Socialism was compatible with loyalty to Austria and end all discrimination against the Austrian Nazis; Arthur Seyss-Inquart, a prominent Nazi sympathizer, must be appointed Minister of the Interior and military relations improved by the coordination of staff planning and the exchange of German and Austrian officers. Though these terms were clearly designed to bring both the Austrian army and police under Nazi control, the Austrians saw no alternative but to accept them.

The agreement accelerated the decline of the Schuschnigg regime. Many who had stood aloof hastened to join the Nazis, either from conviction, which they thought they could now safely display, or from opportunism, in anticipation of a Nazi take-over. Schuschnigg tried desperately to stem the tide, seeking even the support of the outlawed Socialists. He soon came to see that his only chance of safeguarding Austria's independence lay in a demonstration that the bulk of the Austrian people wished to remain independent. The Chancellor arranged for a plebiscite by which the country was to decide whether or not it favored "a free and German, independent and social, Christian and united Austria." The plan was made public on March 9, four days before the plebiscite was to be held, to catch the Nazis off guard.

The Annexation. Hitler denounced the plan as a violation of the February agreement and threatened to move into Austria unless the plebiscite were called off and Schuschnigg resigned. Plans for military action were hastily drawn up and troops concentrated along the Austrian border. Under this pressure the Austrians cancelled the plebiscite,[2] and Schuschnigg resigned, to be succeeded by Seyss-Inquart. Nevertheless, Hitler ordered his forces to move into Austria, and in the early morning of March 12, 1938, they crossed the border in response to a plea for help that had been extracted from the reluctant Seyss-Inquart.

Outwardly at least, the German troops were jubilantly received. Under the impact of this enthusiastic reception, Hitler decided to incorporate Austria outright into the German Reich. A plebiscite held four weeks later to "ratify" the merger produced a majority in Austria of 99.73 per cent in favor of it. By then all opposition had been silenced, and there were no impartial observers to watch over the Nazi-controlled counting

---

[2] Whether the plebiscite, if it had taken place, could have provided a convincing demonstration in favor of independence is uncertain. That the plan was legally unauthorized since the constitution made provisions only for referendums on legislative matters might be discounted on the grounds that in the existing emergency the country had to have a chance to make its views known even if the procedure were technically illegal. What was much more serious was the lack of up-to-date electoral lists, because no elections had been held since 1932, and the existence of voting arrangements which endangered the secrecy of the vote and the accuracy of the counting.

of the ballots. What decision the Austrians would have reached in an orderly plebiscite thus will never be known.

The Great Powers acquiesced in the seizure of Austria. The French were embroiled in another cabinet crisis and in any event would not act without Britain's support, and the British did not object to the annexation as such, but only to the way in which it was brought about. Chamberlain was still convinced of the possibility of an understanding with Germany; the best course, he felt, was to suspend all negotiations for the time being and announce "some increase" in rearmament. He also rejected a Soviet proposal for a conference to discuss some possible joint action in the event of another German act of aggression. The League of Nations passed over in silence this disappearance of one of its members.

The annexation of Austria netted Germany a considerable accretion of political, economic, and military power. Apart from the overall enhancement of his prestige and the acquisition of Austria's resources—iron ore, timber, electric power—Hitler had further improved his position to exert pressure on southeastern Europe. Above all, however, Czechoslovakia was now surrounded by Germany in the north, west, and south, and had become much more vulnerable to a German attack.

THE END OF CZECHOSLOVAKIA

Hitler's Plans. With his task thus made easier, Hitler turned his attention to Czechoslovakia. He considered three ways in which he might gain control of that state: (1) by an attack "out of the blue without cause or justification," (2) after diplomatic exchanges that would lead to tension and ultimately to war, or (3) by "lightning action resulting from an incident (as, for example, the assassination of the German Minister [to Prague] after an anti-German demonstration)." The first alternative was discarded as too dangerous; the third was thoroughly canvassed, and the documentary evidence, while not fully conclusive, suggests that in order to provide a pretext for an attack, the murder of the German envoy by Nazi agents may indeed have been considered. At the same time the second alternative was also pursued, with the Sudeten German issue providing the topic for the preliminary exchanges. This approach also had the advantage of misleading the outside world about Hitler's real objective which was not the "liberation" of the Sudeten Germans, but the destruction of the Czechoslovak state. With Czechoslovakia under German control, the task of subduing Poland, Hungary, and the Balkan countries would be greatly facilitated.

With the Sudeten German leader, a one-time gymnastics instructor Konrad Henlein, Hitler arranged that Henlein would put demands to the Czech government which the latter would find unacceptable, and Czech intransigence would then be blamed for the resulting tension. In

April, at the annual congress of the Sudeten German Party, Henlein called for complete autonomy for the Sudeten Germans. As expected, the Prague government rejected his demand; but anxious to come to terms with the Sudeten Germans (and to satisfy the British and French who kept pressing Prague for concessions to the Germans), the Czechs proposed an amnesty for political offenders, the appointment of German officials in proportion to the size of the German population, and new local elections. The negotiations soon were deadlocked, and the British, fearful lest Hitler resort to armed intervention, virtually forced a mediator on the Czech government. The man picked for this task, Lord Walter Runciman, a banker and transportation expert, had no special qualifications for his assignment; actually, as Halifax informed the French government, his task was not so much to mediate as to urge the Czechs, for the sake of peace, to accede to the Sudeten German demands. Runciman's pro-German sentiments were at once evident, and under his prodding, President Beneš expressed his readiness early in September to grant the Sudetenland almost complete autonomy. Since Hitler, however, was not interested in the status of the Sudetenland, he ignored Beneš' offer.

Hitler's military plans were completed by then and the attack on Czechoslovakia was set for early October. To prepare the ground properly, the Sudeten Germans received instructions to create "incidents," and on September 11 and 12, 1938, riots broke out throughout the Sudetenland. But when Prague imposed martial law the next day, order was quickly restored. Yet the German radio and press continued to report clashes and bloodshed (freely invented by a staff member of Propaganda Minister Goebbels who, as Goebbels' press secretary testified at the postwar Nürnberg Trials, "spent whole nights poring over general staff maps, directories, and lists of names, using them to fabricate atrocity reports from the Sudetenland"). In a violent speech at the annual Nazi Party congress, Hitler warned that he would not stand by much longer watching law being perverted into lawlessness. Military preparations, now carried on openly, left no doubt as to what he meant. The French, reluctantly, also began calling up reservists, though they were convinced that no military action on their part could save the Czechs. They also dreaded the prospect of German air raids against which they would be defenseless. Nor did feelers put out to the Soviet government produce a reassuring reply: the Soviet Union would honor its alliance with Czechoslovakia as stipulated, that is, if the French honored theirs. But even in that case it was not clear what help the Russians could give since they were separated from Czechoslovakia by Rumania and Poland, and neither of these two states was prepared to permit the transit of Soviet forces. (Rumania's King Carol suggested, however, that if Soviet planes should fly across Rumanian territory, he would close "all three eyes.")

While the French government fretted over its inadequate armaments and Britain's unwillingness and inability to provide help, some German generals, it will be recalled, worried about Germany's ability to go to war against a coalition of Czechoslovakia, Britain, and France. They completed their plans to arrest the Fuehrer and his closest associates should war break out, but since war, in the end, was averted, these plans were never put into operation.

Chamberlain's Intervention.   At this point Chamberlain decided that only a personal talk with Hitler could save the situation. A meeting was arranged at the Fuehrer's mountain chalet at Berchtesgaden for September 15. There Hitler informed the Prime Minister that in accordance with the principle of national self-determination he must insist on the outright cession to Germany of all predominantly German-settled areas of Czechoslovakia. Chamberlain who thought the demand reasonable passed it on to the Czechs. The latter, however, accepted it only after having been warned by the French that France would not support them in a war against Germany since by rejecting the German demands, the Czechs would be responsible for the war.[3]

Yet Hitler was still determined to gain control of all of Czechoslovakia and prepared to go to war over it. When Chamberlain met him again at the Rhenish resort town of Godesberg to report that the crisis was solved, the Fuehrer told the anguished Prime Minister that in view of Prague's continued persecution of the Sudeten Germans, he must insist on the surrender of all German-settled areas by October 1. He also asked that the principle of national self-determination be applied to the Slovaks, Poles, and Hungarians in Czechoslovakia. This ultimatum the Czechs rejected on the grounds that an evacuation of the Sudetenland by October 1 would not allow them to establish a new defense system before surrendering the heavily fortified Sudeten Mountains.

Both the British and French governments were badly divided as to what course to pursue, but in the end they decided to reject Hitler's terms; should war result, the French would assist the Czechs and the British would stand by the French. France began mobilizing in earnest, and Britain proclaimed a state of emergency and alerted the Royal Air Force and Navy for imminent action. The Czechs already had mobilized a few days before.

Yet both Paris and London were convinced that they were poorly prepared for war, especially in the air,[4] and they knew that their peoples

---

[3] The Czechs, moreover, accepted only on condition that the remaining Czech state be guaranteed by an international undertaking—a condition which was never fulfilled. Thus Czechoslovakia's offer to cede the Sudetenland never became binding and the transfer arranged over Prague's head at the Munich Conference was legally invalid. See Boris Celovsky, *Das Münchener Abkommen von 1938* (Stuttgart, 1958), pp. 371–73.

[4] Actually, they overestimated considerably the strength of the German air force; the Luftwaffe was deficient in bombers and would have been unable to carry out any sustained raids on Paris and London, the greatest concern of the French and British governments.

Mussolini arrives for the Munich Conference. Left to right: Göring, Count Ciano, Hitler, Mussolini. (*Reprinted courtesy Wide World Photos*)

were most anxious to stay out of war. Once more Chamberlain appealed to Hitler and proposed a modified plan: the Sudetenland would be turned over to the Germans in three phases during the first ten days of October while areas where German predominance would have to be ascertained would be transferred by October 31. The French, to make the plan still more palatable to Hitler, suggested that the cession of the Sudetenland be speeded up further. Mussolini was asked to arrange a four-power meeting to discuss these plans and at the Duce's urging Hitler invited him, Chamberlain, and Daladier to a meeting on the following day, September 29, at Munich. The Czechs were not asked to attend, nor were the Soviets, although they were allied to both France and Czechoslovakia.

The Munich Conference.   The four statesmen met in the early afternoon of that day. Chamberlain and Daladier had not worked out any proposals nor had they agreed on a joint strategy. Hitler, on the other hand, had drawn up a plan which, with some minor modifications, was adopted after a confused discussion. Going farther than Chamberlain's plan, it provided for the completion of the German occupation of all of Czechoslovakia's German-settled areas by October 10. In areas of mixed population, plebiscites would be held under international supervision. Supplemental agreements provided for the settlement of the Polish and **321**

Hungarian minority problems within three months and for an international guarantee of Czechoslovakia's new borders against unprovoked aggression, to.be given after the Hungarian and Polish question had been solved.

Except for the hapless Czechs, most people received the agreement with immense relief. The Munich crowds cheered Chamberlain as the harbinger of peace, and he received a hero's welcome on his return to London. The Parisians greeted Daladier as jubilantly, to the Premier's astonishment: "The fools—they do not know what they applaud." Chamberlain also brought home a joint declaration signed at his suggestion by him and the Fuehrer by which they pledged to resolve all mutual problems by consultation. "I believe it is peace for our time," he announced. But in actual fact he was less certain; if Hitler would live up to the agreement, everything would be well, he told some associates; if he did not, at least his guilt would be clearly established. Churchill called Munich a "total and unmitigated defeat": it doomed Czechoslovakia to destruction, shattered the French security system, put all of eastern Europe at Hitler's mercy, and by excluding the Soviet Union from the settlement of the crisis, jeopardized what chance there still was of redressing the balance of power.

The Seizure of Czecho-Slovakia. The implementation of the Munich agreement was quickly completed. By October 10 the German-settled areas were occupied by German forces, but in a number of cases the troops advanced farther, and the line of the farthest military advance was unilaterally fixed by the Germans as the German-Czech boundary line. The Poles helped themselves to the area around Teschen in northeastern Moravia, and the Hungarians were awarded a large slice of southern Slovakia by an arbitrary German-Italian decision without consultation with the British and French. Altogether the Czechs lost over one fourth of their territory and one third of their population. Moreover, they were not given the guarantee against aggression promised at Munich; London and Paris would not give Prague guarantees without the participation of the Axis Powers, and the latter begged off on the grounds that such guarantees were now pointless since Czechoslovakia, in Hitler's words, "must in all things be allied with Germany."

Domestically the rump state was transformed under German pressure into the confederation of Czecho-Slovakia, composed of the Czech part (Bohemia and Moravia) and two autonomous lands, Slovakia and Carpatho-Ruthenia, and all held loosely together by a Czecho-Slovak government and parliament at Prague. Beneš was forced to resign and left the country in fear of his life; as his successor Emil Hacha, Chief Justice of the Supreme Court, was elected President.

The British and French meanwhile took steps to increase their armaments; but whereas Britain expanded its air force substantially, France's

We, the German Führer and Chancellor and the British Prime Minister, have had a further meeting today and are agreed in recognising that the question of Anglo-German relations is of the first importance for the two countries and for Europe.

We regard the agreement signed last night and the Anglo-German Naval Agreement as symbolic of the desire of our two peoples never to go to war with one another again.

We are resolved that the method of consultation shall be the method adopted to deal with any other questions that may concern our two countries, and we are determined to continue our efforts to remove possible sources of difference and thus to contribute to assure the peace of Europe.

[signature: Adolf Hitler]

[signature: Neville Chamberlain]

September 30, 1938.

Anglo-German Consultation Agreement, signed by Hitler and Chamberlain at Munich, September 30, 1938. (*Reprinted courtesy Wide World Photos*)

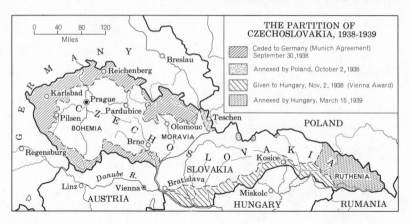

arms output continued to lag. At the same time both countries made new attempts to deal with Hitler "in the spirit of Munich." London proposed closer economic cooperation, and agreements on coal export quotas were reached in January 1939, largely at the expense of the British mining industry. The French on their part concluded an agreement with Germany similar to the Anglo-German declaration signed at Munich by Hitler and Chamberlain. Both countries accepted their common frontier as final and promised to consult on all matters of mutual interest, but when during a preliminary discussion Foreign Minister von Ribbentrop maintained that Czecho-Slovakia was part of Germany's sphere of influence, French Foreign Minister Georges Bonnet did not contradict him.

From all this Hitler concluded that he would run no great risk if he seized rump Czecho-Slovakia. He had never been satisfied with the Munich agreement because it had kept him from seizing the entire Czech state at the time and had denied him the brief war for which he had hoped as a test of German racial vitality. The ink had hardly dried on the Munich agreement when he ordered his generals to lay plans for the seizure of the remaining Czech state. Early in 1939 Slovak separatists were encouraged to call for full independence, and in mid-March, under German prodding, an independent state of Slovakia was established. Hitler was now ready to move against the Czechs. President Hacha was called to Berlin, told that Czech intransigence made further collaboration impossible, and on threat of war was forced to sign away the independence of "Czechia" which became the German Protectorate of Bohemia-Moravia. On the following day, at Germany's bidding, Hungary annexed Carpatho-Ruthenia.

Again the German gains were substantial. Not only did Hitler destroy without firing a shot the excellently trained and equipped Czech army of 400,000 men, entrenched until Munich behind superbly devised fortifications, but he also obtained control of important industrial resources, including the world famous Skoda armaments works, and of fertile agricultural lands. Strategically, Germany's position vis-à-vis Poland was greatly strengthened, for thanks to their control of the new state of Slovakia the Germans could now attack Poland on three sides.

A week after the Czech coup, German naval units seized the German-settled Memelland from Lithuania, and on Good Friday 1939 Mussolini, not to be outdone, annexed the little Balkan kingdom of Albania.

THE UNITED STATES AND EUROPE IN THE 1930's

Drifting Apart. It had been the power of the United States that had made possible the ultimate Allied victory over the Germans in World War I. Aware of the American contribution to the German defeat, Britain and France had made repeated efforts during the 1920's to associate the United States with the maintenance of peace and order in Europe. The Depression put an end to these endeavors, and they were not resumed when the Nazi-Fascist threat to the European order began to make itself felt.

A number of factors accounted for this dissociation. Not only was the full measure of that threat not seen for some time by the European Powers, but when they did see it, those in charge of the British and French governments were men who had lost faith in the effectiveness of collective security. They preferred the bilateral approach to the solution of the problems that endangered their countries, and this approach excluded close collaboration with the United States in order to check Hitler and Mussolini. The European leaders felt that they had good reason not to rely on collective security. The League had been unable to preserve law and order, Soviet Russia was not considered a trustworthy ally for military and political reasons, and the United States did not wish to be an ally at all. "The isolationists there are so strong and so vocal," Chamberlain confided to his diary in February 1938, "that she cannot be depended on for help if we should get into trouble."

Hitler and the United States. Hitler in turn based his strategy on the conviction that he would not have to worry about the United States when he set out on his quest for *Lebensraum*. He saw the United States as a degenerate, corrupt country torn by social and racial strife and far too preoccupied with its internal problems to concern itself with events in Europe. Although he seems to have envisaged the eventual inclusion of the United States into his projected German world empire, he confided this plan only to his immediate entourage. In his prewar speeches and writings he mentioned the United States only rarely, and when he did, he spoke of it with evident contempt. Nor did he ever attempt to improve German-American relations although they began to decline almost from the moment he came to power.

Neutrality Legislation. Both Hitler and the European democracies assumed correctly, though Hitler for the wrong reasons, that the American people were strongly opposed to any active intervention in European affairs. Held back by a deep aversion to war and disillusioned about the benefits to America of joint international action, Americans preferred to dissociate themselves from the non-American world and to devote their energies to their domestic concerns. Moreover, many felt that the United States had been drawn into Europe's war in 1917 by profit-greedy bankers and arms manufacturers and that America's security had not been at stake at all. They considered it inconceivable that the United States, thanks to its fortunate location, could ever be threatened by any European power. In their view, the task of keeping their country out of foreign wars reduced itself to preventing American bankers, shipowners, and armament makers from trading with nations at war.

With the sentiment that the United States should be kept out of war, President Roosevelt and the so-called internationalists were in agreement. They did not believe, however, that this goal could be attained by America's turning its back on all foreign conflicts. In their view, the United States was too much a part of the rest of the world simply to ignore developments which it disliked; thus, it too had a stake in the active promotion of peace. Not to distinguish between aggressors and victims of aggression, Roosevelt feared, might encourage aggression and eventually draw America into war rather than maintain peace. He therefore proposed that legislation be enacted that would give him discretionary powers to impose arms embargoes in time of war. But Congress was fearful lest such distinction between good and bad nations might defeat the purpose of such a law, and in August 1935 it passed a Neutrality Act that compelled the President, on the recognition of the existence of war, to prohibit the sale and transportation in American ships of arms, ammunition, and other implements of war to any participants in that conflict. He also could, at his discretion, warn American citizens against traveling on ships of belligerent nations.

The law was first applied to the Ethiopian war, and in invoking it, the United States acted more quickly against Italy than did the League.[5] But Washington refused to associate itself with the more far-reaching sanctions proposed by the League, and was content with a "moral embargo" on oil, copper, and other strategic materials, which proved ineffective.

The Spanish Civil War.   During the Spanish Civil War the United States assumed officially a "hands off" attitude. Since the Neutrality Act did not apply to civil wars, a special Congressional resolution barred the export of arms to Spain, and passports were ruled invalid for travel in Spain to

---

[5] Despite America's professed neutrality some of the measures taken by Roosevelt were directed specifically against Italy. Thus his warning against traveling on belligerent ships was intended to hurt Italy's passenger trade since land-locked Ethiopia had no ocean-going merchant marine and no submarines to attack Italian shipping.

keep Americans from enlisting in the International Brigades. Similarly the United States refused to participate in any mediation effort and also declined to serve on the Non-Intervention Committee. With American public opinion sharply divided as to the merits of the two Spanish factions, no other course seemed politically possible. American intervention would also have collided with the nonintervention course pursued by Britain and France. When pro-Republic circles concluded that the future of democratic government everywhere would be endangered by the defeat of the Spanish Republic and tried to obtain a repeal of the arms embargo, Chamberlain warned Roosevelt that American arms shipment might serve to spread the war. For a brief moment the President and the State Department seemed to favor repeal, but on Chamberlain's pleas they abandoned the plan.

Isolation vs. Intervention. While Americans followed developments across the Atlantic with increasing concern and felt mounting revulsion at Hitler's brutalities, their growing emotional involvement did not produce any major change in foreign policy. A new Neutrality Act, passed in 1937, maintained the existing restrictions to which an embargo on loans had meanwhile been added. At the same time, Congress wished to avoid a total trade ban in case of a major war lest American business be seriously harmed by such an all-inclusive embargo. The new act authorized the President for a two-year period to permit the sale to nations at war of any materials other than arms and ammunition on a "cash and carry" basis, that is, payment on delivery with the purchases to be taken away by the buyer in non-American ships. Though the "cash and carry" clause suggested that America's well-being was dependent on developments in other parts of the world, this implication was not very widely perceived.

Nor did Japan's invasion of China lead to a change in American attitudes. The sinking of the gunboat *U.S.S. Panay* by Japanese bombers in the Yangtse River did arouse widespread indignation, but also led many to wonder why American ships were patrolling Chinese waters. The incident provided new support for a Constitutional amendment which, except in the case of invasion, would let the United States go to war only if a majority of the electorate so decided in a national referendum. When the measure came to a vote in the House of Representatives, almost half of the members voted in favor of it.

Roosevelt followed the deterioration of the international situation with far greater concern. In October 1937 he warned in a speech at Chicago that "war can engulf states and peoples remote from the original scene of hostilities," and that "mere isolation or neutrality" was no safe protection in a world of disorder. He suggested a "quarantine" against the spreading "epidemic of world lawlessness." Public response to the proposal was not wholly unfavorable, yet Roosevelt did not pursue the matter because he apparently felt that the country was not yet prepared for a more active foreign policy. That winter he also considered calling an international conference on the reduction of armaments, equal access to raw materials, and the law of war, but this plan was dropped when Chamberlain objected to it on the grounds that it would be derided, if not resented, by Hitler and Mussolini and might jeopardize his own efforts to come to terms with the two dictators.

Changing Attitudes.   Hitler's seizure of Austria did more to arouse the United States to the dangers of the international situation than any preceding developments. In January 1938, in the wake of the *Panay* incident, Roosevelt had asked for a billion dollar naval appropriation for the building of a two-ocean navy. The bill had first run into bitter opposition, but two months after the annexation of Austria both houses of Congress passed it by substantial majorities. Nevertheless, American opposition to any involvement in Europe remained unchanged. When the French government, encouraged by what it thought a change in the American position, pleaded with Washington for some gesture of support during the Sudeten crisis, its pleas were rejected. So was an appeal by French Foreign Minister Bonnet that Roosevelt act as an arbiter. When Roosevelt did call on Hitler, Beneš, Chamberlain, and Daladier at the height of the crisis to find a peaceful solution, he stated expressly that he was not abandoning the principle of noninvolvement. To the French the noncommittal attitude of the United States served as further justification of their surrender at Munich.

Like the French government, the British government began to revise its attitude toward the United States. In the summer of 1938 it negotiated a trade treaty with Washington in which it made most of the concessions. "The reason why I have been prepared . . . to go a long way to get this treaty," Chamberlain explained, "is precisely because I reckoned it would help to educate American opinion to act more and more with us, and," as he added in a characteristic display of wishful thinking, "because I felt sure it would frighten the totalitarians."

Though indignant at the dismemberment of Czechoslovakia, the United States acquiesced in the Munich settlement with a genuine sense of relief. As it became evident that Munich had not secured peace, Roosevelt called for a vast armament program, paying special attention to the air force and navy, and the country, thinking in terms of hemisphere defense, approved of his plans. Yet when it transpired that part of the airplane production was to be sold to France and France was allowed to share some top-secret engineering techniques, fears of a secret alliance with France kindled Congressional opposition to the President's program. Opposition increased when Roosevelt was quoted as having told a group of Senators that America's frontier was on the Rhine. The incident also hampered Roosevelt's efforts to obtain an amendment of the Neutrality Act that would have permitted the sale of arms and ammunition to nations at war on a "cash and carry" basis. The amendment was intended to benefit Britain and France which would control the Atlantic in case of war and, it was hoped, deter Hitler from going to war against them. Press reaction and public opinion polls after Hitler's Czech coup in March 1939 showed that a majority of the American people favored the plan. But Congress, still dominated by isolationist elements, refused to enact the amendment and even allowed the more limited "cash and carry" clause to expire. Roosevelt's efforts to help avert the outbreak of war thus were futile.[6] When war did come, the President was compelled to invoke the Neutrality Act, and all arms orders of the British and French were immediately cancelled.

THE SOVIET UNION AND EUROPE IN THE 1930's

The Call for Collective Security. While American foreign policy was being hammered out in broad daylight, as it were, Soviet policy was determined behind closed doors, and any attempt to outline its objectives must therefore remain speculative.

Throughout the mid–1930's Moscow's official spokesmen kept calling for joint measures against all violations of international law. At League meetings, Foreign Commissar Maxim Litvinov urged preventive action against aggression and predicted the grim consequences to which failure to heed this advice would lead. Yet fears of Soviet Russia nurtured over many years could not be easily discarded, and Western statesmen hesitated to collaborate more closely with Moscow. Only a few years earlier Litvinov had argued that cooperation between capitalist and communist countries was impossible; his current claim that such collaboration was indeed feasible seemed the less convincing as the Comintern kept social unrest alive even during the Popular Front period. There was also the question of how valuable an ally the Soviet Union could be even with the best of intentions. Since the purges of the mid–1930's were removing most of the top army leaders, Western military experts had no great confidence in the striking power of the Red Army.

Soviet Russia too had misgivings about the possibilities of a constructive policy of collective security. The reluctance of France to implement the Franco-Soviet military alliance, the inability of Léon Blum's Popular Front government to cope with the French right, were seen as evidence of France's unreliability. Similarly, the failure of Britain and France to stand up to Hitler and Mussolini was interpreted by the Kremlin, not as a sign of weakness or shortsightedness, but as part of a plan to build up Hitler's strength so that one day he might turn against the U.S.S.R.

---

[6] It is very doubtful, however, that if Congress had permitted the sale of arms on a "cash and carry" basis, Hitler would have refrained from attacking Poland. Hitler counted on a short war in which most likely he did not expect American aid to make itself felt.

Towards the end of 1936 Soviet leaders began warning the Western Powers that if the latter continued to ignore Moscow's bid for joint action against the aggressors, the Soviet Union might again withdraw into isolation.

Soviet distrust was further aroused by Britain's attempted rapprochement with Italy and by the dismissal of Eden who favored a rapprochement with Russia. The Kremlin must also have worried when Chamberlain stated in February 1938 that the peace of Europe depended on the attitude of Germany, Italy, France, and Britain, with Soviet Russia ominously omitted. After Hitler seized Austria, Litvinov called once more for collective action against Nazi Germany, but his appeal again was rejected. The Soviet leaders saw in this refusal further evidence of a Western plot to give Hitler a free hand in the East. Alarmed at the growing Russian hostility toward Britain and France, Western observers in Moscow warned that the Kremlin might try to reach an understanding with Hitler and Hitler might agree to an accommodation to secure his rear for an attack on the Western Powers.

The Czech Crisis.   The Sudeten crisis was of special concern to the Soviet Union because of Czechoslovakia's proximity. Moscow announced that it would honor its treaty obligations to Czechoslovakia and render military assistance if France fulfilled its respective commitments. How much help could Soviet Russia provide since it did not border on Czechoslovakia? Questions to that effect Moscow shrugged off as the responsibility of France or Czechoslovakia or the League of Nations, which would have to obtain transit rights for the U.S.S.R. across Rumania and Poland. There is no evidence that the Soviet leaders expected any early call for assistance, if only because they doubted that France would take action, and no preparations were made to prepare the Russian people militarily or psychologically for armed action. This passivity in turn aroused Western suspicions that the Kremlin was mainly interested in pushing Britain and France into a war against Germany.

Whether the Soviets would have aided the Czechs had Prague decided to fight without France's help is equally unclear. One or two tentative offers were made by Moscow, but no clear-cut promise was given since the Czchs never asked for separate Soviet assistance. The Czech government feared that unilateral help by the Kremlin would enable Hitler to declare his attack on Czechoslovakia a "crusade against Bolshevism"; it worried also lest collaboration with Moscow alone might create domestic difficulties.

Of the various moves the British and French made to settle the Sudeten issue, the Kremlin was not informed in advance. Nevertheless, when after the Godesberg meeting Foreign Secretary Halifax stated, without consulting the Soviets, that France, Britain, and Russia would come to the aid of the Czechs, the Soviet Union seems to have welcomed such cooperation. Abandoning its previous reserve, Moscow approached the Rumanians concerning the transit of Soviet forces. The next day, however, the Munich Conference was arranged to which Soviet Russia was not invited.

Stalin's Bid to Both Camps. Moscow's exclusion from the Munich meeting could only confirm its suspicion that the Western Powers wished to divert Germany eastward into a clash with the U.S.S.R. The Anglo-German declaration issued at Munich and the corresponding Franco-German agreement of December 1938 seemed also to point to this strategy. There is some indication that Moscow began now thinking in earnest about playing off Germany against the West. On March 10, 1939 Stalin, addressing the Eighteenth Congress of the All-Union Communist Party, summed up the Soviet position: The "aggressor states," Germany, Italy, and Japan, were having their way, not because they were stronger than the Western Powers, but because the Western Powers hoped to involve the fascist dictatorships in war with other countries—Japan with China, Germany with the Soviet Union—and after the belligerents had bled each other white, Britain and France expected to dictate the peace terms. The Soviet Union, on its part, Stalin declared, would fight off any aggressor and was prepared to support nations which were victims of aggression and fighting for the preservation of their independence. But the Soviets' main interest, he insisted, was to maintain peace and expand economic relations with all countries.

In its combination of accusations and enticements directed at both the Western Powers and the "aggressor states," the speech was obviously meant as a bid to both sides. It was an invitation to the Western Powers to join with the Soviet Union in a common front against the aggressors provided Russia would not be asked to "pull the chestnuts out of the fire for them," and a suggestion to Nazi Germany that there existed no "visible grounds for conflict," and that an accommodation at the expense of the West might be possible. But to judge by the tenor of his speech, Stalin still preferred to reach an understanding with the "nonaggressive" Western democracies rather than with the "aggressor" Hitler.

THE LAST MONTHS

Hitler's Demands on Poland. During the Sudeten crisis Hitler had been anxious to assure himself of Poland's neutrality. He had acted as the champion of the Polish minority in Czechoslovakia and had encouraged the Polish government to seize the region of Teschen, which Poland had long coveted. Yet less than a month after Munich, Foreign Minister von Ribbentrop informed the Polish ambassador to Germany that the time had come for a general settlement between the two countries. He asked for the return of Danzig and for the construction of an extraterritorial highway and railroad across the Polish Corridor to connect East Prussia with the rest of Germany. In return, Germany was prepared to guarantee Poland's frontiers and extend for another 25 years the non-aggression pact signed in 1934. Warsaw rejected the proposals because acceptance would have reduced Poland to the position of a German satellite.

The Germans pursued their demands during the following months, but they put serious pressure on the Poles only after the final destruction of Czecho-Slovakia. The Warsaw government was now given to understand that any further refusal to submit to Berlin's requests might lead to war. Yet the Poles would not yield, and to their relief Britain and France came to their aid, pledging themselves to give all support in their power to the Polish government "in the event of any action which threatens Polish independence and which the Polish government accordingly considered it vital to resist with national forces."

This change of attitude on the part of the Western Powers occurred in the wake of the news of Germany's demands on Poland, the seizure of the Memelland, and the establishment of a German protectorate over the new state of Slovakia. The declaration was made on the initiative of Chamberlain and reveals the measure of his disillusionment. He now offered to help a country ruled by a dictatorial military clique and unlike the Czechs, guilty of serious violations of the rights of its German minority, and he tried to withhold from Germany the city of Danzig whose population was 90 per cent German and which, unlike the Sudetenland, had been part of Germany until 1919. Above all, Chamberlain gave the Poles the unconditional right to determine when Britain was to come to their aid. After Mussolini's seizure of Albania, similar guarantees were given to Greece and Rumania, and in May an Anglo-Turkish declaration on mutual aid in case of aggression was issued. (In each case France took corresponding steps.) In addition, peacetime conscription was introduced and negotiations initiated with the U.S.S.R. for the creation of a united front against the aggressors.

Hitler was little impressed with Britain's stand and issued a secret directive to the *Wehrmacht* to be prepared for the invasion of Poland by September 1. He also denounced the German-Polish Nonaggression Pact and the Anglo-German Naval Agreement in order to frighten both Poland and Britain, and he called publicly for the return of Danzig and the Polish Corridor. In May the Rome-Berlin Axis was transformed into the "Pact of Steel," a military alliance whose offensive character was barely disguised. As the Fuehrer explained to his military leaders at a conference late in May, war had become inevitable to secure adequate living space for the German people. Danzig, he added, was not the objective that mattered; what was at stake was the eastward expansion of Germany's *Lebensraum* to assure its supply of foodstuffs. Hitler's hope was to achieve this goal by a localized war against Poland, but he declared himself ready to fight Britain and France as well if they should come to Poland's aid, and he maintained that he would also take on Russia should Moscow ally itself with the Western Powers. Such a war, he knew well, Germany was not likely to win, and he said as much when he blandly stated that the intervention of Britain and France might turn the war into a life-and-death struggle that could last for ten or fifteen years. He was prepared to burn all his bridges, staking the existence of eighty million people on the fulfillment of what he considered his mission.

The Anglo-French-Soviet Negotiations. The Western commitments to the Eastern European countries were meaningless unless they were supplemented by Soviet military assistance. In April, London and Paris entered into negotiations with Moscow to secure Soviet help to Poland and Rumania should the two countries ask for assistance in the event of a German attack upon them. To the Russians such an arrangement seemed inadequate in terms of their own security. They called for the conclusion of an Anglo-French-Soviet alliance of mutual aid supplemented by a military convention and an unconditional guarantee of all states bordering on the Soviet Union between the Baltic and the Black Sea. The Russians not only wanted to be assured of British and French aid should they go to the help of a victim of Nazi aggression; they also wished to keep the Germans as far away as they could from their own borders.

From a military-defensive viewpoint the Soviet proposals sought to answer legitimate problems. Yet the countries to be guaranteed feared that the demands were made not merely for defensive purposes, but to enable the Soviet Union to take over, under the guise of a rescue action, part or all of their territory. They all had reason to worry about the Kremlin's intentions—Finland and the Baltic States had been part of Russia until 1917, Poland had taken from the U.S.S.R. part of White Russia and the Ukraine during the Russo-Polish War of 1920–21, and Rumania held the one-time Russian province of Bessarabia. Apprehensions increased when Moscow asked also for safeguards against "indirect aggression." The Soviets were particularly concerned about the organization of Nazi fifth columns prepared to help turn over a state to the Germans. They also feared the enforced conclusion of "friendship pacts" by which small border states might be used by the Germans as a springboard for an attack on the Soviet Union; in cases like these Moscow wanted to have the right to send troops into a state without special authorization. Under the circumstances the countries in question rejected the Soviet guarantees, and the Western Powers, sharing their fears, did not press them nor would they approve of Soviet Russia's moving into these states without the latter's permission.

In the course of the negotiations the Western Powers moved closer to the Soviet position, with the French, feeling more vulnerable, generally readier than the British to make concessions. Agreement was reached on the conclusion of the triple alliance, discussions were inaugurated on a military convention, and the guarantees to be given were extended to a number of other states besides Rumania and Poland. But the problem of whether aid was to be rendered only if asked for by these states and the question of "indirect aggression" could not be settled. There are indications that eventually the Western Powers might have accepted the Soviet terms, but negotiations came to an end when Stalin decided to throw in his lot with Hitler.

The Nazi-Soviet Nonaggression Pact. Feelers about a rapprochement between Berlin and Moscow had been put out for some time by both sides. In May Stalin dismissed Foreign Commissar Litvinov, the advocate of collective security and of Jewish background, and replaced him with his close associate Vyacheslav Molotov (1890–   ), thus easing the initiation of any negotiations. In June exploratory talks were held by the two governments. But Chamberlain on his part had not given up hope that a genuine understanding with Hitler might still be achieved, the more so because he disliked intensely the prospect of any collaboration with the Soviets. In July the Prime Minister proposed to Hitler, through intermediaries, Anglo-German cooperation in world trade, colonial adjustments, a nonaggression pact, and Britain's good services in obtaining an eventual peaceful settlement of the Danzig and Corridor problems, provided Hitler desisted from further aggression. The offer merely served to confirm Hitler's conviction that Britain was not willing to fight and that if he could come to terms with Stalin, Poland would be isolated and could be defeated quickly.

In early August Hitler asked for a speed-up of the talks with the Kremlin—if Poland was to be defeated before the autumn rains turned the Polish roads into mud, the attack had to be launched by September 1. Two weeks later Stalin agreed to comprehensive political and economic negotiations, for the talks with Britain and France were deadlocked. Moreover, news of Britain's latest offer to Germany had leaked out, heightening Soviet suspicions about the real intentions of the Western Powers. In addition, Far Eastern concerns may have accounted for the change of fronts. Soviet forces were engaged in a major battle with Japanese troops along the Manchurian frontier, and Moscow was fearful lest an alliance with the West might find Russia fighting a two-front war against both Germany and Japan. An understanding with Germany, however, could possibly discourage the Japanese from further attacks on Siberia.

Under German prodding, the Nazi-Soviet discussions produced quick results. On August 23 Ribbentrop and Molotov signed in Moscow a non-aggression pact by which both countries pledged themselves not to attack each other and to stay neutral if either one should become the "object of warlike action" on the part of a third power. Significantly, the pact did not contain the customary escape clause suspending the treaty should one of the signatories be guilty of an act of aggression; Stalin thus gave advance notice that he would not interfere with a German attack on Poland. In a "Secret Additional Protocol" Germany paid the price for Soviet neutrality: "in case of a political-territorial change" eastern Poland, Finland, Estonia, and Latvia were to become part of the Soviet sphere of interest, and central and western Poland and Lithuania were assigned to Germany's sphere (Lithuania was subsequently also pledged to the U.S.S.R.). Soviet Russia's interest in Bessarabia was likewise acknowledged while Germany declared itself disinterested in that area.

Obviously neither signatory signed the pact in good faith, but for both it bought time—for Hitler, time to fight Poland and, if necessary, Britain and France, without having to concern himself about Soviet Russia; for Stalin, time to strengthen Russia's military power for future action, while Germany and the Western Powers would go to war and, as he hoped, greatly weaken each other.

Hitler Goes to War. On August 22, at the news of Moscow's willingness to sign the pact, Hitler gave orders to launch the attack on Poland on August 26. Meanwhile, a ferocious press campaign was kept up against the Poles, with reports of Polish atrocities against Poland's German minority heightening the tension. Troops had been assembling in eastern Germany for some time under the guise of training exercises and summer maneuvers; now additional forces were openly dispatched to the Polish border. Contrary to Hitler's expectations, the British and French governments refused to be intimidated. Britain called up its reserve units, alerted all civil defense organizations, and promulgated an Anglo-Polish military assistance pact that supplemented the unilateral guarantee of the spring. A special message from Chamberlain warned Hitler of Britain's determination to stand by Poland. France, too, affirmed its readiness to help Warsaw. At the same time Mussolini warned Hitler that Italy had not yet completed its preparations for going to war.

Still hopeful of neutralizing the two Western Powers, Hitler decided to postpone the attack. Both Britain and France had kept urging him and the Poles to settle their difficulties by negotiation; he now offered to negotiate, but on terms so humiliating for the Poles that they were evidently meant only to provide himself—and the West—with an alibi. Even before the Poles, as expected, rejected them, the Fuehrer set September 1 as the day the war would begin. During the night of August 31, some SS men stage-managed a Polish attack on the German radio station at Gleiwitz; using this "incident" as his justification and dispensing with a declaration of war, Hitler sent his forces across the Polish frontier in the early morning of September 1.

The Western Powers stood by their treaties with Poland. On September 3, after some frantic mediation attempts by Mussolini, who hated the prospect of being a mere onlooker while history was being made by others, Britain and, somewhat more reluctantly, France declared war on Germany.

16

World War II:
The European Phase

One of the major problems troubling the post-World War I world was that of the origins of that war. Of more than historical interest, the "war guilt" question became a political issue of overriding importance. No such question arose after World War II; there was general agreement, shared by Germans as well as non-Germans, that the latter conflict was started deliberately and unilaterally by Hitler—it was, as some historians have called it, "Hitler's war."

In spite of this fact, Hitler quickly lost control over the course of the war. Contrary to his expectations, Britain and France entered the conflict, stayed in it after the fall of Poland, and Britain kept fighting on even after France's collapse. Similarly, Hitler failed in his efforts to shield the German civilian population from the grimmer effects of the war. Although more slowly than in the case of Britain and Russia, eventually the war became "total" for Germany too.

It was in this intensity that the Second World War differed most radically from the earlier conflict. The war was total inasmuch as the air war obliterated the distinction between home front and battle front. Mobilization and control of manpower and resources also assumed proportions unequalled in 1914–1918. Finally, the conflict was carried on on all sides beyond the actual fighting. In its most ruthless manifestation, it continued in the form of mass murders of civilians and prisoners of war, and in the willful debasement and economic enslavement of conquered peoples; on a more humane level, it called for the prosecution of war criminals, the removal of Nazis and Fascists from public office, and the re-education of the enemy. Less than any other war was the Second World War merely a military operation.

The fact that the war extended far beyond the military sphere was reflected also in the marked shift of power that occurred almost everywhere in the area of civil-military relations. In World War I most of the belligerents suffered from the autonomy of the military and in the worst cases from military interference in the civilian domain. Except for one or two incidents in France at the time of its collapse, no such intrusions occurred in the Second World War. The authority of the political leaders remained unchallenged. Instead, it was they who intruded on the preserve of the military. Hitler, Stalin, Mussolini, and Churchill too concerned themselves not only with strategy but also determined tactical operations and technical questions and overruled and removed generals who disagreed on such matters. In their judgment, most military decisions had also political implications, and these they wished to control. Conversely, Americans tended to compartmentalize military and political objectives, concentrating on winning the war before worrying about the peace. Hence the most clearcut dividing line between civil and military jurisdiction existed in the United States.

Civilians also made their vital contributions to the fighting of the war. As in World War I, the scientists and technicians helped to shape the course of the conflict by their development of new instruments and new weapons—from bombsights, radar, schnorkel, and sonar detection devices to antiaircraft guns, jet planes, guided missiles, and the atom bomb. Yet the civilians in factory and laboratory, while taking their place side by side with the soldier, did not supersede him. Thanks to motorized transport the soldier moved faster than before, but the machine could not take his place, and he was still needed to fight and win battles. In fact, more men were involved in military operations during the Second World War than ever before. The respective peak strengths of the major armies ran to 10.2 million Germans, 5 million Britons, 5 million Frenchmen, 3.75 million Italians, 12.5 million Russians, 6 million Japanese, and 12.3 million Americans.

THE EARLY MONTHS

The Disspirited Belligerents. In 1914 the European nations had expectantly gone to war, each confident that its side would win and that victory would be attained after only a few months of fighting. No such hopes inspired these nations in 1939—too many people still remembered the horrors and hardships of the earlier conflict, and those who did not had sufficient imagination to envisage the trials that lay ahead. "May God bless you all and may He defend the right," Neville Chamberlain concluded after having told his countrymen that they were at war with Germany. "For it is evil things that we shall be fighting against, brute force, bad faith, injustice, oppression, and persecution. And against them I am certain that the right will prevail." This was hardly a call of the nation to arms, nor did this weary septuaganarian inspire confidence when he pledged himself to devote "what strength and powers I have to forwarding the victory of the cause for which we have to sacrifice so much." Britain set grimly to work to fight the war against Germany, but there was a great deal of uncertainty as to what the country was fighting for and with what chance of success.

Doubts of this kind beset the French even more than the British, and millions of Frenchmen had no answer to that taunting question, "Why die for Danzig?" So great was the prevailing uncertainty that the government preferred not to ask parliament for an express assent to a declaration of war as constitutional law required. Daladier chose instead to interpret as such an assent an earlier parliamentary resolution granting the government special credits to allow it to fulfill "France's obligations resulting from the international situation."[1]

The German people too received the news of the start of the war with misgivings. Despite years of indoctrination, there were no outbursts of jubilation. Hitler took account of this mood when he assured the nation, rather defensively: "I am asking of no German man more than I myself was ready to do throughout four years. There will be no hardships for Germans to which I myself will not submit. . . . I will not take [my uniform] off again until victory is secured or I will not survive the outcome." Göring gave voice to the prevailing uneasiness when he observed at the news of Britain's declaration of war: "May God help us if we lose this war!"

As for the Poles, they had scarcely a chance to express their feelings.

The Polish Campaign.   The war against Poland lasted for little more than a month. The German Wehrmacht had developed new strategic techniques—the Blitzkrieg, or lightning war—for which the Poles were entirely unprepared. Waves of airplanes bombed airfields, destroying the Polish air force on the ground. At the same time, railroad junctions, bridges, and other key points of transportation and communication were also demolished to prevent the Polish forces from completing their mobilization. Those units that managed to assemble at their assigned stations were no match for the fast moving tanks and armored cars of the Germans; relying on horse-drawn artillery and supply trains, the Poles were easily overrun

---

[1] When he first requested the credits, Daladier had explicitly stated that he would not consider an approval of the credits as tantamount to an approval of a declaration of war.

TERRITORIAL CHANGES
IN EASTERN EUROPE
1938-1940

Territories annexed by Germany, 1939
Territories annexed by the U.S.S.R.,
1939-1940
Territories ceded to Hungary,
1938-1940
Territories ceded to Bulgaria, 1940

0   100   200   300   400
Miles

ARCTIC   OCEAN

Murmansk

Arkhangelsk

NORWAY

Bergen

Oslo

NORTH

SEA

FINLAND

Helsinki

Stockholm

Leningrad

Tallinn
ESTONIA

Volga

Riga
LATVIA

Moscow

DENMARK   Copenhagen

Memel   LITHUANIA
Königsberg   Kovno   Vilna

Smolensk   Tula

NETHERLANDS   Hamburg   Danzig   EAST
Amsterdam   Bremen   PRUSSIA

Minsk

WHITE
RUSSIA

Berlin
Brussels   Leipzig   GOVT.
BELGIUM   Cologne   Lodz
LUX.   GERMANY   Warsaw
Luxembourg   Prague   GENERAL
POLAND   Cracow

Kharkov

Kiev   Dnieper R.

Strasbourg   Munich   PROTECTORATE
Basle   Vienna   Bratislava   SLOVAKIA
SWITZERLAND   AUSTRIA

Lvov
BUKOVINA

Dnepropetrovsk

UKRAINE

Lyons   Milan

Budapest

HUNGARY

BESSARABIA   CRIMEA

Odessa

Po
Genoa   Bologna

Zagreb

Belgrade

Bucharest   R.

Sevastopol

RUMANIA

Danube

BLACK   SEA

ITALY

CORSICA

Rome

YUGOSLAVIA

BULGARIA
Sofia

DOBRUJA

Istanbul

Naples

Tirana

Saloniki

Ankara

SARDINIA

ALBANIA

Izmir

Palermo

GREECE

Tunis

Athens

MALTA I.

MEDITERRANEAN   SEA

by their motorized adversaries. Within two weeks organized Polish resistance came to an end; Warsaw held out until September 27, and on October 5 the last two pockets near Lublin and Lvov surrendered.

On September 17, at the invitation of the Germans, the Russians moved into eastern Poland. Two days later the two governments fixed the exact demarcation line by which they divided the "former Polish state" between them. The partition allotted to the Germans a somewhat larger share than originally envisaged in return for the cession of Lithuania to the Soviet domain. The Germans incorporated the western half of their booty—Danzig, the Polish Corridor, Poznan, and Polish Silesia—into Germany; out of the remainder they created a nominally separate territory, the Government-General of Poland. The Russians annexed their newly acquired lands (an area somewhat larger than that assigned to them after World War I by the Curzon Line) to the Ukrainian and White Russian Republics.

On the very day on which Poland was being partitioned Soviet Russia also set out to consolidate its position in the remainder of its sphere of interest. Estonia was forced to sign a mutual aid and trade pact with the U.S.S.R., giving the Russians the right to establish military, naval, and air bases on Estonian territory; two days later Latvia and Lithuania had to submit to similar demands. Designed to strengthen Soviet defenses against a German attack, the moves were suggestive of the brittleness of the newly formed Nazi-Soviet association.

The Soviet-Finnish War.   Of even greater concern to Moscow was the position of Finland. Leningrad, some twenty miles from the Russo-Finnish border, was within range of Finnish artillery, and the Finnish army was known to have close ties with the German Wehrmacht. In early October the Soviets requested from the Finns the cession of part of the Karelian Isthmus to place Leningrad beyond Finnish artillery range. They also asked for some islands flanking the approaches to the fortress of Kronstadt, a thirty-year lease of the port of Hangö which they wished to use as a naval base, and a strip of territory along the Arctic coast. In return for these concessions, Moscow offered Finland some land, both strategically and economically valueless, along the Soviet-Finnish frontier. The Finns were willing to accept some of the Soviet demands, but they rejected the lease of Hangö on the grounds that its proposed conversion into a naval base would jeopardize their neutrality. They also refused to surrender the Karelian territory on which their main line of defense had been constructed.

Taking advantage of a frontier incident (which conceivably they themselves manufactured), the Soviets, without declaration of war, attacked Finland late in November 1939. The offensive had been poorly prepared and the Finns, inured to the severe climate and the densely wooded, snow-covered terrain, put up a skillful and highly effective resistance. Encouraged by worldwide sympathy with their cause, they appealed for help to the League of Nations, but had to content themselves with the expulsion of Soviet Russia from the League. Limited amounts of military and other supplies did reach them, however, from a number of countries, and some foreign volunteers joined their army. France and Britain assembled a small expeditionary force to come to Finland's aid; yet in the end it could not be sent because Norway and Sweden, frightened by German and Russian warnings, would not grant it passage across their territory.

In February 1940 the Russians began pouring some of their best forces and their most powerful artillery into the campaign, for an all-out attack on Finland's Karelian defenses, and in mid-March, after the Russians broke through the fortifications, the Finns had to give up the fight. The peace terms which they were forced to accept were considerably more severe than the original Soviet demands: Finland lost the entire Karelian Isthmus, substantial territory along Lake Ladoga, and a sizable strip of land on the Arctic coast. But Finland's gallantry did not go entirely unrewarded— the country retained its independence.

The Phony War. While in eastern Europe the first months of war were filled with military activity of one kind or another, military action in the west remained negligible. The French army leaders were guided by the experiences of the First World War in which frontal attacks had invariably resulted in useless mass slaughter. Their strategy was based on their resolve to fight the new war as "economically" as possible. They planned to lay siege to the Germans behind the Maginot Line until, worn out and half-starved by the Allied blockade, the Germans could be defeated by a few knock-out blows. The plan was approved by the British who in any event had no choice but to follow the lead of the French. No attempt was made to ease German pressure on Poland by an attack in the west despite Poland's desperate pleas for relief.

The Allied plan contained serious flaws. The success of the proposed strategy was in doubt as long as the Maginot Line did not protect all of France's eastern frontier. Yet after Belgium had denounced its alliance with France, the Franco-Belgian frontier had been fortified only thinly. The decision had been made partly because of the cost involved and partly because the French general staff considered it in the French interest to go to Belgium's defense should Belgium be attacked. The most serious error in the Allied war plan, however, was its assumption that the Germans would let Britain and France pursue that very strategy of attrition that had led to the German defeat in 1918.

Hitler on his part seems to have believed that Britain and France would be willing to conclude peace once Poland had been defeated, and Allied inaction during the Polish campaign served to encourage this expectation. But the peace proposals that Hitler made at the end of the Polish campaign implied his retaining his gains, and this the British and French governments would not accept. Fired by his speedy victory over Poland, Hitler welcomed the opportunity to continue the war, and the date for

Allied War Council in Paris, February 1940. Left to right: Lord Halifax,
Daladier, Chamberlain, Churchill, Oliver Stanley (British Secretary for
War), Sir Kingsley Wood (British Secretary for Air). (Reprinted courtesy
Wide World Photos)

the western offensive was set for November 12. For various reasons the
campaign had to be postponed a number of times—much to the relief of
the army leaders, who felt that they needed more time to mount a successful attack.

Thus both sides, each for its own reason, avoided any action that might
plunge them prematurely into an all-out struggle. Except for some desultory air raids on remote bases like Scapa Flow or Helgoland and some
more spirited U-boat activity, the western front remained quiet during the
autumn and winter months of 1939–40.

The Home Fronts.   Neither in Britain nor in France did the war restore
a sense of national purpose. Chamberlain tried to form a "national" government by inviting some Liberals and Laborites into his cabinet, but was
rebuffed; Daladier did not even try to create a new *union sacrée*. The most
important cabinet change in Britain was the appointment of the militant
Churchill as First Lord of the Admiralty; Eden received the Dominions
Office. In France Daladier took over the foreign ministry from Bonnet,
the most appeasement-minded of all the French ministers; but Bonnet
remained in the cabinet as Minister of Justice. Nothing was done to

strengthen the fighting spirit of the British and French; if anything, Daladier deepened France's internal rifts by suspending the few reforms of the Popular Front that were still in effect. Similarly, the French government intervened relentlessly against Communist antiwar propaganda, but allowed the activities of rightist defeatists to go unpunished.

The Germans tried to capitalize on the confused mood of the Allied peoples by a concentrated campaign of psychological warfare. Their radio broadcasts beamed at the French strengthened the doubts of many a Frenchman about the purposes of the fighting. The Germans also managed to learn of some of the secret comings and goings of Allied leaders, and by revealing them over the air, created the impression that German agents had infiltrated the top layers of the French government. They failed, on the other hand, to undermine British morale; the British were merely amused by Nazi broadcasts attacking their government and society and predicting Germany's imminent victory.

In March 1940 Daladier was forced to turn over the premiership to the more energetic Paul Reynaud; but Reynaud, having only a one-vote majority in the Chamber of Deputies, had to retain the spiritless Daladier as War Minister. He could inaugurate merely limited changes, and of these, few had been implemented when the Germans attacked. Chamberlain was swept out of office after the disastrous Norwegian campaign and replaced by the indomitable Churchill.

The German people accepted the war in glum resignation; even the victory over the Poles did not arouse much enthusiasm. Peace rumors, on the other hand, were received with genuine rejoicing. Hitler acknowledged this unbellicose mood when he complained to his generals that people were reproaching him for "fighting, always fighting." Nor was the fighting spirit of the troops what it had been in 1914: where German infantry was forced to engage in close-range combat with Polish forces, they were often reluctant to go forward. To arouse the nation's passions, the Gestapo manufactured (or utilized) an attempt on Hitler's life: on November 8, 1939, the beer hall cellar from which Hitler had launched his ill-fated putsch in November 1923, was blown up while that event was being commemorated by the Nazi Party's "Old Fighters." Hitler and other top party leaders had left before the explosion went off, but seven of their less fortunate party comrades were killed and 63 wounded. The next day, blazing headlines blamed the attempt on Chamberlain and the British Secret Service.[2]

Yet if the bulk of the German people had no enthusiasm for the war, neither were they openly discontented. Living conditions did not decline notably; food had been rationed even in peacetime, and shipments of

---

[2] The complicity of the Gestapo has never been conclusively proven, but it is hard to see how anyone could have installed the bomb mechanism in a pillar close to the speaker's platform without official assistance. Hitler's speech, moreover, was unusually brief, and contrary to custom, he and his chief associates left immediately after his address.

foodstuffs from Soviet Russia and the Balkan states helped to offset the effects of the blockade. Thus the nation went doggedly about its business, resigned to the fact that it was in any case powerless to change the course of events.

ACTION IN THE WEST

The Campaign Against Denmark and Norway. In the plans of the Nazi war economy Sweden played a key role as Germany's main supplier of high grade iron ore. During the warm season the ore could be ferried across the Baltic Sea beyond the range of the British navy and air force, but during the winter months part of that route was blocked by ice, and the Germans were forced to ship the ore down the Norwegian coast. Here German shipping was exposed to the perils of mines and to air and naval attacks by the Allies. There was also the danger that the British might try to seize the Swedish mines—a prospect recently underscored by the Anglo-French plan of dispatching troops across Sweden to Finland.

Hitler's fears were not unjustified. Since the fall of 1939 Churchill had been urging the British war cabinet to let him lay mines in Norway's territorial waters in order to block German ore shipments. The government had rejected his pleas on legal as well as political grounds, but when it resolved to send troops across Sweden to Finland, it decided to occupy the ore fields of northern Sweden. No troops were dispatched, however, and the Allied Supreme War Council yielded to Churchill, and in March 1940 it ordered the mining of the Norwegian waters. The British also made preparations to take over the Norwegian ports flanking the ore route should the Germans attempt to seize these harbors. On April 8 the mine-laying operation got under way; on the following day the Germans invaded Denmark and Norway.

Denmark surrendered almost without firing a shot, but Norway fought back. The German plans, however, had been prepared with great care whereas Norway had made no specific defense preparations. German troops were debarked in key ports along the coast; at Oslo coastal defenses inflicted heavy losses on the German fleet as it advanced on the capital, but German air-borne forces quickly secured control of the city. Norwegian Nazis, led by a one-time War Minister, Major Vidkun Quisling, assisted the Geman invaders in a few places. Quisling, however, failed in his most important assignment—that of persuading King Haakon VII to appoint him Prime Minister of a pro-German government which would have lent at least a semblance of legitimacy to the Nazification of Norway. King and government succeeded in making their way to northern Norway where the British were staging a counterinvasion. That venture ended in dismal failure; after some weeks the British forces were forced to withdraw, and the King and government of Norway left with them for exile in Britain.

The benefits that Germany derived from the Scandinavian campaign were considerable. Apart from safeguarding their access to Sweden's ores, the Germans obtained the foodstuffs and raw materials of Norway and Denmark, considerable control over those of Sweden, and valuable naval and air bases for an attack on Britain and the British blockade. They failed on the other hand to block the escape to Britain of large parts of the Norwegian merchant marine. Joining the British war effort, Norwegian merchantmen made an important contribution to Britain's survival by ferrying in vital supplies.

The Campaign in the West. On May 10, 1940 the oft-delayed invasion of France and the Low Countries got under way. The Netherlands was overrun within five days; the advance through Belgium proceeded quickly after the key fortress of Eben Emael, which guarded the approaches to Liège, Brussels, and Antwerp, had been captured by parachute forces. The outcome of the campaign was decided when German forces broke through the supposedly impassable Ardennes Mountains just above the northern end of the Maginot Line. The plan had been adopted by Hitler himself over the objections of some of his army commanders; he was attracted to it by the element of surprise on which it was based and which in his judgment outweighed all the risks it involved. The breakthrough did take the French by surprise; the Germans overran the few French forces stationed west of the Ardennes, and from there their armored columns raced on to the Channel coast, cutting off in the process the whole Belgian army and a sizable Anglo-French force.

Caught in a vise between the German columns strung out across France from Sedan to the Channel and others pressing down from Holland and Germany, the encircled Allied forces were compelled to retreat to the sea. After two weeks of continued fighting the Belgian army under King Leopold III abruptly laid down its arms, leaving the flank of the trapped Anglo-French troops without protection. The latter withdrew toward Dunkirk, the one Channel port still under Allied control; their annihilation seemed certain when Hitler suddenly ordered his tanks to a stop. Why he did so has never been clearly established; remembering his World War I experiences, he may have thought the terrain unsuitable for armored warfare; he may have hoped to come to terms with Britain more easily by sparing it a humiliating defeat; or he may have wished to let his air force rather than the "reactionary" army get the credit for destroying the entrapped Allied forces. If this was his hope, it was not fulfilled. Britain's Royal Air Force managed to drive off the Luftwaffe, and under its protective umbrella the British evacuated 338,000 men, 224,000 of their own, the remainder Frenchmen and Belgians, in a hastily assembled flotilla of destroyers, minesweepers, trawlers, ferries, life boats, and yachts.

In a desperate effort to avert France's defeat, Premier Reynaud had meanwhile replaced the French commander-in-chief, Gamelin, with

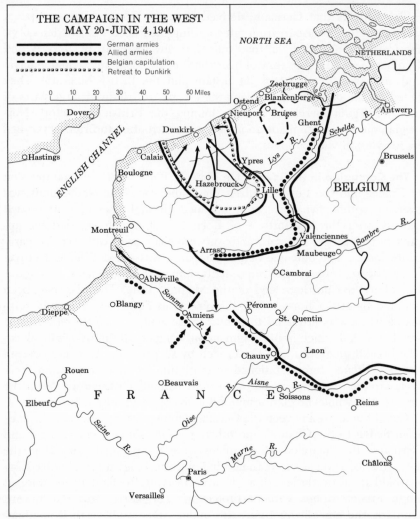

THE CAMPAIGN IN THE WEST
MAY 20-JUNE 4, 1940

━━━━━━━━━━ German armies
●●●●●●●●●●●●●● Allied armies
━ ━ ━ ━ ━ ━ Belgian capitulation
◻◻◻◻◻◻◻◻◻◻◻◻◻ Retreat to Dunkirk

0   10   20   30   40   50   60 Miles

NORTH SEA

NETHERLANDS

Dover

Zeebrugge
Ostend   Blankenberge
Nieuport   Bruges
Ghent   Schelde R.   Antwerp

ENGLISH CHANNEL

Dunkirk

Hastings   Calais   Ypres   Lys   Brussels

Boulogne   Hazebrouck   Lille   BELGIUM

Montreuil   Valenciennes   Sambre R.

Arras   Maubeuge

Abbéville   Cambrai

Dieppe   Blangy   Somme   Amiens   R.   Péronne   St. Quentin

Chauny   Laon

Rouen

Beauvais   Aisne R.

Elbeuf   F R A N C E   Soissons   Reims

Seine R.   Oise

Marne R.

Paris   Châlons

Versailles

General Maxime Weygand, the favorite disciple of Marshal Foch. At
the same time Reynaud invited Marshal Pétain into the government as
Vice-Premier, hopeful that the appointment of the "hero of Verdun"
would bolster the morale of the country. He himself took over the
Ministry of War from the morose Daladier; as Under-Secretary he chose
Brigadier General Charles de Gaulle (1890–   ), long-time advocate of
motorized warfare and one of the few military leaders who had held up
the German advance in the sector under his command along the Aisne
River.

But these changes could not ward off the collapse of the army. Weygand was unable to fight his way through to the Allied forces trapped
in Belgium, and Pétain, who thought that the war was lost, did nothing
to raise the morale of the nation. When the German forces advanced
southward early in June, they had no difficulty piercing the line of de-

fense that Weygand had hastily strung across France from the Somme River to the Maginot Line. Paris was declared an open city and surrendered without a fight; by June 20 Hitler's armies had seized Lyons and were approaching Bordeaux where the French government had taken refuge. Compounding these troubles, Mussolini on June 10 declared war on France and Britain to share in the spoils of victory.

To keep France in the war, the British government proposed a merger of the two countries into a Franco-British Union, but it refused to commit Britain's Air Reserve to the rescue of France. Reynaud resigned and was succeeded by Pétain who asked at once for an armistice. It was concluded on June 22 in Marshal Foch's dining car in which the armistice ending World War I had been signed; on Hitler's orders the car had been brought from the Musée des Invalides in Paris to the very spot where it had stood on the earlier occasion. The terms gave the Germans the right to occupy northern and central France and the entire coastline down to the Spanish frontier—altogether about two-thirds of metropolitan France, including the most important industrial regions, all Atlantic naval and air bases, and, of course, Paris. The cost of the German occupation was to be borne by France. The French army was to be disbanded, except for a small force needed to maintain public order, the air force abolished, and the navy interned. All German prisoners of war were to be released, but French prisoners were to remain in captivity until the end of the war. The Germans, on the other hand, promised not to use the French navy in the war and not to occupy the French colonies. By these promises they hoped to keep the French navy and colonies from going over to Britain. At the same time they created an unoccupied zone in France to permit the establishment of a French government on French soil; its existence, it was hoped, would make it difficult, if not impossible, to set up a French government-in-exile. In keeping with this policy, Mussolini was prevented from occupying more of unoccupied France than the few square miles his forces had seized during their short-lived campaign. Neither was the Duce allowed to take over any of France's Mediterranean possessions.

The collapse of France, as the historian Gordon Wright has written, "was far more than defeat: it was utter humiliation, almost too deep for any Frenchman to comprehend." The nation set out at once in search of traitors and saboteurs whose misdeeds could be made to account for the disaster. Yet treachery played no decisive role in the debacle, as a series of subsequent investigations determined—the collapse was primarily a military disaster caused by the failure of the French generals to prepare for the kind of warfare they were to face. On the whole their forces had not been underequipped; except for planes, German superiority in matériel was not great, and France's inferiority in fighter planes was made up by the British contribution. Apart from Germany's unmatched bomber force, what proved decisive was the more effective use to which the Germans put their equipment—their concentrated use of planes and tanks and their close coordination of ground and air forces. The French, on the other hand, had dispersed the bulk of their tanks and planes in defensive positions along the entire front in keeping with their defense strategy that called for a continuous line of fire. Yet the disaster cannot be blamed solely on the military. If the French military leaders proved incapable of adjusting their strategy to the new techniques which the Germans were developing, their inertia was part and parcel of that general spiritual paralysis that had seized most Frenchmen during the interwar years.

The Battle of Britain.   Hitler had not planned an invasion of Britain, but had assumed that the British would sue for peace once France had been defeated. He also had doubts about the feasibility of an invasion and feared that even if successful, it would seriously weaken Germany vis-à-vis Soviet Russia. Finally, a successful invasion was bound to precipitate the breakup of the British Empire, a development that would benefit the United States, Japan, and, again, Soviet Russia rather than Germany. The Fuehrer was anxious therefore to end the war against Britain. Through various neutral capitals he transmitted his peace terms to London: the British could have peace if they accepted Germany's conquests on the Continent and returned Germany's former colonies. The terms seemed lenient; yet to leave Germany in control of the Continent would have put Britain forever at Germany's mercy. It would have allowed the Germans to draw upon Europe's manpower and resources to build up a navy and air force far exceeding anything that the British could ever assemble in defense of their islands.

No one knew this better than Churchill, who had succeeded Chamberlain as Prime Minister on the very day Hitler launched his attack on France and the Lowlands. Now 66 years old, Winston Churchill, the aristocrat with the common touch, the parliamentarian with dictatorial instincts, had been waiting for this moment when he might take charge of the conduct of the war. To this veteran of British colonial campaigns, military historian and amateur strategist, war had never seemed the irrational catastrophe that it appeared to most of his countrymen.[3] He had thrown himself with gusto into his responsibilities as First Lord of the Admiralty in the First World War and had chafed at Britain's reluctance to risk a confrontation with Hitler. His readiness to do battle had made him suspect to many Britons who thought him irresponsible and impetuous. But these misgivings were discarded in this hour of crisis when Churchill's combativeness was the quality most needed to save the country. He was in the true sense the choice of the people. With characteristic self-confidence Churchill entered his new office under circumstances that would have frightened a lesser man; of his reaction to his

---

[3] Characteristically, Churchill was the only British Prime Minister who wore a military uniform while in office.

appointment as Prime Minister he wrote in an oft-quoted passage of his memoirs:

I cannot conceal from the reader of this truthful account that as I went to bed about 3 A.M., I was conscious of a profound sense of relief. At last I had authority to give directions over the whole scene. I felt as if I were walking with Destiny, and that all my past life had been but a preparation for this hour and for this trial. . . . I thought I knew a good deal about it all, and I was sure I should not fail. Therefore, although impatient for the morning, I slept soundly and had no need for cheering dreams. Facts are better than dreams.

For Churchill, acceptance of Hitler's terms was out of the question. He had bitterly criticized his predecessor who had abandoned Britain's traditional policy of maintaining a balance of power on the Continent. If such a balance was ever to be restored, Hitler must not be allowed to consolidate his gains, and the war must go on. Nor did this seem a hopeless undertaking; Churchill's advisers informed him that Germany's economic collapse could be expected within less than two years. After this, the Continent could be easily liberated with the help of the local populations. All depended on gaining time and beating off the invasion which seemed imminent, and here again Churchill and his advisers were hopeful that this could be done.

However illusory many of these calculations were, Churchill succeeded in communicating his confidence to the nation and arousing its fighting spirit. Laborites and Liberals joined his government, thus making it a truly national one, and under its leadership the country drilled and trained, built up its defenses, and steeled itself for the German invasion.

The confidence of the military leaders that they would be able to repel an invasion was based on a number of factors. Britain's naval superiority over Germany had been further increased by the losses the German navy had suffered during the invasion of Norway. The Royal Air Force was numerically smaller than the German Luftwaffe, but its striking power was greatly enhanced by the development of a highly efficient radar detection system which precluded surprise attacks, and by ground to plane communications that made it possible to redirect planes in the air. Both naval and air forces had been reinforced by French, Polish, Norwegian, and other units that had made their way to Britain. (To prevent the Germans from reinforcing their navy with French warships, a British naval force sank or disabled a sizable part of the French navy anchored at Oran, Algeria, in early July.) General de Gaulle, now an exile in London, was trying to keep France in the war through a newly organized Free French movement, and the Dominions also continued to stand by their mother country. Above all, there was growing evidence of America's readiness to extend to Britain as much help short of war as it could.

American sympathies had lain overwhelmingly with the Western

Powers since the beginning of the war. In November 1939 Congress had yielded to President Roosevelt's pleas and had authorized the sale of arms and ammunition to belligerents on a "cash and carry" basis. But confident of the Allies' ability to defeat Hitler and still isolationist in its sentiments, the United States had taken no other steps to assist them. In fact it was hampering the flow of supplies to Britain and France by barring American ships from entering belligerent ports. The defeat of France shocked Americans out of their certainty, and many gave up Britain as lost. Roosevelt, knowing that Britain was America's first line of defense, decided to give that embattled country what help he could spare. Beginning in June 1940, close to a million rifles of World War I vintage, 200,000 revolvers, 87,500 machine guns, and large amounts of ammunition were rushed across the Atlantic to replenish Britain's depleted stores. "When the ships from America approached our shores with their priceless arms," Churchill recalls in his memoirs, "special trains were waiting in all the ports to receive their cargoes. The Home Guard in every county, in every town, in every village, sat up all through the nights to receive them. Men and women worked night and day making them fit for use. By the end of July we were an armed nation so far as parachute or air-borne landings were concerned. We had become a 'hornet's nest.' "

Hitler meanwhile had ordered that preparations be made for an invasion of Britain. But he pursued these plans with obvious reluctance, and he seemed plagued by misgivings. "The invasion of Britain is an exceptionally bold undertaking," he admitted with unusual wariness, "even if the way is short, this is not just a river crossing, but the crossing of a sea that is dominated by the enemy." The fact was that he had a deep-seated aversion to being on water (an early associate later recalled that the Fuehrer was terrified when he took him on a boat ride on one of the Bavarian lakes), and this phobia also intruded on Hitler's strategic plans. "On land I am a hero," he confided to his naval chief, Admiral Raeder, "but at sea I am a coward." For once he listened patiently to his advisers when they pointed out the risks and difficulties of the enterprise. Perhaps because he had not much faith in it, he turned his attention to Soviet Russia and had plans drawn up for a Russian campaign the following spring.

Obviously the invasion could not succeed until Germany had control of the skies over Britain, and early in August German air raids on Britain were launched on a massive scale. The attacks continued through August into mid-September; they caused much destruction, but they failed to establish Nazi supremacy in the air, and they did not break the spirit of the British people. In the end German losses in pilots and aircraft were such that the Luftwaffe shifted from daylight to nighttime bombings. Other preparations for the invasion also ran into difficulties. The Royal Air Force kept bombing the transports and barges assembled in the Channel ports and prevented the Germans from bringing their invasion fleet up to full strength. In one such raid in mid-September the British succeeded in destroying or damaging 21 transports and 214 barges, some 12 per cent of the assembled shipping. In view of these losses and the Luftwaffe's failure to secure air supremacy, the invasion, originally scheduled for September 15, was postponed several times and finally was put off indefinitely.[4] Nightly bombing raids on Britain continued, however, until the spring of 1941.

The Battle of the Atlantic. The war at sea had been fought with fierce intensity since the early days of the conflict. By reviving the convoy system of the First World War, the Allies were able to limit the depredations of the U-boats, and British merchant ship losses (from all causes) averaged 90,000 tons a month from September 1939 through May 1940. In June, however, after the Germans had acquired new naval and air bases along the Norwegian and Channel coast, sinkings claimed 282,000 tons and by September monthly losses exceeded 300,000 tons. Temporarily, they were made up for by the accretion of Allied merchant ships put at Britain's disposal, but Allied shipping too was reduced by some 65,000 tons each month between July and December 1940.

Since the French navy was no longer available for escort duty and a large part of Britain's destroyers were consigned to home waters to guard against an invasion, convoys could no longer be adequately protected. Churchill asked Roosevelt for the sale of fifty or sixty destroyers of World War I vintage that had recently been refitted for use by the United States navy. Such a sale was permissible only if the two service chiefs certified that the destroyers were not needed for the defense of the United States. This the two chiefs would not do. In the end an arrangement was made by which fifty destroyers were turned over to Britain in exchange for a number of air and naval bases in British possessions in Newfoundland, Bermuda, and the Caribbean.[5] Guarding the approaches to the United States and the Panama Canal, these bases were considered more essential to national security than the destroyers. In addition, the British promised never to sink or surrender their navy but, if necessary, carry on the fight from other parts of the Empire. Early in September the fifty destroyers were turned over to British crews. (Most of them, alas, turned out to be in need of major repairs due to their age and condition, and only nine of them were in active service in December 1940.)

With the bases-destroyers deal the United States gave up all pretense

---

[4] Some historians have suggested that Hitler never intended to invade Britain, but staged his preparations only in the hope of frightening it into peace negotiations.

[5] Actually the British were also to receive twenty torpedo boats, five bombers and five naval planes, and 250,000 rifles with ammunition, but due to an oversight these items were not listed in the final text of the agreement. Except for the rifles which could be released as nonessential to American defense purposes, the British received none of these items lest an amendment of the formal agreement lead to charges of secret deals.

to neutrality and became a "nonbelligerent" participant in the war. In spite of this implication, the agreement had the approval of the bulk of the American people. Americans were becoming increasingly conscious of the direct threat to American security that Nazism presented. At that very time, Nazi intrigues aiming at the overthrow of the Argentinian and Chilean governments were discovered; in that same vein, Berlin, predicting Britain's defeat, warned the Latin American governments to desist from unfriendly actions if they wished to do business with a Nazi-controlled Europe. As a result, some of these governments were very reluctant, if not outright opposed, to joining the United States in taking measures for the defense of the hemisphere. There was also the danger that the Nazis might take over the American possessions of the French and the Dutch and use them as bases for attacks on the Panama Canal or as a springboard for subversive activities. Should Britain fall, northern and western Africa was expected to come under Nazi domination; to frightened minds this was an alarming prospect and the West African port of Dakar, some 1,500 miles from the bulge of Brazil, seemed suddenly very close to the South American continent. "For the first time," observes the historian Thomas A. Bailey, "[Americans] fully understood the relationship of the British fleet to the Monroe Doctrine." Finally, there was great fear that Britain's collapse would give further impetus to Japanese aggression in the Far East.

More perceptive observers understood that the real threat to the United States did not lie in an invasion, but in the fact that an America, facing a Nazi-dominated Europe, Africa, and Latin America and a Far East controlled by Japan, would have to give up many of its cherished traditions and institutions. Americans would have to curtail their living standards, for they might lose markets and vital supplies (such as rubber and tin) and would, on the other hand, have to allow for a vast expansion of armaments. At the same time they would also have to accept many political restrictions to combat the growth of domestic fascism that would result from the confrontation with a victorious Germany and Japan. And not a few of these observers wondered whether American independence could long be maintained under such circumstances.

Lend-Lease. Some months later the United States took another step to assure Britain's survival. The British were approaching the moment when they would no longer be able to pay for their purchases on the cash basis required by the Neutrality Act. To provide the needed supplies as a gift was politically impracticable; to grant loans was bound to lead to the same kind of difficulties that had plagued Anglo-American relations after the First World War. Roosevelt proposed to lend Britain arms and other needed material—in the same way, as he put it, in which one would lend one's garden hose to a neighbor whose house was on fire, without worrying about the price of the hose. Congress approved, and an "Act Further to Promote the Defense of the United States," passed in March 1941, authorized the President to "sell, . . . lease, lend, or otherwise dispose of" any "defense articles" to countries whose defense he considered vital to the defense of the United States, with payment to be made on any terms he deemed satisfactory. This law, Roosevelt proudly announced, made the United States the "arsenal of democracy"; Churchill, in a more sweeping but less felicitous phrase, called lend-lease the 'most unsordid act in the history of any nation."

American Aid Short of War. The Lend-Lease Act was passed at a time when Britain's need for help had become especially urgent. During the winter of 1940–41 the Germans had been able to increase their ocean-going submarine fleet and U-boats now attacked British convoys in groups. To these highly effective "wolf-pack" tactics was added an increasing number of long-range aircraft which posed an additional threat to British shipping. British, Allied, and neutral losses rose from 320,000 tons in January 1941 to 401,000 in February, 537,000 in March, and 654,000 in April (which included, however, the exceptional losses suffered in the Greek campaign). The attempt to starve Britain into surrender placed that country in deadly peril.[6] To arouse American public opinion to the gravity of the crisis, Roosevelt made an immediate demonstrative gesture. Within three hours after he had signed the Lend-Lease Act he turned over to Britain 28 motor torpedo boats, 3,000 depth bomb charges, and some naval guns for the arming of merchant vessels. Obviously such limited aid was wholly inadequate to cope with the U-boat menace, but at the time the United States had little to spare. To provide more effective assistance, the President ordered the navy to help Britain ferret out, but not attack, German submarines which were operating in the less well-guarded western Atlantic, and to warn Allied ships of their presence. In mid-July, American warships began convoying lend-lease goods to Iceland to relieve Britain of part of the escort burden; in September, after the sinking of some American merchant vessels, there followed the arming of American merchant ships and the order to "shoot at sight" on any U-boats, and in November the Neutrality Act was repealed, making it possible to send supplies to Britain in American ships. American help combined with improved British defense measures brought quick results. From July to December 1941 shipping losses were reduced to a monthly average of 224,000 tons.

The Atlantic Charter. Midway through these developments, in August 1941, Roosevelt and Churchill met secretly aboard two cruisers off Newfoundland. The main purpose of the rendezvous was to establish personal

---

[6] Britain would have been in still graver danger had Hitler been able to persuade Franco to attack Gibraltar, for without Gibraltar the task of safeguarding British convoys would have been even more difficult. But Franco, impressed by Britain's continued resistance and dependent on overseas oil and wheat which Hitler could not provide, refused to enter the war.

contact between the President and the Prime Minister, but the meeting proved useful also for the discussion of lend-lease and naval problems and the growing menace of Japanese aggression. The conference is mainly remembered, however, as the birth hour of the Atlantic Charter— an informal agreement on the postwar objectives of the United States and Great Britain. The Charter disclaimed any expansionist ambitions of the two countries, renounced territorial changes without the consent of the people affected, and called for national self-determination, international collaboration on social and economic reforms, peace, freedom from fear and want, and disarmament. Whether the Charter served as a source of encouragement to the conquered peoples of Europe and the underprivileged in all parts of the world, as it was hoped it would, is hard to say; its main importance undoubtedly was that even without any specific pledges it acknowledged America's moral commitment to the defeat of the Axis Powers and the establishment of a democratic postwar order.

PERIPHERAL DEVELOPMENTS

German-Soviet Relations. As France's resistance collapsed, the Soviet Union at once took steps to reinforce its defenses. On the day Pétain asked Hitler for an armistice, the Red Army occupied Lithuania and a day later took over Latvia and Estonia as well. Pro-Soviet governments were installed in all three countries and under their auspices the three states voted themselves as member republics into the Soviet Union. Similarly, the U.S.S.R. forced Rumania to surrender the strategically important provinces of Bessarabia and northern Bukovina. At home, in order to step up the output of arms, the Kremlin introduced the eight-hour working day with full work on Saturday and froze all workers in their jobs.

The Germans had urged the Rumanians to comply with the Soviet demands lest the Russians go to war against Rumania and seize or destroy its oil wells, which helped fuel Germany's motorized forces. Berlin was greatly alarmed by the Soviet moves and during the next few months consolidated its own position in the Balkan Peninsula. To prevent a new "Balkan War," Rumania was forced to return to Bulgaria and Hungary the provinces of Dobrudja and Transylvania which it had taken from these two neighbors after World War I. The cession of Transylvania led to the overthrow of King Carol II (who was succeeded by his 18-year-old son Michael) and the establishment of a fascist dictatorship under General Ion Antonescu, which assured Rumania's subservience. Shortly afterwards a German military mission was dispatched to Bucharest to prepare Rumania as a base for the war against Soviet Russia. The mission was followed by a Panzer division and antiaircraft units assigned to safeguard the oil fields.

The Nazi and Soviet moves were indicative of the deterioration of relations between the two countries. There were other sources of friction —among them large-scale arms sales to Finland by Germany and the passage of German troops across Finnish territory. Above all, Germany, Italy, and Japan concluded a tripartite pact of mutual aid in 1940 which was directed primarily against the United States, but which the Soviets assumed was aimed at them. To allay Moscow's misgivings, Molotov was invited to Berlin; but when he came in November, he refused to be diverted into a discussion of the partition of the British Empire and insisted on guarantees that Germany would leave Bulgaria, Turkey, and Finland untouched and would withdraw from Rumania.[7] These promises Hitler would not make, and the meeting came to a deadlock. The impasse resolved whatever doubts the Fuehrer still had about going to war against Soviet Russia and orders went out to the army to complete preparations for an attack by May 15, 1941.

The Italian Campaigns Against Egypt and Greece. Since the campaign against France had won Italy no military laurels or territory, Mussolini hoped to gain both by an attack on Egypt from Italian Lybia. The outlook seemed promising: the Italian forces outnumbered the British by 6 to 1 (215,000 to 36,000). Nevertheless, the Italian commander, Marshal Rodolfo Graziani, refused to move, pleading inadequate preparations. Threatened with removal from his command, Graziani finally launched an offensive in September 1940 that carried him some sixty miles into Egypt. There he stopped for lack of supply and transport facilities; yet when Hitler offered the dispatch of some motorized units, Mussolini proudly declined. Churchill, mindful of the strategic importance of the Suez Canal, rushed to Egypt an armored brigade with 150 tanks. The decision was made early in August at the height of the Battle of Britain when an invasion seemed imminent and Britain could ill spare this force. It was an act both of courage and faith—"at once awful and right," as the Prime Minister wrote in his memoirs. Other reinforcements consisting of Indians, Australians, New Zealanders, and a Polish brigade were assembled from India, Kenya, and Palestine. With their help General Sir Archibald Wavell attacked the Italians in early December, quickly overran their positions, and in just eight days drove the Italians out of Egypt. Pursuing them into Lybia, the British advanced to Benghazi; they would have occupied all of Lybia had Wavell not been forced to dispatch part of his force to Greece which was threatened by a German attack.

If Wavell was not able to expel the Italians from all of Lybia, he did

---

[7] Molotov was the less impressed by the proposal to carve up the British Empire because a part of the talks was carried on in an air raid shelter during a heavy British raid on Berlin.

succeed in driving them from their other possessions in Africa. By mid-May 1941 they were defeated in Eritrea, Somaliland, and Ethiopia.

Italy fared no better when the Duce ordered his troops in Albania to invade Greece late in October 1940. Mussolini was deeply resentful of Hitler's move into Rumania and resolved to stake out his claim in the Balkans before Hitler took all; in his anxiety he overruled his military advisers who warned him against launching a mountain war just before the onset of winter. As they foresaw, the campaign quickly took a disastrous turn for their forces. In the snow-covered Balkan mountains the Greeks proved superior fighters; despite their numerical inferiority they repelled the invaders and drove them back into Albania. The British, rushing to the aid of the Greeks, disrupted the Italian supply lines by naval and air raids, and in an attack on the naval base of Taranto destroyed a sizable part of the Italian battle fleet. There seemed to be every likelihood that the Italians would soon be driven out of Albania altogether.

Hitler's Balkan Campaign. Hitler followed Italy's difficulties with increasing dismay. British planes operating from Greece could now bomb the Rumanian oil fields. The Greek campaign also threatened to interfere with his plans for the invasion of Russia. Churchill, he learned, was trying to forge a Turkish-Greek-Yugoslav anti-Axis front; to foil these efforts, the Balkans had to be brought under Nazi control as quickly as possible. In February Bulgaria was compelled to consent to the entry of German forces in preparation for an attack against Greece, and in March Yugoslavia was pressured into adherence to the Tripartite Pact. Yugoslavia's accession to the Axis led to the overthrow of the Belgrade government by a group of army and air force officers and the establishment of a new regime under the young heir to the throne, King Peter II. The new government promised to maintain Yugoslavia's neutrality, but Hitler, fearful of British designs on Yugoslavia and taking the rising as a personal affront, ordered his military chiefs to draw up plans to "destroy Yugoslavia militarily and as a national unit . . . with merciless harshness." In early April 1941 the Germans, supported by Italian and Hungarian forces, attacked both Yugoslavia and Greece. Once more Blitzkrieg tactics produced immediate results—Yugoslavia, ill-led and ill-prepared, was overrun in twelve days; mainland Greece fell after three weeks, and Crete was seized in an airborne attack at the end of May.

Yet Greece's and Yugoslavia's resistance was not without consequences. Hitler was forced to delay the invasion of Russia by more than a month, and this delay reduced further what chances he had of defeating the Soviet Union.

The Middle East. While the Germans came to Italy's rescue in the Balkan campaign, they also rushed aid to their Axis partner in Lybia. Under the command of General Erwin Rommel (1891–1944), who had spearheaded the dash from Sedan to the Channel in the French campaign, the German Africa Corps drove the thinned-out British forces back to the Egyptian border. Churchill, in desperation, urged the entry of the United States into the war to buttress Britain's Middle Eastern position. If Britain were driven from Egypt and the Middle East, he warned, the war would become a "hard, long, and bleak proposition" even with the all-out participation of the United States. Fortunately for the British, Hitler was preoccupied with his plans against Russia and denied reinforcements to Rommel for a campaign against Egypt and the Suez Canal. Similarly, he sent but inadequate help to Iraq when that country's pro-German government was trying to expel Iraq's British garrison. Iraq not only controlled some of Britain's main oil lines, but also had airfields from which the Luftwaffe could have bombed the Caucasian oilfields so vital to Russia's defense. Owing to Hitler's inaction, the British were able to shore up their Middle Eastern position: they reasserted themselves in Iraq and wrested Syria and Lebanon from the French.

THE ATTACK ON THE SOVIET UNION

Hitler's Strategy. Hitler had pressing reasons for taking on Russia as quickly as possible. With the United States giving the British all aid short of war, Britain was growing increasingly stronger. In consequence the invasion of Britain was bound to require the commitment of all of Germany's resources. This Hitler could not afford as long as his eastern front was threatened by Soviet Russia; only with his rear rendered safe by the defeat of the Soviet Union could he risk throwing his full military strength into the invasion of Britain. Russia, moreover, had the manpower, foodstuffs, and raw materials which he would need to offset America's resources in the final encounter with the "Anglo-Saxon" Powers. Above all, since the days of *Mein Kampf,* he had looked on the conquest of Russia as the main goal of his foreign policy, for only Russia had the vast spaces on which he planned to build up his empire. All else was prelude, and he was happy, therefore, to address himself to this ultimate task even if all preliminary steps had not yet been completed. In fact, with time working against him, he knew that he had no choice in this matter: if he was to win the war, Russia had to be conquered at once.

Hitler had serious doubts that this would be an easy matter. To reassure his hesitant generals, he told them to plan a short swift campaign of annihilation; but when they proposed a concentrated attack on Moscow to achieve this purpose, he insisted that they first get control of the Baltic region to render the Baltic Sea secure for German shipping. Only if Soviet resistance should collapse "unexpectedly quickly," he declared in his famous "Barbarossa" directive to the Wehrmacht, could there be any question of advancing on Moscow at once. Similarly, in the south,

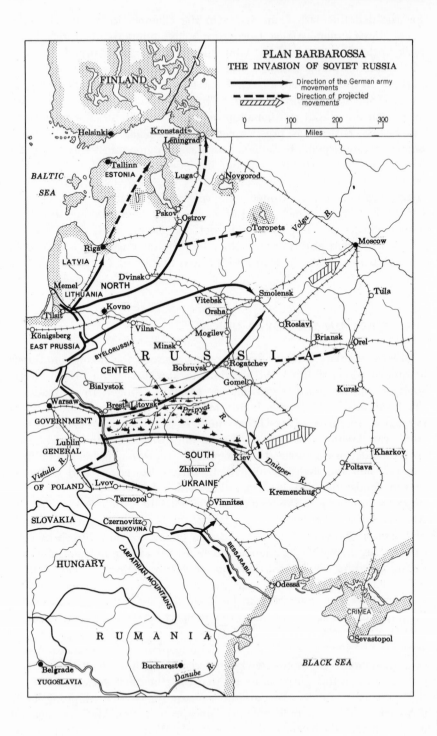

PLAN BARBAROSSA
THE INVASION OF SOVIET RUSSIA

Direction of the German army
movements
Direction of projected
movements

0   100   200   300

Miles

the first objective would be the capture of the Ukraine and the "war economically important" Donets Basin. He clearly was planning for the possibility of a protracted campaign.

The Kremlin received a great many forewarnings of the forthcoming German invasion—some of them from the British and American governments, which in turn had gotten their information from the German Resistance movement. In May 1941, because of the seriousness of the situation, Stalin himself assumed the chairmanship of the Council of People's Commissars. While the Soviet leaders expected an early attack, they were not prepared for it when it did come, on June 22, 1941. The Germans were able to overrun in the first two weeks Lithuania and Latvia, parts of White Russia, and the western Ukraine, and the Finns, who had joined them in the attack, advanced upon Leningrad. After the fall of Smolensk in mid-July, however, Soviet resistance began to stiffen, and the Germans discovered that they had seriously underrated the Russian manpower reservoir.

The Battle of Moscow. The German army leaders proposed once more an attack on the capital. To their mind Moscow was a strategic and psychological prize of the first order and one which the Russians were bound to defend with large forces. A victory over such a concentration of power could well prove decisive. Hitler persisted in his concern with economic objectives. As he confided to his immediate entourage (though not to his generals), he was convinced that the war would most likely be a long one, and he must therefore capture all economic resources within his reach. Only after the occupation of the food rich Ukraine and the coal mines and industries of the Donets Basin did he consent, late in September, to an offensive against Moscow.

The attack started on October 2 and during the first two weeks progressed rapidly. On October 16 most of the Soviet ministries and all foreign missions were evacuated from the capital, and the city prepared for the final German assault. Yet the first snow was already falling, and soon winter set in with unusual severity. The Germans were ill-equipped for a winter campaign; Hitler had thought it bad for the morale of the troops and the nation if preparations suggesting the possibility of a winter campaign had been made in advance. But it was as much sheer exhaustion as the rigors of the Russian winter that brought the German advance to a halt some twenty miles west of Moscow. The Soviets now launched a counteroffensive and during the next few weeks drove the Germans back over distances ranging from 40 to 200 miles on a 500-mile front. Under Hitler's proddings and threats the German retreat was finally brought to a halt and the army saved from complete destruction.

The year ended with Moscow and Leningrad still in Soviet hands, with the Germans pushed back some forty miles from Rostov, their point of farthest advance in the south, and the myth of German invincibility shattered. At this very moment, the United States was drawn into the struggle, confronting the Germans with the prospect of a full-fledged two-front war. Hitler appears to have realized that he could not hope to win such a war militarily and that his only chance of eventual victory lay in some special development—a new miracle weapon, some unexpected turn of events on the political stage, or some ingenious maneuver such as only he could devise. To gain time for such an event to occur, he decided that he would have to protract the war as long as he could. This was bound to become increasingly difficult as the anti-Axis Powers were gaining in strength. What was needed, therefore, was ruthless persistence in holding on to all conquered territory, never retreating regardless of casualties, in order to prolong the struggle at any price. Such a strategy could be pursued successfully only if the army's faith in (or fear of) the Fuehrer was sustained by continuous indoctrination. Hitler was certain that only he could accomplish both tasks, and he took over himself the command in the field of the army. "Those few operations which will be necessary anyone can carry out," he explained. "The main task of the commander-in-chief of the army is to educate the army in National Socialism. I don't know any general of the army who could fulfill this task as I want it done." Or, as he put it on another occasion, he wanted to bind the army to his person and destiny.

HITLER'S EUROPE

The New Order. The realm that Hitler had amassed by this time covered a vaster area than any of the empires built up by the Romans, the medieval German emperors, or more recent conquerors. It comprised not only Germany and the conquered countries, but to all practical purposes included such allied states as Rumania, Bulgaria, and Hungary. Similarly, Italy was being drawn increasingly into the German sphere of domination, and neutrals like Sweden and Switzerland retained little freedom of action. This vast domain, the Nazis announced, would be integrated into a "New Order"—a German-led Europe that would safeguard peace and stability.

The vista of a strong, peaceful Europe was cleverly chosen: since the traditional European state system had failed to bring peace, many Europeans longed for a new order that would end war and social unrest. Pride in national honor and prestige were at a low ebb, and not a few non-Germans were willing to accept Hitler's supremacy if he would provide material security and the protection of their personal rights. They were soon to discover that Hitler did not envisage a European union in which all Europeans would enjoy dignity and security. His plans called for an order that would perpetuate his mastery over Europe and in which Germany, enlarged by French, Belgian, Polish, and other territories, would dominate the rest of Europe either directly or through subservient indigenous governments. Economically, Europe was to be reorganized so as to make Germany the industrial heartland of the continent, with the surrounding states serving mainly as suppliers of foodstuffs and raw materials. This division of labor was to give Germany full economic control of Europe and at the same time assure it of permanent military ascendancy since the satellite states would be deprived of their arms industries. By the transfer of all *Volksdeutsche* (racial Germans) from non-German areas to Germany proper and the expulsion of all non-Gemans from the Reich, the cleavage between master race and servant peoples was to be widened still further.

The Implementation. Some of the proposed measures were taken at once. Danzig and the formerly German parts of Poland were reincorporated into Germany, and so, practically though not formally, were Alsace-Lorraine, Luxembourg, and some Yugoslav areas that had been part of Austria until 1918. The Protectorate of Bohemia-Moravia, the Polish Government General, and the occupied Soviet areas were maintained as separate "associate" units; they were to be Germanized by German settlers, the assimilation of suitable indigenous elements, and the expulsion of those who were unassimilable, especially Jews and intellectuals. Presumably, these lands would in the end be annexed to Germany. Of the so-called occupied territories, Belgium, the Occupied Zone of France, Greece, and the Serb part of Yugoslavia[8] were administered by the German military authorities, whereas the Netherlands and Norway were governed by civil commissioners. Denmark, which was accorded the status of a "model protectorate," retained its own government subject to supervision by the German minister in Copenhagen.

Economic policies were dictated largely by the requirements of the moment, but in the treatment of the eastern territories the ultimate objectives were clearly discernible. Hitler announced at once that he did not wish to rebuild Polish industry, and Göring ordered the removal to Germany of "all Polish plants not urgently required for the bare subsistence of the inhabitants." Another directive concerned with the occupied Soviet territories forbade the development of any important facilities for the production of consumer goods or any other finished industrial products: "It is rather the task of European and especially German industry to process the raw materials and semi-finished products produced in the occupied Eastern areas and to take care of the most urgent requirements for industrial consumer goods and production means of these Eastern areas which are to be exploited like a colony."

In the west deindustrialization proceeded on a more limited scale; wherever possible, industrial facilities were utilized for the German war effort. In 1941 80 per cent of French heavy industry in the Occupied

---

[8] Croatia was set up as a separate state of which a cousin of King Victor Emanuel III of Italy, the Duke of Spoleto, was to become King. Because of strong opposition in Croatia, he never did.

German troops marching down the Champs-Elysées in Paris. In background, the Arch of Triumph. (*Reprinted courtesy Wide World Photos*)

Zone and 50 per cent of the industrial plants in unoccupied France were kept busy on German orders. Much machinery that was not deemed war-essential was confiscated and sent to Germany, as were large stocks of food, raw materials, and rolling stock. France's industrial output in 1941 dropped to 50 per cent of what it had been in 1938. However, when Allied bombings began interfering with industrial production in Germany, the process of concentrating industry in the Reich came to a halt, and more production was shifted to plants in occupied countries.

Labor was recruited from all parts of Nazi-controlled Europe to replace German workers serving in the armed forces. By May 1942, 7,805,-000 men had been drafted into the armed services from the civilian labor force, and 4,224,000 foreign workers were employed in their place (some 3,000,000 jobs were eliminated in handcraft, banking, insurance, and other distributive trades). Recruitment was at first voluntary, but became compulsory in the occupied countries in 1942. It was also used to help consolidate Germany's domination over the continent. Only individual workers, no families, were recruited to reduce the birth rate of the peoples affected. Those of "inferior" racial background got the smallest food rations and the poorest housing facilities, with death taking its expected disparate toll among them.

Germany's Allies. The treatment of Germany's allies resembled in many respects that of the conquered countries. While the allied states retained their own governments, most of these governments functioned on German tolerance (the main exceptions being Finland and Italy). Economically, the southeastern countries had been absorbed into the German orbit even before the war; now their peoples served as sources of manpower. With "racial" considerations overriding all other factors, allied nationals often were treated worse than those who were "enemy aliens." As a result, Italians, Bulgarians, and Rumanians, being supposedly of inferior racial stock, ranged below Danes, Dutch, Norwegians, and Frenchmen.

Italy, in fact, was never more than a junior partner in the Axis alliance; as its military dependence on Germany grew, its economy, too, was more closely aligned with that of the Reich. Increasing numbers of Italian laborers were sent to German in return for large imports of finished goods; at the same time, many Italian factories either were closed or put to work for the Reich. Yet the Germans could not or would not live up to their commitments; whereas Italian exports of goods and labor kept growing, imports from Germany declined steadily, weakening the Italian economy even further.

Vichy France. The Unoccupied Zone of France held a special position in Hitler's Europe—midway between defeated enemy, ally, and neutral. On July 10, 1940 the French Senate and Chamber of Deputies, sitting jointly as a National Assembly at the resort town of Vichy, voted the Third Republic out of existence by giving Pétain full powers to draw up a new constitution. No such constitution was ever drafted, but Pétain, using his new authority, took the title of "Chief of the French State," adjourned both Senate and Chamber indefinitely, and assumed all governmental and legislative powers. Theoretically, the new state included all of France, but in practice Pétain could exercise his authority only in the Unoccupied Zone. A spate of reforms dealing with family, education, and economic and labor relations inaugurated a "national revolution" aimed at all the ills that the democratic liberalism of the Third Republic was supposed to have inflicted on France. The tendency of these reforms was conservative rather than fascist, calling for an increased influence of the Church, a sort of patriarchal corporatism, and a patriotism carrying strong regional overtones.

Ideologically, Vichy France never aligned itself fully with Nazi Germany. On the other hand, its attempt to steer something of a political course of its own ended in failure. Pétain, secretive and noncommittal, maintained a cautious wait-and-see attitude and let himself be pulled along by events. His two main associates, Laval, Vice-Premier until December 1940 and again from April 1942 on, and Admiral François Darlan, acting head of the government in 1941–42, tried to secure for

France the position of an ally. Yet by offering collaboration, they merely increased Vichy's subservience to Germany. For a time, Vichy managed to maintain diplomatic relations with the United States at some economic benefit to the mainland and the French colonies. These ties were broken off, however, after the Anglo-American invasion of French North Africa in November 1942, and from this time on Vichy France was in effect another full-fledged Nazi satellite.

Ideology. Since Nazi plans called for a closely integrated German-dominated Europe in which non-Germans would play a subordinate role, the Germans relied on physical force rather than on an ideological underpinning to maintain the new European order. They ignored the demands of indigenous Nazi movements in the occupied countries, such as the Dutch Nationaal Socialistische Beweging under Anton Mussert, Degrelle's Rexist movement in Belgium, and Quisling's Nasjonal Samling in Norway, which wished to maintain a measure of independence for their peoples. The Germans could disregard the aspirations of these groups because the local fascists had only small followings and contributed little to the consolidation of the New Order. While individual members of these movements received administrative appointments, native governments recruited from them were established only in rare cases and were closely supervised by the Germans.

Even though the ideological alignment of the occupied countries was a matter of little concern to the Nazis, they did demand the adoption of the racial policies they had introduced in Germany. In the implementation of these policies they encountered, however, much opposition and sabotage: Finland never took any anti-Jewish measures, and Italy, Vichy France, Bulgaria, and Hungary, while enacting restrictive laws, refused to deport their Jewish population as long as they retained any freedom of action.

Resistance. From the moment of defeat, there were men and women in the occupied countries who would not resign themselves to the enslavement of their homeland. While some of them managed to escape and continued the fight against Germany from abroad, others stayed in their native land. Their numbers increased as the ultimate defeat of the Nazis became more likely. They carried on a relentless guerrilla war, engaging in sabotage, killings of Germans, Italians, and native collaborators, the destruction of trains, bridges, and other key installations, or hampering the implementation of such Nazi policies as the deportation of Jews. The extent of these activities varied, depending on the degree of oppressiveness of the occupation regime and factors of history and geography. Resistance was strong from the outset in Poland and Yugoslavia; both countries were treated with special brutality by the Germans, and both had a deep-rooted history of conspiratorial activities. Opposition was also widespread in such mountainous or densely forested countries as Norway, Greece, and the occupied Soviet areas.

Resistance generally sprang up on the local level, and the various groups were eventually fused into nation-wide movements. In Yugoslavia, resistance was carried on openly from the beginning—part of the army was never demobilized but under the leadership of Colonel (later General) Draja Mihailovich withdrew into the mountains to continue the fight against the Germans and Italians. Almost at the same time, a Yugoslav Communist, Josip Broz Tito (1892–   ), began gathering an underground army of his own to fight the occupation forces. Efforts to merge these two groups were unsuccessful, and their rivalry was soon to have international repercussions (see p. 376). Tensions between Communists and non-Communists existed also in other Resistance movements;[9] they were shelved temporarily although the Communists insisted on maintaining their separate identity within the underground groups. Courageous and dedicated fighters, well suited for clandestine warfare, the Communists acquired a new respectability, and the Germans, by blaming all sabotage acts on the Communists, helped to confirm this image.

The impact of the Resistance activities is hard to determine. The most effective movement was that of the Russian partisans who were especially successful in interfering with German military operations by blowing up rails, trains, and bridges. The Russian guerrillas were in a more advantageous position than other Resistance movements since they were in close physical contact with their regular army and government. After 1942, they were reinforced with regular troops dropped behind the German lines and equipped even with mortars and heavy guns. They also had a large territory to operate in; as early as 1942 they controlled sizable areas in the vast forest country of Byelorussia and the northern Ukraine, and in the region around Smolensk and Briansk, which served as their bases of operations. Tito's forces, by wrecking bridges and other installations, seriously interfered with the shipment of supplies to Rommel's Africa Corps and helped to bring about its defeat. Other groups by their very existence kept pinned down German forces that were badly needed on the Russian and other fronts. They also did valuable intelligence work for the Allies and helped to pave the way for the invasion of the Continent. Above all, the Resistance movements could claim much of the credit for sustaining the hope for an eventual liberation of occupied Europe. By keeping many from resignedly collaborating with the Axis Powers, they made what perhaps was their most important contribution to Hitler's final defeat.

[9] The Communists became active Resistance fighters only after the German invasion of Soviet Russia had, in their view, turned the "imperialist" war into a "people's war."

17

World War II:
The Global Phase

With the entry of Japan and the United States into the war, World War II expanded into its global phase. As most of the participants saw it, however, the change seemed one of quantity rather than quality, extending the geographical dimensions of the conflict, but barely affecting its strategy. Except for the United States, the belligerent powers found it difficult to envisage the global war as one single contest. The Axis countries did not coordinate their operations in one overall strategy; the Germans concentrated on their struggle with the Russians and their campaign in North Africa and later in Western Europe, while the Japanese were absorbed in their Far Eastern operations. Although the British took part in the Asian campaigns, they, too, viewed the struggle as primarily European. The Soviets of course were preoccupied with beating off the German invaders. Only the United States was fully involved in both Europe and Asia.

Yet if there existed no strategic connection between the two theaters of war, there clearly was a logistic one. From the outset the United States and Britain gave priority to the war in Europe, but because of the American involvement in the Far East, the United States could not throw the entirety of its resources into the war against Hitler. As a result the Western Powers were forced to postpone a direct cross-Channel attack on the Germans far longer than would have been necessary had the United States had no Asian commitments. In its stead they launched peripheral operations which produced no decisive results. It is here that the Far Eastern phase of the war exerted its impact on European developments—an impact that had also its political repercussions. The delays in a direct attack on the Germans accentuated tensions and problems in Western-Soviet relations which a speedier defeat of the Nazis might have precluded.

THE UNITED STATES ENTERS THE WAR

Japan and the War. Japan's attack on the United States was directly related to the course of the European war, and the events leading to the assault on Pearl Harbor form a pertinent part of our story.

Hitler's victories in the spring of 1940 gave new impetus to Japan's expansionist aspirations. The collapse of France and the Netherlands opened up the prospect of seizing Indo-China and the Dutch East Indies, and the seemingly imminent defeat of Britain promised additional spoils. Japan could gain control of Indo-China by the dispatch of troops from adjacent China; on the other hand, it could not take over as easily the Dutch possessions because the United States might block such an undertaking. To neutralize American power, the Japanese proposed to Berlin a mutual aid pact, and Berlin agreed. To Germany the bases-destroyers deal, just concluded, was a warning that the United States might enter the war on Britain's side; the Germans hoped, as did the Japanese, that a German-Japanese alliance would restrain Washington. In September 1940 Germany and Japan, together with Italy, signed a Tripartite Pact, recognizing each other's predominance in their respective domains and promising to assist each other in the event of an attack by a presently nonbelligerent power. The pact stated expressly that it was not aimed at the Soviet Union; whatever the German attitude, Japan was anxious to improve its relations with Moscow, for only if Moscow stayed neutral could the Japanese risk moving southward. Accordingly, in April 1941 the Japanese government signed a neutrality pact with the Russians who were equally anxious to stabilize their Far Eastern front in case of a German attack. When the Germans invaded the Soviet Union two months later, the Japanese refused to come to Germany's aid despite Berlin's urgent pleas.

Pearl Harbor. The United States kept watching Japan with growing concern. Tokyo's activities were wrecking the Far Eastern balance of power and endangering America's access to the tin and rubber of Southeast Asia. Any direct intervention against Japan was precluded by America's lack of military preparedness and the Nazi ascendancy over Europe. Washington therefore resorted to economic pressures: it placed embargoes on high-octane gasoline, scrap metal, iron ore, chemicals, and machine tools, froze Japanese funds in American banks, and closed the Panama Canal to Japanese shipping. The hope was that these steps would serve as a warning strong enough to deter Japan from carrying out its expansionist plans, but not so strong as to provoke it into going to war. The two countries were unable, however, to attain a political settlement that might avert war altogether: the Japanese insisted on a free hand in China, whereas the United States demanded their withdrawal from China to forestall Japan's domination of the Far East. The impasse was ended by the Japanese raid on Pearl Harbor on December 7, 1941; the attack immobilized the Pacific Fleet of the United States and enabled Japan to launch its drive to the south without fear of immediate American intervention.

Hitler declared war on the United States four days later. He need not have done so under the Tripartite Pact since he was obliged to assist Japan only if the Japanese were the attacked. He seems to have acted mainly from hatred and contempt for America and from the wish to declare war on the United States before Washington would declare war on him. Mussolini immediately joined him.

The United Nations.   While the Axis Powers seemed to close ranks— in reality they never achieved any genuine collaboration—the states fighting the Axis moved to strengthen their own coalition, which they now called the United Nations. On New Year's Day 1942 the anti-Axis countries issued a declaration by which they proclaimed their adherence to the principles of the Atlantic Charter, promised to pursue the war with all the resources at their disposal and in cooperation with each other, and pledged themselves not to sign a separate peace. The declaration was at once implemented by an Anglo-American agreement to consider the Atlantic and European area the primary theater of the war: Germany was the main enemy and its defeat took precedence over that of Japan.

Yet collaboration of the United Nations, while better than that of the Axis camp, also was subject to serious strains. Problems of strategy and policy were a source of recurrent tension between Britain and the United States, and they caused almost continuous friction between the Western Powers and the U.S.S.R.

UNITED NATIONS STRATEGY AND DIPLOMACY

Western Strategy.   The months following on America's entry into the war were a period of sharp reverses for the United Nations. In the Far East the Japanese overran Malaya, Burma, the Philippines, and the

AXIS EUROPE, 1942

- Axis states
- Occupied states (by Axis)
- German farthest penetration into the U.S.S.R.

Dutch East Indies; in the Atlantic German U-boats inflicted ruinous losses on Allied convoys; in Russia the Soviet counteroffensive was petering out from lack of supplies, and the Germans were making preparations for a new attack of their own. In North Africa, Rommel's Africa Corps was poised for an assault on the Suez Canal and in June lunged forth to the edge of the Nile Delta.

British and American military planners tried hard to work out a plan that would turn the tide of defeat. Their efforts were hampered by a basic disagreement on the strategy to be adopted against the Germans. The Americans favored a concentrated direct attack—a cross-Channel invasion of France, with a beachhead to be established in Normandy in the fall of 1942 and the main assault to be launched in 1943. The British, remembering the costly Dardanelles campaign of 1915 and the Flanders battles of 1917, insisted that preparations were wholly inadequate for any early large-scale invasion. They proposed a number of peripheral thrusts at the Nazi empire—in Norway, North Africa, and elsewhere—until Germany, weakened by these attacks, as well as by air strikes,

blockade, and the Russian campaign, could be given the *coup de grâce*—
perhaps in 1946, if not later. In the end the British strategy was accepted
for 1942 and plans drawn up for the invasion that fall of French North
Africa.

The Soviet Call for a Second Front. The decision touched off serious
difficulties in Western relations with Moscow. Ever since the Nazi assault
on the U.S.S.R., Stalin had asked for the immediate opening of a second
front, either in France or the Arctic, that would relieve the enormous
pressure on his own front. As Russia's military position became increasingly critical, he became more insistent; he kept reiterating his demand
and at one point proposed that if a second front were unfeasible, twenty-
five or thirty British divisions be sent to the Russian front.

In the spring of 1942 Foreign Commissar Molotov visited London and
Washington to secure the opening of a second front in 1942. He arrived
in London at a moment when the Soviets' military fortunes were once
more at a low ebb; the Russian spring offensive in the eastern Ukraine
had been repelled by the Germans, and the Red Army was being dis-
lodged from its footholds in the Crimea. In June the Germans launched
their own summer offensive that was to take them to Stalingrad and
the Caucasian oil fields. Molotov pleaded for the opening of a new front
in France and warned that the Soviets would be forced to fight a defensive war if they were pushed back behind the Volga. In keeping with
British strategic views, Churchill pointed out the impossibility of an
effective cross-Channel invasion. In Washington, however, Molotov received the impression that a second front would be established that fall.
A communiqué drafted by him and approved by both Roosevelt and
Churchill announced that "in the course of the conversations full understanding was reached with regard to the urgent tasks of creating a second
front in Europe in 1942." Churchill warned Molotov that he could make
no firm commitment and that he agreed to the statement only because
it might worry the Germans and induce them to keep large bodies of
troops in the west. Yet the Soviets insisted that they had received a
definite promise and charged the Western Powers with a grave breach
of faith when the latter, instead, invaded North Africa.

THE MEDITERRANEAN CAMPAIGN

The Invasion of North Africa. Though conceived by the British, the
North African invasion was essentially an American undertaking, under
the supreme command of General Dwight D. Eisenhower. With the
British raid on Oran still rankling in French minds (see p. 349), Americans were thought to have a better chance of negotiating the surrender
of the French garrisons. Yet when General Mark W. Clark put his forces

ashore in November 1942, he encountered some stiff resistance, especially in Morocco. Three days later, however, Admiral Darlan, who happened to be in Algiers, ordered a cease-fire. In return, he was allowed to remain as the provisional governor of French North Africa—an arrangement that caused considerable dismay in the United States and Great Britain. Roosevelt and Churchill approved of the deal with this prominent Vichyite because it spared thousands of lives and prevented the Germans from intervening, but they let it be known that the agreement was a temporary arrangement incurred for tactical military reasons.

Shortly before the invasion the British launched an offensive against the Axis forces in Egypt. Under General Sir Bernard Montgomery, they drove Rommel back into Lybia and advanced on Tunisia. Too far inside the Mediterranean basin, Tunisia had not been an invasion target and had remained under Vichy control; before any Allied forces could reach it, however, Hitler rushed troops into the protectorate to retain a bridgehead. Concurrently, the Fuehrer moved troops into unoccupied France in patent violation of the armistice agreement of 1940. He was not quick enough, though, to prevent the scuttling of the French fleet at the naval base of Toulon.

The Casablanca Conference. The Anglo-American leaders assumed confidently that the Axis forces were close to defeat in North Africa—actually they were not fully cleared out until May 1943—and that it was time to decide on the military operations to be undertaken next. It seemed advisable to have this question decided at a top-level conference, and in January 1943 Roosevelt and Churchill met at Casablanca in French Morocco.

The problem of future operations was settled in favor of a continuation of the Mediterranean campaign; the early part of July was set as the date for the invasion of Sicily. The cross-Channel invasion was postponed until 1944 on the pleas of the British planners who convinced their American counterparts that a large-scale invasion of Northern France would still be unfeasible in 1943.[1]

At Casablanca Roosevelt and Churchill also tried to resolve the political differences that beset French North Africa. Darlan had been assassinated on Christmas Eve 1942 (by a royalist sympathizer who apparently hoped to see the French Pretender, the Count of Paris, take Darlan's place), and the President and the Prime Minister wished to unite the various French factions under one leadership. De Gaulle had had no part in the invasion since it was believed that he had no significant following in the

[1] As always, the main bottleneck was shipping. The Battle of the Atlantic was still going badly; shipping losses averaged 620,000 tons a month and by the end of 1942 exceeded new construction by about one million tons. Moreover, the Far Eastern campaign, even though secondary to the European war, claimed a sizable share of the available ships.

North African territories and that his presence might tend to complicate matters. As Darlan's successor, Roosevelt and Churchill had selected General Henri Giraud. Having escaped from German imprisonment in both World Wars, Giraud was something of a French national hero; he was also emphatically nonpolitical and identified with neither De Gaulle nor Vichy. Yet while Giraud had the support of the non-Gaullist elements in North Africa, he proved sadly incompetent as a proconsul; it was therefore decided to establish De Gaulle and Giraud as joint leaders. De Gaulle, deply offended at having been by-passed, thought the Anglo-American attitude toward him an affront to the French nation and the Resistance; he insisted on negotiating with Giraud directly rather then under Churchill's and Roosevelt's auspices. A vague agreement was arranged between the two men, but it took De Gaulle only a few months to assert himself over Giraud, and the latter disappeared into obscurity.

Unconditional Surrender. The Casablanca meeting is best remembered as the occasion on which the demand for the unconditional surrender of the Axis Powers was first put forth. In calling for an unconditional surrender the Allied leaders hoped to avoid the difficulties that had arisen after the First World War when Germany had surrendered conditionally—on the basis of the Fourteen Points. They also wished to reassure Stalin that they would make no separate deal with the Axis Powers. At the same time, Roosevelt stressed his resolve that unconditional surrender did not imply the destruction of the German, Italian, and Japanese peoples, but was aimed merely at their war-making powers and their despotic regimes and at the punishment of their "guilty, barbaric leaders." Or as Churchill put it, unconditional surrender meant that "the Nazi, Fascist, and Japanese tyrannies . . . must be completely broken, and that they must yield themselves absolutely to our justice and mercy. . . . It does not mean, and it never can mean, that we are to stain our victorious arms by inhumanity or by a mere lust of vengeance."

It has often been claimed that the demand for unconditional surrender served to prolong the war. There is no evidence that it did so to any significant extent.[2] In the case of Italy it does not seem to have had any appreciable effect at all; in the case of Japan it may have delayed negotiations for a few weeks. (In the end neither country surrendered unconditionally.) As for Germany, Hitler's stranglehold on the Reich was such that only he could determine when the war should be ended. Hitler, however, had nothing to gain from a negotiated peace and would in any event have continued to fight to the final collapse of the Reich.

---

[2] The formula has also been attacked as meaningless on the ground that a country cannot be surrendered unconditionally and that specific military, political, and adminstrative agreements must be arranged. What was actually meant by the term was that the long-range substantive policies adopted against the defeated countries would be discretionary with the victors.

The Fall of Mussolini. On July 10, 1943 a British army led by Montgomery and an American army under General George S. Patton landed in Sicily. The Italians, ill-equipped and demoralized, offered little resistance; only the German units put up a determined fight and held out in the northeastern part of the island until mid-August. Their skillful resistance delayed the Allied invasion of the Italian mainland and allowed Hitler to rush reinforcements to Italy. Rather than overrun all or most of Italy in 1943 as they had hoped, the Allied forces could occupy only the southern part, below Monte Cassino.

By that time momentous political changes had occurred in Rome. The country's heart had never been in the war; uneasiness grew into despair when the Axis forces were driven out of North Africa and Italy seemed the next likely target of an Allied attack. For some time Italy's withdrawal from the war had been urged by a dissident faction within the Fascist Party (including Count Ciano and some other of Mussolini's most trusted advisers). The matter was also explored by the high command of the army and even roused King Victor Emmanuel from his customary circumspect lethargy. The hope was that if Mussolini were removed from office, the Western democracies might enter into negotiations with a new government. Fear of Mussolini, lack of initiative, and legal scruples kept the advocates of this course from taking action; they were also restrained by the thought that a withdrawal would bring down on their country the wrath and vengeance of Hitler.

The invasion of Sicily spurred the dissident Fascists into action. Having made certain of the King's support, they attacked Mussolini at a meeting of the Fascist Grand Council on July 24. After a rambling debate, they expressed their lack of confidence in the Duce by voting, 19 to 7, to return to the King his full constitutional powers. Mussolini, plagued by illness and indecision, did not react. Although he had received warnings that he was to be overthrown, he took no steps to protect himself; when he called on the King the next day, he let himself be arrested by a detachment of carabinieri and be spirited away in an ambulance. Nor did the Fascist militia come to his rescue; leaderless and demoralized, this hapless force allowed itself to be placed under the control of the regular army.

Victor Emmanuel had no intention of launching a revolution. His sole concern was to replace the Fascist regime by a royal-military dictatorship. As Prime Minister of his new government he appointed Marshal Pietro Badoglio (1871–1956), the most popular of the generals, who had commanded the Ethiopian campaign, but had fallen out with Mussolini over the war against Greece; the other ministers all were technical experts rather than political leaders—high civil servants, judges, and military men.

Badoglio set out to play an intricate double game, trying to hold off the Germans while approaching the Anglo-Americans in quest of an armistice. He urged the latter to accept Italy as an ally in the war against Germany, but also asked for assurances that the Allies, still fighting in Sicily, would be sufficiently close to help him beat off the Germans once he had broken with them. Badoglio was denied the status of ally, but was promised an alleviation of Italy's lot in proportion to the country's contribution to the war effort. When he was further assured of support in the form of an airborne division, the Marshal concluded an armistice early in September. By that time, the Germans had brought sufficient forces to Italy to occupy almost all of the country as far south as Naples. The Allied invasion, on the other hand, had barely begun and no troops could be spared to help defend Rome. The King and Badoglio managed to escape from the capital and make their way southward to Brindisi in Allied-held territory.

At that very moment, Mussolini was freed from captivity by German glider troops and installed by Hitler as head of a puppet "Social Republic" in northern Italy. To offset the claim of the Duce that he was speaking for Italy, the Allies decided to increase the authority of King Victor Emmanuel and Premier Badoglio: they returned the liberated provinces of southern Italy to the King's sovereignty, and he was urged to declare war on the Germans. The monarch did so in mid-October after trying, without success, to wrest still further concessions from London and Washington.

These dealings with men closely associated with the Fascist regime again caused serious dismay in Britain and the United States. Official assurances that the arrangements were purely temporary, designed to shorten the war and maintain order behind the Italian battle front, did little to allay these widespread misgivings. What was not mentioned officially was the Allied concern that a more democratic government might encourage factional politics and plunge Italy into political chaos.

SOVIET-WESTERN RELATIONS: 1943

The Battle of Stalingrad.   When Hitler launched his Russian summer offensive in June 1942, his main concern was to capture the oil wells of the Caucasus, in keeping with his continued quest for foodstuffs and raw materials to fight a long war. A comparatively small force was dispatched against Stalingrad which flanked the route to the Caucasus while the bulk of the troops was to make its way south to the oil fields of Maikop and Grozny and beyond them to Baku. Their advance was rapid; in mid-August German *Panzers* reached Maikop and later that month Bavarian mountain troops hoisted the swastika on Mt. Elbrus, the highest peak in the Caucasus. Other units were approaching Grozny, the Soviets' chief source of oil, and Hitler began talking of moving on to Iran and the Persian Gulf. There was deep fear in the West that German forces would soon be linked with the Japanese who had reached the Indian-Burmese frontier. In that event the U.S.S.R. would be almost completely cut off from its allies.

Actually the German advance had reached its high water mark by this time. Soviet resistance was stiffening, and the exhausted overextended Germans could barely hold on to their positions. In December they were forced to withdraw to Rostov and the Crimea, their point of departure, to avoid being trapped by the Russians. While the Caucasus army managed to link up with the main German front, the forces engaged in the seizure of Stalingrad were less fortunate. Hitler would not let them withdraw from the city when they were threatened by Soviet encirclement. He knew that the surrender of Stalingrad would put an end to all hopes of seizing the oil fields; Stalingrad, moreover, being named after his principal adversary, had acquired a symbolic significance that impelled him to hold on to the city, whatever the price. After weeks of relentless street-to-street and house-to-house fighting in snow and ice, the

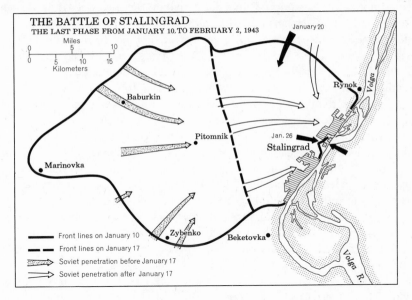

THE BATTLE OF STALINGRAD
THE LAST PHASE FROM JANUARY 10, TO FEBRUARY 2, 1943

dazed, half-starved, frozen survivors of this hopeless battle—91,000 of whom 18,000 were wounded—surrendered on January 31, 1943. During the two-months siege 140,000 men perished; of those who were captured only 5,000 returned to Germany.

Soviet-Western Tensions. The victory of Stalingrad assured the Russians of eventual victory, but a long and arduous struggle still lay ahead. Hence, they continued to call for a second front that would draw away some forty or fifty German divisions from Russia. Soviet reaction was bitter when Stalin was told in June 1943 that the invasion of France would have to be put off until 1944. The Kremlin could not appreciate the immense problems of building up an invasion force of more than one million men across 3,000 miles of ocean; it was equally unable to understand the enormous physical difficulties facing an amphibious cross-Channel operation. Moscow seems to have taken the repeated post-ponements as evidence that the West again was trying to weaken both Germans and Russians before it would enter the fight and dictate the peace terms.[3] Charging the Western Powers with bad faith, Stalin re-called his ambassadors from London and Washington, and a meeting between him and Roosevelt, planned for July in Alaska, was canceled.

Political disputes also continued to strain Soviet-Western relations. Concerned with Russia's future security, Stalin insisted on the recovery of the Baltic, Rumanian, and Polish territories that had been annexed by the Soviet Union in 1939–40. The Western Powers rejected his claims as incompatible with the Atlantic Charter and other commitments, and the Polish government-in-exile announced in London that it would not and could not, without a popular mandate, give up the provinces that Moscow demanded. The Germans added to these tensions with the announcement that they had discovered in Katyn Forest, not far from Smolensk, the mass grave of some 14,000 Polish officers massacred by the Russians in 1940. Without waiting for Moscow's reply, the London Poles accepted a German proposal for an investigation by the International Red Cross. The Kremlin denied all knowledge of the crime; charging the Poles with doing the work of the Nazis, Moscow broke off relations with the Lon-don regime.[4] At the same time a newly organized Union of Polish Patriots, composed of Polish Communists in the Soviet Union, came out in sup-port of the Soviets. To all other problems besetting Russo-Polish relations was now added the likelihood of a Polish Communist government con-testing the authority of the government-in-exile in London.

Like Poland, Yugoslavia faced the prospect of two rival governments contending for leadership after the war. The official government, mon-archist-conservative in character, had also established itself in London and supported General Mihailovich as its spokesman in Yugoslavia. Facing him was the Communist-dominated Partisan movement led by Tito. The issue was complicated by the fact that only Tito was fighting the Axis while Mihailovich arranged local truces, hoping to save his men for a final blow at a later date and meanwhile battling Tito's Partisans. Roosevelt left the solution of this intricate situation to Churchill since

---

[3] Moscow's disappointment was the greater as it had just decreed the dissolution of the Comintern as an ostensible goodwill gesture towards the West. Retrospect has made clear how empty a gesture it was: among the signers of the statement announc-ing the dissolution were such future government heads as Klement Gottwald (Czechoslovakia), Wilhelm Pieck (Germany), Anna Pauker (Rumania), and Matyas Rakosi (Hungary), and the party chiefs Maurice Thorez (France) and Palmiro Togliatti (Italy).

[4] It seems certain, on the basis of the available evidence, that the Russians com-mitted the Katyn murders.

he did not wish to involve himself in what he considered essentially an Anglo-Soviet concern. Churchill would not abandon Mihailovich, but he came to see the military advantages of helping Tito; beginning in the spring of 1943, Britain sent aid to the Partisans.

Divergences, real and assumed, over the treatment of Germany were another source of recurrent friction. Despite all promises to the contrary, both sides suspected each other of plans to conclude a separate peace with the Germans. The Western Powers were greatly alarmed at Stalin's repeated reference to the liberation of Russia as his major objective, suggesting that he might stop fighting once the Germans had been pushed out of Russia.[5] At other times it seemed as if the Soviets were grooming a Communist government to seize power once Germany had been defeated. In July 1943 a National Committee for Free Germany was founded in Moscow by German prisoners of war, former Communist Reichstag deputies, and other political refugees. Its actual purpose seems to have been to appeal to the German army leaders to overthrow Hitler— its official colors were the old Imperial colors of black-white-and-red, designed to appeal to conservative elements. But given Moscow's sponsorship of the Union of Polish Patriots, Western apprehensions did not seem farfetched. (The Committee failed to arouse either the German generals or the German masses against the Nazis and did not survive the war.) The Soviets on their part kept worrying lest the West make a deal with a German Darlan or Badoglio.

The Moscow Conference. The strains and stresses on the Soviet-Western relationship led Churchill and Roosevelt to try to arrange a meeting with Stalin. But Stalin would not leave Russia because of the exigencies of the military situation, and only a meeting of foreign ministers could be arranged. However, by early September the Russians had brought to a halt that summer's German offensive and in a counteroffensive were hurling the Germans back on a 500-mile front extending from Smolensk to the Asov Sea. Stalin now proposed a heads-of-government meeting at Teheran, the capital of Iran, and Roosevelt and Churchill accepted.

The Foreign Ministers, Cordell Hull, Eden, and Molotov, met at Moscow in the latter part of October. From the outset it was apparent that the major concerns of the participants differed markedly from each other. The Soviets were primarily interested in shortening the war; Molotov (and Stalin) kept asking for an ironclad confirmation of the spring 1944 date for the cross-Channel invasion. Eden in turn wished to settle the specific political problems that kept intruding on Russo-

---

[5] Most likely Stalin originally phrased his appeals in this manner to rouse Russian patriotism; but noticing the fears of the West, he may have continued to use this approach to keep apprehensions alive in the hope that they might speed the opening of the second front.

Western relations. Neither Hull nor Molotov cared to take up these questions. Hull feared that such discussions might lead to quarrels that would block agreement on the general principles of present and future collaboration that he hoped to achieve; Molotov on his part wished to retain full freedom of action in eastern Europe. It was decided to establish a European Advisory Commission composed of representatives of the three governments; this commission would work out plans for the administration of the defeated enemy states and the liberated countries. On only one territorial matter did agreement prove possible: Austria was to be restored as an independent state. Here Western and Soviet interests coincided.

Secretary of State Hull came to Moscow in order to lay the foundation for the continued collaboration of the great powers. At his urging the conference adopted a Declaration of the Four Nations (including China). The statement called for the unconditional surrender of the Axis countries and their disarmament, proposed the establishment of an organization of all "peace loving" states to maintain international peace and security, and pledged the signatories to use military power in the territory of other states only to achieve the aforementioned purposes. The Declaration was hailed as a milestone in world affairs since it seemed to assure the postwar collaboration of the West and the Soviet Union. It was also considered a landmark because it put an end to American isolationism and pledged the United States to continued participation in world affairs.

An American proposal for the postwar treatment of Germany was accepted "in principle." It called for Germany's surrender of all territory acquired since 1938 and for the payment of reparations in kind and in services. In addition, it provided for the joint occupation, de–Nazification, disarmament, and democratization of the Reich by the three powers. Similarly, agreement was reached on the prosecution of all individuals who had committed atrocities and other war crimes. The conference thus produced a number of general understandings, but few specific decisions.

The Teheran Conference. The three heads of government met at Teheran from November 28 to December 1, 1943. Again the discussion of the cross-Channel invasion took up much of the time. Churchill was still fearful of the great difficulties facing that operation. To drain off more German strength before launching the invasion, he proposed an extension of the Mediterranean operations. He suggested sorties across the Adriatic into Yugoslavia in aid of Tito, or, after an advance up the Italian peninsula towards Pisa and Rimini, an invasion of northern Yugoslavia that would take Western forces into Austria and southern Hungary. As a third possibility, he mentioned a landing in southern France. Stalin rejected the Balkan operations, as militarily less effective than the cross-Channel invasion and bound to delay it. Possibly the Soviet leader was also concerned that such Allied activities might deprive

Big Three at Teheran, 1943. (*U.S. Signal Corps Photo*)

him of his freedom of action in southeastern Europe. Since American military experts agreed that Churchill's plans were impractical, Roosevelt sided with Stalin. The decision to launch the cross-Channel invasion in May 1944 was reaffirmed, with a supporting landing to be made in southern France. Stalin promised to start an offensive at about the same time to keep the Germans from transferring troops from the east to the west.

No formal political decisions were reached at Teheran, but the question of Poland's frontiers was examined at length. By this time it was clear that the Soviets would soon advance into Poland and be able to make whatever territorial arrangements they wished. In the interest of future relations with Moscow, Churchill considered it wise to accept what could not be prevented in any event. He agreed that Russia should get all Polish territory up to the Curzon Line (whose actual course was, however, a matter of dispute) and part of East Prussia including the port city of Königsberg. Churchill also approved of compensating the Poles with German territory east of the Oder River. Roosevelt, who worried about the Polish-American vote in the forthcoming Presidential election, sidestepped the question. He was also anxious to see Russia join the Pacific war once Germany was defeated, and since Stalin gave a formal assurance at Teheran that his country would do so, the President did not wish to jeopardize this assistance by a direct challenge of the territorial claims of the Soviets.

The future of Germany was discussed only briefly. Roosevelt proposed the breakup of the Reich into several parts; Stalin concurred, but

Churchill objected. The Prime Minister foresaw that with Germany dismembered and France and Italy reduced to impotence, the Soviet Union would be the only major military and political power on the European continent. This situation he wished to prevent. The matter was assigned to the European Advisory Commission for further study.

The conference closed on a note of general contentment. Stalin apparently felt reassured about the invasion of France and the future of Poland; Roosevelt was confident that he had laid the foundation for a friendly relationship with Stalin[6] and for the continued collaboration with Soviet Russia in Europe and later in the Far East; and Churchill, with some reservations, seems to have shared the President's feelings.

THE HOME FRONTS

Britain. During the "phony" phase of the war, life for the British civilian differed little from the life he had led in peacetime. Except for the nightly blackouts and the rationing of some foodstuffs nothing seemed to have changed. Only after the invasion of France was the British economy put on a war footing; but once this was done, the home front mobilization was far more comprehensive than that of Nazi Germany. The government took over the allocation of manpower and raw materials, set prices, rationed a large number of consumer goods, and stopped altogether the manufacture of others. Armaments production more than quadrupled (yet the needs of the armed forces were such that in 1943–44 one fourth of all armaments required by the British and Empire forces still had to be supplied by lend-lease). Along with the arms output, agricultural productivity was sharply increased in order to reduce imports and save shipping space, and farm production grew by one third.

Given the existing restrictions, life in wartime Britain was hard and drab. Yet the demands made upon the country were distributed as equitably as possible to make them more tolerable; while upper and middle classes paid the largest part of the cost of war, the lot of the low-income groups was eased by subsidies reducing the cost of living. The well-to-do showed their patriotism and discipline by refusing to patronize the black market; similarly, tax evasion was minimal, despite steep increases in taxation rates. As a result, morale remained high and the burdens imposed upon the country aroused no serious factional discontent. If anything, they strengthened the social cohesion of the nation.

What also helped to uphold the country's morale was the hope that victory would call forth comprehensive social reforms. They would

---

[6] To attain it, Roosevelt even took to teasing Churchill about his Britishness and his cigars in Stalin's presence. "I kept it up," he later recalled, "until Stalin was laughing with me . . . From that time on our relations were personal."

provide greater social and economic security, improved living standards, and better educational opportunities for all classes. In 1942 a government committee headed by Sir William (later Lord) Beveridge brought out a report on "Social Insurance and Allied Services," outlining a vast social insurance scheme that would assure everyone of some degree of economic security. Other reports proposed ways of maintaining full employment, reforms of the educational system, and urban planning and reconstruction. Except for a few educational reforms, no immediate action was taken on these proposals. The Conservatives, who controlled the House of Commons, opposed many of the projected reforms, and Churchill, preoccupied with the war, did not wish to be distracted by controversial domestic issues. The Labor Party agreed on the need for national unity and refrained from insisting on an immediate adoption; but it backed the reform plans wholeheartedly and made clear that it would demand their enactment as soon as the fighting was ended.

In the interest of maintaining domestic peace, the parties also observed an electoral truce; when a parliamentary seat fell vacant, it was assigned to a representative of the party that had held it before.

The United States. It would be beyond the scope of this book to discuss in detail American domestic conditions during the war. Some points touching directly on European developments should, however, be mentioned. One concerns America's role as the "arsenal of democracy." To discharge its obligations in this capacity and at the same time meet its own needs, armaments production was expanded almost fourfold from 1941 to 1942; by the end of 1942 it equalled the combined output of Germany, Italy, and Japan, and by 1944 it was twice as large. This feat was accomplished by a combination of government plans and controls and negotiated agreements with labor and industry; its success was the more remarkable as the country was not directly exposed to the horrors of war and thus was not subject to the same overwhelming pressures as the other belligerents to forgo "business as usual."

About one-seventh of American war expenditures, estimated at $360 billion, was spent on lend-lease aid; of this amount ($50 billion), $31 billion worth of goods went to Britain and the Dominions, $11 billion to the Soviet Union, $3 billion to France and its possessions, $1.6 billion to China, and the balance to the other 34 beneficiaries. Reverse lend-lease amounted to $7.8 billion, of which Britain contributed $6.7 billion and France $860 million. Returns in kind yielded another $2.5 billion.

If the American people were willing to bear the restrictions imposed by high taxes, rationing, price controls, and wage freezes, one major reason was that the country had learned that its own future was closely tied up with the future of Europe. This change of attitude was also reflected in the growing awareness that the United States must play an active role in the preservation of peace after the defeat of the Axis Powers. Responding to this realization, the House of Representatives passed a resolution, 360 to 29, in September 1943, pledging the United States to participate in a worldwide organization equipped "with power adequate to establish and to maintain a just and lasting peace." The Senate passed a similar resolution, 85 to 5, just after Secretary of State Hull had committed the United States at the Foreign Ministers Conference at Moscow to help set up such a body.

The Soviet Union. Of all the belligerent nations the Soviet people were subjected to the severest hardships. The territory that Russia lost between June and November 1941 produced 38 per cent of its cereals, 84 per cent of its sugar, and raised 38 per cent of its cattle and 60 per cent of its pigs. In the summer of 1942 the Russians lost also the agricultural lands of the Don valley and the Kuban, and while these latter losses were soon recovered, the 1942 crops of the two regions were either destroyed or seized by the Germans. The land that remained under Soviet control, only 58 per cent of all prewar land sown to crops, was worked almost entirely by women, youngsters, and elderly people. Inevitably, production suffered a marked drop, and crops decreased even further as large numbers of tractors and horses were requisitioned by the army and fertilizer became increasingly scarce. Food rations for the civilian population (except heavy workers) thus were appallingly low and not infrequently unobtainable, and deaths from malnutrition ran into the millions. In beleaguered Leningrad where the ordinary civilian had to get by on a diet of some 500 calories a day,[7] those who were fortunate supplemented their rations with dog or cat meat. Over 600,000 and possibly as many as one million people starved to death during the siege of the city.

Industrial output suffered equally serious reverses as a result of the military setbacks of 1941–42. By December 1941 the U.S.S.R had lost 60 per cent of its coal mines; steel production dropped to one-third and overall industrial output to less than one-half of what it had been in June. In 1942 the German advance into the Caucasus wrought similar havoc with the oil production of Russia. Production was further impaired by the evacuation of industrial enterprises from European Russia. Altogether some 1,300 plants, making up close to one million car loads, were transferred to the east. A remarkably successful achievement in itself, it meant nonetheless a serious decrease, for many months, in the armaments output, not to mention machinery, tools, and consumer goods. Again, the civilians were the chief sufferers, and most consumer goods became virtually unobtainable. In Moscow, in 1942, the lucky owner of a cigarette might sell just a drag for 2 rubles (50 cents), and medical supplies were so scarce that teeth had to be extracted without an anesthetic.

It was not until the fall of 1942 that arms output caught up with the

---

[7] The normal daily requirement for men is 3,000 calories, for women, 2,300.

needs of the armed forces, and from then on it expanded rapidly. By the end of the war industrial production in the Ural regions had increased 360 per cent and in Siberia 280 per cent over prewar levels. At the same time lend-lease supplies arrived in growing amounts. The character of the lend-lease shipments was changing, however; whereas tanks, planes, and antiaircraft guns had been the principal items before, now the most important goods were trucks, railway equipment, and oil products. From 1943 on the mobility of the Soviet armies surpassed that of the Germans, owing to the more than 400,000 American trucks, 50,000 other vehicles and motorcycles, almost 2,000 locomotives, and 10,000 freight cars that were delivered to the U.S.S.R.

The civilians' lot, on the other hand, continued to be grim. Working hours remained long and holidays almost nonexistent; steep taxes and compulsory savings cut deeply into the meager pay; food still was scarce, and so was fuel. Above all, work was desperately hard, especially for women and old people who made up the bulk of the labor force; they were often put to work, as in Kazakhastan and Siberia, on opening new coal mines or on the building of electrical power plants and steel furnaces. Children grew up poorly fed, instructed in overcrowded, understaffed schools, and without adequate supervision either at home or at school.

The government tried to improve morale by appealing to the pride and patriotism of the country, and poets and playwrights made Russian heroism, past and present, a major theme of their works. For the sake of national unity, Marxism was played down: the war was called the Great Patriotic War; a "Hymn of the Soviet Union" replaced the "Internationale" as the national anthem; decorations named after military heroes—Alexander Nevsky, Suvorov, Kutuzov—were bestowed on the army. After Stalingrad, gold braid and epaulettes reappeared on officer uniforms. These sartorial changes, however, were intended not only as rewards for military achievements; they were also adopted, as the publicist Alexander Werth has explained with an eye to the future: "The time was drawing close when the Red Army would have its word to say as the greatest national army in Europe; it was only right that its officers should be as smartly dressed as the British and American officers—not to mention the German[s]."

A similar combination of motives accounted for the concessions made to the Orthodox Church. Here again the immediate objective was to promote national unity by allowing the Church some greater scope of activity. But the rehabilitation of the Church was also to improve relations with the West and to enhance Soviet prestige in those countries in which Orthodox Christianity was influential. To further this aim, the election of a new patriarch of the Russian Orthodox Church was allowed, the patriarchate was permitted to publish a journal (while publication of the leading atheist journal was suspended), a number of theological seminaries were reopened and church buildings restored.

The Church on its part urged the faithful to keep fighting the "fascist robbers," and collected funds for the purchase of arms, medications, and other needed supplies.

As eventual victory seemed assured after Stalingrad, official statements placed again greater emphasis on the Soviet system and the Communist Party as the mainsprings of Russia's successes. At the same time Stalin's role as the chief architect of victory was underscored. Even though national unity was still the Kremlin's major concern, care was being taken that neither the party's ascendancy nor Stalin's preeminence would suffer from it.

Germany. Living conditions in Germany remained nearly normal during the first two years of the war. Vast food stocks were requisitioned in occupied countries and rations always were adequate. There was some scarcity of consumer goods, but civilian production was cut much less sharply in Germany than in Britain, let alone Soviet Russia. The comparatively high level of nonmilitary production could be maintained partly because raw materials and production facilities became available in the conquered countries, and partly because Hitler, fearful of the effect on German morale, hestitated to order incisive reductions.

This situation changed after the first serious setbacks in Russia. The increased need for arms and ammunition required a thorough reorganization and reallocation of industrial facilities—a necessity reinforced by Allied air raids whose effects began to be felt in 1942. To cope with this task, Hitler appointed as Minister of Armaments and Ammunition a young architect, Albert Speer (1905–   ) who had assisted him in his building projects. Speer, a capable and resourceful organizer, succeeded in increasing German arms output by 56 per cent within a year, and despite the increasing disruption of the German economy by Allied bombings, kept expanding military production throughout the greater part of 1944. In that year, he testified later, 130 infantry divisions and 40 armored divisions were completely re-equipped. Airplane production continued to grow until September 1944 and ordnance and U-boat production until December 1944. Speer achieved this production record partly by the improvement of production techniques and partly by the concentration of war production in the largest and most efficient plants. His record is the more noteworthy as he had to fight his way through a maze of overlapping government and Nazi Party bureaucracies and Hitler, forever worried about German morale, would not let him cut civilian production as much as Speer thought essential. The price for Speer's accomplishments was paid by the millions of foreign laborers who were drafted into service in Germany under inhuman conditions, and by prisoners of war who were put to work in armament factories in violation of international law. In January 1943, at the conclusion of the battle of Stalingrad, labor conscription was at long last introduced in the Reich for both men and women, but it was never fully enforced.

By May 1944 the number of German women employed had increased by only 182,000 over May 1939 (the corresponding figure for Britain was 2,283,000) while the number of domestic servants stayed at an average of 1.4 million throughout the war (in Britain their number decreased from 1.2 million in 1939 to less than 500,000 in 1944). Speer's efforts became pointless when, beginning in May 1944, Allied bombings destroyed 90 per cent of Germany's fuel stocks and the tanks and planes he was turning out could no longer be operated. Convinced that the war was lost, he tried to salvage whatever he could, and with great personal courage sabotaged Hitler's scorched-earth policy.

In the wake of the setbacks in Russia, Hitler officially assumed the unlimited powers which in effect he had held already for years. He had the Reichstag pass a law in April 1942 that gave him life-and-death power over every German "without being bound by existing legal regulations." He made full use of his new authority, removing at will not only military leaders and party and government officials, but also judges he considered too lenient. Even some of his oldest and toughest associates, like Heinrich Himmler, head of the S.S. and the Gestapo, were now deeply afraid of him.

No law was needed, however, to deal with Jews, and in 1941 Hitler ordered the "final solution of the Jewish problem," which meant the complete annihilation of European Jewry. Between 1942 and 1945 millions of Jews from all parts of Europe were herded into cattle cars and sent to extermination camps, mostly in Poland, of which Auschwitz was the best known. There the victims were gassed, in Auschwitz 6,000 a day, and their bodies cremated—after gold fillings and bridgework had been removed from their teeth. How many Jews perished in the gas chambers will never be known since the camps did not keep death records. Adolf Eichmann, the S.S. officer in charge of the "final solution," estimated their number at four million, adding that two million more had died before firing squads; but these figures are believed to be too high, and Eichmann himself later mentioned a total of five million. This is also the figure at which Raul Hilberg arrived in his standard work, *The Destruction of the European Jews.* By mid-1943 all German Jews had been removed from Germany, except for those who were living in mixed marriages and a few hundred who had gone into hiding, and on June 30, 1943 Germany was proclaimed *judenrein* (free of Jews). Despite mass roundups of Jews throughout German-controlled Europe, the Nazis achieved this goal in few other parts of their empire; local resistance to mass deportations of Jews was widespread, though it was not always dictated by humanitarian impulses.[8]

---

[8] The Rumanian government, for example, refused to allow the deportation of Rumanian Jews as long as Hungarian Jews were allowed to remain in Hungary. Later it blocked deportations in the hope of selling Jews into freedom—at a price of $1,300 per person.

The German Resistance movement remained passive as long as Hitler was winning one victory after another, for under the circumstances his overthrow was a political impossibility. Only when Germany's military defeat seemed certain and Hitler clearly prepared to fight on until the country's total destruction, did the plotters resume their attempts to remove him. Their path was strewn with many obstacles. Headed by Carl Goerderler, one-time major of Leipzig, and Colonel General Ludwig Beck, a retired chief of the general staff, the group included officials and officers, clergymen and professors, one-time labor union executives and political leaders—men spanning almost the entire political spectrum from authoritarian conservatives to socialist democrats. Because of the variety of their political, social, and economic viewpoints, the conspirators failed to agree on a common program. More important, they could not hope to overthrow Hitler unless they had armed support, and such support only the top army leaders could provide. Of these, most were reluctant to commit themselves—some from timidity, others because they felt themselves bound by their oath to Hitler or because they were fearful that a revolt would precipitate rather than avert the final catastrophe. In the end some of the junior officers for whom the moral imperative of removing Hitler overruled all other considerations took matters into their own hands. But ill-luck pursued their several attempts to assassinate the elusive Hitler, and the arrest of some members of the Resistance warned them that the Gestapo was closing in on the plotters.

CAMPAIGN IN THE WEST

The Normandy Invasion. On June 6, 1944—D(ebarkation)-Day—the long-awaited cross-Channel invasion of France was launched under the command of General Eisenhower. The immensity of this undertaking can best be illustrated by a few facts and figures. Within 48 hours some 150,000 men with their equipment were to be taken to Normandy by air and sea. They were to be landed on a heavily fortified and guarded shore, the approaches to which had been blocked by mines and a great variety of ingeniously devised obstacles. An air armada of 12,000 planes would pave the way by mass bombings and by flying in three airborne divisions; over 5,000 ships stood ready to transport to the beaches a first assault wave of five divisions, 1,500 tanks, and thousands of guns, armored cars and trucks along with ammunition, food stocks, and other supplies.

Despite unfavorable weather conditions and a number of unforeseen difficulties, the operation was remarkably successful. The Allies had laid their plans with great care and resourcefulness. For the first time amphibious tanks were used on a major scale; they were equipped with

A scene from the Normandy Invasion.

automatic mine detonators and with large coils of steel strips that
enabled them to negotiate walls and antitank ditches. Two entire
harbors, complete with breakwater and piers, were towed across the
Channel to expedite the unloading of men and supplies. The Allies also
had unchallenged control of both sea and air and, above all were able
to catch the Germans off guard. Misled by bad weather reports, the
German High Command had shrugged off warnings of their own
counterintelligence which had intercepted what it knew was the code
message alerting the French Resistance to the imminence of the invasion.
The Germans lost their last chance of driving the Allies back into the
sea when Hitler hesitated to commit two nearby armored divisions,
uncertain whether the Normandy landings were not merely a feint.
Aided by their opponents' confusion, the Allies consolidated their beachhead and built up their forces for their advance into the interior. Within
three weeks close to one million men were safely brought over to
Normandy.

One phase of the original plans had to be abandoned, however—
there were no simultaneous landings in southern France. No troops
could be spared from the Italian campaign which had come to a virtual
standstill during the winter of 1943–44. From their mountain positions
at Monte Cassino, the Germans had beaten off all Allied attacks, and it
was not until mid-May 1944 that the offensive could be resumed. Allied
troops entered Rome on June 5, Leghorn on June 17, and Florence on
August 4. The invasion of southern France was not launched until
August 15 when an American army and some Free French units landed
on France's Mediterranean coast, between Toulon and Cannes. Aided
by the French Resistance, they quickly gained control of the coast from
Marseilles to Nice and from there advanced northward. By that time

St. Lô, France, July 1944, after both Allied and German shelling had reduced the city to rubble. (*U.S. Army photograph*)

the Allied forces in Normandy, led by Montgomery and General Omar N. Bradley, had broken out of their beachhead and were moving on Paris. As they approached, the French underground in the capital rose and began battling the Germans; a French armored division was rushed to its aid, and on August 25 General De Gaulle made his triumphant entry into the French capital.

The Attempt on Hitler's Life.　None of these setbacks shook Hitler's determination to continue the war. Disaster threatened not only in the west but also in the east where the Russians were advancing through Poland and the Baltic States and were approaching Rumania. Hitler refused to give up voluntarily any territory, fearful lest his generals keep on retreating once he allowed them to abandon a threatened position. While Germany was in imminent danger of becoming the main battleground, forces that might have been used in the defense of the Reich were bottled up in the Crimea, the Baltic States, and the Balkans. The Germans also paid an appalling price in casualties and matériel by holding on to indefensible positions rather than retreating to more suit-

able lines of defense.

What seemed irrational to conventional military thinking made sense, however, to Hitler. In the spring of 1944 German engineers began to mass-produce long-range missiles, and the first V-bomb was fired across the Channel just a few days after the invasion of Normandy. Production of jet planes also was getting under way; both promised to be formidable weapons that might eventually turn the fortunes of war. Above all, Hitler counted on a rapid deterioration of Russo-Western relations that would lead to a breakup of the coalition and allow him to align himself with one side against the other. Thus he was hopeful that he might still avert defeat, but he knew also that all depended on gaining time. On these premises, the inflexible strategy which he pursued may well have been the most effective. It is doubtful that he could have held off Germany's surrender as long as he did in any other way; strategic withdrawals, as proposed by his generals, would most likely have hastened Germany's final defeat. As the English historian F. H. Hinsley has written, "Apart altogether from the political effect of such a policy in Germany and among Germany's satellites, its military consequences, if only because of the saving of effort for the Allies and the more rapid concentration of their strength at Germany's borders, would have been more rapidly disastrous than those which followed on Hitler's choice."

The anti-Nazi Resistance, on the other hand, saw Hitler plunging the country into catastrophe, and it redoubled its efforts to remove him. The plotters had secured the support of some senior generals, among them Rommel, then in command of an army group in France, and their chances of seizing power quickly and smoothly thus seemed greatly improved. On July 20, 1944 Colonel Klaus Count Schenk von Stauffenberg managed to plant a time bomb in Hitler's conference room at his East Prussian headquarters, but the Fuehrer's luck stayed with him, and he was hurt only slightly. (His health, however, already gravely impaired, was weakened further by the psychological shock of the attempt, and he was physically a broken man during the last months of his life.) On learning of Hitler's survival, the plotters lost heart, called off whatever steps they had already taken to take over power, and let themselves be arrested. Some were summarily shot; some committed suicide; others were tried by a so-called "People's Court" and condemned to death; still others awaiting trial were shot before Berlin fell to the Russians the following April. Altogether, as many as 5,000 men and women may have lost their lives; only a handful of those involved in the plot escaped.

A large part of the German people still had faith in their Fuehrer and were deeply shocked; others, numbed by resignation or fear, took the news of the attempt in their stride. The only tangible result of the incident was that Hitler tightened his hold on the army. The Nazi salute was introduced in the Wehrmacht; party officials were attached to all military headquarters where, among other functions, they passed on promotions; Himmler became commander-in-chief of the Reserve Army and began drafting boys between fifteen and eighteen years and men in their fifties into a newly formed people's militia (*Volkssturm*); Goebbels, the Minister of Propaganda, was put in charge of "total mobilization." Although there was some increase in desertions, on the whole civilians and army attended doggedly to their duties. Hitler, though close to a complete physical breakdown and laid up for weeks, was still so completely in control that he could even plan another offensive.

The Ardennes Offensive. During August and September 1944 the Anglo-American armies liberated virtually all of France and Belgium, and in mid-September the first American units crossed the German border near Aachen. Having outrun their supplies, the Allied forces broke off their advance at this point. The Germans used the respite to regroup and re-equip their own forces, and owing to a remarkable recovery, defeated a British attempt to outflank them by a lunge through the Netherlands. But Hitler knew that holding operations could not

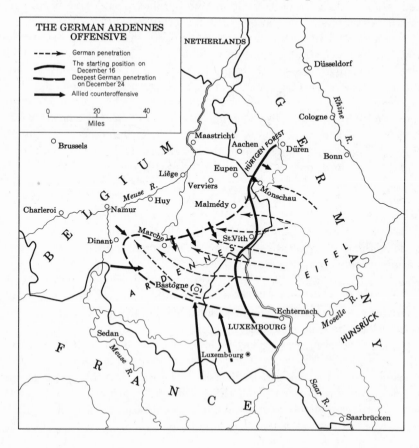

long delay the final defeat, and he decided to risk the bulk of his western forces on another offensive. His plan was to send his columns across Belgium to Antwerp, the one major harbor near Germany that the Allies were able to use. The attack was to cut off the British from the American forces (similar to the strategy used so successfully in 1940), deprive the Allies of their main harbor facilities, and net the Germans the vast supply stores assembled in Antwerp—in particular, oil of which they were desperately short since Rumania had been overrun by the Russians. Concentrating his troops under cover of night, Field Marshal Gerd von Rundstedt succeeded in taking the Allied command by surprise when he struck on December 16. Yet after some notable initial successes, the offensive petered out for lack of manpower and supplies. Eisenhower mounted a counterattack, and three weeks later the remnants of the shattered German forces had been driven back to their point of departure.

TENSIONS IN THE ANTI-GERMAN COALITION

Troubles in the West. While military progress was on the whole satisfactory, the anti-Hitler coalition was troubled by recurrent political difficulties. Friction between De Gaulle and Churchill-Roosevelt increased sharply when De Gaulle's forces were assigned only a minor role in the invasion of Normandy (of which De Gaulle, for security reasons, was informed only one day before D-Day). Relations improved temporarily when a French armored division was given the task of driving the Germans from Paris and De Gaulle's National Committee of Liberation was recognized as the provisional government of France. Yet new difficulties kept arising due to De Gaulle's rigid insistence on the treatment of France as a great sovereign power. In actuality France's liberation depended on military decisions of the United States and Britain that frequently had to be made in disregard of De Gaulle's special wishes.

Britain and the United States on their part found themselves in marked disagreement over the role they would want to play in post-Nazi Europe. As the Red Army moved into Poland and was nearing Rumania, Churchill became greatly concerned over the distribution of power and the spreading of Communism on the Continent. In the east he tried to retain some measure of influence by means of an understanding with Stalin, parceling out responsibility for the administration of the Balkan countries and Hungary between Britain and the U.S.S.R. In the west, in Belgium and Italy, as well as in Greece, which British forces took over as the Germans withdrew, he tried to contain the Communist threat more directly. In all these countries liberation touched off bitter quarrels over the retention of the monarchy and over the future relations between essentially conservative governments and popular movements generated by the Resistance and to varying degrees under Communist influence. Fearful of revolution and looking on monarchy as a mainstay of order, Churchill sided with the existing governments. In Greece, British forces engaged in pitched street battles with the E.A.M., the Communist-led Greek Liberation Front.

The United States followed Churchill's activities with serious misgivings. Washington disliked the partition of the Balkan Peninsula into spheres of influence; this threatened to involve the American people permanently in European disputes and might in the end turn the country against the proposed new worldwide organization. Roosevelt also feared that quarrels with the U.S.S.R. might jeopardize the Soviet entry into the Far Eastern war. In the west the United States dissociated itself from what it considered Britain's unwarranted interference in the domestic affairs of other countries, in violation of the Atlantic Charter. This disapproval was not without effect and helped to persuade Churchill not to force unpopular kings on unwilling peoples. In Italy, Belgium, and Greece, the final decision on the future of the monarchy was postponed and regents appointed to take the place of the monarchs. Following the American lead, the British also acquiesced when the Italians replaced the Badoglio government without consulting the Allies. The new government was headed by the Socialist Ivanoe Bonomi, a pre-Fascist Premier and head of the underground movement in Nazi-held Rome; it included Count Carlo Sforza, a vociferous anti-monarchist, and the Communist leader Palmiro Togliatti. (The British succeeded, however, in having Sforza excluded from a subsequent government.) Similarly they agreed in Greece to the replacement of Premier George Papandreou by a leader of the republican movement, General Nicholas Plastiras.

Soviet-Western Difficulties. Of the issues troubling Soviet-Western relations, Poland remained the most serious. The Union of Polish Patriots, renamed the National Committee of Liberation, had begun to assume governmental functions in the liberated part of the country. Anxious to check Communist influence, the Western Powers sought to prevent the establishment of an all-out Moscow-controlled government. Yet all efforts to effect a rapprochement between the Soviet government and the Polish government-in-exile in London remained unsuccessful. Moscow refused to deal with the London government, some of whose members were bitterly anti-Soviet, and the London Poles would not remodel their government and were still unwilling to sign away the land east of the Curzon Line.

Their enmity deepened beyond repair when Polish underground forces rose in Nazi-held Warsaw in August 1944 as the Red Army was approaching the capital. The rising was timed so as to permit pro-

London Poles to take over Warsaw before the Red Army's entry; it was suppressed by the Germans because the Soviet forces, though less than 25 miles away, did not come to its aid. The London government charged Moscow with deliberate sabotage, and the Russians were indeed most reluctant to let the Western Powers arrange a shuttle airdrop to keep the insurgents supplied. What was decisive, however, was Russia's failure to drive the Germans from Warsaw. This seems to have been due, not to willful intention, but to the unexpectedly stiff defense put up by the Germans and to the exhaustion of the Red forces after two months of an uninterrupted advance over nearly 400 miles.

The expected spread of Communism, in the wake of the Red Army, weighed heavily on Churchill's mind. In August 1944 a Russian army overran Rumania and from there surged into Bulgaria. Having seized Sofia in mid-September, it turned west and in early October crossed into Yugoslavia. Another Soviet army moved from Rumania into Hungary across the Carpathians. After having driven the Germans from the eastern half of that country, its advance was checked temporarily in the suburbs of Budapest. To retain at least a foothold in this part of the Continent, Churchill revived once more his plan of dispatching an expeditionary force from Italy by way of northwestern Yugoslavia into Austria and Hungary; again it was vetoed by the United States as militarily unpromising (as indeed it was, given the difficult terrain through which the troops would have had to make their way).[9] In any event the plan had to be abandoned because of a renewed military stalemate in Italy.

Politically, Churchill tried to retain some voice in eastern European developments by an agreement which he reached with the Soviets on another visit to Moscow. By this arrangement both sides accorded each other varying degrees of influence in several eastern European countries during the immediate postliberation period. Their respective influence was expressed in the following enigmatic percentages:[10]

	Britain (and the U.S.)	Soviet Russia
Greece	90	10
Yugoslavia	50	50
Bulgaria	20	80
Hungary	20	80
Rumania	10	90

[9] Tito, too, opposed the proposal, but Stalin, on consultation, supported it. We can only guess at his change of mind: perhaps he wished to protect his southern flank; perhaps he wanted to use the British to check the expansionist aspirations of Tito who was already disturbingly independent and was demanding Trieste and Austrian Carinthia.

[10] Sir Llewellyn Woodward, *British Foreign Policy in the Second World War* (London, 1962), pp. 307–308.

Exactly how this agreement was to be implemented was never made clear; Churchill himself saw in it "no more than a guide." Its one tangible advantage from the Western viewpoint was that the Russians refrained from supporting the Communist-led E.A.M. when it rebelled against the Greek government in December 1944. No agreement could be reached on Poland, and in late December the Kremlin recognized the Committee of National Liberation as the provisional government of Poland.

The Yalta Conference. Apart from the problems of eastern Europe a number of other East-West issues awaited a settlement on the highest level—among them the postwar treatment of Germany and Russia's participation in the war against Japan. Some questions also had arisen in connection with the establishment of the new world organization for which a charter had been drawn up by representatives of the United States, Britain, the Soviet Union, and China at a conference at Dumbarton Oaks, in Washington, D.C., in the summer of 1944. Roosevelt's anxiety to reach an understanding with Stalin was such that when the latter declined, for reasons of health, to leave Russia, the President decided to go all the way to Yalta, in the Crimea, to meet with him. Churchill who was equally anxious for another meeting with the Soviet dictator deferred to Roosevelt's wishes.

The Yalta Conference took place from February 4 to February 11, 1945. Unlike the Teheran meeting it was concerned more with political than with military issues, but many of the political decisions were shaped by military developments. In mid-January the Russians had launched a new offensive in Poland. By the time the conference opened one army, commanded by Marshal Konstantin Rokossovsky, had cut off East Prussia from the rest of Germany; farther to the south Marshal Georgi Zhukov had swept through Silesia on to the Oder River some forty miles east of Berlin, while a third army, under the command of Marshal Ivan Konev, was moving on Dresden.

With Poland wholly under Soviet control, the Western Powers had no choice but to accept the Curzon Line as Poland's eastern frontier. To their dismay the Russians now called for a western expansion of Poland beyond the Oder to the Western Neisse, a tributary of the Oder. Unable to obtain a change of the Soviet stand, they could only ask for a delay of the final determination of Poland's western frontier until the peace conference. They also failed to secure the replacement of the existing provisional Polish government by a government representative of all political factions. All they could get was an agreement by which "democratic leaders from Poland itself and from Poles abroad" were to be invited into the existing government, thus leaving the latter in power.

Despite Churchill's agreement with Stalin, the Western Powers were even less successful in their efforts to gain a modicum of influence in the other east European countries under Soviet control. In both Rumania and Bulgaria the Soviets refused to consult with British and American representatives, and native Communists seemed poised to take over the government. A similar situation was developing in Hungary which had recently surrendered to the Red Army, and efforts to check Tito's power in Yugoslavia by a merger of his National Committee of Liberation with the London-based Yugoslav government-in-exile also ended in failure. The Western Powers had to take what comfort they could from a Declaration on Liberated Europe that described the existing arrangements as temporary ones to be superseded at the earliest possible moment by "free elections of governments responsive to the will of the people."

The negotiations about Germany produced concrete agreements on some technical points, but only vague ones on substantive issues. An instrument of surrender was drafted; it called for unconditional surrender and, in general terms, for the de-Nazification and demilitarization of Germany and for its dismemberment. During the interim period, in accordance with proposals worked out by the European Advisory Commission, Germany was to be divided into three occupation zones, with the British taking over the northwestern part, the Americans the southwest, and the Russians the east. An Allied Control Council, composed of the commanders-in-chief of the three occupation zones and located in Berlin, would deal with all problems affecting Germany as a whole; its decisions were to be carried out by the zonal commanders. Since Roosevelt had repeatedly stated that American troops would withdraw from Europe within two years after the end of the war, Churchill pleaded that France be admitted to the occupation and administration of Germany. At his urging, Roosevelt and Stalin agreed to the creation of a French occupation zone to be carved out of the American and British zones and to France's participation in the Control Council.

Throughout the discussions, Roosevelt was less ready than Churchill to press issues on which the Russians refused to yield. While the Prime Minister worried about the future power structure of Europe, the President's foremost concern was to ensure Russia's early entry into the war against Japan. Roosevelt's military experts, overrating Japan's remaining strength, had urged on him the need for Soviet assistance, warning that without such help the Far Eastern war might drag on for another two years and cost up to one million American casualties. The President was anxious, therefore, to avoid any serious clash with the Soviets lest such a quarrel jeopardize Russian action in the Far East. To his gratification, Stalin amplified his earlier promise and announced that the Red Army would go to war against Japan within three months of the defeat of the Reich. In return for that pledge the President assented to the Soviets territorial and other claims in the Far East, in part at China's expense.

Agreement was also reached on some basic problems concerning the new international organization; this settlement will be discussed in its appropriate context (see p. 400). Suffice it to state here, in further explanation of the President's attitude toward Stalin, that he was hopeful that once that organization had been set up with Russia a member, such issues as the freedom and independence of the eastern European countries could be settled more easily by this new body.

In this expectation President Roosevelt was mistaken—the reality of Soviet power could not be outflanked so easily. Nor was what was happening in eastern Europe merely a matter of power. The Western Powers themselves had approved of the Soviet demand for governments friendly to the U.S.S.R. in the neighboring countries, but there was little indication—least of all in Poland—that free elections would produce such governments. Correspondingly, Marxist precepts decreed the overhauling of the social and economic systems of the east European countries because no state founded on a capitalist economy could be expected to be "friendly" to the Soviet Union. Yet it is evident that even a more "realistic" stance on Roosevelt's part would not have changed the course of events. "As a result of the military situation," Edward R. Stettinius, Secretary of State at the time of Yalta, has written, "it was not a question of what Great Britain and the United States would permit Russia to do . . . but what the two countries could persuade the Soviet Union to accept." There is no reason to assume that a more skeptical attitude would have extracted greater concessions from Stalin. The only other alternative would have been a break-off of the talks. As matters looked at the time, with the Western armies still stalled along the German border, lack of a zonal occupation agreement might have allowed the Russians to seize a much larger part of Germany than the agreement accorded them. It might also have led to Russia's refusal to enter the war against Japan or to delay until the Anglo-American forces in the Far East had suffered substantial losses. This was a price which neither Roosevelt nor Churchill was willing to pay.

THE FINAL PHASE

The Defeat of Germany.   In early February the Red Army resumed its assault on Budapest, and on February 14 the Hungarian capital was in Soviet hands. The Red forces pressed on to Vienna, and eight weeks later, after some bitter fighting, they entered the Austrian capital. Early in March Eisenhower's armies advanced on the Rhine. At Remagen, halfway between Koblenz and Bonn, Bradley's forces managed to seize a bridge before the Germans could blow it up; they poured over the river, and German resistance crumbled. Bradley swept on through the Ruhr Basin and in mid-April reached the Elbe River. Montgomery's armies surged into northern Germany while the armored columns of

Patton and a French army under General Lattré de Tassigny crossed the
Rhine into southern Germany. At about the same time, Anglo-American
forces under British Field Marshal Sir Harold Alexander broke through
the German defenses in the Appennines and moved into the Po Valley.
At their approach the Italian Partisans rose and swept away Mussolini's
puppet "Social Republic." One Partisan band captured and shot the
Duce as he was trying to flee to Switzerland.

Though not much farther from Berlin than the Red Army, Eisenhower
made no attempt to move on Berlin. The German capital no longer
seemed an important strategic objective, and thinking in military terms, the
General was not concerned with its value as a political prize. On the other
hand, he had had reports for some time that the Germans were fortifying

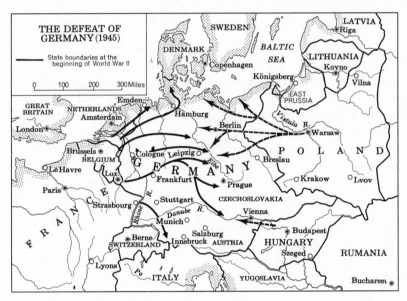

THE DEFEAT OF GERMANY (1945)

State boundaries at the beginning of World War II

the Bavarian and Austrian Alps into a redoubt from which to carry on a
protracted guerrilla war; he therefore decided to dispatch Bradley's army
group to southern Germany to squelch this plan (which, as it turned out,
had not gone far beyond the blueprint stage). The task of taking Berlin
was left to the Russians; on April 17 Zhukov resumed his offensive, and
eight days later his forces encircled the German capital.

Among those still in the city was Hitler. He had kept hoping for a
break in the enemy front; when Roosevelt died on April 12, he firmly
believed that President Truman, scornful of Russia, would take the
United States out of the war (just as during the Seven Years War, when
King Frederick the Great of Prussia seemed on the verge of defeat, Tsar
Peter III had made peace with Prussia after the death of his mother,
Tsarina Elisabeth). When Hitler finally had to admit that all was lost,

he decided to stay in Berlin to the end. There still was no question of surrender: the German people had shown themselves unworthy of his leadership, he explained, and did not deserve to survive. Despite the hopelessness of the struggle, his hold on the country remained unbroken, and even after he had been cut off from his troops by the Soviet advance, the German armies fought on. Until he shot himself on April 30, 1945, when the Russians had fought their way within a few hundred yards of the Reich chancellery, he remained the unchallenged master of Germany.

Distrustful of most of his party associates, Hitler had appointed Grand Admiral Karl Dönitz as his successor. Dönitz tried to conclude an armistice with the Western Powers in order to continue the fight with the Russians, but was rebuffed by the West. On May 8—VE-Day—Germany surrendered unconditionally to the United States, Britain, and Soviet Russia.

Japan's Surrender.   In the Far East the tide of war had been turned in June 1942 when American air and naval forces inflicted a heavy defeat upon the Japanese navy in the battle of the Coral Sea. Similar American victories in encounters off Midway Island and in the Bismarck Sea in 1943 had put an end to Japan's expansionist aspirations. Having stopped the advance of Japan, United States forces, with some British and Dominion support, began dislodging the Japanese from their island strongholds in the southwest Pacific. In a series of "island hopping" campaigns they advanced into the Philippines; meanwhile British, American, and Chinese units drove the Japanese from Burma. At the same time, aerial assaults on the Japanese homeland laid waste the industrial centers which produced Japans' war matériel.

By the spring of 1945 it was evident that Japan had lost the war, but the Japanese military leaders still insisted that determined resistance could secure a compromise peace, and refused to agree to any surrender, either unconditional or conditional. The dropping of two atomic bombs on Hiroshima and Nagasaki on August 6 finally put an end to the fighting in mid-August 1945. By that time the hopelessness of Japan's situation had been underscored by another event. On August 8, three months to the day after VE-Day and two days after the detonation of the first A-bomb, the Soviet Union declared war on Japan and sent its forces into Manchuria. On August 14—VJ-Day—Japan surrendered, after the victors had agreed to Tokyo's demand that it be allowed to retain its emperor.

18

Europe–Battleground
of the Cold War

As late as 1940 Europe had still been the center of world affairs, and the non-European world had adjusted to, rather than left its imprint on, European developments. In 1945, with the European state system shattered, Europe's fate lay essentially in the hands of the United States and the Soviet Union. The uncertainty of its future was heightened by the fact that these two powers disagreed sharply as to the policy to be applied to the battered continent. Both were determined to prevent the recurrence of Nazism and Fascism, but there their agreement ended. The Soviet Union wished to achieve this goal by means of vast social and economic changes that would at the same time sweep eastern Europe into the Communist orbit (and thus also strengthen the Soviet Union vis-à-vis the West). The United States on its part believed that Nazism could best be suppressed by the rehabilitation and reinforcement of international law and order and a decentralized private enterprise system (which would also provide the best bulwark against any further advances of Communism). The contest over the reconstruction of Europe thus was part of a much larger struggle between East and West in which traditional balance of power considerations and differing ideol-   **399** ogies clashed with each other. In this contest Europe became one of the crucial battlegrounds, and during the immediate postwar period the deepening conflict between the United States and the U.S.S.R. overshadowed and largely shaped European developments.

THE LIQUIDATION OF THE SECOND WORLD WAR

The United Nations. In keeping with its domestic experience the United States considered the preservation of international law and order the best safeguard of peace. It made itself the foremost advocate of the new international organization that was to take the place of the League of Nations, and served as host to the several conferences that led to the establishment of the United Nations.

In an earlier chapter considerable space was devoted to the discussion of the organization and activities of the League of Nations (Chapter 4). Dominated by the European Powers and concerned primarily with European problems, the League was for all practical purposes an essentially European body. The United Nations, on the other hand, has been active primarily in non-European areas—Israel, Kashmir, Korea, the Sinai Peninsula, the Congo—and has been unable to exert any significant influence on European issues. This was partly due to the fact that the United Nations Charter exempts all questions relating to the settlement of the Second World War from United Nations jurisdiction, and this bars the United Nations from participating in the solution of such problems as the reunification of Germany. But the main reason is that the United Nations lacks the strength to assert itself in areas of a direct American-Soviet confrontation, such as Berlin. It can be effective only in regions like Africa or the Middle East which are of marginal interest to the great powers. We need, therefore, but briefly survey the organization and activities of the United Nations and pay special attention only to those aspects that have had an immediate bearing on European developments.

The chief organ of the United Nations is the Security Council, composed of what were in 1945 the "Big Five"—the United States, the Soviet Union, Britain, France, and China—and orginally six, now ten, of the smaller countries elected for two-year terms. The Security Council, charged with the maintenance of international peace and security, acts if all five permanent member and at least four of the nonpermanent ones support a motion; the "nay" of one permanent member is sufficient to block any action—an arrangement made in deference to the fact that to enforce a decision over the opposition of a Big Power might either prove impossible or lead to the breakup of the United Nations. The question of the voting rights of a permanent member that is a party to a dispute before the Security Council was solved at Yalta by depriving that member of its vote while efforts at a voluntary settlement were being made, but letting it veto any enforcement measures.

The plenary body of the United Nations is the General Assembly in which each member nation is represented. Each member was to have but one vote, but the Soviet Union was granted at Yalta two additional votes for Byelorussia and the Ukraine. These two Union Republics were admitted as separate members despite their lack of sovereignty—a concession of symbolic rather than practical significance made in the hope that it might facilitate the settlement of the mutiplying difficulties in central and eastern Europe. The Assembly can, by a two-thirds majority, make recommendations. (One of the first recommendations passed by the General Assembly proposed that all members of the United Nations withdraw the heads of their diplomatic missions from Spain as an expression of their disapprobation of the Franco regime.)

A number of other organs and affiliated agencies—the Economic and Social Council, the Trusteeship Council concerned with what in League parlance was called mandated territories, the International Labor Organization, the World Health Organization, the Food and Agricultural Organization, and the United Nations Education, Scientific and Cultural Organization (UNESCO)—work for worldwide improvements in their respective fields. As in the case of the League, these nonpolitical agencies have made important contributions to the improvement of social, educational, health, and nutritional standards.

The United Nations was formally established at a conference at San Francisco on June 26, 1945; it came into effect on October 24, 1945 after ratification of the Charter by the majority of the signatories, including the Big Five.

Friction Over Eastern Europe. While the United Nations was being set up at San Francisco, Soviet-Western differences over events in central and eastern Europe continued to deepen. To the dismay of the Western Powers, the "friendly" governments to which both Britain and the United States agreed the Soviets were entitled in that area were weighted increasingly in favor of Communists. In Rumania an inefficient coalition government of bourgeois members and Communists was replaced by a predominantly Communist one after the personal intervention of Soviet Deputy Foreign Commissar Andrei Vyshinsky. In Bulgaria and Hungary, too, the Communists were being given increasing power. In Austria the Soviet commander in control of Vienna recognized a provisional Social Democratic-Communist government without prior consultation with the Western Powers. In Poland the Soviets would consent only to the inclusion of four non-Communists in the existing 18-man government of Communists and Communist sympathizers. In March 1945, moreover, the Russians turned over to the Poles most captured German territory east of the Oder and Western Neisse, and the Poles administered these lands as an integral part of their state.

Difficulties arose also in Yugoslavia where again a few non-Communists were taken into Tito's government, but far too few to assure that 50–50 distribution of influence that Churchill had negotiated in Moscow some months before. The Yugoslavs, moreover, made preparations to seize Trieste, thus trespassing on an area which the Western Powers considered part of their sphere of influence. (In this, however, Tito acted against the wishes of Moscow, which was not prepared at the time to engage in an open conflict with the West.) To this dismal picture, there was only one exception: in March 1945 the Finns were allowed to hold free elections.

For Washington and London these were disturbing developments. Both capitals felt a moral and political responsibility toward the peoples of eastern Europe. They were concerned about the fate of these countries which had been freed from one totalitarian regime apparently only to fall prey to another. They also worried about the increase of power that would accrue to the Soviet Union should it establish complete control over eastern Europe. Similarly, they feared that the Communization of eastern Europe might prevent the restoration of the economic interchange between eastern and western Europe on which the rehabilitation of all of Europe depended. Finally, looking to the more remote future, they wondered whether they were to be barred from trade and investment opportunities in this entire region. Washington tried to compel Moscow to change its policies by cutting off lend-lease supplies and by refusing to withdraw to its own German occupation zone American forces which in the course of the fighting had advanced into areas assigned to the Soviet zone. The Western Powers also refused to recognize the Rumanian and Bulgarian governments installed by the Russians.

To the Soviets the measures they had taken seemed justified by their need for what they considered "friendly" governments on their borders. They resented the West's objections the more because they had refrained from intervening when the British had moved against the Greek Liberation Front. The Soviets struck back by barring the Western Powers from their occupation zones in Austria and also denied them entry to Berlin and Vienna, from which the four powers were to direct the administration of Germany and Austria.

Whereas the German and Austrian differences could be settled a few weeks after VE-Day, other issues could not be resolved. If Western-Soviet collaboration was to survive into the postwar era, these problems had to be settled at once on the highest level. In June 1945 arangements were made for another heads-of-government conference.

The Potsdam Conference. The conference, the longest of the Big Three gatherings, met at Potsdam near Berlin from July 17 to August 2, 1945.[1] Again, it accomplished little beyond reaching agreements on

---

[1] Berlin had originally been proposed as the seat of the conference but because of war-time destruction lacked adequate office and living accommodations.

some technical matters. Western efforts to ease the lot of the east European states failed. The Soviets rejected all requests for a more adequate governmental representation of non-Communist elements as an unwarranted interference. They pointed out that they on their part had recognized the French and Italian governments which were not democratically elected either, and had refrained from interfering in Greece where the Communists were being suppressed. Unpersuaded, the Western Powers refused to recognize the east European governments. They refused also to accept the incorporation into Poland of German territory up to the Western Neisse. At their insistence, the official agreement left the determination of the German-Polish boundary to the future peace treaty, but this, as its ambiguous wording suggests, was rather a face-saving formula. Part of East Prussia, including the city of Königsberg, was turned over to Russia which thus acquired a Baltic sea port that was ice-free most of the year. In their own sphere of interest the Western Powers warded off Soviet claims to a United Nations trusteeship over one of Italy's North African colonies and to Russian participation in the administration of the Ruhr industries.

The discussion of the postwar treatment of rump Germany took up less time, partly because here the bargaining powers of East and West were more evenly distributed and partly because the agreements reached were almost all rather general ones—the disarmament, de-Nazification, and democratization of Germany. A few guiding principles were evolved: economically, Germany was to be treated as a unit, and while no central German government was to be established for the time being (this function being assumed by the Allied Control Council), essential central administrative departments would be set up. Self-government on the local, provincial, and state level was to be revived as soon as possible. A complicated reparations arrangement tried to reconcile Soviet demands for large reparations with Western determination to prevent the stripping of the German economy to an extent that would plunge the country permanently into chaos. A year before, a plan proposed by Secretary of the Treasury Henry Morgenthau had been briefly considered that wished to reduce German to a "pastoral" economy, but by now it was fully realized that any excessive spoliation of the German economy would wreak havoc and endanger the rehabilitation of all of Europe.

The Nürnberg Trials. One of the agreements arrived at at Postdam concerned the speedy prosecution of the major German war criminals. The first trial opened before an International Military Tribunal at Nürnberg on November 1. Among the 22 defendants were Göring, Ribbentrop, and other leading Nazis, the army and navy chiefs, and various government members such as Schacht, Speer, and ex-Chancellor Papen. The charges were crimes against the peace (preparing or waging a war of aggression), war crimes (murder and ill-treatment of prisoners of

war, killing of hostages, pillage), and crimes against humanity (genocide, deportation, slave labor). The charges were carefully prepared and
thoroughly documented, and the accused were given considerable leeway in their defense. Nevertheless, the trial was deprived of what "educational" effect on the Germans it might have had by the fact that the
tribunal was composed of the victor powers. Moreover, since military
aggression had never been codified as a punishable offense, the prosecution of some of the defendants for crimes against the peace gave rise
to charges of *ex post facto* legislation. Twelve of the defendants were
condemned to death,[2] seven received prison sentences ranging from 10
years to life, and three were acquitted, among them Papen and Schacht.
Whatever the shortcomings of the trial, the tribunal was not a kangaroo
court, and while the proceedings failed to impress many Germans, the
documentary record which was assembled provides once and for all
irrefutable evidence of the crimes of the Nazi era.

The Struggle Over Germany. The prosecution of war criminals was
one of the few instances of constructive four-power collaboration in
Germany. In every other area difficulties arose. The Allied Control Council passed a great many laws abolishing Nazi legislation or institutions,
it took care of technical matters such as the interzonal validity of legal
documents, but it settled few substantive issues. Disarmament could
be decreed easily enough and could be implemented by the seizure of
armaments and the destruction of military installations, but sharp disagreements arose over the dismantling of arms factories that could be
converted to civilian production. As for de-Nazification, the Council did
not agree on procedures for many months, and meanwhile each zonal
commander evolved his own system. It proved impossible, for example,
to dismiss every Nazi from his post if public administration and the
economy were to keep operating; the various zones dealt with this
problem therefore on the basis of political considerations and practical
needs, inevitably giving rise to bitter charges and countercharges. Each
zone also pursued its own policies of democratization: the Western zones
followed the path of multiparty parliamentary representation, but the
Russians, after similar beginnings, threw their weight behind the Communist Party and in the spring of 1946 sponsored the enforced merger
of Communists and Social Democrats into a Socialist Unity Party that
quickly became the dominant force in the Soviet Zone.

Economically too the four zones went their separate ways. The Soviets
inaugurated sweeping land expropriations and nationalized all major
business enterprises, the British toyed with plans for the socialization
of large industries, the Americans and the French upheld a decentralized
private enterprise system. Economic reintegration of the zones proved

---

[2] Among them was Göring who cheated the gallows by swallowing poison a few
hours before he was to be hanged.

GERMANY AFTER WORLD WAR II
OCCUPATION ZONES

impossible due to French and Soviet opposition. The French, having been excluded from the Potsdam Conference, did not feel bound by its agreements. They therefore opposed the establishment of centralized administrative agencies, which in their view were liable to pave the way for the resurgence of a strong Germany. The Russians, desperately short of foodstuffs, claimed large amounts as reparations and shipped them home. This made impossible the equitable distribution of available food-stuffs among the zones, as agreed to at Potsdam in order to assure the Germans a minimum living standard. As a result the United States and Britain were compelled to underwrite the food deficits of their zones, which had always depended on shipments from eastern Germany.

In March 1946 the Control Council agreed finally on a level-of-industry plan for the entire German economy and also determined which indus-trial installations were to be available for reparations as in excess of that level. Yet owing to continued French and Soviet opposition, the agree-ment did not lead to the restoration of Germany's economic unity, and the American and British zones were thereupon merged into one eco-nomic unit in January 1947. A year later, under American pressure, the French joined "Bizonia" after having been permitted to link the coal-rich Saar Basin in an economic union with France.

By 1948 the chasm between East and West had deepened so far that the reunification of all of Germany no longer seemed a practical pos-sibility. The foreign ministers of the occupation powers, meeting in a series of conferences, were unable to close the widening rifts. The Russians continued to claim as reparations large amounts of foodstuffs and goods produced in their zone, forcing the Western Powers to continue shipping food and other necessities to their own occupation zones. The Kremlin demanded also a voice in the control of the Ruhr industries to make certain that the Ruhr would not become a new basis for German aggression. This request the United States and Britain found equally unacceptable for they were determined to keep Moscow from interfering in the economy of West Germany. In view of the fate of other Communist-bourgeois coalition governments, they also rejected the establishment of a central German government for which the Soviets were calling. Instead, they began discussing the establishment of a separate West German state. To this plan the Russians reacted by withdrawing from the Allied Control Council.

As there seemed to be no prospect of German reunification on terms the West could accept, the Western Powers proceeded with the plan of building up "their" Germany into a sovereign self-governing state. By this step they hoped to lighten their own responsibilities, expedite Europe's economic rehabilitation, and strengthen the West's position in the eyes of the world. There was also the chance, though admittedly slim, that the establishment of a West German state might force the Soviets to loosen their hold on their zone. The Germans hesitated, however, to set up a separate West German state that was likely to perpetuate the division of Germany. They were warned that refusal might delay indefinitely the return of government to German hands, and in the end agreed to proceed. But they insisted on stressing the temporary nature of the new state and would adopt only a provisional "basic law," pending the reunification of Germany after which a permanent constitution would be enacted.

The Berlin Blockade.   The Soviets tried to block these plans by imposing a blockade on the Western-occupied sectors of Berlin. The Western Powers, they charged, had forfeited their right to remain in the capital since the four-power administration of Germany had come to an end. The Western Powers refused to leave, contending that they were in Berlin by right of conquest; they also felt that they had a moral commitment to protect the two million West Berliners. Above all, they knew that the faith of Germany and Europe in America's willingness to stand up for its principles depended on their remaining. The now-famous airlift, organized by the American zonal commander, General Lucius D. Clay, kept the city supplied with the needed amounts of food, fuel, and other necessities. By the spring of 1949, the Soviets realized that the blockade only served to strengthen Western and West German unity and thus aided the very developments it was meant to stop. In

The Berlin Airlift. *(Reprinted courtesy The Bettmann Archive, Inc.)*

May they called off the blockade in return for a new four-power conference on Germany. That conference met from May 23 to June 20 at Paris, but accomplished as little as all earlier ones.

The Two Germanys. Meanwhile a "Parliamentary Council," composed of delegates of the eleven states that had been established in the three Western zones, drafted the "basic law" for the new West German state. When it was approved by the three zonal commanders and ratified by ten of the eleven states,[3] the Federal Republic of Germany was formally established. West German sovereignty was restricted, however, by an Occupation Statute that left the occupying powers in charge of foreign policy, disarmament, reparations, and various economic controls, and gave them the power of veto over all German legislation.

Unable to prevent the formation of a West German state, the Russians followed the Western lead. In the fall of 1948 a "People's Council" sponsored by the Socialist Unity Party was charged with drafting a constitution for an East German state. The document was adopted by a "People's Congress" elected on the basis of a single slate of names in May 1949, and a few days after the establishment of the (Western) Federal

[3] Bavaria considered the "basic law" too unitarian and did not formally ratify it; Bavaria accepted it, however, as binding after it had been ratified by two thirds of the other states.

Republic of Germany, the (Eastern) German Democratic Republic came into being. The division of Germany was complete.

The Occupation of Austria. Austria too was divided into four occupation zones, but unlike Germany, the country retained its political and economic unity. From the outset it had an indigenous central government; originally sponsored by the Soviets, it was subsequently recognized by the Western Powers as well. The first elections were held in November 1945 and gave the Communists no more than 5.4 per cent of the vote. The Russians accepted the formation of a new government coalition of the Austrian People's Party, successor to the one-time Christian Social Party, and the Social Democrats. After the democratic pre-Dollfuss constitution had been revived, the occupying powers contented themselves essentially with the supervision of its implementation. Despite their cooperation in political matters, the Russians refused to sign a peace treaty with Austria. They derived substantial economic benefits from their occupation zone which contained some valuable oil fields; but perhaps even more important, they wished to keep their armed forces on Austrian soil—the more so because their withdrawal from Austria would have deprived them of the right to keep troops in Hungary and Rumania (see p. 409).

The Paris Peace Conference, April 1946. Left to right: Soviet Foreign Commissar Molotov, U.S. Secretary of State Byrnes, British Foreign Secretary Bevin, and French Foreign Minister Bidault.
(U.S. Information Agency)

The Peace Treaties with Italy and the Axis Satellites. Negotiations of peace treaties with Italy, Finland, Rumania, Bulgaria, and Hungary extended over many months. In the end they did produce treaties, which were signed in Paris in 1946–47. Italy lost some minor Alpine territories to France, surrendered its Aegean island possessions to Greece, and the province of Venezia Giulia to Yugoslavia. The changes corresponded to ethnic conditions in the territories concerned. The Yugoslavs, backed by the Soviets, demanded also the Italian port of Trieste which was the major Adriatic-Mediterranean outlet for the Danube states. This demand the Western Powers rejected on both ethnic and strategic grounds. In the end Trieste and its immediate hinterland were established as a Free State (like Danzig in 1919) and placed under United Nations protection. (The arrangement proved unworkable since the Security Council could not agree on a governor for the territory, and in 1954, after relations between the West and Yugoslavia had improved, the city proper became part of Italy while the adjacent rural areas were incorporated by Yugoslavia.) The disposal of the Italian colonies was left to the United Nations, which after protracted debates accorded them various degrees of autonomy. The Italian army was reduced to 250,000 men and the navy to little more than a coast guard. Reparations in the aggregate amount of $360 million were to be paid to the Soviet Union, Yugoslavia, Albania, Greece, and Ethiopia.

Peace treaties with the Axis satellites reconfirmed the U.S.S.R. in the territories obtained from Finland and Rumania in 1939–40 and added to them Finland's Arctic district of Petsamo. Hungary was forced to return Transylvania to Rumania, and there were other minor territorial changes. The treaties provided for arms limitations and reparations to go to the Soviet Union, Yugoslavia, Czechoslovakia, and Greece. Moscow also retained the right to keep troops in Hungary and Rumania to protect its lines of communication with its occupation forces in Austria. In turn, the Russians bowed to Western predominance on two other issues: they gave up their demand for a trusteeship over one of the Italian colonies and allowed the Dodecanese Islands to be turned over to Greece.

Japan. The settlement concerning Japan need be discussed here only in so far as it touched on European developments. In the deepening conflict between the West and the Soviet Union, the future of Japan was of crucial importance. Since American forces occupied the Japanese islands, the United States insisted on retaining the ultimate power of decision. Various Allied commissions were established to help develop policies for postwar Japan, but their role was merely advisory, and the Soviets refused to take part in them. So as not to bar permanently all cooperation with the U.S.S.R., conclusion of a peace treaty with Japan was postponed. It was finally negotiated during the Korean War in 1951 on American terms. The Kremlin refused to sign the treaty.

THE COLD WAR

The Underlying Causes. With the conclusion of the Paris peace treaties, Russo-Western collaboration came virtually to an end. The United States and Britain were fearful that the Soviet Union was preparing to gain control over Western Europe. Plagued by economic misery and torn by internal dissension, the European states seemed easy targets for a Communist takeover. To Anglo-Americans, moreover, Soviet ambitions constituted not only a threat to their countries' security, but also a brutal violation of elementary human rights. The Russians, on the other hand, were convinced that the capitalist West was approaching another depression and that it would go to war in search of new markets. In Moscow's view Western insistence on the protection of individual freedoms and property rights in eastern Europe was merely an attempt to retain capitalist, i.e., anti-Soviet bases within the Soviet domain. In February 1946 Stalin warned his countrymen that they ought to prepare themselves "against any eventuality."

As a result Moscow kept tightening its hold over those parts of eastern and central Europe which it controlled, and the West began consolidating its own position and keeping the Soviets out of areas over which it held sway, such as the Italian colonies and Japan. Of even greater importance was Germany. Control of that country, centrally located, highly industrialized, and endowed with a hard-working, resourceful people, was bound to tip the scales of political power in Europe in favor of the controlling side. For this reason neither side would accept the other's terms of reunification lest Germany be drawn into the opponent's camp, and each side held on to the part it controlled. At Yalta Roosevelt had maintained that American troops would remain in Europe for no more than two years after the end of the war; in September 1946 Secretary of State James F. Byrnes announced that American forces would not be withdrawn from Germany as long as other occupation forces remained on German soil.

Whatever each side's fears, neither side was prepared to go to war against the other. It was highly doubtful in any event whether the conflict, rooted as much in issues of ideology and economics as in a contest for power, could be resolved militarily. While both camps increased their armaments and formed new alliances, actual operations in the East-West conflict were carried on mainly on the ideological and socioeconomic plane (except for some strictly localized peripheral military action). It is to its predominantly nonmilitary nature that the conflict owed its name, the Cold War.

The Quest for Atomic Control. One of the factors responsible for the special character of the Cold War was the development of nuclear power as a military weapon. Its devastating effectiveness had been demonstrated by the two atomic bombs dropped on Hiroshima and Nagasaki in August 1945. The first had laid waste four of Hiroshima's seven square miles and had killed over 200,000 of the city's 343,000 inhabitants, 88,000 instantly and the remainder subsequently as a result of radioactive reaction. The even more powerful bomb dropped on Nagasaki had wiped out six square miles of that city's area.

Of the immense military significance of the A-bomb there could be no doubt. Possession of the atomic bomb was of special importance to the United States because soon after the war it began trailing the Soviet Union in most other categories of military preparedness. The difference was especially marked in land armaments; by 1947, owing to their rapid demobilization, American forces in Europe had dwindled to 400,000 men, mostly administrative personnel. (British and French forces stationed in Germany amounted to an additional 60,000 men, to whom could be added another 200,000 home-based troops not committed on colonial or occupation assignments.) The Russians, on the other hand, maintained a combat-ready army of 400,000 men in Germany, and could draw on several million more in eastern Europe and the U.S.S.R. This overwhelming preponderance of Soviet land power was balanced off only by American nuclear power.

It was clear, however, that the United States would not long retain its monopoly on atomic power. For this reason, it was important to subject the production of atomic power to international control before other countries would be able to produce nuclear bombs. The United States submitted a plan to the United Nations which outlined procedures for the establishment of such control; at the same time it offered to turn over all American bombs to this international control authority once it was operating effectively. To ensure prompt discovery of anyone producing nuclear weapons, the investigating activities of that agency were not to be subject to any veto. The Soviets countered with a plan by which all existing bombs would first be destroyed after which an international control agency would be set up. Fearful of a pro-Western majority in that agency, they also insisted on retaining the right of veto. The United States plan was predicated on Soviet faith in American good will; the Soviet plan, on American faith in the Kremlin's sincerity. In the prevailing atmosphere of deep mutual distrust, neither plan could serve as the basis for an agreement.

The Truman Doctrine.   One of the peripheral areas in which the Cold War exploded into military action was Greece. In 1946 civil war flared up again in that country. This time the Communist-led insurgents received help from Yugoslavia, Bulgaria, and Albania, and at least indirectly from the U.S.S.R. They were soon in control of large parts of northern Greece. Britain supported the Greek government both financially and militarily, but in February 1947 London warned Washington that Britain's own economic plight was such that it would have to withdraw its forces from Greece and end its financial support of Greece, as well as of Turkey, by March 31, 1947.

The Greek insurgents were not all Communists, and they owed much of their domestic support to a widespread dissatisfaction with the existing corrupt and reactionary regime. The leaders, however, were Communists and it was clear that if they defeated the government, Greece was likely to be swept into the Soviet orbit. Turkey on its part had been the target of a Soviet diplomatic offensive which demanded the right to build a naval base on the Bosporus and the return to the U.S.S.R. of some strategic border areas that had been Russian until 1918. Without British support Turkey might well succumb to Russian pressures and allow the Soviets to expand their power down to the Mediterranean and into the Middle East.

The crisis was one which fell within the jurisdiction of the United Nations, but the urgency of the matter and the expectation of a Soviet veto blocking action by the United Nations led the American government to step directly into the vacuum left by Britain's withdrawal. On March 12, 1947 President Truman announced what became known as the Truman Doctrine, proclaiming it the policy of the United States "to support free peoples who are resisting attempted subjugation by armed minorities or by outside pressures." He emphasized the close connection between America's future and that of Europe: "If we falter in our leadership, we may endanger the peace of the world—and we shall surely endanger the welfare of our nation." American help given to Turkey and Greece enabled the two countries to withstand Soviet pressures. It took over two years, however, until the Greek civil war was brought to an end.

The Marshall Plan. Britain's financial plight highlighted the enormous economic difficulties that were weighing on postwar Europe. The war had exacted from Europe a frightful toll; of Europe's 28 million combatants, 5.4 million died in action, and if the U.S.S.R. is included, the figures are 40.5 million and at least 8.4 million, respectively. In addition, as has been estimated, 6.5 million civilians died from bombings, starvation, maltreatment, reprisals, and mass extermination, and a conservative estimate of Soviet losses increases that number to 11.5 million.[4] These figures assume added significance if it is kept in mind that all of the combatants and large numbers of the civilians who lost their lives perished at their most productive age.

Since home front and battlefield became one during World War II, material devastation surpassed any earlier wartime destruction both absolutely and relatively. The economic branch that was hit hardest was transportation, due partly to bombings and battle action and partly to

---

[4] Eugene M. Kulisher, *Europe on the Move: War and Population Changes, 1917–47* (New York, 1948), pp. 274–80.

confiscations and the Germans' systematic scorched-earth policy. France lost 75 per cent of its railroad rolling stock, Belgium over 50 per cent, and the Netherlands almost its entire equipment. In addition, bridges and marshaling yards were demolished and railroad trackage torn up. Of the major harbors of continental Europe only two remained in full operation—Bordeaux and Antwerp; Europe's merchant marine was reduced to half its prewar size. Similarly, agricultural productivity hovered around one-half of its prewar yields. Industry, on the other hand, suffered less than expected, and except in the Soviet Union, most plants affected by the ravages of war needed only repairs rather than complete reconstruction.[5] Yet owing to the lack of capital and materials and the disruption of the transportation system, repairs too were difficult to accomplish, and these difficulties were compounded by the exhaustion and demoralization of the peoples of Europe.

The United Nations Relief and Rehabilitation Administration (UNRRA) organized in 1943 and financed largely by the United States could do little more than provide Europeans with food, clothing, and other necessities; it lacked the resources required to spark the recovery of the Continent. Moreover, politically neutral, UNRRA provided relief to all European countries in need, among them Poland, Yugoslavia, and the Ukraine, and this very fact led to its demise in the first half of 1947, since America refused to provide further funds.

Given the limited resources of UNRRA, the United States granted loans on its own to Britain, France, Belgium, and other European countries in 1945–46.[6] Though substantial, they were in effect only stopgap measures wholly inadequate to rehabilitate the economies of the recipient countries. The amounts of foodstuffs, raw materials, and machinery required by the European nations were immense and would obviously have to be supplied on a vast scale over a period of time.

The United States had a vital interest in Europe's recovery. America could not hope to prosper surrounded by misery and despair. Europe, moreover, had long been America's best export market, and failure to restore this market was bound to affect the American economy with particular force. Prolonged misery was also likely to lead to revolt and might drive Western Europe into the Communist camp, making the Soviet Union the master of all Europe. Finally, beyond all considerations of national security and economics, humanitarian impulses urged the granting of aid to the hard-pressed Europeans. Yet while the United States was aware of its stake in Europe's recovery, it was neither willing nor able to continue underwriting this rehabilitation by piecemeal assistance to individual countries.

---

[5] The material losses of the Soviet Union can best be summed up by one figure: they amounted to about one-fourth of all Soviet property. See Sidney Harcave, *Russia: A History* (Philadelphia, 1964), p. 691.

[6] Credits earmarked for Poland and Czechoslovakia were cancelled, however, as tensions mounted in 1946.

The aid plan that was proposed and which took its name from General George C. Marshall, then Secretary of State, was based on the realization that what was needed was not merely the restoration of the productive capacity of the various European countries. It was equally important to revive what Marshall called the "entire fabric of the European economy"—the exchange of goods between town and country and across national boundaries, the European-wide coordination of production and transportation, the restoration of banking, insurance, and other services on the vastest possible scale. The Marshall Plan called on the nations of Europe to work out a comprehensive cooperative rehabilitation program and offered America's help in the drafting of such a plan and in its subsequent implementation.

The plan was addressed not only to western Europe, but to eastern Europe and the Soviet Union as well. Both had long provided western Europe with foodstuffs and raw materials, in exchange for industrial products; the renewal of these exchanges would benefit them as well as the West and speed the rehabilitation of all of Europe. The Soviet Union refused to take part in the plan, however, and barred also the participation of its European satellites. The plan called for the drafting of an overall program which would have compelled the U.S.S.R. to reveal to the West the full scope of its strengths and weaknesses, and this Moscow would not accept. As for the satellites, the Kremlin was fearful lest the plan provide an entering wedge for Western capitalism and whittle away the political and economic transformation of these countries, reducing them again to their former economic dependence on the West.

In consequence, the Marshall Plan was limited to western Europe (except Spain) and Austria, Greece, and Turkey. It proved to be one of the most successful ventures in foreign aid and international economic cooperation. Over a period of four years, from 1948 to 1951, the United States provided credits and goods amounting to $12 billion. The results were impressive; industrial production in western Europe not only attained prewar levels, except for coal, but by the end of 1951 surpassed them by 41 per cent; agricultural production expanded 9 per cent over prewar levels. Even the ruinously battered transportation system was restored to prewar capacity during these four years.

The Marshall Plan did not solve all of Europe's economic problems or relieve its social difficulties (see p. 430), but it did check the spread of Communism in western Europe, it laid the foundation for Europe's subsequent economic prosperity and for further endeavors in European economic cooperation. Last but not least, it restored hope and self-confidence in Europe.

Cominform and COMECON. In September 1947, three months after the launching of the Marshall Plan, the Soviets set up a new international organization of Communist parties, the Communist Information Bureau

(Cominform). It consisted of the Communist parties of the Soviet bloc and those of France and Italy; its principal Soviet spokesman was Andrei Zhdanov (1896–1948), a member of the Soviet Politburo and one of Stalin's closest associates. The Cominform was founded to foil the plans of American "monopoly capitalism . . . for the enslavement of the countries of Europe and Asia" and was to coordinate the activities of its member parties. As Zhdanov explained the strategy of the Cominform, "If the European countries display the necessary fortitude and readiness to resist American enslaving credit, America may be forced to retreat." Given the desperate plight of the west European workers, strikes bordering on insurrections could be organized in France and Italy in the winter of 1947–48 in order to thwart the Marshall Plan. The Kremlin was convinced that the plan was devised as an outlet for American surplus production and that without it the United States would be plunged into an economic crisis. By sabotaging the plan the Soviet leaders hoped to compel the American government to grant credits to both eastern and western Europe on terms acceptable to Moscow.

Defeat of the Marshall Plan was only one of the tasks with which the Cominform was charged; it was this particular function that accounted for the inclusion of the French and Italian parties. Another purpose of the Cominform was to strengthen the hold of the Soviet Union on the east European satellites and thus help to consolidate Soviet power. For the Soviet bloc was beginning to show serious fissures: Yugoslavia pursued domestic policies of its own; Poland and Czechoslovakia had wished to take part in the Marshall Plan; and other bloc members too tended to be preoccupied with their local concerns at the expense of Moscow's overall plans. By means of the Cominform Stalin wished to tighten his hold on the Communist parties of these states and control their policies more closely.

In the same vein a Council for Economic Mutual Assistance (COMECON) was established at Warsaw in January 1949. Its task was to increase the productivity of the Soviet bloc (minus Yugoslavia, which had been expelled from the bloc the year before) and help further to consolidate Moscow's hold on the bloc by adjusting the component economies to the needs of the Soviet Union. COMECON accelerated the industrial development of Soviet Europe, but the subordination of the satellites' national interests to Moscow's plans caused much dissatisfaction. Moscow retaliated by engineering a series of purges in these countries in order to ensure its supremacy (see p. 462).

The Czech Coup. The one state in the Soviet orbit which had not become a Communist dictatorship was Czechoslovakia. Under the leadership of President Beneš the Czechs maintained the essentials of a democratic government, and they conducted their economic affairs with somewhat greater freedom than their east European neighbors. Paying

greater attention to the consumer, Czechoslovakia enjoyed living standards higher than those in any other country in eastern Europe. As a
result, the Communists, who had received 38 per cent of the vote in the
first postwar elections of 1946, were losing ground. Since new elections
were to be held in the summer of 1948, this was a matter of serious
concern to the Kremlin. In view of the deepening East-West conflict,
military control of Czechoslovakia was essential to Moscow, for Czechoslovakia protected the flanks of the Soviet forces in both Austria and
East Germany. The country played an equally important role in Moscow's economic plans since economic progress in the Soviet orbit depended on an increased contribution of Czechoslovakia to the rehabilitation and industrialization of eastern Europe. Yet the Czechs were
reluctant to adjust their economy to these needs. They voiced strong
opposition to a new Communist-sponsored five-year plan designed to
increase Czech heavy industrial capacity by 80 per cent—at the price
of the conversion of 30 per cent of all consumer goods output to the
production of capital goods. Thus, for political, economic, and military
reasons, Czechoslovakia's semi-autonomy obstructed the plans of the
Kremlin. Events played into Moscow's hands when in February 1948 a
government crisis erupted in Prague over the recruitment of police personnel. Under the pressure of mass demonstrations and "action committees," with the police under Communist control and the Red Army
stationed along almost every Czech border, Beneš had no choice but to
yield and to appoint a new Communist-controlled government.

The Soviet-Yugoslav Split. The full integration of Czechoslovakia into
the Soviet bloc was more than offset by the expulsion of Yugoslavia a
few months later. Relations between Soviet Russia and Tito's Yugoslavia,
never entirely smooth, had steadily deteriorated since the war. The
Kremlin objected to Tito's continued demand for Trieste and part of
Austria's province of Carinthia in spite of Moscow's manifest inability
to obtain these lands without going to war. Tito on his part resented
Stalin's unwillingness to press more vigorously for the surrender of these
two territories to Yugoslavia. Difficulties arose also over military and
economic questions. Russia wished to see the Yugoslav army become an
appendage of the Red Army, trained and equipped in accordance with
Soviet requirements; the Yugoslavs insisted on having a separate army,
trained also in the guerrilla-type mountain warfare that had proved so
important in World War II and supplied by a Yugoslav arms industry.
In the economic realm Moscow wished Yugoslavia to remain essentially
a food and raw material producing country, whereas Belgrade was determined to expand its industrialization. In the eyes of the Kremlin, all
this added up to a stance of independence which, if unchecked, was
likely to encourage similar trends in other satellite states.

Early in 1948 Moscow began subjecting Yugoslavia to increasing politi-

Marshal Tito. (*Reprinted courtesy Brown Brothers*)

cal and economic pressures, hopeful that these would lead to the replacement of Tito by a more amenable leader. But Tito refused to yield, and in June Yugoslavia was expelled from the Cominform on trumped-up charges of having delayed its collectivization. Contrary to the Kremlin's expectations, Tito retained the support of party, army, and secret police; moreover, many non-Communists were prepared to support him for he was defending Yugoslavia's national independence. Still, Tito found himself in a highly precarious position, and he tried hard to achieve a reconciliation. Once a reconciliation proved out of the question, however, he became more defiant. Rumors of a forthcoming Soviet invasion he countered with the announcement that he would fight back; by holding out to the Soviets the prospect of a drawn-out mountain campaign he may well have saved his country from a Russian attack. Jointly with its remaining satellites, Moscow contented itself with imposing a tightening economic blockade on Yugoslavia; given the close economic ties that bound Belgrade to the Soviet bloc, this put an enormous strain on the Yugoslav economy. It was tempered by the corresponding dependence of most of the satellites on Yugoslav trade, which precluded the cut-off of all commercial relations. For some months, however, Yugoslavia found itself in almost complete isolation, shunned by the West as a Communist country and branded as a nation of Marxist deviationists by the Communist world.

Yet the picture was not completely bleak. Yugoslavia bordered on several non-Communist countries and on the Adriatic Sea which gave it access to non-Communist sources of supply. What the Yugoslavs needed most, however, was credits. Yet as a Communist, Tito could not accept help from the West if he had to purchase such aid with a return to private capitalism or membership in an anti-Communist military alliance. As it was, Tito's fears were unfounded. The West was anxious not to drive Yugoslavia back into the Soviet camp and came to its aid without such conditions. Beginning in 1949, Western economic and military supplies **417**

started flowing into Yugoslavia. Tito on his part made one concession
to the West (which also served his own interests). He closed his frontier
to the Greek insurgents, thus helping to bring the Greek Civil War to
an end.

The principal long-range gain which the West derived from the
Stalin-Tito split was the fact that the break disproved the monolithic
nature of Communism. Though Stalin managed to tighten his hold on
the remaining satellite states, the very existence of Tito's "national Communism" was a continuous threat to the cohesiveness of the Soviet bloc.

The North Atlantic Treaty. To the West the Czech coup seemed
ominously reminiscent of Hitler's moves against Czechoslovakia. Fearful
that it might have been staged in preparation of an assault on western
Europe, several of the western European states proceeded to strengthen
and coordinate their military resources. In March 1948, under the impact
of the Czech coup, Britain, France, and the Benelux countries (Belgium,
the Netherlands, and Luxembourg) concluded a fifty-year mutual defense pact at Brussels and set up for that purpose a Western European
Union. It was obvious, however, that the Union would have little effect
on the military balance of power unless it were backed by the United
States. The Berlin Blockade that same summer caused the United States
to break with its traditional policy against "entangling alliances." On
April 4, 1949, along with Canada, it concluded its first military alliance
in peacetime, the North Atlantic Treaty. The other signatories were
Britain, France, Italy, the Netherlands, Belgium, Norway, Denmark,
Iceland, Portugal, and Luxembourg. According to this pact, an attack on
one of its members would be considered as an attack against all of them;
in the event of such an attack each treaty partner would take whatever
measures it deemed necessary, including the use of force, to assist the
attacked country or countries and protect the security of the North
Atlantic area. While this did not legally oblige the United States to go
to war in defense of a victim of aggression, it did establish a moral commitment. A North Atlantic Treaty Organization (NATO) was set up,
headed by a council composed of the foreign, defense, and finance ministers of the member countries. One of NATO's main functions was the
development of an "infrastructure," that is, the construction of a network of airfields, harbor facilities, food and arms depots, and other such
installations needed to sustain its military operations; it was also to
draft strategic plans, and coordinate the various national contingents
into unified land, naval, and air forces. If it did not attain sufficient
strength to match the land armies of the Soviet bloc, NATO was expected to acquire at least adequate power to inflict serious injury on
the Red forces in case of war. It was to serve as a deterrent to any
aggressive designs the Kremlin might have. Ultimately American nuclear
power would, if necessary, be brought into play to offset Soviet preponderance in land forces.

The efforts of NATO received an additional impetus from the invasion of American-backed South Korea by the Communist North Koreans in June 1950. The situation of divided Korea seemed sufficiently like that of Germany to arouse strong apprehensions in Europe. It was feared that the Korean War might be a prelude to the outbreak of war in Germany, and these fears were reinforced by the fact that the East Germans were equipping their police force with tanks and artillery. Most Europeans were deeply relieved to see the United States come to the help of the South Koreans; they felt reassured that America would respond with equal promptness to a Communist attack on western Europe. NATO plans for a unified command were quickly completed and General Eisenhower was appointed commander-in-chief of all NATO forces. At the same time, some Marshall Plan funds were diverted to military purposes, and in 1951 the Plan was superseded by the Mutual Security Program in which military expenditures outweighed economic investments.

The Rearmament of West Germany. As the claims on the West's armed forces increased, the available manpower proved insufficient to fulfill NATO's functions. An increase appeared the more urgent because the Soviet Union had exploded its first nuclear bomb in September 1949, depriving the United States of its atomic monopoly. Washington proposed the formation of a West German army to bolster the strength of the NATO forces. The proposal caused deep consternation in Europe; the French in particular balked at the thought of rearming the Germans only five years after Hitler's Wehrmacht had finally been defeated. Yet with the bulk of the French army engaged in the defense of Indo-China, France could not supply the needed reinforcements, nor could any other European state. Caught between strong American pressures for and bitter domestic opposition to German rearmament, the French government proposed the establishment of a European Defense Community (EDC) composed of France, Italy, the Benelux countries, and Western Germany which would absorb all German armed forces into a supranational European defense force and thus keep the Germans firmly controlled. All prospective members of the EDC accepted the plan—except France; when the government, after many delays, submitted it rather half-heartedly to the French parliament in 1954, the latter rejected it by a substantial majority (see p. 478).

In 1955 West Germany became a member of NATO. France agreed to the admission of Germany, after the British had reassured the French that Britain would keep its NATO contingent permanently on the Continent. As an added safeguard, Germany was not allowed to maintain any armed forces outside of NATO, as did other members. The Germans were also barred from the production of nuclear, bacteriological, and chemical weapons, and were prohibited from building tanks, submarines, large warships, and long-range bombers unless requested by NATO. The

West German armed forces were limited to an army of 500,000 men, a tactical air force, and a small navy.

If militarily West Germany remained subject to important restrictions, politically it gained increased freedom of action. In 1951, under the skillful stewardship of Chancellor Adenauer, the West German government recovered the right to conduct its foreign affairs; later that year Britain, France, and the United States declared the state of war with the West German state at an end. In 1952 Allied supervisory rights were further curtailed, and in 1955, when Germany entered NATO, its full sovereignty was restored, except for the Allied right to maintain troops on German soil and the continued exclusion of West Berlin from full integration into the West German state.

Soviet Countermoves.   Ever fearful of German military potentialities, the Soviets tried hard to block West German rearmament. Moscow mobilized the resources of a worldwide "Peace Movement" which the Kremlin had been sponsoring for some time. Originally launched to arouse public opinion against atomic warfare and thus neutralize the West's superiority in nuclear weapons, the movement had been recently used to prevent the conclusion of the North Atlantic Treaty. It acquired its full momentum, however, only in its fight against West German rearmament. Here it could draw on considerable non-Communist support, for fear of German militarism was still deep-rooted throughout Europe and opposition to the rearming of Germany widespread. When the "Partisans for Peace" sponsored a house-to-house drive in France to obtain backing for a protest against German remilitarization, they claimed to have received six million signatures within three months. It is probable that the movement was at least partly responsible for the protracted delay in the rearmament of West Germany.

The EDC plan caused even deeper alarm in the Kremlin and led it in the spring of 1952 to propose the conclusion of a peace treaty with an all-German government that would be formed after nationwide elections supervised by the four occupying powers had been held. According to this proposal, the reunified Germany was to enjoy almost full sovereignty including the right to its own armed forces. The price the Soviets demanded for these concessions was the acceptance of the Oder-Neisse Line as the permanent German-Polish boundary and the neutralization of Germany, meaning specifically no German participation in the EDC or any other "kind of coalition or military alliance directed against any power which took part with its armed forces in the war against Germany." Certain that the plan was intended as a dilatory maneuver by the Kremlin, the West made no attempt to determine whether the plan offered a genuine chance of reunifying Germany. The United States also felt confident that a European army reinforced by West German troops would strengthen the bargaining position of the Western Powers. Washington insisted therefore on proceeding with the rearmament of West

Germany and the establishment of EDC, and the Soviet proposal was sidestepped. The Kremlin itself soon lost interest in it—perhaps because it seemed possible to prevent West German rearmament with the help of the "neutralist" movement.

The Soviets did not rely solely on diplomacy and public opinion to ward off potential threats from West Germany. As early as 1948 they had begun to transform the East German "people's police" into a skeleton army. In 1950 and 1951 they authorized the formation of an East German navy and air force. In 1955, in response to the establishment of the West German army, the East German state set up a National People's Army. According to information issued by the West German government, that army numbered about 110,000 men in the early 1960's. If the paramilitary East German police units of 50,000 men are added to it, the German Democratic Republic had a land army of 160,000 compared to Bonn's 500,000-man army—a number that corresponded roughly to the population ratio between East and West Germany. Following the Western lead, the Soviets also accorded the East German state all attributes of sovereignty. At the same time East Germany became an associate member of the Warsaw Pact, the Soviet-sponsored counterpart of NATO, formed in 1955 on Germany's entry into NATO.

WESTERN EUROPE AND THE COLD WAR

Neutralism. Western Europe's initial reactions to the Cold War varied. Since many countries had large Communist parties, their reception of the Truman Doctrine was reserved. On the other hand, they welcomed the Marshall Plan, except for the Communists, who fought the plan bitterly but failed to block it. The North Atlantic Pact, in turn, did not receive the same strong support on the part of non-Communist Europeans. Switzerland, traditionally neutral, did not join, and neither did Sweden and Eire. Sweden refrained because of its proximity to Russia, Eire because it thought itself sufficiently safe from Russian attacks to forgo sharing the burdens of NATO and enter an alliance that also included Great Britain. Norway and Denmark joined NATO, but barred all foreign troops from their soil in peacetime.

Even in the countries which became full-fledged members of NATO, there existed considerable non-Communist opposition to the Atlantic alliance. This attitude, known as neutralism, maintained that western Europe should not merely follow the American lead in foreign policy, but should steer a course of its own between East and West. Neutralist arguments varied, and not a few of them were mutually contradictory. Some Europeans did not trust the United States to live up to its commitments in case of war, and they attacked the North Atlantic Treaty as a provocation of the U.S.S.R. that might induce Russia to attack western Europe, with the United States standing by passively. Others were fearful lest the United States, carried away by its anti-Communist crusading spirit, might go to war against Soviet Russia, with Europe becoming the main battlefield. Still others worried about the economic effects of rearmament and the hopelessness of matching Soviet land power. Finally, many, especially in Britain, attacked the Atlantic Pact policy as being based upon a gross overestimate of Soviet strength and on a misinterpretation of Soviet plans, which were considered to be based on the belief in the inevitable self-destruction of the capitalist system rather than on military aggression. In a national variation on the neutralist theme, German neutralists saw in NATO and in German rearmament a barrier to the reunification of Germany.

Neutralism was nowhere developed into an organized movement. In Britain neutralist sentiment centered around the left wing of the Labor Party; in Germany it had its main mouthpiece in the Social Democratic Party and other outlets in a few minor right-wing parties and organizations. In France neutralism crystallized around some newspapers such as *Le Monde* and *L'Observateur* and the Catholic monthly *Esprit*. Many French neutralists also supported the Communist-sponsored Partisans for Peace.

Despite widespread support, neutralism failed to have a direct effect on the course of events (except, perhaps, in the case of the defeat of the European Defense Community). Its failure was due in part to the refutation of the neutralist arguments by events and partly to the strength of the political and economic ties with the United States. In addition, such skilled leaders as Chancellor Adenauer outmaneuvered their neutralist opposition by securing substantial political gains in return for West Germany's pro-Western alignment. Still, the efforts of the neutralists may not have been entirely futile. After the death of Stalin in 1953, neutralist pleadings possibly helped to bring about the resumption of East-West negotiations—if only by reinforcing the urgings of such nonneutralist advocates of new negotiations as Winston Churchill.

East-West Trade. Dissent between western Europe and the United States arose also over the question of trade relations with the Soviet bloc. As the Cold War grew in intensity, American aid to other countries was made contingent on the latter's embargo on exports of "strategic" goods to the Soviet bloc and Comunist China. To the European countries, whose economies were more dependent on foreign trade than was that of the United States, these restrictions were a heavy burden. They never observed them as strictly as did the United States, and the American government was forced to relax its controls. Washington also bowed to the argument that an expansion of East-West trade might lead to an improvement of overall relations. This consideration assumed special significance when the death of Stalin appeared to open up new possibilities for a rapprochement.

19

Western Europe from VE-Day to the Death of Stalin: The Internal Transformation

In an earlier chapter, post-World War I Europe was described as an amorphous community held loosely together by cultural ties and some common political and economic concerns. The war drove home to the European nations the need for a greater degree of unity. In retrospect they perceived that Hitler's foreign political successes had largely been due to their self-centered attitude during the prewar years; he had been able to seize one country after another because those not directly affected by his actions had stood by inactively. Only a closer union of the European states could prevent a recurrence of those tragic events. Most Resistance movements called for a European federation after the war, and while the governments on their part were not prepared to go quite as far, some governments-in-exile prepared the way for regional groupings. The Greek and Yugoslav governments planned a Balkan Union; those of Czechoslovakia and Poland proposed common programs in foreign affairs, defense, trade and social policy; and the exiled leaders of the Benelux countries drew up plans for a customs union after the war. Throughout occupied Europe nationalism was giving way to a new spirit of cooperation that transcended national barriers.

THE INTEGRATION OF WESTERN EUROPE

The First Steps.   The ground thus was not unprepared for a unification of Europe when the war came to an end. Yet by that time the deepening East-West conflict precluded the formation of an all-European federation. Hopes for regional unions remained alive, however, in both parts of Europe. Eastern European endeavors in this direction will be discussed in the next chapter; as for efforts in western Europe, they were soon stymied by numerous obstacles. The Resistance movements, split by disputes between Communists and anti-Communists, lacked the strength and the skill to promote their proposals, and governments were either too preoccupied with everyday problems to pursue their more modest plans or began to have reservations about them. Although a number of movements for European unity were organized, almost all of them lacked official sponsors. In 1949 a government-backed Council of Europe was finally organized, but its functions were purely consultative. The one actual step towards integration that was taken was the inauguration of the Benelux customs union in 1948.

European Recovery Program and NATO.   Another impetus to European integration came from an entirely different quarter—the United States. The Marshall Plan, or, as it was officially known, the European Recovery Program, working through the Organization for European Economic Cooperation, tried to draw the participating economies more closely together. It did so successfully in the area of trade. Bilateral trade agreements, import quotas, and exchange restrictions were replaced by a liberalized trade program including the removal of import controls, currency stabilization, and a multilateral payment system. The latter was administered by the European Payments Union, a supranational agency which functioned as the clearinghouse for the trade balances of the member states. The European Recovery Program was not able, however, to coordinate production in a similar manner. While output expanded rapidly, it did so largely within a national framework. Inevitably, there was a great deal of duplication of effort, and once more European governments began to worry about the danger of overproduction.

NATO's contribution to European integration was also of limited significance only. Training and equipment of NATO forces was unified, but lack of a common foreign and economic policy set narrow limits to any efforts at integration.

The European Coal and Steel Community.   In the spring of 1950, owing to the lack of coordination in industrial production, western Europe was faced with a serious recession. Orders for steel were declining, and statistical forecasts indicated that the Continent would have an unmarketable surplus of eight million tons of steel by 1953. Among those concerned over this prospect was Jean Monnet (1888–   ), head of France's industrial modernization program and a man of wide experience in the field of international trade and finance. Monnet was convinced that Europe's economic rehabilitation depended on the creation of a vast European market untrammeled by tariffs and other trade barriers. In such a common market the various national industries would enjoy the advantages of a greatly expanded demand, but would also be forced to improve their production methods to ward off each other's competition. As a first step Monnet proposed the formation of an enlarged market for the coal and steel industries. Both were key industries and of basic importance also in the production of armaments which would make their coordination significant politically as well as economically.

French Foreign Minister Robert Schuman (1886–   ), to whom Monnet submitted his plan, was particularly well suited to translate the project into reality. Originally a lawyer in Metz, the capital of Lorraine, Schuman had served in the German army in World War I, but had opted for France in 1919 and at the age of thirty-three had become a French citizen. He had not turned into a Germanophobe, however, but had always worked for Franco-German reconciliation. Monnet's proposal seemed to offer a way of moving in that direction, and Schuman made himself the advocate of the plan that was to bear his name. As proposed, the Schuman Plan called for the improvement of production techniques

French Foreign Minister Robert Schuman. (*Reprinted courtesy Brown Brothers*)

and for the supply of coal and steel to France, Germany, and other cooperating countries "on identical terms" and under the supervision of a supranational High Authority. The proposal met with serious opposition from both French and German industrialists who feared each other's competition. In the end, however, both countries accepted the plan by large parliamentary majorities. To the French, all possible disadvantages were outweighed by the fact that the plan subjected the German steel industries to international controls that would serve as a check on Germany's military potential. At the same time, the plan assured French industry of permanent access, on terms of equality, to German coking coal; France itself had never produced enough of this resource. For the Germans, the advantages of the Schuman Plan lay in the fact that it required the removal of all remaining production curbs if Germany was to compete with France on equal terms. The Germans hoped also that the proposed rapprochement with France and other western European nations would strengthen their diplomatic position vis-à-vis Soviet Russia. Italy and the Benelux countries accepted the invitation to join; the British, on the other hand, remained outside because membership in the European Coal and Steel Community (ECSC) seemed incompatible with Britain's membership in the Commonwealth and with its special relationship with the United States. The British, moreover, had not yet accepted their decline from World Power status and thus were unwilling to surrender part of their national sovereignty.

The ECSC began operating in 1953; its jurisdiction extended over coal, iron ore, scrap iron, and steel. It took steps to align internal prices and transport charges as well as external tariff rates (but governments still found ways, by means of concealed subsidies, to protect their industries against each other's competition). The ECSC also was given the authority, in periods of "manifest crisis," to impose trade and production quotas. Both iron and steel production expanded by over 50 per cent between 1951 and 1957; coal production, on the other hand, failed to increase, except in Germany. Intra-Community trade in ECSC products more than doubled during the same years. It is questionable, however, whether the increases were due to the existence of the ECSC or to the general expansion of economic activity as a result of the Korean War. Quite possibly, the main importance of the Community lay in its furthering of a common European spirit. In its various organs, the High Authority, the Common Assembly, and the Court of Justice, it developed supranational bodies that accustomed the participating countries to the techniques of close collaboration across national boundaries.

In addition to its economic functions, ECSC was also to promote the improvement and equalization of working conditions in the industries it embraced. Although its powers in the social domain remained undefined and the Authority refrained from intervening in matters of wages or working hours, disparities in coal and steel wages narrowed down more markedly than in industrial wages as a whole, evidently as part of an overall leveling of costs and prices within the common market.

SOCIAL CHANGES

The Political Scene. The early trend toward unity was accentuated by a marked parallelism in the domestic developments of most west European states. Disillusionment with the rightist parties, the leading role played by groups of the left in the Resistance, and above all, the demand for comprehensive reforms produced sharp leftward shifts. This was a time of great expectations—of hopes for a new beginning that would end old injustices and sweep away antiquated institutions. To achieve these goals new leaders were needed to replace the discredited politicians of prewar days. In France a coalition of Socialists, Communists, and left-of-center Popular Republicans dominated the political scene after De Gaulle resigned from office in January 1946. A similar coalition of reform-minded Christian Democrats, Socialists, and Communists governed Italy after the British had relaxed their hold on the country's political life. Belgium, too, had a Socialist-Communist-Christian Socialist government during the immediate postwar period, and the Netherlands was governed by a Catholic-Socialist coalition. The Scandinavian countries, as before, had Socialist administrations, and Britain, for the first time, gave itself an all-Labor government based on a Labor majority.

Postwar Reforms. Plans for a better postwar world were drawn up at an early stage in World War II. After the fall of France, it seemed imperative to rekindle the fighting spirit of the peoples of western Europe by holding out to them the promise of greater social justice and material security once Hitler had been defeated. In Britain's darkest hour in 1940, the government first took up these issues, and some time later a commission was formed under the economist, Sir William Beveridge, to work out plans for a cradle-to-grave social insurance program to be enacted after the war. Most governments-in-exile also began working on plans for postwar social reforms, and so did many of the Resistance movements. A "Charter" drawn up by the French Resistance called for the nationalization of the major means of production, improved social security including the right to work, and workers' participation in the "direction of economic life."

The Resistance plans grew out of a combination of Marxist tenets, lessons learned from the Depression, and social and humanitarian impulses. They envisaged societies in which class differences would be less sharp and the material lot of the masses greatly improved. In calling for the nationalization of all banks, key industries, and utilities, the plans were to assure their operation in the public interest and facilitate the overall economic planning that would be needed to increase production and maintain full employment. There was widespread agreement among non-Marxists as well that the laissez-faire system had lost its validity in the complexities of the industrial mass age and that by the proper allocation of resources, strategic investments, and the control of credits and interest rates, economic productivity could be greatly expanded.

British Reforms.   Of all the countries concerned Britain came closest to carrying out its original reform program. Between 1945 and 1951, under the auspices of a Labor government, the Bank of England, the coal mines, railways and civil aviation, gas and electricity, and temporarily, road transport and the iron and steel industries were nationalized (with liberal compensation for the former owners). In addition, moving toward the "welfare state," Parliament created a National Health Service providing every Englishman with free medical services and financed by a compulsory social insurance system. In the same vein, educational facilities were expanded and a comprehensive housing program enacted. Most of these measures also had the approval of many Conservatives. The need for greater social security was generally accepted, and there was widespread agreement that lack of competitiveness, existing government controls, and dependence on government financing made public ownership imperative for most of the enterprises which were to be nationalized. The matter was different in the case of the well-run iron and steel industries. The issue here was whether because of their very importance these key industries ought to be under public control. Their nationalization thus was strictly a partisan issue; while in control of Parliament the Labor Party nationalized iron and steel in 1949, and the Conservatives denationalized them when their party was returned to power in 1951.

France and the Smaller Countries.   France, too, inaugurated important reforms in the years 1945–1947. The social security program initiated by Léon Blum's Popular Front government in 1936 was expanded, and the Bank of France, the largest deposit banks and insurance companies, gas, electricity, and the coal mines were nationalized. Together with the railways, aircraft, and armament industries, which had come into public ownership in the 1930's, the nationalized enterprises constituted a substantial sector of the French economy. Sometime later shipping, air lines, and Paris' transportation facilities were added to it. In 1946 a General Planning Commission was set up, with Jean Monnet as its head. The Commission was to rehabilitate and modernize French industry so as to increase its production. This it did by concentrating on the development of the "basic sectors" of the economy—coal, electricity, steel, cement, farm machinery, transportation, fuel, and fertilizers. The Commission determined the distribution of scarce materials, authorized new projects, controlled credit policy, and, above all, decided on the allocation of public funds.

Similar changes took place in the smaller west European countries. Belgium inaugurated a comprehensive social security system; the Dutch, the Swiss, and the Swedes expanded theirs. Both Belgium and the Netherlands established a widespread network of government-administered arbitration machinery to safeguard industrial peace. The Belgian government took an active part in the modernization of the industrial region around Liège and Namur. In Norway and Sweden the government helped to underwrite the expansion of several major industrial concerns, among them Norsk Hydro, a huge combine operated by hydroelectric power. (In 1950 Norway produced the world's highest per capita amount of electricity.)

The winds of change affected least the surviving dictatorships. Both Spain and Portugal introduced few reforms, and these were limited in scope, especially in Portugal. Spain launched a modest social security program, but it was financially quite inadequate.

Italy and West Germany. In Italy there was a strong social upsurge after the war, yet the Committees of Liberation, which were the chief advocates of social reforms, quickly lost their political influence. They were dissolved by the Allies, along with the Partisan formations that had helped to liberate northern Italy. The Communists, too, submitted to Allied policy—most likely on orders from Moscow which was anxious to observe the sphere-of-influence understanding in order to bar Western intervention in eastern Europe. Thus, the more conservative forces reasserted themselves, and all major reforms were postponed. (One important change was made, however, in the social insurance system: after June 1946 it was financed exclusively by employers' contributions and government grants.) Italy remained a land of sharp social contrasts where great wealth, concentrated in a relatively small group of industrialists and landed proprietors, confronted a hard-pressed middle class and an industrial and rural proletariat plagued by inflation and unemployment. It was only when serious peasant unrest developed in southern Italy that a breakup of some of the most inefficient estates was undertaken in 1950. An isolated measure, this did little to relieve the plight of the peasantry.

In West Germany, the demand for comprehensive social reforms was also widespread. Not only the leftist parties, but also the middle-of-the-road Christian Democratic Union advocated the nationalization of coal mines and other key industries and called for state planning of the economy. These plans were abandoned, however, as the conservative wing of the party, led by Konrad Adenauer (1876–1967), became the dominant element. Yet while Germany returned to a private enterprise economy under Christian Democratic auspices, the economy was not a laissez-faire system. Ludwig Erhard, the creator of the German "social market economy," insisted that free enterprise could operate effectively only within the framework of social responsibility. By 1954 West Germany set aside a larger percentage of its gross national product for social security programs (14 per cent) than any other nation in western Europe.

Social Problems and the Marshall Plan. In Britain and the Scandinavian countries the reforms introduced were effective enough to safeguard domestic peace. Life was not easy in Britain in the immediate postwar period, but hardships were shared equitably by all. The austerity program imposed by the need for restricting imports was readily observed, and there were no black markets of any significance to offset price and rationing controls. Nor did the workers rebel against their difficult lot; they were satisfied that they did not bear a disproportionate share of the sacrifices that had to be made.

In France and Italy, on the other hand, inequitable taxation, inflation, and food shortages frequently aggravated by flourishing black markets canceled out any social gains. Life for the French and Italian worker was hard, and the burdens he had to bear were made even heavier by the knowledge that he was the victim of grave social injustices. His discontent was expressed in the large following the Communist parties enjoyed in both countries. Communism seemed the more attractive to many as the Socialists were torn by dissension. Undecided as to whether to work more closely with the Communists or the bourgeois parties, the Socialists thus lacked drive and failed to appeal to new voters. (In Italy the Socialist Party broke up into two separate factions over this issue.)

Communist militancy was at first restrained, in keeping with Moscow's directives, and Communists sat in both the French and Italian governments. Yet when non-Communist unions in France launched strikes to protest labor's plight early in 1947, the Communists joined them so as not to lose control of their own followers. They were promptly dismissed from the government. Their exclusion, it was believed, would also facilitate securing American aid—a hope that also led to the expulsion of the Communists from the Italian government in June 1947. In the deepening Cold War, and urged on by the Cominform, the Communists became more aggressive, and strikes led by them in France and Italy in 1947–48 assumed near-insurrectionary proportions.

At this point, Marshall Plan money began to flow into western Europe. By providing food and employment it helped to meet the most basic needs of the workers. But although the further increase of Communism was checked, the movement did not decline significantly. The major beneficiaries of the European Recovery Program were the upper and middle classes; its benefits, apart from providing the minimum necessities, were slow to trickle down to the workers. Real wages did not increase and the gap between the well-to-do business class and the workers remained wide. Millions continued to support the Communists from a deeply felt sense of social injustice, and this attitude did not change until the mid-1950's when Europe's spreading prosperity brought about a marked improvement in the condition of all classes.

THE CRUMBLING OF EMPIRE

Changes in Sovereignty. Economic difficulties were heightened by the disintegration of many of the colonial empires. Nationalist movements, aiming at independence, had existed in most colonies for some time; these movements gained greatly in strength when the colonial powers suffered crushing defeats in the war. By 1945, with the myth of the white man's superiority shattered, the demand for an end to colonial rule was widespread in Europe's Asian and African possessions.

The British Empire was liquidated under the auspices of the Labor Party which had long been opposed to colonialism. India was the first colony to receive its independence; partitioned along religious lines (Hindu and Moslem), it was divided into two separate states, India and Pakistan. A year later, in 1948, Burma and Ceylon acquired statehood. India, Pakistan, and Ceylon retained some ties with Britain by becoming members of the Commonwealth of Nations—thus renamed to accommodate members of non-British background. Arrangements with Malaya proved more difficult, owing to the conflicting interests of Malaya's mixed population (Malay, Chinese, and Indian), and in 1948 the British found themselves involved in a costly jungle war against Communist-led Malay guerrillas. Only after the insurrection was suppressed in 1953 was Malaya launched on the road to self-government. The League mandate of Trans-Jordan was ended in 1946 and an independent kingdom of Jordan set up in its place. The neighboring mandate of Palestine could not be liquidated as easily because of the rival claims of Jews and Arabs. The issue was submitted to the United Nations which proposed to partition the territory—a plan which neither Arabs and Jews would accept. On the withdrawal of the British in 1948, war broke out between the newly formed Jewish republic of Israel and the adjacent Arab states; after some years the conflict subsided into an uneasy truce.

France granted its colonies some participation in government within a newly formed French Union of mother country and overseas territories; except for the Communists, even the leftist parties were unwilling to let the colonies sever all connections with metropolitan France. However, the demand for full independence did not subside. Algeria, Morocco, and Tunisia were troubled by continuous unrest, and an open rebellion broke out in Madagascar. Although for the time being the French retained control of their African lands, they could not maintain themselves in Indo-China. In December 1947 war broke out in Vietnam between them and native insurgents led by the Communist chieftain Ho Chi Minh, and after some years of intermittent fighting, the French were defeated. In 1954 Vietnam was "provisionally" divided into two parts—the northern sector to be ruled by the Communists under Ho Chi Minh and the southern region set up at least nominally as a democratic republic. The other sections of Indo-China, Cambodia and Laos, had been granted independence in 1949.

The Dutch, on returning to their East Indian possessions after the war, found native forces in control of the islands. The Indonesians, led by the Nationalist leader Sukarno, insisted on obtaining complete independence whereas the Dutch wished to accord them only domestic self-government. War broke out in 1947 and lasted until 1949, when The Hague, unable to carry on, recognized Indonesia as a sovereign state.

Italy lost its colonies as the result of the war, except for Italian Somaliland. This it retained as a United Nations trusteeship until Somalia obtained independence in 1959.

Where no immediate changes in sovereignty occurred, as in the African possessions of France, Britain, and Belgium, economic development programs were initiated to raise living standards and prepare the way for eventual local self-government. Efforts were also made to improve and expand educational facilities and social conditions. Only Spain and Portugal refrained from making any major concessions to the changing times. Their possessions were among the least developed, untroubled as yet by movements for independence.

The Impact on Europe. Self-government could be conceded the more easily to the colonies because of the growing feeling in most mother countries that colonialism had had its day. In Britain large parts of the nation opposed it on moral grounds; moreover, the maintenance of garrisons in India and Palestine until they became independent were a heavy drain on Britain's manpower and financial resources. In France, too, there was an increasing unwillingness to sacrifice lives and money to retain control of the colonies. The French government never dared to use draftees in the war in Vietnam, but had to rely upon volunteers. France also paid heavily for the conflict in Vietnam: the French committed over one-fourth of their army to that war, and half of their military budget was claimed by the fighting. As for the Dutch, their campaign against Indonesia proved a similar burden which they could not long bear, quite apart from the fact that the small Dutch nation was unable to cope with eighty million rebellious Indonesians. On the other hand, Germany's freedom from all colonial responsibilities doubtless contributed to the country's astounding economic recovery, and

Italy's economic upswing was similarly aided by the fact that it was no longer burdened with colonies that had been a liability rather than an asset.

The loss of the colonies saved the mother countries substantial expenditures, but it did also involve severe economic losses. The British and the Dutch, it is true, retained their investments in India and Indonesia, respectively, and the French saved theirs in the non-Communist part of Vietnam, but much property was destroyed in the war and the post-war fighting. Moreover, some of the newly formed countries wished to embark on economic policies of their own rather than supplement the economies of their former European masters. Only in the remaining colonies could development projects be launched to help meet the needs of the mother country.

DOMESTIC POLITICS IN THE COUNTRIES OF WESTERN EUROPE

Britain. Joining the general trend to the left, the British people entrusted their postwar fortunes to a Labor government headed by Clement R. Attlee, long-time leader of the Labor Party and Deputy Prime Minister in Churchill's war government. The parliamentary elections of July 1945 gave Labor 393 seats in the House of Commons as against 189 for the Conservatives and 58 for all other groups including 12 Liberals. This was not a sign of ingratitude towards Churchill; the deep respect and affection in which Churchill was held during the remaining years of his life clearly refute the charge that the country did not appreciate his achievements. Those who turned to the Labor Party simply considered it more responsive to their domestic concerns.

The social reform program on which the new government embarked has been discussed; in the present context it need only be added that the Conservative opposition did not challenge the merits of Labor's program but objected primarily to individual procedural features. For this reason the expanded free medical services and other increased social benefits did not encounter any strong opposition even though they increased the costs of production not inconsiderably.

By rendering Britain less competitive in foreign markets, the new social services added to the country's economic difficulties. These were already serious as a result of the war, postwar commitments, and an exceptionally cold winter in 1946–47 that brought production virtually to a standstill in some parts of the country. Britain's financial position was further imperiled by sudden price rises in the United States after the removal of American price controls in 1946; the price increases reduced by one-third the purchasing power of a $3.75 billion loan that Washington had granted to London a few months before. Throughout the immediate postwar period the government thus was forced to insist on rigid austerity to husband its scant foreign balances and insure the import of foodstuffs and raw materials. The country accepted the need for governmental restrictions and submitted to continued rationing and heavy taxation until with the influx of Marshall Plan aid conditions began to improve.

The one serious political clash that arose between government and opposition developed over the nationalization of steel. The issue, it will be recalled, was political rather than economic. The Conservatives could not prevent the passage of the Steel Nationalization Bill by the House of Commons, but the House of Lords tried to hold up the enactment for two years, which it could do through its suspensive veto. Labor insisted that as undemocratic a body as the Lords ought not to be able to block a decision of the Commons for so long a time and secured an amendment reducing the Lords' veto power to one year. In the end the Lords refrained from delaying the enactment of the bill for even a year because the government promised not to proceed with the nationalization before the parliamentary elections due in 1950. The country was to decide whether the Steel Nationalization Act was to be carried out or repealed.

The elections of 1950 were uneventful. Labor ran on its record, and the Conservatives on their part accepted the welfare state. As for nationalization, they objected primarily to its further extension. On foreign policy there was even less disagreement between the two parties. Labor nevertheless suffered a sharp setback, obtaining only 315 seats (against the Conservatives' 298) and an overall majority of no more than six. While there was no marked disagreement on substantive issues, the electorate was almost evenly divided on who would be more successful in dealing with them.

Attlee's second government lacked the drive and determination of the first. It nationalized the iron and steel industries, but despite its election promises undertook no further social reforms. Under the impact of the Korean War living standards began to decline again, and new price controls, tightened food rations, and higher taxes were imposed. Serious dissension developed in the Labor Party over the government's pro-American foreign policy on the grounds that it was politically unwise and economically ruinous. In October 1951 Attlee went once more to the country; the new elections gave Labor a plurality in the popular vote, but only 295 seats against the Conservatives' 321. The latter formed a new government under the seventy-six-year old Churchill as Prime Minister.

The change inaugurated a marked shift in policy. Steel, as expected, was denationalized but placed under the supervision of an Iron and Steel Board that had jurisdiction over prices, investments, and the importation and distribution of raw materials and steel products. Road transport, too, was returned to private ownership. For the rest, the government tried to encourage private enterprise by the removal of some controls and restrictions. Its policy was successful: production increased, and exports not only caught up with imports, but began to exceed them. As a result taxes could be reduced, and food rationing was gradually abandoned (the last rationed item, meat, was decontrolled in July 1954). Churchill's own efforts, however, were devoted mainly to foreign policy. Here the death of Stalin in March 1953 seemed to offer new opportunities to ease East-West tensions (see Chapter 21).

France. De Gaulle emerged as the unchallenged leader in liberated France and was able to restore order quickly after the retreat of the Germans. Still, during the first few weeks after liberation, local vigilante committees executed a large number of Vichyites and collaborators without proper judicial procedures. Once order had been established, all further purges were handled by special courts. Altogether about 100,000 persons were brought to trial; of these, 80,000 were sentenced to penalties ranging from loss of civil rights to death. Of the 2,000 death sentences, 800 were carried out. Among those executed was Pierre Laval, whereas Pétain's death sentence was commuted to lifetime imprisonment on the Ile d'Yeu, a small island in the gulf of Biscay. (Pétain died in 1951.)

The next major task that awaited the nation was the drafting of a constitution for what became known as the Fourth Republic. Elections for a constituent assembly were held in October 1945; for the first time women were given the right to vote. The Communists emerged as the largest party with 152 seats; the newly founded Republican Popular Movement, a Catholic left-of-center party calling for social reforms and economic planning, followed closely with 151 seats; the Socialist Party took third place with 132 seats. The Radicals and the center and rightist parties together obtained less than 100 seats. The country made clear that it had no wish to return to the middle-of-the-road Third Republic.

The assembly unanimously elected De Gaulle President-Premier, but it refused to draft the kind of constitution for which he called and which would have given him far-reaching executive powers. Instead, Socialists and Communists proposed a strong one-house parliament, without any upper house to serve as a conservative brake. De Gaulle thereupon resigned his office, expecting apparently that the country would soon recall him on his own terms. In a referendum in May 1946 the nation rejected the proposed constitution lest it pave the way to a Communist dictatorship.

New elections gave the MRP a plurality (160 seats); the Communists all but held their own with 146 seats while the Socialist delegation was reduced to 115. The size of the other parties remained largely unchanged. A newly drafted constitution provided for a two-house parliament, with the powers of the upper house severely limited. In its preamble the new constitution assured every citizen of the right to realize his potentialities, and declared him entitled to material security, health protection, and rest and leisure. In all other essentials the new law revived the political system of the Third Republic. Perhaps for this reason little more than one-third of the electorate (9.2 million) voted for it, while 8.1 million rejected it and the remaining nine million abstained from voting.

Throughout this period an MRP-Socialist-Communist coalition governed the country. In May 1947, however, the Communists were forced out of the government. For the next decade France's political destiny rested mainly with a so-called Third Force, a coalition of Socialists, MRP, Radicals, Independents, and Peasants. The Third Force steered a cautious, tortuous course between the Communists on the left and the De Gaulle-sponsored Popular French Rally (RPF) on the right. The RPF had been founded after De Gaulle's retirement to work for his goals; its chief concern was to put an end to political instability by giving the government greater power. Being avowedly authoritarian, the movement was widely suspected of fascist aspirations.

The most immediate threat to the Third Force came, however, from the Communists. A poor harvest in 1947 drove up food prices to new heights and during the second half of that year price increases rose three times as fast as wage raises. Bread rations were reduced from 300 to 250 to 200 grams per day—an amount lower than had been available at any time during the war and a special hardship on a people for whom bread was the basic item on the daily menu. Working-class despair exploded into a wave of Communist-led strikes in the fall of 1947. In fanning the fires of discontent, the Communists also pursued political aims; urged on by the Cominform, they hoped so to disrupt the economy as to jeopardize the success of the Marshall Plan. The strikes thus had clearly revolutionary overtones, culminating in the seizure of town halls, prefectures, and public utilities. After some weeks the government suppressed this near-insurrection with the help of the army and special security forces. The strikes were resumed a year later when a succession of governments failed to alleviate the lot of the workers. Once more army and special police had to be called out to cope with the crisis. The miners' strike alone cost the country five and a half million tons of coal in lost output; this amount had to be bought out of ERP funds that had originally been earmarked for the purchase of industrial equipment.

In 1949 conditions began to improve. The increase in production sparked by the European Recovery Program led to a stabilization of prices and an improvement of living standards. Yet tax and other inequities were not remedied, and the Korean War imposed new strains on the economy.

New elections in 1951 produced a further swing to the right. To isolate Gaullists and Communists, the electoral law had been revised;

electoral alliances of the smaller parties were given the status of a single party to enable them to defeat the two major antidemocratic parties more easily. In this manner the Third Force obtained 253 seats while the Communists, though still the largest party in terms of the popular vote, received only 97 seats, and the Gaullists, now the largest party in the Assembly, 107. A new government was formed with Socialist support, though without Socialist participation. Traditionally anticlerical, the Socialists broke again with the government when the old troublesome Church–State issue was revived with the enactment of a law granting state subsidies to parents who sent their children to parochial schools. A substantial part of the RPF now swung its support behind the government and some of its members accepted ministerial portfolios—much to the dismay of De Gaulle, who angrily broke with the movement.

During the following years a number of governments headed by right-of-center Premiers, of whom Antoine Pinay was the most capable, tried to fight the perennial inflationary pressures by cutting government expenditures and investments. On the whole these efforts were ineffective because of the constantly mounting cost of the war in Indo-China. Yet there were also some hopeful signs. Despite all difficulties, France's industrial and agricultural output continued to grow. Similarly, a marked population increase, after decades of demographic stagnation, was proof that the nation had regained its vitality and was not afraid of the future.

Italy. One of the first major issues that Italy faced after the war concerned the future of the monarchy. The throne had been so closely associated with the Fascist regime that there was a widespread demand for its abolition. A plebiscite was held in June 1946; twelve million voted for the establishment of a republic while ten million favored retaining the monarchy. In the face of these returns, King Humbert II, who had just succeeded his father Victor Emmanuel III in order to improve the monarchist chances, left for exile in Portugal.

Concurrently with the referendum a constituent assembly was elected. It enacted a constitution that resembled in many ways that of pre-Fascist Italy. The major innovations concerned the substitution of an elected president for the hereditary king and an elected upper house for an appointed one. In addition, Mussolini's Lateran Treaty with the Vatican was incorporated into the new document, granting Catholicism the status of "sole religion of the state" and relegating all other religions to second-class status. Finally, women were given the vote, and every citizen was guaranteed the right to economic security and health protection.

Of the parties participating in the elections, the Christian Democrats emerged as the largest with eight million votes (35 per cent of the popular vote). The party called for social and economic reforms, but having close ties also with banking and industrial circles and with the Church, it was essentially a middle-of-the-road party. Thanks to the size of its following and the skill of its leader, Alcide de Gasperi (1881–1954), a pre-Fascist politician who had waited out the Fascist era as a Vatican librarian, it became the determining factor in Italian politics. The Socialist Party, with 4.7 million votes (20.7 per cent), quickly wore itself out in the continued internal wrangle over whether to collaborate with the bourgeoisie or the Communists. In 1947 the moderate minority led by Giuseppe Saragat broke away while the bulk of the party under Pietro Nenni, a veteran Marxist and one-time associate and prison mate of Mussolini in the Duce's Socialist days, aligned himself with the Communists. The Communists, on their part, obtained 4.3 million votes (18.9 per cent). They were led by Palmiro Togliatti, a lawyer who had spent most of the Fascist era in Moscow; under his leadership the party became the largest Communist Party in western Europe. A "Front of the Common Man" (*Uomo Qualunque*), a lower middle class party with Fascist overtones, drew 1.2 million votes (5.3 per cent); it catered to the grievances of its followers, contrasting their patriotism with the selfish maneuvering of the "politicians."

De Gasperi governed at first by means of a coalition with Socialists and Communists. It was an uneasy alliance in which the Christian Democrats, dedicated Catholics and the mainstay of the existing political and economic system, faced a Socialist-Communist bloc that wished to overhaul that entire system and replace it with a socialist state. In the spring of 1947, aided by the split in the Socialist ranks and assured of American economic assistance, De Gasperi managed to form a new government composed of Christian Democrats and some moderate conservatives. During the summer there was some improvement in the economic situation, and the upward trend continued as Marshall Plan aid arrived. Communist strikes directed against the European Recovery Program were suppressed, and businessmen and landowners who had been siding with *Uomo Qualunque* threw their support to the Christian Democrats.

In April 1948 the first elections were held under the new constitution. The campaign became a battle front of the Cold War; the Communists had seized power in Czechoslovakia only two months before, and there was fear that the Italian Communists along with the Nenni Socialists might win the elections and take Italy too into the Soviet camp. Both the Vatican and the United States came to the aid of the Christian Democrats, with Washington hinting broadly that a Communist Italy could not expect any further American help. Italian-Americans organized a letter campaign with official encouragement, asking their relatives in Italy to vote against Communism. Christian Democracy won the elections, gaining an absolute majority with 307 out of 574 seats in the

Chamber, while the Communists obtained 135 seats and the Socialists, 51.

During the following years the country's economic improvement continued. The discovery of natural gas and oil in the Po Valley and the construction of new hydroelectric plants provided additional sources of energy for industrial expansion. Yet unemployment remained a serious problem, and land reform lagged. When the Korean War created new economic difficulties, discontent grew. In local elections in 1951 and 1952 the Christian Democrats suffered setbacks while Communists, monarchists, and a neo-Fascist party, the Italian Social Movement, scored significant gains. As in France, efforts were made to strengthen the position of the democratic parties. A new electoral law provided that any party or group of parties polling more than 50 per cent of the vote would automatically obtain 380 seats instead of the 295 to which it would normally be entitled. The remaining 210 seats were to be divided among the opposing parties in proportion to the votes they received.[1] However, in the elections in 1953 the electoral coalition of Christian Democrats, Saragat's Social Democrats, Liberals, and Republicans received only 49.85 per cent of the vote. De Gasperi, unable to form a majority government, was forced to resign. With his departure from the political stage—he died a year later—Italian politics reverted to their earlier instability.

West Germany.   The Basic Law which inaugurated the West German state in May 1949 established it as a federal republic composed of (at present) ten states. In this as well as in several other respects the Basic Law resembled the Weimar Constitution; like the latter, it provided for a President, a two-house parliament, and a government responsible to the lower house, the Bundestag. Some important changes, however, were introduced to prevent a renewed erosion of parliamentary democracy by a totalitarian movement. The Chancellor can be removed by a no-confidence vote only if the Bundestag is prepared to elect a successor—an arrangement that renders ineffective the formation of purely negative opposition blocs. On the other hand, emergency powers are no longer entrusted to the President, who is not responsible to the parliament, but to the Chancellor, who is. The Bill of Rights, symbolically, heads rather than concludes the constitution as it did in the Weimar document; anti-democratic parties are unconstitutional; the federal flag is black-red-gold.[2] The election system, according to the Electoral Law of 1949, is based on a combination of single member districts and nation-wide

---

[1] The arrangement revived unhappy memories of a somewhat similar arrangement that Mussolini had made in 1924 to secure an absolute majority for the Fascists in the Italian Chamber.

[2] One of the few things East and West Germany share is the national colors, but the East German flag displays a hammer and sickle in the upper left-hand corner.

proportional representation; the states divide the seats allotted to them into the two categories on a (now) fifty–fifty basis. In 1957, to do away with small splinter groups, parties were excluded from proportional representation unless they received 5 per cent of the national vote or won seats directly in at least three districts.

In the first national elections in August 1949 the middle-of-the road Christian Democratic Union emerged as the largest party, with 139 seats. Its leader, seventy-three-year-old Konrad Adenauer, had been an outstanding Lord Mayor of Cologne from 1917 to 1933. During the Nazi era Adenauer had lived quietly in retirement, carefully staying out of all oppositional activities, but had been imprisoned twice by the Nazis as politically suspect. After a brief spell as Cologne's first postwar Mayor he had devoted himself to the organization of the Christian Democrats. Adenauer was an extraordinary mixture of enlightened statesman, shrewd tactician, and cynical autocrat whose high-handedness was tempered by his deep religious commitment. Following closely on the heels of the Christian Democrats were the Social Democrats with 131 seats. A revival of the Weimar party, they were still nominal Marxists, but in practice resembled the British Labor Party in their objectives. Under the leadership of Kurt Schumacher, a former editor and Reichstag deputy who had spent ten of the twelve Nazi years in concentration camps, the party assumed a strongly nationalist stance to wipe out its Weimar image of lack of patriotism and to appeal to middle class voters.

The third largest party, the Free Democratic Party, obtained 52 seats. Its following was an odd mixture of old-time liberals and conservative businessmen whose only connection with liberalism was their faith in free enterprise. The leader of the party was Theodor Heuss, a publicist and Reichstag deputy in Weimar days, who was elected the first President of the Bonn Republic. Under his successors in the party leadership, the Free Democrats became increasingly conservative and eventually were closely identified with big business interests. The other parties ranging from Communists to neo-Nazis elected but a handful of deputies.[3]

The first government of the new state was a coalition of Christian Democrats, Free Democrats, and the German Party, a minor rightist party of farmers and small businessmen whose 17 votes helped to provide the needed majority. Adenauer became Chancellor, and Ludwig Erhard (1897–   ), an economist from Bavaria, Minister of Economics. Their foremost domestic task was the rehabilitation of the economy—a formidable undertaking that seemed even more difficult because of the presence of some ten million refugees and expellees from the Soviet occupation zone and eastern Europe, respectively. As it turned out, the

---

[3] Neo-Nazis and Communists were outlawed as unconstitutional in 1952 and 1956, respectively.

special skills and the industry of the newcomers proved a singular boon to Erhard's "social market economy." Economic revival was also speeded by German disarmament. Without an armed force, Germany was able to concentrate fully on its economic rehabilitation whereas most European countries had to allot substantial parts of their manpower and resources to increased military preparations.

Germany's reunification was at first the dominant political issue. Adenauer, despairing of an early solution, pursued a policy of close collaboration with the Western Powers, especially the United States. For this he was sharply attacked by the Socialists, who accused him of jeopardizing what chances of reunification still existed. As time went on, a growing number of West Germans came to look upon reunification as an increasingly remote goal, the attainment of which depended not on them but on Moscow and Washington.

After the outbreak of the Korean War the problem of reunification became intertwined with that of rearmament. Many Germans rejected the Allied demand for a German military contribution to Europe's defense on the grounds that it would further deepen the division of Germany. Others objected because they considered a military defense hopeless or a dangerous provocation of Russia. Adenauer backed the call for a German army for both political and military reasons. Without such a contribution to Western defense efforts, he was fearful of losing the good will of the United States; at the same time he viewed such a force as a counterweight against the East German people's police. The latter was much more heavily armed than its West German counterpart, and the Chancellor worried that its superiority, if unchallenged, might invite border forays. The Social Democrats and various neutralist groups, on the other hand, opposed the creation of a new German army. In March 1953 parliament finally approved rearmament by a simple majority. The Socialists challenged the move before the Federal Constitutional Court on the grounds that the Basic Law did not provide for an army; for this reason, the formation of such an army could be authorized only by a constitutional amendment requiring two-thirds majorities in both houses. The Bundestag elections in September 1953 produced an impressive victory for Adenauer and the Christian Democrats, who obtained 45 per cent of the vote. With the help of the Free Democrats and several of the smaller parties Adenauer secured the needed two-thirds majority for amending the Basic Law.

The Low Countries. Belgium and the Netherlands, although sharing the same fate during World War II, faced rather different problems at the end of the conflict. Belgium had suffered relatively little physical damage and had accumulated substantial dollar balances in 1944–45. At that time Antwerp had been the only large harbor left intact on the North Sea coast (thanks to the Belgian Resistance, which had foiled

German attempts to destroy the docks), and Antwerp's port facilities thus had earned Belgium considerable foreign exchange. Belgium had also retained full control of its Congo colony; the Congo's rich uranium deposits, of special value in the nuclear age, became an important new source of wealth for the mother country.

The Netherlands, on the other hand, faced grave economic difficulties. Large parts of its agricultural area had been flooded, and the destruction of homes and industrial plants was far more extensive than in Belgium. The country soon found itself involved in a costly conflict with its East Indian colonies. Yet the Dutch set to work with a will; the flooded areas were drained within less than a year, and reconstruction got under way at once. In 1948 industrial production, which had been reduced to half its peacetime capacity by the end of the war, reached prewar levels once more.

That year the Netherlands, Belgium, and Luxembourg established the Benelux customs union. Owing to the existing disparities, the union did not at first remove any internal barriers and created only a common external tariff. During the 1950's, however, internal tariffs, quota restrictions, and tax differentials were removed, and free internal trade and a common labor market were established. By 1960 Benelux foreign trade had doubled and internal trade was three times as large as in 1948.

Politically, Belgium, unlike the Netherlands, had to wrestle with serious troubles after the war. Many Belgians objected to the restoration of King Leopold III on the throne. The King, though calling himself a prisoner of war, had spent the war in a castle near Brussels and to the dismay of his subjects had even remarried, a privilege not ordinarily granted to prisoners of war. A large part of the nation objected also to his capitulation in 1940 and suspected him and his wife of pro-Nazi associations. Since Leopold's supporters and opponents were fairly evenly divided, the issue was not settled until 1950 when the King abdicated in favor of his son Baudoin. In addition, the old rivalries between Walloons and Flemings kept troubling the country and led to a redistribution of parliamentary seats in favor of the Flemish regions.

Compared to these tensions, the disputes between the Dutch parties, mainly Labor and Catholics, seemed very minor. Queen Wilhelmina, who had spent the war years in Britain, retained the respect of her people; however, because of age and ill health, she, too, abdicated in 1948 and was succeeded by her daughter, Juliana.

In foreign affairs both Belgium and the Netherlands abandoned their prewar stance of neutrality and joined the Western European Union and NATO.

The Scandinavian Countries.   Norway, Sweden, and Denmark found it comparatively easy to return to their peacetime ways. Except for some shipping losses Sweden and Denmark emerged intact from the war. Only

Norway suffered extensive physical damage. The country's financial position, however, happened to be rather strong since the Norwegian government returned from exile with substantial funds earned by its merchant marine or received as indemnity for ships that were lost. By the careful use of these holdings in combination with an austerity program of exceptional severity, the country managed to rebuild rapidly what had been destroyed. Yet all three nations depended on foreign trade for the maintenance of adequate living standards, and thus all of them were affected by the plight of the rest of Europe. By its promotion of international trade the European Recovery Program started them back on the road to full rehabilitation.

Politically, the Scandinavian countries experienced none of the difficulties that plagued most other European countries after the war. At home they continued on their moderately socialist course. The most striking departure occurred in the field of foreign affairs when Norway and Denmark gave up their traditional neutrality and joined NATO. In 1952 Norway, Sweden, Denmark, and Iceland established the Nordic Council to facilitate collaboration among them; one of the Council's accomplishments has been to obtain for nationals of a member country residing in another member country the social and economic rights enjoyed by the citizens of the host country.

Switzerland. As a neutral, Switzerland was little changed by the war, and its domestic alignments resembled largely the prewar pattern. Unlike France, Italy, and such other latecomers as Belgium and Greece, the nation rejected proposals to give women the right to vote; on the other hand, the Swiss followed the general trend towards the welfare state and adopted, by referendum, a comprehensive social insurance program. They continued to cling to their traditional neutrality and entered neither the Western European Union nor NATO, nor did Switzerland become a member of the United Nations. However, the Swiss did join some of the affiliated UN agencies.

The Iberian Dictatorships. Spain was the only fascist regime to survive the war intact. To assure the continued support of army and Church, both monarchist strongholds, Franco promulgated an Act of Succession in 1947 which called for the installation of a king upon his death or retirement. Yet the monarchy was only to be restored if a person of royal blood could be found who would maintain the existing political system. A concordat signed with the Vatican in 1953 confirmed Catholicism as the "only religion of the Spanish peoples." It conceded the Church a dominant influence on education. Non-Catholics, on the other hand, could not hold public office or become officers in the armed forces and were barred from editorial positions on newspapers. That same year Franco also proclaimed a general amnesty for all those convicted of political offenses committed during the Civil War, and dropping pending charges against all Republicans, he urged exiles to return to Spain. Yet there was no restoration of civil liberties, and all publications, movies, and radio remained subject to censorship.

Spain's most immediate domestic problem was its desperate economic situation. No major rehabilitation of the areas devastated during the Civil War was possible during World War II. After the war, as an associate of Hitler and Mussolini, the Franco regime was ostracized by the Western Powers and excluded from Marshall Plan aid and other assistance. Given Spain's scant resources, its antiquated land system, and the lack of enterprise of its business class, abject poverty remained widespread. The average annual agricultural production during 1948–1952 was still below the annual average for the years 1931–1935. Industrial production, on the other hand, doubled and in some cases tripled between 1935 and 1954. The workers benefited but little from this expansion. A United Nations survey found that in 1953 the standard of living of Spanish workers and peasants was 10 to 30 per cent lower than before the Civil War (even when allowance was made for increased social benefits).

The masses were still too exhausted by the Civil War to rebel against these conditions, but as that conflict receded into the background in the mid–1950's, discontent began to manifest itself more openly in strikes and demonstrations. At that very time, however, American funds began to flow into Spain in return for the establishment by the United States of naval and air bases on Spanish soil. They injected a badly needed stimulus into the Spanish economy and in so doing, contributed materially to the strengthening of the Franco regime.

In Portugal, Premier Salazar continued to keep a tight grip on the country. To disguise the authoritarian nature of his regime, he permitted opposition candidates to participate in elections, but he either forced them out of the race or annulled the returns whenever they showed unexpected strength. In 1953 Salazar launched a six-year Development Plan to promote electrification and transport as the essential basis for industrial growth; some funds were also allotted for the development of Portugal's African colonies. A second six-year plan was launched in 1959 to develop both agriculture and industry. Owing to the lack of private initiative, an increasing number of the new enterprises were state owned; their earnings provided a substantial part of the government's revenue.

Greece.   In earlier chapters Greece had been viewed as a part of eastern Europe, but in a discussion of the post-World War II scene it must properly be considered as belonging, politically, to western Europe.

Devastated during the war, the country found its plight deepened by the civil war that kept it in turmoil through the late 1940's. The struggle was aggravated by the selfishness and corruption of influential elements in the government camp and by the ineptness and demoralization of the Greek army. Greece had no income tax, which put the bulk of the tax burden on the masses, and no control over foreign exchange, which allowed those who had dollar funds to invest them abroad while the United States was underwriting the dollar deficits of the country. Similarly, a flourishing black market was fed by supplies from UNRRA and other foreign aid sources. Many non-Communists joined the Communist rebels, and the government was afraid to equip the rural population with arms against the guerrillas lest the peasants use the rifles against government forces. The unpopularity of the government was of considerable help to the insurgents, as was the aid and protection given the latter by Greece's Communist neighbors. In December 1947 the rebel leaders felt strong enough to proclaim the establishment of a "Democratic Greek Government" in the "free mountains of Greece." It was not until 1949 that the government forces, retrained and equipped by the United States and aided by Tito's closing of his frontier, defeated the rebels in their main mountain strongholds.

The government camp, however, was plagued by continued political instability. The monarchy was retained by popular decision, but King George II who was brought home from exile in 1946 was not a popular figure. What prestige the monarchy did recover, it owed primarily to Queen Frederika, the energetic social-minded wife of George's successor, Paul I. Yet the influence of the throne was not strong enough to bolster the authority of the government. Cabinets followed each other in rapid succession, and it took a national hero, Field Marshal Alexander Papagos, leader of the Greek army against the Italians in 1940, to form the first stable postwar government in 1952. Under him and his successor, Constantine Karamanlis, the country applied itself to its economic rehabilitation, and in the mid-1950's economic conditions began to improve. Thanks to an effective long-range program inaugurated in 1959, and the large-scale migration of surplus labor to France and West Germany, the economy continued to expand into the mid-1960's. Beginning in 1965, however, political differences began to upset once more the stability of the country. Claiming that Greece was threatened by a Communist coup, a junta of army officers seized power in April 1967 and set up a tight military dictatorship.

Throughout the 1950s' Greece was involved with Britain and Turkey in a fierce dispute over the future of the British colony of Cyprus. The issue was finally settled in 1959 when all three countries agreed on the independence of Cyprus. Even then clashes between the island's Greek majority and Turkish minority kept tension alive between Greece and Turkey, and in 1963 the United Nations had to intervene to prevent the outbreak of war.

THE CULTURAL SCENE

Existentialism. No brilliant cultural flowering burst forth after the Second World War as it had after the first. Many of the great writers and artists who might have launched a renaissance of the arts had gone into exile or perished in concentration camps, and new talents who could have enriched the postwar world with their work had died in battle or as Resistance fighters or were never allowed to develop their creative ability in the stifling atmosphere of totalitarianism.

The most significant cultural phenomenon of the immediate postwar era was existentialism—not an original contribution of the times, but rather the activation of a philosophical attitude that traces back to the nineteenth-century Danish philosopher Sören Kierkegaard and in the interwar period received a strong stimulus from the German philosopher, Martin Heidegger. In the bewildered and anguished atmosphere of Continental Europe it attracted widespread attention, for it seemed to provide answers to the most pressing moral problems of the day. In its most influential postwar version, that of the French philosopher and writer Jean-Paul Sartre (1905–   ) and his disciples, existentialism maintained that man's existence, being propelled by consciousness, was more than mere physical essence. From this it concluded in Sartre's words that "the destiny of man is placed within himself." Thus man, according to Sartre, was not the hapless object of impersonal historical forces. He did have choices, even though they were subject to severe limitations in an alien and hostile world in which he was standing essentially alone. These choices were often difficult and required great courage, and the temptation was great to avoid them (which was also a choice), especially in an age in which mass media of communication and an ever-growing bureaucracy exerted their leveling impact on human existence.

Holding man morally responsible for what he did or did not do, the existentialists also addressed themselves to the problem of responsibility for the crimes of totalitarian dictatorships. The German existentialist philosopher, Karl Jaspers (1883–   ), noted that although crime was an individual act and there could be therefore no collective criminal guilt, the individual German who passively tolerated the Nazi regime, let alone supported it, bore a moral responsibility for the crimes it committed. This moral responsibility was not covered by any law and could be atoned for only by individual moral regeneration. Jaspers recognized also a collective political responsibility of all Germans for the actions of the Nazi government. This latter responsibility, he maintained, imposed upon the nation the obligation to make amends to the victims of Nazism —a responsibility which the West German state acknowledged in a series of restitution and indemnity laws.

Literature. Existentialist themes, mirroring the anguish and soul searching of the postwar era, were also dominant in the literature of those years. Some of the existentialist thinkers like Sartre sought to convey their ideas by means of poems, novels, and plays (*The Wall, The Roads to Liberty, No Exit*) in which their heroes "exist" in a bewildering world, sometimes outwitted by absurd coincidences, sometimes trying to deceive themselves into being something they are not, or to escape responsibility and commitment. In the end they can find inner peace and freedom only by being true to themselves, assuming all the burdens and perils that moral integrity involves.

Sartre's fellow countryman, Albert Camus (1913–1959), also explored the meaning of human existence in a world increasingly mechanized, bureaucratized, and self-destructive. In his novel *The Stranger* the central figure symbolizes the depersonalized nature and loneliness of modern mass man in a world that resents his lack of feelings, but whose own display of emotions is in reality no more than a hollow pretense. In his best known novel, *The Plague,* Camus probed the reactions of a community under severe emotional and physical stress—the childish sensationalism of some, the cowardice and opportunism of others, the resigned fatalism of still others, but also the sense of community, the heroism, the self-denying dedication to help one another that crisis inspires in some men. Similar themes dominate the plays of Jean Anouilh; they also center on the anguish of human "existence," of choosing between right and wrong in a world that wishes to suppress these choices. Anouilh's heroes wrestle in vain with their plight and in the end find their release in assuming a false role, committing suicide, allowing themselves to be sent to the gallows, or by simply withdrawing into themselves. Whether or not these writers had answers to the dilemmas of life, they at least called attention to the predicaments of the human condition.

To Frenchmen writing under the impact of the horrors of war and despotic totalitarianism, the purpose of life and the meaning of human freedom were the paramount issues; to German writers the questions of guilt and moral responsibility were of overriding concern. These issues were discussed in two notable works on life in the concentration camps, Ernst Wiechert's *Forest of the Dead* and Eugen Kogon's memoir, *The Theory and Practice of Hell.* Similar problems were taken up in the novels of Elisabeth Langgässer (*The Quest*) and Werner Bergengrün (*Dies Irae*), whose culprits were redeemed in the end by religious faith. But dissenting voices were not entirely muted, and a one-time Free Corps fighter and nationalist author, Ernst von Salomon, protested in his semi-autobiographical novel, *The Questionnaire,* that not every right-wing opponent of the Weimar Republic was a Nazi and that because of the Western Powers' insistence to sit in judgment on such intangible questions as political guilt and moral responsibility, there was little to choose between Nazism and the democracies. Among the younger writers the physical and psychological wreckage left by war and Nazism called forth frightening pictures of the confusion, the cynicism and sterility of those postwar years. This disillusionment dominated not only the works of German authors, but also those of such Swiss writers as Friedrich Duerrenmatt (*The Visit; The Pledge*) and Max Frisch (*Homo Faber; The Chinese Wall*) and some Belgian and Dutch playwrights and novelists.

Italians, on the other hand, paid less attention to the problem of the individual in relation to his environment—just as politically they looked more leniently on their Fascist fellow citizens than did other nations on theirs. Italian authors, calling themselves "neorealists," were more concerned with social hypocrisy, with the misery of the masses, and with the pervasive terror of a ruthless dictatorship. Nor did they abandon themselves to the glum despair of human nature that haunted so much contemporary German and French writing, but rather saw some gleam of light even in the darkest corners of life. Among the best of their postwar novels were Carlo Levi's *Christ Stopped at Eboli* and Alberto Moravia's *The Conformist*.

English postwar literature also showed little interest in the existentialist concerns of the Continent—perhaps because Britain had not shared the nightmare experience of Nazism. Most English writers did not view moral decay or social alienation as problems posed to the individual by a corrupt or irrational world. To Rebecca West (*The Meaning of Treason*), treason was an individual aberration, not the product of a disintegrating society; and critics of social conventionalism (Kingsley Amis, *Lucky Jim*) and social climbing (John Braine, *Room at the Top*) felt that these problems could best be dealt with in a light vein. Similarly, George Orwell launched his attacks on Communist totalitarianism (*The Animal Farm; Nineteen Eighty-Four*) in the form of satirical fantasies. William Golding, on the other hand, in dealing with fascism in his allegory *Lord of the Flies*, used a more direct existentialist approach to picture the degradation and self-destruction to which people can be driven by terror and bigotry. C. P. Snow saw man as holding his own against the encroachments of technology and bureaucracy in his multivolume sequence of novels, *Strangers and Brothers*.

On the whole the postwar era produced few works of European stature. Next to Sartre and Camus, Thomas Mann must again be mentioned (see p. 245); while living in the United States, Mann continued to write in German and considered himself a European rather than an American author. In his masterful novel, *Doctor Faustus*, he told in allegorical form the story of modern Germany. The book, painting a vast panorama of German social and cultural life since the turn of the century, presents a devastating indictment of the dehumanization of modern civilization. In its artistic sensitivity, its profound psychological insights and political probings, *Doctor Faustus* may well come to be ranked as Mann's greatest achievement. During those dark years, Europe brought forth also some outstanding works of pure art; among these, mention ought at least to be made of the poetry of the Welshman Dylan Thomas and of the beautifully wrought short stories of the Danish authoress Isak Dinesen.

The Creative Arts.   Painters and sculptors, too, concerned themselves with man's vulnerable position in a complex world. This basic human dilemma was strikingly expressed in the sculptures of the Italo-Swiss artist Alberto Giacometti (1901–1966). His figures, reduced to their essence in their bone-thin structure, faceless and without expression, moving about without discernible purpose, seem lost, as it were, in

Alberto Giacometti, *City Square* (La Place). (Collection, The Museum of Modern Art, New York)

nothingness; but as one critic has written, "standing in proximity to each other, [they] seem to exist by virtue of their neighbors. . . . Here is the . . . existentialist . . . paradox: Man exists always in a situation, and yet, another entity, *his own life*, stands in relief, alone."[4] The same questioning mood, tempered, however, by subtle irony, pervades the work of the French painter, Jean Dubuffet. In one characteristic picture Dubuffet painted a man with the head and mane of a lion, but sought to point up his essential helplessness in the bewildered expression of his face and the despairing gesturing of his hands. A similar skepticism about human nature was reflected in the works of the Cobra group (Copenhagen, Brussels, Amsterdam) of Danish, Belgian, and Dutch painters.

[4] Dore Ashton, *The Unknown Shore: A View of Contemporary Art* (Boston and Toronto, 1962), pp. 145–46. Italics in original.

In a strange, puzzling world in which so much defied rational explanation, artists also sought refuge in fantasy, some of them delving back into the probings of a surrealist dream world (Juan Miró, Wolfgang Schulze [Wols]), others returning to ancient myths and beliefs (Marc Chagall). The most desperate expression of postwar disenchantment was the school of *tachisme* (from the French word for *stain*) whose canvasses were torn and singed, symbolizing the destructiveness of the times (for example, the painting-collages of the Italian artist, Alberto Burri). On the other hand, the sculptures of Britain's outstanding artist, Henry Moore (1898–   ), even when they were reduced to near-skeletal proportions, conveyed an inherent vitality, inspiring, in Moore's own words, "a stimulation to greater effort of living." As such, they were suggestive perhaps of Britain's undaunted spirit in those dark years.

Architecture.   As after the First World War, architecture was also the most affirmative of the arts after the Second. Moving away from the functionalism of the prewar era, it assumed a new artistic awareness. If writers and painters concerned themselves with the darker aspects of life, architects sought to show, as a French group announced, that they could create "a world where dreams can still find a place." Murals, mosaics, stained glass windows, sculptures, and bas reliefs came to adorn, not only official buildings and churches, but factories, schools, and apartment buildings as well. Color was no longer considered a decoration, but became an integral part of a building, and brilliant color schemes brightened the exterior as well as the interior of apartment houses from Sweden to Italy. Le Corbusier, who was an architect, painter and sculptor at the same time, developed this synthesis to its greatest perfection. Unlike the other arts, postwar architecture testified from the outset to that astounding vitality that was to burst forth in Europe once the worst after-effects of the war had been overcome.

Motion Pictures.   Of all entertainment media, motion pictures are as a rule the most expensive to produce. This fact put severe limitations on movie production in impoverished Europe after the war. Some of the Italian producers, Roberto Rossellini and Vittorio De Sica, overcame this difficulty by filming their pictures "on location" rather than in studios and drawing on nonprofessionals to act in all lesser roles. In this manner, they added to the realism of their productions and turned out some memorable artistic creations in *Open City, Shoe Shine,* and *The Bicycle Thief.* Dealing with Nazi brutality, partisan warfare, postwar suffering and misery, these films were little appreciated, however: they revived unhappy memories even though their stark realism was tempered by the gallantry, the love and compassion of some of the central figures. On the other hand, a British film, *Brief Encounter,* produced on an equally modest budget in 1945, became a widely acclaimed success—perhaps not only because of its sensitive artistry, but also because this simple story of a brief love affair of two middle-aged married people took the viewers away into a peaceable small-town world untouched by wars and dictatorships.

Italian producers also introduced another new element into movie production: characters of different national backgrounds spoke in their native language, adding to the realism of the production and demonstrating that art, once more, was serving as a unifying link across national barriers. But if this technique was well received, this also showed that art was no longer a last surviving link of the European community, but formed part of a broader movement toward the reinvigoration of that polity.

20

Eastern Europe and
Soviet Russia:
The Stalinist Era

Postwar developments in eastern Europe stood in marked contrast to those in the West. Both areas strove to attain greater unity, but west European endeavors, while at times prodded by the United States, aimed at voluntary agreements, whereas the Soviet bloc was established under the tutelage of the Red Army and by men who had been trained and instructed by Moscow. Moreover, Moscow claimed for itself the controlling role of the bloc, with the political, economic, and military policies of the bloc members adjusted to the needs of the Soviet Union. The satellites, on their part, had to be content with the assurance that the increasing strength of the U.S.S.R. would in turn redound to the strengthening of their own socialist system.

THE SOVIET UNION

The Task of Reconstruction. The Soviet Union emerged from the war with vast areas devastated and its economy in perilous shape. According to official Soviet statistics, 1,700 towns, 70,000 villages, 31,000 factories, and 98,000 collective farms had been destroyed. In addition, 84,000 schools, and tens of thousands of hospitals, libraries, theaters, and other educational and recreational facilities lay in ruins. With 40,000 miles of railroad trackage torn up and most of the bridges in the western part of the country demolished, transportation was in complete disarray in that area. Livestock, which had never been plentiful, was further reduced with the loss of seven million horses, 17 million head of cattle, and twenty million hogs. Industrial output was 25 per cent lower in 1946 than it had been in 1940; industrial expansion in Asian Russia had not kept pace with the devastation that had been wrought in the European parts.

To deal with the most pressing needs, the Soviet government accepted UNRRA assistance and, in its concern to secure such aid, permitted foreign observers to supervise UNRRA relief operations on Russian soil. Yet UNRRA could give help only on a limited scale, and the government set out at once to draw up plans for the full rehabilitation of the Soviet economy. In March 1946 work on the fourth Five Year Plan covering the years 1946–1950 was completed. Its main concern was the restoration of the war devastated regions and the promotion of continued industrial expansion; like its predecessors the plan gave priority to the production of capital goods. In pursuit of these aims the Soviet planners were remarkably successful: coal and oil production almost doubled between 1945 and 1950, electric power output doubled, and steel and rolled metals output was two and a half times as large in 1950 as it had been in 1945. (The following table is based on *Information U.S.S.R.* [1962].)

	1940	1945	1950
Coal (in m.t.)	165,900,000	149,300,000	261,100,000
Crude Oil (in m.t.)	31,100,000	19,400,000	37,900,000
Steel (in m.t.)	18,300,000	12,300,000	27,300,000
Rolled Ferrous Metals (in m.t.)	13,100,000	8,500,000	20,900,000
Electric Power (in kw. hr.)	48,300,000,000	44,300,000,000	91,200,000,000

Raw materials, machines, vehicles, some entire plants were brought in as reparations from the former enemy countries to speed up the reconstruction work, and hundreds of thousands of prisoners of war were retained to help rebuild the economy.

Consumer goods output, on the other hand, remained low. By 1950 it had barely reached the level of 1940—a year during which the manufacture of consumer goods had already been curtailed in the face of the deteriorating international situation. To alleviate the existing shortage, the Russians stripped the occupied countries of whatever goods they could seize as war reparations. An American UNRRA observer saw German bicycles, radios, wine glasses, sewing machines, and goose-feather pillows on sale in the Ukraine in 1946. Agriculture also faced serious difficulties. It was allotted only one-fifth of the funds that were earmarked for industry, limiting severely the output of agricultural equipment. The heavy losses in livestock caused a continuous shortage of dairy products and meat, and also deprived the farms of needed draft animals. A severe drought in 1946 turned the food shortage into a crippling famine. Above all, agriculture continued to suffer from basic organizational problems. During the war the peasants had been permitted to increase and spend more time on their private plots to expand food production in both Soviet controlled and German occupied areas.[1] The recovery of this land for the kolkhozes and the reintroduction of strict working time schedules resulted in considerable tension. The lack of incentives also had its retarding effects.

In 1947 a special Three Year Plan called for an increase in livestock. It had little effect—largely because the peasants who owned a substantial part of the existing livestock had no interest in increased stock breeding. The law allowed them to raise but a limited number of animals on their private lots; they would therefore have had to turn over any additional ones to the kolkhoz. A drive to combine smaller kolkhozes into larger units in order to facilitate their supervision and ensure a better use of the available farm machinery was more successful; the number of farms was reduced from 252,000 to 94,800 in the years 1950 to 1952. On the other hand, a plan to couple the mergers, for the sake of greater efficiency, with the resettlement of the peasants in so called agro-towns of some 5,000 inhabitants ran into so determined an opposition that it had to be dropped. The peasants were equally opposed to the proposal of abolishing their private plots and assigning them a section in a larger plot that could be tilled jointly—a scheme evidently designed to pave the way for the eventual abolition of all private agricultural enterprise. The resulting tensions severely affected agricultural output during those years.

Peasant morale, finally, suffered another grave blow when the currency was revalued in December 1947. The exchange ratio was least favorable in the case of cash, with ten old rubles to be exchanged for one new one. This particular measure was aimed at those individuals who had failed to deposit their cash holdings in bank accounts—presumably wartime black marketeers or "speculators." Among these, the peasants were the most important target, even though the government had encouraged them to grow as much food as possible on their private plots and sell it on what amounted to a legalized black market. Bank accounts and government bonds, on the other hand, were exchanged at a more favorable rate, with the poorest groups receiving preferential treatment:

---

[1] Contrary to expectations, the Germans did not dissolve the collective farms lest the resulting disruption endanger the food supply for the German armed forces.

Bank deposits up to 3,000 rubles	1:1
Bank deposits from 3,000 to 10,000 rubles	2:3
Bank deposits over 10,000 rubles	1:2
Government bonds, depending on type	1:3–5

With the currency revaluation rationing came to an end and prices were lowered on those basic foodstuffs (bread, flour, cereals) now in more plentiful supply. On the other hand, prices for meat, fats, milk, sugar, and eggs were raised, and so were the prices for shoes, clothing, and other essentials.

Social Conditions. To alleviate the hardships caused by the existing shortages, priority was given to the restoration of recreational facilities. Among the first buildings to be repaired in the devasted cities and towns were the theaters and community halls where the hard-working Soviet citizen could relax in his leisure hours (and also be reached more easily by political campaigns). Social services, too, were expanded; medical facilities had been further developed during the war and now provided improved services to the civilian population. The number of doctors and nurses grew from 130,400 in 1941 to 294,200 in 1955, and the number of hospital beds from 661,400 to 1,110,000.

Private housing, on the other hand, remained in desperately short supply. One-half of all homes in the German-occupied towns and cities had been destroyed or seriously damaged; General Eisenhower recalls in his memoirs that when he flew to Moscow in July 1945, he did not see a single house standing between the Soviet border and the suburbs of Moscow. To speed home construction, the Soviet government encouraged the building of private homes (up to five rooms) in the cities, providing sites free of charge in perpetual lease and loans for the purchase of building materials.

Labor's lot was gradually lightened by the reduction of working hours and the cutting of prices, although wages remained unchanged. Still, the average work week continued to run to 46 hours (eight hours on Mondays through Fridays and six on Saturdays), and real wages did not attain the 1937 level until 1952. The effect of the price cuts, moreover, was doubtful since many consumer goods were hard to get—a fact constantly brought to mind by the long queues waiting in front of most stores.

If the ordinary worker's lot was not easy, that of the forced laborer was infinitely harder. Forced labor expanded greatly during the postwar years as a result of the unending roundup of persons charged with disloyalty during the war and of the wholesale arrests of suspected opponents in the newly acquired territories. As Stalin's morbid suspicions grew, additional millions were hauled off to the mines and construction jobs in Siberia and Sakhaline Island where manpower was scarce and forced labor played an important role in the economic development.

Finding the execution of capital offenders economically wasteful, the government also decreed in 1947 that all death sentences be automatically commuted to 25 years of forced labor.[2]

The scarcity of consumer goods contributed also to a further widening of differences in living standards. Preferential food rations, housing priorities, shopping privileges, and choice theater seats were awarded as special incentives or were allowed as perquisites of high-ranking positions in party, civil service, economy, and the armed forces. Wide differentiation in pay scales reinforced this social stratification; an army captain received 24.3 times as much basic pay as a private, and the corresponding ratio between a general's and a private's pay was 114.3 to 1 (15 to 1 in the United States).[3] The practice of allowing less gifted children to attend high school and university against payment of a fee was also continued although it had been originally introduced as a wartime emergency measure. Perhaps the most telling evidence of the emergence of a new managerial class was the predominance of the white collar intelligentsia in the membership of the Communist Party.

Political Developments.   No major political reforms were undertaken after the war. The Supreme Soviet and the soviets of the member republics were newly elected in the spring of 1946. Georgi Malenkov (1902–   ), one of Stalin's most trusted lieutenants, and Andrei Zhdanov, wartime boss of besieged Leningrad, emerged to second and third position in the party, and in 1949 were joined by Nikita Khrushchev (1894–   ), long the top party leader in the Ukraine and now the troubleshooter in agriculture. A nationwide purge expelled those deemed unworthy of party membership. At the same time the political leaders took steps to reassert their ascendancy over the military, and some of the most distinguished (and most popular) Red Army commanders, Marshal Zhukov among them, were removed from the public limelight and transferred to obscure posts. Equally marked was the continued concern with traditionalism as a means of appealing to the unconverted and thus preserving national unity. The Council of People's Commissars was renamed Council of Ministers in 1946, and the Red Army became the Soviet Army. In this same vein the Soviet leaders began to extol the Russian people "as the outstanding of all nations that constitute the Soviet Union" (Stalin)—an approach which a few years before would have been castigated as nationalist chauvinism. The Russians were hailed as "elder brothers" of the other Soviet peoples to whom they were showing the road to greatness as teachers and guides.

The emphasis on the Russians' virtues was underscored by a bitter campaign against the corrupt and decadent West. Both strategies were designed to rally the country behind its leaders and to offset whatever

[2] In 1950, when Stalin's purges gathered further momentum, the death penalty was restored for "traitors, spies, and those seeking to undermine the state."

[3] Similarly some passenger ships had five different classes.

alien influences had contaminated the Soviet people during the war. Among these the most dangerous had been the impressions gathered by Soviet soldiers in central Europe where they discovered, not the capitalist-induced misery that Communist propaganda had pictured, but living standards greatly superior to those in the U.S.S.R. The combination of Great Russian patriotism and anti-Westernism was also designed to strengthen the country for the exertions that present and future demanded. Proud of their own achievements and contemptuous of the corruption and decadence of the West, the Soviet peoples could be expected to suffer more easily the hardships the plans of the government imposed upon them. In this spirit they would also, if necessary, take up arms against the West when the "capitalist contradictions" of the Western economy would turn the West against the U.S.S.R. And to accentuate further the disparity between the Soviet and the non-Soviet world, marriages between Soviet citizens and foreigners were prohibited.

Cultural Developments. Since Soviet culture was as much an instrument of government policy as were the economy and the press, Soviet writers and artists were also enlisted in the campaign of party and government. Their task was to brighten the life of the people, and by demonstrating the superiority of the Soviet system, help them to look with confidence to the future. Plays, novels, and paintings extolling historical deeds and recent wartime exploits were acclaimed (for example, Konstantin Simonov's novel *Days and Nights,* describing the battle of Stalingrad), whereas works of nostalgic reminiscence or melancholy reflection were condemned as harmful to the people's morale (for example, the poems of Anna Akhmatova). Authors also were urged to turn their attention to the workers and farmers since their labors had contributed greatly to the victory over the Germans and thus deserved literary acknowledgment. Doubtless the hope was that workers and farmers would tend to their present duties more vigorously if they knew that their efforts were fully appreciated.

To maintain the momentum of these endeavors, it was essential to exalt the strength and wisdom of Stalin, and here again writers, painters, and sculptors were enjoined to contribute their share. Boris Gorbatov, author of a widely read novel, *The Unconquered,* that centered around the partisan struggle in the Ukraine, described the introduction of a party worker to an underground meeting in what was considered an exemplary approach and was so quoted by Soviet authorities:

"This man has come to us from the Party," and all raise their eyes to Stepan. "This man has come to us from the Party. This means—from Stalin." As Stalin's messenger he walked over this rearing and wrath-swollen earth—and they believed him.[4]

[4] A. M. Egolin, *The Ideological Content of Soviet Literature* (Washington, 1948), pp. 5–6.

Creative artists paid similar tribute to Stalin. Harrison Salisbury, *New York Times* correspondent in Moscow in the late 1940's, noted that of the 95 best works exhibited in 1949 in Moscow's famous Tretyakov Art Gallery, 38 paintings and sculptures depicted Stalin and another 38 showed other Soviet leaders or dealt with some political-ideological theme.

However, given the vagaries of totalitarian regimes, even the choice of "safe" subjects such as Soviet wartime exploits did not always protect an author from political difficulties. Several writers describing the war in a humorous vein were reprimanded for not having done justice to the hardships and dangers which partisan fighters and regular soldiers endured. Sometimes a change in the party line led to trouble. In 1945 the novelist Alexander Fadeyev was awarded the Stalin Prize for his novel, *The Young Guard,* the story of a youthful partisan group; some time later the book was withdrawn for not paying sufficient tribute to the leadership role of the Communist Party.

Writers and artists were also enlisted in the Cold War; as Zhdanov put it, "the task of Soviet literature [was] not only to return blow for blow all [the] vile slander and [the] attacks upon our Soviet culture, upon socialism, but also boldly to attack bourgeois culture which is in a state of degeneration and decay." A representative example of works inspired by this directive was Konstantin Simonov's play, *The Russian Question,* which dealt with the troubles of an American newspaperman who tried to report honestly on Soviet achievements, but was thwarted by his capitalist bosses and abandoned by his fiancée and his friends. Conversely, all artistic trends of which the Soviet leaders disapproved were branded as bourgeois and Western. Such charges were leveled against experimental and modernistic works—creations which the Kremlin considered "undemocratic" since they could not be understood by the masses and thus were socially wasteful. Criticisms were directed especially against nontraditional musical works, among them operas and symphonies by such renowned composers as Dimitri Shostakovich and Sergei Prokofiev. "This music," the Central Committee of the Communist Party decreed, "reeks strongly of the odor of the contemporary, modernistic bourgeois music of Europe and America which reflects the decay of bourgeois culture, the total negative, the impasse of musical art."

While Soviet literature and art were stagnating under these restrictions, Soviet science made significant strides in such fields as mathematics, aerodynamics, and low temperature investigations. The government was lavish in its support of these fields, as it was generous in the support of all scientific research that it thought useful to the implementation of its goals. It subsidized liberally the research of the botanist Trofim Lysenko, who claimed that characteristics acquired due to a change in environment could be inherited, and sided with him against those Soviet biologists who maintained that heredity was not influenced by environmental conditions. The Lysenko thesis was of course the biological corollary of the Marxist axiom that man is socially the product of his environment.[5] Lysenko's theories served, moreover, as the basis for agricultural experiments, and the intervention of the Central Committee may have been an attempt to compel other scientists to assist Lysenko in these endeavors.[6]

Conclusions that were not compatible with the goals of the Soviet leadership were rigorously suppressed. Thus the economist Eugene Varga, long-time director of the Institute of World Economics and World Politics at Moscow, found himself out of favor after 1946 when he predicted—correctly, as it turned out—that Western capitalism was not headed toward an imminent depression and that the capitalist states were likely to introduce far-reaching social reforms without any violent revolution.

The Last Days of Stalin. The tightening of cultural and scientific controls was but another aspect of Stalin's relentless determination to suppress all manifestations of political and intellectual independence. His overriding concern with his own power position was evident also when he called a new party congress in October 1952—the first one in 13 years. One of the main items of business was a revamping of the party organization: Politburo and Orgburo gave way to an enlarged Presidium —a move that, as Khrushchev later maintained, was aimed at the replacement of many experienced administrators with out-and-out sycophants. In his anti-Stalin speech of 1956 Khrushchev suggested also that Stalin may have been planning the liquidation of all the old Politburo members. Possibly in preparation of such a purge, Stalin leveled charges of errors and negligence against such party stalwarts as Molotov and Anastas Mikoyan at a subsequent Central Committee meeting. In January 1953, moreover, it was announced that a group of nine distinguished physicians had murdered Zhdanov (who had died in 1948) and were also plotting the murder of several military leaders to disrupt Soviet defenses. The accused, some of whom were Jewish, had allegedly been recruited into the service of American intelligence by the American Joint Distribution Committee, a Jewish charity organization. The "doctors' plot" climaxed an anti-Jewish campaign that had been under way since 1948 when the establishment of the state of Israel rendered all Jews suspect of divided loyalties. As the Soviet press pointed out at the time, the charges disavowed those who were suggesting that capitalist encirclement was no longer a threat to the Soviet Union. Quite possibly

---

[5] Marx and Engels had themselves been disciples of Jean Lamarck, an eighteenth-century French naturalist who taught that acquired characteristics could be inherited.

[6] The skepticism of many of Lysenko's colleagues (as well as most Western scientists) was borne out by reports, early in 1966, that Lysenko had falsified the records of his experiments.

the arrest of the doctors was to initiate a series of purges aimed at opponents, presumed or real, of Stalin's domestic and foreign policies just as the death of Kirov had touched off the purges of the 1930's. Whatever Stalin's intentions, his death on March 5, 1953 put an end to his plans.

THE SOVIET SATELLITES

The Politics of the Soviet Bloc.   In establishing its ascendancy in eastern Europe, the Kremlin did not follow rigid preconceived plans. Some changes were imposed almost everywhere—in all states occupied by the Red Army, aristocracy and upper bourgeoisie were stripped of their political and economic power on charges of treason and collaboration. No attempt, however, was made to turn these states immediately into outright Communist dictatorships. Communist parlance described the Soviet-sponsored regimes as "people's democracies" rather than dictatorships of the proletariat, stressing the fact that these regimes were different from the Soviet system. Thus the monarchies were not abolished at once, and Rumania remained one, if only in name, until late in 1947. Comparatively free elections were tolerated in Hungary and in the Austrian and German occupation zones in 1945–46, and Czechoslovakia retained considerable leeway in determining its internal policies. In Poland, on the other hand, Communist predominance was established at once, and in Rumania and Bulgaria within a few months after the entry of the Red Army. Even in these states, however, oppositional activities were not immediately suppressed. Only in Yugoslavia and Albania, where native Communists seized power at war's end, Communist control of the political life was virtually unchallenged from the beginning.

Except for Yugoslavia and Albania, extent and tempo of the political transformation of the east European states appears to have been dictated by a combination of Soviet needs, domestic conditions, and Cold War tensions (see p. 410). Speed seemed vital in Poland because of its known hostility to the U.S.S.R. and its strategic position between Russia and Germany; it was considered almost equally important in Rumania which also had a long tradition of anti-Russian and anti-Soviet feelings and shared as long a border with Russia as did Poland. Greater liberality was shown in areas bordering on the West, either because close collaboration seemed assured even without direct control, as in Czechoslovakia, or the presence of the Red Army served as a safeguard, as in Hungary. Intervention, moreover, would have needlessly irritated the Western Powers and in the case of Germany and Austria might have jeopardized the possibility of reunification on terms acceptable to Moscow.

Coalitions with non-Communist parties also had the advantage of reconciling and neutralizing important social and political elements whose voluntary collaboration was bound to facilitate the consolidation of Communist power. Once power was firmly in Communist hands, however, with Communists directing police and army, the alliances were dissolved and replaced by sham coalitions in which the non-Communist members were chosen by the Communists and joined forces with them in groupings known as "National" or "People's Fronts." The non-Communists were politically powerless, but their presence in the government did symbolize the fact that peasants and middle class still constituted separate social and economic elements and that because of the survival of some measure of private enterprise the "people's democracies" continued to differ from the Soviet regime.

While Communist control was established in most of eastern Europe, the emerging Soviet bloc did not coalesce into a tightly integrated unit. Tension developed between Polish and German Communists over the permanence of the Oder-Neisse line; Polish and Czech Communists argued about their respective claims to the Teschen area (see p. 322); and the Rumanian and Hungarian governments quarreled over the border province of Transylvania. Other satellite attitudes also were causing alarm to the Kremlin. Poland and Czechoslovakia wished to take part in the Marshall Plan, and Tito would not abandon his claims to Trieste and southern Carinthia. At the same time the Yugoslav leader and Dimitrov, the Bulgarian Premier, proposed to establish a Balkan Union, eventually to be expanded into an eastern European one. To Moscow the plan seemed inspired by local political and economic needs and by the personal ambitions of the two leaders, without regard for the concerns of the U.S.S.R.

The Consolidation of the Bloc. Beginning in 1947, as the Cold War grew in intensity, the Kremlin sought to tighten its hold on its satellites. The first step it took was the establishment of the Cominform, one of whose tasks was to combat the existing centrifugal tendencies. Tito and Dimitrov were forced to abandon the Balkan Union project, Czechoslovakia came under full Communist control, and efforts were made to remove Tito (which ended, however, in the separation of Yugoslavia from the bloc). Moscow made no attempt, on the other hand, to bring Finland under closer control. Helsinki was asked to sign a friendship and assistance pact with the Soviet Union, but this pact committed Finland only to fight off any attack directed against it "or the Soviet Union through Finnish territory" by Germany or a German ally, and did not impinge on Finland's sovereignty. Located far away from the "people's democracies," Finland could be permitted to retain its political independence and social and economic structure at no risk to the cohesiveness of the Soviet bloc. Moreover, as Finnish resistance in 1939–40 had shown, the price of transforming Finland forcibly into a satellite would have been high, and the attempt might in turn have driven Sweden, which still was neutral, into the Western camp.

In domestic politics, too, the people's democracies became more closely attuned to the U.S.S.R. If earlier the term "people's democracy" had signified differences from the Soviet system, it was now defined as another type of dictatorship of the proletariat. Like its Soviet counterpart, it conceived as its main tasks the winning of the class struggle, which meant the end of all collaboration with bourgeois elements, and the introduction of socialism, which called for full collectivization and the nationalization of all enterprises. New constitutions were enacted to ratify the changed attitude; they borrowed heavily from the Soviet constitution, and the Hungarian and Polish documents paid express tribute to the U.S.S.R. Finally, the east European states purged all Communist factions suspect of sympathizing with Tito's version of communism and of disapproving of total submission to Moscow. The purges were especially bloody in Hungary, Bulgaria, and Czechoslovakia where such old party stalwarts and government members as Laszlo Rajk, Hungarian Politburo member and Minister of the Interior, Traicho Kostov, Bulgarian Politburo member and Deputy Prime Minister, and Vladimir Clementis and Rudolf Slansky, Czech Foreign Minister and Deputy Prime Minister, respectively, were liquidated. Many of the victims were Jews accused of secret ties with the new state of Israel. Purges were also carried out in Rumania, Poland, and East Germany, but except in Rumania, no blood was shed. Among those removed from office was Wladyslaw Gomulka, the Secretary-General of the Polish party and First Vice-Premier in the government, who had long opposed slavish subservience to Moscow; he was imprisoned, but was never brought to trial. The purges were not limited to the leaders—according to one estimate, 25 per cent of the membership of the east European parties were expelled in the years 1949–52.[7]

Priority of Soviet interests over the concerns of the satellites was also reflected in the official relations of the bloc members. They were linked by bilateral mutual assistance pacts with the Soviet Union and concluded bilateral treaties with each other. No multilateral treaties were permitted by Moscow lest they arraign the people's democracies against the U.S.S.R. To keep the satellites separated from each other, even travel from one state to the other was rendered difficult by red tape and restrictions. Soviet control was reinforced by the assignment of Russian military advisers to the armed forces of the satellites—one of the sources of friction between Stalin and Tito. In Poland, always of special concern to the Kremlin, a Polish-born Red Army marshal, Konstantin Rokossovsky, became Minister of Defense. Similarly the secret police was directed

---

[7] Zbigniev Brzezinski, *The Soviet Bloc: Unity and Conflict* (Cambridge, Mass., 1960) p. 97.

by advisers dispatched by the Kremlin. Moscow's supremacy was further enhanced by the increasing dependence of the east European economies on that of the Soviet Union.

Despite this apparent consolidation of the Soviet bloc, it is doubtful that the bloc was gaining in strength. Suspicion and fear were sapping its vitality, and an ever-expanding bureaucracy, slow moving and opposed to change, also exerted its retarding influence. Living conditions still were bleak and beset by severe hardships for the bulk of the people. Blaming the shortcomings on ideological errors, especially in the non-Soviet parties, Stalin warned shortly before his death that these mistakes were undermining the strength of the Communist movement. Death overtook him before he could act on his warnings.

Economic Developments. The economic transformation of the east European states passed through several stages that paralleled roughly the political evolution. The property of Germans and Italians, of native fascists and collaborators was seized; commercial and industrial enterprises were nationalized and landed property broken up into small and medium-sized farms. In addition, all banks and insurance companies were immediately taken over by the state in Poland, Czechoslovakia, and Yugoslavia, and within two years in the other east European countries. With varying speed nationalization was extended to all key industries and to all other enterprises of major proportions—in most cases without compensation. By 1949 all industries of more than local importance had been seized; after this, local industries and handicrafts were brought under state control.

Not all nationalized enterprises became the property of the state in which they were located. According to the reparation arrangements made with the former Axis satellites—Hungary, Rumania, and Bulgaria —and with (East) Germany and Austria, the Soviets laid claim to all German "assets." These included mines, oil wells, and industrial and commercial enterprises that the Germans had acquired in the course of their economic penetration of southeastern Europe. Some of these properties were seized by the Russians and administered by Soviet companies; others were turned over by Moscow, for political and economic reasons, to companies owned jointly by the Russians and the respective satellite country, with a Soviet director, however, in charge of the management. Both categories enjoyed complete tax exemption, extraterritoriality, and other competitive advantages; they provided the Soviets not only with large amounts of raw materials and industrial goods, but also enabled Moscow to exert substantial control over the local economies.

Land Reform. Among the first measures taken by the new east European regimes were land reforms. In addition to property seized from native fascists, Nazi collaborators, and Axis nationals, most large estates were expropriated and redistributed; however, of these, significant numbers existed only in Czechoslovakia, Poland, and Hungary. In fact, almost 90 per cent of the land that changed hands was located in these three countries, and half of this amount consisted of formerly German properties acquired by Poland as the result of its expansion to the Oder-Neisse line.[8]

Economically, the most important result of the land distribution was the large increase in subsistence farms. They covered about 25 per cent of the agricultural area in Czechoslovakia and Poland, roughly 36 per cent in Bulgaria and Yugoslavia, and 50 per cent in Hungary. Inevitably, this atomization of farm land compounded the difficulties of east European agriculture and helps to account for the fact that agricultural yields remained below prewar levels throughout those years. Yet the creation of the new dwarf holdings also had its advantages: it secured the new governments the support of the small peasants, and it permitted the postponement of large-scale investment in agriculture since the small holdings could be worked without mechanized equipment.

Collectivization. When the people's democracies were transformed into dictatorships of the proletariat, collectivization of the farms was an obvious corollary. It was launched on a large scale in 1949. As in Russia, peasant resistance was strong, and the pressures that were exerted on opponents of collectivization were in turn borrowed from Soviet practice —discriminatory taxation, withholding of credits, equipment, fertilizer, and seeds, moral pressures, and, not infrequently, violence. In many of the countries concerned, however, these penalties did not prove very effective. Almost all farms in Bulgaria and three-fourths of all farms in Czechoslovakia were collectivized. Rumania, on the other hand, collectivized only one-half of its arable land, and peasant resistance in Poland, Yugoslavia, and Hungary was such that collectivization comprised less than one-fourth of the land in the first two states and barely one-third in the last.

Nor was the socialized sector of agriculture more productive than its private counterpart. The cooperatives were beset by bureaucratic red tape, lacked adequate equipment, and were further hampered by inefficient management and the lack of incentives. Food thus remained in short supply. Yugoslavia was the first to revise its agricultural policies; it not only allowed independent peasants to stay out of the collectives, but also permitted those who had joined, to withdraw. Stalin's death led to a reappraisal of agricultural policies in the other countries as well; while not going as far as Yugoslavia, most of them did suspend all further collectivization.

---

[8] Figures cited in this and the following paragraph are taken from Nicholas Spulber, *The Economics of Communist Eastern Europe* (Cambridge, Mass., and New York, 1957), pp. 241–42, 245.

Industrialization. By 1949 economic rehabilitation and political con-solidation had made sufficient progress in the east European states to permit the conversion of their economies to socialist ones (in the Soviet sense). Apart from full nationalization and collectivization, the move called for industrial expansion on a large scale. Five Year Plans were drawn up with the help of Soviet advisers. Like their Soviet models, the plans centered on the development of certain key industries—coal, iron and steel, electric power, cement, and machinery. Production in capital goods was to be tripled while consumer goods output was at best to be doubled. The more modest goals in the latter area were dictated not only by the shortage of manpower, equipment, and raw materials, but also by the need to finance reconstruction and develop-ment out of national resources. Because almost 25 per cent of the national income was to be invested in economic development and repara-tions further drained the resources of the former Axis allies, living standards had to be severely curtailed.

The results of the industrialization campaign were substantial even though they did not measure up fully to expectations. By 1953 east European iron and steel production had doubled compared to 1938; oil production was nearly twice as large; and electric power output had almost tripled. Manufacture of cotton and wool products, on the other hand, increased less than half on the average. Consumers felt this lag the more sharply because imports of consumer goods from the West, an important factor in prewar days, were not resumed. Moreover, much of what was being produced was earmarked for export or allotted to the armed forces and the police. What was also disappointing was the failure of industrialization to reduce agricultural overpopulation—a burden that had long weighed on the east European economies. The new workers were recruited chiefly among the young, and industrialization thus absorbed merely the "natural" population increases.

Industrial development was pursued independently in the various states. All of them concentrated on increasing the output of coal, iron and steel, and electric power, and sought to produce whatever they could within their own borders. Except for adjustments to Russia's needs, no effort was made to coordinate the expansion, nor were disparities in development evened out between the more advanced states and the more backward ones. Similarly, when political developments led to a large-scale shift of foreign trade from the West to intrabloc trade, trade treaties, too, were concluded bilaterally. The Council for Economic Mutual Assistance made no significant changes when it was organized in 1949 to promote closer economic cooperation among its members; little coordination was effected and trade continued on a bilateral basis. On the other hand, the adoption of the ruble as the standard currency for intrabloc trade gave the Russians an additional lever with which to exert control over the economies of the bloc members.

Social Conditions. Comparatively speaking, social conditions in the satellite states resembled those in Russia during the early Five Year Plans. Food and other consumer goods were rationed severely, except in Czechoslovakia prior to the Communist coup in 1948. Housing accommodations, which had never been plentiful, were scarcer than ever in the large cities owing to wartime destruction, population increases, and the precipitate growth of the industrial working class. Wages were kept low and working hours long to attain the maximum of production at minimal cost. To get the largely unskilled workers to meet their production quotas, labor discipline was exceedingly strict, and even minor infractions were dealt with severely. As in Russia, however, to many of the workers "the new environment did at first offer an improvement over previous conditions, or at least an opportunity of breaking away from a life which many of them no longer thought meaningful or desirable. Many of them did not have a clear image of what tomorrow would bring, but many did have a vague feeling that today was no longer for them. . . ."[9] Yet poor pay, seemingly unending working days, and incessant pressures gradually had their disillusioning effect.

On the other hand, there were some tangible improvements in the life of the masses. Educational opportunities were broadened by the Communist regimes. The new governments strove hard to wipe out illiteracy, still widespread in some of the east European countries; in Bulgaria one-third of the population was illiterate in the 1930's, and in Albania four-fifths as late as 1944. Special adult classes were organized and elementary schooling made compulsory for an average of eight years (except in Albania where the shortage of educational facilities was such that until 1960 only four years of schooling were required). Higher education was likewise expanded. Given the necessary ability, the children of factory workers and poor peasants could attend, free of charge, high school and university and in fact were encouraged to do so. Upper and middle class youth, on the other hand, lacking the proper social background, were either barred or admitted only in exceptional cases. All education was adapted to Marxist tenets and became exclusively the concern of the state; except in Poland, all private and parochial schools were nationalized by 1949. In view of the shortage of doctors, scientists, and engineers, higher education was strongly oriented towards scientific and technical subjects. Russian became the main foreign language to be taught; in most states instruction began in the fourth or fifth year of schooling, but in Bulgaria, in many ways the most Stalinist of the satellites, some instruction was provided on the kindergarten level.

Social services were similarly expanded. Medical treatment was made available free of charge, and social security was enhanced by new benefits, although here again there was discrimination against those whose "social origin" was suspect. For the actual beneficiaries the significance

[9] Brzezinski, *op. cit.*, p. 102.

of these measures varied: they added little to the arrangements existing in Czechoslovakia, but constituted notable improvements in countries such as Hungary, Bulgaria, and Albania. In many cases their full effect was curtailed, however, by the lack of trained personnel and material resources.

Religion. As Marxists, the leaders of the new east European regimes were anxious to curb all religious influences. Where they were in full control as in Yugoslavia, they took measures at once to check religious activities. Where their position was less secure, they refrained at first from all interference. In Poland, Hungary, and Rumania, as a matter of impartiality, they restored Jewish and other religious rights abolished during the Nazi era. As their power increased, they began to restrict the rights and privileges of the various religious groups.

This intervention occurred as a rule in three phases. The first step was to seize all church property—largely in land which had been exempted from earlier expropriations—thus depriving the churches of their main economic resources. Next the religious schools were nationalized. In the final phase, the government began to persecute the top church leaders. The Orthodox Churches, which had a long tradition of accommodation to government policies, accepted the restrictions imposed upon them with little resistance. The Mohammedans, concentrated mainly in Yugoslavia and Albania, also could be subdued without much difficulty. The Catholic Church, on the other hand, did not submit as readily to government dictates as did other groups. Backed by the spiritual authority of the Vatican, it refused to accept the loss of its lands and its schools, the dissolution of its youth groups, and the censorship of its press. The very fact of the Church's Western basis made it suspect as an outpost of Western capitalism and a seedbed of anti-Communism —a view reinforced by the strongly conservative views which many Church leaders were known to hold personally.

To discredit the Church and intimidate the lower ranks of the clergy, the governments preferred charges of wartime collaboration and/or high treason against the Church's highest leaders. The Yugoslav primate, Archbishop Aloysius Stepinac, was sentenced to 16 years' imprisonment on the former charges, the Hungarian primate, Cardinal Joseph Mindszenty, to life imprisonment on the latter. In neither case did the evidence bear out the conviction. Stepinac's contacts with the Nazi occupation authorities and the Croatian puppet regime had occurred in the course of his official duties, but no proof was adduced that he had voluntarily supported either group. As for Mindszenty, an outspoken, passionate foe of the regime, the most incriminating evidence that could be gathered was that he had expressed the hope to the American Minister to Hungary that the Communists would be overthrown. Pope Pius XII struck back by excommunicating all those connected directly or indirectly with these trials. Fearful of domestic reactions to similar trials, the Prague and Warsaw governments contented themselves with the internment of the Czech and Polish primates, Archbishop Joseph Beran and Cardinal Stefan Wyszynski.

Occasional efforts at a rapprochement produced few results. In 1950 the Polish episcopate and the Warsaw government concluded an agreement by which the former accepted the supremacy of the government in its foreign, social, and economic policies and promised to support the Soviet-sponsored peace movement. The government in turn acknowledged the authority of the Pope in matters of faith, morals, and ecclesiastical jurisdiction. It also agreed to permit religious instruction in public schools, allowed the re-establishment of a Catholic press, of Catholic organizations and charitable activities, and promised not to interfere with public processions and pilgrimages. Yet when the Vatican refused to establish permanent bishoprics in the formerly German territories on the grounds that the Oder-Neisse line was merely a provisional arrangement, the Church-state struggle flared up again. A precarious truce was achieved in 1953 when the bishops swore an oath of loyalty to the state. Similarly, Tito made an attempt in 1951 to improve relations with the West by releasing Archbishop Stepinac. However, when Stepinac was made a cardinal the following year, the anti-Catholic campaign was resumed, though tempered by Yugoslavia's need to maintain tolerable relations with the West and especially with the United States.

Although the Church-state struggle in the people's democracies was impelled by the same Marxist motivations as in the U.S.S.R., the Catholic element in Poland, Hungary, Yugoslavia, and Czechoslovakia was too strong to permit the relentless persecution of Catholics that had taken place earlier in Soviet Russia. Nor did these states introduce that complete separation of State and Church that Marxist doctrine demanded. In Yugoslavia the Catholic Church continued to receive substantial state subsidies and the clergy was included in the social security system. In Poland a Catholic university was allowed to function at Lublin, although constrained by many restrictions, and some religious instruction was provided in public schools. Czechoslovakia, too, permitted a minimum of religious instruction in elementary schools, if only during after-school hours. And while the Czechoslovak party frowned officially on any religious activities of its members, it did not as a rule insist on expulsion, but contented itself with lesser penalties when a party member was found to have retained his church membership or had attended church services or ceremonies. These concessions constituted no serious Communist setbacks, however; by 1954 Communist ascendancy over all churches was no longer in doubt—except in Poland where the authority of the Catholic Church was so deeply entrenched as to be little affected by the attacks of the government.

Culture in the People's Democracies. Cultural developments in the satellite states paralleled the political evolution. After the defeat of the Nazis there was a brief interlude of comparative freedom—shortest in Yugoslavia and longest in Czechoslovakia—after which all cultural life was subjected to the strictures of "socialist realism." Lyricism, emotional moods, the beauty of nature per se were ruled out as legitimate topics of poetic creations. As one East German critic observed, "To be impelled by subjective attitudes is to give up the conscious molding of reality. To submit the guiding idea of a poem to the chance of linguistic euphony, rhythm, rhyme, or an alliteration—this is a survival of the faith in the spontaneity of artistic creation."[10] Instead, subject matter and presentation were carefully planned so that literature (and the arts) would fulfill their social and educational function and not waste themselves in a purposeless individualism.

Inevitably, cultural activities tended to assume a drab uniformity from Bulgaria to Poland. Everywhere books, paintings, and musical compositions extolled the virtues of collective farming and industrialization and the heroism of peasants rising against oppressive landlords or of partisans fighting Nazis and native fascists. Polish novels like *Tractors Conquer the Spring*, by Witold Zalewski, and *No. 16 Has Started Production*, by Jan Wilczek, had their Rumanian and Bulgarian counterparts in *Steel and Bread*, by Ion Calugaru, and *MT Station*, by Andrei Guliashki. Music and painting too dealt with socio-political themes— *A Summer Day at a Collective Farm* (awarded the Rumanian State Prize) and *Song for Stalin* were representative Rumanian compositions; *The New Members Arriving at the Collective Farm*, a typical Rumanian painting; *Farewell of a Partisan* and *The New Bulgarian Village*, characteristic Bulgarian pictures. In architecture Soviet influences were likewise marked: Warsaw built a Palace of Science and Culture modeled on the University of Moscow, and East Berlin's Stalin-Allee (now Karl Marx-Allee) could pass for an avenue in Kiev or Leningrad.

Yet socialist realism did not hold sway fully everywhere. In Poland postimpressionists and abstract painters continued to work and teach, and although their choice of subject matter was increasingly dictated by official policy, they persisted in what was condemned as a "formalist, decadent" style. Nor would they indulge, in depicting farm or factory scenes, in that bland optimism that socialist realism demanded. A modicum of an independent creative spirit survived also in Polish literature: a novel on the life of Chopin, *The Nature of Love*, by Jerzy Broszkiewicz, although picturing the composer as "progressive-minded," stressed also the romantic strain in his character. *The Nature of Love*

---

[10] *Neues Deutschland*, Sept. 3, 1952, quoted in Lothar von Balluseck, *Dichter im Dienst: Der sozialistische Realismus in der deutschen Literatur* (Wiesbaden, 1956), p. 29.

was brought out by one of the few remaining Catholic publishing houses, and this sponsorship may have shielded the book as well as some similar works from government intervention. But the government also allowed the publication in state publishing houses of a number of works which did not measure up fully to Marxist tenets. Even at the height of the Stalinist era the Warsaw regime did not forget that the Polish mind could not be totally regimented without impunity.

On occasion, other governments would allow some measure of freedom to a few authors whose international reputation made it inadvisable to suppress their "deviationist" works. In East Germany the novelist Arnold Zweig, author of the world famous novel *The Case of Sergeant Grisha* (1927), could successfully ignore that basic axiom of socialist realism that man must always be viewed as a product of the processes of dialectical materialism. According to Marxist reasoning, it was wrong to explain the actions of an individual by psychoanalytical probings; rather, it must be shown that "objectively" his attitude was a reflection of his social situation. Arnold Zweig, however, refused to abandon the psychological approach, and the East German editions of his works (*The Axe of Wandsbek; Education at Verdun*) remained essentially unchanged. Thus Stormtrooper Teetjen, the central character of *The Axe of Wandsbek,* was pictured not only as a representative of the German petty bourgeoisie that had contributed so much to the rise of Hitler, but also as the bewildered victim of an omnivorous dictatorship. Communist critics refuted at once this blanket indictment of totalitarian dictatorships and blamed Zweig for creating the impression of an "ineluctable involvement into which Teetjen is drawn seemingly without his fault." Although the book was not suppressed, the movie version was withdrawn immediately after its first showing.

Similarly, the Hungarian literary critic, Georg Lukács, a life-long Marxist, could publicly attack the artificiality of socialist realism and its neglect of human dilemmas. He also turned against the rejection of all bourgeois art and maintained that a bourgeois writer like Thomas Mann could describe social reality as accurately as any Marxist author. What mattered was not the personal views of the author, but his intellectual honesty, analytical penetration, and creative ability. Any work so created would also be socially useful, for political lessons could be drawn from the reality that it pictured. In defense of this view Lukács called on no less a witness than Marx, who had thought highly of the social realism of Balzac's novels, despite Balzac's devout Catholicism and royalism.

Unlike Zweig and Lukács, the German poet and playwright, Bertolt Brecht, author of *The Three Penny Opera* and *Mother Courage,* revised his works in accordance with the ideological dictates of the East German regime. He was permitted, however, to have their original version performed on West German stages. His drama, *The Trial of Lucullus,* was originally an indictment of all wars and was so shown in West Germany;

however, in its East German revision, retitled *The Condemnation of Lucullus,* the play takes the Roman military leader to task for having engaged in wars of aggression.

Despite adjustments, retractions, and recantations, these men, each in his own way, continued to work in an indeterminate twilight zone in which the old literary standards and values were not entirely dead. As Arnold Zweig put it, "The future belongs to the Asians. . . . As for myself, I am glad I could still drink from the springs of Europe, and no one can make me forget this."

DIVERSITY IN EASTERN EUROPE

The Soviet Bloc. The communization of the various east European states appeared to have deprived eastern Europe of its traditional "European" diversity. In view of this apparent uniformity and the predominance of non-European influences, many contemporary observers began wondering whether these states could still be considered part of the European community. There was a growing feeling in the first postwar decade that the European polity was now bounded in the east by the Elbe River and that eastern Europe was outside the pale.

Actually, as we saw, the leveling of eastern Europe was never as complete as it seemed. Within the Soviet bloc there were marked differences in the process of Sovietization. Bulgaria and Albania achieved the highest degree of Stalinism; Poland, the least. Catholicism retained a measure of autonomy in Poland, and contrary to Marxist dogma several of the satellites thought it wiser not to insist on a complete separation of State and Church. Others again were unable to force their writers and artists completely into the Communist mold. In the economic arena, the extent of collectivization varied considerably in the different states, and the lack of coordination in industrialization left the door open for potential diversification. Above all, Finland and Greece never became part of the Soviet bloc, and Yugoslavia belonged to it only until 1948; on its expulsion it began to develop its own type of national communism.

Greece was discussed in the previous chapter as a member of the west European community; it remains to trace briefly the postwar development of the two other outsiders—Yugoslavia and Finland.

Yugoslavia. During the immediate postwar period Yugoslavia advanced more swiftly on the road toward communism than any other east European state. It established at once what amounted to a one-party dictatorship, completed the nationalization of all business enterprises in 1948, and outdistanced all other Soviet satellites in the ruthlessness of its collectivization drive. Ideologically the Yugoslavs were faithful practitioners of Soviet communism, and for a time they even looked forward to the day when—as an equal—Yugoslavia would become a member state of the U.S.S.R. Whatever their differences with Moscow, the Yugoslav leaders considered themselves loyal members of the Soviet bloc and perfectly willing to stay in it. When relations with Moscow worsened in 1948, Tito tried hard to arrive at an amicable settlement with the Kremlin.

Yugoslavia's expulsion from the Cominform came as a deep shock to the Yugoslav leaders.[11] At first they would not accept the reality of the exclusion, and they kept hoping to be taken back into the Soviet camp. They made various conciliatory gestures, even going so far as to salute publicly the Soviet Union and Stalin at their annual party congress some four weeks after their expulsion. But Stalin would not relent.

Once it was realized that there could be no reconciliation, the Yugoslav leaders began to probe for the causes of the break. Since they felt guilt-less, the fault could only be Moscow's. Stalin, they concluded, had proved a poor Marxist; he was wrong to insist that only one road led to socialism and that all Communist states should therefore submit to his dictates. True Marxism, Belgrade maintained, called for full equality between socialist states; rather than prescribe one road to socialism applicable in all situations, it allowed for different paths, depending on the stage of development in individual countries. Given the certainty of its ultimate victory, even non-Communist states could be headed toward genuine socialism. The Titoists thus looked approvingly on the moderate socialist Scandinavian countries and saw promising socialist tendencies in the social reforms and economic controls of the capitalist states.

Applying these views to foreign policy, the Yugoslavs rejected the doctrine of an inevitable war between capitalism and communism and opposed both NATO and the Warsaw Pact. On the other hand, once they had reached this conclusion, their rapprochement with the West presented no ideological problems. Nor did they see any difficulty in concluding a treaty of friendship and cooperation with anti-Communist Turkey and Greece in 1953. Steering a cautious course between the Western and Soviet camps, they preferred nonetheless to align them-selves with such uncommitted countries as India and Egypt. As Marxists, they still saw, of course, as their ultimate goal the worldwide establish-ment of communism. But while not ruling out revolutions to achieve this objective, they believed that this goal could best be attained by a peace-ful transformation and that the prospects for such a transition were better now than they had been ever before.

Domestically, too, the Yugoslavs moved away from tight centralization.

---

[11] The traumatic impact of the exclusion was such that Tito and some of his closest collaborators were stricken with ailments that were apparently psychosomatic: Tito had a first gall-bladder attack; Deputy Premier Milovan Djilas lost his hair; Boris Kidric, a member of the Politburo, developed ulcers and a skin rash. Cf. George W. Hoffman and Fred Warner Neal, *Yugoslavia and the New Communism* (New York, 1962), p. 140.

A new constitution promulgated in 1953 gave greater autonomy to Yugoslavia's member republics and granted considerably wider powers to local governments. The effects of this diffusion of power were limited, though, by the fact that all basic decisions were still made by the ubiquitous League of Communists, as the Communist Party was renamed in 1952 to distinguish its somewhat more flexible structure from Soviet-type parties. In the economy, administrative powers over the means of production were transferred to workers councils on the grounds that socialist ownership of a factory was meaningless if the plant were run by the state. The workers councils were subjected, however, to various party and state controls, and the day-to-day management was entrusted to directors appointed by commissions on which government and party were represented. While the councils were to determine production, wages, prices, investments, and distribution of profits, their decisions were circumscribed also by the annual economic plans, by government wage and price controls, and by the fact that a large part of the available investment capital was allotted by the state. The resulting mixture of government planning and free competition did not at first achieve the hoped for increase in productivity—perhaps because the changes were made too precipitately and led to abuses. After 1952, however, the situation improved, and while the annual growth rate of the economy had been 2.4 per cent between 1948 and 1952, it climbed to 10.4 per cent between 1953 and 1959.

This rise was partly accounted for by the decollectivization of agriculture. The government consented to the dissolution of the collective farms in 1953 after agricultural production had dropped to less than two-thirds of the average prewar output. The only limitation imposed upon private farming was that no individual could own more than 25 acres. The Titoists did not abandon their hope for eventual full collectivization (13 per cent of all farm land remained collectivized); they expected time to work in their favor and ultimately convince the peasants of the advantages of socialized agriculture. Titoism was confident that it was riding the wave of the future.

Finland. Although geographically in the Soviet orbit, Finland managed to remain a parliamentary democracy. That it would be able to do so did not seem likely at first. In the first postwar election in March 1945, the Finnish Communists, received almost 25 per cent of the vote. They were given five seats including the strategic Ministry of the Interior in the newly formed government headed by the Conservative Juho Paasikivi. In March 1946, a Communist, M. Pekkala, became Premier, with the Communists occupying one-third of all cabinet posts. They brought the special security police under their control, but failed to extend their control over the army and the bulk of the regular police. In 1948, incensed by his abuses of power, the parliament removed the Communist Minister of the Interior by a vote of no-confidence; when the Communists lost one-fifth of their seats in the elections later that year, Pekkala was also forced to resign. The Kremlin stood passively by, and for the next 18 years, no Communist sat in any Finnish cabinet. The Finns were careful, however, to pursue policies that Moscow would find unobjectionable. Having previously rejected the invitation to take part in the Marshall Plan, they kept aloof also from the proposal of a Scandinavian neutrality bloc (which was abandoned on the formation of NATO), and they also declined to participate in the Nordic Council.

Finland's economy was burdened with the usual postwar difficulties. Reparation deliveries amounting to $225 million weighed heavily on the country until completed in 1952; added to them were "German assets" of more than $50 million that had to be turned over to the Soviet Union. In addition, the country was faced with the task of resettling some 400,000 persons displaced from the areas ceded to Russia and of restoring the war devastated regions. By rigorous taxation the various needs and programs were met; land redistribution involving some five million acres made possible the resettlement of the expellees and the offer of farm land to war veterans. Some American and United Nations loans were made available to Helsinki, but on the whole the country accomplished its tasks out of its own resources. In retrospect, the reparation deliveries proved a boon inasmuch as they forced the Finns to expand greatly their ship building, machinery, and metal industries in order to meet their obligations. The large-scale investment in these industries had to be paid for, of course, with a scarcity of consumer goods, and the resulting hardships produced serious unrest and a wave of nation-wide strikes in 1948. In the 1950's, however, after reparation deliveries had come to an end, the expanded industries helped to supply both domestic and foreign markets. Finnish living conditions improved rapidly, and with three-fourths of Finland's foreign trade centered outside the Soviet orbit, the country came to share the growing prosperity that spread across the non-Communist world.

21

The Reassertion of Europe

The death of Stalin in March 1953 constituted a landmark in the history of postwar Europe. Until that time the basic decisions concerning Europe were made in Washington and Moscow; London, Paris, and Bonn had little more than a consultative voice, and Prague, Warsaw, and East Berlin frequently were accorded not even that. There were, to be sure, exceptions, as in the matter of East-West trade, but in general the European states were objects of the Soviet-American confrontation rather than independent participants. After Stalin's passing from the international stage, both eastern and western Europe began to reassert themselves as autonomous factors in world affairs, the former slowly and within narrowly defined limits, the latter more rapidly and more effectively. The less militant attitude of Stalin's successors helped allay fears in the West of an imminent war, and western Europe thus felt less dependent on American military protection than it had earlier. Its growing prosperity also ended its need for American economic aid, and this fact made it still easier for west European governments to assume a more independent position on international issues. In the East, the striving for greater autonomy followed on the weakening of Moscow's **475** controls over the satellite states in the post-Stalin era. It derived further momentum from the official acceptance of Titoism by Moscow and from the deterioration of Sino-Soviet relations.

These developments were accompanied by a gradual *détente* in East-West relations. Contributing also to this relaxation of tension was the nuclear striking power of both the United States and the Soviet Union, which seemed to remove war as a serious possibility in Europe. At the same time the emergence of China as a world power shifted the attention of the two superpowers to the Far East. Europe's reemergence as an independent factor in world affairs was helped importantly by the fact that during the 1950's Asia became the major arena of internal unrest and external clashes.

THE EASING OF EAST-WEST TENSIONS

The Berlin Conference of 1954. The improvement of East-West relations that followed on Stalin's death evolved only slowly after the distrust and bitterness which the preceding years had engendered. The men who took Stalin's place in the Kremlin—Malenkov; Molotov; Beria, the Minister of the Interior and head of the secret police; Bulganin, the Minister of Defense; and Khrushchev, newly appointed First Secretary of the party—tried to improve the atmosphere by some conciliatory gestures. The armistice negotiations in Korea, deadlocked for months, were resumed on Communist initiative; a seemingly hopeless stalemate in the United Nations over the election of a new Secretary General was ended with Moscow's acceptance of the Swedish banker-diplomat Dag Hammarskjöld (1905–1961). Similarly, trade between East and West Germany was expedited and controls relaxed on the routes connecting Berlin with West Germany. Finally, in May 1953 Moscow also dropped formally its territorial claims against Turkey (see p. 412). Europe's response to these moves was not unfavorable. Churchill, who had hoped for some time for an East-West rapprochement, proposed a security pact on the model of the Locarno Treaty and called for an immediate Big Four conference on the highest level ("at the summit"). American reaction was less positive; President Eisenhower who had assumed office a few months before, and his new Secretary of State, John Foster Dulles, dismissed the Soviet overtures as unconvincing. Their attitude reflected the prevailing climate of American public opinion that had been aroused to fever pitch by the anti-Communist crusade of Senator Joseph McCarthy. In the end the United States agreed to an exploratory meeting of the three Western Powers, but when it was held, Churchill was incapacitated by a stroke and could not himself plead his case. All that Dulles would concede was a four-power meeting of foreign ministers to discuss the German and Austrian peace treaties.

This conference was held in Berlin in January 1954. Like all previous meetings dealing with these treaties, it failed to accomplish anything.[1] The basic issue concerning the German treaty was whether it should be concluded with a German government formed on the basis of all-German free elections (as the Western Powers demanded) or with a government created out of a merger of the East and West German regimes (as the Soviets requested). Whatever changes Stalins' death had called forth, the struggle over Germany continued unabated. The Russians insisted on their proposal, fearful lest free elections produce a pro-Western majority in East Germany—a concern reinforced a few months before by an East German uprising that had to be put down by Soviet forces. If Russian fears could be allayed at all, only a Western commitment to neutralize a reunified Germany could do so. Such a concession the United States considered too hazardous, nor would it abandon its plan of bringing West Germany into NATO. On these disagreements the conference foundered.

Centrifugal Trends in East and West. Although Germany's reunification still depended entirely on the decisions of Moscow and Washington, the two capitals had to take into account divergent European positions on other issues. Increasing restiveness in the satellite states led the Kremlin to relax its controls of the Soviet bloc. It insisted on the installation of a more moderate regime in Hungary, another center of discontent. All satellite states were encouraged, moreover, to initiate comprehensive economic reforms in accordance with their national needs. The cohesion of the Soviet bloc could no longer be upheld simply by force; instead, it was to rest to a greater extent on ideological ties and mutual economic and security interests.

The Kremlin also decided to seek a reconciliation with Yugoslavia. To woo Tito back into the Soviet camp was imperative lest any of the satellites abuse their new freedom of action and turn Titoist too. At the very time that Moscow loosened its grip on the satellite economies, it proposed to Belgrade the resumption of full diplomatic relations. This done, trade was quickly expanded with Yugoslavia. The rapprochement culminated in a visit to Belgrade of the two top Soviet leaders—Khrushchev, the head of the Soviet Communist Party, and Bulganin, now Chairman of the Council of Ministers. Tito, however, could not be coaxed back into the Soviet camp and insisted on retaining his independence; whereas Khrushchev described his visit as that of one Communist leader to another, the Yugoslav leader treated it as a state visit of two foreign dignitaries. He made it clear that he would not abandon his neutral position.

In the Western camp, too, ties were beginning to loosen and Wash-

---

[1] Even the question as to where in Berlin the conference was to meet could only be solved by holding sessions alternately in East and West Berlin.

ington's leadership in the East-West struggle was challenged more frequently. In the spring of 1954 France was facing military disaster in Vietnam. Washington considered rushing naval and air support to the French, but Britain, hopeful that a forthcoming conference would end the fighting, refused to join the United States, and the plan was abandoned. Similarly, Foreign Secretary Anthony Eden would not side with the more inflexible Dulles at the conference table. Together with French Premier Pierre Mendès-France he agreed to a settlement of the Vietnamese war on terms that Dulles found unacceptable (see p. 432).

The most striking example of this reassertion of western Europe was the refusal of the French National Assembly to approve the establishment of the European Defense Community (see p. 419). A large part of the French people were opposed to German rearmament even within the EDC and to the absorption of their own army into a supranational EDC force. However, American warnings that financial aid might be withheld had led the French government to sign the EDC treaty in 1952. Such warnings were no longer effective two years later when the French Assembly finally voted on ratifying the treaty. Neither was Dulles' threat of an "agonizing reappraisal" of American foreign policy should France fail to approve the EDC. The Assembly rejected the treaty by a substantial majority (319 to 264). In the end the French resigned themselves to West German rearmament within the framework of NATO, where both the United States and Britain could help control the new German army and their own army would remain a separate national force.

Warsaw Pact and Austrian State Treaty. The inclusion of West Germany in NATO led to the signing at Warsaw of a Pact on Friendship, Cooperation and Mutual Aid, the so called Warsaw Pact, by the U.S.S.R. and its eastern European allies in May 1955. The Warsaw Pact superseded the various bilateral military assistance pacts on which the defense arrangements of the Soviet bloc had been based. It was designed to secure Moscow's military supremacy in the bloc as a counterweight to the greater domestic autonomy of the east European states, but was drawn up in forms that appeared to base Moscow's rights on voluntary agreements. The joint command of the Warsaw Pact forces was entrusted to a Soviet marshal; the treaty also provided for the stationing of Soviet forces in the satellite states on the basis of mutual understandings. However, the pact did not only serve Soviet interests; directed against a rearmed West Germany it also reassured the east European states, which were genuinely alarmed at seeing the Bonn Republic acquiring considerable military strength.

Vis-à-vis the West, the Warsaw Pact was intended to balance off a NATO reinforced by a West German army. Yet Moscow also seems to have hoped that the pact might cause the West to keep Germany out of

NATO, for East Germany was not invited into the pact until Western Germany formally became a NATO member. Moscow, moreover, did not rely on military measures alone to prevent the Bonn Republic from joining NATO. Just one day after the conclusion of the Warsaw Pact an Austrian State Treaty was signed at Vienna by the United States, Britain, France, and the Soviet Union.[2] The treaty ended the four-power occupation of Austria in return for an Austrian pledge of permanent military neutrality (and the payment of a terminal indemnity of $150 million to the Soviet Union). The Kremlin was the moving force behind its conclusion—apparently in the hope that the neutralization of Austria might set an example for the settlement of the German problem and thus obviate West Germany's membership in NATO.[3] As further evidence of their peaceful intentions, the Soviets also returned to Finland the Porkalla naval base near Helsinki which they had leased from the Finns for fifty years.

The Summit Conference at Geneva. In the face of these conciliatory moves, European demands for a summit meeting of the United States, the Soviet Union, Britain, and France grew more insistent. It was by now also in the American interest to seek an accommodation with the U.S.S.R., for in 1953 the Soviets had turned out their first hydrogen bombs, portending an early end to American nuclear superiority. In these circumstances the United States dropped its objections to a summit conference, and the Big Four met in Geneva in July 1955. President Eisenhower led the American delegation; Bulganin and Khrushchev represented the U.S.S.R.; Anthony Eden, who had succeeded Churchill as Prime Minister, was Britain's spokesman; and Premier Edgar Faure was France's chief delegate.

The conference revolved around the familiar issues of German reunification, European security, and armaments limitation. Again, no agreements were reached; a proposal by Eisenhower to limit military installations and subject them to mutual aerial inspection was side-stepped at once by the Soviets. The meeting did, however, contribute to a further easing of tensions, and this led later that year to a "package deal" among the great powers by which several east European countries —Rumania, Hungary, Bulgaria, and Albania—and some west European states—Italy, Spain, Portugal, and Eire—were admitted to the United Nations. Along with them, Finland, Austria, and a number of unaligned

---

[2] It was called a state rather than a peace treaty because Austria was not considered an enemy power. No Austrian state existed when war broke out in 1939, and the new Austrian state created in 1945 had not participated in the war.

[3] If earlier the Russians had been reluctant to agree to an Austrian treaty because its conclusion would have deprived them of the right to keep troops in Hungary and Rumania (see p. 409), they no longer needed to consider this factor since the Warsaw Pact provided for the stationing of Soviet forces in the satellite states.

Geneva Conference, July 1955. Left to right: Bulganin, Eisenhower,
Faure, Eden. (Reprinted courtesy Brown Brothers)

Asian nations also were granted membership. Shortly afterwards, the
Twentieth Congress of the Soviet Communist Party acknowledged officially that states with differing social systems need not clash with each
other, but could coexist peacefuly side by side.

The East European Risings and the Suez Crisis.   In the fall of 1956
the Cold War *détente* was threatened by crises in both the Soviet and
Western camps. With the Kremlin bestowing its blessing on Titoism,
some of the east European states were making new efforts to secure a
further measure of independence from Moscow. They were also encouraged by Khrushchev's address to the Twentieth Congress of the
Soviet Communist Party in which he repudiated Stalin's "cult of the
individual." Khrushchev rejected Stalin's claim that Soviet-type socialism
was the only legitimate one, and allowed that socialism could be attained
by various roads. Accordingly, the Cominform, long moribund, was disbanded in April 1956.

The immediate effect of these changes was the discarding of Stalinist
practices in a number of east European countries. Leaders who had been
disgraced a few years before were rehabilitated, if only posthumously,
and their Stalinist foes demoted or dismissed altogether. Various reforms
sought to relieve the unsatisfactory economic conditions and restrict the

powers of the police. They were insufficient to prevent the outbreak of riots in the Polish city of Poznan in June 1956. The disturbances were quickly suppressed, but the demand for economic improvements and less dependence on Moscow persisted. In October, Gomulka, long known as the defender of Polish national interests against Moscow's intrusions, was reappointed First Secretary of the Polish Communist Party. Khrushchev attempted to stem this trend by a personal intervention in Warsaw; to lend greater emphasis to his demands, he gave orders to Soviet forces stationed in Poland to move on the capital. Yet the Polish leaders would not be intimidated; knowing the mood of his countrymen, Gomulka warned Khrushchev that they would fight rather than submit to the Kremlin's dictates. Gomulka promised, however, that Poland would stay in the Soviet bloc—a decision necessitated in any event by Poland's own interests (see p. 547). Thus reassured, the Kremlin accepted the proposed liberalization of Poland's regime.

The Polish revolt touched off risings in long-smouldering Hungary, beset like Poland by economic troubles and police repression. Imre Nagy, a national Communist, was appointed Premier, and sweeping reforms were announced. Shaken by this new act of defiance, the Soviets not only accepted the changes, but at Nagy's request also withdrew their forces from Budapest. They promised to pull their troops out of Hungary altogether and proposed a revision of the Warsaw Pact and a re-examination of economic relations between the U.S.S.R. and the east European states. By this time, however, Nagy was losing control of developments. Less strong and skillful a leader than Gomulka, he bowed to popular pressures and announced the abolition of the one-party system and the transformation of his all-Communist government into a coalition. To Moscow the inclusion of liberals and possibly even conservatives in the government was intolerable; coupled with the promise of free elections, the move seemed to foreshadow Hungary's break-away from the Soviet bloc—a fear confirmed a day later when Nagy proclaimed his country's neutrality and withdrew from the Warsaw Pact. Soviet forces were rushed back into Budapest to overthrow Nagy and crush the rebellion. After some hours of bitter fighting resistance collapsed in the capital; it continued in the countryside sporadically for a few more days. A new Soviet-sponsored government was established with Janos Kadar as Premier; significantly, it retained most of Nagy's economic reforms.

The West stood by passively during these events. Earlier there had been suggestions in the United States about rolling back the Iron Curtain and the liberation of eastern Europe, but these proposals proved wholly unrealistic.[4] One reason given for the West's inaction was its preoccupa-

---

[4] There is no evidence that these statements or the broadcasts of the Voice of America and Radio Free Europe were responsible for the outbreak of the east European risings, but they may have encouraged the Hungarians to carry their revolution beyond the limits the Soviets would tolerate.

tion with a crisis that had arisen in Egypt over control of the Suez Canal; another was the involvement of the United States in its Presidential election. The decisive factor, however, was that intervention by the West would have increased the danger of nuclear war, and this was out of the question. Thus the Soviets were able to suppress the uprising without much difficulty.

If the West remained inactive in the Soviets' hour of crisis, the Kremlin stood by while the West was faced with a Middle Eastern emergency. For some time Western and Soviet influences had been competing for Egypt's favor, and Egypt's President Gamal Abdel Nasser had blandly secured as much aid as he could from each side. In July 1956 Secretary of State Dulles, indignant at Nasser's equivocations, withdrew an earlier promise to help underwrite the construction of a dam on the Nile River at Aswan that was to aid both agriculture and industry in southern Egypt. In retaliation, Nasser seized and nationalized the Suez Canal Company. The British feared that Nasser might bar them from the use of the canal and from direct access to their oil fields, and decided to force him to rescind the expropriation. The French sided with them, hopeful to use this opportunity to cut off any further Egyptian assistance to the anti-French rebels in Algeria. The United States, after some vacillation, opposed armed intervention, but the British and French would not be stopped. Taking advantage of a simultaneous Israeli campaign against Egypt, they launched an attack late in October 1956. By November 6, though poorly planned and ineptly executed, the invasion was close to success. Yet faced with the opposition of the United States, the United Nations, and a large part of British public opinion, London and Paris broke off the attack and negotiated a cease-fire. They withdrew their troops after a United Nations Emergency Force arrived in Egypt to enforce the truce.

Significantly, the Soviets threatened to intervene only after the Kremlin knew that the United States was opposed to the Anglo-French move. Trying to take advantage of this dissension, the Kremlin proposed a joint Soviet-American intervention against Britain and France, but this plan was at once rejected by Washington. Moscow was warned that the United States would repel by armed force any armed Soviet move in the Middle East. If there was any danger of a new East-West confrontation, the armistice put an end to it.

Rapacki Plan, NATO, and Nuclear Armaments. Fearful of nuclear war, the United States and the Soviet Union had both carefully kept out of each other's sphere of interest in the two crises. Thus the door had not been closed to an East-West accommodation. The hope, however, that the nuclear armament race could now be brought to an end was not fulfilled. A series of conferences aiming at a ban of nuclear testing and/or atomic production controls failed to produce an agreement.

Neither the health hazards of radioactive fallout nor the enormous financial burden of nuclear armaments could induce the United States or the Soviet Union to change their positions sufficiently to arrive at an understanding. In the fall of 1957 Polish Foreign Minister Adam Rapacki proposed the creation of a nuclear free zone in central Europe, including the two Germanies, Poland, and Czechoslovakia, in which nuclear weapons would neither be produced nor stockpiled. The plan was rejected by the United States and West Germany as being too narrow to safeguard European security; it would have deprived the West of forward bases in areas which had just then acquired a special significance.

The Rapacki Plan was launched a few months after the Soviets had developed an intercontinental ballistic missile (ICBM) with a range of 5,000 miles and equipped with a nuclear warhead. The United States hoped to offset Moscow's advantage by emplacing intermediate range missiles (IRBM's) in western Europe, and in this strategy West German bases played an important part. Once more the west European nations were reluctant to follow the American lead. The Rapacki Plan was received with considerable interest in Europe where a disengagement of East and West had long been advocated by Churchill, Eden, and others. At a NATO meeting in Paris in December 1957 Dulles had to promise to enter into negotiations with the U.S.S.R. before he could secure the authorization to install IRBM's in those countries that were willing to have them. At that only Britain, Italy, Turkey, and West Germany expressed willingness; France, Norway and Greece refused.

European reluctance to accept the missiles was not only due to the desire to speed the easing of tensions rather than maintain the hazardous status quo. Many European leaders also objected to Washington's insistence that the nuclear warheads remain in the custody of the United States and the decision to use them rest with the American President. American control of the warheads was considered an offense to national pride, and it also gave rise to the question whether nuclear weapons would actually be available in any emergency. Would the United States be prepared to use them in defense of Europe even at the risk of calling forth retaliatory attacks upon New York or Chicago? NATO's Secretary General, Belgian ex-Foreign Minister Paul-Henri Spaak, proposed the formation of an independent west European nuclear force, and France, still smarting under Washington's opposition to the Suez campaign, laid plans to create a national one. Britain, which had such a force, found the American plan least objectionable.[5]

---

[5] Britain's nuclear force was built as much to avoid too great a dependence on the United States as to serve as a deterrent against any would-be aggressors. "The fact that we have it," Prime Minister Harold Macmillan stated in 1958, "makes the United States pay a greater regard to our point of view, and that is of great importance." Hugh Gaitskell, the leader of the Labor Party, agreed: "The real case for our having

The issue assumed a new urgency when De Gaulle took over the government of France in 1958. The General proposed the establishment of a three-power directorate for NATO in which the United States, Britain, and France would each have an equal voice. When the proposal was rejected by Washington, De Gaulle withdrew the French Mediterranean fleet from NATO and accelerated the build-up of France as a nuclear power. Early in 1960, after the United States and the U.S.S.R. had suspended nuclear testing, France tested its first atomic bomb in the Sahara Desert.

The Problem of Germany.   Closely connected with the problem of nuclear arms control was the ever-present question of German re-unification. Chancellor Adenauer had long ago decided that reunification on non-Communist terms was possible, if at all, only if West Germany aligned itself with the West. As a trusted member of the Western community, it would thus be in a position to influence the West's policies concerning Germany and watch that the West's resources would be used to attain the reunion of Germany. In keeping with this policy, Adenauer advocated West German rearmament within the EDC and later in NATO, and he was Dulles' strongest supporter when the latter proposed the emplacement of IRBM's in Western Europe. Adenauer expected the Western Powers not to accept an overall accommodation with Soviet Russia unless the unification of Germany formed part of such an agreement. His fear was that unless Germany were reunited before East and West settled down into some mutually acceptable *modus vivendi*, it might never be reunified.

Whatever the long-term prospects of Adenauer's strategy, its immediate effect was to arouse Soviet Russia's suspicions. West Germany's rearmament revived fears of a renewed aggressive militarism—fears widely shared by the east European states which were also still haunted by their World War II memories. Anthony Eden has told in his memoirs how much these concerns influenced the Soviet position at the Geneva conference in 1955 and how deep-seated these anxieties were. Adenauer's subsequent policies did nothing to dispel Russian fears. He kept warning against any premature agreements on arms controls and test bans lest they jeopardize German reunification. To the Soviets these views merely confirmed their fears of West German "revanchism."

Berlin Crisis II.   If reunification seemed a dead issue for the time being, West Berlin's precarious status inside Communist East Germany served as a constant reminder of its continued existence. Aided by West German and American subsidies, the city had become a Western outpost of bustling activity, the leading German manufacturer of clothing

our own independent nuclear weapons is fear of excessive dependence upon the United States." Quoted in William P. Snyder, *The Politics of British Defense Policy: 1945–1962* (Columbus, 1964), p. 232.

and electrical supplies and an important center of printing and publishing. East Germans had free access to it, and its prosperity kept impressing on them the sharp contrast with the bleakness of their own life. Besides inviting uncomfortable comparisons, West Berlin also was an irritant to the Soviets as a vantage point of Western intelligence and propaganda activities. Above all, it was the one safe escape route to the West that remained open to the East Germans; over 1.5 million East German refugees poured through it between 1949 and 1961, over half of them young people up to the age of 25, and tens of thousands of them doctors, teachers, engineers, and technicians. Clearly the East German economy could not stand indefinitely this continuing drain on its most valuable manpower.

In November 1958 the Kremlin resumed its attempts to drive the Western Powers from Berlin. Khrushchev served notice that, owing to Western violations, Moscow considered the Potsdam Agreement null and void, and he demanded that the Allies withdraw from West Berlin. Rather than incorporate West Berlin into the East German state, he proposed as a concession to the Western Powers that West Berlin be made a neutralized and unarmed free city. Should the West not accede to these proposals within six months, Russia would sign a separate peace treaty with East Germany. The West rejected the plan since it would have left West Berlin at the mercy of Soviet Russia and the East German state. The Soviets allowed the six months deadline to pass,

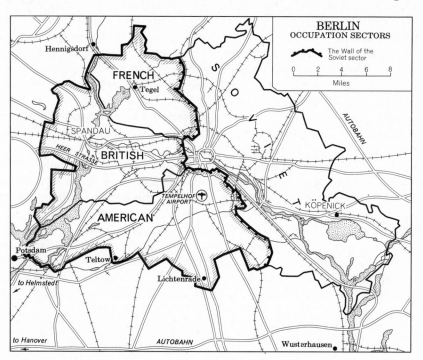

and they did not act either when a foreign ministers conference in the summer of 1959 failed to produce a solution. Subsequent negotiations proved equally futile.

Unable to take over Berlin without resort to armed force, the Soviet and East German leaders decided to bar the East Germans from West Berlin: in August 1961 a wall was built along the border between the eastern and western part of the city to block any further escapes to the West.[6] The Wall settled East Germany's most acute difficulties resulting from the existence of West Berlin, but caused a new decline in East-West relations. However, since the Soviets were careful not to infringe on the rights of the Western Powers in East Berlin and on the *Autobahnen*, the crisis was allowed to subside.

NEW ISSUES AND TENSIONS

Challenges to the United States and the Soviet Union. The United States and the Soviet Union were the more anxious to avoid too deep an embroilment over Berlin because other foreign developments also claimed their attention. The United States was particularly concerned over the transformation of Cuba into an outpost of communism. Just a few months before, Cuban exiles had tried to overthrow the regime of Fidel Castro; the American-sponsored attempt had ended in disaster, and there was serious concern in Washington that the debacle of the Bay of Pigs had not only enhanced the prestige of Castro, but had also injected a new dynamism into the communist drive for Latin America. Similarly the unstable situation in Southeast Asia gave Washington cause for worry: efforts to neutralize Laos to prevent a communist takeover were dragging on inconclusively while neighboring South Vietnam was plunged into a civil war in which communist elements were steadily gaining ground. Finally, the United States was faced with trouble in the Western camp itself. President De Gaulle was proceeding with the development of his own nuclear force, thus jeopardizing American hopes of stopping the proliferation of nuclear armaments. At the same time, De Gaulle made it clear that he did not only look upon France's nuclear power as a military imperative; by rendering the defense of his country less dependent on the United States, he also hoped to curb America's political and economic influence in France and in Europe.

Soviet Russia's difficulties arose above all from the deterioration of its relations with China. These tensions resulted from basic differences over the tempo and objectives of the world communist drive. Moscow wanted to concentrate on the development of the communist countries in the

---

[6] Despite the Wall, almost 3,500 East Germans managed to escape from East to West Berlin between August 1961 and the end of 1964. The most important escape routes were subterranean tunnels dug by enterprising West Berlin students.

conviction that the emerging nations could best be converted to communism by a demonstration of its superiority over capitalism. Peking, on the other hand, considered support of revolutionary movements in Asia, Africa, and Latin America of greater importance and urged the aggressive promotion of the communist cause in the underdeveloped countries. Alarmed at China's militancy, the Kremlin attempted to curb it. In 1959 Khrushchev repudiated an agreement with Peking by which the U.S.S.R. was to share with China its knowledge of nuclear arms production.

The Sino-Soviet conflict boded trouble not only on the global plane, but threatened also Soviet Russia's position in the communist camp. In fact, China soon made one convert in eastern Europe: since 1958 Albania, long fearful of its big neighbor, Yugoslavia, and uncertain of post-Stalin Russia, began shifting its allegiance from Moscow to Peking. In 1961 the break between Moscow and Tirana became complete. Nor did the other European states support Moscow wholeheartedly in its dispute with China. Rumania remained pointedly noncommittal; other countries, while siding with the U.S.S.R., criticized Khrushchev for allowing the quarrel to be aired openly before the non-communist world.

The Cuban Crisis and Europe. In the fall of 1962 the Cuban problem erupted into the most serious of all Soviet-American confrontations. This new crisis grew out of Moscow's attempt to install on the island medium-range (500–1,000 miles) and intermediate-range (up to 2,000 miles) ballistic missiles. The MRBM's would have covered Washington, St. Louis, and Dallas, and the IRBM's would have brought Boston, Chicago, Omaha, and Santa Fé—that is about half of the United States—within firing range. Owing to the United States' vast superiority in ICBM's, American nuclear striking power would still have remained at least twice as large as that of the Soviet Union; thus the installation of the missiles would have affected the political more than the military balance of power.[7] But this was reason enough for the United States to bar the missiles from Cuba. A blockade was established around the island and Moscow was warned to remove the weapons or else face the risk of war. Faced with America's determination to prevent the emplacement of the missiles in Cuba, even at the price of nuclear war, the Kremlin gave up the attempt.

The Cuban crisis had its implications for Europe as well. Had America permitted the Kremlin to proceed with its plan, it might have encouraged Khrushchev to resume his efforts to drive the Western Powers out of Berlin. American inaction in the face of the Soviets' activities would

---

[7] Militarily, the main advantage of the MRBM's would have been that, unlike ICBM's, they allowed almost no warning time between their launching and arrival on target.

also have had a considerable psychological impact on Europe. Nonetheless, the immediate European reaction to the crisis was mixed. Having lived for so long in the shadow of Soviet missiles, many Europeans found it difficult to appreciate America's alarm at the installation of missiles in Cuba. The British response was one of skeptical reserve, and Italy, too, felt misgivings over the American reaction. But there were those who understood the difference between Europe's acceptance of Soviet-based missiles for lack of a realistic alternative, and an American acceptance of missiles in Cuba, which was not a matter of life and death to the Soviets. Among those who saw this most clearly was De Gaulle. "If there is war, I will be with you. But there will be no war," he replied on being informed of the American plan. Adenauer, too, immediately sided with Washington.

The Test-Ban Treaty. The Cuban crisis was the culmination of East-West tensions. Having won his victory, President Kennedy played it down so as not to humiliate Moscow beyond all hope for a rapprochement. Khrushchev accepted his defeat and addressed himself to the task of shoring up the faltering Soviet economy. In January 1963 he announced that because of the Wall there was no immediate need for the conclusion of a separate peace treaty with East Germany, and the problem of Berlin receded farther into the background.

In this atmosphere of diminishing tensions, the hope revived that agreement might now be reached on a nuclear test ban. The Soviet Union had resumed atmospheric testing in September 1961; in reply to the Soviet move, the United States had made some underground tests that same month and had followed them up with atmospheric explosions the following April. Increasing public concern over the dangers of fallout made action imperative. After an auspicious start, the discussions threatened to flounder on the question of on-site inspections; monitoring systems located outside the Soviet Union could detect all atmospheric and underwater tests, but there was some doubt whether these devices could distinguish between earthquakes and underground tests. The Soviet Union denied this difficulty and, always fearful of espionage, would allow only three inspections a year on its soil whereas the United States insisted on seven. In the end, agreement was reached on a limited test ban outlawing tests in the atmosphere, in outer space, and under water, and a Test Ban Treaty was signed in Moscow in August 1963.

During the following weeks over a hundred other countries acceded to the treaty, but there were some notable omissions. Among them were Red China and France, neither of which would sign because both were determined to acquire their own nuclear power. An American offer to supply France with the technical data which the French might obtain from any tests of their own failed to change De Gaulle's mind. To overcome the objections of countries which did not wish to be associated with some of the other signatories, official texts were made available for signing in Washington, Moscow, and London. Thus West Germany signed the Washington document, whereas East Germany put its signature to the Moscow copy.

The assassination of President Kennedy in November 1963 brought to a halt all further attempts at a Soviet-Western rapprochement. In October 1964 Khrushchev was removed from office (see p. 538), and his successors, Aleksei Kosygin, the new Soviet Premier, and Leonid Brezhnev, First Secretary of the Soviet Communist Party, concentrated on improving Moscow's relations with China. Subsequently, American intervention in the war between the government and Communist-led guerrillas in South Vietnam and Soviet aid to North Vietnam impeded any new efforts toward a further *détente*.

The Multilateral Nuclear Force. Another obstacle to improved East-West relations was the fear of nuclear proliferation. We do not know whether the Soviet Union made any further attempt to keep China from developing its own nuclear weapons; Washington, on its part, made a number of efforts to restrain the western European Powers from developing nuclear forces of their own. The Eisenhower Administration proposed in 1960, shortly before its departure, the creation of a mixed-manned, missile-equipped submarine force to be turned over to NATO if a feasible system of joint control could be worked out.[8] With some important modifications, the Kennedy Administration pursued the proposal. To improve Europe's military capabilities and coordinate its policies, it coupled the plan with a call for greater European economic and political unity: the Common Market (see p. 497) was to be expanded by the inclusion of Britain, and political unity obtained by the federation of Europe. Anxious to keep Western defense strategy flexible, the Kennedy plan also made the creation of the multilateral nuclear force (MLF) dependent on the completion of NATO's conventional armaments. However, American insistence on the need for conventional weapons together with America's retention of a veto over the use of the MLF, created new difficulties. More than ever Europeans were wondering how reliable a deterrent that force would be.

The situation was further complicated by the fact that the United States, in fulfillment of an earlier commitment, reinforced Britain's preferential nuclear position by promising to equip Britain with the same Polaris missiles (though without nuclear warheads) which the other European nations were to have only by way of the MLF. To satisfy De Gaulle, France, too, was offered Polaris missiles, but Paris rejected the offer on the grounds that France had neither the nuclear

---

[8] The form of a mixed–manned seaborne force was chosen to prevent any nation from claiming proprietary rights to land-based missiles.

warheads nor the submarines to make use of the missiles. Going further, De Gaulle vetoed Britain's entry into the Common Market. He maintained that because of the special Anglo-American relationship, Britain's membership would open the door to American domination of the Common Market, thus increasing European dependence on the United States. The General also announced that France would continue to develop its own nuclear striking force since "no one in the world . . . can say if, where, when, how and to what extent the American nuclear weapons would be employed to defend Europe." De Gaulle did not underestimate the importance of American nuclear power; he hailed it as the "most powerful of all" and the "essential guarantee of peace." But being himself a strong believer in the supremacy of the nation-state, he was convinced that America would use its nuclear weapons only in defense of its own national interests. He did not believe that the defense of Europe at any price was one of these.

The difficulty was a very genuine one. The United States was anxious to give its partners in NATO a sense of participation in nuclear strategy; at the same time it wished to avoid the proliferation of nuclear power which would render even more difficult an agreement on nuclear arms limitations. Genuine joint control of the MLF would also present complex technical and strategic problems; how, for example, would multilateral decisions be reached on the use of nuclear weapons in emergencies in which every minute would count? On the other hand, given America's veto, its nuclear near-monopoly in the West would not be affected by the proposed MLF, and the creation of that force would have symbolic rather than real significance. Those who accepted the plan most readily were the West Germans. Pledged not to produce any nuclear weapons, they saw here a chance to obtain at least some influence on nuclear strategy. Yet Bonn's receptivity to the proposal aroused fears about West Germany's ultimate designs in both eastern and western Europe and caused the Soviet Union to block all further discussions of nuclear disarmament. The risks and difficulties of the MLF thus proved so formidable that it soon was relegated to the bottom of NATO's agenda. In 1965 the plan was dropped altogether by Washington.

EUROPE ON THE MOVE

The Gaullist Concept of Europe.   Meanwhile, De Gaulle addressed himself to the task of realizing his long-cherished plan for a French-led Europe holding its own between the United States and the Soviet Union. It was to rest on close Franco-German ties; as a first step, the General concluded a friendship treaty with West Germany providing for intensified collaboration between the two countries. The arrangement was vague, but Adenauer might have given effect to the pact had he stayed longer in office. His relations with Washington had grown notably cooler since the Eisenhower era, for Kennedy disagreed with Adenauer's conviction that an East-West *détente* would perpetuate the division of Germany. Chancellor Erhard, who succeeded Adenauer in October 1963, shared Washington's view that a *détente* would aid rather than hinder reunification. Accordingly, Erhard set out to improve relations with the United States. In particular he insisted on close cooperation with Washington in nuclear questions—a policy that put some strain on Bonn's ties with Paris. Neither De Gaulle nor Adenauer accepted this passively. In November 1964 the General invited the ex-Chancellor for a well-publicized visit, and on his return, Adenauer and other "Gaullist" leaders in Germany called for Germany's participation in a European nuclear force not subject to an American veto.

De Gaulle's aspirations looked beyond the union of western Europe under the leadership of France. Ultimately he envisaged the re-creation of a Europe that extended once more, politically as well as geographically, "from the Atlantic to the Ural Mountains." Such a development presupposed a complete break between the Soviet Union and China, and De Gaulle could point to the fact that developments seemed to be moving in this direction. In March 1966, in pursuit of his goals, the General withdrew France's armed forces from the integrated defense system of NATO (though he did not withdraw from the Atlantic alliance as such). This step was not only a declaration of independence from the United States, but also an expression of his conviction that Europe was no longer the center of the major international crises. In his view, that center had shifted to Asia, and he wished to retain a free hand in the struggles in that part of the world. Dissociating himself further from American policies, he resumed diplomatic relations with Peking in the fall of 1963.

Whether these were the inspired visions of a farsighted statesman or the fantasies of a French supernationalist, only the future could tell. Even if De Gaulle's predictions should come true, there remained the question whether France had the capabilities to play the role of grandeur he assigned to his country and whether, after his departure from office, his countrymen would wish to continue to play it. Meanwhile, the General threw into disarray the Western defenses and the containment of Germany's armed forces within the framework of NATO. Similarly, his policies were hampering the further unification of Europe—a result which was not unwelcome to him (see p. 500).

West Germany and Eastern Europe. As the eastern and western European countries assumed a more independent attitude, they also began to develop increased contacts with each other. The time was auspicious because Soviet Europe by itself was unable to meet the growing demand for better living conditions. Because of its need for economic assistance, trade between the two regions grew markedly in the mid-1960's. West Germany and Italy were especially active in eastern Europe, which had traditionally been one of their major markets. On the eastern side, Rumania took the lead in this commercial rapprochement; in 1963 over half of its trade was with the West, and the Western share increased as time passed. However, in absolute terms, Poland ranked as the West's main partner in trade, while Hungary took third place. This growing exchange of goods was accompanied by an increasing amount of technical and managerial collaboration. A steel mill was built in Galati, Rumania, by English engineers and equipped with German machinery; it was to process iron ore brought in from Brazil and India. In Poland, the West Germans provided the know-how, skilled labor, and capital, and the Poles provided the manpower, raw materials, and factory grounds for the joint manufacture of such items as road building equipment, kitchen stoves, men's wear, and tape recorders. A similar arrangement between Fiat, Italy's leading car manufacturer, and the Warsaw government led to the establishment of the first automobile plant in Poland. The west European partners shared in the profits and risks, but not in the ownership of these enterprises.

For the West Germans these ventures were more than mere business transactions. During the Adenauer era, political contacts with eastern Europe had been held to a minimum since the Bonn government did not wish to have dealings with countries that had recognized the East German regime. The Erhard government viewed the trade expansion as a first step toward a general rapprochement with the Eastern countries that might help it to outflank and weaken the German Democratic Republic. At the same time, Bonn tried to increase East German dependence on the West German economy by encouraging increased interzonal trade. (By tying all trade agreements to undisturbed traffic between Berlin and West Germany, it also hoped to ensure continued access to West Berlin.) To reassure the east European countries of its peaceful intentions, the West German government also offered to sign nonaggression and disarmament pacts with them. There were suggestions that the Oder-Neisse Line might be negotiable as the price of reunification. In an official statement accompanying the pact proposals, the Bonn government declared that it would not give up its claims to the lost lands east of the Oder-Neisse line "until such a time as a freely elected *all-German* government recognizes *other* frontiers." (Italics added). Whether or not this strategy could lead to reunification, West Germany seemed determined not to wait any longer for Washington's lead. Like De Gaulle, the West Germans felt that they must act on their own.

They also agreed with De Gaulle that Europe ought not to involve itself in the conflict between the United States and Communist China. Beginning in 1963, West Germany began expanding its trade with Communist China: German exports increased from $25 million in 1964 to $79 million in 1965, and in 1966 a German-led consortium contracted to build a steel processing plant in China. In doing so, the West Germans quickly overtook the East Germans as trade partners of Red China. Because of East Germany's close association with Moscow, its trade with China had been falling off for some time, and by 1965 was reduced to one-fifth of that of the Bonn Republic.

The government of Kurt-Georg Kiesinger which succeeded that of Chancellor Erhard in December 1966 pursued the policy of a rapprochement with the East with even greater vigor. Under the guidance of the new Foreign Minister, Willy Brandt, the long-time Mayor of West Berlin, West Germany resumed diplomatic relations with Rumania and planned to normalize its relations with other east European countries as well. Similarly, it seemed prepared to enter into high-level talks with East Germany on economic and other matters of mutual interest—a marked departure from the previous West German policy of rejecting any such contacts. The East Germans, however, insisted on being recognized as a legitimate government by West Germany before entering into major negotiations. They also persuaded other east European governments not to resume diplomatic relations with the Bonn government as long as Bonn did not recognize East Berlin. Since West Germany was not prepared to take this step, the Kiesinger-Brandt policy of a rapprochement with eastern Europe appeared to have run into a stalemate after some months.

Britain and Europe. The resurgence of continental western Europe could also be measured in terms of the declining prestige of Britain. Owing to its ties with the Commonwealth and its special relationship to the United States, Britain continued to look upon itself as a major power in world affairs, somewhat apart from Europe, yet sharing many of its concerns. As such, it saw itself as a connecting link and a mediator between Europe and the United States. During the Cold War, it played this role with a modicum of success, conveying to Washington Europe's dismay at America's policies, acting as an intermediary between the United States and the Soviet Union, and attempting to ease Soviet-American tensions. On balance, however, Britain's advice did not carry much weight with Washington, for the special Anglo-American relationship was far less important to Washington than it was to London.

This fact was driven home to the British when the United States refused to back Britain and France in the Suez crisis. Britain, however, reacted differently to the American attitude than did France. Whereas the French concluded that they ought to attain a greater degree of independence from the United States, the British continued to accept the principle of American leadership in the Western alliance. On the other hand, Britain remained determined to retain formally its full national sovereignty. Accordingly, it did not join the European Economic Community, better known as the Common Market, when it was organized in 1957, for EEC membership would have meant submission to the decisions of supranational agencies and the abandonment of Britain's preferential tariff arrangements with the Commonwealth countries. But soon the question arose whether in staying out of the EEC Britain had not overestimated its economic resources and potentialities. In 1961, beset by severe economic difficulties, the British government had a change of heart and applied for membership in the Market. It was prepared to make important concessions on its trade with the Commonwealth nations, but to France the issue was no longer a purely economic one, and De Gaulle vetoed Britain's admission (see p. 490).

Britain accepted the rejection with notable equanimity. Public support of the bid for EEC membership had been lukewarm, and the prospect of retaining a measure of aloofness from the European continent and preserving the special ties with the Commonwealth was pleasing to many. There were those, however, who wondered whether Britain could still afford to retain this traditional stance. The Polaris agreement of 1962 had put an end to Britain's development of its own strategic nuclear weapons; in the spring of 1966 its military limitations became even more evident when it decided to cut by one-third its overseas forces, frankly conceding that it was no longer able to undertake any major military operation without the support of the United States. Yet there was no corresponding tightening of the Anglo-American relationship as Britain grew more dependent on American backing; never as close as the British liked to believe, the ties had in fact grown weaker since the death of President Kennedy. On the economic level, too, there was cause for concern. British foreign trade was shifting increasingly from the Commonwealth to Europe:

	1956	1964
Commonwealth	40%	30%
EEC	13%	18%
EFTA[9]	12%	14%

The aggregate trade with the EFTA and EEC nations was larger in 1964 than that with the Commonwealth nations, with the increase largest in the case of the Common Market. Yet few Britons seemed to worry about these facts; they were not an issue in the elections of October 1964 and March 1966.

However, in the fall of 1966 Prime Minister Harold Wilson decided that Britain's economic difficulties could not be solved permanently unless Britain joined the EEC. As before, the main obstacle to Britain's membership was De Gaulle; he still seemed doubtful that Britain was sufficiently independent of the United States to pursue the "European"

[9] EFTA is the British-led European Free Trade Area (see p. 499).

policies which he advocated. Perhaps in order to reassure the General, Wilson made a number of statements suggesting his dissociation from too close a relationship with the United States. Yet when he submitted Britain's application for membership in May 1967, De Gaulle still seemed opposed to Britain's admission.

Western Europe and the United States. If Britain was loosening its ties with the United States, it was not alone. An important cause of Chancellor Erhard's removal from office in November 1966 was the feeling* among West German leaders that the orientation of Erhard's foreign policy toward the United States was proving too costly. (At issue was a West German commitment to purchase American arms in partial compensation for the maintenance of American forces in Germany.) Consequently, one of the first moves of Erhard's successor, Chancellor Kiesinger, was to strengthen his country's ties with France and to coordinate his foreign policies more closely with those of De Gaulle.

Yet this loosening of European-American ties could not be explained simply in economic terms. With the Soviet Union no longer viewed as a threat to the peace of Europe, Europeans felt less dependent on the United States than they had in the past. As they saw it, moreover, America's involvement in the war in Vietnam distracted the United States from giving its full attention to Europe's concerns, forcing western Europe to stand increasingly on its own feet. To Europeans this conclusion seemed also confirmed by the fact that the United States was planning the reduction of its NATO contingent to replenish its forces in Vietnam. Evidently western Europe and the United States were entering a new phase in their relationship.

22

Western Europe:
Economy, Society,
Culture in the Era
of Affluence

The internal history of Western Europe during the 1950's and 1960's was on the whole a tribute to the industry of its people and to the resourcefulness of its leaders. Not since the days before World War I had Europe enjoyed as protracted a period of prosperity as it did during these years. They were also years of political and social realignments, characterized by an increasing willingness to resolve existing divergences peaceably rather than by violence. All in all, they were years of expanding opportunities, of greater social justice, and of improved living standards, opening up vistas of future possibilities that would have seemed utopian only a decade before.

Yet the blessings of affluence carried within them also the seeds of new social dangers—an excessive preoccupation with material concerns, a widespread readiness to accept authoritarian political leadership, a growing indifference toward moral and spiritual issues. As always, the artists were the first to sense these tendencies: the contemporary literature of western Europe testified with alarming near-unanimity to the pervasive presence of these problems. Man's cynicism and materialism were ever recurring themes of novels and plays.

PROBLEMS OF INTEGRATION

Further Steps Toward Unity. The European Coal and Steel Community was looked upon by its founders as a first step toward the full political and economic integration of its six members. These hopes suffered their first serious setback when France rejected the establishment of the European Defense Community. In the circumstances, any further integration seemed possible only in the economic domain, and it was here that the next steps were taken: in June 1955, meeting at Messina, Italy, the foreign ministers of the six ECSC nations—West Germany, France, Italy, and the Benelux countries—agreed to expand their economic collaboration. The negotiations gathered speed when the Suez Crisis drove home to the six their vulnerability and the need for closer cooperation. By endangering their access to the oil of the Middle East, the Suez episode underlined also the growing importance of nuclear energy. As a result, two new institutions were set up by the treaties of Rome in 1957—the European Economic Community or Common Market and the European Atomic Energy Community (EURATOM). EURATOM was a joint undertaking designed to develop nuclear energy for peaceful uses and assure a level of productivity which none of the Six could hope to attain if it were to proceed by itself.

The European Economic Community. The EEC was to give wider scope to the economies of the Six by removing, within fifteen years, all tariff and other trade barriers between them. Cooperation was to be furthered also by the free movement of labor and capital within the Common Market and by the creation of a uniform external tariff between the Market and the rest of the world. Special institutions were established to implement these policies: an Investment Bank was to aid the less developed parts of the EEC and a Social Fund underwrote the retraining and resettlement of workers affected by the removal of tariffs and quotas. Provisions were made to coordinate monetary policies, stabilize prices, equalize wages, and harmonize working and living conditions in the Market area. Supranational organs similar to those of the ECSC were set up to administer the Community, with a Council of Ministers representing the national interests of the members. The EEC could admit new members by the unanimous vote of the present membership; it could also admit "associate" members which enjoyed free access to the Market, but retained their own tariffs. The former Belgian and French colonies became the first associate members; in 1961 they were joined by Greece. As the preamble to the EEC treaty stated, economic integration was eventually to be supplemented by political federation.

On the whole, the EEC nations experienced a remarkable expansion

Meeting of Common Market members at Bonn, July 1961. Left to right:
Spaak (Belgium), Werner (Luxembourg), Fanfani (Italy), De Quay
(Netherlands), Lefevre (Belgium), De Gaulle (France), Luns (Netherlands),
Adenauer (West Germany). (*Reprinted courtesy Wide World Photos*)

of their economies, but it was impossible to say to what extent this could
be attributed to their membership in the Common Market. Most of them
were growing rapidly before the EEC came into being; the sluggish
economies of Belgium and Luxembourg, on the other hand, were proof
that EEC membership did not automatically guarantee rapid growth.
The most noteworthy increase was in intra-Market trade of industrial
goods; as a result, internal industrial tariffs were lowered more rapidly
than had been anticipated. By July 1, 1963 they had been reduced to
60 per cent and by 1966 to 80 per cent of their 1957 level. In July 1968
internal tariffs were to end altogether. Important adjustments were
also made in external tariffs; by 1966 they had been adjusted 60 per
cent of the way toward full uniformity.

Agriculture, on the other hand, was beset by serious difficulties. Cus-
tomarily the most heavily protected sector of any economy, it was also
the most national-minded. To France the expectation of finding a large
market for its exploding agricultural output had been a major incentive
for joining the EEC, but in this hope it was disappointed. The German
farming community, more heavily subsidized than its French counterpart, did not wish to be exposed to French competition. It forced the
Adenauer government, which needed its vote, to delay any changes in
EEC farm policy. By mid-summer 1961, harassed by peasant riots and

furious at seeing Germany reaping huge benefits from tariff reductions on industrial goods, France threatened to block any further lowering of industrial tariffs until common price levels had been established for agricultural products. Again the discussions dragged on endlessly, but a deadline set by De Gaulle forced a showdown. "After 140 hours of negotiations, two heart attacks, and one nervous collapse,"[1] agreements were reached on a large number of farm products, satisfying the French for the moment. During the following years little further progress was made. Dissatisfied, De Gaulle withdrew from the negotiations in July 1965, thus holding up all further advance toward integration. Domestic pressures forced him to return to the conference table, and in July 1966 agreements were reached eliminating all internal agricultural tariffs by July 1968.

Britain, the Common Market, and EFTA.   Britain, it will be recalled, did not enter the Common Market when it was first formed. London's refusal to join was dictated not only by political considerations but also by economic concerns. One of the mainstays of the British economy was cheap food; however, as a member of the EEC Britain would have had to accept the Market's external tariff and this would have put an end to the duty free importation of foodstuffs. Yet unhindered access to the vast market of the EEC was of crucial importance to a country as dependent on exports as Britain. London therefore proposed the creation of a loose all-European free trade arrangement in which other west European nations would be linked with the Common Market. It would require only the removal of internal tariffs, but would not involve a surrender of sovereignty or the creation of a common tariff wall against nonmembers. This proposal was rejected by the French, who objected to Britain's insistence on continuing food imports from Commonwealth countries. In 1959 the British established a more modest European Free Trade Area (EFTA) with Norway, Sweden, Denmark, Portugal, Switzerland, and Austria. (Finland became an associate member in 1961.) It called for the gradual abolition of tariffs between EFTA members, but made no provision for economic unification. By 1967 it had eliminated all internal industrial tariffs.

EFTA proved of little benefit to the British. The Scandinavian countries and Portugal had always been among their good customers, and British exports to EFTA members increased more slowly than those to the EEC nations. In 1961 Britain applied, therefore, for admission to the Common Market, ready to make important concessions in matters of agriculture and food imports. But this was no longer sufficient to overcome French opposition. To De Gaulle, Britain's membership in the EEC

[1] U. W. Kitzinger, *The Politics and Economics of European Integration: Britain, Europe, and the United States* (New York, 1964), p. 35.

was much more a political than an economic issue, for behind Britain he saw lurking the threat of an American hegemony.

European Union in Suspense.   After France's veto the EEC encountered many obstacles. Whereas the governments of the Six had adjusted most differences with comparative ease until then, they now tended to follow De Gaulle's example and upheld their national interests much more rigidly. De Gaulle, moreover, was opposed to political integration and would accept political coordination only on the government level. Political union he envisaged as a loose union of states rather than peoples, with the EEC basically a technical organ concerned with economic affairs. In the spring of 1967 it seemed unlikely that any genuine political unification could be achieved in the foreseeable future.

Yet there were pressures pointing to the need for greater political unity. European industrialists were conscious of the vast technological gap existing between their operations and those of their American counterparts. They knew that this gap could be closed only by the creation of European-wide enterprises subject to one single system of taxes and social security, one legal code, and one monetary policy, and sparked by scientific and technological research drawing on resources of continental dimensions. Since De Gaulle and other political leaders were anxious to fight off American competition, these were facts they could not lightly dismiss. As much as the General opposed the political unification of Europe, it remained to be seen whether he would in the long run be able to resist the economic pressures calling for political integration.

THE REVOLUTION IN ECONOMIC POLICY

The New Government-Business Relationship.   One of the striking developments of the 1950's and 1960's was the almos⁺ uninterrupted economic prosperity that continental western Europe enjoyed. "Growth of output and consumption, productivity, investment and employment [surpassed] any recorded historical experience."[2] The continued boom was especially notable in view of the vulnerability from which the European economies had suffered throughout the interwar period (except for the fully insulated Nazi economy).

If these economies now showed an unexpected vitality, their structure and management differed sharply, however, from the prewar system. The largest part of all the economies still was in private hands, but private enterprise was hedged in by far-reaching government powers and con-

[2] Angus Maddison, *Economic Growth in the West: Comparative Experience in Europe and North America* (New York, 1964), p. 25.

trols. The sources and methods of the new government role varied in different countries—in Italy and Austria the government's powers rested on the extensive public ownership of industrial enterprises; in Germany they were derived mainly from vast powers of taxation and extensive social insurance programs that put at the disposal of the government huge funds for investment purposes; in Sweden and Holland they derived from governmental authority to plan centrally key aspects of economic development; in France they grew out of a combination of these factors.

Government Planning. The objectives of governmental activity changed in the course of time, in keeping with changing needs. On the whole, governments were at first concerned with meeting short-term emergency situations—unemployment, inflation, an upset in the balance of payments. Only France embarked on a long-range program directing the country's development over a period of years, but neglecting in turn such immediate difficulties as inflation. As time went on, governments faced new tasks; in an era of continuing prosperity they no longer worried about recessions or unemployment, but about maintaining the economic momentum. Their task was now to sustain a steady rate of productive growth and prevent violent price fluctuations. There was no question of freezing either profits or wages but of imposing restraints in order to correlate them to the tempo of the increase in production. From slump control many governments thus were turning to boom control. (Conversely, France, under De Gaulle, tackled such immediate emergencies as its spreading inflation.) By the mid-sixties Britain, France, Italy, Spain, Sweden, Norway, Belgium, Holland, and Austria were engaged in some measure of central economic planning. Of these countries, France went farthest in government planning (but even the French plans were modest by Soviet standards), while Italy's was the least systematized. Britain was a comparative latecomer in developing long-term economic plans; they were initiated in the early 1960's by the Conservative government of Prime Minister Harold Macmillan but were still in an experimental stage in 1965. Spain's Economic Development Plan was launched in 1964.

French planning, it will be recalled, was originally devised to encourage the rapid expansion of certain key industries. Since the mid-1950's, however, the planners saw their main task in spotting prospective bottlenecks of production—a task that they sought to fulfill by anticipating future demand on the basis of national income forecasts. In the case of private firms, the planners implemented their programs by agreements on output for which they offered tax relief or low interest loans.

Sweden's planning sought to maintain full employment, and rapid economic growth by channeling labor into those regions and industries that offered the greatest economic opportunities. This the government accomplished by means of public investments (relatively among the highest in Europe), tax concessions, and carefully allocated subsidies. In addition, it relied on collective bargaining on a nation-wide scale based on forecasts of the growth of the national product. Centrally established wages prevented competitive bidding for labor with its inevitable rise in wages and prices; by removing local inequities, this arrangement also helped to preserve industrial peace. Finally, by forcing less efficient enterprises out of business, it released labor to where it could be utilized to better advantage.

Italy and Austria, finally, steered their economies by means of the pressures they could exert through their publicly owned enterprises. Although Italy did develop overall plans, they remained on the whole ineffective; efforts to industrialize the southern part of the country and to expand the ship building and metallurgical industries in the north were carried out by the Fascist-inherited Institute of Industrial Reconstruction which controlled about 30 per cent of Italy's industry. The situation was similar in Austria whose nationalized industries produced roughly one-fourth of the country's industrial output.

West Germany's Market Economy. The German government did not draw up any long-term program to sustain full employment and growth of production, but planning was not absent from the West German economy. To a large extent this function was assumed by private business itself, which undertook to police itself to guard against the abrupt changes and violent fluctuations associated with a free market economy. This kind of direction was made possible by the authority enjoyed by Germany's industrial associations. Since 1953 many of these bodies compiled annual forecasts of productive capacity and probable future demands in their industry to provide guidance to member firms in their planning. The associations also encouraged their members to collaborate on long-range development projects. Similarly, Germany's major banks served as coordinators of investment plans, and generally sought to foster collaboration within industrial areas in which they were interested.

The government's role in the economy was far from negligible, however. Publicly owned enterprises accounted for one-third of Germany's output of iron ore, one-fourth of its coal, and almost one-half of its zinc. Like the Monnet Plan in France, the government favored the expansion of certain key industries—coal, iron, steel, and electricity—and these were among the chief beneficiaries of the government's cheap loans and tax allowances. On the average, the government spent about 25 per cent of its budgetary expenditures on tax concessions and subsidies to direct the country's economy. Beginning in 1962, it also sponsored an annual national forecast of business trends and prospects. Although this was no plan in the French sense, the apparatus was being created that would allow, if need be, to shift without difficulty from an economy still essentially self-regulated to one guided by an overall plan.

Private Enterprise. The growing economic role of the governments did not curtail the initiative of private enterprise, but did in fact strengthen it. Manufacturers faced more confidently the challenge of foreign competition; thus, French and Italian industrialists, traditionally slow in adjusting to new conditions, learned to live with the tariff reductions of the Common Market. Similarly, the knowledge that the fluctuations of the business cycle could be controlled had its psychological impact on European businessmen. Their plans no longer were based on the certainty of periodical setbacks, and they were willing to engage in longer-range projects. In this same spirit, they accepted the expanding social insurance programs that most European governments were promoting. They found that they could still do well despite the increasing social expenditures, which a short time before they would have considered intolerable burdens.

During 1966 this confidence gave way to new caution, however. Inflationary pressures, a falling off of demand, and reductions in public investments led to a decline in business activities in West Germany, France, and the Low Countries. Unemployment began to increase, if only moderately, suggesting that these countries were facing a temporary recession rather than a more serious crisis. Even a comparatively minor decline was alarming, however, because any increase in unemployment in West Germany, France, and Belgium—all three large-scale employers of foreign labor—was bound to create problems also in the homelands to which the foreign workers would be forced to return.

There were other clouds on the economic horizon. Long-range plans required comprehensive and highly sophisticated research into anticipated technological developments and large scale investments that would not pay off for some time. Only very large enterprises could embark on such ventures, and there was a marked increase in mergers and concentrations. They raised the question of the public control of these industrial giants, just as the question of democratic control arose in regard to the government's economic planners. To these problems the answers had still to be found. They may prove difficult to develop because of widespread public indifference (see p. 510).

SOCIAL CHANGES

Population Movements. If further proof was needed of Europe's vitality, it could be found in the growth of its population during the 1950's and 1960's. The increase was more notable in the case of countries whose birth rate had either been stagnant or had been declining during the interwar years. France's birth rate had dropped steadily during the prewar period, but it rose rapidly after the war. The French population increased from 42,752,000 in 1953 to 47,853,000 in 1963 and continued to grow at a rate of almost 500,000 per year. Britain, whose birth rate had remained stationary in the 1930's, recovered its wartime losses with remarkable speed and expanded its population from 50,880,000 to 53,-812,000 during the 1953–1963 period. Other countries whose birth rate was on the ascendant in contrast to prewar years were Austria, Belgium, Norway, and Switzerland. But the trend was not uniform. Italy and Greece, long plagued by overpopulation, were witnessing a decline of their birth rates. In both countries the effects of an advancing urbanization and modernization were beginning to make themselves felt.

On the labor market the effects of these trends could, of course, not be felt for some time. Beginning in the mid-1950's, the expanding economies of the countries of northwestern Europe began suffering from an increasingly serious manpower shortage; conversely, the south European countries still found themselves burdened with large numbers of unemployed. This led to the largest peacetime migration of workers recorded in modern Europe. The bulk of the migrants came from Italy; they were joined by tens of thousands of Spaniards, Portuguese, Yugoslavs, Greeks, and Turks who went north in search of employment. By the end of 1965, France had absorbed 1,250,000 of them (and would have taken more if it had not been for the influx of 500,000 Algerian refugees); West Germany hired a similar number (supplemented in this case by millions of East German refugees). Some of the smaller countries also relied on a large influx of foreign labor to maintain their economic momentum: in Switzerland in August 1964 the number of foreign workers amounted to 820,000, about one-third of the country's entire labor force. Sweden recruited abroad one-third of the 25,000 new workers needed each year, and foreigners held one-fourth of all jobs in Norway's merchant marine.

What the overall impact of this migration would be, it was too early to say. Inevitably, tensions developed between the native population and the newcomers; as a result the Swiss passed laws in 1965, 1966, and 1967 reducing the number of foreign workers by an aggregate of 12 per cent. Most governments sought to prevent serious clashes by providing special housing, educational, and recreational facilities for the foreign workers, and assigned social workers to assist them; the supplying countries on their part provided briefing courses on the host countries for their departing citizens. Much, of course, would depend on whether the foreign laborers would remain permanently in their new homes; most seemed to plan to return to their native country. As economic activities began to decline in 1966, many foreign workers did go back to their homelands.

The labor shortage provided also increasing economic opportunities for women; many continued to work after they were married and had children. In Austria women made up 36.5 per cent of the labor force—one of the highest percentages in Europe. The growing importance of women in the economic life of their country was also reflected in their improved legal status; in 1965 French wives, of whom 53 per cent were working, were given legal equality with their husbands, enabling them to sign contracts, own property independently, and run their own business. Germany, in 1961, included for the first time a woman minister in its government.

Structural Changes. Another outstanding feature of postwar western Europe was its progressing urbanization. Between 1950 and 1963 the number of agricultural workers declined by over 25 per cent, from 51,000,000 to 38,000,000. Because rural overpopulation had long been a serious problem in most European countries, this exodus, touched off by the rapid industrial expansion, was on the whole a salutary development. Still, the influx of rural laborers into cities that were ill-prepared to absorb them created severe housing and other difficulties—especially in Italy and France.

The economic boom also enhanced social mobility, at least for the younger generation. In an increasingly complex society, the need of business and government for white collar help was steadily growing, opening up new opportunities for persons of working class background. In the late 1950's one out of three sons of industrial workers were employed in some type of nonmanual work in West Germany. Yet there were clear limits to their advancement, and few of them rose above the lower strata of the white collar class. Changes within the middle class itself were of greater immediate significance. Here the most important development was the recruitment, primarily from its ranks, of a new social group of administrators, lawyers, scientists, and technicians who kept the governmental and economic machinery running. This new "service class" had a considerable impact on European politics and society in the 1950's and 1960's. Concerned with efficient accomplishment, its members had little interest in political parties and ideologies. As professional men they were in search of new opportunities, but as employees they sympathized also with the workers' concern for social security. This gave them a great deal of flexibility, and they had no difficulty in reconciling their faith in competitive advancement with the demands of the welfare state. Even the choice between democracy and authoritarianism began losing its meaning for many of them: they would support whoever would protect them from political interference and offer them the best chance for speedy efficient performance. They could work as easily with a conservative like De Gaulle as with a "socialist" like British Prime Minister Harold Wilson.

Educational Problems. The growing complexity of a sophisticated, highly industrialized society put a premium on education and special skills; conversely, education and specialized training were the gateway to social and professional advancement. As one observer has written, the school was replacing the family as an avenue to the top. Thus the needs of government, economy, and society, and the ambitions of an aspiring citizenry called for a vast expansion of educational facilities. The results were impressive: the number of students in secondary schools in western Europe grew from 9.7 million to 13.9 million between 1950 and 1960. Put differently, while in 1950 only one child in three had gone beyond primary school, the ratio was better than two out of five in 1960.[3] The increase was especially large in the enrollment of girls, attesting both the growing equality of the sexes and the increasing need for an education. How conscious students were of that need was demonstrated in Italy where they repeatedly went on strike in protest against the poor quality of the instruction offered to them.

Although significant progress was made in the physical expansion of educational facilities, little was done to adjust the educational system to the new social needs of the times. The European school system had been designed originally for the benefit of a selected social elite; for this elite it provided a thorough and well-rounded education whereas the masses had to be satisfied with a minimum of instruction. Secondary schools were usually divided into two kinds, with one type offering a wide choice of educational opportunities and the other leading at best to some technical training in a trade school. As a rule the division occurred at an early age, somewhere between ten and twelve years, thus barring a large majority of all children from acquiring an advanced education. Italy was the first to put an end to this waste of human potential; in 1963 it unified all schools up to the age of fourteen, postponing by three years the decisive choice. Similarly, Britain set out in 1965 to fuse its various kinds of secondary education into one overall system of "comprehensive" schools. Another obstacle blocking a genuine democratization of higher education in western Europe was the scarcity of financial assistance available to children of low income groups. Compared to prewar conditions, the situation was somewhat improved, particularly in Britain, but the fact remained that the child of a worker continued to have a much slimmer chance of attending a university than did the child of a business or professional man or of an official.

Labor in the Affluent Society. The working class did not only find itself at an disadvantage in the matter of educational opportunities. Although its members enjoyed the benefits of greater social security, better wages, and enhanced political rights, their share in Europe's prosperity was still disproportionately small. The bulk of the new cars, washing machines, and refrigerators (though not TV sets!) went to the middle and upper classes. Much of what came to be considered a normal appurtenance of middle class life remained beyond the reach of the worker.

[3] Frank Bowles, "Education in the New Europe," in Stephen R. Graubard, ed., *A New Europe?* (Boston, 1964), p. 445.

Among the most disadvantaged were the elderly who depended upon their fixed pensions. In France at least one-third of those over 65 lived in a state of abject poverty, and in Italy the proportion was close to one-half. Payments to the ill and disabled were equally inadequate. (In Germany, on the other hand, all pensions were correlated with the rate of economic growth and were automatically readjusted every two years.) Such disparities continued to breed discontent; yet thanks to the improvements that labor did enjoy, this discontent was expressed in less violent forms in the 1960's than it had been during the preceding decade. Strikes there still were, but they now served as economic weapons used to attain economic objectives such as higher wages or shorter hours, and because of their nonpolitical character they no longer led to violence and bloodshed.

The "Americanization" of Western Europe. As much of the aforesaid suggests, conditions in western Europe came to resemble in many respects American ways and values. The "Americanization" of Europe could be most easily traced in the adoption of such Americana as Coca-Cola, breakfast cereals, and frozen foods, motels and milk bars, self-service stores and cafeterias, but the impact of these foods and facilities was at best superficial. Of much greater importance, socially and psychologically, was the acceptance of American production and business methods, fostered since the days of the Marshall Plan. They made their great contribution to the economic prosperity of western Europe and guided it toward a consumer civilization on the American model.

Beyond this, the extent of American influences was hard to determine. As in the United States, political life in Europe was characterized by the decline of ideology, the emergence of a few catch-all parties, and an increasing concern with men rather than issues. Similarly, the beginning reorganization of the secondary school system brought European education closer to the American concern with education for the many rather than the few. Above all, there were indications that large numbers of Europeans saw their life's goal avowedly in the realization of their own potentialities rather than in a struggle for national grandeur and power.

This shift in views and values may in part have been due to the cultural cross-fertilization engendered by the close formal and informal contacts between the United States and Europe. To what extent these contacts accounted for this social and cultural "Americanization," and how much of it was simply the result of an inevitable adjustment to changing conditions was and would always remain an unanswerable question.[4]

[4] This cross-fertilization operated also in the opposite direction as America moved towards the welfare state and assigned to the government an increasing role in the guidance of the economy.

THE CHANGING POLITICAL SCENE

The Pacification of Politics. In prosperous times public interest in politics slackens. Not surprisingly, then, political conditions became more quiet and stable as western Europe attained new levels of economic growth. Ideologies began to lose their importance as an increasing number of citizens came to agree on fundamentals. Most socialist parties bowed to the conciliatory effects of full employment and social security and gave up their class struggle doctrines. They also dropped their demands for the all-out nationalization of the means of production and for all-encompassing economic planning; in fact, in many countries their programs differed but little from those of their bourgeois opponents. The bourgeois parties in turn reconciled themselves to the permanence of the welfare state and to the growing role of the government in the shaping of economic decisions. With both camps in basic agreement on the social and economic policies that should be pursued, their divergences concerned mainly the speed and extent of these measures. Collaboration between bourgeois parties and Socialists thus proved possible not only in the Scandinavian countries, long noted for their political moderation, but also in Austria whose Socialist Party had been one of the most militant movements before it was crushed by Chancellor Dollfuss in 1934. After Austria's liberation in 1955, the Austrian Socialists formed a government coalition with the conservative Austrian People's Party that lasted for almost ten years. Representatives of both parties worked also closely together on the boards of directors of all publicly owned enterprises. In 1963 Italy's Socialist Party, after years of collaboration with the Communists, formed a coalition government with the Christian Democrats, and in 1966 it united again with the moderate Democratic Socialists, largely on the terms of the latter. Similarly, West Germany's Social Democrats joined bourgeois coalitions in some of the states within the Federal Republic and on the national plane. In 1959 they adopted a new program that cut all remaining ties to the Marxist origins of the party (see p. 523).

Extremism did not entirely disappear from the political stage, but in most west European countries was not important politically. Neofascist groups continued to exist in Germany, Austria and Italy. However, until 1965, except for brief local flare-ups, the post-Hitler Nazis had only a small following in the Bonn Republic. In 1966 a National Democratic Party appeared on the scene with a strongly nationalist platform marked by some barely disguised Nazi overtones. Aided by the deteriorating unemployment situation, the National Democrats scored some successes in state and local elections, reviving fears of a possible Nazi resurgence. Neofascists in Austria and in Italy had greater support from disgruntled lower middle class elements in small towns and villages who saw themselves bypassed by the new affluence and derived little benefit from the welfare state. Yet only in Italy did neofascists have any political weight; however, when they seemed to have a chance to enter the government in 1963, they were barred at once by a nation-wide upsurge. In France, fascism had a brief revival during the Algerian crisis, but it receded into obscurity as soon as that crisis was settled. Even in Spain it kept losing ground as Franco transformed his government into an old-fashioned dictatorship.

Communism. Communist parties, on the other hand, still had a mass following in France and Italy where some 25 per cent of the voters continued to cast their ballot for them. Here persistent social and economic grievances and the inertia of political habits assured Communism of a continued appeal. There were indications, however, that only a minority of the Communist voters still believed in the Marxist program; most of them seemed to vote Communist either because they considered this an especially effective form of protest or simply from force of habit. This slackening of ideological commitment was also reflected in the decline of party membership, most notably in the French party, and in the poor attendance record at party meetings and functions.

These conditions made a reassessment of domestic Communist strategy necessary; at the same time the thesis that "socialism" could be attained by different roads made changes permissible. The Italian party tried to adjust to the changed spirit of its followers by initiating a process of transformation that was converting it into a more pluralistic and flexible movement, open to contacts with non-Communists. On occasion it even supported a political opponent; in 1964 it thus helped elect to the presidency the Social Democrat Giuseppe Saragat. The Communist parties in the Scandinavian countries, in Belgium, and Austria underwent similar realignments in the hope of recouping their fortunes. The French Communists, on the other hand, shied away from so basic a reversal, but they, too, lost some of their militancy. In parliamentary elections they entered local alliances with the Socialists, and in the presidential elections in 1965 they united with the Socialists and Radicals to support the Socialist candidate, François Mitterand.[5] Similarly, they collaborated with the other parties of the left on a nation-wide basis in the Assembly elections of March 1967, thus helping to inflict a serious setback on the Gaullist regime. Perhaps even more significant and indicative of the changing political climate, in a number of districts the Communist candidate received considerable rightist support in the run-off elections.

How far this evolution would go and how lasting it would be remained to be seen. The answer depended not only on developments in western Europe.

[5] Nevertheless, one million normally Communist voters were believed to have voted for De Gaulle.

The Decline of Parliamentarism.   Postwar western Europe witnessed a widespread rehabilitation of parliamentary democracy. Yet if parliamentarianism was recovering lost ground, its revival also brought forth new problems. Germany's "chancellor democracy," the formation of De Gaulle's "Presidential Republic," a spate of alarmed books in Britain (*Can Parliament Survive?, The Passing of Parliament, Parliament in Danger!*) indicated that parliamentary institutions were endangered by new challenges that kept whittling away their prestige and their powers.

This decline of status and jurisdiction resulted in part from earlier experiences of parliamentary ineffectiveness; memories of this kind accounted for the curtailment of parliamentary powers in the Bonn and French Fifth Republics. Both states wanted to guard themselves against the parliamentary vagaries that had beset the Weimar and Fourth Republics. But parliaments had also to struggle against a growing political indifference. Essentially content with existing conditions, most people were more concerned with efficient administration than with adequate parliamentary representation. Long-range planning that involved long-range commitments, the superior expertise of the governmental bureaucracy in regard to complex technical, social, and economic issues, and above all, the increasing consensus of conservatives and socialists and the concomitant lack of alternative policies—all tended to limit the importance of parliamentary activities. Finally, governments could establish direct visible contact with the people by television, thus bypassing parliaments as public platforms even more effectively than had been possible by radio. The decrease of plenary sessions and increasing absenteeism of deputies in some countries indicated that parliamentarians, too, were aware of their declining role. Those who believed in democracy thought this decline the more serious because the growing social and economic role of most governments called for stronger rather than fewer parliamentary controls.

THE END OF EMPIRE

Fade-Out of Asian Colonialism.   The disintegration of the colonial empires continued through the 1950's and '60's. British rule in Asia came virtually to an end with the establishment of an independent Federation of Malaysia in 1963. The federation included Malaya (independent since 1957), Singapore, Sabah (British North Borneo), and Sarawak; on its formation Malaysia entered the Commonwealth. Since Singapore still served as Britain's main naval base in the Far East, Indonesia and the Philippines assailed the federation as a product of British neocolonialism, and Indonesia launched raids on Sarawak from its own part of Borneo. To ease the situation, Singapore withdrew from the federation in 1965, but the future of Britain's base was in doubt, and London made clear that the base would be maintained only as long as Britain was welcome. Except for the British protectorate of Brunei on Borneo and a few islands in the southwest Pacific, Hongkong remained Britain's only Far Eastern dependency, and Britain's presence in Hongkong depended on Chinese sufferance. The Dutch lost their last Far Eastern possession when they surrendered their part of New Guinea (West Irian) to Indonesia.

The Breakup of the African Empires. During the first postwar decade several of the colonial powers granted their African territories greater self-government, but physically their colonial domains remained intact. By the mid-1950's this situation was changing. Aroused by the success of the Asian peoples, African leaders increased their efforts to gain independence for their lands. Mass demonstrations and riots lent additional force to their demands, and in the end they could not be ignored any longer. In 1956 Britain (and Egypt) granted full independence to the Sudan, that same year France relinquished what control it still had over Tunisia and Morocco, and a few months later Spain allowed Spanish Morocco to be merged with the newly independent state of Morocco. The French refused, on the other hand, to withdraw from Algeria since it was legally part of metropolitan France and the home of a large number of European settlers. The issue was complicated by French domestic concerns, and it was only in 1962, after a protracted bitter war with the Algerian National Liberation Front, that the territory was given its independence (see p. 517).

Spreading south, African nationalism won its first sub-Saharan victory in British West Africa's Gold Coast, which was recognized as the sovereign state of Ghana in 1957. Nigeria followed in 1960. By 1967 British control of its African territories was about to come to an end. On the whole, the transition was quiet and smooth and with the exception of the Sudan, all of the new states joined the Commonwealth. In Kenya, however, the British were drawn into a savage guerrilla war with the nationalist Mau Mau movement which they defeated only after four years of fighting. Difficulties developed also in Southern Rhodesia where 239,000 white settlers ruled 3,600,000 Africans. The British were unwilling to accord independence to Southern Rhodesia as long as the white minority refused to share political power with the African population. In 1965, Rhodesia, as it now called itself, unilaterally proclaimed its independence. London refrained from armed intervention, but imposed an economic blockade on the new state in the hope of thus forcing it to abandon its policy of white supremacy. Late in 1966 the United Nations, urged on by its African members, also imposed some economic sanctions on Rhodesia.

French "decolonization" south of the Sahara Desert followed a somewhat similar pattern. The French Union, set up after the war, no longer corresponded to the reality of the clamor for untrammeled self-government. In 1956 the Fourth Republic enacted a series of liberalizing reforms to satisfy these demands, but these measures were overtaken by events before they could be applied. To save what he could when he took over the government, De Gaulle dissolved the French Union and invited its members to join a newly formed Community. (In keeping with its multiracial character, the Community was not called "French.") All participating members were promised democratic self-government and their citizens full legal equality, regardless of race or religion. Except for Guinea, all former sub-Saharan colonies joined the Community, but in the end only six remained in it—after having been granted unlimited sovereignty. Whether in or outside the Community, most of the new states continued to maintain close ties with France and also became associate members of the Common Market.

Unlike the British and French colonies, the Belgian Congo showed little interest in independence during the early postwar years. When such demands were first voiced in the mid-1950's, the Belgian government responded with vague and dilatory promises. Yet the emancipation of the neighboring French colonies had its effect on the Congolese, and in 1959 demands for independence led to risings in the capital of Léopoldville. Later that year new riots broke out, culminating in massacres of hundreds of white settlers; frightened, Belgium precipitately granted the Congo full independence in June 1960. The Congolese were quite unprepared for the tasks that awaited them. Racial clashes, tribal wars, political rivalries, and a threatening East-West confrontation plunged the new state into chaos. Thanks to the intervention of the United Nations, an uneasy peace was finally restored. With some difficulty, it survived the withdrawal of the United Nations forces for lack of funds in 1964.

The Remaining Colonies.   By the mid-1960's the British, French, Dutch, and Spanish possessions had shrunk to a fraction of their one-time expanse. Britain still controlled Gibraltar, Hongkong, and Aden (until 1968), part of Borneo (Brunei), a number of islands in the Atlantic, Indian, and Pacific Oceans—among them St. Helena, Tristan de Cunha, Mauritius, and Pitcairn—and in the Western Hemisphere, British Honduras, the Bahamas, Bermuda, and the Falkland Islands. France's possessions, now called Overseas Territories, included the islands of St. Pierre and Miquelon off Newfoundland, French Somaliland, the Comoro Islands off Southeast Africa, Polynesia, and New Caledonia. The former French colonies in the Western Hemisphere, on the other hand—Guadeloupe, Martinique, and Guiana—and the island of Réunion in the Indian Ocean were joined to metropolitan France as overseas departments. Their inhabitants became French citizens who elected representatives to the French National Assembly and the Senate. Spain clung to a few territories on the east coast of Africa. Similarly, the Dutch still retained control of their possessions in the Western Hemisphere, but legally the Dutch Empire came to an end when the Caribbean possessions, now known as the Netherlands Antilles, and Dutch Guiana, renamed Surinam, became integral parts of the mother country.

The one empire that remained almost intact was that of the Portuguese. They suffered only one minor loss—the annexation of Goa and two other tiny enclaves by India in 1961. Besides the small trading base of Macao, south of Hongkong, Portugal's realm included part of the island of Timor in the Southwest Pacific, Angola, Mozambique, and Portuguese Guinea in Africa, and two island groups in the Atlantic. In 1961 opponents of Premier Salazar plotted to launch a rising in Angola, but failed—the attempt is best remembered for the seizure by co-conspirators of the Portuguese luxury liner *Santa Maria* on the high seas. The *Santa Maria* was to be sailed in triumph to liberated Angola, but since the colony remained under Lisbon's control, the ship had to be taken to Brazil, and the incident remained a bizarre episode. In the mid-1960's, however, unrest was increasing in Angola and Mozambique. The Portuguese were still able to contain it, but they were not relying on armed force alone to curb the native rebellions. Apart from dispatching economic aid to the colonies, they seemed confident that, given time, Portugal's traditional racial tolerance would so blur the dividing lines between Portuguese and Africans that the call for independence would lose its meaning.

The Impact on Europe. As during the first postwar decade, the colonial losses had their salutary effects on the European powers concerned. With their military and administrative expenditures greatly reduced, they could utilize their resources more economically. France doubtless was the main beneficiary; not only were the French freed of the crushing financial burden of the Algerian war, but the release of several hundred thousand draftees and the influx of over half a million Algerian refugees also helped ease France's manpower shortage. Portugal's continued poverty, on the other hand, was at least partly due to the heavy outlays in money and men which its colonial possessions exacted. At the same time it was seen that trade with the former colonies could be maintained without political rule; commercial patterns that had developed over a long period of time remained on the whole unaffected by the political changes.

Economic ties were not the only links between one-time mother country and colonies that survived the severing of the colonial relationship—other bonds were also preserved and even expanded. Often the former colonial powers were drawn back into the lands they had just abandoned to help maintain or restore internal order. The liberation of the colonies did not automatically open the gates to progress and peace; many of the new states were torn by tribal and personal feuds, inexperience, corruption, and economic difficulties. Their plight called for economic, technical, and educational aid, and such aid became even more important when Soviet or Chinese influences began to make themselves felt in the (formerly French) Congo Republic, Guinea, Ghana, and Zanzibar. The French, who poured some $700 million a year into their one-time African colonies, were so successful in maintaining close ties with the latter that their success gave rise to charges of neocolonialism. The British, unable to match this effort, retained a more precarious relationship with their one-time possessions.

Britain's ties with its former Asian and African colonies imposed upon London some special obligations. In most cases these ties had been formalized by Commonwealth membership, and as members of this multiracial association the new states expected to be accorded full racial equality by all other Commonwealth members. This was one reason why Britain could not countenance Rhodesia's insistence on white supremacy (the other being fear of eventual violent uprisings). This same consideration led London not to dissuade the Union of South Africa when that state decided in 1961 to withdraw from the Commonwealth rather than give up its policy of *apartheid*. (On the other hand, Britain ignored the concerns of the Commonwealth when it limited the right of Commonwealth citizens to enter Britain in order to guard against racial friction at home.)

For a time at least, Britain and France also remained concerned militarily with the areas that had once belonged to their empires. Apart from helping the new states to train and equip their armed forces, both joined the South East Asian Treaty Organization (SEATO), the Far Eastern equivalent of NATO, and Britain became also a member of the Middle Eastern Central Treaty Organization (CENTO). As time went on, however, it became doubtful whether either London or Paris still was able or willing to honor these commitments.

DOMESTIC POLITICS

Britain. In keeping with the temper of the times social and economic concerns dominated the political climate in Britain during the 1950's and into the 1960's. Meeting the expectations and needs of the country, Churchill's second administration ran on in placid stability. Industry benefited from a sharp drop in the world prices for raw materials; as exports increased, imports could be expanded without upsetting the balance of payments. However, the credit for what was achieved belonged, not to Churchill, but to his Chancellor of the Exchequer, R. A. Butler. Churchill himself was frequently incapacitated and when he was up and about, showed signs of increasing senility. Yet, ignoring the pleadings of his family and friends, he clung to his office until April 1955.

Anthony Eden, since 1940 his heir-designate, succeeded him. Eden was not a man of strong will and action, and he was in poor health himself. Satisfied with riding along on the existing economic momentum, he held office for less than two years; his mishandling of the Suez crisis and ill health led to his resignation in January 1957.

The new Prime Minister, Harold Macmillan (1894–   ), came from an old and distinguished publishing family. He had established an outstanding record as Minister of Housing in 1951–1954 and more recently had been Eden's Chancellor of the Exchequer. Macmillan was able to inject further vigor into the economy, and although its growth could not compare with that of some of its Continental rivals, the British people were enjoying more of the benefits of an affluent society. In the elections of 1959 they showed their appreciation to "Supermac," as they called him affectionately, by giving him a majority of one hundred over all other parties. But industrial productivity kept lagging behind that of Britain's foreign competitors, and a year later exports began declining again.[6] Domestic demand aggravated the resulting inflationary pressures, and to add to the government's difficulties, there were pressing social responsibilities that it was pledged to discharge. The need for hospitals was still far from satisfied, and in the field of higher education the shortage of high school and university facilities continued to be serious. To cope with these problems, the government reduced its military expenditures. The chief victim of this policy of retrenchment was Britain's independent nuclear deterrent. Abandoning its own production of missiles, London obtained Polaris missiles from the United States—on condition that they would be assigned to NATO except in special emergencies. Similarly, sharp cuts were made in land and sea armaments, in tacit acknowledgment of Britain's declining power.

The country's continued economic difficulties induced Macmillan to apply for Britain's admission to the Common Market. The rejection of Britain's bid by De Gaulle was a serious setback for him. His position was weakened further when his Secretary for War, John Profumo, was found to have had unsavory associations while in office and had lied about them to Parliament; the scandal was aggravated by fears, later proved unfounded, that Profumo might have endangered national security. Macmillan's mistake had been his quick dismissal of the evidence against Profumo in the face of the latter's denials. He appeared to have ridden out the storm, however, when illness forced him to resign in October 1963. Macmillan had been in office for almost eight years and in all left behind a distinguished record as Prime Minister.

By contrast, his successor, Lord Home, most likely will be remembered primarily as the first Prime Minister to renounce his peerage in order

---

[6] During the period 1955–1964, Britain's annual increase of productivity per man averaged 2.3 per cent as against 4.7 for France, 4.8 for West Germany, and 5.8 for Italy.

to become eligible for a seat in the House of Commons.[7] In doing so, Home took advantage of a recently enacted Peerage Act that enabled British peers to aim at the prime ministership, otherwise closed to them, by renouncing their peerage and running for the House of Commons. Lord Home became Sir Alec Douglas-Home and was elected to Commons in a by-election in Scotland. Perhaps through no fault of his own, he was unable to reverse the trend of the sagging economy, but to the country he gave the impression of lacking energy and imagination. After barely a year in office, he lost the elections in 1964. Once more a Labor government took over.

Labor had done some soul searching during its years out of power. Like other socialist parties it had had to contend with a growing tendency on the part of its followers to make their peace with the private enterprise system. What increase in production there had been, moreover, had occurred chiefly in the private sector of the economy—automobiles, chemicals, machinery, and electrical equipment. Though there was no evidence that coal, gas, or transport would have fared better under private management, many advocates of nationalization lost interest in it—among them not a few of the workers who were themselves employed in the nationalized industries. Labor's election program thus was not focused on the traditional issue of nationalization vs. private enterprise—except for a pledge to renationalize the iron and steel industries (enacted into law in 1967)—but on the more systematic promotion of economic growth and the correlation of incomes and productivity.

The Labor Party won the election by the slimmest of margins—a four-seat majority. Evidently, it owed its victory less to any confidence in its ability to master the economic difficulties than to the prevailing disillusionment with the Conservatives. Under these circumstances, the new Prime Minister, Harold Wilson (1916–   ), a forty-eight-year-old economist, embarked on no major changes in policy. He tried to restore the trade balance by tax reductions on exports and tariff increases on imports; to reduce domestic consumption, he also raised income taxes and taxes on cars, tobacco, and alcohol. A $3 billion loan arranged by the International Monetary Fund tided him over his immediate difficulties and helped spark the economy into greater activity. In all this, Wilson proceeded with notable aplomb despite his precarious majority, which eventually dwindled to two seats. When he called for new elections in March 1966, the country was sufficiently impressed with his record to give him a majority of 97 seats. Yet economic recovery was slow and seemed once more endangered early in 1967 when eco-

[7] Since the turn of the century no peer had become Prime Minister. What at first may have been accidental eventually became an established tradition on the grounds that a peer could not appear before the House of Commons.

nomic difficulties began to make themselves felt in other parts of western Europe.

France. Unlike most European countries, France, during the 1950's, seemed less preoccupied with economic growth and social security than with political problems. This, however, was a deceptive impression. While France's political troubles commanded the headlines, the country modernized and reorganized a large sector of its economy and greatly increased its production. However, this vast process of overhauling the economic machinery went on outside the political arena—the Monnet Plan, for example, was never discussed by the National Assembly. That body was in fact dominated by economic conservatives who were deeply suspicious of any government intervention in the economy. It drove Premier Mendès-France from office when, fresh from his settlement of the war in Indo-China, he proposed to curb the spiraling inflation by a tightening of the tax laws and a series of reforms designed to improve industrial and agricultural productivity.

Significantly, the only other effort made to mobilize the Assembly on behalf of an economic policy was an attempt by a vociferous demagogue, Pierre Poujade, to end all large-scale planning, modernization, and government controls. The Poujadist movement appealed to small farmers, shopkeepers, and other disgruntled elements who felt that their economic survival depended on a return to a system in which the government's main economic function would be the protection of the small entrepreneur against the competition of big business. In the elections of 1956 the Poujadists won 52 seats in the Assembly; Poujade, however, proved sadly inept as a political leader and the movement quickly distintegrated.

Socialists and Radicals had joined forces during the election campaign and had run on a platform promising economic reforms and a settlement of the Algerian crisis. Guy Mollet, the head of the Socialist Party, became Premier of a left-center coalition, but his government introduced few reforms. Its energies were soon so fully absorbed by the Algerian problem that it found little time for anything else. It did, however, negotiate France's membership in the Common Market and laid the plans for an independent nuclear deterrent.

The Algerian crisis grew out of a Moslem rebellion that broke out in 1954. By 1956 it had expanded into a costly, savagely fought guerrilla war which a French army of close to 500,000 men was unable to end. As the war wore on, increasing numbers of Frenchmen came to favor a settlement with the rebels. Such a settlement would have granted self-government to the Algerian Moslems. This was opposed by the European settlers whose families had lived in Algeria for generations, who had helped build it up, and who feared that they would lose everything if Algeria became independent. The Europeans had an ally in the French officer corps which, after almost twenty years of military defeats, was determined to make a stand in Algeria and thus restore France's military honor. Supported by many Gaullists and other rightists in mainland France, these groups compelled the government to continue the war. As a Socialist, Premier Mollet was opposed to all imperialist ventures, but because his government was dependent on rightist support, he kept on fighting and even drew France into the Suez campaign in order to cut off Egyptian help to the rebels.

For his militant stand Mollet earned little thanks from the right. When he attempted to overhaul the tax system to check the worsening inflation and distribute the tax burden more equitably, his conservative supporters turned against him, and he was forced to resign. There followed a number of makeshift governments, each of which foundered on the Algerian issue. In May 1958 rumors reached Algiers that a new government about to be formed by a moderate conservative, Pierre Pflimlin, would enter into negotiations with the rebels. Determined to block any talks, a group of civilian extremists seized power in Algiers and obtained the support of the local high command of the army. The National Assembly in Paris responded by granting Pflimlin emergency powers by the impressive vote of 475 to 100, but this closing of ranks came too late. The rebellion had meanwhile spread to the island of Corsica, and a parachute attack on Paris was said to be imminent. With the loyalty of the Parisian police and army in doubt, attention turned once more to De Gaulle. There was a growing demand that he take over the government to preserve order. The General was prepared to accept the call provided he were given a free hand in overhauling the country's political and constitutional structure. Since he seemed the only one able to save the country from a fascist-military dictatorship, the Assembly accepted his terms. On June 1, 1958 it approved De Gaulle's appointment as Premier; it also gave him special decree powers for a six-month period and authorized him to draft a new constitution.

The appointment of the sixty-eight-year-old General was an act of faith more than a matter of informed judgment. Little was known of De Gaulle beyond what has been told about him in this account. This was no accident because De Gaulle had long cultivated a mystique about himself, convinced that a leader, to have prestige and authority, must keep aloof from his following. Few Frenchmen knew that the General was a complex personality, standing with one foot in the last century and with the other in the next, as one observer has noted. He was a fierce patriot and a traditionalist, self-centered and authoritarian, and deeply imbued with an almost religious sense of mission. Yet he also had a keen flair for political trends, for the subtleties of international power politics, and above all for the potentialities of technological developments. To these attributes must be added an artistic strand most clearly reflected in De Gaulle's marked literary skill that made his *Memoirs* a major contribution to recent French writing. To this enigmatic personality the French entrusted their fate.

The General set to work, confident that France, "this marvelous country, [held] in its hand all the cards for an extraordinary regeneration." The new constitution which was approved in September by almost 80 per cent of the electorate satisfied De Gaulle's old demand for a strong executive. It gave the President special powers and in turn restricted those of parliament. The latter's sessions were limited to six months per year and its authority narrowly circumscribed. Parliamentary elections in November provided the newly founded Gaullist Party, the Union for the New Republic, and the parties allied with it, with a comfortable majority in the Assembly. In December De Gaulle was elected President of the Fifth Republic; Michel Debré, one of his oldest supporters, took his place as Premier.

With similar dispatch De Gaulle addressed himself to France's financial problems. By a policy of severe deflation—tax increases, wage and price controls, cutting of government expenditures, currency revaluation—he was able to ease the inflationary pressures. The burden of these measures, however, weighed most heavily on the low income groups: the reduction of government expenditures included the lowering of social insurance benefits, the suspension of veterans' pensions, and the abolition of farm subsidies that had kept food prices down. Although minimum wages and family allowances were increased, the raises did not compensate for the aforementioned losses. Prices, moreover, continued to rise some 4 per cent annually, and the economic gap between labor and middle and upper class kept growing wider. As the economy expanded, it is true, the workers' lot also improved, but recurring wage disputes and strikes and the continued large Communist vote were indications of labor's persisting dissatisfaction.

In the Algerian issue De Gaulle felt his way. He pursued the war against the Arab rebels, but at the same time dismissed or transferred all officers whose loyalty to the government seemed in doubt. When European extremists rioted in protest against his dilatory tactics, the army suppressed the rising. In January 1961 he secured a mandate for negotiations by means of a referendum. Three months later several discharged generals staged a new putsch in Algiers and prepared to overthrow his regime, but once more the bulk of the armed forces remained loyal to De Gaulle. In May the talks with the Moslem rebels got under way. They touched off a campaign of terror and sabotage by European extremists and dissatisfied military elements who hoped to provoke the Arab community into an all-out civil war and frighten off Frenchmen supporting De Gaulle. Some months later the plotters also made an attempt on the life of the President.

De Gaulle would not be intimidated; the talks continued and in March 1962 led to an agreement, subject to a popular vote, granting Algeria full independence. The treaty provided also for the indemnification of departing European settlers, and arranged for economic and technical collaboration between France and Algeria. Sweeping majorities of both nations approved the settlement.

In October, De Gaulle suffered a brief, but distinct setback. He proposed a constitutional amendment providing for the popular election of the President (rather than by some 80,000 "no·ables"); wishing to turn the occasion into a demonstration of confidence in his regime, he had his newly appointed Premier, Georges Pompidou, bypass the constitutional amendment procedures and call for a referendum. In protest against the dubious legality of the plan, the Assembly overthrew the Pompidou government, whereupon De Gaulle dissolved the Assembly. The referendum was held, and although the amendment was passed, it was endorsed by only 46 per cent of the eligible voters, with considerable numbers abstaining. In the parliamentary elections, however, Gaullist deputies won 267 out of 482 seats. The gains were made at the expense of the middle parties whereas both Socialists and Communists, who entered electoral alliances in a number of districts, returned with substantially larger delegations. Moreover, the Communists' 41 seats were

Charles De Gaulle. (Reprinted courtesy Wide World Photos)

not representative of their popular vote which still amounted to almost four million or 21 per cent of the total.

With the Algerian issue out of the way, De Gaulle devoted himself more fully to his coveted goal—raising France to the leadership of a Europe independent from both the United States and the Soviet Union. The various steps he took to attain this goal have been discussed and need not be retold. What should be noted, however, is the ambiguous response of the French people to his diplomacy of *grandeur*. When they were called upon to pass judgment on him in the Presidential election in 1965, a majority gave their vote to candidates other than De Gaulle. Only in the run-off election against the Socialist François Mitterand did the General obtain a majority, but it was not a very large one (55 per cent). Most observers attributed this result to widespread misgivings in France about the wisdom of De Gaulle's foreign policy.

There was growing concern, too, about the increasingly undemocratic character of the regime that allowed De Gaulle to make basic decisions on his own without consulting or even informing his ministers, let alone parliament. Many Frenchmen also objected to the government's control of radio and television from which oppositional speakers were barred except on special occasions. Admittedly, these spokesmen were free to air their views in the press and in meetings, but none of these media reached audiences comparable to those of radio and television. The government thus enjoyed great advantages over the opposition in keeping in touch with the country. Though Gaullist France was not a totalitarian police state, its authoritarianism was marked. This fact became one of the central issues of the parliamentary elections of March 1967. It accounted for the serious setback of the Gaullist regime, which retained a bare one-vote majority in the National Assembly.

Italy. Conditions in Italy during the 1950's resembled those of the French Fourth Republic. Like the latter, Italy was plagued by political turbulence while its economy seemed barely affected by this instability and enjoyed an unprecedented expansion. Throughout that period the Christian Democratic Party continued to dominate Italian politics. The party was torn, however, by incessant internal feuds; lacking a parliamentary majority, it wavered between coalitions with the smaller democratic parties and gentleman's agreements with some of the rightist groups. Each arrangement aroused bitter opposition within the party: its conservative backers—businessmen, landowners, Vatican—looked askance at alliances with the liberal left and the liberal wing objected to any collaboration with antidemocratic elements such as the monarchists. Under the circumstances most governments were short-lived. The one exception was that of Premier Antonio Segni, a left-of-center reformist, who stayed in office from July 1955 to May 1957. Segni initiated a number of economic reforms, trying especially to accelerate the industrialization of the southern provinces. He also was instrumental in the establishment of a constitutional court that set to work purging Italian law of its remaining Fascist ingredients.

After this interlude successive governments tended more toward the right, and one Premier, Fernando Tambroni, even accepted the support of the neo-Fascists in parliament. The fear that Tambroni might open the door to a Fascist resurgence touched off a nation-wide wave of demonstrations and strikes that swept Tramboni from office. His successor, Amintore Fanfani, renewed the alliance with the minor democratic parties, and to enhance the prestige of his cabinet, included in it several former Premiers. This, however, was merely a stopgap measure and a more permanent solution had to be found. For some time liberal elements in the Christian Democratic Party had been advocating an "opening to the left"; with the right seriously discredited, they pressed more urgently for a coalition with the Socialists. They could point to the fact that the Socialists had been moving away from their alliance with the Communists since the Hungarian revolt and had for some time been collaborating with the Christian Democrats in the government of some of the major cities. Still, in both camps there was strong opposition to such collaboration on the national level. Christian Democratic objections were overcome when the Vatican, now headed by the reform-minded Pope John XXIII, hinted its approval; Socialist opponents gave in when their veteran leader, Pietro Nenni, persuaded them that the workers could not hope to secure a fair share in Italy's economic expansion unless the Socialists collaborated with the liberal element of the Christian Democratic Party.

After a year of informal cooperation, the Socialists entered the government in December 1963. New parliamentary elections had produced a marked shift to the left—chiefly in favor of the Communists who gathered 25.3 per cent of the vote. The coalition was not a happy one; plagued by mutual distrust and by quarrels over state subsidies to Church schools, it broke up after a few months only to be renewed again. The new government succeeded in slowing down the spreading inflation, but the deflationary measures it had to adopt forced it to postpone the realization of some of its major objectives—agrarian reforms, better housing, and more adequate education. Here much remained to be done. The improving financial situation gave reason to hope that these policies could soon be implemented.

West Germany. The Bonn Republic continued to enjoy the benefits of its "economic miracle" in the 1950's. Unlike France's and Italy's, West Germany's affluence was spread more equitably among the various classes, and German workers were among the best paid in Europe. The most patent inequities were further reduced by a complex arrangement known as "equalization of burdens"; it provided for the payment of indemnities to war refugees and expellees, to those who had suffered heavy property losses during the war, and to victims of Nazi persecution. The program was financed by a special tax amounting to half the possessions a taxpayer had owned in 1948, a poor year, and to be paid over a period of thirty years.

As attested by two events, the nation was fully recognizant of the achievements of Chancellor Adenauer. In the Bundestag elections of 1957, 50.2 per cent of the voters cast their vote for the Christian Democrats, giving the Chancellor an absolute majority in the parliament (270 out of 497 seats). The opposition paid its tribute to him when the Social Democrats bowed to the success of the "social market economy" and adopted a new program that repudiated the party's Marxist heritage and pledged itself to protect private ownership of the means of production "as long as it does not impede social justice." The Social Democrats also abandoned their advocacy of Germany's demilitarization and neutralization and came out in support of NATO.

These successes, however, marked also the zenith of Adenauer's chancellorship. In the spring of 1959 he declared himself ready to relinquish the chancellorship and be a candidate for the presidency, as the successor of President Heuss. Yet when he discovered that as President he would have far fewer powers than he had thought, he overruled the wishes of his party and insisted on remaining Chancellor. He questioned the political competence of Erhard, his designated successor, and he also seems to have felt that after the recent death of Secretary of State Dulles he was the only one left in the Western camp who knew how to deal with the Soviets. He had his way and retained the chancellorship, and the Minister of Agriculture, Heinrich Lübke, became President.

The contemptuous disregard with which Adenauer treated his party's wishes left painful wounds. Opposition to him increased when the Christian Democrats lost 10 per cent of their vote in the elections of 1961 while the Social Democrats and the Free Democrats increased theirs by almost 15 and 67 per cent, respectively. The following year his position was further shaken by the *Spiegel* affair. This incident grew out of the arbitrary arrest of the editors of *Der Spiegel*, a widely read newsweekly modeled on *Time* in makeup and style. The arrests had been ordered by the Defense Minister, Franz-Josef Strauss, on the dubious charge that the magazine had published secret military information. The resulting uproar forced Strauss to resign, but Adenauer's defiant defense of Strauss' action affected his popular standing. A year later, under constant pressure from the Christian Democratic leadership, he finally resigned his office, and Erhard succeeded him.

Under the affable leadership of the new Chancellor, the style of government changed from Adenauer's "Chancellor democracy" to a cabinet type of administration in which the individual ministers were allowed greater freedom of action and parliament was able to have its say on the shaping of policy. This led to considerable in-fighting and intriguing, encouraged by Adenauer, who remained fiercely critical of Erhard, and by Strauss, who was preparing the way for a comeback. Yet Erhard managed to ward off the attacks on him and went his way. Over Adenauer's objections he allowed German foreign policy to shift its direction in both East and West (see p. 491). He was vindicated in the elections of 1965 in which the Christian Democrats defeated the Social Democrats by almost as large a margin as they had under Adenauer in 1961.

Erhard's triumph was short-lived. In foreign policy his rapprochement with the United States proved a liability when the United States would not agree to a reduction of West German debts incurred through purchases of American arms. Domestically, the Chancellor had to contend with a declining economy and an increasingly restive coalition partner, the Free Democratic Party. By withdrawing their support from the government, the Free Democrats forced Erhard to resign in November 1966.

The government of Kurt-Georg Kiesinger, who succeeded Erhard, broke new ground, resting as it did on a coalition of Christian Democrats and Social Democrats. In bringing together Christian and Social Democrats, Kiesinger's cabinet reflected the prevailing pragmatic approach to politics that had come to supersede ideological commitments. The new government was notably active in foreign affairs, but it did not display a similar initiative on the domestic scene. It remained to be seen what it would do to stop the decline of the country's economy.

CULTURAL LIFE

Literature. Inevitably the affluence of the decade 1955–1965 produced an artistic counterreaction. Playwrights and novelists were sensitive to the materialist preoccupations of their contemporaries and tended to focus their attention on the seamier side of Europe's prosperity—the bureaucratization, conformism, and moral indifference it seemed to engender. Some carried their message in the traditional form of the straightforward social protest; others clothed their critiques in bitter satires; still others sought a refuge in the surrealist dreamworld that was now revived, or vented their malaise in new linguistic and literary experiments.

Some of the most striking pioneering efforts were made in France. Here the disenchantment of the artist expressed itself in a pervasive sense of futility. The newer writers took up the old existentialist themes of man's role in an irrational world, but they no longer called for that commitment to independent courageous action which Sartre and his disciples had demanded. Samuel Beckett, the Irish author living in

France, viewed man as incapable of mastering his predicaments. In a revealing passage of his novel *Molloy*, Beckett gave voice to his disillusion by having his protagonist cry out: "I have been a man long enough. I shall not put up with it any more. I shall not try any more." His most widely acclaimed play, *Waiting for Godot*, dramatized the impasse man had reached in his existence and the illusions in which he looked for solutions. Throughout the play, the central figures keep waiting for Godot, but it is never made clear what he can do for them nor are they certain that Godot exists—it is the very waiting for his arrival that gives meaning to their otherwise purposeless life. The Franco-Rumanian playwright Eugène Ionesco had many of his characters speak in time-worn clichés or in an incomprehensible babble in order to express the banality of human existence and man's inability to communicate with his fellows. He also relied heavily on visual effects to demonstrate man's inability to live a meaningful life—a room overcrowded with furniture, castigating the senseless accumulation of possessions; a stage overflowing with eggs, as a slap against the incessant drive for greater production; the population of a town turning themselves into rhinoceroses, to assail the spreading tendency toward an inane and cowardly conformism.

Although Beckett's and Ionesco's plays may not rank as great literature, their style did have an important impact on the theater of the 1950's and 1960's. Their influence along with that of other practitioners of the "Theater of the Absurd" made itself felt in Britain, Germany, and the United States. Their plays, moreover, drew large audiences; in the mid-1960's Ionesco was possibly the most widely performed of all contemporary playwrights. Evidently he struck a responsive chord in audiences throughout the Western world.

At the other pole of the existentialist world, the novelist Raymond Queneau saw the absurdity of the universe not as tragedy but as a subject matter for comedy. His novels were peopled with simple souls who in their innocence remained untouched by their evil environment and led happy and independent lives. In a more traditional vein, the melancholy novellas of Françoise Sagan (*Bonjours, Tristesse; A Certain Smile*) were widely read because of their escapist nostalgic mood.

In Germany the poet and novelist Günter Grass emerged as Germany's and perhaps Europe's most talented novelist. His two major works, *The Tin Drum* and *Dog Years*, were explorations of middle class life during Germany's recent past, from the late 1920's to the days of the "economic miracle." In their skillful combination of straightforward narrative, surrealistic techniques, and linguistic experiments they were works of remarkable craftsmanship. Grass' satire allowed him to view the vicissitudes of the times with notable detachment, but even in their funnier passages his novels conveyed a grim picture of human cynicism and weakness. Heinrich Böll's novels (*Billiards at Half Past*

Nine, The Clown) were similar indictments of moral cowardice and opportunism. The playwright Peter Weiss, in turn, tried to arouse his audiences by painting a frightening picture of the loneliness of human suffering in a drama about Jean-Paul Marat, the French revolutionary, and the Marquis de Sade. On a somewhat different plane, the involved novels of Uwe Johnson (*Speculations about Jakob*) were concerned with the individual caught up in the contest between East and West Germany and trying to retain his integrity.

The novels and essays of Alberto Moravia, Italy's greatest living writer, also continued to deal with the problems of human integrity and moral purpose. Moravia, too, was deeply concerned with man's apathy and indifference and his tendency to consider himself as a means rather than an end (*The Empty Canvas; Man as an End*). Some of his fellow novelists sought release from the present by turning to the past. The success of *The Leopard*, by Giuseppe di Lampedusa, an old-fashioned romance laid in nineteenth-century Sicily, indicated that a large reading public was prepared to follow them into the seemingly simpler world of bygone days.

British authors shared the concerns of their Continental confreres, but were less interested in devising new literary or theatrical techniques to convey them. John Osborne's drama, *Look Back in Anger,* was a mordant attack on middle class values and a grim picture of individual maladjustment; his *Luther,* an outcry against prejudice and hysteria. Colin Wilson's *The Outsider* assailed the materialism of modern civilization and urged those who refused to conform to it to "seek power over it": "The Outsiders must achieve political power over the hogs." The Hitler-like ring of this conclusion was at first overlooked in the enthusiasm over Wilson's trenchant critique of contemporary attitudes, but later contributed to the decline of his reputation. The cruelty of which a distorted mind may be capable was dissected in John Bowle's novel *The Collector.* Much social and moral stocktaking, however, was done in conventional novels providing vast panoramas of British life, among them the multivolume narratives of C. P. Snow, Anthony Powell, and Evelyn Waugh which continued to command large faithful audiences.

Movies and Television. Movie producers also took up some of the themes that haunted the literature of the 1950's, and they too engaged in experiments of style and technique. The brooding productions of the Swede Ingemar Bergman (*Wild Strawberries; The Sorcerer*) probed the dark recesses of the human mind; the surrealist productions of the Italian director Federico Fellini depicted the corruption of Italian society and the difficulties of human communication (*La Dolce Vita; 8 1/2*). The same topic of human isolation and bewilderment was taken up in such French productions as *Last Year at Marienbad* and *Hiro-*

shima, Mon Amour. Some acid closeups of social climbing and cynicism were presented in the British movie, *Room at the Top,* and the German film, *Rosemarie,* the story of a prostitute who doubled as an industrial spy—a plot that was based on an actual occurrence.

Film-makers were anxious to improve their productions not just for artistic reasons, but also to fight off the growing competition of television. As a medium of mass communication, television was gaining ground rapidly in the 1950's and 1960's. It had not yet found its artistic bearings, and most of its entertainment was insubstantial and stereotyped. On the other hand, it was making its distinct contribution as a source of information—by means of documentaries, news forums, and broadcasts of important events. What the effect of this contribution was, socially and politically, it was still too early to say.

Scientific Developments. World War II constitutes a watershed in the development of European science. Until that time Europe had held the center of the stage in scientific endeavors as it had in world politics. The bulk of all basic scientific discoveries had come from European experiments and speculations. This changed radically during and after the war. By then science's center of gravity had shifted to the United States. Many European scientists had found in America a refuge from war and fascism and joined forces with their American colleagues in the development of such fields as nuclear physics (Niels Bohr, Enrico Fermi, Edward Teller) or mathematics (John von Neumann, Hermann Weyl, Kurt Gödel). Others came after the war, attracted by generous research funds and unequaled laboratory facilities.

To put an end to this trend and become once more competitive in science and technology, government and industry began underwriting scientific research continuously and systematically in almost every west European country. (Partly because of this sponsorship and partly because of changing European attitudes, scientific efforts shifted noticeably from basic to applied research.) Yet even governmental support proved inadequate to meet the equipment needs of nuclear physics, especially in the smaller countries. In recent years a number of supranational enterprises were launched—among them a boiling heavy water reactor in Norway, a high temperature, gas-cooled reactor in Britain, and a Eurochemic Company, treating irradiated nuclear fuels, in Belgium. For the development of nuclear energy for peaceful purposes EURATOM established a Joint Nuclear Research Center with branches in Germany, Italy, and the Low Countries. To deal with problems of theoretical physics, a European Council for Nuclear Research was set up at Geneva; fourteen European countries became members. In the same vein, supranational agencies were established for space research and rocket development. In the realm of science European integration was moving ahead.

RELIGIOUS LIFE

Protestantism. The Lutheran Churches in Europe had been notably strengthened by their struggle against the encroachments of Nazi totalitarianism. This spiritual revival subsided, however, once the strains and stresses of the wartime years were forgotten. Church attendance fell off again, and the prosperity of the 1950's contributed further to the growing religious indifference. For a time the German Lutheran Church commanded some attention as one of the few operative links between East and West Germany. This mediating role led it to oppose German rearmament and induced part of its clergy to favor a neutralist policy for the Bonn Republic. In consequence, it lost some of its standing as West Germany moved towards closer alignment with the West. Internally, the ties between the Church and its followers grew looser as the Church became more bureaucratized; in the 1950's it substituted clerical hierarchies for the lay "councils of brethren" that the Confessional Church (see p. 232) had set up in the Nazi era. The change reflected the decline of religious concern among German Protestants.

Catholicism. The Catholic Church could continue to count on the devotion of large parts of its faithful, but it, too, was confronted with critical challenges. In France, Belgium, and Italy many Catholics, if they were not Communist Party members, supported Communism in the elections; conversely, the Church's association in several countries with conservative, or outright reactionary, elements also caused serious social and political difficulties. On the nonpolitical plane the Church's stand on birth control, mixed marriages, and divorce became a source of growing concern as these matters gained increasing social acceptance.

Local attempts were made to cope with some of these problems. Archbishop Giovanni Montini of Milan, the future Pope Paul VI (1897–), developed special missionary programs for the slum districts of his archdiocese. In France the worker-priest movement dispatched priests as laborers into the factories to revive the workers' flagging interest in religion; this program ran into trouble when some priests, rather than making converts to Christianity, were themselves converted to Marxism. It was abandoned on orders from the Vatican, but was subsequently revived. In Spain the Catholic Church had been one of Franco's original supporters, but in the 1950's a growing faction of the clergy, appalled by the social backwardness of the country, found that they could no longer reconcile such support with their religious responsibilities. They backed the workers in their struggle for social justice, and sided with university students who were calling for intellectual freedom. Some of the more militant priests participated in antigovernment demonstrations, and at one point Barcelona witnessed the man-handling by the police of hundreds of protesting clerics.

Vatican II. Shortly after his election in 1958, Pope John XXIII (1881–1963), an earthy, worldly wise prelate, called an Ecumenical Church Council in an attempt to adapt Church doctrines and practices to the needs and realities of the twentieth century. The second such council to be held at the Vatican—the first met there in 1869–70 and proclaimed the dogma of papal infallibility—it became known as Vatican II. It

Pope John XXIII. (*Reprinted courtesy Wide World Photos*)

was attended by some 2,300 bishops who gathered for four sessions during the years 1962–1965. In order to stress the Church's desire for renewed Christian unity, some sixty Protestant and Orthodox observers were invited to the council's deliberations.

The decisions of the council were designed to pave the way for the modernization and liberalization of the Church. The most important liturgical change provided for the celebration of parts of the Mass in the vernacular, with the priest facing the communicants to give them a greater sense of participation. Organizationally, the principle of episcopal collegiality was adopted: although nominally the Pope retained his vast powers, the bishops were to share responsibility with him in the government of the Church. (Pope Paul announced later the establishment of an elective synod of bishops to serve as an advisory body.) The most significant substantive change was embodied in a declaration on religious liberty that insisted not only on the spiritual independence of the Catholic Church, but also on the *neutrality* of the state towards *all* religions. Similarly, a declaration on non-Christian religions acknowledged their spiritual importance. In another declaration, the council adopted a resolution absolving the Jewish people of collective guilt for the crucifixion of Jesus. On the other hand, Vatican II sidestepped such issues as birth control, divorce, and clerical celibacy. (In the matter of mixed marriages Pope Paul relaxed some of the more onerous rules in a subsequent statement.) Dealing with social and economic matters, the council contented itself with some general statements. It took no stand for or against capitalism or communism, and while rejecting atheism, expressed hopes for "fruitful and prudent" discussions with the governments that supported it. It also came out in support of international organizations striving for peace—a stand underlined by Pope Paul's trip to New York to address the General Assembly of the United Nations in the fall of 1965.

Vatican II thus tried to enhance the influence of the Church by making it more flexible and world-minded (both in a spiritual and geographical sense). As one observer wrote, thanks to the council's labors, the Church became more Catholic and less Roman. In this it followed an overall trend—as Europe ceased to be the center of the secular world, it also ceased to be the pre-eminent domain of the spiritual realm of the Church.

23

The Soviet Orbit After Stalin

A system closely geared to the personality of one man cannot survive his death without change. Stalin's departure thus touched off a gradual transformation of the spirit and structure of the Soviet regime. The process was aided by the inability of any one individual to assert himself as Stalin's successor; one-man rule was replaced by collective leadership. Shared power, however, meant lessened power—a development that had in any event become necessary. The country needed an easing of pressures to inject new vigor into its economy and society after the oppressive curbs of the Stalin era.

If the new Soviet leaders were prepared to relax the stifling checks to which their people had been subjected, they were also determined to set clear limits to the alleviations they were prepared to concede. They retained full control over all basic policy decisions and over the means to enforce their decisions. They also watched closely all intellectual and artistic activities; although writers and artists were allowed greater leeway than during the Stalin era, they were brought up short whenever they exceeded what the Soviet leaders considered tolerable liberties. As time went on, however, these checks lost in effectiveness; **531** similarly, the nation as a whole, despite its outward docility, began moving away from that cowed subservience to which it had been relegated in the days of the Stalinist terror.

Corresponding changes occurred in the east European states although the extent and tempo of the liberalization varied in accordance with local conditions. The same process of loosening controls also reshaped the relationship between the Soviet Union and these states; the weakening of the ties between the U.S.S.R. and its one-time satellites brought forth possibly the most incisive and lasting changes.

THE SOVIET UNION

De-Stalinization. Stalin seems to have chosen Malenkov as his successor, and immediately after Stalin's death Malenkov became both Premier and Party Secretary. A week later, however, in mid-March 1953 he was forced to surrender the party position to Khrushchev. The emphasis was now on "collective leadership" on the grounds that no one man ought to concentrate in his hands all the powers that Stalin had held. To undo some of Stalin's abuse of these powers, an amnesty was proclaimed for all those imprisoned for less than five years (unless convicted of "counterrevolutionary crimes"). The Kremlin doctors only recently charged with assassination plots (see p. 459) were found innocent and released, and full protection by "Soviet socialist legality" was promised to every citizen.

Some months later Beria, the Minister of the Interior and head of the security forces, was removed from his offices and executed after a secret trial on charges of treason and abuse of his powers. Large numbers of political prisoners were publicly rehabilitated and released from the forced labor camps and the camps either closed or conditions in them improved. The power of the security forces was curbed and the entire apparatus subjected to stricter control by the party. A final result of this process of "de-Stalinization" was that Stalin's name was from then on rarely mentioned in public.

Economic Developments. A similar easing of government curbs took place in the economic field. The Soviet economy had made impressive advances in some industrial areas, but it was lagging behind in the output of consumer goods and in agriculture. This uneven development threatened to affect the entire economy as the decline of overall economic growth indicated. To remedy the existing imbalance, Malenkov announced that consumer goods production would receive greater encouragement, and its expansion in 1953 did indeed surpass that of capital goods production. To increase food production, agricultural prices were raised and farmers were urged to grow more on their personal plots. Early in 1954 Khrushchev reported that 5.7 million acres of virgin lands in Siberia and Kazakhstan would be brought under cultivation in 1954 and an additional 26.4 million acres in 1955 in order to meet the needs of the country and expand Soviet food exports.

Yet consumer goods output could not be maintained on the expected level. Plant managers, used to giving priority to capital goods, continued to do so when the production of consumer goods threatened to interfere with the turnout of capital goods. The success of the virgin lands program, moreover, depended on the large-scale manufacture of harvesting combines, tractors, and other agricultural equipment, creating additional conflicts and rivalries. Finally, West German rearmament was to be countered by a vastly expanded armament effort which put an even heavier strain on the country's industrial resources. A faction headed by Khrushchev insisted on curbing the consumer goods program, and in February 1955 drove Malenkov from office. Bulganin, until then Minister of Defense, took his place as Premier while Malenkov was demoted to Deputy Premier and put in charge of the Ministry of Power Stations. Throughout the year government and party officials kept busy devising new ways of improving economic conditions; plant managers were allowed greater freedom of action, and other decentralizing measures were taken to improve both industrial and agricultural productivity.

The Twentieth Party Congress. For a time, however, these economic concerns were overshadowed by a sensational turn in political developments. In February 1956 the Twentieth Congress of the Soviet Communist Party convened in Moscow. The congress ratified the de-Stalinization of government, economy, and ideology that had taken place. Following Khrushchev's lead in his opening address, a number of speakers affirmed that socialism could be attained by different roads and that countries with different social systems could coexist side by side. Several speakers also were openly critical of Stalin (in contrast to the previous practice of assailing him only by implication). The attacks on the dead dictator culminated in Khrushchev's final report, behind closed doors, "On the Cult of Personality and Its Consequences." This seven hour long address painted a shocking picture of Stalin's self-idolization, his ruthless abuse of power, and his errors of judgment as a political and military leader, although Khrushchev hastened to add that the dictator also deserved credit for many constructive achievements.

Why Khrushchev made these disclosures, which were bound to embarrass him and many another leader who had worked closely with Stalin, remained a matter for speculation. Addressed to the party leadership, the report was most likely meant to destroy any remaining preferences for Stalinist policies, and to this extent it reflected the views and intentions of the bulk of the leadership. In its specific form, how-

May Day at Moscow, 1957. Left to right: Marshal Zhukov, Khrushchev,
Bulganin, Kaganovich, Malenkov, Molotov, Mikoyan. (*Reprinted
courtesy Sovfoto*)

ever, it bore Khrushchev's personal imprint and was doubtless inspired
by personal aspirations. The pudgy, ebullient Party Secretary had
rapidly risen to prominence since Stalin's death; after the removal of
Malenkov, he was clearly aiming at adding the top government post
of Premier to that of First Party Secretary. Given this goal and the fact
that the bulk of his audience would welcome further measures of de-
Stalinization, Khrushchev evidently wished to establish himself as the
most outspoken critic of Stalin. What he failed to foresee was that his
report could not be kept secret for long, but became soon widely known.

The speech had a profound effect on Communists everywhere. In the
Soviet Union (where only party members were told of the speech)
Khrushchev's disclosures raised hopes for further liberalizing reforms;
in the satellite countries they encouraged demands for political and
economic changes and for greater national independence; in the non-
Communist world they led to substantial defections of disillusioned
party members and calls by many of the local Communist leaders for
greater political and ideological independence. Not since the early 1920's
had the Communist leaders faced similar threats to their rule from
within their own camp.

Khrushchev's Ascendance.   The leader most directly affected by this
reaction was Khrushchev himself. He still faced important opponents
among his fellow leaders. Molotov, as ever a hard-line Stalinist, and
several others blamed his "softness" for the existing difficulties. Malenkov
and his supporters charged that he had been too rigid. In the face of the
adverse reaction to his revelations, the two groups united. Their opposition drew new strength from the Polish and Hungarian revolts in the
fall of 1956.

The dissension that divided the party leaders was reflected in the
various policy shifts that occurred in 1956–57. In immediate response to
Khrushchev's disclosures, workers were accorded greater mobility, working hours were reduced and pensions increased. The economy was further decentralized and the security forces were subjected to a new purge.
Intellectuals and artists were allowed to voice criticisms and demands
for change with comparative freedom. To satisfy the new spirit of independence in the east European states, the Cominform, long moribund,
was dissolved altogether. Yet beginning in July 1956, after the Poznan
riots in Poland, the attacks on Stalin were toned down, and later that
534 year the dead leader was gradually rehabilitated. At the same time artists

and writers were subjected again to stricter controls and talk of political reforms was discouraged.

If on these matters the Soviet leaders could reach agreements, this proved impossible in the matter of economic reforms. In December Khrushchev called for a further decentralization of the economy, proposing the division of the country into semiautonomous economic regions. These regions were to be developed under local party auspices while part of the centralized government machinery that had supervised the economy would be dismantled. Khrushchev's plan involved not only a streamlining of the economic apparatus, but also a strengthening of the party, his special preserve, at the expense of the state. It was bitterly opposed by Khrushchev's opponents led by Malenkov and Molotov, who at one point came close to unseating Khrushchev. Khrushchev succeeded in marshaling a majority of the party's Central Committee—and the leadership of the army—behind him, and in June 1957 his opponents were stripped of their party and government posts. In March 1958 came the turn of Premier Bulganin, who was expelled from his various posts for being a member of the "anti-party group of Malenkov [and others] who had resisted the Leninist policy of the party." Khrushchev had himself elected Chairman of the Council of Ministers, uniting now both the top party and government posts in his hands.[1]

Khrushchev's Economic Policies. A few days after Khrushchev had become head of the Soviet government, the Indian Ambassador to Moscow jotted down this description of him:

Khrushchev is already 64 and is not likely to last long enough for absolute power to absolutely influence him. Also, he is temperamentally different from Stalin. Stalin was inaccessible, secretive, dogmatic and suspicious. He depended for his power on the secret police and on the sense of awe and mystery which he inspired. Khrushchev, on the other hand, is a born extrovert and would die from boredom if he had no one to talk to. He knows his country and the needs of its people, and, unlike Stalin, is more interested in raising standards of living in the U.S.S.R. than in launching grandiose projects to immortalize his name. Above all, the Soviet Union in 1958 is no longer the backward peasant country that Stalin took over and fashioned to his heart's content. Sputniks and Stalinism go ill together, and Khrushchev is well aware of the fact.[2]

It was a perceptive sketch of the new Soviet leader. Tough and cold-blooded, this one-time miner and metal worker was endowed with a shrewd agile mind and inexhaustible energy behind an uncouth exterior.

---

[1] If Khrushchev thus followed Stalin's example, none of his opponents, however, had to pay with his life or personal freedom for his opposition. Molotov was appointed Ambassador to Outer Mongolia and Malenkov and Bulganin were given administrative posts.

[2] K. P. S. Menon, *The Flying Troika: Extracts from a Diary* (London, 1963), p. 205. The first sputnik had been launched in October 1957.

At the same time Khrushchev was earthy and open-minded, a compulsive talker with a marked talent for histrionics. He had fought his way up through the ranks and had risen successively to party head of Moscow and the Ukraine, member of the Politburo, and First Secretary of the party. What was most notable about Khrushchev, however, was the fact that despite his long-time association with Stalin, his ruthless maneuvering and in-fighting in the party, and his participation in the blood purges of the 1930's, he had retained a strain of humanity in his personal makeup. Whatever the seamier side of his record, he had an evident concern for his country and its people.

Khrushchev at once took steps to increase industrial and agricultural productivity and improve living standards. The economy was decentralized further and labor unions were enjoined to pay greater attention to the material needs of the workers. To ease the work of the collective farms, they were authorized to buy their own mechanized equipment while the state-owned machine tractor stations which had serviced them were dissolved. The current (sixth) Five Year Plan was discarded as unrealistic and a new Seven Year Plan launched in 1959. The new plan called for an 80 per cent increase in industrial output, which was to be speeded by the progressive automation of manufacturing processes. Heavy industry was again accorded priority, but provisions were made for a substantial expansion of consumer goods output, especially in food, clothing, and housing. Wages and pensions were to be raised by almost 100 per cent during the seven year period and educational, social, and health services greatly expanded. The plan, Khrushchev predicted, would enable the Soviet Union to overtake the United States in productive capacity by 1970.

The continuous concern with the improvement of living conditions indicated the extent to which Soviet conditions had changed. A new generation had grown up that would no longer resign itself to continual hardships and shortages. However amorphous and unorganized, the pressure it put up was too strong and widespread to be ignored, let alone suppressed. The government, on the other hand, could yield to these demands the more readily because it came to understand that there existed a close relationship between labor productivity and living standards: the more consumer goods were available, the greater would be the incentive to work harder and earn more money in order to buy these goods.

While the output of clothing and furniture, of radios and television sets was expanding, agricultural productivity remained a perpetual problem. Khrushchev's early reform measures—increased agricultural prices, larger investments, cultivation of virgin soil—produced substantial results; grain crops increased by almost 40 per cent between 1954 and 1958, and meat sales rose by nearly 50 per cent. After 1958, however, the increase in agricultural productivity barely kept step with the increase of the population. The decline was due to decreasing investments, a drop in prices, a series of droughts, and the perpetual inadequacy of incentives inherent in the system of collectivist agriculture. Moreover, virgin soil cultivation had to be abandoned in many areas owing to the rapid erosion of the soil; wheat production in the newly planted territory, which had amounted to over 25 per cent of total production in 1956, declined to less than 15 per cent in 1962. In 1963, as a result of an exceptionally serious drought, the food situation deteriorated to a point where the government had to resort to large-scale imports of breadstuffs. Though on a reduced scale, these imports continued through 1966.

The Party Program of 1961. The growing concern with living conditions was also reflected in the new program issued by the Soviet Communist Party in 1961—the first such program since 1919 and the third since the party's formation. Unlike its predecessors, the document devoted much space to the raising of living standards and promised the attainment by 1980 of "abundance of material and cultural values for the whole population." Specifically, it envisaged a five-fold increase in industrial production, a 2.5-fold expansion of agricultural output, and a similar 2.5-fold growth of per capita real income. The housing problem would be solved, working hours reduced to 35 hours per week, and rent-free housing, free education, and other free public services provided, including free local transporation. All in all, the program reaffirmed, American productivity would be surpassed by 1970.

Politically, the document codified the major ideological adjustments that had been made during the preceding years. The principle of collective leadership was confirmed; its permanence was to be ensured by a greater turnover of party leaders who could from then on be elected only for a limited number of years (with exemptions, however, for party workers of "generally recognized authority and high political, organizational, and other abilities"). The program also confirmed the possibility of peaceful coexistence between socialist and capitalist states, but pledged the Soviet party and people "to support the sacred struggle of the oppressed peoples and their just anti-imperialist wars of liberation."

The program emphasized that there was no inconsistency between the two positions. Peaceful coexistence, according to it, did not signify the end of the contest between capitalism and socialism: "Peaceful coexistence serves as the basis for the peaceful competition between socialism and capitalism on an international scale and constitutes a specific form of class struggle between them." Against the major capitalist powers of the world this contest would have to be fought out within the framework of peaceful coexistence, but this did not preclude the support of local struggles of national liberation in which the Soviet Union would not be directly involved (and which presumably would be fought without resort to nuclear weapons).

In picturing the material abundance that the future would bring, the program hailed it as the foundation for a truly communist society where goods would be distributed according to needs rather than work. It still envisaged the "withering away" of the state, but made clear that this would mean, not the disappearance, but merely the transformation of administrative bodies into organs of "public self-government." The program foresaw an enhanced role for the party in building the full communist society and paid considerably more attention to the party's future functions than either of the previous two programs. This it did in an evident effort to refurbish the party image, for the standing of the party had seriously suffered from its failure in recent years to fulfill its role as the directing force of Soviet society. The creative innovating impulses had come mainly from the intellectuals, economists, artists, and scientists whereas the party, run by bureaucratized *apparatchiks*, had acted as a brake rather than a guide. The program sought to tackle this problem when it called for a "new, higher stage in the development of the party itself and of its political, ideological, and organizational work that is in conformity with the full-scale building of communism."[3]

These plans were designed not just for domestic consumption. Their promise of material abundance was meant to demonstrate to the outside world the superiority of Soviet communism over Western capitalism; the pledge of help to the peoples of Asia, Africa, and Latin America was to counteract the influence of the Chinese; the acceptance of the possibility that socialism could be attained by parliamentary means was to please the Italian and other like-minded west European Communists. At the same time the program addressed itself to the Chinese in an attempt to impress them with its picture of the abundant society of the future and with its open support of wars of national liberation. Yet the hope of the Soviet leaders for a reconciliation with China was not fulfilled; after an angry debate about the program, Chinese Premier Chou En-lai abruptly left Moscow, and the political and ideological gap between the two countries grew wider.

The Fall of Khrushchev. In October 1964 Khrushchev was suddenly removed from power by the Central Committee of the Communist Party. The immediate cause of his downfall appears to have been the Sino-Soviet dispute which had been growing more bitter and clamorous. To deal with it, Khrushchev had called a world congress of Communist parties to meet in November. At this gathering he expected the bulk of the parties to side with him against the Chinese and by thus discrediting Peking render it harmless. The plan encountered much opposition both

---

[3] Most likely in order to strengthen the ties between people and party and inject fresh blood into the party apparatus, party membership was allowed to increase by over 20 per cent, from 8.9 million to 10.8 million, between October 1961, when the party program was issued, and January 1965.

in the U.S.S.R. and abroad lest it should further weaken the Communist camp, and this most likely precipitated Khrushchev's removal.[4] His inability to halt the deterioration of Sino-Soviet relations was one of the charges made later against him in the official explanation of his dismissal.

That statement charged him with a long list of errors and setbacks. In agriculture he was held responsible for the failure of the virgin soil project on which he had embarked against the advice of most experts, and he was also blamed for the serious imbalance in agricultural crops. In industry he was accused of vacillating between decentralization and recentralization, of continuous changes in planning procedures, and of the excessive favoring of consumer goods industries (a charge reminiscent of the criticism by which he had helped engineer Malenkov's downfall). In foreign affairs, apart from the Sino-Soviet dispute, he was criticized for his precipitate reconciliation with Yugoslavia, his inept handling of the Cuban crisis, and the deterioration of relations with Rumania (see p. 549). Khrushchev was also accused of the "cult of personality," of nepotism and undignified bearing in public. The charges added up to a picture of him as an egocentric, impetuous, and irresponsible individual, a man lacking in balance and statesmanship to whom the fate of the country could not be entrusted any longer.

The coup by which Khrushchev was removed from his posts was carefully planned and the preparations completed while he was vacationing in the Crimea. His opponents lined up against him a majority of the Central Committee and secured the support of the army; confronting him with this hostile coalition of party and army, they forced him to resign as Premier and First Secretary of the Communist Party.

The Era of Brezhnev and Kosygin. Khrushchev's duties were once more split up—Leonid Brezhnev (1906–   ), an agricultural engineer, who had been once one of Khrushchev's protégés and had held a great number of important party and government positions became First Secretary of the Communist Party, and Aleksei Kosygin, a top executive with governmental and business experience, was appointed Chairman of the Council of Ministers. Compared to Khrushchev, both were quiet, colorless men, although not as withdrawn as Stalin had been. It was indeed in the manner in which they conducted the business of party and government that the contrast between them and their predecessor was most marked. Substantively, their policies differed little from Khrushchev's. They were unable to improve relations with China, they failed to keep Rumania from going its own way, and they were equally unsuccessful in their efforts to strengthen the Soviets' hold over most of the other east European countries. Relations with the West remained unchanged, neither improving nor worsening.

[4] After Khrushchev's dismissal the meeting was promptly called off.

After signing Soviet-Polish Friendship and Aid Pact in Warsaw, April 8, 1965, left to right in foreground: Kosygin, Gomulka, and Brezhnev. Behind Kosygin (partly hidden): Polish Premier Josef Cyrankiewicz. Behind Brezhnev (partly hidden): Soviet Foreign Minister Andrei Gromyko. (Reprinted courtesy Sovfoto)

Domestically, too, the new men continued to wrestle with the very same problems that Khrushchev had faced. Heavy industry was accorded new priorities, but the improvement of living standards remained high on the agenda of party and government. Agriculture, as always, received special attention, with additional funds allotted to the output of chemical fertilizer and farm implements and further incentives provided for farmers. To encourage production on their small private plots, farmers were permitted to increase their individual livestock holdings and charge higher prices for their produce. These measures were considered of special importance, for the plots, in spite of their smallness, constituted a significant source of foodstuffs. In the mid-1960's they produced 70 per cent of the country's potatoes, 42 per cent of its vegetables, 41 per cent of all meat, 45 per cent of all milk, and 76 per cent of its eggs. Thus any increase of production on the private plots would help to improve the food situation. To put a halt to the flight from the land, farmers were given pensions and other social security benefits in 1965 and guaranteed wages in 1966.[5]

Some significant changes were made in planning procedures. In accordance with proposals made by a Soviet economist, Yevsey G. Liberman, more attention was paid to economic calculations and the proper ratio of interest on and amortization of capital to investment and

[5] How much worse the economic status of the average farmer was compared to the city dweller can be seen from the fact that between 1952 and 1965 the townsman bought 3.8 times as many goods per head as his rural counterpart. See Timothy Sosonovy, "The New Soviet Plan: Guns Still Before Butter," *Foreign Affairs*, July 1966, p. 627.

profits. More important, in the light industries planning was to be guided by consumers' preferences since it was found that unpopular products would not sell even if nothing else was available. Although the Communist Party retained the final decision on all policy questions, the decisions were based less on ideological principles than on the businesslike calculations of managers concerned with concrete results—a development that paralleled trends in western Europe.

The Party Congress of 1966. This attitude of a sober matter-of-fact approach to existing problems pervaded the deliberations of the Twenty-Third Party Congress that met in Moscow in the spring of 1966. Its main concern was to keep conditions stable and orderly, avoid the disturbing improvisations and experiments of the Khrushchev era, and proceed with the business at hand. One of the first tasks it tackled was to end the policy of overt, blatant de-Stalinization which Khrushchev had pursued in his days of power and which had been the cause of much restiveness, especially among younger people. This was done, not by rehabilitating Stalin whose name was not even mentioned, but by rehabilitating the period in which he had ruled. In the speeches dealing with those years, emphasis was put on that era's constructive achievements, whereas its terror, purges, and labor camps were now played down. In a symbolic gesture the title of First Secretary of the Communist Party was changed back to Secretary General on the grounds that Lenin had created that title (though Stalin had been the only one to hold it), and that of the party's Presidium to the time-honored one of Politburo.

In this same vein the congress stressed the need for peaceful coexistence. The call for peace was constantly reiterated although no doubt was left that this did not include national wars of liberation and that the Soviet Union would continue to support North Vietnam in its struggle against the United States. The strictures of China were severe in substance, but moderate in tone, in accordance with the new leaders' determination to avoid the noisy brawling in which Khrushchev had liked to indulge. Proposals to read China out of the world Communist movement were bypassed and the door left open for an eventual reconciliation.

It was evident that the main concern of the party leadership was the domestic development of the U.S.S.R. As Brezhnev put it, in a pointed rebuke of China, "Our class brothers all over the world hold that the successful building of communism in the Soviet Union constitutes the main support, the main contribution to their revolutionary struggle." Thus the congress' main order of busines was the inauguration of a new Five Year Plan.

This plan (the eighth), covering the years 1966–70, was considerably more modest in its goals than Khrushchev's Seven Year Plan of 1959 which had not been fulfilled in most of its major objectives. Whereas under the former plan grain production was to have reached 180 million tons by 1965 (as against an actual harvest of 120.5 million tons), under the new plan the goal for 1970 was set at 167 million tons—a figure which might still turn out to be unrealistic. Forecasts of industrial expansion, although surpassing the goals of the previous plan, were considerably below the hopes held out by the party program for 1970. The latter had envisaged an output of electric power of between 900 and 1,000 billion kwh., but the new plan aimed only at 850 billion. Nor was there any more mention of overtaking the United States in industrial and agricultural productivity.

The lion's share of investments still went to heavy industry to enhance the country's economic and military strength. Although living standards were to be raised, the main expansion was to be in the production of items that required a comparatively small outlay of capital—television sets, washing machines, refrigerators—rather than housing, automobiles, or public utilities.[6] Premier Kosygin explained the limitations imposed on the improvement of living conditions as being necessitated by the war in Vietnam that was forcing the U.S.S.R. to increase its defense allocations at the expense of the consumer industries.

Education.   The Soviet educational system underwent a number of changes during the post-Stalin era. Most of the innovations were initiated by Khrushchev whose reforming zeal inevitably extended to the educational domain. One of his aims was to render Soviet education more democratic than it had been during the latter years of the Stalin era. In 1956 the fees charged in secondary schools and universities were abolished. New nighttime and correspondence courses were set up for those who were unable to complete their secondary education to allow them to prepare for the university entrance examinations while holding a job. The second major change initiated by Khrushchev concerned the inclusion of extended practical work experience in the curriculum of all secondary schools. There was a great need for technicians and other highly skilled workers; the hope was that if students became acquainted with farm or factory work at an early age, it would be easier to steer high school graduates into agricultural and industrial jobs. To prepare them for the complex duties that awaited them in these jobs in the age of mechanization and automation, the number of secondary schools specializing in fields such as electronics and radio engineering were greatly expanded.

Few of these reforms were retained without change by Khrushchev's successors. The admission to the universities of people who had attained their high school education in evening classes or correspondence courses was severely curtailed because this kind of preparation was often found to be insufficient. At the same time funds were provided to enable needy young people who were gifted to study full time until the completion of their secondary education. And although Khrushchev's decision to

[6] *Ibid.,* p. 623.

combine practical work experience with academic studies was not abandoned, compulsory factory work was reduced to one month in the ninth grade. The new leaders did not merely modify Khrushchev's reforms, but also introduced changes of their own. The most significant, in keeping with the trend of the times, was the creation of alternative programs concentrating on the humanities or the sciences. Students in the nonspecialized secondary schools could choose between these—a noteworthy departure from the rigid uniformity that had so far prevailed.

Religion. The general loosening of checks and controls that characterized post-Stalin Russia did not extend to the sphere of religion. In 1958 Khrushchev launched a new antireligious campaign to counteract the growing number of church weddings and baptisms and the increasing attendance at church services. This notable growth of religious activity resulted from the more relaxed atmosphere of the post-Stalin era which made it less dangerous to profess one's religious beliefs. A bitter press campaign sought to discredit some of the Orthodox Church leaders by accusing them of criminal offenses and charging the lower clergy with deception and licentiousness. The number of churches, which had risen from 4,225 in 1938 to 20,000 in 1955, declined to about 10,000 by 1965; seminaries were reduced from ten to five during that same period. Similar measures were taken against other denominations, with Jews and Catholics among the chief sufferers.

These repressive policies continued into the Brezhnev-Kosygin regime. As in the case of the Sino-Soviet dispute, however, the fight was carried on in much subtler forms after Khrushchev's removal. Thus the leading atheist journal, *Science and Religion*, stated in 1966 that Christianity could not be dismissed as the invention of charlatans and that many of the moral and ethical views expressed in the Bible were correct and could be answered only by increased attention to moral issues. An Institute of Scientific Atheism was founded to help provide guidance on these problems. The new leadership understood also that the churches satisfied certain emotional needs for color and ritual on important occasions and that these needs should not be ignored. In consequence, the government developed special ceremonies for such state functions as the registration of newly born children, civil marriages, and funerals in the hope of thus being able to compete more successfully with the color and solemnity of religious rites.

How effective these measures were remained to be seen. There were indications that in the face of the new repression, religious believers were once more driven underground to practice their beliefs more covertly.

Literature. Writers and artists had been especially sensitive to the rigid controls of the Stalin era; thus the impact of de-Stalinization was reflected almost at once in their work. Authors claimed the right to choose their own topics and stressed the need for individual self-expression. Novels and plays began probing some of the darker aspects of Soviet conditions, castigating the lack of ethics and imagination of party and government bureaucrats. The speed with which such critical works appeared suggests that they were part of that underground literature that was written in Stalin's time, but could not be published then. Some of these problems were dealt with in Ilya Ehrenburg's novel *The Thaw*, brought out in 1954, which gave this period its name: two of the novel's characters were painters—one a prosperous Stalinist mechanically turning out his pictures of collective farm life and other approved subjects; the other, a genuine artist, half-starved and unknown, working in semi-secrecy on his unorthodox landscapes until, after Stalin's death, his work was appreciated. Writers purged in Stalin's day were rehabilitated and their work, long banned, was reprinted or published for the first time. Translations of foreign literature also were made available on a larger scale than before. But although the "thaw" produced a spate of new works dealing with topics that had long been taboo, it produced nothing of outstanding artistic merit. The best known of the new novels *Not By Bread Alone* by Valdimir Dudintsev, pitted an idealist inventor against a dull, unimaginative Soviet official; it was a pedestrian, badly organized narrative, utterly lacking in grace and style. The book was nevertheless eagerly read—evidently because its protest against bureaucratic red tape and restrictions touched a responsive chord in millions of readers.

Like other areas of Soviet life, literature did not undergo these changes without encountering opposition. That opposition came from the Stalinists within the writers' own ranks and from the party which retained control of all creative activities and insisted that writers adhere to the rules of "socialist realism." Although these rules were now interpreted somewhat more flexibly, the party leadership was concerned lest widespread criticism of Soviet institutions in novels and plays undermine their authority. In the fall of 1956 party spokesmen began warning writers against abusing their new freedom. Khrushchev attacked Dudintsev as "a calumniator who took a malicious joy in describing the negative side of Soviet life . . . in an unhealthy, tendentious, and obnoxious work."[7] When the Hungarian revolt occurred a few weeks later, censorship was tightened again and the more liberal writers were subjected to scathing attacks in the press and in public meetings. In the wake of this campaign a number of novels appeared, designed to counteract "decadent bourgeois tendencies" and the "corrupted intelligentsia." A typical example, *The Brothers Yershov*, by Vsevolod Kochetov, revolved around the struggle between "good workers" and "bad engineers" in an industrial plant; in one passage the book warned against granting writers too much freedom lest they foment revolution.

---

[7] Quoted in Marc Slonim, *Soviet Russian Literature: Writers and Problems* (New York, 1964), p. 304.

These repressive endeavors culminated in the attacks on Boris Pasternak (1890–1960), author of the novel *Dr. Zhivago*. The novel dealt with the life of a physician who was neither a Communist nor a defender of the bourgeois-capitalist order, and merely wished to devote himself to his work, and live his own life. Despite his lack of political commitment Zhivago kept being drawn into the turmoil of revolution and civil war, the tragic victim of forces beyond his control. The editors of the monthly *Novy Mir* (*New World*) rejected the manuscript on the grounds that it sought to show that "far from having any positive significance in the history of our people and mankind, the October Socialist Revolution brought nothing but evil and hardship." The matter might have rested there if the book had not been awarded the Nobel Prize in 1958. The award was considered an anti-Soviet gesture by Moscow and touched off a spate of attacks on Pasternak; he was given to understand that if he went to Sweden to receive the prize, he might not be allowed to return. Pasternak thereupon withdrew his acceptance because, as he wrote to Khrushchev, he could not bear living out his life as an exile. Although the public clamor thereafter died down, Pasternak did not publish anything further.

Despite such pressures the new movement lived on. Its most prominent representatives in the 1960's were the poets Evgeny Yevtushenko and Andrey Voznesensky, who both called for the purification of Soviet life and as authors were deeply interested in linguistic and rhythmic experimentation; the novelist Alexander Solzhenitsyn, author of *One Day in the Life of Ivan Denisovich,* a novel about life in a Siberian forced labor camp based on the author's personal experiences; and Alexander Tvardovsky, also a poet but best known as the editor of *Novy Mir,* which became, within the limits permitted by the censors, an outlet for the new spirit of self-assertion among Soviet writers. How narrow these limits still were, was shown by the fact that Soviet Russia continued to have an underground literature that was circulated clandestinely in manuscript form or in small mimeographed magazines, or smuggled out of the country to be published abroad. In 1966 two writers, Andrei Sinyavsky and Yuri Daniel, were sentenced to seven and five years hard labor, respectively, for having published abroad works that were considered anti-Soviet in spirit.

But Soviet authors were not engaged in rebellion against party and government. Many of them accepted willingly the existing restrictions —among them as prominent a figure as the novelist Mikhail Sholokhov. Critics like Yevtushenko and Tvardovsky, on the other hand, were loyal Communists who merely felt that the Soviet system would benefit from being more flexible and allowing the artists greater independence. It was a feeling shared by other artists as well. "The time has come," wrote the composer Aram Khachaturian "to revise our established system of institutional guardianship over composers. . . . Creative problems cannot be solved by bureaucratic methods. . . . Let the composer and the libretto writer work carefully on their composition, on their own responsibility."

The composer would of course have to do this, Khachaturian added, "in the light of the great vital tasks which our party has set him." Yevtushenko and the other new writers fought their fight within that same framework.[8]

SOVIET EUROPE IN THE POST-STALIN ERA

Economic De-Stalinization. The death of Stalin led to some changes in the top echelons of party and government in most of the satellite countries, but on the whole these changes were less incisive than in the U.S.S.R. Gradually all of the people's democracies ended the union of the top party and the top government post in the hands of one individual, but in every case a Stalinist retained at least one of these positions— usually the more important one of First Secretary of the Communist Party.

In the economic domain the death of Stalin touched off more significant changes. Following the Soviet lead, the people's democracies began to pay greater attention to the improvement of living conditions and shifted production from the earlier overriding emphasis on capital goods to an expansion of consumer goods industries. In some cases the leadership undertook the changes on its own initiative. In Hungary, whose industrialization had been especially hurried and violent, the Kremlin called for a slowdown. In Czechoslovakia riots in the wake of a stringent currency reform forced the government's hand. In East Germany a statewide uprising in June 1953 caused the regime to make concessions beyond those it had granted already on its own.

The steps taken varied in the various countries. In addition to shifts in investments, the corrective measures consisted of price and tax reductions and for farmers in the decrease of delivery quotas. The Soviet Union also transferred its share of jointly owned enterprises to the country concerned (on unknown "favorable" terms), and in the case of East Germany it gave up all remaining reparation claims. Czechoslovakia allowed farmers to withdraw from collective farms, but rescinded this policy when some 500 collectives (out of 7,000) broke up within a year. East Germany and Rumania, on the other hand, stepped up their collectivization drive in 1953 as a counterweight to the economic concessions. On the whole, the alleviations did improve living standards, especially in East Germany and Czechoslovakia.

In order to speed the economic growth of the Soviet camp, Moscow also sought to inject new life into the moribund Council for Mutual Economic Assistance (COMECON). Its plans called for a division of

---

[8] Yevtushenko described the role in which he saw himself in his *Precocious Autobiography* (1963)—in many respects a remarkable little book full of revealing insights into life in Stalinist and post-Stalinist Russia.

labor and industrial specialization of the east European countries—a sharp departure from the Stalinist practice of discouraging any joint ventures. Apart from its material benefits, the strengthening of COMECON was to reinforce the ties binding the members of the Soviet bloc to each other and to the U.S.S.R. (Similarly, the Warsaw Pact which all bloc members joined superseded the bilateral military agreements of Stalin's day.)

Political De-Stalinization. Political Stalinism suffered its first major setback in the satellite countries as the result of the rapprochement between the Soviet Union and Yugoslavia in 1955. The rehabilitation of Tito came as an unpleasant shock to the satellite leaders all of whom owed their position to their avowed anti-Titoism. They were reluctant therefore to restore official relations with Belgrade lest new contacts with Yugoslavia would serve as an encouragement to Titoist forces in their own countries. On Moscow's prodding they did restore diplomatic relations and signed some trade and cultural exchange agreements, and after Khrushchev's disclosures of Stalin's misdeeds, they half-heartedly rehabilitated domestic Titoists who had been purged; yet they were careful at the same time to impose firm restrictions on any domestic critics.

In most of the east European countries the leaders retained control of political developments; in Poland and Hungary, however, pent-up discontent could not be contained and exploded into internal upheavals. Living conditions had sharply declined in both countries when they had followed the Soviet lead after the fall of Malenkov and had once more shifted the major emphasis of their production to capital goods. A rising of workers in Poznan in June 1956 could be suppressed by the Polish government, but made a reshuffling of government and party leadership necessary. As a result the Stalinists were replaced by moderates in all top positions. In October, with the re-emergence of Gomulka, the protagonist of "national" Communism, the new course took on a markedly anti-Soviet flavor. Khrushchev tried to block Gomulka's ascendancy, but accepted Gomulka's election as First Secretary of the party when Gomulka assured him that Poland would stay in the Soviet camp. Moscow accepted Gomulka's assurances because it knew him to be a devoted Communist who might modify, but would not abolish the existing political and economic system. Moreover, Poland was bound to remain in the Soviet orbit if only because it depended on Moscow's support in the defense of the Oder-Neisse Line against German revisionist claims.

In Hungary developments ran a different course. As in Poland, economic hardships were at the root of the difficulties. They had been somewhat alleviated when Imre Nagy, a moderate, became Premier in 1953 and introduced some economic reforms. However, in 1955, in the wake of Malenkov's demotion, Nagy had been removed by his Stalinist rivals, and both economic and political controls had been tightened again. Yet during the "thaw" of the Nagy era, a new spirit of independence had been aroused that could no longer be suppressed. Shocked by the dismissal of Nagy, groups of intellectuals and workers gathered around the former Premier. The Stalinists, led by Matyas Rakosi, wished to disband them, but were restrained by Moscow, which was fearful of the outbreak of risings such as had occurred at Poznan. Rakosi was forced to resign. His successor, Ernö Gerö, another Stalinist, made some half-hearted concessions, but they were too inadequate to satisfy the Nagy faction. Encouraged by the success of the Polish uprising and Moscow's passivity, the students and workers of Budapest rose against the Gerö regime in October 1956, and the Central Committee of the Communist Party hastily reinstated Nagy as Premier. The course of the revolt and its crushing by Soviet tanks, when it threatened to uproot Communism altogether in Hungary, has been described in a previous chapter (see p. 481).

The Reforging of the Soviet Bloc. With the Hungarian revolt suppressed, the Soviet leaders addressed themselves to the task of reinforcing once more their control over eastern Europe. Since the tightening of political bonds would have smacked too much of Stalinist methods, they concentrated on providing economic aid to Poland, Hungary, and East Germany—the regimes most in need of support against anti-Soviet elements in their countries. Further steps were taken to render COMECON more effective and speed up the specialization of its east European members, making them more dependent on each other and on the Soviet Union, their chief source of raw materials.[9] In the case of Poland these measures were taken also to keep Warsaw from seeking economic aid in the West. (In the summer of 1957 Poland was granted two American credits of $95 million and a year later it received additional credits in the amount of $98 million.)

Further Economic Reforms. The people's democracies acknowledged once more the leadership role of the Soviet Union—explicitly in a joint declaration at Moscow in 1957 which spoke of the "Socialist camp headed by the Soviet Union," implicitly by assuming a more rigid political stance at home and by resuming the persecution of skeptics critical of their actions and policies. They also followed the Soviet example when they revised their industrial program, scaling down heavy industrial projects and allowing an increase in consumer goods production. When these steps did not produce the hoped-for improvements, the eastern European states overhauled their economic systems more thoroughly in the following years. Following Khrushchev and in some cases overtaking him,

[9] From an economic viewpoint such specialization was of course sound and could, if properly implemented, contribute substantially to the material improvement of the states involved.

they too reduced central planning in varying degrees, giving individual industries or branches of industries a substantial degree of autonomy and relating wages more closely to productivity.

In some respects the reforms of the east European countries departed, however, from Soviet practices. In the mid-1960's Poland, Czechoslovakia, Hungary, and Bulgaria gave new encouragement to private craftsmen and small entrepreneurs, allowing them also to hire a limited number of helpers. Again the extent to which this was done varied—from small repair shops and handicrafts in Bulgaria to restaurants, service stations, and furniture stores in Poland. These concessions were made to meet the growing demand for better services in areas and activities where state-owned enterprises could not have been operated efficiently; the hope was also that the expansion of catering services would help to promote tourist trade.

In the agricultural sector too most people's democracies deviated from the Soviet approach. Bulgaria alone speeded the liquidation of private farming after 1956 and by 1958 had collectivized 92 per cent of its arable soil. Czechoslovakia followed with 70 per cent, but East Germany and Rumania trailed far behind. Poland and Hungary, on their part, allowed their farmers to withdraw from the collectives; in Poland land worked collectively declined from 24 to 14 per cent between 1956 and 1957 and in the case of Hungary, from 33 per cent to 22 per cent.

In the late 1950's the collectivization drive was renewed in Czechoslovakia, East Germany, and Rumania in order to shore up the political power of their governments. In the former two states the drive was completed by 1961, whereas in Rumania it covered 73.5 per cent of the land. Collectivization differed, however, in various countries. In most of eastern Europe both land and livestock became public property; on East German collective farms, on the other hand, only the land was cultivated in common whereas the cattle remained the personal property of the individual farmers. As in the U.S.S.R., collective farmers in the east European states were given the use of a small plot of land for private farming, and in these states, too, private farming made a decisive contribution to the total output of meat, eggs, and dairy products.

COMECON. COMECON made little progress during these years. The projected integration and specialization of the member economies encountered serious difficulties, due to national rivalries and the poor quality of the goods produced. In 1963 the Rumanians began fighting the plan openly. They objected to the proposed division of labor between COMECON members, fearful lest Rumania remain permanently a predominantly agricultural and oil producing country.[10] Taking advantage

---

[10] By this time, however, Moscow was probably no longer as much concerned with perpetuating the economic dependence of the east European states upon the U.S.S.R. as with the fact that Russia's role as the chief supplier of raw materials to these

of Moscow's preoccupation with the Sino-Soviet dispute, the Rumanians forced Khrushchev to abandon the integration of the east European economies.[11] At the same time Rumania, and in its wake several other east European countries, expanded their trade with the West.

Some steps towards closer collaboration were taken, however. In January 1964 a COMECON bank was established as a clearinghouse to facilitate intrabloc trade and put an end to the bilateral barter trade that had prevailed until then. A "Friendship" pipeline furnished oil from wells near Kuibyshev in the Volga valley to Poland, East Germany, Czechoslovakia, and Hungary; a vast electric power grid served as an important additional source of power for these same countries, and eventually was to include all COMECON members. Other cooperative ventures such as a freight car pool were also expected to stimulate trade among member states.

Diversity in the Soviet Orbit. Despite all efforts of the U.S.S.R. to align the economic and foreign policies of the east European states, national divergences became more marked in the 1960's. Moscow could no longer resort to coercion to achieve its objectives, and although on the whole the east European governments considered cooperation in their own interest, collaboration was modified by their need to consider the specific demands and requirements of their own people. Several of the people's democracies began to go their own way domestically, but some of them also embarked on foreign policies of their own. Of these latter, Albania withdrew altogether from the Soviet camp; its further development will be discussed in another part of this chapter. But even the states remaining in the Soviet camp came to differ sufficiently from each other in their actions and policies to warrant a separate discussion of at least some of them in the 1960's.

Poland. Gomulka had been swept into power in 1956 because he was the leading "national" Communist. He was, however, by nature conservative and authoritarian, and as he consolidated his position, his regime became considerably more inflexible than it had been when he first came to power. He replaced the original more liberal cabinet members by more orthodox Communists, the powers of the security police were expanded, some magazines discontinued, and several writers put on trial for having

---

countries was not very profitable and required heavy investments in the development of new sources of oil and ores. (In 1965 the Soviet Union met 75 per cent of the raw material requirements of the east European states.) Of all the countries in the Soviet orbit, Rumania was the only one well endowed with natural resources and hence best equipped to help relieve Moscow's difficulties.

[11] While Moscow failed to make COMECON the basis of a comprehensive "socialist" division of labor, it did conclude bilateral agreements with some of the east European states by which both partners bought certain types of industrial products from each other rather than manufacture them themselves.

"slandered" party and government in their writings. Poland did not return to the days of Stalinist terror, however, and its citizens still enjoyed greater freedoms than those of any other state in the Soviet orbit; but compared to the liberties gained in the "Polish October," the country was retreating a considerable distance from the early days of the Gomulka era. Only in the field of agriculture did Gomulka refrain from withdrawing any concessions made to the Polish farmers. He was convinced that for the time being private farming was more productive than collectivization (which officially remained the ultimate goal), and the bulk of the land remained in the hands of independent farmers, with its agricultural output superior to that of any other state in the Soviet camp.

That Gomulka allowed the farmers to retain the land may also have been necessitated by the fact that State-Church relations deteriorated again after a brief truce in 1956–57. Given the strong position which the Church enjoyed in the countryside, Gomulka would most likely have lost all support in the rural areas had he not left the farmers in control of their land.

In foreign affairs Poland sided as a rule with the Soviet Union, mindful that Soviet support might some day be needed against German territorial claims. However, Gomulka opposed Khrushchev's attempt to expel China from the Communist camp, perhaps from fear lest the same fate might befall deviationist Poland. As for the West, he was willing to trade with it, but politically he remained deeply distrustful of it.

Hungary. While Poland retreated from a more relaxed political regime to a more restrictive one after the upheaval of 1956, Hungary moved in the opposite direction. After a period of severe repression in which he broke the power of the two groups mainly responsible for the revolution—the intellectuals and the workers—the new party chief, Janos Kadar, tried to rally the nation in an effort to rehabilitate the country socially and economically. Personally much less of an autocrat than Gomulka, Kadar listened to the advice of his associates and kept in close touch with public opinion. The power of the secret police was sharply reduced, social discrimination discouraged, and nonparty experts given an important role in the development of the economy on the principle that "he who is not against us is with us." Kadar also improved relations with the Catholic Church, although the continued presence of Cardinal Mindszenty, a refugee in the American legation in Budapest since the 1956 rising, precluded any permanent settlement of the State-Church relationship.

Czechoslovakia, Bulgaria, East Germany. Despite their different economic development, Czechoslovakia and East Germany, the two most highly industrialized countries in the Soviet camp, and Bulgaria, economically the most backward, evolved along fairly similar lines during the 1960's. All three retained governments that tolerated little political relaxation, and all three, though for different reasons, remained much closer aligned with Moscow than any other state in the Soviet orbit. The Czechoslovak leadership did so because its continuous political and economic difficulties required Soviet support for its survival, Bulgaria's economic backwardness kept it dependent on Soviet aid, and the East German government, forever threatened by the existence of the West Grman state, could not afford to fend for itself. Unpopular though the East German regime was, the building of the Berlin Wall in 1961 did strengthen its position. With the escape route to the West barred, the drain on its manpower came to an end and non-Communists resigned themselves to the fact that they would have to make the best of their situation. To improve their lot, they went to work with a will and took pride in their state's ability, after liberalizing economic reforms, to attain sixth rank among Europe's industrial powers and tenth among the world's —a position achieved against formidable odds and without significant outside aid.

Rumania.   Next to East Germany, Rumania remained the most tightly governed of the east European states. Economically, too, it undertook fewer reforms in the 1960's than any other country in the Soviet orbit. The essential conservatism of the Rumanian leadership was aided by the country's natural wealth—oil and other mineral resources, fertile soil, large forests, a temperate climate—which provided it with that basis for industrialization the lack of which accounted for the recurring difficulties of East Germany, Poland, and Czechoslovakia.

The tight control the Communist leaders exercised over party and country enabled them also to defy successfully the U.S.S.R. on the issue of industrial specialization within COMECON. Khrushchev's "socialist division of labor" proposed that Rumania concentrate on the manufacture of oil pipes and drilling equipment, but otherwise assigned it the task of supplying the COMECON members with foodstuffs and raw materials. Party chief Gheorghe Gheorgiu-Dey took advantage of the quickening Sino-Soviet dispute, playing off Peking against Moscow. He calculated that Khrushchev could not afford losing Rumania as he had lost Albania, and that he would have to accept the Rumanian position to keep Rumania in the Soviet camp. As he expected, Moscow did give up the attempt to fit the Rumanian economy into its plan. Rumania remained in the Soviet camp, but as an ally rather than a satellite, maintaining also friendly relations with Albania and China and displaying a special proficiency in developing closer ties with the West. As a sign of its new independence, Bucharest ended the compulsory study of Russian in all schools and universities and changed Russian street and place names. A new constitution adopted in July 1965 omitted mention of the Bolshevik Revolution and the liberating role of the Red Army which the old document had lavishly praised in a lengthy preamble.

In 1966 the Rumanians also made an attempt to challenge Moscow's predominance in the Warsaw Pact. Nicolae Ceausescu, who had become party leader on Gheorgiu-Dey's death in 1965, challenged Moscow's prerogative to provide the commander-in-chief of the Warsaw Pact forces and called for a periodic rotation of the command. He also demanded the joint control by the pact members of the use of nuclear weapons stationed outside the Soviet Union. Finally, following Tito's lead, he proposed the scrapping of both NATO and Warsaw Pact and the establishment of an all-European security system. Ceausescu made it clear, however, that despite its reservations, Rumania would not withdraw from the Warsaw Pact as long as NATO remained in existence.

In its attitude toward COMECON and Warsaw Pact, Rumania had no support from other members of these organizations. The highly industrialized countries, Poland, East Germany, and Czechoslovakia, welcomed industrial specialization, and the Hungarian and Bulgarian regimes, fearful of domestic repercussions of Rumania's "nationalist" attitude, also rebuked Bucharest's stand. Similarly, most of these countries, ever fearful of West Germany, did not wish to reduce Moscow's role in the Warsaw Pact. If there was no longer a Soviet "bloc" in the mid-sixties in which east European satellites did the Kremlin's bidding, there was still a Soviet camp of countries held together by common interests and fears.

Cultural Developments. The east European literature of the post-Stalin period reflected the political trends of the times. Plays, novels, short stories revolved around the cruelty and injustices of the Stalinist period, the rigidity and incompetence of the bureaucracy, and such traditional themes as the class struggle and the conflict between the generations. The extent to which these topics could be discussed varied— Hungary permitted a great deal of freedom; Poland frowned on criticisms of the Stalinist era (and withheld newsprint to force recalcitrant writers into line); East Germany, Czechoslovakia, Rumania, and Bulgaria steered a cautious course, sometimes loosening cultural controls and subsequently tightening them again as the political atmosphere changed. Given the vagaries of the party line, many writers preferred to take refuge in nonpolitical themes—in itself a noteworthy change from earlier years when every literary work had to carry an ideological message.

The changing literary scene was perhaps best symbolized in a German novel, *The Divided Sky* by Christa Wolf, which enjoyed official approval as attested by the award of East Germany's Heinrich Heine Prize. The central characters are two young people, a chemist who eventually moved to West Berlin (in pre-Wall days), and his fiancée who joined him there, but unhappy in the Western environment, returned to East Germany. What was of interest in this otherwise undistinguished book was the fact that the young man was dealt with in pity rather than anger as would have been the case a few years before. Of greater literary merit was the novel *Ole Bienkopp* by another East German author, Erwin Strittmatter.

Its story revolved around the efforts of a farmer to establish a collective farm in his village—an undertaking hampered by the shortsightedness of local party officials. This in itself was a marked departure from rigid orthodoxy, but what was perhaps as significant was the subtle irony with which this and other political and ideological themes were handled.[12]

Another interesting example of this greater sophistication was the work of the Polish satirist, Slawomir Mrozek (*The Elephant*), who, in his short stories, poked fun gently at the inanity of ideological doctrinairism and the pomposity of the party bureaucracy. On a more serious plane, Jan Kott, professor of theater arts at the University of Warsaw, questioned altogether the rationality of human existence. Echoing familiar Western themes, Kott in a study of Shakespeare, *Shakespeare Our Contemporary*, viewed the English dramatist as a forerunner of Brecht, Beckett, and Ionesco, primarily concerned with the absurdity of the human condition. To Kott Shakespeare is the chronicler of the cruelty of history in which men get caught up as in a relentless mechanism that devours both rulers and ruled. Shakespeare's works thus are considered directly relevant to the present. In this interpretation the dramas of the kings are accounts of intrigues and conspiracies, of the knock at dawn at the door ("Who has not been awakened at least once in his life in this way at four o'clock in the morning?" Kott asks). *Hamlet* becomes the story of a country in which everyone spies on everyone else, where politics is all-pervasive and everyone is haunted by anxiety, and where there is no room left for human warmth and love. *Macbeth* tells of a man to whom murder becomes a normal function of life and who must go on killing: "History is reduced to its simplest form, one single picture, one single division—those who kill and those who get killed." What Macbeth experiences, Kott points out, can be called the "Auschwitz experience." but it is evidently just as much the experience of the Stalinist blood purge. Although Kott occasionally cites Marx in support of some statement he makes, it is a very un-Marxist, irrational world which he describes. Nonetheless, his book was published in Poland.

THE OUTSIDERS

Albania.   Albania had been fearful of a Yugolsav take-over ever since the end of the Second World War. The Albanian Communist Party, organized by Yugoslav Communists in 1941, continued to be treated as a ward by Belgrade, the Albanian economy was being developed by joint Yugoslav-Albanian companies, and for a time Yugoslav forces were stationed on Albanian soil. Albania welcomed the break between Stalin

[12] A throwback to the earlier clumsy techniques was the habit of the novel's chief villain, a sawmill owner, to talk in what apparently was meant to be American slang.

and Tito and after 1948 looked to Moscow to protect it against any aggressive designs on the part of the Yugoslavs. When Khrushchev effected a reconciliation with Tito, Albania's old fears revived. Party Chief Enver Hoxha, a hard-line Stalinist, continued to denounce Tito's "revisionism"; he also came to the defense of Stalin, whose misdeeds he did not deny but which he excused as due to Stalin's erroneous assumption "that they were necessary for protection of the revolution." As China became more critical of Khrushchev's policies, the two countries moved closer towards each other, and in 1960 Albania began staying away from Soviet bloc conferences. The Kremlin retaliated by witholding economic aid, and withdrew technicians and other advisers. So did East Germany and Czechoslovakia, the other two sources of financial and technical help.

China now came to Albania's assistance, and although its help did not equal the aid that the Soviet camp had provided, it was sufficient to tide Albania over its worst difficulties. Moreover, from 1963 on, as the people's democracies began to go their own way economically, Albania's trade with Rumania and other east European countries increased again. To these states Albania's considerable mineral wealth (oil, coal, copper, chrome) and its need for industrial products offered attractive trade opportunities which they were not prepared to forego for ideological reasons.

Politically, Albania continued to draw its main strength from its association with China, which was anxious to support this bridgehead in Europe in its conflict with the U.S.S.R. Albania was fortunate also in its geographical location which placed it beyond Moscow's physical reach. Nor were any of the Balkan states separating the U.S.S.R. from Albania interested in a forcible showdown with the Albanians—the less so as it might affect their own independence. Thus Albania continued on its defiant course—another reminder of the decline of Moscow's authority in the Communist world.

Yugoslavia. In the international domain Yugoslavia maintained its uncommitted position between the Soviet and Western camps after its reconciliation with Moscow. Although it joined COMECON in 1964, it remained an outspoken opponent of both NATO and Warsaw Pact.

Domestically, Tito continued to steer his liberalized course. Most land was farmed individually, workers councils played some role in the management of industrial enterprises, and small business kept operating with the right to hire up to five workers. Increased emphasis on the production of consumer goods served as an incentive to labor to work harder in order to be able to purchase more, and production grew at a rapid pace. By Communist standards the country enjoyed also a considerable measure of freedom. Since the enactment of a new constitution in 1963, the Federal Assembly ceased to be a mere rubber stamp for Tito's decisions, and became a public forum in which government bills could be discussed. Similarly, public discussion was encouraged at the grassroot level. But there were limits to this freedom; whereas individual measures of the regime might be questioned, no criticism of Tito or of basic institutions and policies was tolerated. Former Vice President Milovan Djilas, who violated this rule, paid for his defiance with long years in jail. Within the same limitations, artists and writers were free to pursue their work, although some of them learned that the dividing line between what was permissible opposition and was not was uncertain. The quest for "socialist realism" was abandoned soon after the break with Moscow in 1948; since then both literature and the arts showed a marked preference for non-Marxist themes. In 1966 Yugoslavia re-established diplomatic relations with the Vatican.

Yugoslavia was not without its economic and political problems, however. The concern with expanding the industrialization of the country and at the same time improving living standards led to overinvestments, inflation, and a recurrent balance-of-payments problem. The government was faced with the choice of either again tightening its control over the economy or allowing greater leeway to the market mechanism to rectify the existing difficulties. Tito opted for the latter alternative, giving individual plants the right to decide on investments, letting them fend for themselves in the market, and relegating the Five Year Plans from binding instructions to "moral and political commitments." This involved further depolitization of the economy, with the technocrat increasingly superseding both party leader and government official. As Tito stated in 1965, "We must absolutely discontinue the practice of political people deciding where and what should be built, and how much. This is something the enterprises and factories should decide. . . . We political people can give only general lines of an investment policy; you must make the decisions."[13]

The program ran into strong opposition in party and government when the reforms impinged on old vested interests. Opposition asserted itself also in another quarter. Slovenia and Croatia, the most highly developed of Yugoslavia's member states, welcomed the reforms, but the less developed states, Bosnia, Macedonia, and Montenegro, worried lest their development suffer under the new arrangement, and Serbia wavered between the two camps. Thanks to the newly granted freedom of discussion, the opposition could make itself heard more effectively, and oppositional party and government officials felt encouraged to slow down or sabotage the reforms. In the summer of 1966 Tito expelled the leading advocate of greater centralization, Vice President Alexander Rankovic, from party and government and removed some of Rankovic's closest associates to enforce a speedier implementation of the reforms.

[13] *Borba*, Dec. 31, 1965, quoted in *Foreign Affairs*, July 1966, p. 638, n.2.

Finland. Finnish policy in the post-Stalin era continued to be dominated by the need to maintain friendly relations with the U.S.S.R. On the whole, Finland maintained a tolerable *modus vivendi* with its powerful neighbor, though keeping its own Communists out of the government. Occasional troubles in Soviet-Finnish relations could be settled without major disturbances.

The elections of March 1966 produced a sharp swing to the left, with the moderate Social Democrats emerging as the largest party and the Communists as the second largest. The Social Democrats had long been subject to Soviet attacks for being pro-Western, and since Soviet pressures had forced a Social Democratic Premier, Karl August Fagerholm, out of office in 1958, the Social Democrats had not been represented in any government. Nevertheless, in May 1966, after extended negotiations, a new cabinet was formed under the leadership of the Social Democratic party head, Rafael Paasio. In addition to five other Social Democrats it included three Communists, one left-wing Socialist, and five members of the agrarian Center Party. The arrangement was clearly a product of the East-West *détente:* in Finland itself it was accepted as constructive and realistic; abroad it did not create any serious concern in either the West or the Soviet camp.

With ideological precepts giving way in both East and West to the growing concern with efficient achievement, the prospects of the new coalition seemed better than those of earlier alliances between Communists and non-Communists. The success or failure of the new Finnish government could well prove of significance beyond Finland's borders. Conceivably, its record might serve as some indication as to whether Europe, after a half-century of continued turmoil, might gradually arrive at a new order in which the European peoples in spite of all differences could deal more easily with the many problems for which solutions had still to be found.

Suggested Readings

Chapter 1. The Crisis of the European State System

Hajo Holborn, *The Political Collapse of Europe* (1951), provides a perceptive survey of the history of the European state system. A. J. P. Taylor's *The Struggle for Mastery in Europe: 1848–1918* (1954) is a scintillating account of diplomatic developments during the pre-World War I period. The works of Sidney B. Fay, *The Origins of the World War* (2 vols., 1928–30),* Bernodotte E. Schmitt, *The Coming of the War of 1914* (2 vols., 1930), and Luigi Albertini, *The Origins of the War of 1914* (3 vols., 1952–57), are detailed discussions of the causes of World War I. Fritz Fischer, *Germany's Bid for World Power* (1964), assigns to Germany the main responsibility for the war. John U. Nef, *War and Human Progress: An Essay on the Rise of Industrial Civilization* (1950), examines European attitudes toward war, and Michael Curtis, *Three Against the Republic: Sorel, Barrès, and Maurras* (1959), and Andreas Dorpalen, *Heinrich von Treitschke* (1957), deal with the social and intellectual background of some of these attitudes in France and Germany, respectively. Barbara W. Tuchman, *The Proud Tower* (1966), provides in a somewhat rambling account a great deal of material on the emotional climate of prewar Europe.

Chapter 2. World War I: The European Phase

Two useful military histories of World War I are: B. H. Lidell Hart, *The War in Outline: 1914–1918* (1936), and Cyrill Falls, *The Great War 1914–1918* (1959).* Alfred Vagts, *A History of Militarism* (1965), and Edward Mead Earle, ed., *Makers of Modern Strategy: Military Thought from Machiavelli to Hitler* (1943), are informative on civil-military relations. Frank P. Chambers, *The War Behind the War* (1939), contains much material on domestic conditions in the belligerent countries. Arthur Rosenberg, *Imperial Germany: The Birth of the German Republic 1871–1918* (1931),* is still the best source on wartime Germany despite a somewhat unsatisfactory translation, and Jere Clemens King, *Generals and Politicians* (1951), is a perceptive study of civil-military relations in wartime France. Bernard Pares, *The Fall of the Russian Monarchy* (1939),* is informative on the disintegration of wartime Russia. Illuminating discussions of staff planning and frontline action can be found in Barbara W. Tuchman, *The Guns of August* (1962),* Alistair Horne, *The Price of Glory: Verdun 1916* (1963), and Leon Wolff, *In Flanders Field: The 1917 Campaign* (1958).* William Henry Chamberlain, *The Russian Revolution, 1917–21* (2 vols., 1935),* is a standard work on its topic. E. H. Carr, *The Bolshevik Revolution, 1917–1923,* Vol. 1 (1951), analyzes the doctrinal aspects of the revolutions of 1917.

Chapter 3. World War I: The Atlantic Phase

The problems of Wilson's neutrality policies are discussed in Robert E. Osgood, *Ideals and Self-Interest in America's Foreign Relations* (1953),* Ernest R. May, *The World War and American Isolation, 1914–1917* (1959),* Arthur S. Link, *Wilson the Diplomatist* (1957),* and Daniel M. Smith, *The Great Departure: The United States in World War I: 1914–1920* (1965).* Arno J. Mayer, *Wilson vs. Lenin: Political Origins of the New Diplomacy, 1917–1918* (1959),* provides a suggestive account of political developments for this period. Harry R. Rudin, *Armistice 1918* (1944), analyzes the last months of the war. Victor S. Mamatey, *The United States and East Central Europe, 1914–1918* (1957), lucidly surveys a complex problem.

Chapter 4. The Search for a New Order

The best brief survey of the period under discussion is Holborn's *Political Collapse of Europe.* Paul Birdsall's *Versailles: Twenty Years After* (1941) provides a helpful concise analysis of the issues dealt with at the Paris Peace Conference. Seth P. Tillman, *Anglo-American Relations at the Paris Peace Conference* (1961), is a valuable more recent addition to the vast literature on the conference. Of first-hand reports, Harold Nicolson, *Peacemaking 1919* (1933),* and Stephen Bonsal, *Unfinished Business* (1944), are especially informative. Gordon A. Craig and Felix Gilbert, eds., *The Diplomats: 1919–1939* (1953),* offer a great deal of material on the main actors on the diplomatic stage, and Walter R. Sharp's and Grayson Kirk's *Contemporary International Politics* (1940) still is useful as a rich source of facts and figures. Anglo-French relations are dealt with perceptively in W. M. Jordan, *Great Britain, France, and the German Problem: 1918–1939* (1943), and Arnold Wolfers, *Britain and France Between Two Wars* (1940).* Soviet-Western relations are analyzed in George F. Kennan, *Russia and the West Under Lenin and Stalin* (1960),* and for the early 1920's, in Carr's *History of the Bolshevik Revolution,* Vol. III (1953). Material on United States-European relations can be found in Richard W. Leopold, *The Growth of American Foreign Policy* (1962). Robert H. Ferrell, *Peace in Their Time: The Origins of the Kellogg-Briand Pact* (1952), is an informative, readable study of its subject. The standard work on the League of Nations is F. P. Walters, *A History of the League of Nations* (2 vols., 1952), a fact-laden study by a one-time League official.

Chapter 5. Economics, Society, Culture in the 1920's

Paul Alpert, *Twentieth Century Economic History of Europe* (1951), provides a useful introduction into postwar Europe's economic problems. J. B. Condliffe's *The Commerce of Nations* (1950) is a superb analysis of international trade relations. George L. Ridgeway, *Merchants of Peace: Twenty Years of Business Diplomacy Through the International Chamber of Commerce: 1919–1938* (1938), and Lord (Arthur) Salter, *Memoirs of a Public Servant* (1961), are informative on the diplomacy of international economics. America's role is discussed by George Soule, in *Prosperity Decade: From War to Depression: 1917–1929* (1949) and in Cleona Lewis, *America's Stake in International Investments* (1938). Harold G. Moulton and Leo Pasvolsky, in *War Debts and World Prosperity* (1932), have the standard work on its subject.

The social scene of the 1920's is analyzed in Carl Landauer's *European Socialism: A History of Ideas and Movements from the Industrial Revolution to Hitler's Seizure of Power* (2 vols., 1959), Peter F. Drucker's *The End of Economic Man* (1939), Erich Fromm's *Escape from Freedom* (1941),* and Hannah Arendt's *The Origins of Totalitarianism* (1951).* Joseph A. Schumpeter, *Capitalism, Socialism, and Democracy* (1950),* is suggestive. Cultural developments are examined by H. Stuart Hughes in *Consciousness and Society* (1961),* William Barrett, *Irrational Man* (1959),* and Edmund Wilson, *Axel's Castle* (1931).* John Canaday, *Mainstreams of Modern Art* (1959), and Everard M. Upjohn, Paul S. Wingert, and Jane G. Mahler, *History of World Art* (1949), are informative surveys of their subject.

Chapter 6. Domestic Politics in the 1920's: The Western European Democracies

British developments are surveyed in D. C. Somervell, *British Politics Since 1900* (1950), a brief but very useful account, Alfred Havighurst, *Twentieth Century Britain* (1965),* a more comprehensive analysis full of facts and figures, and A. J. P. Taylor, *English History: 1914–1945* (1966), a continuously stimulating knowledgeable work. Robert Graves' and Alan Hodge's *The Long Weekend: A Social History of Great Britain, 1918–1939* (1953)* is a readable social history of the period. Duff Cooper, *Old Men Forget* (1954), Hugh Dalton, *Call Back Yesterday: 1887–1931* (1953), and E. L. Woodward, *Short Journey* (1946), are three of a great number of informative memoirs, representing the Conservative, Labor, and independent viewpoint, respectively. Woodward is particularly good on British intellectual life. Of biographies of the main actors, Thomas Jones, *Lloyd George* (1951), and George M. Young, *Stanley Baldwin* (1952), are probably the most useful although neither one is very satisfactory. Alan Bullock, *The Life and Times of Ernest Bevin*, Vol. I (1960), provides valuable information on British labor and on the general strike.

Gordon Wright, *France in Modern Times* (1960), and Paul A. Gagnon, *France Since 1789* (1964), contain good surveys of the French political and social scene. David Thomson, *Democracy in France Since 1870* (1964),* and Edward M. Earle, ed., *Modern France* (1951), also provide much useful material. Val. R. Lorwin, *The French Labor Movement* (1954), is a thorough and dependable standard work; Richard D. Challener, *The French Theory of the Nation in Arms: 1866–1939* (1955), is a prime source on French military thought. There are no adequate biographies in English of any of the leading statesmen of the period.

Among works on the smaller countries Ingvar Anderson, *A History of Sweden* (1956), and T. K. Derry, *A Short History of Norway* (1957), deserve mention. The volumes on Belgium, ed. by Jan-Albert Goris (1945), and on the Netherlands, ed. by Bartholomeus Landheer (1943), in the United Nations Series are useful. J. Christopher Herold, *The Swiss Without Halos* (1948), is a sprightly, fact-laden account.

Chapter 7. Domestic Politics in the 1920's: The Western European Dictatorships

Cecil J. S. Sprigge, *The Development of Modern Italy* (1944), and René Albrecht-Carrié, *Italy from Napoleon to Mussolini* (1950),* are useful historical surveys. William Ebenstein, *Fascist Italy* (1939), is still helpful. Frederico Chabod, *A History of Italian Fascism* (1963), is brief, but valuable as the product of a combination of scholarly research and personal experiences. Dante L. Germino, *The Italian Fascist Party in Power: A Study in Totalitarian Rule* (1959), is a balanced factual examination of its subject. Gaetano Salvemini, *Under the Axe of Fascism* (1937), though poorly organized and polemical, contains much valuable information. A fully satisfactory biography of Mussolini still remains to be written; but Laura Fermi, *Mussolini* (1961),* and Ivone Kirkpatrick, *Mussolini: A Study in Power* (1964), are serviceable.

Gerald Brenan, *The Spanish Labyrinth* (1943),* provides a balanced picture of Spain during World War I and in the 1920's. Salvador de Madariaga, *Spain: A Modern History* (1958), though somewhat impressionistic, also contains much useful information. H. V. Livermore, *A History of Portugal* (1947), offers a factual survey of Portuguese developments.

Chapter 8. Domestic Politics in the 1920's: Central and Eastern Europe

Good surveys of the political history of the Weimar Republic are available in S. William Halperin, *Germany Tried Democracy: A Political History of the Reich from 1918 to 1933* (1946),* and Erich Eyck, *History of the Weimar Republic* (2 vols., 1963–64). Klaus Epstein, *Matthias Erzberger and the Dilemma of German Democracy* (1959), relates the melancholy story of one of the leaders during the early period of the republic, Andreas Dorpalen, *Hindenburg and the Weimar Republic* (1964), discusses the role of the second Reich President against the political and social background of the republic's declining years. No satisfactory biography of Stresemann is yet available, but Henry L. Bretton, *Stresemann and the Revision of the Versailles Treaty* (1955), offers a perceptive analysis of one major aspect of Stresemann's foreign policy, and Henry Ashby Turner, *Stresemann and the Politics of the Weimar Republic* (1963),* provides insights into the domestic problems which he faced. Robert G. L. Waite, *Vanguard of Nazism: The Free Corps Movement in Postwar Germany: 1918-1923* (1952), presents a carefully documented exploration of his subject. John W. Wheeler-Bennett, *The Nemesis of Power: The German Army in Politics: 1918–1945* (1953), and Gordon A. Craig. *The Politics of the Prussian Army: 1640–1945* (1954),* are rich storehouses of information on the political role of the Reichswehr. Konrad Heiden, *Der Fuehrer: Hitler's Rise to Power* (1944), is still the best biographical study of Hitler during the Weimar period. For a briefer account Alan Bullock, *Hitler: A Study in Tyranny* (1964),* is useful. Gustav Stolper, *German Economy 1870–1940: Issues and Trends* (1940), is a convenient introduction to economic developments in the Weimar Republic.

Charles Gulick, *Austria from Habsburg to Hitler* (2 vols., 1948), is a standard work on its subject. Raymond L. Buell, *Poland: Key to Europe* (1939), remains one of the best sources on Poland during the interwar period. J. Taylor, *The Economic Development of Poland: 1919–1950* (1952), is a useful supplement in the economic domain. Hugh Seton-Watson, *Eastern Europe Between the Wars* (1962), and Robert L. Wolff, *The Balkans in Our Time* (1956), are informative readable accounts.

Chapter 9. Soviet Russia in the 1920's

E. H. Carr, *History of Soviet Russia* (1951–   ) at present covers its subject until 1926. Leonard B. Schapiro, *The Communist Party of the Soviet Union* (1960),* offers a comprehensive analysis of the party, full of perceptive insights. Pitirim A. Sorokin, *Leaves from a Russian Diary* (1950), Allan Monkhouse, *Moscow: 1911–1933* (1934), and S. Libermann, *Building Lenin's Russia* (1944), offer interesting details on the early years of the Soviet era. Sir John Maynard, *Russia in Flux* (1948),* though dated in parts, is still useful. Louis Fischer, *The Life of Lenin* (1964),* and I. Deutscher's biographies of Stalin (1949)* and Trotsky (3 vols., 1954–63)* are important. So are Trotsky's autobiography, *My Life* (1930),* and his *History of the Russian Revolution* (1 vol. ed. 1957). Alexander Baykov, *The Development of the Soviet Economic System* (1946), John S. Curtiss, *The Russian Church and the*

Soviet State (1953), and R. Schlesinger, ed., *Changing Attitudes in Soviet Russia: The Family in the U.S.S.R.* (1949), are valuable on their respective subjects. Marc Slonim, *Modern Russian Literature* (1953),* provides a readable survey.

Chapter 10. The Great Depression

In addition to the works of Alpert, Condliffe, and Sharp and Kirk (see Ch. 5), consult Wladimir Woytinski, *The Social Consequences of the Economic Depression* (1936). A. J. Youngson, *The British Economy: 1920–1957* (1960), also offers a concise and useful analysis of the general causes of the Depression. British developments are covered well, apart from Youngson, in Havighurst, Somervell, and A.J.P. Taylor (see Ch. 6). Keith Feiling, *The Life of Neville Chamberlain* (1946), contains significant details, as does Vol. II of Hugh Dalton's *Memoirs* (1957). On France, see Wright and Gagnon (Ch. 6), and Alexander Werth, *The Twilight of France* (1942); on Italy, Ebenstein (Ch. 7), and Frances Keene, ed., *Neither Liberty Nor Bread: The Meaning and Tragedy of Fascism* (1940); on Germany, Eyck and Dorpalen (Ch. 8). International developments are analyzed in Walters (Ch. 4), G. M. Gathorne-Hardy, *A Short History of International Affairs: 1920–1939* (1960), and with special regard to their American aspects, in Robert H. Ferrell, *American Diplomacy in the Great Depression: Hoover-Stimson Foreign Policy* (1957). The World Disarmament Conference is discussed in John W. Wheeler-Bennett, *The Pipe Dream of Peace: The Story of the Collapse of Disarmament* (1935). A. C. Temperley, *The Whispering Gallery of Europe* (1939), contains an interesting eyewitness report of the conference.

Chapter 11. Nazi Germany

In addition to Heiden and Bullock (Ch. 8), consult on Hitler's youth the the revealing reminiscences of August Kubizek, *The Young Hitler I Knew* (1955), and Franz Jetzinger, *Hitler's Youth* (1958), a mine of factual information. Craig and Dorpalen (Ch. 8) examine the relations of the Nazis with the army and Hindenburg, respectively. William Ebenstein, *The Nazi State* (1943), is still useful on the internal organization of the Nazi regime; William L. Shirer, *The Rise and Fall of the Third Reich: A History of Nazi Germany* (1960),* though somewhat uneven in its coverage, offers a readable account of political developments. Franz Neumann, *Behemoth: The Structure and Practice of National Socialism* (1944), continues to be valuable on the organization of the Nazi economy, but should be supplemented with Burton H. Klein, *Germany's Economic Preparations for War* (1959). Oron J. Hale, *The Captive Press in the Third Reich* (1964), offers a thorough survey of Nazi press policies. William Sheridan Allen, *The Nazi Seizure of Power: The Experience of a Single German Town, 1920–1935* (1965),* is illuminating on Nazi infiltration techniques on the local level. The standard work on the Jewish issue is Raul Hilberg, *The Destruction of the European Jews* (1961).

Chapter 12. Economy, Society, Culture in the 1930's

Good surveys of the European economic scene can be found in Condliffe, *Commerce of Nations* (Ch. 5), and his earlier study, *The Reconstruction of World Trade* (1940). British and French economic policy is discussed in Youngson and Werth (Ch. 10); a good discussion of Swedish policy may be found in *The Annals of the American Academy of Political and Social Science*, Vol. 197 (May 1938). The German trade drive is described in Barbara Ward *et al.*, *Hitler's Route to Bagdad* (1939). The most accessible comprehensive discussion of Keynes's ideas, although not wholly satisfactory, is available in Roy F. Harrod, *The Life of John Maynard Keynes* (1951).* Robert Lekachman, *The Age of Keynes* (1966), provides a brief readable survey. Eugene M. Kulisher, *Europe on the Move: War and Population Changes 1917–47* (1948), presents a comprehensive analysis of population problems; Sir John Hope Simpson, *The Refugee Problem: Report of a Survey* (1939), is equally helpful on the refugee issue. *The Statistical Year-Book of the League of Nations: 1938–39* (1939) contains a wealth of data on European developments during the 1930's.

Analyses of English literary developments in the 1930's are available in Julian Symons, *The Thirties: A Dream Revolved* (1960), and Leonard Unger, *T. S. Eliot: A Selected Critique* (1948)*; the French literary scene is discussed in Henri Peyre, *The Contemporary French Novel* (1955), and David Caute, *Communism and the French Intellectuals: 1914–60* (1964). Richard Crossman, ed., *The God That Failed* (1950),* contains accounts of their association with Communism by André Gide, Arthur Koestler, and other writers. On scientific developments Sir William Cecil Dampier, *A History of Science and Its Relation with Philosophy and Religion* (1961), and Julian Huxley, *Man in the Modern World* (1955),* ought to be consulted.

Chapter 13. Domestic Politics in Non-Nazi Europe

In addition to the works listed in Chapters 6 and 10, Thomas Jones, *A Diary With Letters: 1931–1950* (1954), provides important insights into the Baldwin and Chamberlain administrations and into the rationale of their policy of appeasement. A. L. Rowse, *Appeasement: A Study in Political Decline: 1933–1939* (1961), * is the memoir of a bitter opponent of that policy. Of the multitude of memoirs which the leading participants in that period have written, the most interesting are Vol. I of Winston Churchill's magisterial *The Second World War* (1948–53)*; Viscount Templewood (Sir Samuel Hoare), *Nine Troubled Years* (1954), one of the best accounts of the appeasement years by a leading insider; Vol. II of Hugh Dalton's *Memoirs* (1957); and Harold Macmillan, *Winds of Change: 1914–1939* (1966), which is informative on the economic policies of the younger Conservatives. Anthony Eden, *Facing the Dictators* (1962), and Harold Nicolson, *Diary and Letters: 1930–1939* (1966), contain interesting details, but are, on the whole, disappointing. Colin Cross, *The Fascists in Britain* (1961), though journalistic in its approach, contains valuable information. As before, A.J.P. Taylor (Ch. 6) is stimulating and informative; he is less critical of Neville Chamberlain and considerably more so of Anthony Eden than is usually the case.

Besides the titles cited in Chapters 6 and 10, John T. Marcus, *French Socialism in the Crisis Years: 1933–36* (1958), and Peter J. Larmour, *The French Radical Party in the 1930's* (1964), are perceptive studies of their respective subjects. Joel Colton, *Léon Blum: Humanist in Politics* (1966), tells a melancholy story with insight and sympathy; Val R. Lorwin, *The French Labor Movement* (1955), discusses the general setting of the Popular Front era. James Joll, ed., *The Decline of the Third Republic* (1959), examines several specific developments of the period. Of the few memoirs available in English, Paul Reynaud, *In the Thick of the Fight* (1955), deserves mention.

The two standard works on Spain in the 1930's are Hugh Thomas, *The Spanish Civil War* (1961),* and Gabriel Jackson, *The Spanish Republic and the Civil War: 1931–1939* (1965). An interesting eyewitness report of a Spanish noblewoman turned Socialist is Constancia de la Mora, *In Place of Splendor* (1939).

Apart from the works on Italy mentioned in Chapter 7, Hugh Gibson, ed., *The Ciano Diaries: 1939–1943* (1946), are an informative source.

Chapter 14. The Soviet Union in the 1930's

The works cited in Chapter 9 should be supplemented with John Scott, *Behind the Urals* (1942), and John D. Littlepage and Demaree Bess, *In Search of Soviet Gold* (1937), both informative American eyewitness reports. Merle Fainsod's *Smolensk Under Soviet Rule* (1958) * is an invaluable account based on captured Communist Party documents, covering all aspects of Soviet life in the Smolensk area. Robert Vincent Daniels, *The Conscience of the Revolution: Communist Opposition in Russia* (1960), is a thorough and balanced study of its topic. Donald R. Hodgman, *Soviet Industrial Production 1928–1951* (1954), contains a wealth of data on industrial output.

Chapter 15. The Destruction of the European Order

Many of the works listed in the preceding Chapters 11–14 contain material relevant to diplomatic developments. Of specialized studies, in addition to Craig and Gilbert (Ch. 4), the following are helpful: Elizabeth Wiskemann, *The Rome-Berlin Axis* (1949); E. Allison Peers, *Spain in Eclipse: 1937–1943* (1943); Jürgen Gehl, *Austria, Germany, and the Anschluss* (1963); John W. Wheeler-Bennett, *Munich: Prologue to Tragedy* (1963).* Lewis Namier, *Diplomatic Prelude: 1938–1939* (1948), though dated in parts, is still useful. Namier's collected essays, *Europe in Decay,* (1950) and *In the Nazi Era* (1952), also contain interesting analyses and interpretations. Good surveys of American foreign policy in the 1930's can be found in Leopold (Ch. 4), William E. Leuchtenburg, *Franklin D. Roosevelt and the New Deal: 1932–1940* (1963),* and above all for the last years of the decade, in the superb study by William L. Langer and Everett Gleason, *The Challenge to Isolation: The World Crisis of 1937–1940 and American Foreign Policy* (1952).*

Chapters 16–17. World War II: The European and Global Phases

The best sources for military and political developments are Churchill (Ch. 13), Shirer and Bullock, (Ch. 8), Kirkpatrick (Ch. 7), and Langer and Gleason (Ch. 15), which must be supplemented by the same authors' *The Undeclared War: 1940–1941* (1953). Alexander Werth, *Russia at War: 1941–1945* (1964),* though journalistic in its approach, contains useful materials. Harry L. Coles, ed., *Total War and Cold War: Problems in Civilian Control of the Military* (1962), includes essays on Roosevelt, Churchill, and Hitler as war leaders. Arnold and Veronica M. Toynbee, eds., *Hitler's Europe* (1954), is an informative, fact-laden symposium; additional data can be found in Alpert (Ch. 5).

William H. McNeill, *America, Britain, and Russia: Their Cooperation and Conflict: 1941–1946* (1953), and Herbert Feis, *Churchill, Roosevelt, Stalin: The War They Waged and the Peace They Sought* (1957),* are informative judicious surveys of diplomatic developments. John L. Snell, ed., *The Meaning of Yalta: Big Three Diplomacy and the New Balance of Power* (1956),* is helpful.

Individual aspects of the war are discussed in F. H. Hinsley, *Hitler's Strategy* (1951); Alan Clark, *Barbarossa: The Russian-German Conflict, 1941–1945* (1965)*; Cornelius Ryan, *The Longest Day: June 6, 1944* (1959),* and *The Last Battle* (1966)*; John Toland, *The Last 100 Days* (1965)*; Raul Hilberg, *The Destruction of the European Jews* (1961).

Chapter 18. Europe—Battleground of the Cold War

McNeill (Ch. 17) covers the first postwar year with great thoroughness. Herbert Feis, *Between War and Peace: The Potsdam Conference* (1960),* is a detailed account, parts of which have been challenged, however, by Gar Alperovitz, *Atomic Diplomacy: Hiroshima and Potsdam* (1965). Martin F. Herz, *Beginnings of the Cold War* (1966), also is helpful. The Cold War is covered well in the sprightly account by John Lukacs, *A History of the Cold War* (1961).* W. Phillips Davison, *The Berlin Blockade: A Study in Cold War Politics* (1958), is the standard work on its subject. Lucius D. Clay, *Decision in Germany* (1950), John T. Marcus, *Neutralism and Nationalism in France* (1958), and Marshall D. Shulman, *Stalin's Foreign Policy Reappraised* (1963), are other important sources on the Cold War. D. F. Fleming, *The Cold War and Its Origins: 1917–1960* (1961), is a detailed survey highly critical of American policies. Howard K. Smith, *The State of Europe* (1949), is an informative eyewitness report by a perceptive newspaper correspondent.

Chapter 19. Western Europe from VE-Day to the Death of Stalin: The Internal Transformation

Hans A. Schmitt, *The Path to European Union: From the Marshall Plan to the Common Market* (1963), provides an informative survey which should be supplemented with William Diebold, *The Schuman Plan* (1959). Apart from Havighurst (Ch. 6), British developments are discussed perceptively in William A. Robson, *Nationalized Industries and Public Ownership* (1960), and Hugh Dalton, *Memoirs*, Vol. III (1961). France's postwar history is covered well in Gagnon and Wright (Ch. 6), and Herbert Lüthy, *France Against Herself* (1955). John Ford Golay, *The Founding of the Republic of Germany* (1958), may usefully be supplemented with Richard Hiscocks, *The Adenauer Era* (1967),* Paul Weymar, *Adenauer: His Authorized Biography* (1957), and Lewis J. Edinger, *Kurt Schumacher: A Study in Personality and Political Behavior* (1965). H. Stuart Hughes, *The United States and Italy* (1965), provides a concise history of postwar Italy.

William Barrett, *Irrational Man* (1958),* is an excellent introduction into the intricacies of existentialism. Dore Ashton, *The Unknown Shore: A View of Contemporary Art* (1962), Vernon Jarratt, *The Italian Cinema* (1951), and Paul Damaz, *Art in European Architecture* (1956), are convenient introductory surveys.

Chapter 20. Eastern Europe and Soviet Russia: The Stalinist Era

Zbigniew K. Brzezinski, *The Soviet Bloc: Unity and Conflict* (1960), is a fact-laden survey. Schapiro (Ch. 9), as always, is highly informative on party developments. Nicholas Spulber, *The Economies of Eastern Europe* (1957), Hugh Seton-Watson, *The East European Revolution* (1951),* and C. E. Black, ed., *Challenge in Eastern Europe* (1954), also are helpful. Edward Taborsky, *Communism in Czechoslovakia: 1948–1960* (1961), and Wolff, *Balkans* (Ch. 8), provide additional material. George W. Hoffman and Fred Warner Neal, *Yugoslavia and the New Communism* (1962), is a standard work on its subject. Milovan Djilas, *Conversations with Stalin* (1962), is one of the few first-hand accounts on the Soviet dictator which seems trustworthy. Marc Slonim, *Soviet Russian Literature: Writers and Problems* (1964), offers a convenient survey of the postwar literary scene.

Chapter 21. The Reassertion of Europe

In addition to Lukacs (Ch. 18) and Brzezinski (Ch. 20), Evan Luard *The Cold War: A Re-appraisal* (1964),* and George Lichtheim, *The New Europe* (1963),* offer perceptive analyses of developments in the 1950's and early '60's. Jack D. Dowell, ed., *The Unity of Western Europe* (1964), is a concise informative symposium. Anthony Eden's memoirs for that period, *Full Circle* (1960), are of interest for the Geneva Conference of 1955 and the Suez crisis. Arthur M. Schlesinger, Jr., *A Thousand Days: John F. Kennedy in the White House* (1965),* contains a great deal of valuable background information on European developments in the late 1950's and early 1960's.

Chapter 22. Western Europe in the Era of Affluence: Economy, Society, Culture

Stephen R. Graubard, ed., *A New Europe?* (1964), is a rich source of information on recent European developments. It should be supplemented with Lichtheim's book (Ch. 21). U. W. Kitzinger, *The Politics and Economics of*

European Integration: Britain, Europe, and the United States (1964),* is also informative. Andrew Shonfield, *Modern Capitalism: The Changing Balance of Public and Private Power* (1965),* is a superb analysis of recent economic developments in western Europe. Individual countries are surveyed in Havighurst, Gagnon, and Thomson (Ch. 6); Hughes, Hiscocks, and Weymar (Ch. 19); also Dorothy Pickles, *The French Fifth Republic: Institutions and Politics* (1962)*; Stanley Hoffmann *et al.*, *In Search of France* (1963); Alfred Grosser, *The Federal Republic of Germany: A Concise History* (1964).* Kenneth Allsop, *The Angry Decade* (1958), and John Cruickshank, *The Novelist as Philosopher: Studies in French Fiction, 1935–1960* (1962), are convenient surveys of literary developments.

Chapter 23. The Soviet Orbit after Stalin

Schapiro (Ch. 9) and Brzezinski (Ch. 20) should be supplemented with Luca Pietromarchi, *The Soviet World* (1965); Wolfgang Leonhard, *The Kremlin Since Stalin* (1962); and Robert C. Tucker, *The Soviet Political Mind: Studies in Stalinism and Post-Stalin Change* (1963).* Edward Crankshaw, *Khrushchev: A Career* (1966) is an informative balanced account. Myron Rush, *The Rise of Khrushchev* (1958), is an interesting piece of Kremlinology. K. P. S. Menon, *The Flying Troika: Extracts from a Diary* (1963), provides perceptive first-hand observations by an Indian ambassador. J. F. Brown, *The New Eastern Europe: The Khrushchev Era and After* (1966), though less scholarly than Spulber (Ch. 20), is valuable in bringing the latter's work up to date. Slonim (Ch. 20) surveys literary developments into the early 1960's.

Index

Dorpalen

EUROPE IN 1968

Miles
0 100 200 300 400 500

ATLANTIC OCEAN

SHETLAND IS.

Bergen

NORWAY
Oslo
(Christiania)

THE HEBRIDES

ORKNEY IS.

SCOTLAND

SWE

UNITED

NORTH SEA

DENMARK

Glasgow

Edinburgh

Coper

N. IRELAND

Belfast

KINGDOM

HELGOLAND

Kiel

Lübeck

EIRE

IRISH SEA

Liverpool

Manchester

Birmingham

ENGLAND

Hamburg

EAS

Dublin

Weser

Elbe

Bremen

Hanover

Magdeburg

Ben

Pots

NETHERLANDS

Amsterdam

The Hague

GERMAN

Essen

Düsseldorf

Cologne

Bonn

Frankfurt

GERMA

Leipzig

Dresc

50°

Thames

London

ENGLISH CHANNEL

Str. of Dover

Ghent

Antwerp

Lille

Brussels

BELGIUM

Magdeburg

Pra

CHANNEL IS.

Brest

Le Havre

Rouen

LUX.

Rhine

FEDERAL

Nürnberg

Reims

Metz

Danube

REP.

Munich

Versailles

Paris

Orleans

LORRAINE

Strasbourg

Nantes

Loire

Seine

ALSACE

Basel

Boden See

Zürich

Berne

AUS

Innsbruc

BAY OF BISCAY

FRANCE

Bordeaux

Lyons

SWITZERLAND

A l p s

Garonne

Rhone

Milan

Venice

R.

Po

Bilbao

Toulouse

Genoa

Bologna

SAN MARINO

AD

Oporto

PORTUGAL

Valladolid

Duero

Pyrenees

ANDORRA

Marseilles

MONACO

Florence

ITALY

40°

Ebro

Zaragoza

CORSICA

Rom

SPAIN

Madrid

Tagus

Toledo

Barcelona

Lisbon

Guadiana

Valencia

MEDITERRANEAN

MINORCA

TYRRHENIA

SEA

Cordova

Guadalquivir

Seville

Malaga

Granada

MAJORCA

BALEARIC IS.

SEA

SARDINIA

Strait of Gibraltar

Tangier

Gibraltar (Br.)

Ceuta (Sp.)

Melilla (Sp.)

Palermo

Rabat

Fez

Oran

Algiers

Tunis

MOROCCO

ALGERIA

TUNISIA